The Edinburgh Critical History of Nineteenth-Century Christian Theology

The Edinburgh Critical History of Christian Theology
Series Editors: Russell Re Manning, Bath Spa University and Tom Greggs,
University of Aberdeen

The Edinburgh Critical History of Christian Theology presents the history of Christian theology in an innovative way with critical essays addressing the emergence and development of the themes and problematics that characterise each period. Particular attention is given to the diffusion of themes across disciplinary, geographical and historical boundaries, and to the changing practices of Christian theology.

A key concern of the series will be to explore the ways in which themes and clusters of themes can be traced within and across historical periods, leading to a new and informative way of conceptualising the development of Christian theological thinking. In so doing, a guiding methodological assumption of the series is that the history of Christian theology is one of a series of encounters and negotiations between traditions and contexts. The thematic *foci* of the volumes range broadly across creedal and doctrinal *loci* as well as historical particularities.

The Edinburgh Critical History of Christian Theology reflects on how the dominant themes and problematic of a period took shape, were developed, and were bequeathed to subsequent generations; enabling both a re-evaluation of the dynamics of historical Christian theology and a *ressourcement* for contemporary Christian theologians and critical thinkers.

Volumes available
The Edinburgh Critical History of Nineteenth-Century Christian Theology
Edited by Daniel Whistler

Forthcoming volumes in the series
The Edinburgh Critical History of Apostolic and Patristic Christian Theology
The Edinburgh Critical History of Medieval Christian Theology
The Edinburgh Critical History of Renaissance and Reformation Christian Theology
The Edinburgh Critical History of Early Modern Christian Theology
The Edinburgh Critical History of Twentieth-Century Christian Theology
The Edinburgh Critical History of Contemporary Christian Theology

Visit the series webpage at
edinburghuniversitypress.com/series/echct

The Edinburgh Critical History of Nineteenth-Century Christian Theology

Edited by Daniel Whistler

EDINBURGH
University Press

Edinburgh University Press is one of the leading university presses in the UK. We publish academic books and journals in our selected subject areas across the humanities and social sciences, combining cutting-edge scholarship with high editorial and production values to produce academic works of lasting importance. For more information visit our website: edinburghuniversitypress.com

© editorial matter and organisation Daniel Whistler, 2018, 2025
© the chapters their several authors, 2018, 2025

Edinburgh University Press Ltd
13 Infirmary Street
Edinburgh, EH1 1LT

First published in hardback by Edinburgh University Press 2018

Typeset in 10/12 Goudy Old Style by
Servis Filmsetting Ltd, Stockport, Cheshire

A CIP record for this book is available from the British Library

ISBN 978 1 4744 0586 7 (hardback)
ISBN 978 1 3995 4674 4 (paperback)
ISBN 978 1 4744 0587 4 (webready PDF)
ISBN 978 1 4744 0588 1 (epub)

The right of Daniel Whistler to be identified as the editor of this work has been asserted in accordance with the Copyright, Designs and Patents Act 1988, and the Copyright and Related Rights Regulations 2003 (SI No. 2498).

Contents

Notes on Contributors	vii
Editor's Introduction **Daniel Whistler**	1
1. *The Death of God* **Lissa McCullough**	7
2. *The Outside* **Daniel Whistler**	27
3. *Society* **Susan Curtis**	45
4. *The University* **Gerard Loughlin**	64
5. *Freedom* **Regula Zwahlen**	85
6. *The Fetish* **Roland Boer**	105
7. *Evolution* **Bennett Zon**	124
8. *Miracles* **Ruth Barton**	143
9. *Transcendence and Immanence* **Johannes Zachhuber**	164
10. *Mediation* **Andrew W. Hass**	182

11. *The Historical Turn*   203
    George Pattison

12. *Tradition*   219
    Thomas Pfau

13. *The Human*   247
    Steven Shakespeare

14. *The Wisdom of the East*   265
    Joseph P. Lawrence

15. *Homiletics*   283
    Joshua Cockayne

16. *Deification*   300
    Katya Tolstaya

17. *Mysticism*   320
    Benjamin Dawson

18. *Language*   339
    Katie Terezakis

Index   359

Notes on Contributors

Ruth Barton is an honorary research fellow in the School of Humanities at the University of Auckland. She is a historian of science and technology whose major work has been on science and culture in Victorian England. She has written on elites (Huxley, Tyndall, the X Club) and on popular science journalism. Her interests extend to colonial science (controversies over the moa) and domestic technology and women's work. Two books are in press, the co-edited *Correspondence of John Tyndall*, vol. 3, *1850–1852* (University of Pittsburgh Press, 2017) and *The X Club: Power and Authority in Victorian Science* (University of Chicago Press, 2018).

Roland Boer is Research Professor at the University of Newcastle, Australia, and Xin Ao International Professor at Renmin University of China, Beijing. His main research area is Marxism and religion. To that end, he has written numerous works, the latest of which include *The Sacred Economy of Ancient Israel* (2015), *Idols of Nations* (2014, with Christina Petterson) and *In the Vale of Tears* (2014), which won the Isaac and Tamara Deutscher Memorial prize.

Joshua Cockayne is Research Fellow at the Logos Institute for Analytic and Exegetical Theology at the University of St Andrews. His research focuses on Søren Kierkegaard and philosophical theology, particularly the philosophy of the spiritual life. He has written articles on Kierkegaard published in *The British Journal for the History of Philosophy* and *Religious Studies* and was awarded the *Religious Studies* postgraduate essay prize in both 2015 and 2016.

Susan Curtis is Professor of History and American Studies at Purdue University. She is the author of *A Consuming Faith: The Social Gospel and Modern American Culture* (University of Missouri Press, 1991; 2nd edn, 2001), three books on aspects of African American culture and performance, and numerous book chapters and essays on American social reform and religion.

Benjamin Dawson is Lecturer in Romanticism and Critical Theory at Queen Mary University of London. Before this, he was a researcher at the Berlin Institute for Cultural Inquiry (2010–12) and academic assistant in the Media Faculty of the Bauhaus-Universität Weimar (2012–14). He has published essays on Hegel, Mary Shelley and the Romantic scientist J. W. Ritter, and is currently writing a book on the philosophy of science in the Romantic period.

Andrew W. Hass is Reader in Religion at the University of Stirling. His interests and publications operate at the intersection of religion, theology, literature, art and philosophy, with recent interest in the idea of nothing (*Auden's O: The Loss of One's Sovereignty in the Making of Nothing*) and negation (*Hegel and the Art of Negation*). He is Secretary of The International Society for Religion, Literature and Culture.

Joseph P. Lawrence is a professor at the College of the Holy Cross, Massachusetts. He is the author of *Schellings Philosophie des ewigen Anfangs* (1989) and *Socrates among Strangers* (2015). In addition, he has written a number of essays on German philosophy and literature. He is currently working on an alternative reading of Schelling that will accompany his translation of the 1811 version of the *Ages of the World*, which will be published in 2017 by SUNY Press. He regards it as part of a larger ongoing project on philosophical religion.

Gerard Loughlin is Professor of Theology at Durham University. He is the author of *Telling God's Story: Bible, Church and Narrative Theology* (Cambridge University Press, 1996) and *Alien Sex: The Body and Desire in Cinema and Theology* (Blackwell, 2004), and the editor of *Queer Theology: Rethinking the Western Body* (Blackwell, 2007). He co-edits the journal *Theology and Sexuality* (Equinox), is an Associate European Editor of *Literature and Theology* (Oxford University Press), and has published a number of essays on nineteenth-century theology, including in *The Cambridge Companion to John Henry Newman* (Cambridge University Press, 2009) and *The Blackwell Companion to Nineteenth-Century Theology* (Wiley-Blackwell, 2010).

Lissa McCullough teaches at California State University Dominguez Hills and has previously taught religious studies at Muhlenberg College, Hanover College and New York University. She is author of *The Religious Philosophy of Simone Weil: An Introduction* (I.B. Tauris, 2014) and editor of *The Call to Radical Theology* and *Thinking through the Death of God* (with Brian Schroeder), as well as *Conversations with Paolo Soleri*.

George Pattison is 1640 Chair of Divinity at the University of Glasgow. He is the author of many books on Kierkegaard and on a range of topics in modern theology and philosophy of religion, including, most recently, *Kierkegaard and the Theology of the Nineteenth Century* (Cambridge University Press, 2012), *Kierkegaard and the Quest for the Unambiguous Life* (Oxford University Press, 2013), *Heidegger on Death* (Ashgate, 2013) and *Eternal God/ Saving Time* (Oxford University Press, 2015). He is co-editor of *The Oxford Handbook of Theology and Modern European Thought*.

Thomas Pfau is Alice Mary Baldwin Professor of English at Duke University, with secondary appointments in Germanic Literature and the Duke Divinity School. He is author of *Wordsworth's Profession* (Stanford University Press, 1997), *Romantic Moods* (Johns Hopkins University Press, 2005) and *Minding the Modern* (Notre Dame University Press, 2013), as well as numerous essays.

Steven Shakespeare is Senior Lecturer at Liverpool Hope University. He is author of *Kierkegaard, Language and the Reality of God* (Ashgate, 2001), *Radical Orthodoxy: A Critical Introduction* (SPCK, 2007), *Derrida and Theology* (T&T Clark, 2009) and *Kierkegaard and the Refusal of Transcendence* (Palgrave Macmillan, 2015). He is also co-editor (with

Claire Molloy and Charlie Blake) of *Beyond Human: From Animality to Transhumanism* (Continuum, 2012) and (with Katharine Sarah Moody) of *Intensities: Philosophy, Religion and the Affirmation of Life* (Ashgate, 2012).

Katie Terezakis is Associate Professor at Rochester Institute of Technology. She is the author of *The Immanent Word: The Turn to Language in German Philosophy 1759–1801* (Routledge 2007). She is the editor of *Engaging Agnes Heller: A Critical Companion* (Lexington Books, 2009) and of Lukács' *Soul and Form* (Columbia University Press, 2010). Her most recent essays and current book project focus on the twentieth-century American thinker, John William Miller.

Katya Tolstaya is the director of INASEC (Institute for the Academic Study of Eastern Christianity) at the VU University in Amsterdam. Her publications include *Kaleidoscope: F.M. Dostoevsky and Early Dialectical Theology* (Brill, 2013). She is also a laureate of the prestigious NWO Innovational Research Incentives Scheme Grant (VENI) for a research project 'From Orthodoxy to obscurantism? Theological frictions in the contemporary Russian Orthodox Church'.

Daniel Whistler is a senior lecturer at the University of Liverpool. He is the author of *Schelling's Theory of Symbolic Language: Forming the System of Identity* (Oxford University Press, 2013) and co-author of *The Right to Wear Religious Symbols* (Palgrave Macmillan, 2013). He is co-editor of *The Feminist Philosophy of Gillian Howie: Materialism and Mortality* (Bloomsbury, 2016), *Moral Powers, Fragile Beliefs: Essays in Moral and Religious Philosophy* (Continuum, 2011) and *After the Postsecular and the Postmodern: New Essays in Continental Philosophy of Religion* (CSP, 2010), as well as special issues of the *International Journal of Philosophy and Theology* ('Schelling's Afterlives', 2017), *Angelaki* ('Nature, Speculation and the Return to Schelling', 2016), *Political Theology* ('Speculative Philosophies and Religious Practices', 2012) and *Literature and Theology* ('Attending to Others', 2011).

Johannes Zachhuber is Professor of Historical and Systematic Theology at the University of Oxford. He has worked in patristics, modern theology, philosophy of religion, and the reception history of Christian theology. Publications include *Human Nature in Gregory of Nyssa: Philosophical Background and Theological Significance* (Brill, 2000), *Theology as Science in Nineteenth-Century Germany: From F.C. Baur to Ernst Troeltsch* (Oxford University Press, 2013) and (as co-editor with J. Meszaros), *Sacrifice and Modern Thought* (Oxford University Press, 2013).

Bennett Zon is Professor of Music at Durham University, Director of the Durham University Centre for Nineteenth-Century Studies and a Director of the International Network for Music Theology. He is General Editor of *Nineteenth-Century Music Review* (Cambridge University Press) and the Routledge book series, 'Music in Nineteenth-Century Britain'. He is an editor of the *Yale Journal of Music and Religion* as well as the Routledge book series, 'Congregational Music Studies'. His research triangulates music, theology and science from the long nineteenth century to the present. His monographs include *The English Plainchant Revival* (Oxford University Press, 1999), *Music and Metaphor in Nineteenth-Century British Musicology* (Ashgate, 2000), *Representing Non-Western Music in Nineteenth-Century Britain* (University of Rochester Press, 2007) and *Evolution and Victorian Musical Culture* (Cambridge University Press, 2017).

Regula Zwahlen is a postdoctoral research assistant at the University of Fribourg, Switzerland. She is the author of *Das revolutionäre Ebenbild Gottes. Anthropologien der Menschenwürde bei Nikolaj A. Berdjaev und Sergej N. Bulgakov* (LIT Verlag, 2010) and co-editor of the German edition of Sergii Bulgakov's work (volume 1: *Die Philosophie der Wirtschaft*, Aschendorff Verlag, 2014). She co-edits the journal *Religion und Gesellschaft in Ost und West*, and has published a number of essays on Russian and Soviet concepts of personality and on Russian Orthodox human rights discourse.

Editor's Introduction

Daniel Whistler

From the scars of the Kantian critique to the aftershocks of the 1860 Oxford debate over Darwinism, from the advent of death-of-God thinking to the rise of new Evangelical movements, theology during the nineteenth century was fundamentally reshaped by both internal struggles and external encounters. The following critical history charts some of these processes of reshaping by means of a focus on the conceptual developments of the period that cross authors, disciplines and nations, by means, that is, of surveys of theological interactions with anthropology, art, industry, literature, philosophy, politics, science and society. The essays contained herein aim to disclose the various material and intellectual conditions of theological discourse in the nineteenth century and, in consequence, hope to show how the problems and themes of the nineteenth century have in turn given shape to later theological thinking.

Late eighteenth-century life in Western Europe (in particular) was a period of turmoil. Lacoue-Labarthe and Nancy speak of 'the profound economic, social, political and moral crisis of the latter years of the eighteenth century' ([1978] 1988: 5), and, more specifically, identify a 'triple crisis' for thought in the 1790s: 'the social and moral crisis of a bourgeoisie, with new-found access to culture . . . who are no longer able to find positions for those sons traditionally destined for the robe or the rostrum', 'the political crisis of the French Revolution, a model that disturbed some and fascinated others' and 'the Kantian critique . . . unintelligible for some, liberating but destructive for others' (ibid. 5). Over the coming century, there were further social crises, such as the acceleration of the industrial revolution with consequent anxieties over automatism and unbridled innovation, as well as urbanisation, the formation of a mass proletariat and widespread poverty. In many nation-states, politics consisted of waves of revolution and restoration, of the freedoms, terrors and reactions of 1814, 1830, 1848, 1871. The academy was similarly marked by revolutionary systems of idealisms, naturalisms and historicisms, as well as very unsystematic exercises in scepticism, fideism and irony. And, of course, the nineteenth century witnessed great scientific ferment too: not merely that which followed in the wake of the publication of *On the Origin of Species* in 1859, but also that occasioned by debates over the nature and speed of geological formation, the inviolability of natural laws and the distinction of life from the inorganic.

What is more, the above contributed to a further crisis that could be more properly called theological: the loss (at least, partially) of the self-evidence of Christian revelation.[1] The nineteenth century was the first since the Moorish occupation of Spain in which the intellectual classes of Western Europe did not take their own commitment to Christianity for granted. Whether or not this anxiety over the ebbing of Christian faith was in fact an accurate representation of the facts on the ground, the spectre of the loss of religion haunted theoretical productions of the period: only now could it be so uncontroversially confessed that 'the old opinions in religion, morals and politics are so much discredited in the more intellectual minds as to have lost the greater part of their efficacy for good' (Mill [1873] 1981: 246–7).[2] Fascination with heterodoxy, agnosticism and atheism was not, as in previous epochs of Christianity, the lone pursuit of a marginalised few, but rather a significant component of the self-understanding of many educated Christians. However negligible such scepticism may have been from a sociological perspective, its voice was heard and demanded a theological reaction.

Theology thus attained modernity in the nineteenth century, and this modernity was constituted out of anxiety over its own foundations. The original ground of Christianity – the immediate, indubitable sufficiency of revelation – was felt to have withdrawn and been replaced with external foundations, both real and ideal (capitalism, the university, the idea of historical progress, etc.). On the one hand, this fracture bred a new sense of untethered freedom, a series of theological experiments let loose from the normative chains of orthodoxy. On the other hand, the same lack of self-sufficiency led to a restorationist pursuit of legitimacy – whether it be legitimisation by means of the university, confessional norms, or even the promise of incontrovertible facts at the end of the quest for the historical Jesus.

Notwithstanding such restorationist tendencies, theological purity was rare in the nineteenth century. The attempt to remain faithful to the kerygma not only had to stretch backwards across nineteen hundred years of history, but was also to be mediated through the frameworks of other sciences. In order to secure Christian truths, the theologian must become archivist, metaphysician, anthropologist and natural scientist; she must fragment herself across scientific disciplines for the sake of the integrity of theology. In other words, during the nineteenth century, what mattered were not so much internal disputes and controversies within Christian theology – although of course they still mattered too – but theology's relation to what was outside of it (the arts, history, philosophy, politics, science). What mattered was how theologians made use of these external discourses, as well as, conversely, how theological material was itself redeployed for extrinsic ends. The essays that follow describe Christian theology's struggles during the nineteenth century to situate itself in relation to external conditions; they survey its ongoing negotiations with an outside, whether that outside consisted in speculation, scientific discovery or material transformations in urban populations and forms of labour. Theology was formed and reformed by these forces that transcend, engulf, fracture and resist it.

The essays, then, detail various encounters between the theological and non-theological, and so their subject matter is not so much the traditional topoi of Christian theology (the doctrine of God, Christology, Eschatology, Soteriology), but meta-theological points of contact between Christian theology and its external conditions – points at which such traditional topics transform and are transformed by developments in the arts, the natural sciences, philosophy, politics and social conditions. The aim is thereby to analyse concepts illustrative of theology's constant dialogue with the social (Society, The University), natural science (Evolution, Miracles), art (Language, Mysticism), philosophy (Mediation, Immanence and Transcendence) and other religions (the East). More concretely, the volume is broadly structured such that, after an initial two essays that exemplify the above meta-theological approach, it treats nineteenth-century theology's encounter with political, social and institutional changes, then with contemporary scientific developments, before tending to consider theology in relation to other philosophical and historical viewpoints, non-Christian religions and ultimately nineteenth-century writing practices.

Lissa McCullough begins the volume with a survey of the ways in which the concept of God was reinvented, transformed and perverted over the course of the long nineteenth century – or, in her own words, how 'the nineteenth century rescued God from the death of God – at least partially and ambiguously – by the advent of death-of-God thinking'. Such death-of-God thinking, she points out, is not solely limited to usual suspects like Hegel and Nietzsche, but motivates the poetry of Blake, the novels of Dostoevsky, the music of Berlioz, the philosophies of Maimon and Schelling, the historiography of Overbeck, as well as the political atheisms of Stirner and Bakunin. Transformations of the concept of God, accomplished through various emphases on God's death and resurrection, were, McCullough shows, a constant refrain throughout the period.

The second chapter considers how theologians in the nineteenth century fictionalised an a-Christian outside from which to peer back in at the workings of Christianity. Tracing this logic through popular novels of conversion of the period (Charles Kingsley's *Hypatia* and J. H. Newman's *Callista*), George Eliot's heterodox rewriting of this genre in *Romola*, as well as Schleiermacher's *Speeches* and Coleridge's writings on race, I argue that apologists in the nineteenth century confronted the increasing diversity of religious attitudes in Western European societies by describing ever more vividly what it would mean to stand outside the claims of the Christian theological tradition.

Susan Curtis provides an overview of the relation between social changes and the shape of Christian theology in the nineteenth century. In particular, she focuses on American social theology, looking to the intricate entangling of social reform movements and theological thinking at this time. Citing the Settlement House Movement, the Working Men's College, the Fabian Society, New York's Labor Temple and the Brotherhood of the Kingdom, she shows how theologians such as Rauschenbusch and Gladden provided orientation to a generation for whom Christianity was often equivalent to a kind of socialism.

The birth of the modern university and the place of theology within it is the topic of Gerard Loughlin's conceptual genealogy. He focuses on the founding of the University of Berlin and its legacy – with constant reference to Newman's *Idea of a University* – as a case study for the ways in which theology can be excluded and equally fostered in the quest for *Wissenschaft*, as well as, more significantly, the ways in which theology can bear and has borne witness 'to a different way of being university; asking the questions that are not otherwise posed'.

Regula Zwahlen contextualises the Orthodox discourse of *sobornost'* and Solov'ëv's 'free theocracy' in the social and intellectual ferments of the Russian nineteenth century. Charting diverse conceptualisations of freedom as they arose out of liberal, Marxist, Slavophile and populist projects, she shows how theological accounts of freedom were indelibly marked by contemporary political and social debate. In so doing, she demonstrates the problems with ahistorical constructions of theologies of freedom severed from their reference to social context: the Orthodox concept of freedom, for one, is an effect of a cumulative build-up of competing social movements in nineteenth-century Russia.

Roland Boer looks not to the effect of theology on social structures or the effect of social structures on religion, but how theological imagery – specifically the concept of the fetish as formulated in seventeenth- and eighteenth-century histories of religion – affected the theorisation of society or, more precisely, Marx's critique of capitalism. He charts in detail the migration of the concept of fetish from the study of religions to its instantiation as the very form of capital itself (*Kapitalfetisch*). In so doing, he shows how, in Marx's own words, 'capital thus becomes a very mystic being', and also how 'the theological dimension is never far from the surface' in Marx's descriptions of it.

Nineteenth-century debates over divine impassibility and kenotic Christology, the origins of the psychology of emotion and evolutionary genealogies of music are some of the wide-ranging contents of Bennett Zon's study of the effects of theories of evolution on nineteenth-century theologies of art. Zon points to the importance of Herbert Spencer's and Charles Darwin's evolutionary theories in musicological contexts as a means of detailing the slow emergence of theories of divine passibility in modernity, and the roles of an impassible scientist and nature in that genesis.

Ruth Barton argues that the problematisation of the miraculous in Victorian England was not so much due to the triumphant march of a wave of scientist-heroes sweeping away old superstitions, but rather emerged out of a struggle played out in the works of many theologically *and* scientifically inclined thinkers. Barton embarks on three case studies (the Unitarian thinker, Charles Hennell; the Oxford controversialist, Baden Powell; and the Metaphysical Society debates) to show the complexity of the negotiations between the miraculous and the secular in mid-nineteenth-century Britain, concluding that growing scepticism towards miracles was not a result of the authority of specific scientific theories, but a popular, cultural shift that requires further historiographical investigation.

Johannes Zachhuber provides a rigorous *Begriffsgeschichte* of the conceptual opposition of immanence and transcendence, which was a product of nineteenth-century German theology. Charting its emergence in the wake of Kant's critical project and the pantheism controversy, he provides two detailed case studies of its application: in F. C. Baur's historical theology and Albrecht Ritschl's recovery of 'the primacy of the practical'. The point is to reveal – in a way that exemplifies this volume as a whole – the contingent processes of conceptual formation that resulted in ways of thinking about religion that are 'today usually taken for granted and conventionally applied'.

Andrew W. Hass begins his study with the classic theological assertion, found in Paul, Aquinas and elsewhere, that 'when it comes to mediation, only something with difference can act "in between"', and he goes on to consider the production of this internal difference as mediator in regard to the various Romantic and Idealist systems propounded at the beginning of the nineteenth century. That is, Hass considers the implications of the specifics of Fichte, Schelling, Schleiermacher and Hegel's thinking of mediation for Christology. And he argues in particular that while Hegel's valorisation of 'the restlessness of the negative' in all its convolutions is the high point of this theorisation of mediation in the nineteenth century, the subsequent Hegelianisms of the left and the right could not remain faithful to it in their characterisation of the God–human relation.

In his chapter, George Pattison interrogates the commonplace that Christian theology was complicit in the advent of the nineteenth-century historical turn. While theological motivations may have contributed to such a historical turn – indeed, while such a historical turn may well be a secularisation of Christian eschatological templates – Pattison points to the radicalisation of this historicisation in Kierkegaard, Schweitzer, Nietzsche and Burckhardt as a challenge to theological thinking. That is, if the very conditions of understanding history are themselves historicised, then the unified narrative that Christianity tells is put into question. Nineteenth-century theology has, therefore, a much more uneasy relation to history than is usually claimed.

Newman's idea of tradition is the subject of Thomas Pfau's chapter. Pfau sets into context Newman's reaction to romantic sentimentalism (especially as mediated through restoration theologians such as Coleridge, Chateaubriand and de Maistre) and to historicism; he delimits Newman's working out of an idea of tradition through comparison with the Catholic Tübingen School and the work of Franzelin; and finally he evaluates it with constant reference to Hegel, Nietzsche, Blondel and Gadamer; and he does so in order to show the richness and cogency of Newman's position. The result, for Pfau, is a 'reappraisal of tradition that put pressure on modernity's (neo-Stoic) ethos of detached objectivity and critical prevarication'.

Steven Shakespeare's chapter operates in a critical key, putting to the test the vindication of the white, male, Christian, human subject in a range of nineteenth-century theologies. He points to the discursive abjection of the figures of the Jew and the animal as evidence for the violence out of which nineteenth-century theological anthropology is born. Shakespeare writes in a passage that is crucial for the ethos of the volume as a whole:

> The nineteenth-century human is a bridge; however, the ends which tether that bridge are no longer fixed or well understood. The human is stretched between the animal and the divine, but these categories are themselves falling into dispute . . . It is not therefore a matter of deciding for or against the human, any more than it is of deciding for or against the animal and/or God, since there is no pure secular or theological ground on which to do so. Indeed, dreams of such a ground often turn out to be fantasies concealing another violence.

Joseph P. Lawrence considers the ways in which the recuperation of texts from Eastern religions during the nineteenth century provided a challenge to Christian theology. He notes that the 'turn to the East', just like the eighteenth-century fascination with 'the spirit of the Hebrews' which gave birth to it, had good as well as bad consequences. On the one hand, it was caught up in the discourses of colonialism, particularly in Britain and France, leading to a violent othering of the East. Moreover, in Germany particularly, it fed into a growing anti-Semitism that insisted on bypassing Jewish contributions to modern Europe in the name of the Orient. On the other hand, however, Lawrence writes, it fostered a non-sectarian reconception of religion as a practice, rather than a set of dogmas.

The question motivating Joshua Cockayne's chapter concerns the exact nature of the transformation of theories of preaching in nineteenth-century Denmark. He argues that a general reaction against understandings of the sermon as imparting dogma rationalistically led to new models in homiletics, such as the sermon as performance. However, Cockayne provides a sustained study of Kierkegaard's criticisms of many of these developments and suggests that such criticisms are a particularly salient example of Kierkegaard's difference from much theology of the period, especially in regard to his radical distrust of the church.

Katya Tolstaya looks to literature – specifically, Dostoevsky's novels – as the medium through which aspects of Orthodox hesychastic practices were communicated in the nineteenth century. For her, what is particularly significant about the passing references to deification in Zosima's speeches in *The Brothers Karamazov* is that they eschew the anthropocentric interpretation which this doctrine was given elsewhere in the nineteenth century and which has become hegemonic in the twentieth. That is, Dostoevsky grounds Zosima's religious convictions in 'the idea of the unity of creation', which is productive not merely of a community of humans sharing a project of redemption but of an all-inclusive 'world' involved in the soteriological process. This, she concludes, points forward to late twentieth-century ecotheologies.

The language of modern mysticism is the topic considered by Benjamin Dawson in his contribution. He probes the efficacy of kinds of nonsense – or, following William James, 'onsense' – as modes of writing the ineffable, and surveys the relation of such nonsense to the derangement of empiricism, on the one hand, and the rapture of speculative dialectics, on the other. The chapter begins with a discussion of James's uses of the mystic writings of Benjamin Blood, particularly in his rejection of Hegelian monism, before spiralling into a series of considerations that include Böhme's role in nineteenth-century theological thinking and Hegel's invocation of the Eleusinian mysteries. The aim of all Dawson's reflections is to describe the various ways of writing what James in *The Varieties of Religious Experience* calls, 'the mystery of fact'.

Katie Terezakis's chapter concludes the volume. She implicitly takes her cue from von Balthasar's claim in his *Theological Aesthetics* that J. G. Hamann provides a vision of an alternative nineteenth century, that 'he could have become the intellectual and spiritual father of his age', but that 'no one else followed him on his way back to the Fathers', for 'his vision was neglected by German Idealism' ([1961] 1982: 49, 81). Terezakis's contribution, then, envisages the half-acknowledged provocations and subterranean influences that constitute Hamann's impact on nineteenth-century theologies of language. She thus argues that 'Hamann's thinking plots some of the defining predicaments of nineteenth-century thought', even while his name remained conspicuously absent throughout.

Notes

1. I justify in more detail many of the claims made in the following paragraphs in Chapter 2 of this volume, 'The Outside'.
2. This passage is discussed in a similar context in Taylor 2007: 377–8.

References

Lacoue-Labarthe, Philippe and Jean-Luc Nancy [1978] (1988), *The Literary Absolute: The Theory of Literature in German Romanticism*, trans. Philip Barnard and Cheryl Lester, Albany: State University of New York Press.
Mill, John Stuart [1873] (1981), *Autobiography*, ed. John M. Robson and Jack Stillinger, Toronto: University of Toronto Press.
Taylor, Charles (2007), *A Secular Age*, Cambridge, MA: Harvard University Press.
von Balthasar, Hans Urs [1961] (1982), *The Glory of the Lord: A Theological Aesthetics*, vol. 1, trans. Erasmo Leiva-Merikakis, Edinburgh: T&T Clark.

1

The Death of God

Lissa McCullough

Drive your cart and your plow over the bones of the dead. (William Blake, 'Proverbs of Hell', 1793)

The comprehensive story of the death of God is almost too intricate, elaborate, ambitious and ambiguous to be told. It is certainly presumptuous to try. If the referent *God* as redefined repeatedly in religious history offers a multitude of distinct meanings, the *death* of God layers in as many involutions of those meanings. In terms of the hermeneutic demanded to tell this tale, we must concede this to be as elusive a topic as can be raised, involving as it does not merely historical, metaphysical or semiotic dimensions, but all these at once in fractious, unstable concert and dissonance. As soon as we get past the jingoism of the phrase 'death of God' that dates back to debates of the 1960s – a legacy interesting in its own right – we face a thousand decisions and indecisions, ironies and reversals. Symbols are born in human history, live out their meanings, and die carrying with them the most significant and portentous values under the sun. Who contributed more to 'killing' the God of Jesus: Clement of Alexandria, William of Ockham or Friedrich Nietzsche? What contributed more to dooming modern faith: Descartes' theism, Hume's empiricism or Kant's ineffectual bid to make room for faith? When was God most alive in the first place: in the time of Jesus and his followers, before theology got hold of him; in the golden age of Thomas Aquinas, when God was most majestically articulated but already sinking into the abyss of the nominalist challenge; or only today, released at last (in theory) from the delusory entrapments of ontotheology (Heidegger [1927] 1976)? Is the death of God essentially a revenge of Christian Aristotelianism on Christian Platonism? Or is it rather a victory to be celebrated of rising global Christianity over the dying star of imperial-colonial Christendom? 'Then how should I begin?' asks J. Alfred Prufrock wisely, 'And how should I presume?'

Unless the Seed Dies ...

In a sense, historical theology tells the history of thoughtful disavowal of a given God to make room for a God-reconception or God-idea more worthy and adequate, more *actual* in the Hegelian sense. The sociologist of religion, Jacob Taubes, posited this as a key principle when he wrote: 'The progress in theological interpretation throughout history runs parallel with a gradual withdrawal of divine presence. Theological "re-presentation" and theological interpretation are driven deeper and deeper into the web of dialectics because the divine presence is more and more veiled' (1954: 25). Arguably – and Nietzsche's lifelong friend Franz Overbeck did argue this – the fateful withdrawal of God occurred already at the dawn of nascent Christianity. Marcel Gauchet offers a complement to Taubes, arguing that with the death of God in Western Christendom, the system of religion – *religiousness* in its most robust original form – has self-declared the end of its dominion; we Westerners today are inhabitants of a world that 'at a certain point completely turned its back on the reign of the gods', not at the level of personal belief but at the level of effective social organisation (1985: 199).

For Gauchet, the French Revolution only completed this millennial process, which began during the Axial Age with the rise of the state. The end of religion's dominion became possible because religion reached the end of its power as a system built on collective *denial* or *refusal* – a response to something 'unbearable' – because this dread has been gradually mitigated in the course of history precisely by the axial transformation (ibid. 199, 22, 25–6). This unbearable actuality was, apparently, the terrifying freedom of facing an absolutely an-archic world of experience. If relative freedom is a blessing, absolute freedom has been forefended historically by religiousness as an intolerable abyss, an existential black hole. But according to Gauchet's thesis, Christianity has proven to be 'a religion for departing from religion' (ibid. 4); the gradual emancipation from and death of God has trained and conditioned us Westerners to withstand the asphyxiating terror of freedom. Western Christendom is uniquely a civilisation of apostates, per this interpretation.

The import of Nietzsche's famous madman passage in *The Gay Science* ([1882] 1974: §125) is that the 'murder' of God, though it has *long* since occurred, is 'still on its way' in the late nineteenth century, more distant from the murderers themselves 'than the most distant stars'. Cultured despisers in the marketplace mock the madman's distress because none have awakened to the corrosive ramifications and consequences about to devastate their Enlightenment values, purported to be universal. The full terror qua loss, the abyssal implications have yet to be played out, indeed, to be abjectly suffered. Just as passengers on the *Titanic* continued to dine as the unsinkable ship took on water, so by analogy was the death of God a fait accompli long before the structures of civilisation were able to absorb its absolute consequentiality. An omnipotent God of ultimate concern is invasive of every single relative concern and presupposition of a civilisation. Even if an instant is sufficient to complete the thought-deed in an individual mind, the social-political-moral layers of society, habituated by vested interests and grounded *ab origine* in religious axioms, ensure that historically the deed can only be effected very slowly: during that time the thought-deed will almost certainly be converted by the enchainments of tradition and entrenchments of the status quo into something fatefully resembling the old idea, and not merely once but again and again. To offer only one example, Kant's religion 'within the limits of reason alone' drew all its key terms from the Bible: it consists in 'a way of living with the Fall, according to the Law, in the Hope of attaining the Kingdom of Freedom' (O'Neill 1991: 4).

The point to be taken is, even if overt language of the death of God first occurred in the nineteenth century, the nineteenth century did not kill God. God was banished from this world virtually overnight as an epochal consequence of late medieval nominalism, commencing in the late thirteenth century, giving rise to the autonomous domain of modern natural science and its correlative philosophy, and undermining the conceptual foundations of the revealed God of *sacra doctrina* – a disjuncture that proved inexorable and irreparable (Knowles 1962: 265–306; Oberman 1963; Huizinga [1919] 1996; Fabro 1968; Gillespie 1995, 2008; Depoortere 2007). On the heels of this 'exile' of God from nature, the 'death' of God was effectively confirmed in the scientific-critical revolutions of the seventeenth and eighteenth centuries. By the early nineteenth century, God had been demoted to a deistic hypothesis at best – whether a helpful or harmful one remained open to polemical debate. The century's most resolutely atheistic humanists and political thinkers (Feuerbach, Stirner, Proudhon, Marx, Bakunin) were already impatient to banish all residual vestiges of Christianity, even while the cultural-humanistic-pathetic implications of God's banishment had hardly begun to be absorbed *within* religious, philosophical and imaginative-poetic thought – that is, as a devastation of value to be responded to with creative energy and insight. What came to birth in Blake, Schelling, Hegel and – most paradoxically – in Kierkegaard were new-found conceptions or envisionments of God as self-transfiguring in relation to nature and history, rather than eternally impassible and immutable.

A complex either/or faced nineteenth-century post-theism: either reconstruct human relatedness to God on new philosophical-theological grounds (Schelling, Hegel, Schleiermacher, Kierkegaard) or prophesy a new creative vision to supplant the dead divinity (Blake, Nietzsche) or turn away from God towards a chaste atheistic scepticism (Overbeck) or define a bold transvaluation of material existence without God (Stirner, Feuerbach, Marx, Comte). Sceptical-deconstructive and creative-constructive dimensions of this mandate operated in tandem. Sceptical thinking worked to negate the outdated divine presuppositions, purging the received God of tradition from all equations. Constructive thinking advanced to posit a new hope: a new God or humanism or egoistic individualism conceived as better or truer or more vital and defensible than the defunct God whose time has passed.

If the progress of modern philosophy under the relentless pressure of scepticism can be regarded as an 'ingenuity of failures' (Preuss 1987: vii), nineteenth-century philosophy's importance consisted in the creative ways it confronted and prosecuted an already late moment in the death-of-God historical process. With considerable degree of success it rescued, retrieved and transfigured God, reviving and reconceiving the unique intentionality of that concept-word in ways that are experienced even today – more than a century later – as live options. It makes perfect sense, in retrospect, to pose our leading question in full irony: how did nineteenth-century thinking rescue God from the death of God by means of death-of-God thinking?

Blake and Stirner

Although Hegel and Nietzsche are first to be mentioned when explicit language of the death of God is broached, alternate forerunners deserve to be cited in the same breath. The English poet William Blake, in identifying God with human imagination and postulating divine-human imagination as transcending Lockean sense perception, envisioned an intimate co-embodiment of human and divine, a God fully incarnate in humanity; expressed in Blake's own words, 'God is Man & exists in us & we in him', a coincidence that Blake names elsewhere as 'The Eternal Great Humanity Divine' (Frye 1947: 30). Half a century before Feuerbach offered his theory of God as human projection in *The Essence of Christianity* (1841), this far more sophisticated alternative to Feuerbach shone in the darkness. Blake's conception of the divine was inseparable from the 'death' or dissolution of God as traditionally conceived. Indeed, the contemporary death-of-God theologian, Thomas Altizer, consistently credits Blake with having been the first visionary to depict the death of God in his 1793 poem *America*: 'The Heavens melted from north to south; and Urizen ... emerg'd his leprous head / From out his holy shrine, his tears in deluge piteous / Falling into the deep sublime! ... Weeping in dismal howling woe he dark descended howling' (Blake 1982: 'America', plate 16, lines 2–9).

So momentous is Blake's poetic vision of the 'Self-Annihilation of God', melting away and emptying out his 'stored snows' and 'icy magazines', that Altizer closely correlates Blake with Hegel on the basis of this parallelism: 'The "Divine Image" dies in Jesus so as to abolish the solitary God who is the source of judgment and bring about an apocalyptic brotherhood that is a full coming together of God and man' (Blake 1982: 'Jerusalem', lines 23–8; Altizer 1967: 207). But the self-annihilation of Urizen, the abstract God of Enlightenment reason, cannot be understood as a simple nullification of divine presence; it is rather the self-transfiguration of God to become present in human form. Blake wrote quite earnestly, 'I am in Gods presence night & day / And he never turns his face away' (1982: 481). God is transmuted into creative-poetic spirit incarnate, or in terms of Blakean prophesy, the fiery Los.

A profoundly nihilistic counterpoint to Blake's 'Human Form Divine' surfaces with Max Stirner, another who deserves mention when explicit language of the death of God is broached. Almost forty years before Nietzsche's madman announced the death of God, Stirner professed his radical atheist position in *The Ego and His Own* (1844). It was Stirner's conviction, against the highest hopes of naïve humanism, that the death of God means inexorably that the *man* in the God-man equation also must die:

> At the entrance to the modern time stands the 'God-man.' At its exit will only the God in the God-man evaporate? And can the God-man really die if only the God in him dies? They [Man] did not think of this question, and thought they were through when in our days they brought to a victorious end the work of the Enlightenment, the vanquishing of God: they did not notice that Man has killed God in order to become now – 'sole God on high.' The *other world beyond us* is indeed brushed away, and the great undertaking of the Enlighteners completed; but the *other world within us* has become a new heaven and calls us forth to renewed heaven-storming: God has had to give place, yet not to us but – to Man [*nicht Uns, sondern – den Menschen*]. How can you believe that the God-man is dead before the Man in him, besides the God, is dead? ([1844] 1971: 109; translation modified)

For Blake, God is embodied in human imagination so as to live on in human form; thus both are saved. Neither true God nor true humanity is lost. For Stirner, in diametric contrast, it is not only God who must die but the humanity who loved and lived for him, and indeed who holds anything sacred apart from the individual (*der Einzige*) since '*everything sacred is a tie, a fetter*' (ibid. 142).

Homo religiosus must die. God is a fixed idea that has subjected the individual to itself; once you recognise this fixed idea to be a folly, you shut up its slaves in an asylum. God will only be truly dead when the last shadow of the sacred is foresworn in each individual heart and mind, and this includes every moral conceit since 'moral people skimmed off the best fat from religion, and ate it themselves'. Every nation-state holds itself sacred, higher than the individual, demanding patriotic self-sacrifice, tyrannical towards the one. For the state, every one *in himself* is indifferent, a nothing. But 'when mankind is buried, I am my own, I am the laughing heir [*der lachende Erbe*]!' (ibid. 59, 64, 142–3). With a Kierkegaard-like conviction that the individual is what counts above all else in the world, Stirner stands absolutely for the anarchistic an-arche of the existing individual: 'Up with me!' (ibid. 143). Instead of making the leap of faith with Kierkegaard, he makes the resolute plunge to the dissolution of God without remainder. God and state are zeroed out and I am the laughing heir.

Political Implications

The arc of ascending Christian Platonism (in the Greek Fathers, Augustine, Eriugena) vaunted and perfected the doctrine of God's absoluteness, aseity and essential immutability. As it reached systematic apogee, Aristotelian criticism pressed a descent into immanence (in Thomas Aquinas, Duns Scotus, Ockham). Aristotelian thinking was brought to bear in conceptualising the implications of divine incarnation in relation to the world. The gradual collapse of God qua transcendent asserted pressure and opportunity to reinvent and re-establish God qua immanent. Thus the death of God is susceptible of being interpreted as the emergence, insistence and triumph of a commitment to incarnation, enacting the full actuality and palpability of incarnation in the material flesh of the world (Leahy 2003). The nineteenth century was to take up its portion of this task: God as immutable metaphysical transcendent was vanquished by God as empirical change. The century was to generate various this-worldly reformulations of God as self-manifesting in time and history rather than as known speculatively and metaphysically as he is necessarily in himself.

Descartes banished the *biblical* God by philosophising a purely rational deity in relation to material nature (*extensio*) and the human mind (*cogitatio*) in an inquiry conducted entirely, he presumed, on natural, strictly non-biblical grounds. In so doing, philosophy enacted an epochal liberation of thinking, fostering radical *tabula rasa* thought-projects that would restlessly reinvent and recast this material–spiritual dualism in new terms with extraordinary persistence, initiating a repetition-compulsion of sorts that ended only with Husserl. The radical Cartesian diremption between *extensio* and *cogitatio* meant that, after the close of the seventeenth century, natural science took charge of material nature and philosophy took charge of cogitating minds (Whitehead [1925] 1953: 145). The new cosmology unveiled a universe infinite in extension and duration in which eternal matter moves endlessly and aimlessly in eternal space in accordance with necessary and eternal laws (Brague 2007; Funkenstein 1986; Becker 1932: 33–70).

This universe inherited all the *ontological* attributes of deity, but *only* those – 'all the others the departed God took away with him' (Koyré [1957] 1958: 276). The universe under the aspect of *extensio* was understood to embody the will of God, but blotted out all moral and spiritual values, the orienting divine teleology that gave human life purpose and meaning. Descartes' famous contemporary Pascal witnesses in *Pensées* to the trembling dread of existing between two gaping abysses: infinity and nothingness. Having been charged with superabundant value and meaning, God now had to be radically reconceived if this supreme value was not to perish in the mechanistic indifference of the new godless cosmos. The absolutely transcendent God vaunted by Western monotheism, a deity who does not and cannot change, had to be transformed or perish of existential irrelevance. Human existence suddenly had too much of impassibility.

God's metaphysical scaffolding collapsed in the transition from late medieval to early modern with a swiftness comparable to the collapse of a speculative financial bubble – a telling analogy that merits elaboration (McCullough 2014). This collapse fomented not only spiritual and intellectual crises but also crises of political authority that played out in the wars and repressions of the Reformation and the modern European revolutions. Carl Schmitt's often-cited claim that the authority of God is the basis of all authority became increasingly evident as divine authority began to erode and decay. Schmitt traces out how deism and the banishment of miracle arose in parallel with the modern constitutional state; a 'battle against God' by the likes of Proudhon, Comte and Bakunin ensued. For Proudhon, 'mankind had to be substituted for God' (Schmitt [1934] 1985: 36, 50, 53). Proudhon and Bakunin excoriated God, the former inveighing that 'God is hypocrisy and falsehood; God is tyranny and misery; God is evil'; the latter seconding, 'we believe it our duty to recover from heaven the goods which it has stolen and return them to earth', for 'God being master, man is the slave' (Bakunin [1871] 1882: 36, 24, 25). Bakunin's epigraph to his major work reverses Voltaire's famous dictum, asserting: 'If God really existed it would be necessary to abolish him' (ibid. 3).

While pure anarchists like Stirner and Bakunin were single-mindedly coherent due to their ideological clarity, the liberal bourgeoisie was two-faced. Schmitt notes the dual front fought by the rising bourgeoisie: it was driven leftwards by its hatred of monarchy and aristocracy, yet its fear of being divested of property drove it rightwards towards monarchy backed by military might – a 'curious contradiction'. In effect, it wanted 'neither the sovereignty of the king nor the people'. The bourgeoisie wanted a God, but its God could not become active; liberal constitutionalism permitted the king to remain on the throne, but sought to paralyse him through parliament. The conservative monarchist Donoso Cortés (d. 1853) compared this with the inconsistency committed by deism when it excluded God from the world but held onto his existence (Schmitt [1934] 1985: 59–60). Once victorious over the old regime, the bourgeoisie was happy to annex both clergy and nobility as soon as they accepted its political, economic and moral direction; but hardly having come to power, it betrayed its allies in the very bottom strata of society by 'shoving them back into the gulf' (de Ligt 1938: 40). This theopolitical double-face – 'authority is dead, long live authority!' – has predominated in Western liberal societies ever since.

Maimon and Hegel

The generation opening with Kant brought forth the German idealist movement in the universities, which Randall Collins declares in his monumental study of the sociology of global philosophies to be 'one of the most intense outpourings of philosophical creativity in world history'. The movement's ebullient creativity flew in the face of the dominant themes of the Enlightenment – the death of the supernatural, the termination of metaphysical speculation and the replacement of philosophy by empirical science – and swooped in to wrest theology away from the churches into secular hands (Collins 1998: 613–18, 622). Kant's response to Hume, in particular, provoked a renewal not only of epistemology but also of metaphysics. Despite his valiant effort to refute Hume's sceptical demolition of causality – a refutation indispensable for making the world safe for natural science – Kant failed to convince. He did not succeed in accounting for how two utterly heterogeneous faculties, understanding and sensibility, could cooperate with one another; his strenuous effort to do so ultimately begged the question: he did not have a criterion to determine when synthetic a priori concepts apply to a posteriori intuitions. He described what conditions would be needed (*quid juris*), but did not demonstrate whether or when it actually occurs (*quid facti*). This unbridgeable understanding–sensibility dualism in Kant was patterned on the intractable mind–body dualism in Descartes (Beiser 1987: 288–9, 291, 325; 1993, 11). In fact, far from curtailing Cartesian doubt, Kant '*extends* it infinitely along the new divide between all transcendental ideas [including God] and the possibility of their realization in time and space' (Leahy 2003: 42; Franks 2000: 108). This failure of

Kant's transcendental deduction to bridge a priori and a posteriori knowledge was demonstrated most decisively by Kant's obscure contemporary Solomon Maimon (d. 1800), who thereby raised one of the fundamental problems of post-Kantian idealism – as Beiser, Franks and Socher separately argue – and who also proposed the most tenable solution. If the highest formal principle is maximally indeterminate, a maximally determining 'lowest principle' was needed to bridge the gap between form and matter (Franks 2000: 108).

Maimon found the breakthrough in Spinoza, whose thought constituted an early modern revolution unto itself, an utterly radical abolition of the Cartesian dichotomy; in a single stroke, at least when read monistically, Spinoza conflated *extensio* and *cogitatio*, God and world, and in so doing struck a fatal blow against the biblical-historical God and the transcendent-deistic God alike. Maimon's breakthrough recuperated an aspect of Spinoza's monism to defeat Kantian epistemological dualism, though whether with an intention to destroy or reconstruct Kant remains ambiguous (Socher 2006: 106; Beiser 1987: 286–7; Franks 2000: 109). Spinoza had already posited that mental and physical, subjective and objective, are different attributes of a single infinite substance, and human thought, insofar as it arrives at adequate ideas, approximates the *cogitatio* of God qua *natura naturans*. It is in fact the same *act* of knowledge by which we and God know something; this means that the difference between divine and human knowledge is no longer qualitative, as previously thought, but only quantitative (Funkenstein 1986: 290–1). This co-knowing of God and human *cogitatio* made possible the main principle of Maimon's theory: the idea of an infinite subjective understanding that is immanent in materiality, or in Beiser's characterisation:

> If synthetic a priori concepts are to apply to experience, then it is necessary to postulate Leibniz's and Malebranche's idea of an infinite understanding that is present within our finite understanding and that creates not only the form but also the content of experience. . . . Thanks to Maimon, the Kantian transcendental ego acquired a new metaphysical status: it became a single universal subject present within the consciousness of every individual, unifying the finite subject and object. Maimon's infinite understanding is thus the forerunner of Fichte's *Ich* and Hegel's *Geist*. (1987: 286–7)

The immanent infinite understanding posited by Maimon made him 'the great philosopher of immanence' in the context of the critical tradition, in the judgement of Daniel W. Smith, since almost all Maimon's critiques of Kant are aimed at eliminating the illegitimate vestiges of transcendence that still remain in Kant, the most vexing example of this being the thing-in-itself (Smith 2000: 125; Beiser 1987: 303). Construing insights from Spinoza, Leibniz and Maimonides' adaptation of Aristotle, Maimon posited a holistic solution to the Kantian impasse as to how a priori concepts can apply to experience, one that was accepted by all the key thinkers of early German idealism: Fichte, Schelling, Hegel and perhaps the Kant of the third *Critique* as well. (Kant admired Maimon, Fichte confessed a respect for him that 'knows no bounds', Schelling clearly read him and for Hegel indirect influence is established; Socher 2006: 104–6.) All sought to resolve this irremediable dualism through development of the infinite intuitive intellect (*intellectus archetypus*) (Beiser 1993: 11; Socher 2006: 89–92).

It would seem hard to overemphasise what happens in the metaphysical movement that takes place at this moment on the eve of the nineteenth century. From the status of being an *essentially* acosmic God *a se* – who nonetheless de facto created – a perilous crossing is achieved, an immanental passage, and from here forward it is not only that God's laws or ideas imprint the world from outside as a consequence of creation; now, for the first time in mainstream Western thought, divine understanding essentially bursts into, occupies and indwells the world, and the world becomes, in a qualified sense, God's body. 'Without *Godhead* the world cannot be *thought*', Maimon wrote, 'but, without the world, the *Godhead* cannot be known' (Franks 2000: 109). Spinoza's rationalistic conflation of God and nature, *Deus sive Natura*, is transfigured from an acosmism (an insight that Hegel credited to Maimon) into an incarnationalism. The world, rather than merely *depending* on God, *expresses* materially the essential nature of God. God *requires* the substance of the world to become freely revealed to himself. God's transcendence, independence and invulnerability vis-à-vis the world is now breached absolutely – the old Christian God perishes in this transition – and God now becomes absolute Subject creatively imbuing all existence, the absolute inhabitant of historical time. This transition marks the historic eclipse or 'death' of God conceived in terms of aseity and the advent of a modern new God-idea.

The God-thinking of Schelling and Hegel hinged on this immanental passage. They regarded their own new approach to metaphysics as a form of scientific naturalism, insisting that the metaphysical principles of their philosophies can and should be confirmed through experience. Both a priori and a posteriori are products of *natural* reason. All we need to know is nature; the sum total of human knowledge of God is encountered through experience in the this-worldly context of nature. Both young thinkers appreciated how Spinoza naturalised God, conceiving God as nothing other than *natura naturans*, the universe as a whole, making a religion out of nature itself. Nature is not a mere mechanism, nor is spirit (*Geist*) a ghost emanating from outside the machine, but a life sprung up within it. Since natural laws consist not only of the mechanistic physics of the seventeenth century but also the vitalistic biological science of the eighteenth and nineteenth centuries – concerned with generation, growth, stages of development and death – the striving of an absolute subject realising itself in and through nature became thinkable (Beiser 2003: 138–41).

In his essay on freedom (1809), Schelling wants to put aside completely the concept of immanence that expresses a 'dead conceptual inclusion of things in God' in favour of seeing things as having their basis 'in that within God which is not God himself' but is God's basis for *becoming* himself (Schelling [1809] 2006: 33–4). For Schelling, intellectual intuition is an experience-based form of perception that can provide the basis for a purely immanent metaphysics. The young Hegel absorbed and critically recast this Schellingian stance in his *Phenomenology of Spirit* ([1807] 1977), which attempted an immanent metaphysics based on experience alone, but one that claimed to follow the path of rigorous *science* (*Wissenschaft*) (Beiser 1993: 15–16, 20; Harris 1993: 45). Although science at its first beginning was bound to have a visionary quality, 'intuition' must be resolved into a truly *speculative* method of rigorous discursive reasoning (Harris 1993: 44). His entire philosophical career thereafter proposed a post-critical take on how the unconditioned truth of scientific reason can be achieved by, as Orrin F. Summerell puts it, propounding the complete conceivability of reason's autonomy, and therewith its unconditional ground in and as the necessary movement of self-thinking thought: 'Bearing itself in itself, self-thinking thought . . . supplies itself with its own Whence and Whither' (Summerell 2002: 180–1). Adapting Maimon's immanent infinite understanding, Hegel's finite spirit (*der endliche Geist*) qua immanent within infinite Spirit (*der unendliche Geist*), is able to tap into the Absolute's unconditioned contact with the world, which is identically its contact with itself (Leahy 2003: 54).

Hegel was the first thinker to propose an organic philosophical interpretation of the global history of religions and to embark on a vast, painstaking scholarly documentation of the subject (*Lectures on the Philosophy of Religion*, [1821–31] 1988); Schelling made a similar effort in the same era. They were concerned not only with reconstructing the history of religions but with addressing the question of their relative truth (Pagano 2012: 53). Presumably, the ecumenical spirit of their research was subtended by the new metaphysics they embraced: religions evolve organically as the self-knowledge of God – *Geist* – emerges historically from the matrix of nature. Thus, rather ironically, after Descartes had purged from the domain of reason all adversion to the historically revealed God of the Bible, Hegel instituted a God who is essentially the self-revelation of reason in history, telling the old Christian story again but within a truly omni-comprehensive tale.

History, indeed, becomes the universal theatre of divine self-sacrifice in Hegel. This is because incarnation implies the assumption of finitude, and to achieve finitude to the furthest extreme implies – even necessitates – death; kenosis in the form of death is thus the climax of incarnation, wherein God's divinity is accomplished (ibid. 65). It is precisely by virtue of this incarnational principle – which sources our life and our death – that we qua finite spirit are related to God (Yerkes 1983: 116–17, 136–7). And yet, despite the explicit pathos-laden language of the death of God in Hegel's work (Carlson 1999: 22–49; Kosky 2004), it is important to note that Hegel's God cannot die *in principio*: given that the beginning of God is not essentially historical – not actual – the absolute cannot *actually* die (Leahy 1996: 596). In Hegel, death is sublated into the infinity of the divine life by God's taking death upon himself, as William Franke notes, and thereby death is negated and overcome, achieving 'the death of death' (Franke 2007: 217). Hegel's God renders the world intrinsically necessary for God's free self-realisation on de facto grounds, and in so doing Hegel's God sacrifices absolutely the orthodox God of transcendent aseity. Yet Hegel's God himself – *der absolute Zombie* – can never and will never die. As Alain Badiou expresses this infinite immanence of God, in Hegel 'the infinite is merely the void in which the repetition of the finite operates' (Badiou [1988] 2005: 173); hence:

> the bad infinity is bad due to the very same thing that makes it good in Hegelian terms: it does not break the ontological immanence of the one; better still, it derives from the latter. . . . The pure multiple detains in itself the count-as-one. (Ibid. 169)

The primordial privilege of the Infinite-cum-Totality is the raison d'être of every particular.

Overbeck and Nietzsche

In 1873, Nietzsche wrote to his Basel colleague, Franz Overbeck, 'Two twins from the one house went bravely out into the world to tear the world's paper-tigers [*Welt-Drachen*] to pieces', making reference to the boarding house they cohabited at the time (Overbeck [1873] 2005: 26). Odd twins in lifelong fellowship, their temperaments formed a diametric contrast. While Nietzsche was empowered to thought by the bracing energy of detestation, Overbeck held close to the Spinozist credo: *non ridere, non lugere, neque detestari, sed intelligere*. He was intensely yet dispassionately curious, quietly but radically sceptical, a strictly scrupulous scholar, indeed, 'a self-mortifying monk of scholarship', his Basel colleague attested, 'an absolutely honest mind', in Löwith's estimation (O'Neill 1991: 180; Löwith 1964: 388). An outsider with no clear religious conviction, he drifted into the study of theology where, among fellow theology students, he felt 'like a Hottentot'. He was appointed at Basel expressly to represent the liberal tendency in modern Protestant theology, to help the University of Basel keep current with the hottest new trends, and from then forward, on the grounds of a painstakingly scrutinised historical record, he worked with keen diligence to expose the critical untenability of that very liberal tendency. His work was not only a challenge to liberal theology but to all theology per se, and to the possibility of reconciling authentic Christianity with authentic modernity (Gossman 2000: 419–20).

Overbeck's methodological approach as church historian was to presuppose that scholarship and religion are mutually destructive ([1873] 2005: 42); therefore, his only theological function as a professor of theology, he acknowledged in his memoir, was to pronounce the Last Judgment on Christianity (O'Neill 1991: 179). Having no positive theological agenda of his own, Overbeck demonstrated an extraordinary and rare fidelity to Christianity by means of the perfectly unbiased scrupulosity of his historical research. He came to view Christianity as a religion whose original expression was sealed in the past, an inaccessible enigma. He claimed that historical investigation reveals that Christianity in its original form was fundamentally apocalyptic in character, and he regarded all later centuries of Christian history as a betrayal of early Christianity. 'Original Christianity no more expected to have a theology than it expected to have any kind of history on this earth', he wrote. 'Indeed, Christianity entered this world announcing its imminent end' ([1873] 2005: 34; cf. Law 2012: 224–5). *Urchristentum* has not existed, has not been possible or retrievable, since the imminent apocalypticism of the original first-century communities – unrequited by God, let us say – was abandoned.

Overbeck opined that the earliest testimonies of Christianity were created in a kind of literary vacuum for internal consumption within the community, not for a wider exoteric public; though drawing on Jewish traditions, these communities showed no tendency to grow into or fuse with the surrounding Roman-Hellenic culture. There was no call to codify the teachings or create institutions since there would be no future for the world as they knew it. But the actual contexts and themes of this *Urliteratur* were soon occluded in the process of canonisation for the sake of transhistorical and universal applicability, and thenceforward they ceased to be understood. Thus Overbeck considered Christianity a historically obsolete phenomenon, a religion of crisis and immediate decision; he pointed to the unrepeatability of its origins and the impossibility of extracting any timeless substance from them (Sommer 2003: 81, 102).

Based on this view, Overbeck showed the inherent contradictions between the primitive church and the manifold forms of its subsequent secularisation in ancient and medieval worlds. A theology was elaborated only when it became necessary to take account of the fact that the world was not coming to an end, at least not immediately (Gossman 2000: 421). The struggle between faith and knowledge was fought out in the very cradle of Christianity, when Gnosticism destroyed all the historical presuppositions of early Christian faith, turning it into a metaphysical system instead of a popular religion, and doing so by quasi-violent means; rational theology was forced on the church by the earliest Alexandrians through an act of violence (Overbeck [1873] 2005: 34–5). Monasticism, by establishing an alternative to literal martyrdom in the form of the *martyrium quotidianum*, managed to ensure the church's survival into the medieval period, saving Christianity from obsolescence, but only by changing it at the core (ibid. 84).

This unbridgeable distance of *Urchristentum* held a fortiori for all modern manifestations of Christian faith (Sommer 2003: 88). Again, religious faith and the critical theology that seeks to construe it conceptually are mutually destructive in Overbeck's eyes:

While rational knowledge can no doubt destroy a religion, it can never restore it to what it was before. In the modern period [Christian theology proves this], though not so much by the devastation science has wrought in the area of Christian faith, as by the sterility of theology's own attempt, undertaken in response, to reconstruct the Christian religion by means of pure, unfettered scholarship. . . . Of all people, it is the theologians who can turn Christianity into something which – whatever else it may be – is no longer Christianity. ([1873] 2005: 45–6)

Overbeck and Nietzsche shared the judgement that contemporaries in modern Christendom are actually incapable of grasping the true nature of Christianity (Henry 2005: xxxi), but the two differed between themselves on this very question. While Overbeck honoured the limits of the historical record and the social-political communitarian nature of original Christianity, Nietzsche's quest for transvaluation and his faith in the *solitaire* destiny of the super-creative individual skewed his perspective tendentiously beyond the limits of the historical record.

Religiously speaking, Nietzsche shared with Hegel an impatience to transition from the *unglückliche Bewußtsein*, the alienated unhappy consciousness of Christian legacy, to what Nietzsche evokes as *geistreicher und glückliche übermut* ([1901] 1967: §1019), a happy spirited exuberance of post-Christian joyful wisdom (*fröhliche Wissenschaft*). Nietzsche sought to define a double-edged nihilistic-creative praxis; what we find lauded in his work is not the will to believe, but 'the will to create – the will to put meaning into the chaos of existence, and certainly not to find it there' (Leahy 2003: xi). Nietzsche invented his own version of the historical Jesus: a quasi-Buddhist Jesus who liberated himself from *ressentiment*, who conquered suffering and achieved 'blessedness' by resisting nothing, reacting to nothing ([1888] 1990: §27–41, [1901] 1967: §207), whose teachings exemplify a '*way of life*, not a system of beliefs' ([1901] 1967: §212). The life and teachings of Jesus exemplified a praxis of *amor fati*. Nietzsche did not embrace Jesus's 'blessedness' as his own highest ideal because he considered it a decadent (passive) rather than a creative (active) form of this praxis. His Zarathustra, by contrast, embodies the creative form, exercising abundant strength rather than hypersensitivity, passivity and withdrawal. Yet Nietzsche does admire Jesus for having lived a life free of *ressentiment*, likewise free of the illusion of a transcendent world or metaphysical final cause to justify life. Jesus taught a mode of existence that would render moot and useless everything that later Christianity came to propagate as 'divine truth'. There has been only one Christian, Nietzsche wrote famously, and he died on the cross ([1888] 1990: §39).

The way in which Nietzsche execrated Paul for turning Christianity into a religion (e.g. [1888] 1990: §42) stems from his contact with Overbeck (as well as the source criticism of Julius Wellhausen, published in 1878), though Overbeck certainly cannot be held responsible for its crudity or its vehemence. The perishing of metaphysics and dogmatic theology, Nietzsche thought, makes possible a recovery of the Christian ideal that was exemplified in Jesus's life, but then misconstrued and perverted by Paul into a metaphysical doctrine of Jesus's death. Hence the pre-Pauline meaning and value of Jesus's ideal, the actual witness of Jesus's life, is available for the first time only in our era: Christianity has 'only now attained to approximately the state of culture in which it can fulfill its original vocation . . . in which it can show itself pure' ([1901] 1967: §219). For Nietzsche, 'Christianity is still possible at any time' (ibid. §212).

So then, long before Heidegger posited the possibility of a post-ontotheological Christianity, Nietzsche did so. An authentic Christianity 'has absolutely no need of metaphysics' (ibid. §212). An original Christian ideal not only remains possible after the death of God, but the death of God actually opens up a post-dogmatic horizon in which Jesus's life and teachings may at last receive a non-metaphysical interpretation, viewed from a non-religious perspective: 'a Christianity is possible, but without the absurd dogmas', 'not tied to any of the impudent dogmas that have adorned themselves with its name' (ibid. §§239, 212). Christian value judgements have not by any means been overcome by either modern natural sciences or modern values: '"Christ on the cross" is the most sublime symbol even today' (ibid. §219).

Anti-Christianity diatribes became Nietzsche's spur to envision a new religious praxis, a passionate faith in overcoming a decadent, domesticated, declining humanity, whether in accordance with the creative self-sacrificial ideal of Zarathustra ('abundant strength wants to create, suffer, go under', ibid. §222), or another ideal. But let us take notice: these are *ideals*, highly individualist *solitaire* ideals. Nietzsche validated the heroic overcoming of the exceptional individual; Overbeck did not. Distrusting what he considered to be Nietzsche's megalomaniac egoism, Overbeck regarded Nietzsche's *übermensch* as a residue of the very philosophical idealism Nietzsche so tirelessly lambasted. 'What an idea cannot achieve', Overbeck wrote, 'the idea of an idea is even less able to achieve.' Humanity is marked by its solidarity, for Overbeck – 'humanity [*Menschlichkeit*] is still our highest title to glory' (Gossman 2000: 435–6) – and humanity has far more use for the heroism of everyday acts than for superhuman drama. A quietly stoic knight of infinite resignation, Overbeck forged his career into a remarkable witness to historical Christianity in the full range of its paradoxicality. Meanwhile, he wrote of the spiritual darkness he experienced as a modern:

> Our defection from the old and our falling away from it are irreparable. . . . Having come so far, we have no option but to press on further. . . . If our falling away has truly extinguished all light for us, we can least expect to receive new illumination by turning back, and we can be sure that it can only lie ahead of us. (Ibid. 422)

Schweitzer and Kierkegaard

The more comprehensively the banishment of the metaphysical God registered in modern sensibility, the more the quest for the historical Jesus heated up. As God qua Father, first person of the Trinity, underwent profound assault and radical reconceptualisation, one of the burning questions of the day took shape: can Jesus be retrieved as the Truth and the Way; can he, qua God incarnate, become the saviour of God, by means of whom God will be returned to us via history's backdoor? The cherished bid was to get close to the God who once walked on earth, to carry his kerymatic message straight into the present, uncompromised by metaphysical interventions and undefiled by 'the inventions of men' (as Luther called all unbiblical sacerdotal hocus pocus). As John O'Neill wryly notes:

> even German theologians who openly or covertly accepted that God was dead and the crucial events 'mythical' – Semler, Eichhorn, David Friedrich Strauss, Ferdinand Christian Baur, above all Bultmann – showed that the Bible retained its authority by devoting the enormous scholarly energy of their lives to expounding it. (1991: 3)

Albert Schweitzer, in 1906, published the definitive book on the nineteenth century's quest for the historical Jesus, ultimately pronouncing the quest a failure: 'Those who are fond of talking about negative theology can find their account here. There is nothing more negative than the result of the critical study of the life of Jesus' ([1906] 1960: 398). Schweitzer's explanation for the failure closely paralleled the critique of liberal Protestant theology set forth by Overbeck, though the latter is not mentioned. Through 'forced and arbitrary interpretations' of the life of Jesus, creating a 'historical Jesus in its own image' using 'artifice, art, artificiality, and violence', modern theology was determined to find its world-affirming ethic in the teaching of Jesus, and therein lay its weakness; but finally 'it could not keep him in our time, but had to let him go' (ibid. 398–9, 402). The liberal questers, in their naïve self-satisfaction, sought to know Jesus after the flesh, Schweitzer judged, whereas his spirit lay hidden in his words.

Jesus's sayings, speaking as an apocalyptic prophet, were heterogeneous to the world, Schweitzer insisted, and all the religious force of Jesus lay precisely in this world-negation: 'that which is eternal in the words of Jesus is due to the very fact that they are based on an eschatological worldview'. The world-negating prophet 'comes to us as One unknown' (ibid. 402–3). But while Schweitzer still believed that a radical eschatological faith can undergo conversion and choose to 'follow' the apocalyptic Jesus, Overbeck stood for an extreme pyrrhonist doubt with respect to the historical Jesus: he asked whether Jesus's teachings were not only strange and unapproachable, or demanding and formidable, but utterly foreign and actually inapplicable – offering not an unearthly challenge to faith but a historical surd, an irrecoverable anachronism.

Søren Kierkegaard's position, as pseudonymously outlined by Johannes Climacus in *Philosophical Fragments* ([1844] 1985) and *Concluding Unscientific Postscript* ([1846] 1992), is remarkably like Schweitzer's in retrospect. Schweitzer hoped that as a consequence of the failure of the quest for the historical Jesus, 'history will force Christianity to find a way to transcend history' ([1906] 1960: 401). For Kierkegaard, likewise, any expectation that historical grounds might help to support or justify faith can only fall short and never arrive at the core groundlessness of faith; hence the need for a leap, an ultimately groundless history-independent decision of faith. On the one hand, the claim that God 'has entered into time' and become incarnate historically is an axiom of Christian faith; on the other hand, no historical fact – nothing in the eighteen hundred years of Christian history – can offer or constitute legitimate grounds for believing that the Jesus of history, who claimed he was God, was God. Far rather, for Kierkegaard, the eighteen hundred years have only confused the issue, falsifying the faith-conditions of authentic New Testament Christianity (the requirement of a strenuous spiritual *metanoia*), while establishing a pseudo-Christianity and making a fool of God. Kierkegaard was confident that no historical fact or discovery could ever stand between the God who entered into time – making the simple claim on earth that he was God and asking others to follow him – and the faith of the individual follower that this man was indeed God. But Overbeck cast historical doubt exactly where Kierkegaard did not question: he denied that the historical Jesus ever claimed to be God, which shifts the core premise of Kierkegaard's dialectical paradox off its foundation, leaving it in the lurch on historical grounds.

Even now, today, a critical faith may experience this question as a living quandary: whether to honour a decisionist faith in line with Kierkegaard–Schweitzer or a pyrrhonist doubt in line with Overbeck, who believed that Christianity has long since had its day and should be left to die in peace (Law 2012: 238). Certainly, though, the apocalyptic Jesus professed by Schweitzer on the threshold of the First World War – the Unknown One who commands 'Follow me!' – provides a closing bracket for the long nineteenth century of our present inquiry.

Berlioz and Dostoevsky

Besides the 'historical' Jesus depicted in the Bible, a wholly-other-than-historical Jesus – the God-man as figured in art – also reveals dimensions of the death of God. Jesus in art registers the death-of-God trauma profoundly, as we see in the dramatic legend *The Damnation of Faust*, with music and libretto composed by Hector Berlioz, first performed in 1846. When Part 2 opens, Faust is enveloped in the throes of a suicidal depression, alone and abandoned by the empty heavens: 'Oh, how I suffer! And the starless night, which extends from afar its silence and veils, intensifies my oppressive sorrows [*Oh! je souffre! et la nuit sans étoiles, / Qui vient d'étendre au loin son silence et ses voiles, / Ajoute encore à mes sombres douleurs*]'. Engulfed in melancholic despair, Faust hears the church bells of Easter sounding and a hymn being sung by the chorus as they anticipate Christ about to be raised from the tomb. The believers sing plangently of their sorrow as they watch Christ, their beloved master, leaving the tomb and advancing *à grands pas* towards heaven while his faithful disciples 'remain languishing here below': 'Alas! He is leaving us behind under stinging barbs of misery. O divine master! Your joy is the cause of our sorrow. O divine master! You are leaving us behind under stinging barbs of misery [*Tu nous laisses sous les traits brûlants du malheur*]'. Hearing the sacred liturgy as a chance bystander, Faust exclaims with anguish – 'Ô souvenirs!' – overwhelmed with nostalgia for the joy of Easter, now recalled as a distant memory of youth, inaccessible to him, locked away in a past he cannot recapture.

In Faust's keenest moment of anguish, Mephistopheles appears and snarks ironically on all this nostalgic piety. He makes an irresistible offer that Faust accepts, taking Faust on a journey 'to learn about life'. Their first stop is in a raucous tavern where they witness a ribald 'Requiem for a Rat'. The drinking song tells the story of a kitchen rat who, after living so high on the hog 'as to make fat Luther jealous', is poisoned and roasted, then solemnly laid to rest to the strains of a beautiful sacred requiem. The moving solemnity of the chorale gives way to Mephistopheles's song about a flea who organises an infestation of the royal court by his whole family. Faust interrupts the song and demands to leave the saloon, disgusted by the baseness of it all.

The juxtaposition of genuine religious anguish and nostalgic longing for the sacred with blasphemous ribaldry and mockery of the sacred is the striking feature of Berlioz's *Faust*. After the death of the rat, blessed are the fleas, for they shall inherit the royal court. If one dares the comparison, the second part of the opera may be set in parallel with Nietzsche's madman passage of 1882, in which God, rich in substance (like the overfed rat), has 'bled to death under our knives' and is laid out to decompose, for 'Gods, too, decompose'; now the churches are but sepulchres of God, a place to sing a *requiem aeternam Deo*. But it is notable that Berlioz, writing more than a generation earlier than Nietzsche, is if anything more acutely sacrilegious. Both, in effect, plunge the glib Voltairean embrace of God's demise into the ominous pathos of authentic religious dread and remorse. If the mourning is ironic, the dread is not; the death of God has finally reached the human heart, provoking it to ask: whither are we moving now? Away from all suns?

Dostoevsky's Russia – as 'backward' in the East as Berlioz's France was an epicentre of the Zeitgeist in the West – received the impact of modern Western atheist ideas in a highly compressed timeframe as an alien import from abroad rather than a force arising within. Dostoevsky visited Europe and became a sensitive bellwether of this moral-spiritual shock, which he expressed in sundry ways in each of his major novels – quintessentially in Ivan's story of the Grand Inquisitor in *The Brothers Karamazov* (1880), in which Christ returns to visit his flock during the Inquisition but is sent away by his ecclesiastical lieutenant on earth, the Grand Inquisitor, and warned not to meddle again in human affairs or he will suffer a repetition of the fate he met long ago.

When he viewed it in Basel, Dostoevsky was so shocked by Hans Holbein the Younger's painting *Dead Christ* (1521) that he later incorporated it into his novel *The Idiot* (1869). The painting asserts an eerily quiet but aggressive power. In an elongated and compressed horizontal space, which appears to be the confines of a sarcophagus, a gaunt male body is depicted in greyish-green tones, frozen in the rigor of violent death. Art historians remark on the singularity of the painting not only within Holbein's oeuvre but as a peculiarly horrific work of religious art. Although the Christ figure of Grünewald's *Crucifixion* (1512) is more gruesome at first glance, with its sickening bodily sores and torturously twisted hands and feet, precisely these exaggerations, along with the massive size and spatial extension of the body, mark it out as a more-than-human sacred figure. No ordinary man's suffering flesh is depicted in the Grünewald, but the God-man's suffering flesh.

By comparison, the ghastly corpse depicted by Holbein is more disturbing in that it 'contains hardly any religious thought' (Reinhardt 1938: 21–2). Offering no visible sign of God or spirit, this Christ is simply a lifeless body on a slab, a cold tortured flesh. It has seemingly nothing to do with God, or has to do with God only insofar as all organic nature animated by the ceaseless contest of life against death – with death eventually triumphant – has to do with God. Before us is a particular in which the facticity of death has won, leaving no room for the symbolic. 'All is done with a horrible realistic power' producing 'altogether a most revolting effect' (Wornum 1867: 131–2). And yet, far from being closed up in death, the face lies entirely open and exposed by invasive reverse lighting. The eyes that recently served for seeing are open and turned upward. The mouth rests agape, as if having just uttered a cry. The head, neck and shoulders retain the tension of upward supplication.

It has been speculated that Holbein painted an anatomical study of a cadaver, then at some point converted it into Christ in the tomb by the addition of stigmata and a religious title. If so, an unidentified dead man was re-envisioned by the artist as Christ in the tomb – 'christening' a corpse. Was this an act of sacrilege? One searches the length of the emaciated body, the extruding navel, the nasty gash in the hand and vacated green-grey face, passively imploring, for an interpretive clue. The painting seems to pose an antinomy or contradiction for which there is no possible resolution. It is the very picture of godlessness, the inconceivability of resurrection, the frankness of death everlasting.

Three principal characters in *The Idiot*, Prince Myshkin, Rogozhin and later Ippolit, reflect on the painting's religious meaning as provoked by a copy that hangs over the door in one of Rogozhin's rooms. Myshkin, who has seen the original while travelling abroad, unable to forget it, recognises the copy. While Rogozhin and Myshkin hesitate before it, the reproduction induces a dark exchange concerning religious faith. Rogozhin asks Myshkin, 'Tell me, Prince, I've long wanted to ask you, do you believe in God?' then mutters offhandedly, 'I like looking at that picture.' Myshkin exclaims, 'At that picture! Why, some people may lose their faith by looking at that picture!' 'Aye, that also may be lost', Rogozhin replies (Dostoevsky [1869] 1956: 236). The painting's resonance in the novel extends far beyond explicit mentions of it, as the characters' collective subconscious is gripped by its abysmal implications. Each finds himself haunted by the painting as an image and an idea. Only much later in the novel does a full exposition of these implications occur in the brooding confession of Ippolit, who has seen the painting hanging in Rogozhin's place and is consumed with the Christ image as he prepares for his suicide:

> In Rogozhin's picture there was no trace of beauty. It was a faithful representation of the dead body of a man who has undergone unbearable torments.... Looking at that picture, you get the impression of nature ... as some huge machine of the latest design, which has senselessly seized, crushed, and swallowed up – impassively and unfeelingly – a great and priceless Being, a Being worth the whole of nature and all its laws, worth the entire earth, which was perhaps created solely for the coming of that Being!... And if, on the eve of the crucifixion, the Master could have seen what He would look like when taken from the cross, would He have mounted the cross and died as He did? This question, too, you can't help asking yourself as you look at the picture. (Ibid. 418–20; translation modified)

Ippolit espies in the painting a depiction of nature as an insensible force that cannot be personified because it is essentially machine-like. Applying Edwin Panofsky's quip that 'the man who is run over by an automobile is run over by mathematics, physics and chemistry' (Panofsky [1955] 1982: 23), we might infer that what Ippolit sees in *Dead Christ* is a God who has been run over by mathematics, physics and chemistry. Precisely as such, the painting is an incomparable icon for Dostoevsky of the God-man as re-envisioned by the apostate modern mind: a God crushed and conquered by the 'nature' of modern science in an anonymous dead body – a Christ-mask of absolute suffering behind which there is nothing. The shock value of the painting is that *we* are already participant in the symbolic reality depicted: a wholly ironic revelation in which graphic realism is the only 'symbol', or rather the naked *sign*, the positive mark of what is symbolically negated.

Emerson and the New World

Ralph Waldo Emerson, surveying this intellectual-spiritual history from the New World in the early nineteenth century, confident in new beginnings, lamented that his age is retrospective; it writes histories, biographies and criticism, thus building the 'sepulchers of the fathers':

> Foregoing generations beheld God and nature face to face; we, through their eyes. Why should not we also enjoy an original relation to the universe? Why should not we have a poetry and philosophy of insight and not of tradition, and a religion by revelation to us, and not the history of theirs?... There are new lands, new men, new thoughts. Let us demand our own works and laws and worship. ([1836] 1982: 35)

Why should we not enjoy an original relation to the universe, indeed? We are free to turn our faces forward, to seek the new, to pray for revelation and to prophesy new gods; but the past is nonetheless a momentously freighted train, making this easier said than done. The story of God in the twilight of Christendom – which takes the form of the death of God – is a millennial event still unfurling and still charged with unexpected depths of joy and woe.

Denizens of the nineteenth century, chastened by three centuries of internecine religious wars, revolutions and counter-revolutions, occupying a beleaguered post-Enlightenment climate, still harboured steadfast faith in progress at the level of society, a trust in gradual social amelioration through advancing humanism and scientific positivism – the paragon here being Auguste Comte with his 'religion of humanity' in which sociology replaces theology as the queen of the sciences. In the latter half of the century, the Darwinian theory of evolution wrought a decisive *coup de grâce*, setting in place an alternative naturalistic account for the origin of life – including the latecomer *Homo sapiens* – and positing a vast new geologic time that consigned human presence to a miniscule fraction of earth's history. Initially, the main impact of Darwin's theory, however, was to catalyse the transition to a non-Darwinian evolutionism that preserved the old teleological view of things, a pseudo-Darwinism in continuity with Romantic and pre-Romantic *Naturphilosophie* (Moore 2002: 24–6). Once again, the impact of the death of God was mitigated by a far less radical, fall-breaking compromise or stopgap measure.

The waves of transformation that were widely anticipated to bring human liberation and deliverance rolled out the battlegrounds, gulags, famines and death factories of the twentieth century in which an estimated 262 million souls suffered democide worldwide (Rummel 2016; Koning 1987). The slow absorption of the demise of God into broader society – enacted through tumultuous waves of scientific-technological, social-political, economic-legal, spiritual-psychological, moral-religious transformation – has exposed the nerve values of the West and brought forth fierce reactions for and against, creating cognitive dissonance and societal conflicts. The Emersonian–Nietzschean will to innovate, armed with naïve optimism, has faced down a Pandora's box of conservative, nostalgic and reactionary inclinations: white Christian imperial supremacism, schizophrenic bricolage belief systems, longing for 'old time religion', anti-scientism, new age spiritualism, narrow-minded axiological faith and moral-religious hypocrisies of all sorts. The unbridled nihilistic worship of quantum money and world-historical military hegemony beyond the reach of any symbolic value system also has its wellspring in the quest to fill this yawning God-void.

Considering the overwhelming seriousness of the task, we must admire how deliberately the creative minds of the nineteenth century 'broke the new wood', as Ezra Pound wrote of Walt Whitman's poetry (in 'A Pact', 1916). They were compelled to undertake daring new experiments in negating, unthinking and rethinking God. Unthinking God, negating all the way down in order to reconstruct, became not only possible but an intellectual duty. This epochal thinking was boldly carried out primarily by secularising philosophers in universities rather than theologians beholden to the church (Collins 1998: 618–63). Through them, a new theological potency was opened up for secularising theologians of the twentieth century, who built on the breakthroughs of these philosophical forerunners along lines that remain at least partially creative today: Barth the Kierkegaardian, Tillich the Schellingian, Bultmann the Schweitzerian, Altizer the Hegelian–Nietzschean and John B. Cobb the process thinker, to name only a few.

Although it was strictly *inconceivable* for fundamental Christian thinkers of earlier eras – from Athanasius to Augustine to Aquinas – to think in these terms, the nineteenth century deeply grasped that if God is Becoming and Life, then God is equally Negation and Death. It registered the final collapse of an arche and confrontation with a void that we cannot yet claim to be resolved in any way. And yet the new world *post mortem Dei* is aborning, its promises and perils astir, along with the new intuition of a passible God who lives, suffers and dies in unreserved ontological solidarity with us and indeed with all sentient existence. Thus the nineteenth century rescued God from the death of God – at least partially and ambiguously – by the advent of death-of-God thinking.

References

Altizer, Thomas J. J. (1967), *The New Apocalypse: The Radical Christian Vision of William Blake*, East Lansing: Michigan State University Press.
Badiou, Alain [1988] (2005), *Being and Event*, trans. Oliver Feltham, New York: Continuum.
Bakunin, Michael [1871] (1882), *God and the State*, trans. unknown, New York: Dover, 1971.
Becker, Carl L. (1932), *The Heavenly City of the Eighteenth-Century Philosophers*, New Haven: Yale University Press.
Beiser, Frederick C. (1987), *The Fate of Reason: German Philosophy from Kant to Fichte*, Cambridge, MA: Harvard University Press.
Beiser, Frederick C. (1993), 'Hegel and the Problem of Metaphysics', in Frederick C. Beiser (ed.), *The Cambridge Companion to Hegel*, Cambridge: Cambridge University Press, 1–24.
Beiser, Frederick C. (2003), *The Romantic Imperative: The Concept of Early German Romanticism*, Cambridge, MA: Harvard University Press.
Blake, William (1982), *The Complete Poetry and Prose of William Blake: Newly Revised Edition*, ed. David V. Erdman, Berkeley: University of California Press.
Brague, Rémi (2007), *The Law of God: The Philosophical History of an Idea*, trans. Lydia G. Cochrane, Chicago: University of Chicago Press.
Carlson, Thomas A. (1999), *Indiscretion: Finitude and the Naming of God*, Chicago: University of Chicago Press.
Collins, Randall (1998), *The Sociology of Philosophies: A Global Theory of Intellectual Change*, Cambridge, MA: Belknap.
de Ligt, Bart (1938), *The Conquest of War: An Essay on War and Revolution*, trans. Honor Tracy, New York: Dutton.
Depoortere, Frederiek (2007), *The Death of God: An Investigation into the History of the Western Concept of God*, London: T&T Clark.
Dostoevsky, Fyodor [1869] (1956), *The Idiot*, trans. David Magarshack, New York: Penguin.
Emerson, Ralph Waldo [1836] (1982), *Nature and Selected Essays*, ed. Larzer Ziff, New York: Penguin.
Fabro, Cornelio (1968), *God in Exile: Modern Atheism; A Study of the Internal Dynamics of Modern Atheism, from Its Roots in the Cartesian Cogito to the Present*, New York: Paulist Press.
Franke, William (2007), 'The Deaths of God in Hegel and Nietzsche and the Crisis of Values in Secular Modernity and Post-Secular Postmodernity', *Religion and the Arts*, 11: 214–41.
Franks, Paul (2000), 'All or Nothing: Systematicity and Nihilism in Jacobi, Reinhold, and Maimon', in Karl Ameriks (ed.), *The Cambridge Companion to German Idealism*, Cambridge: Cambridge University Press, 95–116.
Frye, Northrop (1947), *Fearful Symmetry: A Study of William Blake*, Princeton: Princeton University Press.
Funkenstein, Amos (1986), *Theology and the Scientific Imagination: From the Middle Ages to the Seventeenth Century*, Princeton: Princeton University Press.
Gauchet, Marcel (1985), *The Disenchantment of the World: A Political History of Religion*, trans. Oscar Burge, Princeton: Princeton University Press.
Gillespie, Michael Allen (1995), *Nihilism before Nietzsche*, Chicago: University of Chicago Press.
Gillespie, Michael Allen (2008), *The Theological Origins of Modernity*, Chicago: University of Chicago Press.
Gossman, Lionel (2000), *Basel in the Age of Burckhardt: A Study in Unseasonable Ideas*, Chicago: University of Chicago Press.
Harris, H. S. (1993), 'Hegel's Intellectual Development to 1807', in Frederick C. Beiser (ed.), *The Cambridge Companion to Hegel*, Cambridge: Cambridge University Press, 25–51.
Hegel, G. W. F. [1807] (1977), *The Phenomenology of Spirit*, trans. A. V. Miller. Oxford: Clarendon Press.
Hegel, G. W. F. [1821–31] (1988), *Lectures on the Philosophy of Religion*, 3 vols, ed. and trans. Peter C. Hodgson, Oxford: Oxford University Press.

Heidegger, Martin [1927] (1976), 'Phenomenology and Theology', in *The Piety of Thinking*, trans. James G. Hart and John C. Maraldo, Bloomington: Indiana University Press, 3–21.

Henry, Martin (2005), 'Translator's Introduction', in Franz Overbeck [1873], *How Christian Is Our Present-Day Theology?*, trans. Martin Henry, London: T&T Clark, xvii–xli.

Huizinga, Johan [1919] (1996), *The Autumn of the Middle Ages*, trans. Rodney J. Payton and Ulrich Mammitzsch, Chicago: University of Chicago Press.

Kierkegaard, Søren [1844] (1985), *Philosophical Fragments/Johannes Climacus*, ed. and trans. Howard V. Hong and Edna H. Hong, Princeton: Princeton University Press.

Kierkegaard, Søren [1846] (1992), *Concluding Unscientific Postscript to Philosophical Fragments*, 2 vols, ed. and trans. Howard V. Hong and Edna H. Hong, Princeton: Princeton University Press.

Knowles, David (1962), *The Evolution of Medieval Thought*, London: Longman.

Koning, Hans (1987), 'Notes on the Twentieth Century', *The Atlantic*, (September): 90–100.

Kosky, Jeffrey (2004), 'The Birth of the Modern Philosophy of Religion and the Death of Transcendence', in Regina Schwartz (ed.), *Transcendence: Philosophy, Literature, and Theology Approach the Beyond*, New York: Routledge, 13–29.

Koyré, Alexandre [1957] (1958), *From the Closed World to the Infinite Universe*, New York: Harper.

Law, David R. (2012), 'Franz Overbeck: Kierkegaard and the Decay of Christianity', in Jon Stewart (ed.), *Kierkegaard's Influence on Theology*, Tome 1: *German Protestant Theology*, Burlington, VT: Ashgate, 223–40.

Leahy, D. G. (1996), *Foundation: Matter the Body Itself*, Albany: State University of New York Press.

Leahy, D. G. (2003), *Faith and Philosophy: The Historical Impact*, Burlington, VT: Ashgate.

Löwith, Karl (1964), *From Hegel to Nietzsche: The Revolution in Nineteenth-Century Thought*, trans. David E. Green, New York: Columbia University Press.

McCullough, Lissa (2014), 'Twilight of an Axial God', in Daniel J. Peterson and G. Michael Zbaraschuk (eds), *Resurrecting the Death of God: The Origins, Influence, and Return of Radical Theology*, Albany: State University of New York Press.

Moore, Gregory (2002), *Nietzsche, Biology and Metaphor*, Cambridge: Cambridge University Press.

Nietzsche, Friedrich [1901] (1967), *The Will to Power*, ed. and trans. Walter Kaufmann and R. J. Hollingdale, New York: Vintage.

Nietzsche, Friedrich [1882] (1974), *The Gay Science*, trans. Walter Kaufmann, New York: Random House.

Nietzsche, Friedrich [1888] (1990), *Twilight of the Idols* and *The Anti-Christ*, trans. R. J. Hollingdale, New York: Penguin.

Oberman, Heiko A. (1963), *The Harvest of Medieval Theology: Gabriel Biel and Late Medieval Nominalism*, Cambridge, MA: Harvard University Press.

O'Neill, John C. (1991), *The Bible's Authority: A Portrait Gallery of Thinkers from Lessing to Bultmann*, Edinburgh: T&T Clark.

Overbeck, Franz [1873] (2005), *How Christian Is Our Present-Day Theology?*, trans. Martin Henry, London: T&T Clark.

Pagano, Maurizio (2012), 'Hegel as Interpreter of Religious Experience', in Paolo Diego Bubbio and Paul Redding (eds), *Religion after Kant: God and Culture in the Idealist Era*, Cambridge: Cambridge Scholars, 47–69.

Panofsky, Erwin [1955] (1982), *Meaning in the Visual Arts*, Chicago: University of Chicago Press.

Preuss, Peter (1987), 'Translator's Introduction', in Johann Fichte [1800], *The Vocation of Man*, trans. Peter Preuss, Indianapolis: Hackett, vii–xiv.

Reinhardt, Hans (1938), *Holbein*, trans. Prudence Montagu-Pollack, New York: FEP.

Rummel, Rudolph J. (2016), 'Twentieth-Century Democide', <https://www.hawaii.edu/powerkills/20TH.htm> (last accessed 5 March 2016).

Schelling, F. W. J. [1809] (2006), *Philosophical Investigations into the Essence of Human Freedom*, trans. Jeff Love and Johannes Schmidt, Albany: State University of New York Press.

Schmitt, Carl [1934] (1985), *Political Theology: Four Chapters on the Concept of Sovereignty*, trans. George Schwab, Chicago: University of Chicago Press.

Schweitzer, Albert [1906] (1960), *The Quest for the Historical Jesus: A Critical Study of Its Progress from Reimarus to Wrede*, trans. W. Montgomery, New York: Macmillan.

Socher, Abraham P. (2006), *The Radical Enlightenment of Solomon Maimon: Judaism, Heresy, and Philosophy*, Stanford: Stanford University Press.

Sommer, Andreas Urs (2003), 'On the Genealogy of the Genealogical Method: Overbeck, Nietzsche, and the Search for Origins', *Bulletin of the Institute of Classical Studies*, 46 (Supplement 79): 87–103.

Smith, Daniel W. (2000), 'Deleuze, Hegel, and the Post-Kantian Tradition', *Philosophy Today*, 44 (Supplement 26): 119–31.

Stirner, Max [1844] (1971), *The Ego and His Own*, ed. and trans. John Carroll, London: Jonathan Cape.

Summerell, Orrin F. (2002), 'Identity, Subjectivity, and Being Other than the Same: Thinking beyond Hegel and Heidegger', *The New Yearbook for Phenomenology and Phenomenological Philosophy*, 2: 179–95.

Taubes, Jacob (1954), 'On the Nature of the Theological Method: Some Reflections on the Methodological Principles of Tillich's Theology', *Journal of Religion*, 34.1 (January): 12–25.

Whitehead, Alfred North [1925] (1953), *Science and the Modern World*, New York: Free Press.

Wornum, Ralph Nicholson (1867), *Some Account of the Works of Hans Holbein, Painter, of Augsburg, with Numerous Illustrations*, London: Chapman and Hall.

Yerkes, James (1983), *The Christology of Hegel*, Albany: State University of New York Press.

2

The Outside

Daniel Whistler

The fate of thought depends on its relation to exteriority . . . (Zourabichvili [1994] 2012: 44)

The Conditions of Theological Insufficiency

This chapter concerns one feature of Christian apologetics during the nineteenth century: the acknowledgement that one need not be doing Christian theology. The idea that 'Christian theology is not everything' comes to be distinctively embedded within the theological thinking of the period. Accordingly, other scientific pursuits and theoretical frameworks are seen not only as independently valuable, but also as key tools for theology's self-determination. Theology comes to itself mediated by an outside.

An initial example of this logic is provided by a passage from Schleiermacher's *Speeches* (to which I return at length later in the chapter):

> This is the great evil, that good people believe their activity is universal and exhaustive of humanity and that if one would do what they do, one would then need to have no sense except for what one does. ([1799] 1996: 62)

Schleiermacher identifies a significant epistemic vice in intellectual narcissism or, more specifically, in a lack of awareness of scientific pursuits that are genuinely different from one's own. Conversely, to recognise the potential alterity (and so contingency) of ways of thinking is an essential virtue that makes good theology possible: successful theologising acknowledges that there is more to thought than itself. There are, therefore, both epistemological and ethical benefits to this line of thinking, as Gjesdal identifies:

> It is at one and the same time expressive of an epistemological commitment that has to do with a finite being's ability to expand its own horizon of understanding and knowledge, *and* an ethical commitment having to do with the fact that such understanding is based on a will to recognize the other as a somebody whose perspective might be as valid as my own. (2014: 104)

Furthermore, there is a specifically theological benefit too: tracing the contours of an outside to theology allows for a more determinate and self-reflexive understanding of the shape of theology itself – and it is this additional boon that forms the subject matter of what follows.

This chapter, then, concerns the possibility of an intellectual space that is outside Christian theology but generated from within, the methodological utopia of an Archimedean point. It concerns, that is, the theological fantasy of a non-theological position from which to view and judge Christianity. This is, in part, a symptom of a crisis of theological absolutes, a crisis of 'the principle of sufficient theology': what appears to break down at this moment is, in words borrowed from Anthony Paul Smith's reworking of François Laruelle's 'principle of sufficient philosophy',[1] the idea that 'everything is theologizable because theology's non-object, God, is related or even meta-related to everything that is' (2013: 102; see also 2010: 295–7). No longer can it be taken for granted that scientific inquiries into politics, language or the functions of organisms are ultimately to be situated in relation to the divine. Theology is just one more conceptual framework among many, and this necessitates that theologians acknowledge the idea that Christian theology is not all there is.

My argument bears similarities to elements of Charles Taylor's project in *A Secular Age*, described as follows:

> The change I want to define and trace is one which takes us from a society in which it was virtually impossible not to believe in God, to one in which faith, even for the staunchest believer, is one human possibility among others. I may find it inconceivable that I would abandon my faith, but there are others, including possibly some very close to me, whose way of living I cannot in all honesty just dismiss as depraved, or blind, or unworthy, who have no faith . . . Belief in God is no longer axiomatic. There are alternatives . . . This has been a recognizable experience in our societies, at least since the mid-nineteenth century. (2007: 3)

That is, Taylor's story of secularisation is one that narrates a shift in Western modernity from a world-picture in which Christianity was absolute – in which all discourse was ultimately and implicitly discourse about God – to one in which Christianity was not everything, 'one option among others, and frequently not the easiest to embrace' (ibid. 3). At some point, an outside to the Christian framework became conceivable. Taylor dubs this 'the modern condition' and defines it thus:

> We live in a condition where we cannot help but be aware that there are a number of different construals, views which intelligent, reasonably undeluded people, of good will, can and do disagree on. We cannot help looking over our shoulder from time to time, looking sideways. (Ibid. 11)

Even to embrace Christianity whole-heartedly in modernity, he continues, is to do so in a 'reflective', rather than a 'naïve' manner:

> There has been a titanic change in our western civilisation. We have changed . . . from a condition where most people lived 'naïvely' in a construal as lived reality . . . to one in which almost no one is capable of this, but all see their option as one among many. We all learn to navigate between two standpoints: an 'engaged' one in which we live as best we can the reality our standpoint opens us to; and a 'disengaged' one in which we are able to see ourselves as occupying one standpoint among a range of possible ones, with which we have in various ways to coexist. (Ibid. 12)

Taylor's story, then, is of the 'breach of naïveté' (ibid. 13) in the modern West.

My interests are, unsurprisingly, much more limited: the emergence of a 'reflective' stance towards religion *within Christian theology itself*. My topic is how, specifically, the Christian theologian in the nineteenth century began to conceive Christianity as non-absolute, as having a non-theological outside. Of course, this is not to deny that there were numerous developments before the nineteenth century that made this possible; indeed, one can say, as Lacoue-Labarthe and Nancy do of other intellectual crises at the turn of the nineteenth century, 'Undoubtedly a long history was necessary before it' ([1978] 1988: 1). Nevertheless, my thesis is that this fracturing of the principle of sufficient theology fully broke out *within theology* during this era, even if, as I will argue at the end of this essay, what went on to happen was not the breakdown of the principle of sufficient theology at all, but a more covert reaffirmation of it.

In what follows, I attempt to illustrate the above through a series of examples: three drawn from mid-nineteenth-century theological fictions of conversion and deconversion (Kingsley's *Hypatia*, Newman's *Callista*, Eliot's *Romola*) and three drawn from theory (Schleiermacher's *Speeches on Religion*, Nietzsche's critique of Eliot, Coleridge's notes towards his *Opus Maximum*).

Conversion

The nineteenth century witnessed the growth of 'a long special tradition of English and American historical fiction set in the early days of Christianity, based on antiquarian research concerned with moral, philosophical, and religious ideas, and dealing in historical disguise with religious and philosophical issues of the [day]' (Dahl 1973: 2). A selective list of representative titles from this genre helps set the scene: *Tales of the Early Ages* (Horace Smith, 1832), *Antonina; or the Fall of Rome* (Wilkie Collins, 1850), *Mary, the Handmaid of the Lord* (Elisabeth R. Charles, 1954), *Ben Hur; A Tale of the Christ* (Lew Wallace, 1880), *Arius the Libyan: An Idyll of the Primitive Church* (Nathan C. Kouns, 1883) (see Dahl 1973: 2–10). As the titles suggest, these novels frequently combine Scottian historical romance and post-gothic sensationalism with pious didacticism. However, most significantly for our purposes is the intent of many of these novels to dramatise 'the ancient clash between pagan philosophy and early Christianity [as] an ideal analogy to the struggle between intellectual doubt and Christian faith in the nineteenth century' (ibid. 5). In other words, authors and readers keenly felt the fragility of the early church as their own: Christianity was once more best described as under siege from an array of threatening non-Christian forces.

It was into this context that theologians were drawn, and one of the first theological appropriations of the genre was Charles Kingsley's 1853 *Hypatia or, New Foes with an Old Face*. Kingsley draws on the above precedents, staging a fable of conversions, redemptions and martyrdoms in fifth-century Alexandria, in order to carry on a theological polemic concerning the nature and value of the early church. The novelist is explicitly styled as a 'Christian apologist' ([1853] 1975: 1:vii), whose main target is the growing influence of Anglo-Catholicism in 1850s Britain, one of the 'new foes' represented under the 'old face' of the Alexandrian Church, which 'sanctioned those habits of doing evil that good may come, of pious intrigue, and at last of open persecution, which are certain to creep in wheresoever men attempt to set up a merely religious empire' (ibid. 2:363). According to Kingsley, the fifth-century church, anticipating the excesses of Catholicism, ended up

> a mere chaos of idolatrous sects, persecuting each other for metaphysical propositions, which, true or false, were equally heretical in their mouths, because they used them only

as watchwords of division. Orthodox or unorthodox, they knew not God, for they knew neither righteousness, nor love, nor peace. (Ibid. 2:363)

The novel's dramatisation of early Christian conversions is thus intended to function as a didactic allegory, and the moral of the story is made clearest in the closing words:

And now, readers, farewell. I have shown you New Foes under an Old Face – your own likenesses in toga and tunic, instead of coat and bonnet. One word before we part. The same devil who tempted these old Egyptians tempts you. The same God who would have saved these Old Egyptians if they had willed, will save you, if you will. Their sins are yours, their errors yours, their doom yours, their deliverance yours. There is nothing new under the sun. The thing which has been, it is that which shall be. (Ibid. 2:377)

Kingsley's novel demanded a response from the Catholic establishment, and that which was forthcoming reappropriated the very genre of Kingsley's apologetics: 'The Catholic Popular Library', established by Cardinal Wiseman in 1854. The Library's stated aim was to provide 'a series of tales illustrative of the condition of the Church, in different periods of her past existence' (Wiseman 1854: vii) – the implication being that of countering 'false' depictions of Catholicism in novels like *Hypatia*. Wiseman inaugurated the series with *Fabiola, or the Church of the Catacombs*, a story of ecclesiastical fortitude in the face of Diocletian persecution. Crawford writes of it, '*Fabiola*, if not the entire series, was probably intended to correct from a Catholic point of view the picture of Church history presented in Kingsley's *Hypatia*' (1950: 219). The intent of the Catholic Popular Library can be gleaned from the frontispiece to *Fabiola* which is representative of many of the twenty-two volumes that were to follow over the next eight years, such as *Heroines of Charity*, *The Patriots of the Tyrol* and *Pictures of Christian Heroism*. It reads:

A Historical Picture of the Early Church in Pagan Rome illustrating the Glories of the Christian Martyrs as exemplified in the lives of the fair young Virgin, St Agnes; the heroic Soldier, St Sebastian; the devoted Youth, St Pancratius; etc., etc. (1854: i)

The success of Wiseman's venture is evidenced by the book's rapid translation into ten European languages, including seven times into Italian (see Chapman 1970: 150).

The most direct response to Kingsley in the Catholic Popular Library was subsequently given by John Henry Newman with the publication of his *Callista: A Tale of the Third Century*, another fable of conversions and martyrdoms in the midst of political persecution, 'specially addressed to Catholic readers, and for their edification' ([1855] 1888: ix).[2] That is, Newman attempts to dramatise 'the portentous stubbornness of a Christian' (ibid. 82) in the face of worldly tribulation: 'O wisdom of the world! And strength of the world! What are you when matched beside the foolishness and the weakness of the Christian?' (ibid. 274). Newman saw his task, in part at least, as the reassertion of the value of early Catholic ascesis against Kingsley's 'muscular Christianity' – that is, he saw it somewhat as a fictional analogue to 'A Library of Fathers of the Holy Catholic Church' begun by Pusey in 1838. This 'initial skirmish' (Dorman 1979) between Newman and Kingsley's competing understandings of the early church went on to form the backdrop to their later controversies, culminating in the outbreak of hostilities in 1864 that led directly to the publication of *Apologia Pro Vita Sua*.[3]

The scholarship on these novels tends to interpret them entirely through the prism of the conflict between 'no Popery' and Anglo-Catholic sentiment in early Victorian Britain, such that the differences between Kingsley's and Newman's accounts are seen to 'embody the philosophical assumptions and practical consequences of two quite opposite Christian ideologies' (Dorman 1979: 173; see further Chapman 1970: 161–5; Poggi Johnson 1999). If nothing else, such interpretations do violence to the texts of the novels: they are seen *in toto* as polemical interventions into late Tractarian politics; hence, Chapman's hermeneutic rule, 'For "Christianity" read "Roman Catholicism"' (1970: 164). In contrast, I want to explore how these novels work as conversion narratives. *Fabiola*, *Hypatia* and *Callista* all situate the Christian experience in a hostile, indifferent or robustly non-Christian society (fourth-century Rome, fifth-century Alexandria and third-century Roman North Africa, respectively); of course, the non-Christian Other – whether pagan, Jew, Muslim or demonic – has always dominated the Christian imagination, but what seems different about the role of the Other in these nineteenth-century narratives is twofold. First, these others are ineluctably present *within* the very social fabric described, as figures who cannot ultimately be expelled, dominated or ignored, but who must be lived with in increasingly complex, if fragile networks of relations. Second, these others are not typically representatives of alien belief systems, but cynics and sceptics who refuse all religion in the name of either 'the received usages of society' (Newman [1855] 1888: 82) or a Promethean individualism. The following sentiment towards Christianity from Newman's *Callista* is representative: 'It's an opinion: there have been other opinions before . . . and there will be other opinions after' (ibid. 44).

In all conversion narratives, a non-Christian becomes Christian – and, for this reason, the initial non-Christian identity of the protagonist needs to act as the starting point for the novel, the assumed background out of which change occurs. The reader is immediately immersed in a social, intellectual and emotional environment that is, by necessity, hostile or indifferent to Christianity and – in order for the conversion narrative to have power and traction for this reader – she must to some extent engage sympathetically with it. Again, such statements are evidently true of conversion narratives in general, but the point holds that, for their conversion narratives to function effectively, Kingsley, Wiseman and Newman needed to rely, to some extent, on their readers' familiarity with the idea of viewing Christianity *from outside*, as one more worldview among others, as a set of beliefs faithfully adhered to only by a section of society and sceptically attacked by others. My interest is in how these novels generate such familiarity and sympathy with the non-Christian position.

This is particularly significant, since it is at such moments that these novels become most explicitly interventions into nineteenth-century theological debates. As already noted, Kingsley frames his fable as an unmasking of 'new foes', and, in a similar fashion, Newman explicitly compares third-century and nineteenth-century behaviours and dogmas (see ibid. 18–19, 20–1, 72).[4] The Christians inhabit a world permeated by strident irreligion, sceptical free thinking and worrying innovations in speculative philosophy – and, what is more, these challenges share the very same social and intellectual space as orthodoxy: they cannot but be negotiated. These novels, whatever their differences, rely on a Christian imaginary constituted at its very core by relations with social, philosophical and ideological others.

Wiseman's engagement with the non-Christian Other stands at one end of the spectrum. The Preface to *Fabiola* explicitly states, 'It was necessary to introduce some views of the morals and opinions of the pagan world, as a contrast to those of the Christians. But their worst aspect has been carefully suppressed' (1854: vii). That is, his response to the ongoing debate over how sympathetically one should present a non-Christian outside is to explicitly suppress the cogency of sceptical and irreligious voices in the name of Christian taste. He refuses the modern 'reflective' attitude outlined by Taylor. For Wiseman, the novel of conversion must only narrate what appears 'decent' to a Christian reader; everything else is to be diluted to the point of euphemism.

Kingsley's *Hypatia* stands at the other end of the spectrum. When Hypatia herself remarks, for instance, 'It is the Christians now, and not the heathens, who are idolaters' ([1853] 1975: 1:316), some readers were scandalised. In 1863, Kingsley was refused an honorary doctorate at the University of Oxford, notwithstanding his nomination by the Prince of Wales, because of 'the heretical and immoral character of [his] works, more especially of *Hypatia*' (*The Times*, 8 June 1863, quoted in Chapman 1970: 160). An 1855 review of *Hypatia* had already worried 'that a clergyman of the Church of England might occupy his leisure more usefully than in writing books of this kind ... There are many parts and passages of history which, out of respect for public morals, had much better be left unexplained' (*Blackwood's Magazine*, June 1855, quoted in Chapman 1970: 158). In the terminology of this chapter, Kingsley's problem was that he seemed to sympathise too much with the non-Christian, to orient his novel too far outside of Christian norms, and so immerse the reader too vividly in the beliefs and practices of fifth-century Alexandrian Neoplatonists. Such sympathy often read, it seems, like a sustained critique on contemporary Christianity as such.

Hence, the fifth-century Christians already live belatedly, looking back with nostalgia from a 'modern' viewpoint 'to the times of persecution, when Christians died like brothers, because they lived like brothers. You will see very little of that now' (Kingsley [1853] 1975: 1:153). In these late times, Alexandrian Christians have developed addictions to a 'strange brood of theoretic monsters' (ibid. 1:xx), for 'the minds of men, cut adrift from their ancient moorings, wandered wildly over pathless seas of speculative doubt' (ibid. 1:xii). Moreover, Kingsley does not merely describe these intellectual voyages into the speculative as external challenges to Christian orthodoxy, but also as something that infects the very framing of theology itself. Hence, in *Hypatia*, theology sometimes degenerates into a kind of eighteenth-century deism ('regard[ing] Deity as the maker of a dead machine, which, once made, will move of itself thenceforth ... [a] dead, barren, and sordid conception of the glorious all' [ibid. 1:313–14]), sometimes into relativism (Christianity 'arrogates to itself the exclusive revelation of the Divine, and cannot see, in its self-conceit, that its own doctrines disprove that assumption by their similarity to those of all creeds' [ibid. 1:318–19]), or sometimes even into a repudiation of Christianity's this-worldly mission ('a generation who were forgetting His love in His power, and practically losing sight of His humanity in their eager doctrinal assertion of His Divinity' [ibid. 2:216]).

In the sympathy it exhibits for non-Christian beliefs and practices, Newman's *Callista* unsurprisingly exists somewhere between Wiseman's *Fabiola* and Kingsley's *Hypatia*. Newman treads carefully; nevertheless, he still gives significant voice to anti-Christian sentiment. Juba, a central character in Newman's original conception of the novel ([1855] 1888: vii–viii), is exemplary of this tendency; for example, when he encounters his brother in prayer, he reacts thus:

> 'O, everyone to his taste, of course,' said Juba; 'but to an unprejudiced mind there is something unworthy in the act.'
> 'Why, Juba,' said his brother somewhat sharply, 'don't you profess any religion at all?'

'Perhaps I do, and perhaps I don't,' answered Juba; 'but never shall it be a bowing and scraping, crawling and cringing religion. You may take your oath of that . . . I won't give an account of my actions to anyone, god or man, devil or priest.' (Ibid. 24–5)

Juba continues:

'Yes, certainly, I once had a conscience. Yes, and once I had a bad chill, and went about chattering and shivering; and once I had a game leg, and then I went limping; and so, you see, I once on a time had a conscience. O yes, I have had many consciences before now . . . they were all bad; but they are all gone, and now I have none . . . The truth is,' continued Juba, with the air of a teacher, 'the truth is, that religion was a fashion with me, which is now gone by. It was the complexion of a particular stage of my life . . . I acted according to the feeling, while it lasted.' (Ibid. 28–9)

Juba represents a strident voice from outside Christianity that subjects Christian dogma and cult to scrutiny and judgement. He personifies the possibility of a point of view external to Christianity – outside the religion looking in, as it were – and it is just such a possibility that I want to elucidate in what follows. While such an external viewpoint may be assumed whenever one speaks of conversion, it can still be asked: what conditions had to be in place for it to be possible for this specific type of outside to Christianity to be imaginatively envisaged by Kingsley and Newman? In other words, what *Hypatia* and *Callista* appeal to in the form of a novel has its analogue in a theological thinking that is not all-engulfing or hegemonic, but which is, on first blush at least, 'reflective' in Taylor's sense outlined above. It recognises that there is an outside to the Christian worldview and that the view from this outside determines Christianity, at least in part. Christianity is partially constituted by stepping outside itself to look back in.

Deconversion

The example of another novel helps develop the above logic of an appeal to the outside. George Eliot's *Romola* has been read as a heretical contribution to this Victorian genre of historical conversion romance, as, that is, a kind of contemporary mutating of the sort of fictional apologetics exemplified by Kingsley's *Hypatia* and Newman's *Callista* (Carroll 1998).[5] While *Romola* may be set in Renaissance Florence rather than an early Christian community, it still immerses the reader in a significantly a-Christian society riddled with scepticism and irreligion.

The novel opens onto a wholly anti-religious atmosphere: the first third of *Romola* is dominated by, initially, the thoughts and actions of its antihero, a hedonist 'of Epicurean levity' (Eliot [1863] 1996: 6), and, subsequently, by the scholarly Stoicism accepted by Romola and propounded by her father. In this environment, Christianity is only invoked to be condemned as 'barbarism' (ibid. 33), the offspring of 'fanatical dreams' (ibid. 52) and 'monkish visions' (ibid. 176), a kind of 'servitude' taught by 'insect-swarms of besotted fanatics or howling hypocrites' (ibid. 66). Eliot expects her reader to immediately make the imaginative jump into this intellectual space outside of Christianity, a space where common sense equates to irreligious scepticism.

From this initial background imaginary, the novel then slowly takes the reader into the Christian consciousness of late fifteenth-century Italy. Romola gradually comes 'to learn the thoughts of men who sank in ecstasy before the pictured agonies of martyrdom' and so acknowledge a 'supreme fellowship with suffering' (ibid. 324) – something that was not an option during the early pages of the novel. In thrall to Savonarola's spiritual counsel, she becomes 'a pious Piagnone' (ibid. 374): 'She had submitted her mind to his and entered into communion with the Church, because in this way she had found an immediate satisfaction for moral needs which all the previous culture and experience of her life had left hungering' (ibid. 388). Savonarola's 'arresting voice had brought a new condition into her life' (ibid. 361). She is converted: 'the chill doubts all melted away' (ibid. 362). Nevertheless, this conversion to Christianity is short-lived, for almost immediately the novel begins to dramatise Romola's alienation from such a worldview: she rediscovers Christianity's 'jarring notes' (ibid. 440) and 'fanaticism' from which she now shrinks 'with newly-startled repulsion' (ibid. 445). Eliot sums up this stage in her protagonist's development as follows:

> Romola had lost her trust in Savonarola, had lost that fervour of admiration which had made her unmindful of his aberrations . . . She [now] saw all the repulsive and inconsistent details in his teaching with a painful lucidity which exaggerated their proportions. (Ibid. 501)

Out of this disillusionment comes 'a new baptism', one in which Christian concepts are made use of and Savonarola's example venerated, but free of a 'strictly religious discipleship' (ibid. 560). Romola embarks on a life of good deeds in secularised imitation of those Christian exemplars who were dedicated to 'struggling against a powerful wrong, and . . . [to] trying to raise men to the highest deeds they are capable of' (ibid. 582).

Carroll summarises this deconversion narrative as follows:

> Romola's education, which is a series of struggles and renunciations, enables her to come to an eventual understanding of Savonarola's martyrdom and its implications for the future of humanity . . . In each case, Romola is appropriated by powerful male visions until she comes to discern, in turn, their inner contradictions . . . In a complex series of permutations she is first appropriated, then resists and finally rebels . . . Their views are both subsumed and superseded . . . [in] a series of personal renaissances. (1998: 115–16)[6]

For Carroll, Romola is a secular heroine who, like Eliot herself, attempts 'to recast the lexicon of Christianity in terms applicable to an age about to embrace the religion of humanity' (ibid. 105).[7] To put it bluntly, Romola has a complicated relation to Christianity: theological images are both, in Eliot's words, 'lifeless barbarisms' and 'living ideas' (1992: 18–19), meshed together in a 'confusion [of] tangled threads' ([1863] 1996: 500). As Taylor has put it of such Victorian 'cross-pressures', 'One thus has to be both against Christianity and for it' (2007: 380). Romola's assessment of Savonarola exemplifies this confusion: his fate betrays 'the struggle of a mind possessed by a never-silent hunger after purity and simplicity, yet caught in a tangle of egoistic demands, false ideas, and difficult outward conditions' (Eliot [1863] 1996: 490). As Eliot puts it early in the narrative:

> The mysteries of human character have seldom been presented in a way more fitted to check the judgments of facile knowingness than in Girolamo Savonarola; but we can give him a reverence that needs no shutting of the eyes to fact. (Ibid. 235)

Eliot's use of Savonarola in *Romola* is indicative, moreover, of a wider reappropriation of him in nineteenth-century European culture, whether it be the 'San Marco cultism' of the New Piagnoni and Risorgimento which discerned in Savonarola's preaching the seeds of 'a great spiritual and moral regeneration of the Italian people'; or Burckhardtian scepticism towards his 'self-delusion' and 'vanity'; or, again, Savonarola's redeployment by Catholic Modernists in the first decade of the twentieth century; or even Ranke's scholarly interest in his role in the prehistory of the Reformation (Weinstein 1970: 3–8). In all these cases, Savonarola's life was never a mere pattern to be contemplated, but material to be utilised for polemic: the nineteenth-century consciousness cuts up, retools and repurposes tradition for contemporary ends – it acts *on* religion. The logic here is very similar to that which led to the birth of the fields of philosophy of religion, history of religion, sociology of religion, and so on. Each of these fields acts on religion; their operations share a structural similarity: they are all made possible by treating religion as material to be interpreted through non-religious terminologies and conceptual schema. On such accounts, religion is to be scientifically elucidated only through an alien medium (philosophy or history or sociology, etc.).

Eliot redeploys Savonarola, variously, for the purposes of assessing the legacy of republicanism in Italy (Santangelo 1972), commenting on 'debates about electoral reform in Victorian England' (Wihl 2009: 259) and 'engag[ing] in a dialogue with Comte' (Shuttleworth 1984: 99). It is this latter redeployment that has garnered most critical attention, for the influence of Comte's reading of human history on *Romola* has long been acknowledged (most fully by Bullen 1975). In this Comtean framework, Savonarola has a double function. On the one hand, he symbolises the limits of Comte's 'monotheistic age': such an age is formed out of Catholic reactions to pagan materialism, but at the same time the seeds of its downfall are to be found in the church's unwillingness to separate religion from politics. In Bullen's reading of the novel, such a weakness is allegorically alluded to in the fate of Savonarola:

> Sure enough, it is through the political actions of Savonarola that the weakness of Catholicism becomes apparent . . . [They] give George Eliot the opportunity to expound on a cardinal Positivist principle – the necessity of distinguishing spiritual and temporal authority – and the ensuing acrimonious debate between Savonarola and Romola hammers home the importance of keeping religion and politics apart . . . By transcending the Catholicism of Savonarola, Romola has outgrown her age and has moved into the future. (1975: 432)

On the other hand, Savonarola also takes up the role of Comte's Priest of Humanity, preaching the value of altruism as a social bond that transcends specific religious dogma: 'Savonarola, as embodiment of Comte's Priest of Humanity, preaches the doctrines of positivism to Romola, stressing primarily her duty not to God, but to Florence' (Shuttleworth 1984: 100). On this reading, Savonarola – as well as Eliot herself – points to the future, rather than highlighting the limitations of the past.

Whether or not *Romola* should be read as a strictly Comtean novel,[8] Eliot's uses of Savonarola are to be differentiated from those of her contemporaries merely to the extent that her ambivalent attitude towards him adds layers of complexity to the set of abstractive operations she is applying to the religious source material. The reader is led to sympathise with Savonarola's nobler ambitions at the same time as she is brought to despise his egoistic practices. Movements of identification and alienation occur in rapid succession.

This repeats the more general logic of Romola's conversions and deconversions rehearsed above: the reader is slowly guided into the Christian worldview from outside, only to once more be brought out into a liminal position, consisting of the secularised appropriation of religious concepts shorn of religious garb. This proliferation of entries into and exits from the Christian position only makes sense if one can think of Christianity as something non-absolute, something that has an outside.

Bildung

This oscillation of exits from and entries into Christianity is repeated in the more theoretical productions of the era. Schleiermacher's 1799 *On Religion: Speeches to Its Cultural Despisers* [*Über die Religion: Reden an die Gebildeten unter ihren Verächtern*] inaugurates a century of Christian theology precisely by recourse to a dialectical method that moves outside the religious point of view, only to return within it. Such movements of ascent and descent, alienation and identification, mark a new stage in the stratagems of Christian apologetics, further developed by Kierkegaard, among others. The latter's project in *Philosophical Fragments* to defamiliarise Christianity for the 'well-informed man' of contemporary Christendom – 'as if [one] took his knowledge away from him, at least provisionally, until by having overcome his opposition to the form he succeeds in assimilating it' ([1846] 1992: 1:246) – has a very similar rhetorical structure to Schleiermacher's *Speeches*. The 'cultured' reader, overfamiliar with religion, is positioned at a distance from Christianity and subjected to 'alienation-effects', in order to bring about a kind of re-conversion to the Christian faith within Christendom. But such conversion from within is only made possible by the experimental creation of a temporary, external reference point – a fictitious Archimedean place to stand from which the religion looks different.

As David E. Klemm notes (2005: 255), the very title of *Über die Religion* evokes – however allusively – the idea of rising 'above' the claims and practices of Christianity, of finding a transcendent 'beyond-religion' from which to describe and judge the Christian tradition. Indeed, the opening words to the *Speeches* designate the intended recipients as 'just those persons who have *raised themselves above* the herd, and are saturated by the wisdom of the century' (Schleiermacher [1799] 1996: 3; my emphasis). The metaphors of 'rising above' and 'looking in from outside' go on to pervade the text: it apostrophises 'you who are capable of raising yourselves above the common standpoint of humanity' (ibid. 11) and demands that 'with your contemplation rise higher'; it looks to 'principle[s] we can discover only from a higher standpoint' (ibid. 36) and concludes that 'I have shown you a higher standpoint' (ibid. 95). Indeed, the average priest and theologian is denigrated precisely because 'what I intend lies almost completely outside their sphere and would hardly resemble what they want to see and hear' (ibid. 4). Schleiermacher opens up an outside, a 'higher standpoint' raised above traditional theological conceptions

Moreover, as Klemm also goes on to spell out (2005: 255–62), such methodological transcendence is fashioned as an exercise in *Bildung*, another concept alluded to in the very title to the work (*die Gebildeten*) (as well as forming the title of the third speech, *Über die Bildung zur Religion*). In Gadamer's influential account of *Bildung* (variously translated as formation, education, cultivation or even inculturation):

> [It] was perhaps the greatest idea of the eighteenth century, and it is this concept which is the atmosphere breathed by the human sciences of the nineteenth century, even if they are unable to offer any epistemological justification of it. ([1960] 2011: 8)

On the model of *Bildung*, 'the essential character of human rationality as a whole' is a 'rising to the universal', and so 'whoever abandons himself to his particularity is *ungebildet*': *Bildung* 'requires sacrificing particularity for the sake of the universal' (ibid. 11). Or, to put it in the terms of the chapter, rationality is attained by moving outside of the particular claims of positive religions, by acknowledging their relativity and insufficiency. Education consists in the rejection of theological absolutes. To quote Gadamer once more:

> The general characteristic of *Bildung* [is] keeping oneself open to what is other – to other, more universal points of view. It embraces a sense of proportion and distance in relation to itself, and hence consists in rising above itself to universality. (Ibid. 15)

It is precisely this movement that Klemm discerns in Schleiermacher's text: 'Schleiermacher wants his audience to rise above both the historical religions and natural religion in order to ascend to philosophical theology as a self-conscious and reflexive way of thinking about and experiencing religion in its truth' (2005: 259). On this model, the 'cultured despisers' of religion have not sufficiently risen above particularity, and Schleiermacher, as 'a philosopher who stands above [them]', employs 'the dispassionate indifference and openness of a philosophical attitude [to] save the mind from the particularism and exclusivism into which its cultured despisers themselves have fallen through their disdain' (ibid. 257).

Nevertheless, Klemm's reading completely misses the whole point of Schleiermacher's invocation of the process of *Bildung*, which is to remake it in a theological image. In Gjesdal's words, Schleiermacher proposes an 'alternative conception of Bildung ... deserving of rehabilitation' (2014: 93).[9] The *Speeches* completely refashion the orthodox conception of *Bildung* from an ascent to the universal at the expense of the particular to a process of self-formation that *also* necessitates a descent into the particular. At the same time as goading its *gebildete* readers to rise higher, the text progressively immerses them in specifically religious networks of meaning. Schleiermacher starts off with the most universal claims of general revelation (in Speeches I and II), before slowly funnelling them down into the more particular aspects of Christian cult and dogma in Speech V. Through 'a process of intellectual seduction' (Crouter 1996: xxx), the *gebildete* reader is persuaded to renounce the transcendent outside of universality for particular revealed truths. For example, after rehearsing a list of typical complaints against Christianity (as 'poorly stitched together fragments of metaphysics and morals' and the 'meaningless fables of barbarous nations'), Schleiermacher asks, 'But why have you not *descended* any more to the particular?' ([1799] 1996: 12–13; my emphasis). Alongside the metaphorics of ascent and height, there is one of descent and depth (see, for example, ibid. 65, 79), and Schleiermacher is repeatedly critical of those 'superficial indifferentists' (ibid. 113) who remain outside a worldview and understand it merely externally:

> To become aware of [a religion] one must have considered [it] not only from an external point of view but from its own center outward ... To know only one point of view for everything is exactly the opposite of having all points of view for each thing; it is the way to distance oneself directly from the universe and to sink into the most wretched limitedness, to become a true serf, bound to the place on which by chance one may be standing. (Ibid. 62)

As Foreman puts it, 'Knowledge is the business of the insider' (1978: 96). Indeed. Foreman uses this passage, among others, to argue that 'Schleiermacher consistently attacked the notion that the would-be knower should seek an "Archimedean point" outside the phenomena from which to control them. That is the flaw in the so-called natural religion' (ibid. 96).

It must be stressed, however, that the movement of Schleiermacher's text is just as little *merely* a 'top-down' deductive progress from universal to particular as it is 'bottom-up' ascent from particular to universal. Instead, it turns out in Speech V that the most universal claims only make sense *through* the particular, and vice versa. *Speeches* is structured as a very Schleiermacherian hermeneutic circle: general and specific revelation are mutually dependent. Natural religion is only understandable in light of the particular, and Christian doctrine only in light of the universal. Hence, while Speech II enumerates the universal characteristics of the 'essence' of religion, such an essence exists in a state of 'indefinite ambiguity' lacking 'determinate form' ([1799] 1996: 109), until it is embodied in the specific claims and practices of a positive religion.[10] In positive religion, Schleiermacher writes, 'the whole suddenly takes on a determinate spirit; everything that was previously ambiguous and indeterminate is fixed', and this, he adds, is the very movement of *Bildung* (ibid. 104). The mind must move unceasingly between the universal and the particular 'until it becomes dizzy and can distinguish neither . . . any longer' (ibid. 43), just as, when reading a text (like the *Speeches* itself), the mind moves back and forth between the meaning of the individual words and those of the whole sentence without cease. In this way, the inside and outside of Christianity are, according to Schleiermacher, mutually constituting: the transcendent starting point '*über*' religion is only made possible by Christian theological thinking, while Christian theology itself requires an outside, an other through which it is to be determined. Such is the refiguration of dialectics in Schleiermacher's *Speeches*: theologising takes place in virtue of mediation by the non-theological; it requires non-theological conversion and re-conversion.

What all the above examples (Kingsley, Newman, Eliot, Schleiermacher) have in common is the imaginary production of a scene of theological non-absoluteness, a place outside of Christianity from which theological conversion can take place. This locating of an outside allowed the theologian, as novelist or theorist, to return inside the Christian worldview, however ambivalently.

Colonisation

The above examples describe the constitution of a non-theological space from within theology. Later in the century, however, the very possibility of such a non-theological outside was fundamentally put into question. A concern surfaced whether such an outside was really the outside of theology as such or just a new, more covert theological inside – whether, that is, it was in fact a space too easy for theologians to recolonise and reappropriate for their own ends. Nietzsche's criticisms of Eliot are precisely along these lines: her attempts to exit Christianity are not successful, he argues, but merely repetitions of Christianity in all but name. She fails to liberate herself substantially from the theological. The relevant passage from Nietzsche's *The Twilight of the Idols* reads thus:

> G. *Eliot*. They are rid of the Christian God and now believe all the more firmly that they must cling to Christian morality. That is an English consistency; we do not wish to hold it against little moralistic females à la Eliot. In England one must rehabilitate oneself after every little emancipation from theology by showing in a veritably awe-inspiring manner what a moral fanatic one is. That is the penance they pay there. We others

hold otherwise. When one gives up the Christian faith, one pulls the right to Christian morality out from under one's feet . . . By breaking one main concept out of it, the faith in God, one breaks the whole. ([1889] 1990: 69–70)

While Eliot might think she is exiting from Christianity by secularising its ethical concepts, much more is required, Nietzsche here argues, to genuinely get out of the Christian framework which has so thoroughly permeated every structure of Western thought. For example, Romola's secular vocation is at bottom nothing more than a repetition of Christian virtues.

From *Beyond Good and Evil* to *On the Genealogy of Morals*, Nietzsche's own increasingly convoluted and violent attempts to forge a full-blown escape from the theological lay bare the challenge posed by the idea of an outside to Christianity. During the twentieth and twenty-first centuries, this challenge comes to be reformulated in many different terminologies: as the thinking of the end of metaphysics, as the deconstruction of phallocentrism, as deterritorialisation. All of these tasks have shared a similar imperative to find a utopian position outside of the Christian tradition, to 'get beyond' the theological categories passed down to us. The most powerful articulation of the difficulty of such a task has proven to be the 'secularisation thesis', the idea that all our attempts to forge a new discourse outside of the trappings of Christianity are doomed to failure, because everything new ends up a repetition, reoccupation or mutilation of Christian theological categories. This logic is found equally in Löwith's claim that systematic visions of historical progress are 'Christian by derivation and anti-Christian by consequence' (1949: 202) and Milbank's argument that 'secular discourse . . . is actually constituted in its secularity by "heresy" in relation to orthodox Christianity' (2006: 3). And, as the example of Nietzsche illustrates, this kind of scepticism towards the possibility of an intellectual outside to Christian theology was common in the nineteenth century itself. As early as 1846, one finds the following: 'Rousseau, Pestalozzi, Fichte, Saint-Simon, every new theory – socialism, communism, all are only trying to restore abandoned Christianity' (Varnhagen von Ense, quoted in Blumenberg [1966] 1983: 120).

A reading of Coleridge's notes towards his unfinished magnum opus helps bring out further some of the problems attendant on this vision of a theological outside.[11] Coleridge envisaged this magnum opus as the 'great work' that would serve as 'the reservoir' for his 'researches and reflections concerning God, Nature and Man', 'the harvesting of his life's labours', his 'system of Philosophy and Faith' (McFarland 2002: xli–xlii, lxxix). As such, it was to have encyclopedic scope, a synthesis of all sciences unified by a central Christic intuition. Among the plans for the *Opus Maximum* and for a proposed lecture course on anatomy are found a series of fragments on race and the origins of racial difference. In these notes, Coleridge offers an explanation of the origins of racial difference partly on the basis of 'dependence on "Circumstantial Nature"' (1995: 1400), but more fundamentally he sees it as a consequence of differences in 'a spiritual goal of moral perfection, "the ideal of being" concomitant with the "moral law" inherent in [man's] possession of reason' (Haeger 1974: 342–3). Hence, 'the whole process [of racial differentiation] is an affair of the Moral Will & for this reason alone belongs to *History*' (Coleridge 1995: 1400). Difference is thereby converted into hierarchy, and Coleridge's theory becomes a 'degeneration thesis' (Haeger 1974: 343): he posits a 'central race', the Caucasian, and various 'poles' of degeneration, 'the Negro', 'the Mongolian', 'the Malay' and 'the American' (Coleridge 1995: 1398) – a scheme that owes much to late eighteenth-century German anthropology. Coleridge goes on to suppose that 'a far higher state of moral and intellectual energy [is found] in the central Race' (ibid. 1404), such that 'we may unhesitatingly assert – Human Species consists of an Historic Race – and other Races' (ibid. 1401). In other words, the Caucasian 'is so evidently less degenerate, as to establish as it were an interspace between these & all others' (ibid. 1401).

The point of Coleridge's speculations on race becomes clearer when he considers the relations between the Caucasian centre-point and the degenerate 'poles', for he imports a Christian eschatological schema as the framework to make sense of them. The historical role of the Caucasian race is that of 'ameliorating – nay, subliming' the others, so as to reconstitute the unity 'of the species = Mankind' as 'one Moral Being in reference to an Ideal fulfillment (= Kingdom of God, Dies Messiae)' (ibid. 1402). Such unification will bring about 'a new Earth & a new Heaven' (ibid. 1403). Coleridge writes elsewhere:

> In the *idea* of the Historic Race we have presented a Vision of Glory . . . the fact that its realization is the final cause of our existence in the world cannot but wonderfully raise and ennoble our nature & the Race to which we belong in our own eyes. (Ibid. 1405–6)

Coleridge's words are reminiscent of traditional justifications for colonialism as, in Said's words, a 'Christian mission to revive a dead world, to quicken in it a sense of its own potential, one which only a European can discern underneath a lifeless and degenerate surface' ([1979] 1994: 172).

In a fragment that forms a projected part of the *Opus Maximum* itself, Coleridge is even clearer about the Christian nature of this 'regeneration of the races' (Haeger 1974: 348). He describes his theory as a 'consideration of the Races relatively to the Goodness of God and the Redemption of Men', and specifies Christ's work as 'preparing for and gradually establishing an opposition of quality in the different Families of the Earth' (quoted in ibid. 350; see McFarland 2002: ciii). McGee unpacks the entire schema as follows:

> Redemption occurs through God's providential ordering of this Central Race: it is through the Central Race that all other races are elevated . . . The Central Race, on its own natural power, could not redeem the other races. It is only through grace, through Christ, that the Central Race can perform its salvific purpose. As Coleridge says, 'Man can only solve the natural by the Supernatural'. Through Christ (supernatural grace), the Central Race becomes the Historic Race, the ideal humanity, and draws all degenerate and decaying others into its own, vibrant life. (2014: 2–3)

Coleridge's writings on race bear witness to what Jennings has labelled 'modern Christianity's diseased social imagination' (2010: 7), as well as to Carter's claim that 'modern racial discourse and practice have their genesis inside Christian theological discourse and missiological practice, which themselves were tied to the practice of empire in the advance of Western civilization' (2008: 3).

For the purposes of the current chapter, my interest is in how Coleridge's very literal advancement of colonialism is shadowed by a more metaphorical colonial enterprise: the subjection of all scientific discourses to an overriding Christian eschatological narrative. In analogy to the manner in which the 'Central Race' is figured as the saviour of the degenerate races in the above, the science of theology colonises other sciences, unifying and ameliorating them. Christian theology offers discursive redemption, or, more fully, salvation from the fragmentation and insufficiency of the sciences in the nineteenth century is promised by Coleridge's 'harmonizing of human knowledge under the final authority of Christian orthodoxy' (Haeger 1974: 353). Theology provides the solution to intellectual *dispersio*. This is not incidental: to borrow Barber's words, in this chapter 'in talking about conversion, or religion, we have all along been talking about coloniality, or race' (2014: 247). Speculations on race do not merely provide one illustration of the hierarchies of domination and appropriation that sometimes hold between Christian theology and its outside; rather, race is the 'primordial scene' of such Christian logic. To quote Barber once more, 'The capacity to establish structures of racialized domination through conversion, and to continue converting while leaving in place these structures, is a capacity established – prior to the colonial period – by Christianity' (ibid. 149).[12] Christian conversion may presuppose an outside, something genuinely non-Christian, but, Barber argues, it does so only on the presumption that such a space of alterity has always already been colonised: from the beginning, in its very conception, it has been converted back to Christianity.

What Coleridge sees in the supremacy of Christian theology is therefore the restoration of the principle of theological sufficiency. To repeat Smith's refrain, everything becomes theologisable, because God is to be related or even meta-related to everything that is. There should be no outside to Christianity, for Christ provides the transcendent meaning that encompasses all scientific, philosophical and historical findings. Every science (exemplified in the above by racial anthropology) should, on this line of thinking, be understood as an offshoot of the theological enterprise, should be conceived *within* theology. What Coleridge's notes indicate is the power of the idea of an absolute theology in the nineteenth century. While stories of conversion or theories of *Bildung* may have fantasised an outside to Christian thinking, the urge to recolonisation in the name of theological supremacism was equally strong.[13] Nietzsche was thus proven right (in part, at least): what at first seemed non-theological was often a covert, even pernicious repetition of theology.

During the nineteenth century, the two movements of exiting and entering from Christian theology coexisted side by side. When theologians envisaged an outside to Christian theology, they often did so merely as an apologetic device, as a means of sucking the reader back into the Christian worldview that much more authentically. This model is so powerful that it becomes difficult to imagine any non-theological outside that could not be retooled for theological ends: even in its positing of a radically non-theological Other, the principle of sufficient theology still frequently remained in force.

Notes

1. Smith summarises Laruelle's position as follows: 'The principle of sufficient philosophy can be summed up in the belief that everything is philosophizable. In this way philosophy gives itself a fundamental or necessary status in the discourses in which it shares (philosophy of art, political philosophy, philosophy of science, philosophy of religion, etc.)' (2013: 100).
2. Newman explicitly mentions Walter Scott's historical romances as a model for these novelistic experiments in apologetics ([1855] 1888: viii).
3. The later 1864 controversy was similarly framed around the issue of the normative value of the early church, and Newman's description of his own conversion experience at that time is remarkable for its parallels to the novels discussed above. Both are founded on the strict analogy between early Christian and mid-nineteenth-century life (see Poggi Johnson 1999: 132–3). Newman writes in the *Apologia*, 'My stronghold was Antiquity; now here, in the middle of the fifth century, I found, as it seemed to me, Christendom of the sixteenth and the nineteenth centuries reflected. I saw my face in that mirror . . . There was an awful similarity, more awful because so silent and unimpassioned, between the dead records of the past and the feverish

chronicle of the present ... It was like a spirit rising up from the troubled waters of the old world, with the shape and lineaments of the new' ([1864] 1950: 133–4).
4. For further discussion of these parallels in the novels between the early church and nineteenth-century life, see Dorman 1979: 175–6; Wolff 1977: 68–71, 273–82.
5. As he does with Walter Scott, Newman also makes reference to Eliot's *Romola* in his Preface to the 1888 edition of *Callista* as a model for the kind of historical romance he had been attempting ([1855] 1888: viii).
6. The gendered nature of this resistance to various worldviews, including Christianity, as mediated through 'a proliferation of father figures' (Shuttleworth 1984: 106) should be evident, even if there is no space to develop it in this chapter. On gender in *Hypatia* and *Callista*, see Lankewish 2000: 247–53.
7. On the idea of Eliot's 'religion of humanity', see the classic commentary, Paris 1962.
8. Bullen (1975) argues for this reading most forcefully. For Shuttleworth, on the contrary, 'George Eliot dramatizes the dangers of the Comtean priesthood' in *Romola* (1984: 102–4), while Schiefelbein (1995) insists, against the Comtean reading, that Eliot's 'emotional attraction to Catholicism' should be taken on its own terms.
9. Gjesdal (2014) goes on to stress the roots of this account in Schleiermacher's *Hermeneutics* and *Dialectics*, thus bringing out the fact that the *gebildete* believer is ultimately a good reader and a virtuous agent. See also Mariña 2008.
10. Schleiermacher continues, 'Just as no human being can come into existence as an individual without simultaneously, through the same act, also coming into a world, into a definite order of things, and being placed among individual objects, so also a religious person cannot attain his individuality without, through the same act, also dwelling in a determinate form of religion' ([1799] 1996: 108).
11. In what follows, my reading of Coleridge is heavily influenced by Carter 2009.
12. On this critique of the category of conversion, see further Barber 2015.
13. On race in *Hypatia*, see Walker 2007.

References

Barber, Daniel C. (2014), 'The Immanent Refusal of Conversion', *Journal of Cultural and Religious Theory*, 13.1: 142–50.
Barber, Daniel C. (2015), 'Nonrelation and Metarelation', in Edia Connole and Gary J. Shipley (eds), *Serial Killing: A Philosophical Anthology*, New York: Schism, 39–52.
Blumenberg, Hans [1966] (1983), *The Legitimacy of the Modern Age*, 2nd edn, trans. Robert M. Wallace, Cambridge, MA: MIT Press.
Bullen, J. B. (1975), 'George Eliot's *Romola* as a Positivist Allegory', *The Review of English Studies*, 104: 425–35.
Carroll, David (1998), 'George Eliot Martyrologist: The Case of Savonarola', in Caroline Levine and Mark W. Turner (eds), *From Author to Text: Re-reading George Eliot's* Romola, Aldershot: Ashgate, 105–21.
Carter, J. Kameron (2008), *Race: A Theological Account*, Oxford: Oxford University Press.
Carter, J. Kameron (2009), 'Creation, Imperialism, and the Aesthetic Imagination: Radical Orthodoxy's Postcolonial Melancholy', paper delivered at the American Academy of Religion, Montreal, 7 November 2009.
Chapman, Raymond (1970), *Faith and Revolt: Studies in the Literary Influence of the Oxford Movement*, London: Weidenfeld & Nicolson.
Coleridge, Samuel Taylor (1995), *Shorter Works and Fragments*, vol. 2, ed. H. J. Jackson and J. R. Jackson, Princeton: Princeton University Press.
Crawford, Charlotte E. (1950), 'Newman's *Callista* and the Catholic Popular Library', *The Modern Language Review*, 45.2: 219–21.
Crouter, Richard (1996), 'Translator's Introduction', in F. D. E. Schleiermacher, *On Religion:*

Speeches to Its Cultural Despisers, trans. Richard Crouter, Cambridge: Cambridge University Press, xi–xxxix.
Dahl, Curtis (1973), 'Pater's *Marius* and Historical Novels on Early Christian Times', *Nineteenth-Century Fiction*, 28.1: 1–24.
Dorman, Susann (1979), '*Hypatia* and *Callista*: The Initial Skirmish between Kingsley and Newman', *Nineteenth-Century Fiction*, 34.2: 173–93.
Eliot, George (1992), *Selected Critical Writings*, ed. Rosemary Ashton, Oxford: Oxford University Press.
Eliot, George [1863] (1996), *Romola*, ed. Dorothea Barrett, London: Penguin.
Foreman, Terry H. (1978), 'Schleiermacher's "Natural History of Religion": Science and the Interpretation of Culture in the *Speeches*', *The Journal of Religion*, 58.2: 91–107.
Gadamer, Hans-Georg [1960] (2011), *Truth and Method*, 2nd edn, trans. Joel Weinsheimer and Donald G. Marshall, London: Continuum.
Gjesdal, Kristin (2014), 'Hermeneutics, Individuality, and Tradition: Schleiermacher's Idea of Bildung in the Landscape of Hegelian Thought', in Dalia Nassar (ed.), *The Relevance of Romanticism: Essays on German Romantic Philosophy*, Oxford: Oxford University Press, 92–109.
Haeger, J. H. (1974), 'Coleridge's Speculations on Race', *Studies in Romanticism*, 13: 333–57.
Jennings, Willie James (2010), *The Christian Imagination: Theology and the Origins of Race*, New Haven: Yale University Press.
Kierkegaard, Søren [1846] (1992), *Concluding Unscientific Postscript to* Philosophical Fragments, 2 vols, ed. and trans. Howard V. Hong and Edna H. Hong, Princeton: Princeton University Press.
Kingsley, Charles [1853] (1975), *Hypatia or, New Foes with an Old Face*, 2 vols, New York: Garland.
Klemm, David E. (2005), 'Culture, Arts, and Religion', in Jacqueline Mariña (ed.), *The Cambridge Companion to Schleiermacher*, Cambridge: Cambridge University Press, 251–68.
Lacoue-Labarthe, Philippe and Jean-Luc Nancy [1978] (1988), *The Literary Absolute: The Theory of Literature in German Romanticism*, trans. Philip Barnard and Cheryl Lester, Albany: State University of New York Press.
Lankewish, Vincent A. (2000), 'Love among the Ruins: The Catacombs, the Closet and the Victorian "Early Christian" Novel', *Victorian Literature and Culture*, 28.2: 239–73.
Löwith, Karl (1949), *Meaning in History: The Theological Implications of the Philosophy of History*, Chicago: University of Chicago Press.
McFarland, Thomas (2002), 'Editor's Prolegomena', in Samuel Taylor Coleridge, *Opus Maximum*, Princeton: Princeton University Press, xli–ccxl.
McGee, Timothy L. (2014), 'Liberation and "Emergent Situations": Theological Discourse between (Christ's) Life and Death', *Journal of Race, Ethnicity and Religion*, 5.3: 1–28.
Mariña, Jacqueline (2008), *Transformation of the Self in the Thought of Friedrich Schleiermacher*, Oxford: Oxford University Press.
Milbank, John (2006), *Theology and Social Theory: Beyond Secular Reason*, 2nd edn, Oxford: Blackwell.
Newman, John Henry [1855] (1888), *Callista: A Tale of the Third Century*, 3rd edn, London: Burns and Oates.
Newman, John Henry [1864] (1950), *Apologia Pro Vita Sua*, New York: Random House.
Nietzsche, Friedrich [1889] (1990), *The Twilight of the Idols*, trans. R. J. Hollingdale, London: Penguin.
Paris, Bernard J. (1962), 'George Eliot's Religion of Humanity', *ELH*, 29.4: 418–43.
Poggi Johnson, Maria (1999), 'New Foes and Old Faces: Fiction, Interpretation, and Integrity in Newman and Kingsley', *Logos: A Journal of Catholic Thought and Culture*, 2.3: 117–35.
Said, Edward [1979] (1994), *Orientalism*, rev. edn, New York: Vintage.
Santangelo, Gennaro A. (1972), 'Villari's *Life and Times of Savonarola*: A Source for George Eliot's *Romola*', *Anglia*, 90: 118–31.
Schiefelbein, Michael (1995), 'Crucifixes and Madonnas: George Eliot's Fascination with Catholicism in *Romola*', *The Victorian Newsletter*, 88: 31–4.

Schleiermacher, F. D. E. [1799] (1996), *On Religion: Speeches to Its Cultural Despisers*, trans. Richard Crouter, Cambridge: Cambridge University Press.

Shuttleworth, Sally (1984), *George Eliot and Nineteenth-Century Science*, Cambridge: Cambridge University Press.

Smith, Anthony Paul (2010), 'What can be done with Religion? Non-Philosophy and the Future of Philosophy of Religion', in Anthony P. Smith and Daniel Whistler (eds), *After the Postsecular and the Postmodern: New Essays in Continental Philosophy of Religion*, Newcastle: Cambridge Scholars, 280–98.

Smith, Anthony Paul (2013), *A Non-Philosophical Theory of Nature: Ecologies of Thought*, Basingstoke: Palgrave Macmillan.

Taylor, Charles (2007), *A Secular Age*, Cambridge, MA: Harvard University Press.

Walker, Stanwood S. (2007), '"Backwards and backwards ever": Charles Kingsley's Racial-Historical Allegory and the Liberal Anglican Revisioning of Britain', *Nineteenth-Century Literature*, 62.3: 339–79.

Weinstein, Donald (1970), *Savonarola and Florence: Prophecy and Patriotism in the Renaissance*, Princeton: Princeton University Press.

Wihl, Gary (2009), 'Republican Liberty in George Eliot's *Romola*', *Criticism*, 51.2: 247–62.

Wiseman, Cardinal [Nicholas] (1854), *Fabiola, or the Church of the Catacombs*, London: Burns.

Wolff, Robert L. (1977), *Gains and Losses: Novels of Faith and Doubt in Victorian England*, London: Garland.

Zourabichvili, François [1994] (2012), *Deleuze: A Philosophy of the Event*, ed. Gregg Lambert and Daniel W. Smith, trans. Kieran Aarons, Edinburgh: Edinburgh University Press.

3

Society

Susan Curtis

Dramatic technological developments and economic arrangements in the nineteenth century brought equally staggering social upheavals that eroded confidence in traditional ideas about culture and religion, humankind and the Almighty. Lived experience, whether in the heart of the industrialising world or at its edges, changed, and with those changes came new ways of thinking about life and its ultimate meanings. Perhaps more than any other single domain, society, as it hurtled towards an industrialised form of modernity, brought new understandings of old concepts in theology.

The nineteenth century was not the first era in which men and women experienced transformational social developments – indeed, every century is marked by departures in the way people live, what they use to provide for their individual and communal sustenance, and how they interact with one another. Nevertheless, the social changes wrought by the harnessing of steam and electricity to generate power and by the envisioning of large-scale production and national as well as international networks of transportation and communication occurred at such an accelerated pace that intellectual and theological traditions lagged behind and often failed to provide satisfying justification for the ways of the world. Both workers in secular culture industries as well as Christian clergymen and theologians struggled to craft ideas and practices that restored a sense of equilibrium to a world turned upside down.

The essay that follows explores more deeply the social changes wrought by advancing industrialism and the concentration of population in urban areas and demonstrates how society in the late nineteenth century contributed to theological change. In order to appreciate the dramatic impact of large-scale industrialisation on people's social and spiritual experience, it is imperative first to examine some of the common-sense ideas that structured their experience of religion before the onset of systemic transformations later in the century. Thus the chapter will begin with an overview of theological themes that emerged under the influence of early nineteenth-century Romanticism and a burgeoning system of market exchange. It will then focus on the social developments of the second half of the nineteenth century that brought about disorienting conditions in which the religious consensus of previous decades rapidly unravelled. Large-scale industrial production and the accelerated erosion of community that accompanied it left Christian theologians floundering to make religion relevant to masses who felt both alienation from the church and social betrayal by secular leaders as well as the clergy.

Theology in an Age of Industrialism: Moral Free Agency and the Christ of Love

The beginnings of industrialisation lay in the eighteenth century when factories and mills began taking advantage of new forms of power to produce finished goods such as textiles on a large scale. These new forms of production required significant capitalisation as well as a labour force disciplined by time clocks rather than by season and task. Even as unfree slave labour came under attack in the Western Hemisphere, labour forces in proto-industrial states and communities found their experience of work increasingly oppressive and poorly remunerated. Relations with employers underwent new strains as former master craftsmen organised their shops on an impersonal, more efficient basis and displayed a willingness to sacrifice artisanship in exchange for profits. These new work arrangements, in many locales, resulted in living arrangements that increasingly segregated workers from their employers. Indeed, working people faced new insecurities around food and shelter as shopkeepers traded their status as patriarchal figures for their families and employees for a new position based on wealth and class. As opportunities opened in these factories and mills, the unfolding process of urbanisation began, and with the increased concentration of people came greater anonymity and anomie.[1]

In the early decades of the nineteenth century, the evolving conditions of work and relationships between employers and employees resulted in distinctively new religious practices. Some churches offered Sunday school classes for the children of the working class to achieve literacy and to be exposed to a set of moral imperatives that would help them socialise into the new reality of market exchange and wage labour. Christian entrepreneurs and successful businessmen also privately funded the publication and dissemination of reading materials that made the case for individual responsibility and temperance for both success and salvation. They pressed religious tracts and Scriptures into the hands of working people, regardless of their interest in or connection to the church. Bible societies, thus, helped to embed certain religious ideals into the wider culture.[2]

The basic theological message in the reading matter and Sunday schools emphasised the concept of moral free agency. In the simplest terms, proponents of moral free agency insisted that God gave every individual the will and the capacity to choose a life free of sin and vice, and that as 'free agents', individuals had the responsibility of accepting the consequences of their decisions. Social crimes such as violence against others or stealing – crimes that occurred more frequently in crowded urban situations where workers lived apart from the oversight of a patriarchal master – were obviously targeted (as they always had been). But even more subtly, the message of individual will to choose the right course of action became focused on once sanctioned social practices such as drinking alcohol. It would be a mistake to see the temperance crusade of the early nineteenth century as a cynical project of shopkeepers to exercise control over an intemperate, inefficient working class. One really could see efforts by the entrepreneurial, shopkeeper class to control the consumption of alcohol as an effort to empower workers to have a better life. Either way, temperance as a virtue and as an essential practice for those destined to achieve a modicum of success in this life and salvation in the next, inflected Protestant theology in the early nineteenth century.[3]

The theology of moral free agency actually found many enthusiastic adherents among the working classes as well as the middle classes. In a rapidly changing world, in which their experience of work and crowded, sometimes squalid, urban living was filled with uncertainty and unfamiliar social relationships, some working people found a sense of control in the idea of being a moral free agent. Indeed, exercising self-control over consumption habits could lead to a slightly better material situation. Other forms of self-control – such as less frequent sexual contact within marriage and a grain-based diet, as recommended by American reformer Sylvester Graham – also gave individuals a greater sense of controlling their destiny. While proscriptions against large families and gluttony were hardly theological mandates, they nevertheless dovetailed with the idea of moral free agency. Similarly, the feeling of empowerment extended to working people and women as they assumed new roles in Sunday school teaching and lay leadership. Thus the ascendance of Arminianism from its marginal position in early seventeenth-century Calvinist circles to its place of prominence (especially in England and in the United States) served well societies in the nineteenth century that were being remade by the splintering forces of industrialism.[4]

Theology embraced by plain folks in Europe and the Americas tapped into continental developments from the late eighteenth and early nineteenth centuries in which philosophers/theologians like Immanuel Kant and Friedrich Schleiermacher sought new understandings of religion that would modify or displace the purely rational with an emotional connection to God. Kant's critiques (1781–90) emphasised human beings' innate capacity to do their duty to God willingly and not merely because it is commanded from on high. Kant also insisted on free will and on the idea that virtue should result in earthly happiness and was connected to the notion of a benevolent, personal God. Schleiermacher advanced Christocentrism, because he believed Christ reconciled the finite with the universal, the here and now with the hereafter. Such a reconciliation could not result from a purely intellectual relationship with religion, he argued in *Christian Faith According to the Principles of the Evangelical Church* (1822); it had to be felt on a powerful emotional level. Emotionalism as a reaction against rationalism also partook of and fostered cultural Romanticism, which was ascendant in the midst of profound social transformations. As various Romantic artists and social reformers saw it, the breakdown of traditional lines of authority inherent in the rise of industrial/market society could liberate individuals from hierarchy, traditional forms of oppression and the supremacy of rationalism.[5]

Among ordinary people, Christocentrism took the form of radical primitivism, that is, the reliance on the New Testament for guidance on theological questions and on institutional organisation. Existing denominations, including the Methodist, Baptist and Presbyterian Churches, all developed primitive factions, and new churches, like Thomas Campbell's Disciples of Christ, emerged in the early nineteenth century. Primitive theology shredded traditional theological speculation on such matters as the nature of the Trinity, the existence of angels and demons, or God's intervention in earthly affairs in favour of more practical interpretations of the life and death of Jesus of Nazareth and his followers' efforts to create a truly 'Christian' church, and the requirements for Christian living in the present. Thomas Campbell famously asserted the basic principles of the Disciples of Christ: 'When the Scriptures speak, we speak; and where the Scriptures are silent, we are silent' (quoted in Walker 1970: 512). Moreover, while God sat in the judgment seat of those individuals choosing sin and error over the gift of eternal life, Christ symbolised love for and acceptance of his followers – theologians like Schleiermacher saw Christ as the emotional connection to a God of vengeance, and in the popular culture, Jesus appeared as an androgynous figure, 'meek and mild'.[6]

By the middle of the nineteenth century, the widespread acceptance among Protestants of the idea of moral free agency and the loving figure of Jesus as a buffer against the harsh exigencies of an industrialising market-oriented society indicates a meaningful correspondence between theology and lived reality. Reform movements – from temperance and anti-slavery to prison and dietary reform – reflected the focus on individual will and the power to control one's ultimate destiny by one's actions. Indeed, groups like the Church of Jesus Christ of Latter-Day Saints (Mormons) and communitarian utopianists that sought collective ways to challenge the vagaries of market society were marginalised by the majority that had embraced an individualistic conception of life in the here and now and as a way of attaining eternal salvation in the hereafter.[7]

Individualism in an Age of Corporations

Industrial and commercial developments that originated in the late eighteenth and early nineteenth centuries in various parts of the world experienced a take-off period after the middle of the nineteenth century. Technological innovations in transportation and communication and the harnessing of new forms of energy – predominantly steam and electricity, but eventually also the gas-powered combustion engine – contributed to the expansion of industrial production and the growth of corporations. International banking and stock exchanges, which were fostered by the revolutions in communication and transportation, similarly underwrote new modes and a larger scale of production. Mechanised agriculture across the industrialising world, like large-scale manufacturing of finished goods, resulted in surplus commodities that fuelled the quest for international markets. In order to compete successfully in this vastly expanded marketplace, producers looked for every possible way to reduce the cost of production. Choices made by industrial entrepreneurs seeking profits in this increasingly competitive marketplace radically transformed the societies in which they occurred. Corporate industrial societies turned the world on its ear for working people, for families, for communities, and for the religious institutions in which they found meaning in social and spiritual ways.[8]

Perhaps the most disorienting effect of rapid, large-scale industrialisation was the devaluation of work. The de-skilling of workers that began in the mills and 'bastard' workshops of the early nineteenth century accelerated in the new context of international competition after mid-century, and the increasing size of the workforce in individual sites of manufacturing or mineral extraction diminished the significance of individual workers and the possibility of a personal relationship with those who employed them. Moreover, a shift away from small-scale agriculture and/or rural, peasant communities towards commercial agriculture and urban concentration left millions of men and women displaced from their traditional homes. Seasonal migrations across national borders in Europe and the Americas as well as more permanent trans-oceanic migrations resulted in a larger labour force struggling to survive in what must be seen as a labour-buyer's market. Labour came increasingly to be seen as little more than a cost of production – one cost among others that had to be reduced to make manufactured goods and other commodities competitive and profitable.

Opportunities to find work typically meant moving to cities – and native-born as well as immigrant wage labourers found themselves living in parts of cities that were congested, unsanitary and unlike the villages or countryside they had left behind. The old cultural rules continued to prevail – that is, individuals were held responsible for their own well-being, and if poverty and squalor were one's lot, then the fault must lie in the individual's bad choices, vices or frivolous expenditures. Social scientists reinforced this view by misapplying Charles Darwin's conclusions about evolutionary survival of particular species to the human population. Thus Social Darwinists' 'survival of the fit' seemed to offer scientific justification to the religious imperative to accept responsibility for one's actions, and the political corollary was a refusal to intervene with programmes to alleviate suffering, to insist upon a living wage or to regulate the practices of corporations in any way. But success did not necessarily seem to be tied to the effort one put into work – wageworkers toiled without stint in factories, mines and mills for ten or twelve hours and barely earned enough to support a family while investors earned fortunes from stock speculation, from living parasitically off the labour of others and from performing little physical labour at all. The limited liability corporation, by its very definition, diffused responsibility for failure among hundreds of stockholders.

Under these circumstances, many families were forced to sacrifice fealty to a gendered social ideal – men engaged in remunerative work outside the home while women managed the children and household – as women sought employment as domestics, laundresses or piece-workers at home or in sweatshops in order to contribute to the family coffers. The children of the poor also contributed to the family income in jobs that put them in a world dominated by adults and by often dangerous machinery or unhealthful environments. These new social arrangements within families raised questions about what it meant to be a father, a child, a woman and a family.

In virtually every industrialising society in the late nineteenth century, a widening chasm separated working people from those who employed them, and social observers began to worry about the rising tension between the social classes. In countries like the United States, France, Germany and Italy that had just emerged from wars to consolidate the nation state, the spectre of 'class warfare' was frightening, but more and more frequently violent clashes between working people and the forces of order occurred. The united interests of capitalists and the state appeared to be conspiracies against the masses, just as labour unions and organised strike actions appeared to be dangerously radical attacks on the status quo. Mistrust of those on the other side of the capital/labour divide called into being scepticism about any shared cultural or religious values.

As a consequence of these massive social upheavals, any semblance of religious consensus evaporated and in fact, many working people found themselves alienated from organised Christianity. After all, the promise of some modicum of success coming from hard work and individual responsibility could not be fulfilled under the conditions prevailing in the late nineteenth century. But to make matters worse, most churches defended the status quo and, at least in the initial phases of industrial expansion in the 1860s and 1870s, few addressed the social disequilibrium. Until later in the century, Christian churches were prone to supporting the middle- and upper-class members of their churches and were simply baffled by the withdrawal of the working class. This seeming indifference led working men to wonder why they should pray on Sundays with those who preyed upon them the rest of the week (Perry 1899).

Withdrawing from churches and refusing to attend Sunday services, however, did not mean that workers had abandoned Christian teachings. As Herbert Gutman demonstrated decades ago, working people in the United States identified strongly with Jesus of Nazareth and justified their struggle for social justice by noting that Jesus had been a carpenter who appealed to the people of his day who worked with their hands. The historical Jesus had chided the publican and had insisted that the rich young man abandon his wealth if he wanted to be a follower. These passages from the New Testament convinced many workers that their sense of betrayal by the church was well-founded (Gutman 1977). Churches increasingly realised that they needed to respond to the injustices and disillusionment exposed by movements for social justice and social change.

The Son of Man and God the Father

One way that Christians in the late nineteenth century addressed the anger and despair of working people and the bewilderment of others was to think about how Jesus could speak to the modern conditions. Curiosity about the historical Jesus not only fed higher critics and church historians, but also inspired ordinary people who could not accept the notion that the Nazarene would turn his back on them. The emphasis on Jesus as the Son of God and Son of Man forced churchmen to acknowledge the social commitments of Jesus in his own day and to assert them as guidelines for modern Christians.

Interest in the Jesus of history was not new. David Friedrich Strauss's path-breaking *Das Leben Jesu, kritisch bearbeitet* appeared in 1836 and had been translated into English as *The Life of Jesus* by the 1840s (Strauss 1902), but it was roundly denounced because of the author's insistence that the miracles attributed to Jesus could not possibly have happened and were nothing more than myths used by early gospel accounts to instantiate Jesus of Nazareth as the Messiah of Scripture. Nevertheless, given the emergence of positivism and the study of history as a social science, a host of scholars, popular writers and even theologians sought the Jesus of history in the second half of the nineteenth century. And while much of this body of work is, as John P. Meier has argued (1991: 6), 'a more modern form of christology masquerading as a historical quest', it nevertheless produced an important shift in thinking about Jesus as man and as Christ. Biographers of Jesus eschewed the 'gentle Jesus, meek and mild' and embraced the burly, bearded he-man he must have been as a carpenter and friend of fishermen. Even a scholar as respected as Walter Rauschenbusch wrote in 'Jesus and the Social Problems of Our Age' that 'There was nothing mushy, nothing sweetly effeminate about Jesus. He was the one that turned again and again on the snarling pack of His pious enemies and made them slink away.'[9] The historical Jesus appealed to working men as well as to those in the upper and middle classes at a time when modern conditions called into question what it meant to be manly.

Social movements of the late nineteenth century identified the historical Jesus as their ideal and as a symbol of the values now compromised by a competitive capitalist ethos. Labour activists and Christian Socialists, like George E. McNeill, believed in the revolutionary potential of Jesus. 'The influence of the teachings of the Carpenter's Son still tends to counteract the influence of Mammon', he wrote in 1890:

> Though the Mammon-worshippers may cry, 'Crucify Him! Crucify Him!', the promise of the prophet and the poet shall be fulfilled . . . by the free acceptance of the Gospel that all men are of one blood. Then the new Pentecost will come, when every man shall have according to his needs. (*Labor Leader*, February–March 1890, quoted in Gutman 1977: 100)

The *United Mine Workers' Journal* revised the Sermon on the Mount for union members:

> Blessed are the union men. They are the salt of the earth which keeps uncontaminated the pure principles of brotherhood in the breast of their fellow toilers, and which, if allowed to die, would make us doubt the fatherhood of God. (*United Mine Workers' Journal*, 30 September 1897, quoted in Gutman 1977: 94)

Railway workers likewise insisted that their members 'are true followers of Christ and are striving to establish upon earth the Kingdom of God, for which disciples are taught to pray' (*Railway Times*, 15 January 1894, quoted in Gutman 1977: 94). In the economic crisis of 1893–4, tens of thousands of American workers joined with Jacob Coxey to form a mass movement known as the Commonweal of Christ. 'Coxey's Army', as the workers came to be known in the popular press, offered a potent critique of the captains of industry who, they argued, had abandoned Christian convictions (Schwantes 1985).

This theological shift occurred at the intersection of a crisis of faith and a crisis of masculinity. As men increasingly found themselves part of a collective – whether located somewhere on the corporate ladder or on a shop floor with hundreds of other workers – the old individualistic ideal rang false. Writers imagined Jesus not only as a strong physical type, but also as a leader among equals. The Jesus of the late nineteenth century led men as a 'captain' or older brother – indeed, it was in part his very status as a 'son' that made Jesus approachable and worthy of emulation and that made Christocentrism an antidote to the crisis of faith. In social organisations such as the Ancient Order of Free Masons, the Benevolent and Protective Order of Elks, and the Red Men, some of which had religious dimensions, men found meaning in collectivity and community. Rituals of membership may have been applied individually, but once they were accepted, members' identities came from the group. Likewise, joining with Jesus as a Christian meant becoming part of a church led by a 'peer'.

Religious writers began to employ new metaphors to describe one's relationship to Christianity. Josiah Strong, for example, argued that any individual worker profitably could be compared to 'a little pin' in a piece of complex machinery; as a 'pin' one was relatively insignificant, but as an integral part of a machine, the cog was indispensable. 'Our lives may seem very insignificant, but when we remember that because we belong to the Kingdom they are part of a vast plan, they at once assume importance', he wrote in 1893 at the beginning of a decade-long depression (Strong 1893: 300). Others, like Washington Gladden, used baseball as a way of explaining what it meant to become a Christian. One must strive to do his best as an individual, but the team effort was unquestionably more important (Gladden 1908: 219–20). Furthermore, within church circles organisations such as the Brotherhood of the Kingdom and, later, the Men and Religion Forward Movement emphasised the importance of being brothers/sons, and striving for a kind of manliness of which Jesus would approve (and which also, it turns out, would serve one well in the industrial/corporate world). Looking to others, gaining rewards from team effort, and subordinating the individual will to that of the collective – these became the guiding lights for following Jesus's path.

In the popular imagination, the 'golden rule' stood in for basic Christian belief. Thanks to popular writers, social commentators and noted social reformers, the mandate from Christ – 'So whatever you wish that men would do to you, so do to them; for this is the law and the prophets' (Matthew 7: 12; Luke 6: 31) – became the theological key to salvation. Not surprisingly, Walter Rauschenbusch and George Herron, prominent Christian Socialists, invoked the golden rule as a way to simplify and readily disseminate a theological position meant to critique modern industrial society. Such writers as Henry Demarest Lloyd and William D. P. Bliss, more known for social reform than for theological writing, couched their creeds for the good society and their exposé of un-Christian behaviour in the marketplace in the terms of the golden rule. The term was so ubiquitous that even Edward Noyes Westcott's enormously popular novel, *David Harum*, made use of it with a bowdlerised version that was actually illustrated through Christ-like acts of kindness and justice. Figures like Samuel Jones, a reform Mayor of Toledo, Ohio, showcased the scriptural ideal by taking 'Golden Rule' as a nickname. Jones drew inspiration from Leo Tolstoy and Giuseppe Mazzini as well as from the Sermon on the Mount as he sought through his example 'to teach larger views of life and duty' (Jones, quoted in Frederick 1976: 244).[10] In these ways, such men saturated American culture with religious ideals that came to be widely embraced as popular theological imperatives.

As the historical Jesus and Christocentrism took centre stage, God as father similarly underwent a transformation. Immanence gave God an important role of being invisibly present in the lives of men, but neither interfering in the daily affairs of humankind nor acting primarily as stern, uncompromising judge. As early as 1868, Elizabeth Stuart Phelps published a novel, *The Gates Ajar*, which presented God as a loving father who welcomed his children to reside with him for all eternity – whether or not they had met the arbitrary litmus test of a church. The daughter of Austin Phelps and granddaughter of Moses Stuart, both traditional stalwarts in the Congregational Church, Phelps found herself caught between a grateful and adoring readership, eager to be free of the vengeful God of the day, and traditionalists like her father, who in 1868 saw her writing as heretical.[11] Within two decades, however, the fatherly figure of God in *The Gates Ajar* had become a standard representation of the Almighty. One theologian in the 1890s even insisted that one of the consequences of Christocentrism was that 'God was gradually and rather unceremoniously bowed out of his universe' by those who could more readily identify with his son (Strong 1910: 44). Immanence drew attention away from the personage of God, as a final judge or as a father disappointed in his creation, and it emerged in a good deal of late nineteenth-century theological writing.

Mid-century Christian Socialists contributed to the reformulation of the images of God and Jesus by insisting that Jesus as Christ had brought humanity out from under the curse of God. Christian Socialists welded the demands for equality and justice in the world to an ideal of Jesus as the bearer of this truth. John F. D. Maurice, for example, used his position as founder of the Working Men's College in London to advance the idea that as sons of God, working men needed no other form of reconciliation with God; they simply needed to follow Jesus's example. Like the Commonweal of Christ or the labour movement in the United States, the Working Men's College sought to prepare workers to participate in the political life of the present in a context in which Christianity fuelled the quest for justice. The overarching aim was to create and extend democratic institutions through education. In short, the social movements and theology of the late nineteenth century reinforced one another.

The new understandings of Jesus and God mirrored men's lived experience in the late nineteenth century. Unions protected working men more ably than their fathers could, even though the view of fathers as loving pals to their children became sentimentalised in popular culture and in advice literature. Group activities – in work and in recreation – gave individuals the opportunity to strive but also to succeed or fail as part of a collective. New hymns celebrated Christ and new editions of hymnals in the late nineteenth century banished many of the old standards that featured an angry, judgemental God (see Sizer 1978; Blumhofer 2005; Cope 1906). The Religious Education Association in the United States revised the Sunday school curriculum in order to socialise the next generation into the Jesus-centred, group-oriented thinking that gave Christianity a place of relevance in the urbanised, industrialised world.

Settlement House Movement and the Laws of Service, Sacrifice and Love

While Christocentrism addressed the crisis of masculinity in crucial ways, it had an equally powerful impact on women. Industrial reality blurred the line between work and home that once had been clearer (although never entirely distinct), and women also questioned what it meant to be a woman and a Christian in the industrial era. Women of the upper classes performed few of the duties once assigned to 'true women' or 'angels in the home' earlier in the century – duties such as caring for children, preparing food and keeping house. Many of these tasks were performed by women seeking to augment their families' incomes. But in caring for other people's children, washing other families' laundry, preparing and serving food in others' homes, or perhaps working in factories and sweatshops that enabled other families to hire domestics, women of the working class could hardly live up to the ideal woman of the past. Moreover, middle-class women's educational opportunities prepared them for professions from which they often were barred or offered only grudging access. A crisis of femininity as intense as the crisis of masculinity prompted women to establish a new relationship to Christianity.

The challenges facing women and their families in the poorest classes of the industrial world developed because of the growing chasm between the rich and the poor and because of the concentration of the urban poor in urban slums. Christian reformers recognised that the spiritual needs of people living in urban squalor could not be met without first recognising the economic, social and physical deficiencies in their lives. The theological and religious shift in the late nineteenth century occurred when middle-class church people refused to blame impoverished people for their poverty and recognised the need for a neighbourly helping hand as well as a sense of 'brotherhood' in Christ. Theologians referred to the impulse behind this new thinking as the desire to obey the three great laws of life: service, sacrifice and love.[12] One of the most important manifestations of this shift was the emergence and rapid development of the settlement house.

The first settlement, Toynbee Hall, opened in 1884 as an experiment initiated by Samuel and Henrietta Barnett. To distinguish the settlement from a private hand-out or from mere charity, Toynbee Hall was opened in the East End of London precisely where the greatest need for social and spiritual redemption was felt. The Barnetts and the Oxford University students who took part eschewed the role of missionary to the benighted and instead adopted the role of a neighbour 'to learn as much as to teach; to receive as much as to give' (Barnett 1884). Like many of the men and women who followed their example, the residents of Toynbee Hall advanced the idea that spiritual renewal and reward was available to the reformers as well as their neighbours and that the reformers had a good deal to learn from those around them. They combined practical solutions with a collaborative spirit to make settlement houses vital resources to denizens of the industrial world's most blighted neighbourhoods.

After visiting Toynbee Hall in 1888, two American women, Jane Addams and Ellen Gates Starr, returned to Chicago where in 1889 they opened Hull House for the purpose of bringing the philosophy of Toynbee Hall to the United States. In short order the movement spread across the country. While most settlements were not strictly sectarian, most proceeded on spiritual grounds to offer a holistic approach to poverty – tending to the day-to-day needs of working families and providing nourishment to the soul (Stebner 1997; Deichmann Edwards and Gifford 2003).

Jane Addams penned one of the most eloquent explications of the need for a meaningful

Christian role for women and men in the settlement house movement. She argued in 'The Subjective Necessity of the Social Settlement' that girls dutifully went to church, listened to sermons, and longed to do something about the injustice and/or suffering in their communities only to be told that they ought not to place themselves in such potentially dangerous situations. What good, she wondered, was religious training if it could not lead to direct action? 'Our young people feel nervously the need of putting theory into action, and respond quickly to the Settlement form of activity', she wrote. Settlement house work, as Addams saw it, involved 'keeping house' in working-class and ethnically diverse neighbourhoods and living as Christian neighbours to help and support those who lived next door. Addams took as her model the early Christian communities that focused on fellowship, social relationship and 'a deep enthusiasm for humanity'. Early Christians, she insisted, 'believed in love as a cosmic force'. University-educated women like Addams brought professional knowledge to everyday problems, and they considered it a Christian duty to address environmental concerns that affected everyone in the neighbourhood, to provide wholesome and safe programmes for neighbourhood children whose mothers and fathers worked outside of the home, and to provide intellectual, cultural and educational tools for people denied a proper education so they could better comprehend their place in the new industrial, urban order and to more effectively respond to the challenges that order posed. Above all else they brought love to their fellow men and women as a 'simple natural expression' of the revelation inherent in Christ's message (Addams 1910: 121–2).

The settlement house movement offered meaningful outlets for women to refashion their identities as Christians and as women. As time passed, women and men who worked in settlements brought Christian ethical concerns to the public square and often provided the statistical and empirical data needed to persuade law makers of the need for social legislation. For women, the engagement in public discourse represented a new opportunity that was nevertheless grounded in traditional female domains. Women simply amplified the meaning of 'home' and enlarged the spiritual frame to include their responsibility to friends and neighbours as well as to themselves. The refusal to insist on a hierarchy of social worth led to a pragmatic approach to truth and to a realisation that all truth is contingent and a result of a process – ideally, for Addams and others, a democratic and inclusive process.[13]

Social Salvation

Across the industrialised world, social changes wrought a need for greater collectivity. As all of the theological and churchly responses discussed so far make clear, the older individualist understanding of sin and salvation gave way to social definitions of both. If working people had abandoned organised Christianity because they refused to pray alongside their employers who preyed upon them during the rest of the week, then many people of the cloth decided the problem lay in large part with the way churches defined sin. Some began to classify as sin such social wrongs as the exploitation of workers, despoliation of the natural world, and indifference to poverty and suffering. They thus challenged those who ostensibly broke no laws to consider whether their actions reflected what Jesus had expected of his followers and whether they had broken a higher law. Emblematic of this new way of thinking was Charles Monroe Sheldon's *In His Steps* (1897), which enjoined Christians to ask, 'What would Jesus do?' before making basic decisions in their lives. Sheldon's novel, translated into more than a dozen languages and pirated by publishers around the world, only popularised an idea that was taking shape in more formal statements of theology and in Christian organisations. As a Congregationalist, Sheldon clearly had shed historic ties to his Puritan and Calvinist forebears, for he placed responsibility for receiving God's grace squarely in the hands of the individual (see Boyer 1971).

More than two decades before Sheldon's *In His Steps* took Christendom by storm, clergymen and theologians had begun to formulate a theology best known as 'applied Christianity'. The title referred to the *living* of a Christian life, not merely *believing* like a Christian. Maurice's Working Men's College and articulation of Christian Socialism were important efforts to harness Christianity to movements for social justice. Other less radical manifestations of applied Christianity appeared in the last three decades of the nineteenth century. Washington Gladden's *Applied Christianity: Moral Aspects of Social Questions* (1886) exemplifies work aimed at stirring the consciences of middle- and upper-class Christians in light of economic volatility, which left so many people living in poverty.

The social view of Christianity built upon a theological foundation provided by the work of Albrecht Ritschl and Adolf von Harnack, who influenced at least two generations of Christian seminarians at the end of the nineteenth century. Both Ritschl and Harnack rejected church dogma that obscured the essential message of Christianity. Harnack, in particular, insisted upon historical analysis in which Scriptures were treated as scientific evidence. As a historian, he believed that the late Hellenic influence on the early church had led to dogmas that helped fledgling Christians define boundaries between their worldview and that of non-believers. But the effect, Harnack insisted, had been the obscuring of the fundamental message of Christ. He and Ritschl held an ethical understanding of the Christian gospel and argued that the basic impulse behind submission to God lay in a longing for meaning. Moreover, the act of submission was accompanied by a desire to act ethically. It was this ethical foundation on which Christianity should be built.[14]

The appeal to conscience, however, proved insufficient. Beginning in the 1890s, theologians expressed new ways to discuss salvation that placed a premium on collective thinking and behaviour. Social salvation required Christians to work ceaselessly for the betterment of the poorest in their communities, for as long as they failed to consider the needs and well-being of others, they could not truly be saved. This position grew out of social gospellers' and Christian socialists' new emphasis on Christ's demand for taking care of those in need, expressed in Scripture: 'Truly, I say to you, as you did it to one of the least of these my brethren, you did it to me' (Matthew 25: 40). Shouldering these social responsibilities came to be seen as evidence of a saved soul.

Walter Rauschenbusch, who had travelled to Berlin to study with Harnack, incorporated the German's conclusions in *A Theology for the Social Gospel*. Rauschenbusch saw a connection between salvation and love for others. A genuine religious experience was not Christian, he insisted, unless it 'binds us closer to men'. At the same time, social salvation permitted believers to 'lean back on the Eternal' and to 'draw from the silent reservoirs' for comfort and strength. The ethical impulse became manifest in Rauschenbusch's theology as the quest for salvation could never end as long as there were people in need of love and service (1917: 105). Similarly, Washington Gladden, in a volume entitled *Social Salvation*, argued: 'The bread and water of the spiritual life are the doing of one's duty and the service of our fellows; and without these elements one can never have the life of fellowship with God' (1902: 13).

The social gospel, with which social salvation is associated, took many forms, but all pushed for social reform in the secular realm as the duty of Christ's followers. Industrialisation and technological innovation brought positive change into many lives – they fostered greater sociability, intercultural contact and understanding, and commerce. But at the same time, these notable achievements came at the expense of many working people and racial and ethnic minorities. As Henry Demarest Lloyd noted in *Wealth against Commonwealth* (1894), there had once been a time when scarcity made suffering for some an unfortunate reality, but modern man's capacity to produce the necessities of life made such suffering unconscionable. Lloyd wrote:

> between this plenty ripening on the boughs of our civilization and the people hungering for it step the 'cornerers,' the syndicates, trusts, combinations, with the cry of 'overproduction' – too much of everything. Holding back the riches of earth, sea, and sky from their fellows who famish and freeze in the dark, they declare to them that there is too much light and warmth and food. They assert the right, for their private profit, to regulate the consumption by the people of the necessaries of life, and to control production, not by the needs of humanity, but by the desires of a few for dividends. (1894: 9)

Exposés such as William Booth's *In Darkest England and the Way Out* and Jacob Riis's *How the Other Half Lives*, both published in 1890, made it difficult to ignore the need for serious social reform, if not full-on structural change.

Among the many movements that embraced aspects of the social gospel were the Fabian Society in London, founded in 1884. Led by Thomas Davidson, the men and women who gathered in London on a fortnightly basis, beginning in 1883, ultimately resolved 'That an association be formed whose ultimate aim shall be the reconstruction of society in accordance with the highest moral possibilities' (Pease 1916: 31). They sought a path forward that subordinated material interests to spiritual needs and that avoided the pitfalls of unworkable utopianism on one side and purely economic equality on the other.[15] The Fabians attracted those interested in gradualist approaches to social reform and who chose to set an example of Christian living under modern conditions as a strategy for garnering support for political solutions to social questions. Elsewhere, courses in the recently founded disciplines of sociology and political economy were introduced into schools of theology to better prepare seminarians for the challenges that awaited them in the world and to introduce them to interpretations of Scripture and theology that would help address those challenges. Looking back on the emergence of the social gospel, Walter Rauschenbusch observed in 1904 the transformation in religious thought that occurred:

> Within our own memory the fear of hell and the desire for bliss in heaven have strangely weakened, even with men who have no doubt of the reality of heaven and hell. On the other hand, the insistence on present holiness and Christian living has strengthened. Good men give less thought to their personal salvation than our fathers, but their sympathy for the sorrows of others is more poignant. (1904: 1055)

Another outgrowth of the emerging social gospel was the institutional church movement. Instead of the traditional Sunday services and perhaps a handful of midweek gatherings of young people, women's organisations and the like, institutional churches kept their doors open throughout the week. They became hives of social activity – providing wholesome alternatives to saloons and dance halls at night, day nurseries and medical services for working families by day. They provided inexpensive meals for single men and industrial education courses for young people hoping to improve their chances at employment. Those involved in the institutional church movement believed that the church could become a vital force in the lives of the impoverished urban poor if it addressed all of their needs, spiritual as well as physical. At a time when some congregations fled to the newly established suburbs, institutional churches remained committed to the urban centre and sought to serve the people who lived in the neighbourhood as brothers and sisters in Christ.

Among the more notable of the institutional churches in the United States, one finds Charles Stelzle's Labor Temple in New York City as an effort to attract working people by reducing theological tenets to a simple belief in Christ's power to save and by fostering an ecumenical spirit where all – regardless of creed or political stance – were welcome. Stelzle's minimalist theological approach reaped a harvest of souls, resulted in renewed interest in the church by once alienated working people, and introduced innovative approaches to worship borrowed from successful vaudeville productions. Once the service began, Stelzle left no dead air between 'acts' of worship – prayers, hymn-singing, the sermon and the collection of offerings. In spite of the success of the Labor Temple, the Presbyterian Church that authorised Stelzle's experiment withdrew its support because of what they regarded as too many theological and liturgical compromises with the world (Curtis 1991: 258–70).

The principles underlying Stelzle's experiment, however, were not extinguished when the Labor Temple closed its doors. Christians in many denominations began to incorporate popular cultural forms and celebrities into their church activities in order to remain relevant to men and women of all classes bombarded with seductive messages about entertainment and self-realisation through consumer goods. They also sought common cause with other denominations – through ecumenical services, Ministers' Alliances, and organisations such as the Federal Council of Churches and eventually the World Council of Churches. Perhaps the most powerful statement made by members of the Federal Council of Churches was the Social Creed adopted in 1908. In its opening lines, the Social Creed called for churches to be concerned 'directly with certain practical industrial problems', and to stand for 'equal rights and complete justice for all men in all stations of life', for 'the right of workers to some protection against the hardship often resulting from the swift crises of industrial change' and for 'a living wage'.[16] This show of solidarity with working people signalled the adoption of social salvation and the social gospel by the mainstream of Protestantism.

Although not precisely a part of the social gospel movement, the Catholic Church staked out important policy ground in the late nineteenth century consistent with the ideals expressed by Protestant social gospellers. In response to class conflict in the industrialised world, Pope Leo XIII issued *Rerum novarum* in 1891 in order to spell out the 'Rights and Duties of Capital and Labor'. He scolded both capitalists and labourers for their refusal to find common ground and to treat one another in the spirit of Christian brotherhood. He worried that 'a small number of very rich men have been able to lay upon the teeming masses of the laboring poor a yoke little better than that of slavery itself' (*Rerum Novarum*, On Capital and Labor, Encyclical of Pope Leo XIII, 15 May 1891, in Carlen 1981: 243). The Pope likewise chastised working men who, in the thrall of socialist leaders broke their contracts with their employers and resorted to violence in labour disputes. *Rerum novarum* endorsed the commitment of those Catholic leaders pursuing social justice and an end to class warfare. In the United States, some Catholic bishops used the Pope's instruction as licence to support 'gas and water' socialism at the municipal level, compulsory arbitration of labour disputes, and the nationalisation of railroads and telegraphs. Thus, in the United States, the Pope's efforts to nip radicalism in the bud led, perhaps unintentionally, to the embrace of socialist political action (see Curtis in Stein 2012: 504–6).

The Kingdom of God on Earth

Ameliorative social legislation emerged in Europe, England and the United States as a result of the pervasive transformation of Christian practice at the turn of the twentieth century. From relatively conservative figures like Adolf Stöcker and Friedrich Naumann in Prussia to Christian Socialists in England, the push for reform gained strength at the end of the nineteenth century. In the United States, some clergy ran for office in order to advance a Christian social agenda in the public sphere, but even their allies in politics and journalism adopted a Christian position as they advocated for reform. Washington Gladden famously asserted that 'if the kingdom of heaven ever comes to your city, it will come in and through the City Hall' (Gladden 1905: 243–4). Investigative journalists in the United States embraced the moniker 'muckrakers', which referred to John Bunyan's *Pilgrim's Progress* character who was so focused on the filth before him that he never lifted his eyes to behold the glory of God's creation. Twentieth-century muckraking journalists adopted as their motto the biblical passage: 'And you shall know the truth and the truth shall make you free' (John 8: 32). They essentially set the agenda for social reform legislation.

The idea of passing laws to limit the power of corporations and the wealthy capitalists, to provide for the welfare of working people, to protect children from industrial labour and to construct a social safety net for every citizen arose in part from the desire to see the Kingdom of God on earth. The notion that humankind could help build God's kingdom drew upon a theological disposition towards postmillennialism. Jean Quandt has defined postmillennialism as 'the faith that the Kingdom of God would be gradually realized in this world; justice, peace and love would eventually reign supreme'. It is contrasted with pre-millennialism, 'with its catastrophic notion of the second coming of Christ'. Those remaining loyal to pre-millennialism resisted efforts to improve conditions; God, they believed, would wait until the final collapse of human civilisation to sweep away the wicked and reign for a thousand years over a peaceful kingdom filled with his believers. Because postmillennialists believed in the 'gradual redemption of the world under the influence of Christ's spirit rather than his physical presence', they saw it as their duty to move towards that state of godliness of which Jesus was the only perfect example (Quandt 1973: 391). The postmillennial impulse gained a sizeable following in the years spanning the nineteenth and twentieth centuries.

In 1892 Walter Rauschenbusch and Leighton Williams founded the Brotherhood of the Kingdom dedicated to better understanding what the Kingdom of God on earth would be and to 'assist in its practical realization in the world' (White and Hopkins 1976: 73). The ecumenical organisation endeavoured to make the Kingdom of God the focus of their work with their underlying impulse being to transform the social realm. Increasingly the devotion to earthly social reform led to less attention on the hereafter. Indeed much of the inspirational literature penned by Christian advocates of social reform urged readers to find salvation in the here and now. Similarly in early twentieth-century Switzerland, Leonhard Ragaz and Hermann Kutter founded a Christian socialist movement grounded in the belief that God's kingdom promised justice and peace in this world. In support of the Swiss labour movement, Ragaz added a pacifist perspective as well as a rallying cry for worker-owned cooperatives. Ragaz believed that if capitalists resorted to violence to reach their objectives, one should not be surprised. Were socialists to do so, however, they would be committing treason to their basic ideals.

As the Western world careened towards war in the 1910s, the hope for establishing a

Kingdom of God on earth began to diminish. The high-water mark of this remarkable era of theological innovation was reached in 1917 with the publication of Rauschenbusch's *A Theology for the Social Gospel*, but within a year many of the most outspoken advocates for these theological positions were gone from the scene. Indeed, even the staunchest advocates of social salvation, Christian socialism and the three great laws of life fell silent in the din of war or found ways to make them integral to the conflict.

The Great War and the Death Knell of Social Theology

From the middle of the nineteenth century to the eve of the Great War in Europe, social movements and social change in the industrialised world sparked a major reorientation of Christian theology. In these transformative decades, church leaders and theologians reconsidered the nature of sin and the means of salvation. They began to see how the individual experience was always contingent upon the social and that the line separating the sacred and secular was permeable. Socialist political philosophy and a variety of social movements fostered a creative intellectual and spiritual climate for theological innovation.

In the face of industrial conditions, which produced unprecedented – and many believed, unconscionable – levels of suffering and privation, Christians felt compelled to step away from business as usual in their churches, communities, schools of theology and cultural life. They felt they must intervene in their societies in order to press for social justice, an imperative they regarded as part of their duty as Christians. Concentrated wealth and industrial power proved to be tenacious opponents to those seeking refuge from the competition, greed and social conflict they felt had been spawned by industrial capitalism. So, even though the new, socially based Christian teachings gained ground in the years spanning the nineteenth and twentieth centuries, they were increasingly disseminated and received in circuits and modes of mass communication dominated by capitalistic forces. By the time war came to Europe and eventually to the United States, ideals such as 'service' and 'sacrifice' had become harnessed to secular patriotism and the mobilisation for war.

With a few notable exceptions, proponents of the new theology convinced themselves that the war against the Austro-Hungarian Empire was a just cause. Once the slaughter began, it became increasingly difficult to support the 'law of love' and pacifism as antidotes to chemical warfare and machine-gun fire. George Herron believed that the Great War had brought about the betrayal of Christian ideals. His postwar lament, *The Defeat in the Victory* (1921), captured his sense that even though the victors had couched their war aims in Christian terms, their resort to violence meant only defeat of those principles. By contrast, Harry Emerson Fosdick became increasingly bellicose as war approached. On the cover of *The Challenge of the Present Crisis* (1917), published in the year the United States entered the fray, Fosdick's editor had designed a mailed hand wreathed by a crown of thorns, a none-too-subtle way of suggesting that Jesus would have approved of the war. Two years later, after having spent time at the front ministering to soldiers, Fosdick used the very terms of the social theology to justify organised violence. He argued that soldiers had fought to 'save the world' by making a 'social sacrifice' that would lead to 'innermost salvation'. The war had stripped away all but the bare essentials of religion: 'service', 'sacrifice', 'courage', 'unconquerable cheer' and 'fidelity to comrades'. As civilians, these soldiers would have no patience with what now seemed namby-pamby do-goodism (Fosdick 1919: 27).

Much of the zeal for social justice and social salvation was thus consumed by the conflagration of war. While remnants of the theological innovations of the preceding six decades lived on (in some cases into the post-Second World War period), important aspects of the social gospel faced critical challenges from the Christian mainstream. Even theologians like Reinhold Niebuhr and his circle, who thought they were only correcting the flaws in the social theology, nevertheless left many believers with the impression that neo-orthodoxy had little room for the socialistic ideals of the past.[17] But in the dawn of the twenty-first century as the chasm between the world's wealthiest and poorest denizens grows apace, we have much to learn from the pioneering theologians of the turn of the twentieth century.

Notes

1. For a good case study of this process, see Johnson 1978.
2. Two classic works on nineteenth-century American reform efforts are Walters 1997 and Brion Davis 1967.
3. For an exceptionally strong case study of the impact of early industrialisation on religious ideas and practice in the American context, see Johnson 1978. For an excellent socio-cultural analysis of the onset of market society in the United States, see Watts 1987. Finally, Leigh Eric Schmidt, in *Holy Fairs* (2001), explores connections between seasonal religious gatherings in seventeenth- and eighteenth-century Scotland and later revival practices in the United States.
4. Walters (1997) connects the flurry of reform movements, including Graham's regimen of dietary reform, to the changes accompanying market capitalism. Edward P. Thompson's classic work, *The Making of the English Working Class* (1966), offers a compelling analysis of the important role played by participation in the Methodist Church in the empowerment of working people and thus in the moulding of a kind of class consciousness. See also Boylan (1990) for a study of the impact of the Sunday school movement on women's experience.
5. John W. Stauffer's *The Black Hearts of Men* (2004) establishes connections between European Romanticism and various reform efforts and religious ideals in the United States in the middle third of the nineteenth century. Tyler (1962) and Wood (1993) both argue that the United States in the years immediately following the war for independence and the establishment of a constitutional government in 1789 was marked by the flowering of movements that took seriously the idea of freedom and that rebelled against existing hierarchies. For a study of one of the social and religious rebels, Elias Smith, see Kenny 1994.
6. The reference here is to a children's poem and prayer written by Charles Wesley in the 1740s. The poem was later set to music and became a well-known hymn in the twentieth century.
7. Scholarship that connects outsider groups – especially the Mormons – to the larger American culture includes Quinn 1988; Hansen 1981; Curtis Mernitz 1982; Hatch 1991; Moore 1987.
8. Many of the changes that took place in the nineteenth century were intertwined, as many scholars have demonstrated. For excellent large-scale studies that provide perspective on these massive transformations, see Black 1960; Brown 1976; Taylor 1951; Sellers 1994; Geisst 1997.
9. This quote is from a galley proof of the article in the Walter Rauschenbusch Papers, American Baptist Historical Society, box 41. See also Sharpe 1942: 322.
10. The book as a whole offers an examination of ten individuals Frederick demonstrates as popular proponents of the golden rule. Westcott's title character (1899) was so widely known that he was invoked in the early twentieth century by Carroll D. Wright, Secretary of Labor in the United States, as he pushed for social justice from his position of power.
11. For a discussion by the author of accusations of heresy, see Phelps 1896: 119. On her father's response, see Bennett 1939: 1.
12. For two examples of the articulation of these laws, see Gladden 1893: 176; Rauschenbusch 1907: 271.

13. For an intellectual history of the thinkers who insisted upon a liberal perspective and upon applying Christian principles in everyday life, see Kittelstrom 2015; see Chapter 7 for a discussion of Jane Addams as a 'social democrat'.
14. Ritschl 1908, translated into English by Thomas Bailey Saunders, is the best presentation of his historicist perspective and of his insistence that even members of a Christian community can know Christianity only by subordinating themselves to Christ. Similarly Harnack, in *What Is Christianity?* (1900), offers historical knowledge of Christianity as an essential way to understand the meaning of Christian community.
15. For a first-hand account, see Pease 1916: 13.
16. What became the Social Creed of the Churches began as a speech by Frank Mason North to the Federal Council of Churches. See North 1908; Ward 1912.
17. For a recent provocative analysis of Niebuhr and other twentieth-century theologians, see Edwards 2012.

References

Addams, Jane (1910), *Twenty Years at Hull House*, New York: Macmillan.
Barnett, Samuel (1884), 'Universities and the Poor', *Nineteenth Century* (February).
Bennett, Mary A. (1939), *Elizabeth Stuart Phelps*, Philadelphia: University of Pennsylvania Press.
Black, Cyril (1960), *The Dynamics of Modernization: A Study in Comparative History*, New York: Harper & Row.
Blumhofer, Edith (2005), *Her Heart Can See: The Life and Hymns of Fanny J. Crosby*, Grand Rapids: Eerdmans.
Boyer, Paul (1971), '*In His Steps*: A Reappraisal', *American Quarterly*, 23 (Spring): 60–78.
Boylan, Anne M. (1990), *Sunday School: The Formation of an American Institution, 1790–1880*, New Haven: Yale University Press.
Brion Davis, David (ed.) (1967), *Ante-Bellum Reform*, New York, London: Harper & Row.
Brown, Richard D. (1976), *Modernization: The Transformation of American Life, 1600–1865*, New York: Hill & Wang.
Carlen, Claudia (ed.) (1981) *The Papal Encyclicals*, vol. 2: 1878–1903, Wilmington, NC: McGrath.
Cope, Henry F. (1906), *One Hundred Hymns You Ought to Know*, New York: Revell.
Curtis, Susan (1991), *A Consuming Faith: The Social Gospel and Modern American Culture*, Baltimore: Johns Hopkins University Press.
Curtis Mernitz, Susan (1982), 'Palmyra Revisited: The Book of Mormon and Nineteenth-Century American Culture', *John Whitmer Historical Association Journal*, 2: 30–7.
Deichmann Edwards, Wendy J. and Carolyn De Swarte Gifford (eds) (2003), *Gender and the Social Gospel*, Urbana: University of Illinois Press.
Edwards, Mark Thomas (2012), *The Right of the Protestant Left: God's Totalitarianism*, New York: Palgrave Macmillan.
Fosdick, Harry Emerson (1919), 'The Trenches and the Churches at Home', *Atlantic Monthly*, 123 (January).
Frederick, Peter J. (1976), *Knights of the Golden Rule: The Intellectual as Christian Social Reformer*, Lexington: University of Kentucky Press.
Geisst, Charles R. (1997), *Wall Street: A History*, New York, London: Oxford University Press.
Gladden, Washington (1886), *Applied Christianity: Moral Aspects of Social Questions*, Boston: Houghton Mifflin.
Gladden, Washington (1893), *Tools and the Man: Property and Industry under the Christian Law*, Boston: Houghton Mifflin.
Gladden, Washington (1902), *Social Salvation*, Boston: Houghton Mifflin.
Gladden, Washington (1905), *Christianity and Socialism*, New York: Eaton & Mains.
Gladden, Washington (1908), *The Church and Modern Life*, Boston: Houghton Mifflin.
Gutman, Herbert G. (1977), *Work, Class, and Society in Industrializing America*, New York: Vintage.

Hansen, Klaus J. (1981), *Mormonism and the American Experience*, Chicago: University of Chicago Press.
Harnack, Adolf von (1900), *What Is Christianity?*, Edinburgh: T&T Clark.
Hatch, Nathan O. (1991), *The Democratization of American Christianity*, New Haven: Yale University Press.
Herron, George (1921), *The Defeat in the Victory*, London: C. Palmer.
Johnson, Paul E. (1978), *A Shopkeeper's Millennium: Society and Revivals in Rochester, New York, 1815–1837*, New York: Hill & Wang.
Kenny, Michael G. (1994), *The Perfect Law of Liberty: Elias Smith and the Providential History of America*, Washington DC: Smithsonian Institution Press.
Kittelstrom, Amy (2015), *The Religion of Democracy: Seven Liberals and the American Moral Tradition*, New York: Penguin Press.
Lloyd, Henry Demarest (1894), *Wealth against Commonwealth*, New York: Harper & Brothers.
Meier, John P. (1991), *A Marginal Jew: Rethinking the Historical Jesus*, New York: Doubleday.
Moore, R. Laurence (1987), *Religious Outsiders and the Making of Americans*, New York, London: Oxford University Press.
North, Frank Mason (1908), 'Report of the Church and Modern Industry', *Christian Advocate*, (24 December): 2139.
Pease, Edward R. (1916), *The History of the Fabian Society*, New York: E. P. Dutton.
Perry, H. Francis (1899), 'The Workingman's Alienation from the Church', *American Journal of Sociology*, 4.5 (March), 620–9.
Phelps, Elizabeth Stuart (1896), *Chapters from a Life*, Boston: Houghton, Mifflin.
Quandt, Jean B. (1973), 'Religion and Social Thought', *American Quarterly*, 25.4 (October): 390–409.
Quinn, D. Michael (1988), *Early Mormonism and the Magic World View*, Salt Lake City: Signature Books.
Rauschenbusch, Walter (1904), 'The New Evangelism', *The Independent*, 56 (12 May): 1055–61.
Rauschenbusch, Walter (1907), *Christianity and the Social Crisis*, New York: Macmillan.
Rauschenbusch, Walter (1917), *A Theology for the Social Gospel*, New York: Macmillan.
Ritschl, Albrecht (1908), *The Christian Doctrine of Justification and Reconciliation*, New York: G. P. Putnam's Sons.
Schmidt, Leigh Eric (2001), *Holy Fairs: Scotland and the Making of American Revivalism*, Grand Rapids: Eerdmans.
Schwantes, Carlos A. (1985), *Coxey's Army: An American Odyssey*, Lincoln: University of Nebraska Press.
Sellers, Charles (1994), *The Market Revolution*, New York, London: Oxford University Press.
Sharpe, Dores Robinson (1942), *Walter Rauschenbusch*, New York: Macmillan.
Sheldon, Charles Monroe (1897), *In His Steps*, Chicago: Advance.
Sizer, Sandra (1978), *Gospel Hymns and Social Religion: The Rhetoric of Nineteenth-Century Revivalism*, Philadelphia: Temple University Press.
Stauffer, John W. (2004), *The Black Hearts of Men*, Cambridge, MA: Harvard University Press.
Stebner, Eleanor J. (1997), *The Women of Hull House: A Study in Spirituality, Vocation, and Friendship*, Albany: State University of New York Press.
Stein, Stephen (ed.) (2012), *Cambridge History of Religions in America*, vol. 2: 1790–1945, New York: Cambridge University Press.
Strong, Josiah (1893), *The New Era*, New York: Baker & Taylor.
Strong, Josiah (1910), *My Religion in Everyday Life*, New York: Baker & Taylor.
Taylor, George Rogers (1951), *The Transportation Revolution, 1815–1860*, New York: Harper & Row.
Thompson, Edward P. (1966), *The Making of the English Working Class*, London: Vintage.
Tyler, Alice Felt (1962), *Freedom's Ferment: Phases of American Social History from the Colonial Period to the Outbreak of the Civil War*, New York: Harper Torchbooks.

Walker, Williston (1970), *A History of the Christian Church*, New York: Charles Scribner's Sons.
Walters, Ronald G. (1997), *American Reformers, 1815–60*, rev. edn, New York: Hill and Wang.
Ward, Harry (1912), *Social Creed of the Churches*, New York: Eaton & Mains.
Watts, Steven A. (1987), *The Republic Reborn*, Baltimore: Johns Hopkins University Press.
Westcott, Edward Noyes (1899), *David Harum*, New York: Appleton.
White, Ronald C. and Charles H. Hopkins (ed.) (1976), *The Social Gospel: Religion and Reform in Changing America*, Philadelphia: Temple University Press.
Wood, Gordon (1993), *The Radicalism of the American Revolution*, New York: Vintage.

4

The University

Gerard Loughlin

In 1910, the University of Berlin celebrated its centenary with lavish festivities that had been ten years in the planning. Max Lenz (1850–1932) had been hired to write a history of the university, copies of which were sent to fellow institutions throughout the world by order of the Emperor, Wilhelm II (1859–1941). The heads of these institutions, along with eminent professors and other dignitaries, were invited to Berlin for three days of laudation that began on 10 October with a service in Berlin Cathedral. This was followed with other gatherings and processions, with addresses and the bestowing of honorary degrees, and with banqueting.

The University could congratulate itself in this way because it could think its achievements of the 'utmost moment' in the progress of the world. 'Every civilized nation owes a debt to German scholarship', the President of the still young University of Chicago, Harry Pratt Judson (1849–1927), declared in responding to Berlin's invitation (Howard 2006: 336).[1] It was a view that Julius Kafton (1848–1926), professor of systematic theology at Berlin, did not fail to elaborate in his sermon at the opening service.

Kafton's sermon sets before us the difference that was the University of Berlin, the achievements of German scholarship in the course of the nineteenth century, and the place of theology therein. Kafton pointed to the development of *Wissenschaft* in the university, and of the university in relation to the state. *Wissenschaft* can be translated as 'science', but this may mislead, especially if one is used to distinguishing between the sciences and the humanities, imagining there to be at least two cultures in the university (Snow 1959). For *Wissenschaft* aimed to be universal in its scope, an approach for all university disciplines, to which all are subject.

The text that Kafton took for his sermon was 1 Corinthians 12: 4–12, which likens the members of the church to those of a body, the one body of Christ. Likewise, in the one body of the university there are many academic disciplines – different but united in and through the scientific approach. Kafton warned that the university might splinter and become a 'bundle of specialized schools'. But this would not happen if it heeded the goal of unity, the ideal of *Wissenschaft*. The German university could be maintained, and would be maintained, 'with God's help'. Moreover, the unified university is but one member of a larger body, which is the nation, 'assembled in the order of the state'. The university plays its part by pursuing science for its own sake, and by educating the young in that pursuit, the two being intimately linked. 'No one can think of German culture and German intellectual life without the German universities. Their downfall would mean a collapse of the German nation – so important are they for the whole' (Kafton, quoted in Howard 2006: 337–8).

The ideal of the German university, as presented by Kafton, had developed in the course of the nineteenth century. It had become increasingly influential throughout the world, and would become more so in the twentieth century. As Jacques Derrida remarks, the University of Berlin, 'even now, remains the most imposing reference for what has been handed down to us of the concept of the university' ([1990] 2004: 85). But Kafton also highlighted what many had and have come to see as a problem for that ideal: the threat of fragmentation, of a disordered body, with members pulling in different directions. One of those members was theology, and for many its place in the body of the university had become questionable by the end of the nineteenth century.

Max Lenz, who had written the history of the University of Berlin (1910–18), also lectured on the subject at the closing of the University's celebrations. Like Kafton, Lenz had a high regard for *Wissenschaft* and for the intimacy of university and state – science being the bedrock on which the 'bond of monarchy and university rests' (Lenz, quoted in Howard 2006: 339). But unlike Kafton, Lenz questioned the place of theology in the university. For theology seemed the one discipline that resisted the spirit of *Wissenschaft*, of disinterested enquiry. For theology is bound by dogma and church, answering to 'revelation' and ecclesial requirements. Science is either historical or natural (empirical), and so theology must become the former if it is to continue in the university committed to *Wissenschaft*. University theology must become – and was already becoming – the history or study of religions (*Religionsgeschichte* or *Religionswissenschaft*).

Lenz's argument against an unreformed, ecclesial theology was not new. It had been around from the start of the nineteenth century, and – as we shall see – it had been affecting theology throughout the century, with theology trying to become ever more *wissenschaftlich*. But for Lenz it had not been trying hard enough. Kafton and Lenz were at one in their enthusiasm for the ideal of the research university, a community pressing forward through the disinterested study of history and nature to an ever more united society. But for Lenz, theology had to become much more of a historical science than already achieved, and in that becoming put itself in question. These arguments have been strangely replayed at the beginning of the twenty-first century, with people again arguing that theology has no place in the university, or that if it has, it must become something else – study of religion or religious studies. But the fact that these arguments were being made at the beginning of the nineteenth, twentieth and twenty-first centuries testifies to the fact that theology has remained in the university, stubbornly resisting.

It is with the story of theology's resistance that this essay is concerned. And it is largely concerned with this in regard to the German university, where a distinctly modern idea of scientific theology was first formed and questioned. It is from Prussian universities, and above all the University of Berlin, that such an idea spread, especially to Britain and North America. As a consequence – though also because the field of theology in the nineteenth century is so vast – there are only passing references to those other places and the theologies that developed in them. There are only passing references to what is undoubtedly one of the key nineteenth-century texts to address the question of theology in the university, namely, John Henry Newman's *The Idea of a University* (1873).[2] There are interesting differences and similarities between Newman's conception of theology and that which developed in the German universities, and there are equally fascinating similarities and differences between Oxford and Berlin, not the least of which is that there was no undergraduate course in theology at Oxford before 1870. There was, however, theology, with professors in the subject, but only because students were required to show knowledge of divinity – of the Gospels in Greek, the Thirty Nine Articles of Religion, and

Bishop Butler's *Analogy of Religion* (1736) – if they were to obtain a BA, and because most of them were contemplating a career in the church (Chapman 2014: 46).

Theology persisted and developed in the course of the nineteenth century, responding to the political, economic and social changes that transformed society. However, there are those who, while acknowledging theology's persistence, question its identity: the form remained the same, but the substance changed. One such person is Gavin D'Costa, who thinks that theology is now but a masquerade (2005: 20), and it is by way of his reading of theology in the university that we will move our consideration from the end to the beginning of the long nineteenth century. We will then consider the development of theology in the German university, the relationship of the university to the state, the proliferation of subjects in the university, and the relationship between prayer and university theology. We will finally consider the supposed eclipse of theology by religious studies and the secularisation of university and theology.

D'Costa starts his study of *Theology in the Public Square* by likening the place of theology in the modern university to that of Israel in Babylon; a place where theology, 'properly understood, cannot be taught and practiced' (ibid. 1). He cites two people – Richard Dawkins and Donald Wiebe – who think that theology should not be taught in the university, which is a rather weaker claim than D'Costa's own. The latter – which can be rendered more personally: that D'Costa cannot teach theology proper in his own University of Bristol[3] – is advanced for a number of reasons. First, the university is no longer where it was, for it no longer exists under a 'sacred canopy'; and second, it no longer has an 'organic vision' of its disciplines, nor a common understanding of what is good and true (ibid. 2).[4] Kafton's fear of a fragmented university has come to pass. For D'Costa, the university has changed throughout its history, increasingly becoming a less comfortable place for theology – or theology proper. There are a number of periods in which these changes occurred, but the 'nineteenth century was the decisive turning point' (ibid. 5). And the decisive turning point in the nineteenth century was the creation of the University of Berlin in 1810.

Berlin

The University of Berlin was founded in the shadow of the French Revolution and then of Napoleon's invasion of Prussia and defeat of its army at Jena and Auerstädt in 1806. The new university was an assertion of Prussian values in the face of military defeat,[5] but also the fruition of reformist tendencies in the Prussian state itself. Many saw a need for civil institutions that would better serve the interests of the state than had the old universities, with their debauched and riotous students. Indeed, the extensively named Julius Eberhard Wilhelm Ernst von Massow (1750–1816), minister of state with responsibilities for universities, wanted to follow the French example and get rid of universities altogether, replacing them with technical colleges. The French revolutionaries had closed the University of Paris in 1793, and it was not until the ascent of Napoleon (self-crowned emperor in 1804) that a new system of higher education began to emerge in France. This separated research from teaching, establishing institutions such as the Collège de France for the former and from 1808 a new Université impériale for the latter. A few faculties of Catholic theology reopened under Napoleon, but they were tied to the state and so shunned by the church.

It was Karl Friedrich Beyme (1765–1832) who was to take forward the development of the university at Berlin, and while he was leery of the name, he was also influenced by those who imagined the university a place for thinking rather than training. Beyme sought guidance from J. W. H. Nolte (1767–1832) on whom to approach for the teaching of theology, and it was Nolte who suggested Friedrich Schleiermacher (1768–1834), newly fled from Halle to Berlin. Schleiermacher had moved because of the closing of Halle University, and he greeted enthusiastically the prospect of a new post within a new university. The fruit of this enthusiasm was the publication in 1808 of his *Gelegentliche Gedanken über Universitäten in deutschem Sinn* [*Occasional Thoughts on Universities in the German Sense*] ([1808] 1991).

Beyme was not to see his project through to completion. That honour fell to Wilhelm von Humboldt (1767–1835), who took over from the interim figure of Karl Freiherr von Stein. Humboldt became the first Head of the new Department of Ecclesiastical Affairs and Public Education, and it was he who finally got the King to found the university in 1809, with its first senate meeting in the following year, on the tenth day of the tenth month, a few days after its first students heard their first lectures. It was also Humboldt who decided to retain the old name of 'university' for the new undertaking in Berlin. It was to be the university reborn.

There were those – such as J. B. Erhard (1766–1827) – who thought that theology should have no place in the new university (Erhard 1802). Johann Gottlieb Fichte (1762–1814) also thought it should be removed from the academy, becoming a practical rather than a scientific art, with pastors trained in other institutions. To remain in the university as a scientific art, theology would have to give up its 'claim to the sole knowledge of secrets and charms, frankly explaining and openly acknowledging that the will of God can be known without any special revelation' ([1807] 1956: 155). Scientific theology would become a merely historical study, eschewing the speculative and interpretative. Indeed, Fichte thought that a scientific theology could be housed within history. It did not need its own faculty.

However, in Berlin's early years, it was Schleiermacher, rather than Fichte, whose ideas of theology and the university were to prevail. Schleiermacher was more respectful of the university's older forms. He retained the name of university, and was suspicious of the French stress on the technical over the speculative. Yet he was also committed to *Wissenschaft*, and to philosophy as the 'lord' (*Herrin*) of the other disciplines. But more importantly, he maintained the connection between speculative science and practical outcome, insisting that practical theology – on the ministrations of the church – was the culmination of a theological education, the 'crown' of both philosophical and historical theology, as he wrote in the first edition of his *Brief Outline of Theology as a Field of Study* ([1811] 2011: 12, §31). Theology is a practical science, like law and medicine. In this way, Schleiermacher kept together what Fichte would have sundered.

The university was to be a place for research and teaching, where students would learn to learn – *das Lernen des Lernens* (Schleiermacher 1980: I/4: 35) – and come to understand the unity of knowledge and the power of the science by which it is brought to light. Students would be encouraged to become researchers themselves, but first and most importantly they were to learn the 'unity and connectedness of all knowledge' (Schleiermacher [1808] 1956: 245). Yet while *Wissenschaft* seeks the whole of knowledge, the whole of knowledge can never be wholly found, but is, as Schleiermacher's colleague, Wilhelm von Humboldt, wrote in an unpublished memorandum of 1809, 'always to be searched for' ([1809] 1956: 379). For Humboldt, both teaching and research were subordinate to the furthering of *Wissenschaft*, which was never finished, but always pushing on. Schools teach what is known, but the university seeks the unknown. 'This difference completely changes the relationship between teacher and student. . . . [T]he teacher no longer exists for the sake of the student; both exist for the sake of *Wissenschaft*' (ibid. 377–8).

State of Knowledge

Both Humboldt and Schleiermacher wrestled with the relationship between the university and the state, coming to recognise the involvement of the latter as a necessary evil, since it alone could provide the infrastructure for a university in pursuit of *Wissenschaft*. Yet the latter – the pursuit of a knowledge never fully to be attained – requires a freedom that the state will always resent and seek to circumvent. But the granting of such freedom serves the state, since the fruits of the university benefit all. It is a matter of 'freedom *from* the state *for the sake of* the state' (Higton 2012: 69). Nevertheless, tensions between government and academia would persist throughout the century and are to be found wherever universities are publicly funded. Such tensions are also found in private institutions, when the funders are not also the academics.

The one aspect of Humboldt's programme that now seems perplexing and proved problematic at the time was his suggestion that the state, and not the university, should appoint the professors. It would seem that though Humboldt had a high regard for what professors did, he had a low view of those doing it, and seemed to have imagined that state ministers would rise above the petty squabbles of the professoriate. Needless to say, the state proved less wise than Humboldt hoped, its commitment to *Wissenschaft* less secure than its interest in political gain and advancement.

In 1817, Karl Sigmund Franz von Altenstein (1757–1840) became chief of the newly established Ministry of Culture (Kultusministerium), from which position he continued to reshape Prussian universities in line with Berlin. The purpose of theology in the university was the training of clergy. 'A learned character is deeply embedded in the character of Protestantism. It is the surest means of maintaining an able clergyman; only serious intellectual activity keeps one vital and protects against indolence' (Altenstein, quoted in Howard 2006: 246).

It was under Altenstein that the University of Bonn was established in 1818, a Prussian outpost in a largely Catholic region, that as a consequence was established with two theological faculties, Protestant and Catholic. Though resisted by the Catholic hierarchy, the Catholic faculty – under Georg Hermes (1775–1831) – was for a time a centre for Catholic liberalism.[6] As with Hermes, the Protestant professors appointed by Altenstein were committed to developing a scientific theology, along Schleiermacherian lines. In the same year that Bonn was founded, Altenstein successfully persuaded Hegel, then but newly arrived in Heidelberg, to take up Fichte's chair in Berlin. There Hegel's responsibility for *Wissenschaft*, as Altenstein put it, could be exercised to its fullest extent.

Altenstein – along with Johannes Schulz (1786–1870) – worked tirelessly to promote the university as the home of *Wissenschaft*, its different disciplines unified by philosophy's commitment to the unity of knowledge; hence the importance of securing Hegel for Berlin. Perhaps more importantly, Altenstein worked tirelessly to increase the number and quality of professors in the universities. The Prussian professoriate, between 1800 and 1830, grew by a remarkable 147 per cent (Howard 2006: 251). At the University of Berlin, between 1820 and 1840, the number of theology students increased by 146 per cent, and their professors by 66 per cent (ibid. 252). However, it should be noted that in other parts of the university, the increase in professors outstripped that of students, a pattern that would be accentuated at the end of the century, as the prestige of other sciences grew at the expense of theology, with its scientific nature increasingly in doubt. Nevertheless, for Altenstein, theology was at the heart of the university, albeit an idealist theology that would serve a church bound ever more closely to the state, as was the university itself. It was said of Altenstein that all that mattered for him was 'scientific excellence irrespective of theological colour or party' (Tholuck, quoted in Howard 2006: 260). And this marks him as a harbinger of the university to come, the university of excellence, as lauded by Stanley Fish (2005, 2008). Or to put it the other way, it shows us that the research universities of the twenty-first century – seeking the academic stars of the day and rewarding 'output' and 'impact' – repeat those of the nineteenth. These are universities where – as for both Altenstein and Fish – theology can flourish so long as it does what it does excellently.

Thomas Howard (2006: 297–8) argues that by the end of the nineteenth century the state had so annexed the university that it could be thought a *Wissenschaftsstat*, with Protestantism the catch-all for the modern values of 'freedom, progress, and scientific inquiry', opposed to those of Catholic medievalism. Moreover, appointments to faculty positions were now firmly in the gift of the state, of the minister for education. The nature of the relationships between the Prussian state, Protestant church and university at the end of the nineteenth century is well indicated by the case of Adolf von Harnack (1851–1930), in his opposition to the appointment of Martin Spahn (1875–1945) to a Chair at the University of Strasbourg, and in the opposition of others to Harnack's own appointment at the University of Berlin.

Alsace was still coming to terms with its annexation by Germany, when, in 1901, the minister for education, Friedrich Althoff (1839–1908), decided to inaugurate a Catholic professorship within the University of Strasbourg as a way of enticing the Catholic population of Alsace to think better of German learning. But his appointment of Spahn drew the ire of those who did not think confessional allegiance consonant with the ideals of a university pursuing disinterested research. One of those who protested was Harnack, who in a public letter reminded the government of its duty to protect 'the sanctuary of the university from the disturbing encroachment of confessional and related forces' ([1901] 1984: 155). Harnack himself had been the beneficiary of the state's high-handedness in making professorial appointments against the wishes of other interested parties. For it was indeed Althoff who had, in 1888, brought Harnack to Berlin from Marburg against the wishes of many in the church who doubted Harnack's orthodoxy. Althoff argued that 'the freedom of scientific inquiry would be undermined and the standing of the theological faculties diminished' if these concerns were to prevail (Althoff, quoted in Howard 2006: 300).

Proliferation

Gavin D'Costa, among others, laments the fragmentation of knowledge in the modern university, a loss of the whole that he follows Prudence Allen (1985) in tracing back to the founding of the University of Paris in the thirteenth century, and the creation of its faculties. But needless to say, this splintering of subjects was made definitive in the University of Berlin, the place where theology was finally 'toppled' (D'Costa 2005: 19), though – as we have seen – such fragmentation was but in prospect for Max Lenz at the end of the long nineteenth century. And for Lenz theology was still standing, perhaps a little too sturdily.

The fragmentation of knowledge was very far from being in prospect at the beginning of the nineteenth century. Indeed, the University of Berlin was founded upon the opposite expectation, with its originators looking to an ever fuller and more cohesive ordering of knowledge. Their grounding texts (*Grundschriften*), which informed the aspirations if not always the practice of the new university, were saturated with an idealist philosophy that assumed the unity of human thought, and the possibility of its comprehension and articulation. Thus F. W. J. Schelling, in his *Vorlesungen über die Methode des akademischen Studiums* of 1803, argued for the organic unity of the sciences, and urged that the vision of this unity was vouchsafed to philosophy, 'the science of all science' – *Wissenschaft aller Wissenschaft* ([1803] 1956: 6).

For Schelling, all other sciences, including theology, were positive sciences (*positive Wissenschaft*), aimed at particular goods – eternal life in the case of theology, security in regard to law, and health in relation to medicine. The university serves to produce pastors, lawyers, doctors, 'instruments of the state', but does so through the disinterested pursuit of their respective sciences, pursued for their own sake and yet thereby achieving the good of a scientific state (*Wissenschaftsstat*), a state devoted to disinterested truth (ibid. 17).

There was no fragmentation of knowledge here. Of course, the key to this unity was philosophy and not theology, though theology was a 'higher' faculty in traditional schemata. Philosophy was now the faculty to rule the historically higher faculties of theology, law and medicine. Philosophy might have been ranked lower than these other disciplines, but it was now the one that led into them and ordered them. This idea was also propounded by Schleiermacher, for whom philosophy was a lower faculty in the sense of being the foundation for all the rest, the underlying and unifying point of each: 'Everyone must first of all be a student of philosophy' ([1808] 1956: 260).

When Fichte came to imagine the university he did so by invoking philosophy as the one discipline that could realise the unity of knowledge. And the means for expressing this unified knowledge was the encyclopedia, the 'circle of knowledge' as the name properly intends. As such, the encyclopedia was not a mere accumulation of knowledge, a list of names and topics, but a systematic introduction to the sciences, to their relationships and unity. The encyclopedia, as Schleiermacher said of the true scholar, shows 'the whole in every particular and every particular only in the whole' (ibid. 230).

No less than the inspirers and architects of Berlin, so John Henry Newman (1801–99), in his reflections on *The Idea of a University* (1873), insisted on the unity of the sciences, the university as the place where they are taught, and on philosophy as the ruling science, the 'science of sciences', as if echoing Schelling ([1873] 1996: 45). For Newman, 'all knowledge forms one whole because its subject-matter is one', namely, the 'universe in its length and breadth', which must include the Creator, who, 'while infinitely separate from it', is also so implicit in it, 'that we cannot truly or fully contemplate it without in some main aspects contemplating Him' (ibid. 45). Newman was fully aware that there were those who doubted or denied the existence of a Creator, but while offering some considerations in defence, he for the most part relied on the incredulity of his audience towards such beliefs to venture that natural theology – to say nothing of revelation – establishes itself as a science equal to any other.[7] 'Religious doctrine is knowledge, in as full a sense as Newton's doctrine is knowledge. University Teaching without Theology is simply unphilosophical. Theology has at least as good a right to claim a place there as Astronomy' (ibid. 40).[8]

It was not, then, the arrival of *Wissenschaft* and the encircling of knowledge in the encyclopedia that led to the fragmentation of knowledge and the diminishing of theology in the university. For *Wissenschaft*, as first conceived, was the child of an idealist desire for a unified knowledge that repeated differently the earlier medieval pursuit of the whole.[9] That ideal persisted in what became a monumental, though not enduring, achievement of nineteenth-century German university theology. This was the theological encyclopedia, which like the general one, was not – as already noted – an alphabetical listing of topics, but a comprehensive encircling of theological knowledge. It was a form that began to develop in the eighteenth century (see Purvis 2016: 60–3), but was most enduringly achieved in Schleiermacher's *Kurze Darstellung des theologischen Studiums* of 1811 ([1811] 1910), which he comprehensively revised in 1830, and which was first translated into English by William Farrer as *Brief Outline of the Study of Theology* (1850).[10] There were numerous such works produced throughout the nineteenth century, and – as Farrer's translation indicates – they had an effect beyond the German-speaking world, where however they were never fully naturalised.

Within Germany, Schleiermacher's work was highly influential, and not only in Protestant circles but also Catholic, inspiring the work of the Tübingen scholar, Johann Sebastian Drey (1777–1853).[11] More importantly, Schleiermacher inspired the *Encyklopädie und Methodologie der theologischen Wissenschaft* (1833) of Karl Rudolf Hagenbach (1801–74). This work – which was dedicated to de Wette and Schleiermacher – propelled the ideal of a unified, scientifically ordered theology through the course of the nineteenth century, being translated into several languages and going through twelve editions by 1889. Thomas Howard compares its 'pedagogical success' to that of Peter Lombard's *Sentences* in the medieval period (Howard 2006: 311).

Hagenbach taught at the University of Basle, where he worked tirelessly to make the university and theology fully scientific in the Prussian sense. His encyclopedia aimed to make Schleiermacher's thought more accessible to 'beginning students of theology' (Hagenbach 1833: 1). Apart from striving for the unity of theological knowledge – the theological encyclopedia being part of the general encyclopedia – Hagenbach's book also established the fourfold division of theology into exegesis, historical and systematic theology, and practical theology, and it promoted theology's historicisation, the realisation that theology is as much prone to historical happenstance as any other subject. Like Schleiermacher, Hagenbach insisted that practical theology was the crowning moment in theological progress, the point at which theology became directly relevant in serving the church. But the preceding scientific stages were required. 'Only that theologian who has passed through a preliminary scientific training ... is qualified to dispose and utilize the possession he has acquired' (ibid. 363–4).

If the medieval scholar sought the unity of God's mind, early promoters of *Wissenschaft* thought the human mind – individual human minds – could encompass all knowledge. But it quickly became apparent that such knowledge could at best be held by a community.[12] As the sciences proliferated, becoming more specialised, so the ideal of *Wissenschaft* became more positivistic, more concerned with the one small domain that any particular science was given to know, but to know it objectively, without contamination by the knowing mind. The ideal of knowing all did not go away, but it was postponed: 'perpetual striving for unity came to matter most, not unity itself, which receded as quickly as scholars approached it' (Howard 2006: 278). This new approach was not necessarily opposed to the earlier, more idealist notion of human thought in its unity, for it could be understood as a necessary process within the coming to be of that unity, within a wider movement of human thought towards its telos. It is an idea that perhaps persists today in the fantasy of the 'theory of everything', of a science that someday will know the mind of God.

There were a number of different forces that worked to bring about a more positivistic *Wissenschaft*. One was the rise of philology, the careful, meticulous study of ancient texts, including those of the Bible. Philology sought to establish their origins, the course of their transmission, their errors and contradictions. Everything was to be proved, nothing assumed. The church's Scriptures were to be treated like any other texts,[13] subject to the same degrees of suspicion and criticism (*Kritik*).[14] One of the early and most influential proponents of the science was Friedrich August Wolf (1759–1824), teaching at the University of Halle. Nietzsche would later hail him as having 'freed his profession from the bonds of theology' ([1875] 1988: 8:68). Wolf did not admit to his seminar those training for the ministry, for the truth they were seeking in Scripture was not the truth he had to offer.

But more than philology itself, it was its attitude to texts that was most influential, as this approach spread into historical studies and indeed theology. It was an attitude of painstaking research, one that sought to know a given subject ever more precisely, in ever greater depth, and so was ever more excluding of the generalist. In this way, specialisation occurred across the university, creating divisions between subjects and within them. A fragmentation of knowledge was perceived at the time and subsequently.[15] But in truth it was not the fragmentation of a previous unity but the making and proliferation of ever new knowledges, which might yet have a unity, not in the present but in the future, not in the knowing subject but in the object known.

Another factor in the rise of ever more specific disciplines was the decline of an earlier natural philosophy, *Naturphilosophie*, which was replaced by newer natural sciences (*Naturwissenschaften*). This development came to Germany from France and Great Britain, where an interest in natural theology led to the promotion of natural science by Christian ministers, keen to find in nature evidence of the Deity who had made it (Turner 2014: 106). St David's College, Lampeter, was one of the first places in Great Britain to have a Chair of Natural Philosophy and Chemistry from 1828 onwards, though quite who, if anyone, filled it is obscure (Price 1977: 55). But it was in the same year that Alexander von Humboldt (1769–1859) returned from France to Germany, bringing with him, in the words of Rudolf Virchow (1769–1859), an interest in 'sober observation and common sense', marking a 'transition to the time of the natural sciences' for German *Wissenschaft* (Virchow, quoted in Howard 2006: 282).

We have already noted the centrality that philosophy came to enjoy as the unifying science, and its prestige was further enhanced when it became the means to a career in secondary education. A university education became mandatory for all who wished to teach in a Gymnasium, and students passing the newly introduced *Arbitur*, the final examination of the Gymnasium, were entitled to a place at a Prussian university. Thus the faculty of philosophy became more attractive than theology for those pursing an educational rather than ecclesial career. And in time, the increase in numbers, and in subjects covered by philosophy, led to the division of the faculty. This was resisted in Berlin for longer than elsewhere. Faculties of natural science were created at Tübingen in 1863, at Strasbourg in 1872, followed by Munich in 1873, Heidelberg in 1890 and Freiburg in 1909 (Howard 2006: 283–5). New faculties, with new departments, and attendant research institutions and laboratories, required new buildings, and so new separations of colleagues, architectural as well as intellectual. This burgeoning proliferation could be seen as splintering and fragmentation, the loss of that unity at the heart of *Wissenschaft*, and of an earlier theological coherence, rooted in the world's createdness.

To think knowledge fragmented is to suppose that there was once a unified knowledge, now lost to us. But such a knowledge never existed. Instead we find a history of proliferation, of new knowledges emerging from old, appearing through sidesteps from previous domains, repeating them differently, newly. Thus it was imagined, at the beginning of the nineteenth century, that encyclopedic learning, in the sense already explored, would lead students to actively engage and not passively receive, and so intensify and extend the circle of knowledge, and this is what happened in the course of the century.

To invoke a fragmented knowledge – a proliferation of knowledges – is not to advocate a fragmented university. On the contrary, it is to imagine a community brought together through its commitment to know the whole it can know only in parts. On this reading, we should embrace the university vouchsafed by the nineteenth century. But this university is not Babylon, the 'Berlin-Babylonian university' that holds theology 'captive' (D'Costa 2005: 215). Nor is it Troy that theology must take from within (ibid. 217). It is rather the university as imagined by Newman, when he imagined the city, the metropolis – London or Paris – as a virtual university: 'The newspapers, magazines, reviews, journals, and periodicals of all kinds, the publishing trade, the libraries, museums, and academies there found, the learned and scientific societies, necessarily invest [the city] with the functions of a University' ([1872] 1909: 13; see further Loughlin 2011).

Prayer

An American observer of German university theology, Edward Robinson (1794–1863), was both impressed by the rigour of German *Wissenschaft* and dismayed by its impiety. Professors and students alike seemed 'destitute of any personal religion' (Robinson 1831: 211).[16] Robinson was also dismayed by the interference of the state in the life of the universities. Robinson went to Germany in 1826, and attended the universities of Berlin, Göttingen and Halle, before returning to the United States in 1830 with his German wife. Similar admiration and disdain was expressed by the Swiss theologian Philip Schaff (1819–93), who emigrated to the United States in 1844. Like Robinson, he extolled the separation of church and state in his adopted country, but also praised the freedom enjoyed by German theologians in pursuit of their studies, even when this freedom resulted in absurd impieties (Schaff 1857: 105ff.). He held that the proper response was not to deny *Wissenschaft*, but to embrace it, pass through its investigations and so 'come out more firmly grounded in orthodoxy than before' (Schaff 1847: 512–13).

These observations, from the first half of the nineteenth century, appear to confirm the view that when theology became more scientific – became *wissenschaftliche Theologie* – it became less ecclesial, less situated within practices of prayer and contemplation appropriate for an undertaking that is often acknowledged, after Anselm, as faith seeking understanding. Theology without prayer is also said to be less humble and more presumptuous, for only a 'prayerful theology "declines the attempt to take God's point of view (i.e. a 'total perspective')"' (D'Costa 2005: 114–15, quoting Williams 1991: 143). Gavin D'Costa argues that theology only flourishes when undertaken by virtuous people who pray and enjoy the sacramental life of the church (ibid. 5, 19). Prayer is an 'epistemological requirement' for theology, an 'indispensable prerequisite', along with virtue, for the study of God and church (ibid. 123, 126).[17]

D'Costa quotes the Anglican Newman on Mary as a model of the theologian (ibid. 131–2):[18]

> St Mary is our pattern of Faith, both in the reception and in the study of Divine Truth. She does not think it enough to accept, she dwells upon it; not enough to possess, she uses it; not enough to assent, she developes [sic] it; not enough to submit the Reason, she reasons upon it; not indeed reasoning first, and believing afterwards, with Zacharias, yet first believing without reasoning, next from love and reverence, reasoning after believing. And thus she symbolizes to us, not only the faith of the unlearned, but of the doctors of the Church also. (Newman [1872] 2006: 211–12)

But it is important to note that while Newman does not doubt that the theologian will have faith, he also distinguishes that faith from reasoning about it, which is the work of the 'doctors of the Church', who

> have to investigate, and weigh, and define, as well as to profess the Gospel; to draw the line between truth and heresy; to anticipate or remedy the various aberrations of wrong reason; to combat pride and recklessness with their own arms; and thus to triumph over the sophist and the innovator. (Ibid. 212; see further Loughlin 2011: 226–7)

For Newman, reason will not bring you to faith, but faith will invite you to reason about it, and so such reasoning is distinguishable from faith. Newman's own discussion of the nature and relationship of faith and reason is itself an example of such reasoning.[19]

Can we consider prayer and virtue causative and not merely correlative of (some) *academic* theology? As D'Costa notes, prayer is no substitute for 'intellectual rigor and accountability' and will not magically provide what comes from the 'painful, laborious slog of research' (2005: 114). But if no substitute, is prayer yet necessary for the rigours and labour of theology? Does it tutor humility and guard against idolatry? And then, if we think it desirable or even necessary, must we think it required of the formal structures and culture of the university, as opposed to the lives of individual theologians, who need not leave prayer at the door when they enter the university, but nor need parade it in their teaching and academic endeavours? Finally, we must consider whether the university of the nineteenth century, the German university, and above all the university of Berlin, was somehow the place where an earlier tradition of contemplative theology came to ruin.

It seems unlikely that prayer in and of itself leads to good theology. We need only recall the acrimony of theological disagreement both within and outside the university, the willingness of opponents to call down anathemas on one another, developing theologies in justification, and praying for the enemy's defeat. In 1860, the publication of *Essays and Reviews* – a collection of essays in liberal theology by six priests and one layman – led to the trial of two of its clerical contributors (Rowland Williams and H. B. Wilson) on charges of heresy, and for another contributor – Benjamin Jowett – to decry the 'abominable system of terrorism' unleashed by the orthodox (Abbott and Campbell 1897: 1:275).[20] Of course, one might say that good theology requires the right kind of contemplative prayer, the wordless 'deep prayer' of which Sarah Coakley writes in this regard (2015: 51). But this is to invoke an attitude rather than the practice of prayer in public. From the evidence there is no reason to think that such prayer will lead to better (or worse) theology and ecclesial polity.

Equally, there is no reason to think that prayer fosters non-presumptive theologies. No one doubts that Hans Urs von Balthasar (1905–88) was a prayerful person, and yet his 'kneeling theology' (see Balthasar [1964] 1989: 206–11) seems anything but reticent on the nature of divinity. As Karen Kilby notes, Balthasar 'seems very well to know his way around, to have a view – even sometimes something that seems remarkably like an insider's view – of what happens in the inner life of the Trinity' (2012: 112). Kilby does not find in Balthasar 'anything of the questing, wrestling, dialogical style of the classic works of theology in prayer of an Augustine or Anselm' (ibid. 160), and yet this would seem imperative for theology in the university, where everything is put to the question.

But putting to the question does not mean that prayer has to be driven from the university, for prayer itself puts the one who prays in question. Schleiermacher did not seek to separate university theology from the life of the church. Both were intimately linked, bonded in 'an eternal covenant between the living Christian faith and an independent and freely working science, a covenant by the terms of which science is not hindered and faith not excluded' (Schleiermacher, quoted in Welch 1972: 63). Schleiermacher sought to live this covenant in his own person. For forty years, he preached most Sundays at Trinity Church in Berlin. But he also sought to bring worship within the university, believing that a university church, with a university chaplain leading university worship, would unite church and academy – faith and science – through the common celebration of the Eucharist. This is particularly noteworthy, as Thomas Howard observes, because Berlin is so often presented as the 'prototype of the modern secular, research university' (2006: 188).

However, Schleiermacher's desire to unite the university around the communion table was not realised until after his death, with the holding of the first university service in 1847, and with Karl Immanuel Nitzsch (1787–1868) appointed as the first university chaplain. This office and regular university worship continued until 1870, when both ceased. In 1916, the holding of services returned, but without the office of university chaplain.

Thus the university of Berlin retained the careful distinction between faith and theological science that we find in Newman and, indeed, Thomas Aquinas. But this distinction is also a relationship, since theology answers to the church – as Schleiermacher always maintained – while also retaining its own integrity, answering also to the pursuit of the question, wherever it might lead. Undeniably, there is a tension here, even a diremption in the nature of academic theology: the need to draw close and push away at the same time. We might think it the tension in outlook between Fichte and Schleiermacher. But it would be a mistake to think that at the beginning or ending of the long nineteenth century, Berlin had excluded faith from its pursuit of knowledge, for the possibility of that pursuit was itself held in faith.

While the University of Berlin – in its provisional Schleiermacher-drafted statutes – had no 'confessional identity' and promised freedom from censorship for its professors,[21] Clemens Brentano (1778–1842) composed a cantata – 'Universitati Litterarie' – to celebrate the opening of the university. It placed the university and its pursuit of *Wissenschaft* under God; dedicated to God's understanding:

All-knowing God
We follow the traces of your understanding,
And what we too understand
and what we always teach
is at root only your Being.
The king has established
a house of *Wissenschaft*,
[And] we men stand bound
under his grace and strength.
God, bless our desires,
Let us fulfil the promise . . .
to teach the truth faithfully.
(Quoted in Howard 2006: 180)

The Science of Religion

Newman, in *The Idea of a University*, warns that 'You will soon break up into fragments the whole circle of secular knowledge, if you begin the mutilation with divine' ([1873] 1996: 29). Today we might be a little surprised to think divinity part of secular knowledge. But Newman is talking of natural theology, which he calls the 'science of Religion'. His usage of 'science' now startles, but at the time it was fully consonant with that of his German contemporaries. But a different science of religion would begin to prevail by the end of the nineteenth century.

The fate that awaits theology in the modern university is to become the study of religion or 'religious studies'.[22] Indeed, perhaps it is a fate that has befallen theology already, since D'Costa suspects that very little would change if overnight departments of theology were to become religious studies departments (2005: 21).[23] While D'Costa allows that there may be more than one way to study religion, more than one methodology or set of them, he nevertheless focuses on the phenomenology of Ninian Smart as paradigmatic of what religious studies is about, while yet noting that 'few today follow Smart' (ibid. 21). The phenomenon of religion is to be studied from a neutral, though empathetic, standpoint, from outside the religion in question, and without any consideration of its claims to articulate the world aright. One must bracket one's own beliefs and practices so as to adopt an impartial approach to the object of one's study, which can be observed all the more clearly for such bracketing. It is of course this ideal of objectivity – of the view from nowhere – that marks Smart's phenomenology as a thoroughly nineteenth-century undertaking, since it is an ideal that had developed within the tradition of *Wissenschaft*.

The advent of religious studies in the 1960s was really the repristination of an earlier appearing, namely, the science of religions – *Religionswissenschaft* – that developed in the latter part of the nineteenth century. In part it developed in response to those – such as Paul de Lagarde (1827–91) and Franz Overbeck (1837–1905) – who renewed the call of Fichte from earlier in the century for the removal of theology from the university. Though theology had become *wissenschaftliche Theologie*, it still retained relations with revelation and church, with the particularity of the Christian tradition and its claim to witness the truth of the world's creator in creation. But the claims – the worldviews – of other ancient and contemporary religious traditions were increasingly known and studied; and increasingly Christianity was seen as but one among them. *Religionswissenschaft* was an inherently German development, but oddly not so much in Germany as through the German emigré, Friedrich Max Müller (1823–1900).

It was as the Taylorian Professor of Languages at the University of Oxford (appointed 1854) that Müller made his mark as a Sanskritist, while helping to establish *Religionswissenschaft* through a series of lectures given at the London Institute in 1870 and published in 1873 as an *Introduction to the Science of Religion*. Here he announced the

> duty of those who have devoted their life to the study of the principal religions of the world in their original documents, and who value religion and reverence it in whatever form it may present itself, to take possession of this new territory in the name of true science. (1873: 34)

Christianity too, should be subject to 'true science', studied as but one religion among others. And Müller's call was heeded. Chairs in the history of religion were established in the following years across Europe (Uppsala in 1878, the Collège de France in 1880,

Brussels in 1884) and in the United States (Cornell in 1891, Chicago in 1892). The one country where such chairs did not so readily emerge was Germany, though the subject was being pursued there by an increasing number of individuals. One of their number was Lagarde, who in 1873, published an essay calling on faculties of confessional theology to give way to ones of comparative religion, a historical discipline that would seek the truth in all traditions, with no privilege accorded Christianity. In this way, Lagarde argued, a truly Germanic religion would be discerned.

Gavin D'Costa replays hopes and fears from the end of the nineteenth century when he argues that theology has become too much like religious studies. Franz Overbeck charged theology with losing its soul in becoming *wissenschaftliche Theologie*. In so doing, it destroyed Christianity. Scientific theologians were 'traitors', their theology the 'Satan of religion' ([1873] 1981: 236). However, unlike D'Costa, and others today who would be equally scathing of scientific theology,[24] Overbeck thought that Christianity had an 'aversion to science' because Christianity was an eschatological, world-denying faith ([1919] 1963: 22). 'World-denial is the innermost soul of Christianity' (ibid. 91). Only secluded monastics live the true faith. Though having lost his own faith, Overbeck taught theology at the University of Basle, where he had become good friends with Friedrich Nietzsche,[25] who encouraged Overbeck's thinking and the publication of his *Über die Christlichkeit unserer heutigen Theologie*. Needless to say, Overbeck's denunciations of liberal theology – then regnant at the University of Berlin – hampered the success of the comparative religion he advocated.

Another reason why *Religionswissenschaft* fared less well in Germany than elsewhere was a continuing loyalty to the nature and place of theology in the university that Schleiermacher had established at the start of the century. Harnack's rectoral address of 1901 to the University of Berlin gave both expression and renewed impetus to that inheritance. In 'The Task of the Theological Faculties and the General History of Religion', Harnack carefully considered the call for the advance of *Religionswissenschaft* over *wissenschaftliche Theologie*, but concluded that matters should remain as they were. Christianity should retain its pre-eminence in the theological faculty because Christianity was pre-eminent among the religions. The faculty should continue to serve the church but only because it had first served *Wissenschaft* without let or hindrance from the church. At the same time, *Religionswissenschaft*, which needed to draw on so many other disciplines to fully understand the religions it studied, would find a better home in the faculty of philosophy.

Thus, theology's full ruination was postponed until at least the second half of the twentieth century. But there is an irony in D'Costa's diagnosis of theology's present predicament, one that again echoes themes from the end of the nineteenth century. For the very thing that ruins theology – religious studies – has itself come to ruin. For it was always a fallacy – in the nineteenth century or the 1960s – to suppose that there could be a neutral standing point, outside of all tradition and cultural presumption. The bracketing of belief was always the bracketing of the other as 'other', the assumption of a cultural superiority. There was nothing neutral about the stance of objectivity, and the view from nowhere was always from somewhere, though unacknowledged. This became increasingly apparent towards the end of the twentieth century, as the theory and culture of postmodernity took hold in the humanities and social sciences, with inroads into the natural also. As D'Costa notes, these disciplines 'have tended to eschew objectivity and neutrality, and increasingly acknowledge that the role of the investigator and his or her socio-political location is crucial to the production of knowledge' (2005: 25). But where does this leave theology, and D'Costa's argument about it?

According to Gavin Hyman, the arrival of postmodernity has unexpectedly benefited theology. It is no longer possible to criticise theology for its commitment to particular axioms – narratives of revelation – for now all disciplines have to acknowledge a similar partiality (Hyman 2004: 196–7; see also Loughlin 1999). All are founded upon unfounded principles. As Ludwig Wittgenstein long ago observed, one can be persuaded for or against such principles, but there are none more basic that can adjudicate between them (Wittgenstein [1969] 1975: 81e, §612). This puts religious studies and theology on the same level, and one can no longer usurp the other, or if it can, it is now a returning theology that seeks the rout of religious studies, or at least religious studies as envisaged by Smart (Hyman 2004: 202–3).[26] But then it would seem that theology is no longer captive in the way that D'Costa has proposed. And this would seem to be the case from much earlier, from the ending of the nineteenth century.

The long nineteenth century came to grief in the disasters of the First World War, in the trenches of the Somme. And there died also the theology of people like Adolf von Harnack, the *wissenschaftliche Theologie* that he had so persuasively defended in 1901. At least it died for people like Karl Barth (1886–1968), who, as often retold, turned his back on a science that had not prevented his teachers, Harnack and others, from endorsing the Kaiser and his war. But this did not mean that theology succumbed to the *Religionswissenschaft* that so many thought should take its place. It meant the return of the very kind of theology that Overbeck had thought overcome; a theology that was not entirely world-denying but certainly world-judging, rooted in revelation. From his reading of Overbeck's posthumous *Christentum und Kultur*, Barth embraced eschatology as the truth of Christianity, but a truth that was not obsolete, as Overbeck had thought, but a challenge to the present, including the present church. Moreover, as well as developing a dialectical theology that scandalised Harnack, making him fear for the place of scientific theology in the university, Barth went on to build a highly successful career as a theologian, and did so within the university – first at Göttingen, then at Münster and Bonn, and finally at Basle. Barth maintained a commitment to theology in the secular university that D'Costa rejects (albeit having found a home there himself), a commitment to the sort of theology that D'Costa thinks impossible in such a place.[27] It is to D'Costa's alternative to such a university that we now turn in order to find again a nineteenth-century predecessor.

Sects

D'Costa sketches three possible futures for the study of theology in the university. The first sees theology (and religious studies) dissipated into other disciplines – into history, literature or anthropology. The second future sees religion retained as the subject of a specific discipline, but one that is now entirely religious studies, a purely socio-historical study. And then there is the third future – the one that D'Costa champions – which sees theology not dissipated or subsumed, but dispersed, like the dragon's teeth strewn by Cadmus and Jason, with new and diverse departments springing up everywhere in equally diverse universities. Theology needs to get out of the secular university and into Christian ones, and not just Christian ones, but denominational universities – Anglican, Baptist, Catholic, Methodist, Orthodox. In each, theology will flourish according to the tradition it serves.

It is only in a Christian university that theology can be theology. In such a university, it is not questioned but supported by 'liturgies, upright lives and committed staff' (D'Costa 2005: 216). It is only in a Catholic university that theology can be properly Catholic;

only in an Anglican that it can be properly Anglican; and so on. If theology is otherwise placed, in a secular university, it will become secular theology.[28] For all learning is tradition-specific, and the secular is one such tradition, as sectarian as any other (ibid. 217). Its secularity will seep into the bone of the theology it harbours.

The problem of sectarianism, of different Christianities allied with different political interests, has long troubled Ireland, and it was there in the nineteenth century that something like D'Costa's model was suggested but not fully realised. At the beginning of the century, the only Irish university was Dublin, its only college Trinity. Though dissenters and Catholics had been admitted from 1793 onwards, it remained an Anglican – Church of Ireland – institution, and Catholics were discouraged from entering by their bishops.

Thus it was proposed to establish new colleges – the Queen's Colleges – at Belfast and Cork, and later at Galway, which in due course would form a university – Queen's University. However, because of the 'peculiar and unfortunate character of the religious differences' in Ireland, as Sir Robert Peel put it, the colleges were to be secular institutions (Barr 2003: 29). The precedent was the secular University of London, that had come into being in 1836, constituted of University College, established as a secular undertaking in 1828, and King's College, established in opposition as an Anglican institution in 1829, opening in 1831 (ibid. 29–30). While London University was to expand and flourish, the Irish proposal fared less well, being denounced by Sir Robert Inglis as 'a gigantic scheme of godless education' (quoted in McGrath 1951: 44). Inglis opposed the colleges because they were not to be Anglican, while in Ireland they were opposed by some though not all of the Catholic bishops because they were not to be Catholic. They were also opposed by Daniel O'Connell, who – in a speech on 12 May 1845 – outlined what is in effect D'Costa's model for tradition-specific, sectarian universities:

> While I ask education for the Catholics, I freely and gladly concede it to the Protestants and Dissenters. . . . Let the Protestants of the Establishment have the full use of Trinity College for the education of their youth. Let the Presbyterians have the completest control over the education of their children in the Belfast institution;[29] but for the purposes of Catholic instruction, let two more colleges be instituted, one at Cork, the other at Galway, and let the Deans of those establishments be Catholic clergyman, whose appointment shall be vested in the Catholic bishop of the Diocese. (O'Connell, quoted in McGrath 1951: 44)

In due course Rome would suggest the establishment of a Catholic university in Dublin (Barr 2003: 39–44), and Newman called to be its first rector (ibid. 63–72). Lecturing in 1852, Newman scorned the idea of Catholics attending a secular university. But in 1864, having left Dublin, he sought to establish an Oratory – an outpost of the Birmingham Oratory that Newman had founded in 1849 – and a hall of residence for Catholics attending the University of Oxford. The Bishop of Birmingham, William Ullathorne (1806–89), gained the approval of Rome for the Oratory, but with the caveat – unknown to Newman – that Newman himself would not move to Oxford: 'the intention was to grant Newman sufficient scope to influence Protestants there, but not enough to attract Catholics' (Shrimpton 2014: 428). It was when this stricture came to public knowledge in 1867, that Newman abandoned the project.[30] The proposed hall of residence had already been rejected by Ullathorne.[31] Of course, Oxford was not then a secular university. But that Newman could promote the idea of Catholics at Oxford suggests the possibility of mixing sects; living as a Catholic in a non-Catholic nation, one can become an educated

Catholic through a non-Catholic university. In such a place, one might even be educated in Catholic theology.[32]

The withdrawal of theology from the secular university seems oddly unevangelical. Given the pious nature of D'Costa's 'theological theology',[33] why would it want to get out of the secular university? Why would it not rather remain for as long as it can, bearing witness to the faith, to a different way of being university; asking the questions that are not otherwise posed? D'Costa affirms that the 'Catholic university must serve the Church, so that [the Church] can serve society' (2005: 215). But might society not be best served by retaining theology within the secular university, within the very place that asks the question of the whole?

The universities of medieval Europe did not need to think themselves Christian universities because they were the universities of a Christian society. To replicate such today is to have secular universities. To have Christian ones is to have something new, a break with tradition. Modern Christian universities can never be Christian in the manner of the medieval Oxford or Paris. At best, they are a pastiche of such institutions. And if society and its universities have become secular, might we not expect and want a secular theology also? Which is to say a theology that can speak in and to a world with a secular rather than a sacred canopy. What use is a theology that speaks only to those huddled beneath their sacred umbrellas, while all around a secular rain is falling?

Notes

1. The University of Chicago was founded in 1892. It was a Baptist foundation, and funded by John D. Rockefeller (1839–1937). Judson was a historian and served as the second president of the university from 1903–27. For a study of theology at Chicago, see Chapman 2014: 79–98.
2. I have addressed Newman and his idea of the university more fully in Loughlin 2009, 2011.
3. D'Costa notes that this self-reflective quandary – that he teaches theology in a place where it cannot be taught – is 'uncomfortable' (2005: 5). For it is a place where he still has leave to write his books and teach his students that they are 'prisoners to mammon' (ibid. 215).
4. The image of the canopy derives from Peter Berger (1967).
5. The King reportedly approved the proposal to found Berlin by declaring: 'That is right, that is good! The state must replace with intellectual strength what it has lost in material resources' (Köpke 1860: 37).
6. Hermes' theological system – 'Hermesianism' – was condemned by a papal bull of 1835, *Dum acerbissimas*, and Hermes' writings were placed on the Index.
7. Newman expressly states that he does not prove but assumes the existence of a 'Supreme Being'. His chief defence of this assumption, in the *Idea* as elsewhere, is to suggest that the opposite assumption – that there is no supreme being – is equally a matter of belief that begs the question. See Newman [1873] 1996: 50.
8. Newman insisted that theology was as much a science as any other discipline, defining theology as 'the Science of God, or the truths we know about God put into system; just as we have a science of the stars, and call it astronomy, or one of the crust of the earth, and call it geology' ([1873] 1996: 52).
9. Mike Higton also notes the continuities as well as discontinuities between medieval and enlightenment conceptions of the university. See Higton 2012: 52–4.
10. The most recent translation is by Terrence N. Tice (2011). Of course, the modern systematising of theology may be said to date from the early seventeenth century, with Bartholomäus Keckermann (1572–1608), one of the first to use the term *theologia systematica*.
11. On Drey, see Purvis 2016: 161–2; for theology at Tübingen, see Zachhuber 2013.

12. For an account of the sociality that enabled the ideal and practice of *Wissenschaft*, see Higton 2012: 54–65.
13. Benjamin Jowett (1817–93) notoriously urged readers to 'interpret the Scripture like any other book' (Jowett 1860: 458). '[I]n the externals of interpretation, that is to say, the meaning of words, the connexion of sentences, the settlement of the text, the evidence of facts, the same rules apply to the Old and New Testaments as to other books' (ibid. 407–8).
14. For accounts of these approaches in regard to the Old and New Testaments, see Clements 1985; O'Neil 1985.
15. Jacob Burckhardt in 1840: 'Due to the enormous expansion of *Wissenschaft* one is obliged to limit oneself to some definite subject and pursue it single mindedly' (quoted in Howard 2006: 277).
16. Mark Chapman observes that 'through the nineteenth century an often somewhat vague piety was usually sufficient to convince theologians that what they were doing remained theological' (2014: 17).
17. Sarah Coakley also argues for the necessity of prayer for theology, for 'if one is resolutely *not* engaged in the practices of prayer, contemplation, and worship, then there are certain sorts of philosophical insight that are unlikely, if not impossible, to become available to one' (2013: 16). This of course begs the question, since such insights must remain unavailable to anyone not reading Coakley's book in a prayerful way. Likewise, is prayer necessary for understanding D'Costa's theological study?
18. Newman left the Church of England for the Church of Rome in 1845.
19. Newman's distinction between faith and reason, and his refusal to collapse the latter into the former, is long-standing in Christian theology. Thomas Aquinas makes the same distinction between faith (*fides*) and knowledge (*scientia*). In his discussion of Christian theology (*sacra doctrina*), Thomas distinguishes between two kinds of judgement. One is, as it were, intuitive, the judgement of a virtuous person, while the second is arrived at by reasoning, 'as when a person soundly instructed in moral science can appreciate the activity of virtues he does not himself possess'. In matters of theology, the first is that of the 'spiritual man', gifted by the Spirit, while the second is 'taken by sacred doctrine to the extent that it can be gained by study' on 'premises held from revelation' (Aquinas [1274] 1964: 1a, 1, 6 [p. 25]). The second is the way of theological science, which by implication could be undertaken by people who appreciate the faith they do not themselves possess. D'Costa discusses this passage (2005: 127–8; with unreliable referencing), but focuses on the first kind of judgement, that of the virtuous and spiritual, and makes it more central to Christian theology than I think Thomas requires.
20. On Rowland Williams (1817–70) and H. B. Wilson (1803–88), see Crowther 1970: 82–106, 107–26, respectively. On *Essays and Reviews*, see Chapman 2014: 59–60, 65–77; Crowther 1970: *passim*.
21. These statutes were modified in 1817 to stop professors from speaking on political matters or against the laws of the land, and from 1819 onwards professors had to refrain from anything that might upset the peace and undermine the state. Though not always separated, the concern was with political rather than religious heterodoxy.
22. The term 'religious studies' can make (some) theologians shudder. When it was proposed that the Department of Theology at Durham University should change its name to acknowledge the arrival of new colleagues from the former Department of Religious Studies at Newcastle University, it was agreed on condition that the new name should not include the despised term. Thus the Department of Theology and Religion was born in 2004.
23. D'Costa describes the relationship of religious studies to theology as Oedipal, though he also describes theology in this relationship as a 'dead mother' (2005: 23), which suggests that we should think more in terms of Electra, with seemingly religion – or even 'the divine' – the paternal object of desire, with whom theology had once been sleeping (ibid. 20). Religious studies is now cavorting with religion, and theology is abandoned if not expired or nearly so – a 'nearly dead mother' (ibid. 36).

24. See, for example, Stanley Hauerwas, who welcomes D'Costa's critique (2007: 181–5).
25. Nietzsche was Professor of Classics at Basle from 1869–78.
26. The setting free of theology in postmodernity is also the setting free of religious studies. Hyman proposes a new kind of religious studies that is betwixt and between how it was and how theology is now. It is a less ideological and more *ad hoc* form of religious studies. See Hyman 2004: 214–17. See also Rogers 2006 for how theology and religious studies benefit each other.
27. It might be noted that Stanley Hauerwas (2007), who reiterates D'Costa on prayer, does not follow D'Costa in removing theology from the secular university. Hauerwas remains closer to Barth in this regard.
28. 'God and such a university cannot coexist', as Newman put it in a letter of 16 April 1851 to Bishop Paul Cullen (quoted in Barr 2003: 87).
29. This was the Belfast Academical Institute, founded in 1810.
30. An Oxford Oratory was eventually established in 1993.
31. The opposition of the English bishops to Catholics going to Oxford led Newman to privately denounce the bishops' 'dreadful jealousy of the laity'. Newman to Thomas Allies (30 November 1864) in Newman 1961–2008: 21:327.
32. The University of Durham was founded as an Anglican institution in 1837, partly in response to the spread of 'Godless' education in London. Today it is a secular university, but with a flourishing Centre for Catholic Studies (2008–) in its Department of Theology and Religion. See further Murray 2013.
33. The term is borrowed from Webster 1998.

References

Abbott, Evelyn and Lewis Campbell (1897), *The Life and Letters of Benjamin Jowett*, 2 vols, London: John Murray.

Allen, Prudence (1985), *The Concept of Woman: The Aristotelian Revolution 750 B.C. – A.D. 1250*, Quebec: Eden Press.

Aquinas, Thomas [1274] (1964), *Summa Theologiæ*, vol. 1: *Christian Theology* (1a I), trans. and ed. Thomas Gilby OP, Oxford: Blackfriars.

Balthasar, Hans Urs von [1964] (1989), 'Theology and Sanctity', in *Explorations in Theology I: The Word Made Flesh*, trans. A. V. Littledale and Alexander Dru, San Francisco: Ignatius Press, 181–211.

Barr, Colin (2003), *Paul Cullen, John Henry Newman, and the Catholic University of Ireland, 1845–1865*, Notre Dame: University of Notre Dame Press.

Berger, Peter L. (1967), *The Sacred Canopy: Elements of a Social Theory of Religion*, Garden City, NY: Doubleday.

Chapman, Mark D. (2014), *Theology and Society in Three Cities: Berlin, Oxford and Chicago, 1800–1914*, Cambridge: James Clarke.

Clements, R. E. (1985), 'The Study of the Old Testament', in *Nineteenth Century Religious Thought in the West*, ed. Ninian Smart, John Clayton, Steven Katz and Patrick Sherry, vol. 3, Cambridge: Cambridge University Press, 109–41.

Coakley, Sarah (2013), *God, Sexuality, and the Self: An Essay 'On the Trinity'*, Cambridge: Cambridge University Press.

Coakley, Sarah (2015), *The New Asceticism: Sexuality, Gender and the Quest for God*, London: Bloomsbury.

Crowther, M. A. (1970), *Church Embattled: Religious Controversy in Mid-Victorian England*, Newton Abbot: David and Charles.

D'Costa, Gavin (2005), *Theology in the Public Square: Church, Academy and Nation*, Oxford: Blackwell.

Derrida, Jacques [1990] (2004), *Eyes of the University: Right to Philosophy 2*, trans. Jan Plug et al., Stanford: Stanford University Press.

Erhard, Johann Benjamin (1802), *Über die Einrichtung und den Zweck der höhern Lehranstalten*, Berlin: Braun.
Fichte, Gottfried [1807] (1956), 'Deduzierter Plan einer in Berlin zu errichtenden höheren Lehranstadt', in Ernst Anrich (ed.), *Der Idee der deutschen Universität*, Darmstadt: Wissenschaftliche Buchgesellschaft.
Fish, Stanley (2005), 'Take This Job and Do It: Administering the University without an Idea', *Critical Inquiry*, 31: 271–85.
Fish, Stanley (2008), *Save the World on Your Own Time*, Oxford: Oxford University Press.
Hagenbach, Karl Rudolf (1833–89), *Encyklopädie und Methodologie der theologischen Wissenschaft*, Leipzig: Weidmann.
Harnack, Adolf von [1901] (1984), 'Letter in *National Zeitung* (28 November 1901)', in John E. Craig, *Scholarship and Nation Building: The Universities of Strasbourg and Alsatian Society, 1870–1939*, Chicago: University of Chicago Press, 154–5.
Hauerwas, Stanley (2007), *The State of the University: Academic Knowledges and the Knowledge of God*, Oxford: Blackwell.
Higton, Mike (2012), *A Theology of Higher Education*, Oxford: Oxford University Press.
Howard, Thomas Albert (2006), *Protestant Theology and the Making of the Modern German University*, Oxford: Oxford University Press.
Humboldt, Wilhelm von [1809] (1956), 'Über die innere und äußere Organisation', in Ernst Anrich (ed.), *Der Idee der deutschen Universität*, Darmstadt: Wissenschaftliche Buchgesellschaft.
Hyman, Gavin (2004), 'The Study of Religion and the Return of Theology', *Journal of the American Academy of Religion*, 72.1: 195–219.
Jowett, Benjamin (1860), 'The Interpretation of Scripture', in *Essays and Reviews*, London: J. W. Parker.
Kilby, Karen (2012), *Balthasar: A (Very) Critical Introduction*, Grand Rapids: Eerdmans.
Köpke, Rudolf (1860), *Die Gründung der königlichen Friedrich-Wilhelms-Universität zu Berlin*, Berlin: Schade.
Lenz, Max (1910–18), *Geschichte der königlichen Friedrich-Wilhelms Universitat zu Berlin*, 4 vols, Halle: Verlag der Buchhandlung des Waisenhauses.
Loughlin, Gerard (1999), *Telling God's Story: Bible, Church and Narrative Theology*, 2nd edn, Cambridge: Cambridge University Press.
Loughlin, Gerard (2009), 'Theology in the University', in *The Cambridge Companion to John Henry Newman*, ed. Ian Ker and Terrence Merrigan, Cambridge: Cambridge University Press, 221–40.
Loughlin, Gerard (2011), 'The Wonder of Newman's Education', *New Blackfriars*, 92/1038: 224–42.
McGrath SJ, Fergal (1951), *Newman's University: Idea and Reality*, London: Longmans, Green.
Müller, Friedrich Max (1873), *Introduction to the Science of Religion*, London: Longmans, Green.
Murray, Paul D. (2013), 'The Shaping of Catholic Theology in the UK Public Academy', in *The Vocation of Theology Today: A Festschrift for David Ford*, ed. Tom Greggs, Rachel Muers and Simeon Zahl, Eugene, OR: Cascade Books, 330–42.
Newman, John Henry [1872] (1909), 'Rise and Progress of Universities', in *Historical Sketches*, vol. 3, London: Longmans, Green, 1–251.
Newman, John Henry (1961–2008), *The Letters and Diaries of John Henry Newman*, 32 vols, ed. Charles Stephen Dessain et al., Oxford: Oxford University Press.
Newman, John Henry [1873] (1996), *The Idea of a University*, ed. Frank M. Turner, New Haven: Yale University Press.
Newman, John Henry [1872] (2006), 'The Theory of Development in Religious Doctrine (Sermon XV, 1843)', in *Fifteen Sermons Preached before the University of Oxford between A.D. 1826 and 1843*, ed. James David Earnest and Gerard Tracey, Oxford: Oxford University Press, 211–35.
Nietzsche, Friedrich [1875] (1988), 'Wir Philologen', in *Sämtliche Werke: Kritische Studienausgabe*, ed. Giorgi Colli and Mazzinno Mantarini, Berlin: Walter de Gruyter.

O'Neil, J. C. (1985), 'The Study of the New Testament', in *Nineteenth Century Religious Thought in the West*, ed. Ninian Smart, John Clayton, Steven Katz and Patrick Sherry, vol. 3, Cambridge: Cambridge University Press, 143–78.

Overbeck, Franz [1919] (1963), *Christentum und Kultur: Gedanken und Anmerkungen zur modernen Theologie*, Darmstadt: Wissenschaftliche Buchgesellschaft.

Overbeck, Franz [1873] (1981), *Über die Christlichkeit unserer heutigen Theologie*, Darmstadt: Wissenschaftliche Buchgesellschaft.

Price, D. T. W. (1977), *A History of Saint David's University College Lampeter*, vol. 1, Cardiff: University of Wales Press.

Purvis, Zachary (2016), *Theology and the University in Nineteenth-Century Germany*, Oxford: Oxford University Press.

Robinson, Edward (1831), 'Theological Education in Germany', *Biblical Repository*, 1–4.

Rogers Jr, Eugene F. (2006), 'Theology in the Curriculum of a Secular Religious Studies Department', *Cross Currents*, 56.2: 169–79.

Schaff, Philip (1847), 'German Literature in America', *Bibliotheca sacra*, 4: 503–21.

Schaff, Philip (1857), *Germany: Its Universities, Theology, and Religion*, Edinburgh: T&T Clark.

Schelling, F. W. J. [1803] (1956), *Vorlesungen über die Methode des akademischen Studiums*, in Ernst Anrich (ed.), *Der Idee der deutschen Universität*, Darmstadt: Wissenschaftliche Buchgesellschaft.

Schleiermacher, F. D. E. (1850), *Brief Outline of the Study of Theology*, trans. William Farrer, Edinburgh: T&T Clark.

Schleiermacher, F. D. E. [1811] (1910), *Kurze Darstellung des theologischen Studiums zum Behuf einleitender Vorlesung*, ed. Heinrich Scholz, Leipzig: Deichert.

Schleiermacher, F. D. E. [1808] (1956), 'Gelegentliche Gedanken über Universitäten in deutschem Sinn', in Ernst Anrich (ed.), *Der Idee der deutschen Universität*, Darmstadt: Wissenschaftliche Buchgesellschaft.

Schleiermacher, F. D. E. (1980), *Kritische Gesamtausgabe*, ed. Herman Fischer et al., Berlin: Walter de Gruyter.

Schleiermacher, F. D. E. [1808] (1991), *Occasional Thoughts on Universities in the German Sense*, trans. Terrence N. Tice and Edwin Lawler, Lewiston, NY: Edwin Mellen.

Schleiermacher, F. D. E. [1811] (2011), *Brief Outline of Theology as a Field of Study*, 3rd edn, trans. Terrence N. Tice, Louisville, KY: Westminster John Knox Press.

Shrimpton, Paul (2014), *The 'Making of Men': The Idea and Reality of Newman's University in Oxford and Dublin*, Leominster: Gracewing.

Snow, C. P. (1959), *The Two Cultures and the Scientific Revolution*, Cambridge: Cambridge University Press.

Turner, Frank M. (2014), *European Intellectual History from Rousseau to Nietzsche*, ed. Richard A. Lofthouse, New Haven: Yale University Press.

Webster, John (1998), *Theological Theology*, Oxford: Clarendon Press.

Welch, Claude (1972), *Protestant Thought in the Nineteenth Century*, vol. 1: 1799–1870, New Haven: Yale University Press.

Williams, Rowan D. (1991), 'Theological Integrity', *New Blackfriars*, 72/847: 140–51.

Wittgenstein, Ludwig [1969] (1975), *On Certainty*, ed. G. E. M. Anscombe and G. H. von Wright, trans. Denis Paul and G. E. M. Anscombe, Oxford: Blackwell.

Zachhuber, Johannes (2013), *Theology as Science in Nineteenth-Century Germany: From F. C. Bauer to Ernest Troeltsch*, Oxford: Oxford University Press.

5

Freedom

Regula Zwahlen

Man is freer than is usually believed. (Alexander Herzen)

Introduction

It is a commonplace of modern political thought that the concept of freedom serves as a basic value and fundamental principle of modern societies. Against this background, both common perception and academic research treat Russia as a space where past and present are dominated by traditions of bondage, despotism and authoritarianism, with the Russian Church often described as a willing servant of such despotism (e.g. Edie et al. 1969: 315). The Russian philosopher in exile, George Fedotov, even claimed that 'the whole process of historical development in Russia took the opposite direction to the Western European one: it was a development from freedom to slavery' (1981: 181–2). So why on earth should we turn to Russian thought – and even Orthodox theology – to learn about the concept of freedom in nineteenth-century thought?

Worse still, the absence of political liberty is often claimed to have led to a fundamental lack of intellectual originality. Even Isaiah Berlin maintained that Russia contributed 'nothing that was not traceable . . . to some ultimate Western root' ([1978] 1998: 141). It seems that still less originality of thought can be expected from Orthodox theology, which, following Peter I's church reform of 1721, not only developed under the conditions of state tutelage, but placed such a strong emphasis on tradition. However, Berlin's claim has not gone undisputed. According to Andrzej Walicki and others, the striking originality of Russian thought is not to be found in 'pure' philosophy, let alone 'pure' theology, but precisely in the context of Russian intellectual history (Walicki 1980: xiv). Obviously, this context is deeply shaped by Russian Orthodoxy, which, like any other major religion, informed the identity, imagination and habitus of Russian thinkers. Far from being a monolithic body, Orthodoxy was (and still is) a multivalent, heterodox religion populated by distinct parties, different personalities and competing forces. None of these remained untouched by social developments 'outside' the church, and conversely none of the 'secular', let alone 'atheist' Russian thinkers remained untouched by their own upbringing within this 'Orthodox frame of reference' (Michelson and Kornblatt 2014: 4, 7), often literally within spiritual schools and academies.[1] That is why in the following both philosophical and theological accounts of freedom, in that order, are presented and contextualised in terms of the historical deployments of the nineteenth century. Such an approach will teach us, for example, to understand the innovative potential of Russian Orthodox theology's 'return' to the Church Fathers and tradition. Most importantly, continual exchange of ideas between secular and ecclesiastical intellectual realms led to the emergence of Russia's most significant religious philosophers, the most famous among them being Vladimir Solov'ëv.

Further justification for turning to concepts of freedom in nineteenth-century Russian thought is provided by its surprising topicality. The editors of one of the most recent books on the *History of Russian Thought* are keen to show that:

> Russian thought has presciently addressed questions of contemporary and universal interest, such as the dilemmas of modernisation in backward nations, the importance to peoples of a sense of community and distinctive identity, the effects of crises of faith and the attractions and dangers inherent in systems of thought that offer comprehensive explanations of human experience. (Leatherbarrow and Offord 2010: viii–ix)

The notion of freedom is inherent to all these dilemmas. If it is true that both the originality of and general interest in Russian concepts of freedom take place against the background of their historical contexts, it is equally true that it would be preposterous to argue that the notion of freedom in Western Europe was a product of 'pure' philosophy or theology and that its development was not affected by historical contexts; still, this seems to have been the underlying assumption until recently. As a matter of fact, in-depth research into the various debates about freedom that took place during the formation of modern Europe have only just begun, for example with Quentin Skinner's and Martin van Gelderen's recent anthology, *Freedom and the Construction of Europe: Religious and Constitutional Liberties* (2013). It goes without saying that confessional backgrounds played a pivotal role in building 'Western' discourse on freedom as well. On that note, one may claim that it is because Russian thought was embedded in an obviously very different context than in Western Europe, that scholars of Russian thought have been forced, as it were, to be among the first to approach Russian intellectual history by methods only recently taken up with regard to Western contexts. It is to be hoped that the legacy of such recent (and future) studies will reshape many of the common dichotomies that still hold between 'Russian' and 'Western' concepts.

That is, the discursive construction and semantic transformation of freedom in Russia has now attracted the attention of a broader community of scholars.[2] In the context of the Russian authoritarian imperial regimes of the nineteenth century, conceptions of freedom crystallised in numerous different discourses, and above all, came to serve an emerging, politically active public in a way that challenged the dominant discourse of power. One of the most famous Russian thinkers of the nineteenth century, Alexander Herzen, suitably described this situation as 'a time of external slavery and internal freedom' (see Polunov 2005: 51).

This appeal to slavery serves as the very link that places Russia within the 'pattern of continuity' connecting modern concepts of freedom to the ancient world, as Orlando Patterson has suggested. In opposition to the view that the notion of freedom belongs exclusively to modernity, Patterson argues 'that freedom was generated from the experience of slavery'. Explaining the origins and rise to prominence of the value of freedom in the Greek world and its large influence in the Roman world, he contends that the third great development in the history of freedom was the rise of Christianity, 'the first, and only, world religion that placed freedom – spiritual freedom, redemption – at the very center of its theology. In this way, freedom was to be enshrined on the consciousness of all Western peoples' (1991: xvi). But what about the 'Eastern peoples'? The fact that almost all Russian thinkers appealed to the Christian message of freedom – whether they saw it as faithfully transmitted by the church or not – may serve as an argument for Patterson's thesis. Whether it is true or not, the origins of the development of the notion of freedom in nineteenth-century Russia must definitely be studied against the backdrop of such factors as the survival of serfdom until 1861, the persistence of absolutism, social and economic backwardness and a growing tension between state and public, at the very time that repressive powers were falling away elsewhere in Europe (Leatherbarrow and Offord 2010: ix). These factors may have contributed to a situation where, in terms of Berlin's *Two Concepts of Liberty*, more thought seems to have been given to the notion of 'positive liberty', associated with the *freedom to* be one's own master, than to 'negative liberty', associated with the *freedom from* 'interference of other human beings within the area in which I wish to act' (1958: 6–7). In what follows, I start from the assumption that the struggle for freedom on many levels (political, social, religious and individual), under the pressure of an absolutist political system, left little room for sophisticated considerations about the legitimacy and the limits of authority – the very core concern of negative freedom, according to Berlin. Hence, emphasis is placed, rather, on the conceptions of positive freedom more commonly propagated by Russian thinkers of the era, who are, in line with such conceptions, often striving for unlimited authority to be placed in their own hands (ibid. 51).

Svoboda, vol'nost' and *volja*

According to Christoph Schmidt (2007), up until the second half of the eighteenth century, three concepts of freedom[3] were common in the Russian language. First, there was that which stems from the semantic fields of *svoboda*, grounded in ecclesial vocabulary (as a translation of the Greek, ἐλευθερία, e.g. in 2 Corinthians 3: 17). *Svoboda* is synonymous with salvation (*spasenie*) and antonymic to slavery. Second, the word *vol'nost'* was mostly used in the penal sphere (as a translation of the Greek, ἑκούσιος); it denoted a kind of 'external freedom' (provided by privileges or laws), which, during the period of the introduction of Enlightenment thought and habits under Peter I, was widely deployed (e.g. in the translation of 'press freedom' as *vol'nost' knigopechatania*). Third, the notion of *volia*, meaning 'wish', 'will', 'freedom of action' or even 'arbitrariness', was largely used by the Cossack Yemelyan Pugachev who led an initially successful revolt against Catherine II in a time of peasant unrest.

Throughout Europe, the political notion of freedom gained currency in both liberal and conservative circles after the French Revolution (Wittram 1954: 378), as it did in Russia too, where Catherine II responded to the French Revolution and Alexander Radishchev's criticism of autocracy and serfdom with the latter's ban to Siberia. His *A Journey from St. Petersburg to Moscow* (1790) clearly marked 'the parting of ways' between the 'enlightened despot' and the educated public (Leatherbarrow and Offord 2010: 9). Earlier, in 1781, he had written his famous ode to *Liberty* (*Vol'nost'*), a forerunner of similar poems by Ryleev, Ogarev, Pushkin and Odoevsky, among others (Wiener 1902: 361–2).[4] In Radishchev's ode, one discovers a key conceptual change: notwithstanding the title, he invokes the 'spirit of freedom' (*duch svobody*) by replacing the somewhat administrative term *vol'nost'* with the stylistically higher term, *svoboda*. Even in legal language, *vol'nost'* was gradually replaced by versions of *svoboda* (Schmidt 2007: 270, 272), and this conflating of all concepts of freedom into forms of *svoboda* is significant in marking the increased political relevance of the concept, but also problematic when attempting to discern the various different concepts of freedom at play.

This observation is confirmed by the *Brockhaus and Efron Encyclopedic Dictionary*, issued between 1890 and 1907 (forty-one volumes), which devotes only a couple of entries to forms of *vol'nost'*. The entry on 'free people' (*vol'nye liudi*) actually mentions that 'in the records of the Muscovite state, *vol'nyi* is equivalent to the word *svobodnyj*' (Yanovsky 1892: 143). As for *volia*, it is not defined in terms of *'freedom'* at all; instead, there are four entries on 'will' in its philosophical, physiological and legal sense (civil and penal law). On the other hand, there are several telling entries on the various semantic forms of *svoboda* – short ones on the Roman goddess *Libertas*, freedom of (mechanical) motion, 'free church in a free state' (referring to the phrase, 'Chiesa libera in libero stato', from the Italian statesman Cavour), free cell formation (botanics), free church movement in Finland (*De Frikyrkliga*), free arable farmers (*svobodnye chlebopashchcy*), the journal *Free Hours* (*Svobodnye Chasy*), free art and the free thinker (*svobodomyslitel'*) in reference to Anthony Collins's *Discourse on Freethinking* (1713). The longer entries treat the 'freedom of the person' (*svoboda lichnosti*) as a civil freedom that includes the entirety of the person's rights with regard to political, material and moral interests; 'freedom of will' (*svoboda voli*); 'freedom of thinking, of expression' (*svoboda mysli, slova*); 'political freedom' (*svoboda politicheskaia*), designating either the independence of a people, tribe or state from foreign power, or a form of state (*gosudarstvennaja zhizn'*), in which citizens actively participate in legislative, executive and judicial powers; and free commerce (*svobodnaia torgovlia*) as an economic system free of state intervention into private economic activity. Two further entries explain two German movements of free congregations (*Freie Gemeinden* in Prussia), and free thinkers (*svobodomysljashchie*) designating certain political parties in Germany (e.g. *Deutsche Freisinnige Partei*).

This short survey clearly shows, on the one hand, the highly politicised context of the use of the term 'freedom', and indeed the register of contributors to this *Encyclopedic Dictionary* proved to be to a large extent identical with the Russian oppositional intelligentsia (Hagen 2002: 102). On the other hand, several entries about free religious communities seem to introduce the question of religious freedom through the back door, thereby emphasising its crucial significance for the larger discourse on freedom.

Freedom of Expression

In order to explore this discourse further, it is important to bear in mind what could actually be said or written at the time. Catherine II's 'Great Instruction for a New Code of Law' from 1767 articulated the principle of freedom of expression for the first time in the history of Russia. And in another first for the whole of Europe, this declaration 'originated from the government side, without any pressure on the part of society' (Papmehl 1971: 54). The new law declared freedom of expression a natural right of each citizen and downgraded the importance of spoken or written words within the category of high treason. Agreeing in principle with Radishchev's (and J. G. Herder's) conviction that 'the best means of promoting good' was non-interference, and that freedom of thought was only to be feared by unjust power (Radishchev [1790] 1958: 165–70), Catherine's views still changed quite rapidly after the French Revolution and the outbreak of the second Turkish war. Now, she considered Radishchev's book an attempt to diminish respect for authority and disturb public peace, well aware of the fact that even in the French Declaration of Human Rights and the US Bill of Rights an emphasis on the maintenance of public peace limited freedom of expression (Papmehl 1971: 125–6). Consequently, Radishchev was banished to Siberia.

Tides of repression of freedom of expression would come and go throughout the nineteenth century, and the periods of relaxation generally remained brief. However, strict police measures could not prevent a surge of intellectual life in Russia as educational and cultural institutions established under Alexander I continued to develop and the idea of 'enlightened autocracy' remained in place. The number of institutions of higher education increased and the size of the reading public grew, even after the Decembrist uprising in 1825, when Nicholas I enforced militarisation, centralisation and 'enlightened bureaucratization'. Under the 'Tsar-despot', intellectual life in Russia became particularly active in the 1830s and the 1840s. For example, current political and social problems, like the Polish insurrection of 1830–1 or the new governmental ideology – summarised by count Sergey Uvarov's formula 'Orthodoxy, Autocracy, Nationality' – were commonly discussed under the semi-disguise of literary and philosophical argument (Polunov 2005: 51–2).

The new Press Statute, enacted in 1865 by the 'Tsar-Liberator' Alexander II, introduced the principle of 'punitive censorship' – that is, prosecution by the courts *after* publishing – at least until 1873, when the minister of the interior was again entitled to ban the publication of certain news. When Alexander II was killed by terrorists in 1881, his successors pledged to revert to severe autocracy, but the task was more difficult than expected: given the huge quantity of published writings, the censors were overwhelmed with work (Hagen 2002: 99–107). The above mentioned *Encyclopedic Dictionary* may serve as an illustrative example of this situation. The entry on 'freedom of expression' openly deplores that, in contrast to Western European and American states, freedom of press still does not exist in Russia, and then refers to the entry on 'censorship' (Vodovozov 1900: 173–4). This latter entry happens to take the form of an extensive critical analysis of the concept over more than fourteen pages, 'which could hardly have been more severe and accusatory in an exile paper' (Hagen 2002: 102). Hence, at the beginning of the twentieth century, with regard to media control, the state found itself in a very defensive position. The October Manifesto of 1905 finally granted 'freedom of conscience, of speech, of conventions and societies', and the first actual concessions were made to the press a week later. Henceforth, the Russian press was to be subject only to the general penal law, and consequently, new papers, journals and books flooded the empire 'like flood rains on arid soil' (ibid. 64).

Freedom of Conscience and Religious Freedom

In the *Encyclopedic Dictionary* the term 'freedom of conscience' (*svoboda sovesti*) is only mentioned in passing within the entry on 'freedom of the person'. By then, the term had already undergone a long history of emergence in several Russian discourses of the nineteenth century, including those of state administration, the radical intelligentsia, as well as within many liberal and even religious discourses (Michelson 2018: 4). Without a doubt, educated Russians had been familiar with the idea much earlier, but the term acquired practical relevance only in the historical context of the Great Reform of the 1860s (Werth 2012: 607).

The idea of 'freedom of conscience' was closely linked to the problem of religious freedom. For example, the term was known to Orthodox communities in the Eastern part of the Kingdom of Poland as early as the sixteenth century (Florovsky [1937] 1979: 34ff.). However, within the Russian empire, religious freedom was more of a problem for non-Orthodox confessions because of whom the state developed a policy of 'religious toleration' (*veroterpimost'*). According to this policy, the Orthodox Church was dominant, and religious toleration was granted to non-Russian religious communities in the interest of controlling their subjects and maintaining stability, but not to provide individuals with a right to religious self-determination (Werth 2012: 590). The same motives provided the rationale for the extension of religious rights to Russian Old Believers, who were thereby treated as a 'solid core of the Russian nationality', even against the resistance of the Orthodox church (Werth 2014: 202, 250). But converting from one denomination to another remained difficult, and conversion from Orthodoxy to another faith was strictly forbidden (Frede 2012: 562).

In the 1860s, mostly non-Russian groups (e.g. Jews, Armenians, Latvians and Estonians) petitioned the government to be allowed to convert to another religion. Moreover, the problem of mixed marriage between different confessions had to be addressed (Werth 2012: 594–9). Disputes about the topic even divided the ranks of the imperial administration, where Interior Minister Petr Valuev described himself as a fighter for the freedom of conscience, while the Holy Synod's Chief Procurator Konstantin Pobedonostsev was eager to defend the dominant position of the Orthodox Church. In the meantime, the concept continued to evolve in intellectual disputes and scholarly publications, where the concern for the individual, rather than the collective, as a religious agent grew (ibid. 593–609).

As for the Russian revolutionary left, its members were rather uncomfortable with the issue of religious freedom and freedom of conscience. While revolutionary movements like *Land and Freedom* (*Zemlia i Volia*) sought to draw peasants and workers, including potential opposition groups like Old Believers and other sectarians, to their cause, they did not share their religious beliefs. They were, in fact, not fighting for religious freedom, but for freedom *from* religion (Frede 2012: 563–4).[5]

Public interest in freedom of conscience gained critical mass by the end of the nineteenth century, and peaked in 1901 when the Orthodox Church condemned Lev Tolstoy (see Orekhanov 2010). Freedom of conscience was finally granted to the subjects of the Russian Tsar in the Manifesto of 17 October 1905, but was never realised in a coherent legislative programme (Werth 2012: 604–10).

Liberal Conservatism

The beginnings of a 'liberal' tradition in Russia stretch back to the early nineteenth century, when the state authorities encouraged young Russians to attend German universities in order to improve the training of future state officials. By inviting German rather than French or English professors to teach courses in Russia, the government was trying to avoid the exposure of Russian students to undesirable ideas (Berest 2011: 3; Berlin [1978] 1998: 136). The German teachers were expected to teach German natural law in the tradition of Christian Wolff,[6] which emphasised the ethos of public duties over individual rights, while approaching Immanuel Kant in a selective manner, leaving aside his most provocative ideas. But nonetheless, at the beginning of the nineteenth century, Kant was among the most frequently read modern philosophers in Russia (Berest 2011: 110, 141–2).[7]

Several so-called early liberal thinkers like Timofey Granovsky, Vasily Botkin, Pavel Annenkov, Aleksandr Druzhinin and Konstantin Kavelin rose to prominence in the 1840s and 1850s, even though they did not consider themselves 'liberal' as such, because at the time the term was associated with the promotion of revolutionary change. Liberalism was considered roughly synonymous with 'freethought' (*vol'nodumstvo*) or 'Voltairianism' – that is, 'a sceptical or careless relation to the dominating ideas or beliefs, especially religious ones' (Solov'ëv 1892: 136). Rejecting such radical ideas, these men desired gradual reform and social and political stability, but put an emphasis on the dignity of the individual (Offord 1985: xii–xiii). Their assumption that history advances in the direction of personal freedom (as Hegel had suggested) profoundly influenced Boris Chicherin, one of the most famous Russian liberal philosophers, whose own 'conservative liberalism' in turn was to have a defining impact on the 'Liberation movement' (*soiuz osvobozhdeniia*) and the Russian constitutionalists at the beginning of the twentieth century (Nethercott 2010: 250). Chicherin was a constitutional monarchist who attacked both absolutist and democratic governments (Hamburg 1992: 335). In his last work, the *Philosophy of Law* (1898–9), Chicherin combined Kantian and Hegelian thinking so as to uphold inner liberty alongside an externally powerful modern *Rechtsstaat*, as the mutual limitation of freedom under a common code of law. Chicherin was among only a few Russian thinkers who sharply distinguished between morality and law as two different spheres of human life. Morality, he argued, concerned freedom of conscience as 'the first and most sacred right of a citizen', whereas law concerned the limitation of external actions affecting others. Hence, personal liberty included civil rights which should be protected by political rights.

But even a liberal thinker like Chicherin had originally sought to reconcile the idea of human liberty with obedience to the divine laws of history, thereby adding a distinctly religious dimension to his thought. According to his *Science and Religion* (1879), God had created human beings as free moral agents. This insight notwithstanding, he elaborated a religious-political Hegelian theory of history that envisioned a multi-stage process leading to ultimate social harmony in a coming age of the Spirit. Nevertheless, even with regard to religion, Chicherin adhered to liberal principles: he claimed that a state should never hinder the free exercise of religion, acknowledging that freedom of conscience leads to religious pluralism, even with regard to different confessions within Christianity, because 'the existence of different confessions satisfies the multiple dimensions of the human soul'.[8] But most importantly – and this thought qualifies him as a liberal thinker – he considered social inequality a logical consequence of freedom, because inequality is rooted in nature but is also a product of freedom of choice (Hamburg 2010: 112–16, 120–9).

Freedom of 'the People'

It has been claimed that the famous act declaring the 'Liberation of the Serfs' in February 1861 was perceived not only as the emancipation of individual serfs, but also as the liberation of the 'Russian people' (Werth 2014: 151). In other words, the notion of freedom became closely linked to nationalist thinking about the Russian people as the country's ruling nationality, and generally about Russia's place in world history. At the same time, the intensifying cultural policy of 'Russification' led to vigorous debates on questions of 'national freedom' among intellectuals of the Jewish, Polish, Baltic, Ukrainian, Finnish and other minority elites throughout the Russian empire (see Kappeler 2001).

Both Westernisers and Slavophiles developed a vision of 'the people' (*narod*) in which individual freedom was not particularly predominant. While Westernisers and 'populists' saw the people either as 'potential beneficiaries of humanitarian improvement' or as just a backward mass, the Slavophiles found in them the 'heart of an apolitical moral organism and the essence of Russia's national distinctiveness' (Leatherbarrow and Offord 2010: 8). The latter perception developed in lockstep with the rise of a romantic 'cultural nationalism', grounded in Herder's organicism, according to which every individual or country serves as an organ with its own purpose within the whole of humankind (Berlin [1978] 1998: 135–6; Rabow-Edling 2006: 101ff.). The search for Russia's purpose in world history was the common ground shared by Slavophiles and Westernisers (Offord 2010: 246). This line of thought harks back to Petr Chaadaev's scandalous *Philosophical Letter* published in 1836, in which he deplored the fact that Providence 'seems wholly to have neglected [the Russian people's] destiny' (Edie et al. 1969: 105). In his later essay *The Apology of a Madman* from 1837 though, he described Russia's lack of culture as an advantage in order to *freely* complete its own, God-given mission in world history (ibid. 115). This idea marks the point of origin of several 'Russian ideas' both secular and religious (Duncan 2000).

In this context, the concept of the free 'unspoilt people' became an indefinite construct fashioned in the minds of intellectuals seeking to build new, distinctively Russian concepts of social life, such as the Slavophiles' Christian moral utopia or Alexander Herzen's and the populists' socialist utopia. Both Dostoyevsky and Tolstoy presented idealised views of the peasants, which were replicated in many other artistic representations of the common people and reinforced by scholarly ethnographic research (Offord 2010: 241–8, 250–8). Meanwhile, the Orthodox Church developed its own concept of the Orthodox Christian Russian People as 'Holy Rus' or 'New Israel' (Strickland 2013: xiii–xviii, 68ff.). In order to illustrate the amalgamation of the discourses on freedom and the people, one may merely cite Dostoyevsky's famous speech on Pushkin:

> If thou conquerest thyself, if thou humblest thyself, then wilt thou be free beyond dreams; thou wilt labor upon a great task; thou wilt make others free and thou wilt find happiness, since thy life will be full, and thou wilt, finally, understand thine own people and their sacred truth. ([1880] 1966: 292)

At the same time, such a view of the people was challenged by the Marxists, who considered the peasantry to be a conservative class (Offord 2010: 255).

Freedom, Necessity and Equality

The Decembrist movement emerged from the officer corps of the Russian army, who, upon returning from France after victory over Napoleon in 1812, perceived a strong discrepancy between Russia's newly gained external power and its internal backwardness. Alexander I's early death spurred the Decembrists' open rebellion on 14 December 1825. The uprising was quickly suppressed, and its proponents executed or exiled to Siberia. Nicholas I subsequently vowed that revolution 'will not cross [Russia's] threshold as long as I still have the breath of life' (quoted in Polunov 2005: 39). In the aftermath of the uprising, a number of conspiratorial student circles were uncovered and outlawed. In 1834, Alexander Herzen, along with other members of a reader circle for socialist literature, was expelled from Moscow (Edie et al. 1969: 274). Other philosophical circles, however, attracted little suspicion in the 1830s and 1840s. Among these were the 'Lovers of Wisdom' in Moscow, who studied the philosophy of Schelling, and later Nikolai Stankevich's circle with its main focus on Hegel's philosophy (Polunov 2005: 51–8).[9] In Berlin's words, the German metaphysical writers 'liberated' Russian intellectuals not only from the dogmas of the Orthodox Church, but also from eighteenth-century rationalism (Berlin [1978] 1998: 145–50). Nevertheless, it was largely in *reaction* to Hegel that many Russian philosophers developed their own ideas. Vissarion Belinsky, for example, expressed his fierce rejection of Hegel's formula that 'freedom is insight into necessity' in his famous *Letter to Botkin* (1840): 'There has developed in me a kind of wild, frenzied, fanatical love of freedom and the independent human personality' (Edie et al. 1969: 306). However, Belinsky's rebellion against Hegel was linked to a social idea:

> Social solidarity (*social'nost'*) or death! That is my motto. What is it to me that the Universal exists when the personality is suffering? What care I if on earth the genius lives as in heaven when the mass is wallowing in dirt? (Ibid. 309)[10]

Belinsky joined the secret Petrashevsky Circle founded in 1845 for the discussion of Western European socialist literature. After the 1848 revolutions, some of its members, among them Dostoevsky, experienced the commutation of their death sentences into incarceration or labour-camp terms to be served in Siberia (ibid. 274).

The failure of the European revolution of 1848 must be considered a turning point in the development of the Russian revolutionary movement. As a response to this growing intellectual ferment, in 1850, the philosophy departments of all Russian universities were closed. Only upon adoption of the University Charter in 1863 could all the branches of philosophy again be taught (Pavlov 2003: 11–12). But whilst in Europe intellectuals experienced disillusion and despair, in Russia revolutionary fervour and the belief in a specific national 'Russian' solution grew stronger. Born from a desire to change the desolate social situation in Russia, the philosophical engagement with problems of freedom and determinism became a pre-eminently political occupation that focused on the possibility – or even moral duty – of engaging in political or revolutionary activity. Hence, Marx's claim that philosophers should not merely interpret, but change the world, fell on fertile ground in Russia.

Marx himself did not reject the concept of individual freedom as such, but its liberal, 'negative' understanding as mere absence of restraints by the actions of others. Marxian freedom consists in *activity* based on the knowledge of necessity. Such activity is based on two concepts of freedom: *self-realisation* of men as individuals (the 'all-round development of the person'), and the struggle of mankind to control his environment, in short, *freedom as power* (O'Rourke 1974: 40–3). The idea that knowledge of necessity will empower man's capacity to *act* and even to 'leap into the kingdom of freedom' was to inspire many Russian socialist thinkers. It engendered first of all a controversy about the pace of change – that is, the question of whether Russia had to embark on the 'capitalist path' or not. Another controversy over the methods of change was directly linked to the question of freedom, and among its participants were two of Marx's most famous Russian contemporaries and opponents, Alexander Herzen and Mikhail Bakunin (Berlin [1978] 1998: 93–129). Herzen defended the 'moral liberty' of each person, while for Bakunin freedom was something to be achieved only after a 'long, cruel historical path' or else after a proletarian revolution (Walicki 2010: 305–8). Again, the interpretational divergence between freedom as an *inherent property of human beings* or as a *historical project* is crucial to understand the differences among socialists such as Herzen and Bakunin, who dedicated their lives to rebellion against every form of oppression (Berlin [1978] 1998: 94), including the Christian tradition and the despotism of Marxism (Edie et al. 1969: 385).

In his exile in London, the 'father of Russian socialism', Alexander Herzen, edited the *Free Russian Press* and the weekly newspaper *Kolokol* (*The Bell*), which exercised an extraordinary influence among Russian revolutionaries in the second half of the nineteenth century. Moreover, it is within these newspapers that freedom of confession was made a core demand (Frede 2012: 567ff.). In his violent rebellion against the metaphysical constructions of German philosophy, Herzen maintained that 'history follows no libretto', except the one of a 'continual emancipation of the human personality . . . up to the greatest harmony between reason and activity – a harmony in which man *feels himself to be free*' (Edie et al. 1969: 377). According to Herzen, the problem with freedom is twofold. First, most people do not really like liberty, and second, one cannot promise freedom tomorrow by 'trampling on liberty today' (Berlin [1978] 1998: 114). But an individual human being is an absolute value in himself, because 'he does not want to be either a passive grave-digger of the past, nor an unconscious midwife of the future' (Edie et al. 1969: 378). With regard to the problem of freedom and necessity, Herzen's approach is very inclusive:

> Man is freer than is usually believed. He depends a great deal on his environment, but . . . a large part of our destiny lies in our hands. . . . The reaction provoked in man by his environment is the response of his personality to the influence of the milieu. . . . The greater the awareness, the greater the independence. (Ibid. 366–8)

Bakunin's concept of freedom was markedly different. Most of all, he disapproved of the formal kind of freedom propagated by bourgeois liberals, because they all believed in the representation of their rights by the state. The state was Bakunin's main enemy indeed, and in this, he differed from what he called 'authoritarian communists' (like Marx) who believed that a social revolution could be *organised*. He rejects any kind of law and legislation, because they always favour a dominant minority of exploiters (ibid. 416). It is for such reasons that Bakunin is considered to be the 'founding father of anarchism'.

Bakunin believes that 'the freedom of each . . . finds in [the freedom of others] its confirmation and its infinite extension', he believes in 'freedom by solidarity' and 'freedom in equality', but that a desire of freedom from nature is absurd, because man is part of nature (ibid. 407–8). Such harmonious balance stands in stark contrast to Bakunin's view that freedom cannot be attained without struggle, because 'order without struggle is death'. In contrast to Herzen, Bakunin does not see freedom as an innate moral principle but as a 'product of life in society'. The break-up of old political friendships, such as Herzen's and Bakunin's, is exemplary of the growing radicalisation and polarisation between different intellectual camps in the years of repression from 1848–56. That is why, in the more 'relaxed atmosphere' of the early reforms by Alexander II, the materialistic nihilists of the 1860s and 1870s were able to comprehensively shape the uncompromising character of the later revolutionary movement (Berlin [1978] 1998: 20–3).[11]

Inner Freedom and Unity of Free Wills (*sobornost'*)

Many of the Russian thinkers mentioned above belonged to a group commonly referred to as 'Westernisers'. Sharing the same philosophical and social background, their antagonists, the 'Slavophiles', found different ways of coping with Hegel, Romanticism and religion (Horujy 2010: 50). Intellectuals like Ivan Kireevsky, Aleksei Khomiakov and Yuri Samarin believed that religion was the source of all enlightenment, and maintained that modernity had to be reconciled with 'sacred tradition' by means of a reformed Orthodox theology. Their arguments followed in the footsteps of Schelling and their concept of God-given 'inner freedom' as freedom from materialistic determinism contained a call to pursue moral perfection. The main features of Slavophile anthropology were thus, first, the claim that God's plan could not be realised by coercion, because that would have contradicted the synergetic tension between God's gracious descent and man's free ascent to his Creator (Michelson 2010: 262); second, the insistence that moral freedom is 'the freedom of choice between the love for God and egoism, or between justice and sin' (Jakim and Bird 1998: 118); and, third, an emphasis on the moral quality of mutual love in personal relationships. Khomiakov and Kireevsky argued that the liberation of the Orthodox Church from political tutelage could return Russia to its divinely ordained historical trajectory. Peter I's earlier church reform of 1721 had replaced the Russian patriarchate with the Most Holy Synod, presided over by an 'Ober-Procurator' who was appointed by the Tsar. Hence, Slavophile discourse about freedom needs to be interpreted not only as a conservative turn to tradition, but also as a case for the institutional freedom of the church.

Khomiakov was an eager defender of free will against what he considered 'infantile' materialistic concepts. But it is the quest for a genuine 'unity of free wills' that underlies Khomiakov's notorious concept of *sobornost'*. Moral autonomy, he argued, was a necessary but not sufficient precondition for individual perfection. The imperfect individual could not accomplish its destiny in the absence of the mutual love that unites Christians (ibid. 120–1). *Sobornyj* is Khomiakov's translation of the word 'catholic': it is derived from the word *sobor* (gathering, council, cathedral), implying that the church is a community of its human members, and not – as he wrote in polemical terms against the Roman church – a geographical unity of all nations under one head. Hence, the *sobornost'* of the church is a unity of 'free believers who longed to fulfil the divinely ordained goal of Providence'. Such an endeavour is – in contrast to coercive or merely formal membership – 'fully grounded in the freedom of Christ' (ibid. 15, 169). Khomiakov expressed his conviction that Orthodox Christianity was uniquely qualified to strike a balance between the ideals of personal freedom and unified society. In this, it allegedly differed from both Roman Catholicism, which he considered to be based on external unity without freedom, and Protestantism, which he believed to rely on freedom without external unity.

Along with secular thinkers such as Herzen and Bakunin, the Slavophiles drew a negative picture of 'the West', where all norms and relationships were said to be artificial and formal. Both secular and religious thinkers shared an excitement for the Russian peasant commune (*mir*) 'as an institution created by the moral freedom of the Russian people' (Edie et al. 1969: 223). Because in a moral community rights would simply be unnecessary, they opposed ethics to rights, but never offered a concrete programme for Russia's spiritual renewal (Horuiy 2010: 33–4). However, despite the many shortcomings and omissions in their thinking, they achieved an innovative 'reconfiguration of Eastern Christianity as a dynamic religion of theocentric freedom and moral progress', and thereby profoundly altered public discourse about Orthodoxy (Michelson 2010: 246, 263–6).

Christ's Freedom and Free Theocracy

When Nikolai Gogol called for a return to ancient religious ways in 1847, Vissarion Belinsky wrote his famous *Letter to Gogol*:

> That you base such teaching on the Orthodox Church I can understand: it has always served as . . . the servant of despotism. But why have you mixed Christ up in this? What have you found in common between Him and any Church, much less the Orthodox Church? He was the first to bring people the teaching of freedom, equality, and brotherhood . . . And this teaching was man's salvation only until it became organized in the Church. (Edie et al. 1969: 315)

Belinsky's juxtaposition of the Orthodox Church and Christ in respect to freedom found a famous follower in Lev Tolstoy. However, it is well known that Tolstoy's teachings were not at all about individual freedom: among other things, he believed human beings to be governed by natural law, even if they tried to see their lives as a succession of free choices (Berlin [1978] 1998: 46). Such ambivalences in Tolstoy's worldview engendered huge debates, and had it not been for his excommunication by the church in 1901, he might never have ended up as a national hero of free-thinking Russia (Michelson 2007: 289).

In contrast to Belinsky and Tolstoy, Vladimir Solov'ëv not only strived to reconcile Orthodoxy with modern society, he also sought to harmonise Christian faith with the 'truth of socialism'. Echoing Belinsky's ideas, in his *Lectures on Godmanhood* (1877–81) he argued that 'freedom, equality, and brotherhood' were genuinely Christian notions. In Solov'ëv's philosophical system, history is tantamount to humanity's self-realisation for the achievement of free union with God. According to his concept of human nature, rational freedom or autonomy is the distinctive human principle along with the divine principle (consciousness of the absolute) and the material principle (consciousness of being part of the natural world) (Poole 2010: 137). Moreover, in his work on Solov'ëv's concept of freedom, Ludwig Wenzler calls him primarily 'a prophetic thinker and advocate of freedom' (1978: 362). Owing to his concept of moral autonomy, his public opposition to the death penalty for Alexander II's assassins, and his defence of religious freedom, Solov'ëv has often been portrayed as the founder of a unique form of Russian religious liberalism. However, liberal values like religious privacy and pluralism were not among Solov'ëv's ultimate goals. His thought was deeply rooted in a universalist Christian narrative that centred on realising 'the Kingdom of God on earth' (Michelson 2014: 31, 36). Thus he envisioned freedom in Christ, instead of mere religious freedom. Nevertheless, he was one of only a few Russian thinkers who broke with the problematic juxtaposition of ethics and law by promoting the liberal principles of moral autonomy and rule of law. In contrast to the Slavophiles and many secular socialist thinkers, in Solov'ëv's conception of society, law played a significant role, because 'law is freedom conditioned by equality'. However, because law is lacking the normative quality of *love*, it is *religion*, understood as truth about God's love, that provides the ultimate ground for universal solidarity. Nevertheless, in Solov'ëv's view, economy, state and society must function in 'relative freedom' from the church (Valliere 2000: 127–37). The fact that Solov'ëv developed his ideas by creating paradoxical terms like 'free theocracy' or a 'triunity of state, church, and society' (Solov'ëv [1888] 1954: 90) makes it quite difficult to understand what the realisation of his 'theocractic ideal' would look like.

In his article on 'freedom of will = freedom of choice [*svoboda voli* = *S. vybora*]' in the *Encyclopedic Dictionary*, Solov'ëv claimed that free will is all about 'the true relation between the individual being and the universal principle'. For Christianity, the problem of freedom and necessity arises from determining the relation between God's absoluteness and human moral self-determination; hence the extensive debates about predestination and grace among Catholic and Protestant thinkers from Augustine onwards. Solov'ëv's article offers a rather surprising conclusion that draws on Charles Secrétan's *Philosophie de la liberté*: divine omniscience does not include knowledge of free human acts before their completion. In the last sentence of his article, Solov'ëv promised a more exhaustive study of the problem in a later entry on 'Philosophy' (Solov'ëv 1900: 169), which never appeared as the respective volume was published only in 1902, two years after Solov'ëv's death. Hence, the relation between individual freedom and universal all-unity in Solov'ëv's theology has remained a much-debated problem (e.g. Oittinen 2003).[12]

One of the most famous elaborations on the subject of Christ and freedom is Dostoevsky's. The Underground Man's glorification of free will is a rejection of any deterministic theory of human behaviour (and particularly of Nikolai Chernyshevsky's influential work *What Is to Be Done?*, 1863); however, Dostoevsky himself does not endorse the Underground Man's claim of boundless freedom, arguing that the human will transcends natural law but not moral law. Thus 'The Legend of the Grand Inquisitor' in *The Brothers Karamazov* takes the form of a powerful assault on both Roman Catholicism and radical socialism in Russia. The tale envisions Christ's return to earth at the height of the Inquisition. He is taken into custody immediately, and charged by the cardinal with the crime of inhumanity for burdening men with the torments of freedom. After all, the cardinal argues, only material well-being and social peace will make people happy. What Dostoevsky, inspired by Slavophile thought and traditional Russian Orthodoxy, is trying to evoke in his narrative is the idea of a moral freedom capable of transcending egoism, the real cause for human distress. Accordingly, man's '"most advantageous advantage" lies not in free choice as such, but in the free acceptance of Christ and His moral message' (Scanlan 2002: 75).

Theocentric Freedom and 'True' Freedom of Conscience

It should not be overlooked that the church took an active part in discourse on freedom. After all, since the beginning of the nineteenth century it had trained hundreds of theologians and thousands of priests who influenced the public sphere and increasingly saw scholarship as a means to fulfil the church's mission to educate society. Hence, the self-consciously Orthodox perspective of most of the above mentioned thinkers has to be taken into account (Michelson and Kornblatt 2014: 3ff.). Most importantly, in 1821, the St Petersburg Spiritual Academy began to translate texts of the Church Fathers into vernacular Russian, and in 1843, the Moscow Spiritual Academy published the first of no fewer than forty-eight volumes of *Works of the Holy Fathers in Russian Translation*, complete with commentaries, analyses and biographies (Michelson 2007: 52, 60–3). Up to this point, the reading audience of the Church Fathers had been limited to the clergy who knew Church Slavonic. The editorial leadership of the project was entrusted to Archpriest Petr Delitsyn, a scholar who had already translated many other works such as Kant's *Kritik der reinen Vernunft*. The same is true of another of the main editors of the series, Archpriest Feodor Golubinsky (ibid. 66–8). Subsequently, the project served as a catalyst for numerous monographs and articles about early Christianity and church history which underpinned the growing self-confidence of the Orthodox Church.

Of particular importance among the translated texts were Gregory of Nyssa's oration on the creation of man in God's image and likeness (Genesis 1: 26) and the translation of some of Irenaeus' most influential works, which taught their reading audiences that for humans 'to participate in salvation' they must be capable of acting freely in the world, as violence and force were contrary to God's salvation plan. Such texts paved the way for the so-called patristic revival, brought about by Orthodox theologians such as Aleksandr Martynov, Dmitry Tikhomirov and Viktor Nesmelov. The idea of man as God's image implied that man was endowed with reason, free will and divine love, but the pursuit of divine perfection in order to achieve Godlikeness, *theosis*, required individual effort. The task of guiding man on his journey towards deification fell to the church. This concept of 'theocentric freedom' shifted the focus from man's sinfulness to his capacity of achieving Godlikeness by free will (ibid. 70–1, 84–90). Elaborating on this line of thought, the Orthodox theologian Konstantin Skvorcov criticised Augustine for his allegedly limited view of human freedom that 'attributed too much effectiveness to evil' (Tataryn 2000: 20–2).

It does not come as a surprise that such an Orthodox understanding of freedom was often contrasted with a negative interpretation of its Protestant counterpart. Aleksei Vvedensky, a professor at the Moscow Spiritual Academy, formulated the main criticisms against Protestant theology. First, he saw Protestant freedom as a freedom to detach oneself from the past and from the faith community, and thus as diametrically opposed to Orthodoxy's esteem for tradition and community. Second, he criticised what he perceived as a startling contradiction among Protestants between the complete freedom afforded to contemporary research and fidelity to Scripture. Such criticisms, however, did not preclude Protestantism being studied in depth at Russian spiritual seminaries around the turn of the nineteenth and twentieth centuries (Wasmuth 2007: 43–7, 57). In contrast to a widely held view which considered Protestantism an irreligious, ultimately atheistic attitude (Michelson 2018: 2), there were theologians like Archpriest Pavel Svetlov who maintained that the three divine principles – freedom, authority and tradition – were represented by Protestantism, Catholicism and Orthodoxy in equal measure, and that true Christianity needed to strive for a harmonious combination of the three. In his seminal work, *God's Kingdom* from 1902, he opposed the rise of nationalist tendencies among the clergy by insisting on a concept of spiritual freedom that was based on individual ethics rather than national-eschatological theories. According to Svetlov, God's kingdom 'is a matter of man's internal moral life and freedom', and has to be understood as a task that is transcendent and immanent at the same time. Such tolerant views notwithstanding, Svetlov nevertheless harboured the suspicion that liberal talk about 'freedom of conscience' all too often meant little more than 'freedom *from* conscience' (Wasmuth 2007: 199–202, 257).

Generally speaking, such discourse on freedom of conscience challenged the teachings of the Orthodox Church on many grounds, and therefore elicited vigorous reaction from many representatives of the clergy. Until the early nineteenth century, the compound *svoboda sovesti* did not exist in the church lexicon: *Sovest'*, conscience, was defined as a God-given moral faculty to distinguish good from evil, while *svoboda* was primarily understood as liberation from sin. The phrase 'freedom of conscience' only gained currency in Orthodox vocabulary during the Crimean War (1853–6), when priests started to use the term in order to defend the freedom of conscience of Eastern Christians living under Ottoman rule. But whereas such use of the term became commonplace among religious minorities and dissenting members of the Russian Church during the decades to come, appeals to 'freedom of conscience' in Orthodoxy went in a completely different direction. This was due to the advent of a 'restorationist consciousness' among the clergy reacting to both the deficiencies of the contemporary church and the rise of atheism in educated society caused by the subordination of church to state in Russia. Therefore, the church had to be restored on the foundations of its 'authentic ecclesiology' (Michelson 2018: 6–10, 18–21). On the one hand, claims in favour of the church's complete independence from the state were partly based on the idea that faith was something that could not be controlled by the state, hence on the concept of the freedom of faith. However, on the other hand, the vision of an independent church as the only divine sanctuary corresponded to a rather totalitarian idea of the church as the one and only institution in possession of complete knowledge of 'God-given laws' and matters of human nature.

Guided by this kind of mindset, Archimandrite Ioann (Sokolov) developed the first Orthodox ecclesiastical account of the concept in *On Freedom of Conscience and Its*

Religious Foundations (1864–5). In this study, he argued that religion was not a 'matter of conscience', but quite the other way round, conscience needed to be considered a matter of religion. According to Ioann, freedom of conscience is tantamount to salvation from sin and a gift of grace, but, alluding to Kant, he also argued that acceptance of salvation from sin was an achievement of individual 'moral will'. As for the church, it could not *grant* freedom of conscience, but rather *forgive* wrong decisions of a free individual conscience (ibid. 28–35).

Even if this account adds nothing new to the Orthodox concept of *freedom as salvation from sin*, it is subversive by virtue of its criticism of existing church–state relations. According to Ioann, the church lost its capacity to expand 'true freedom of religion in the world' as a result of its subordination to the secular authority of Constantine the Great, who, in Ioann's view, created an unchristian state under the guise of Christian symbols (ibid. 36–8). Hence, the Orthodox version of 'freedom of conscience' that emerged in the mid-1860s was simultaneously directed against state coercion *and* intellectual individualism, and in view of the latter, did not resonate well with proponents of a secular freedom of conscience. Nevertheless, Orthodox concepts of freedom hold a certain interest with regard to their somewhat paradoxical emphasis on moral autonomy.[13]

Conclusion

It should have become clear by now that the concepts of freedom developed in nineteenth-century Russia are at least as manifold as the intellectual discourses competing for conceptual dominance at the time. What they all have in common is their highly politicised context. Under absolutist governance in a multi-religious and multi-ethnic empire, discourse on freedom seems to have been more narrowly focused on specific social groups, 'peoples', classes or institutions than on questions of individual freedom in general. Due to political, economic and social circumstances, concepts of freedom were developed in relation to concepts of law, necessity, social equality, love and religion. As mentioned earlier, Russian concepts of freedom seem to fall into the category of positive liberty more often than they align with negative liberty. Granted, this is not an exclusively Russian phenomenon: Berlin himself admits that generally in modern human thinking only a minority of (liberal) thinkers gave more thought to the limits of authority than to pledges of freedom (1958: 46). Apart from very rare exceptions like Boris Chicherin or Alexander Herzen, most of the above mentioned Russian thinkers sought to harmonise their concept of freedom with concepts of equality or brotherhood and tended to prioritise the latter if they had to choose. In addition, Russian intellectuals' general neglect of negative liberty also derived from their disdain of law, which most of them conceived as an imposition from above that restrained freedom, rather than as a limitation of absolutist power.

What is more, ideas of freedom cannot be dissociated from the concept of personality. Thus the positive concept of freedom as self-mastery was associated with the widespread idea of a dual personality split between an ideal autonomous self, capable of weighing and controlling its actions, and an empirical, heteronomous self associated with the passions of 'lower' nature. This concept often tends to derive the 'ideal self' from 'something wider than the individual' – namely, a social whole representing the values or goals that should guide 'self-mastery' in order to achieve some sort of 'higher' freedom (ibid. 16–19). Thus the freedom of a person becomes a *project* in the name of goals rarely compatible with the value of individual freedom. This is in line with recent accounts of the concept of the person as a 'project' in Russian discourse (Plotnikov 2012: 284). The thinkers analysed above conceptualise 'freedom' either as a project that has to be achieved in one's own lifetime or as a task to be realised by future society. Based on these reflections, I suggest that Russian thinkers of the nineteenth century can be distinguished by their tendency to identify freedom *either* as an inherent human property *or* as a historical project in the Romantic sense, with the latter clearly prevailing. This is hardly surprising, given that the current emphasis on freedom as an inherent feature of human dignity in European thought, and especially in human rights discourse, has developed against the backdrop of the historical experiences of the twentieth century.

In one of the earliest accounts on the problem of freedom in Russian history, Reinhard Wittram argued that the Russian history of the nineteenth century was 'one sole extensive answer to the question of freedom posed by the West', despite the dissonances between the political, social and spiritual forces involved in its formation (1954: 378). I can only partly agree with this statement, since there is obviously not 'one sole answer to the question of freedom' to be found, but numerous different conceptions. Echoing Herzen's formula 'Man is freer than is usually believed', one can conclude: Russian discourse on freedom is freer than is usually believed.

Acknowledgements

I would like to thank Stefan Guth and Daniel Whistler for their comments and English language editing. I am also grateful to Vesa Oittinen and the participants of a seminar held at the Aleksanteri Institute at the University of Helsinki for their suggestions. I also thank Patrick L. Michelson for making available some of his unpublished texts.

Notes

1. See, for example, Smith's account of the spiritual hermeneutics of Belinsky (2014: 196–214), as well as Manchester 2008.
2. See the current project 'Freiheitsdiskurse in Russland' at the Ruhr-University Bochum under the guidance of Nikolai Plotnikov, available at <http://www.slavistik.rub.de/index.php?Forschungsprojekte-16> (last accessed 13 July 2017).
3. In what follows, I will use the English terms 'liberty' and 'freedom' interchangeably, since attempts to distinguish between them seem not to have caught on (Carter 2016).
4. See Pushkin's famous poems *To Chaadaev* (1818): 'Minutes of holy freedom we await [My zhdem . . . minuty vol'nosti sviatoi]' and *Exegi monumentum* (1836): 'In my cruel age I extolled freedom [V moi zhestokii vek vosslavil ja svobodu]' (Pushkin 1959b, 1959a).
5. See Marx's critique of the liberal notion of 'religious' liberty of conscience, which fails to liberate conscience from the spectre of religion ([1875] 1973: 31).
6. Christian Wolff's system was known in Russia through the canonical textbook, *Moral Philosophy*, of his disciple Christian Baumeister (Berest 2011: 15). See also Hüning 2016.
7. The law professor and philosopher, Alexander Kunitsyn (1783–1840), was the first Russian thinker to raise a concern over the individual freedom posed by social traditions. In 1821, his book on natural law was removed from all libraries and Kunitsyn banned from teaching. On Kant in Russia, see Kruglov 2009.
8. This is not the only dimension in which Boris Chicherin stood at odds with the religious philosopher Vladimir Solov'ëv. See Hamburg 2010: 118.
9. On Hegel's reception in Russia, see Vadim Sholnikov's and Robert Harris's contributions in Herzog 2013: 17–48.

10. Berlin (1958: 10) criticises Belinsky's preference for solidarity over the value of liberty.
11. It may not have been conducive to the reception of John Stuart Mill's writings that his first book to appear in Russian in 1860, *The Principles of Political Economy*, was translated by the radical materialist Nikolai Chernyshevski. Mill's *On Liberty*, together with *Utilitarianism*, was translated into Russian by Alexander Nevedomsky and appeared in three editions (1866–9, 1882, 1900).
12. A famous follower of Vladimir Solov'ëv was Sergii Bulgakov. On his conception of freedom and its complex relationship with Solov'ëv, see Gallaher 2016: 45ff.
13. One can find traces of moral autonomy in recent documents of the Russian Orthodox Church that speak of the need 'to preserve for the individual a certain autonomous space [*nekuiu avtonomnuiu sferu*] where his conscience remains the absolute master, for it is on the free will that salvation or death, the way towards Christ or away from Christ will ultimately depend' (Russian Orthodox Church 2008: sect. 4, art. 3). The question remains whether the individual choice between salvation and death is tantamount to the notion of moral autonomy in the Kantian sense. Apparently it is not by chance that the 'Basic Teaching on Human Dignity, Freedom and Rights' has a striking dearth of references to juridical rights (Zwahlen 2015: 38–9). On the dissemination of Kantian philosophy in Russian theological academies, see Krouglov 2011.

References

Berest, Julia (2011), *The Emergence of Russian Liberalism: Alexander Kunitsyn in Context, 1783–1840*, Basingstoke: Palgrave Macmillan.
Berlin, Isaiah (1958), *Two Concepts of Liberty*, Oxford: Clarendon Press.
Berlin, Isaiah [1978] (1998), *Russian Thinkers*, London: Penguin.
Carter, Ian (2016), 'Positive and Negative Liberty', in Edward N. Zalta (ed.), *The Standford Encyclopedia of Philosophy*, <http://plato.stanford.edu/entries/liberty-positive-negative/> (last accessed 25 November 2016).
Dostoevsky, F. M. [1880] (1966), 'Pushkin. A Sketch', in Marc Raeff (ed.), *Russian Intellectual History: An Anthology*, New York: Harcourt, 289–300.
Duncan, Peter (2000), *Russian Messianism: Third Rome, Revolution, Communism and after*, London: Routledge.
Edie, James M., James P. Scanlan and Mary-Barbara Zeldin (eds) (1969), *Russian Philosophy: Volume I*, 2nd edn, Chicago: Quadrangle.
Fedotov, G. P. (1981), *Rossiia i svoboda: sbornik statei*, New York: Chalidze.
Florovsky, Georges [1937] (1979), *Ways of Russian Theology*, ed. Richard S. Haugh, New York: Nordland.
Frede, Victoria (2012), 'Freedom of Conscience, Freedom of Confession, and "Land and Freedom" in the 1860s', *Kritika: Explorations in Russian and Eurasian History*, 13.3: 561–84.
Gallaher, Brandon (2016), *Freedom and Necessity in Modern Trinitarian Theology*, Oxford: Oxford University Press.
Hagen, Manfred (2002), *Die russische Freiheit: Wege in ein paradoxes Thema*, Stuttgart: Franz Steiner.
Hamburg, Gary M. (1992), *Boris Chicherin and Early Russian Liberalism: 1828–1866*, Stanford: Stanford University Press.
Hamburg, Gary M. (2010), 'Boris Chicherin and Human Dignity in History', in Gary M. Hamburg and Randall A. Poole (eds), *A History of Russian Philosophy 1830–1930*, Cambridge: Cambridge University Press, 111–30.
Herzog, Lisa (ed.) (2013), *Hegel's Thought in Europe: Currents, Crosscurrents and Undercurrents*, Basingstoke: Palgrave Macmillan.
Horujy, Sergey (2010), 'Slavophiles, Westernizers, and the Birth of Russian Philosophical Humanism', in Gary M. Hamburg and Randall A. Poole (eds), *A History of Russian Philosophy 1830–1930*, Cambridge: Cambridge University Press, 27–51.

Hüning, Dieter (2016), 'Liberty and Determinism: The Approach of Christian Wolff', *Studies in East European Thought*, 68: 119–26.

Jakim, Boris and Robert Bird (eds) (1998), *On Spiritual Unity: A Slavophile Reader*, Hudson, NY: Lindisfarne.

Kappeler, Andreas (2001), *The Russian Empire: A Multi-Ethnic History*, trans. Alfred Clayton, London: Routledge.

Krouglov, Alexej N. (2011), 'Kant and Orthodox Thought in Russia', *Russian Studies in Philosophy*, 49.4: 10–33.

Kruglov, Aleksej N. (2009), *Filosofija Kanta v Rossii v konce XVIII – pervoj polovine XIX vekov*, Moscow: Kanon+.

Leatherbarrow, William J. and Derek Offord (eds) (2010), *A History of Russian Thought*, Cambridge: Cambridge University Press.

Manchester, Laurie (2008), *Holy Fathers, Secular Sons: Clergy, Intelligentsia, and the Modern Self in Revolutionary Russia*, DeKalb: Northern Illinois University Press.

Marx, Karl [1875] (1973), 'Kritik des Gothaer Programms (1875/1891)', in *Karl Marx/Friedrich Engels Werke*, vol. 19, Berlin: Karl Dietz, 13–32.

Michelson, Patrick Lally (2007), '"The first and most sacred right": Religious Freedom and the Liberation of the Russian Nation, 1825–1905', thesis for the degree of Doctor of Philosophy (History), University of Wisconsin-Madison.

Michelson, Patrick Lally (2010), 'Slavophile Religious Thought and the Dilemma of Russian Modernity, 1830–1860', *Modern Intellectual History*, 7.2: 239–67.

Michelson, Patrick Lally (2014), 'Freedom of Conscience and the Limits of the Liberal Solovyov', *Solov'ëvskie issledovanija*, 41.1: 25–46.

Michelson, Patrick Lally (2018, forthcoming), 'Freedom of Conscience in the Clerical Imagination of Russian Orthodox Thought, 1801–1865', in Randall A. Poole and Paul W. Werth (eds), *Religious Freedom in Russia*, Pittsburgh: University of Pittsburgh Press.

Michelson, Patrick Lally and Judith Deutsch Kornblatt (eds) (2014), *Thinking Orthodox in Modern Russia: Culture, History, Context*, Madison: University of Wisconsin Press.

Nethercott, Frances (2010), 'Russian Liberalism and the Philosophy of Law', in Gary M. Hamburg and Randall A. Poole (eds), *A History of Russian Philosophy 1830–1930*, Cambridge: Cambridge University Press, 248–65.

Offord, Derek (1985), *Portraits of Early Russian Liberals: A Study of the Thought of T. N. Granovsky, V. P. Botkin, P. V. Annenkov, A. V. Druzhinin and K. D. Kavelin*, Cambridge: Cambridge University Press.

Offord, Derek (2010), 'The People', in William J. Leatherbarrow and Derek Offord (eds), *A History of Russian Thought*, Cambridge: Cambridge University Press, 241–62.

Oittinen, Vesa (2003), 'Solov'ëvs letzte Philosophie – eine Annäherung an Kant?', *Studies in East European Thought*, 55: 97–114.

Orekhanov, Georgij (2010), *Russkaia pravoslavnaia cerkov i L.N. Tolstoj: konflikt glazami sovremennikov*, Moscow: Pravoslavnyi Svjato-Tichonovskii gumanitarnyi universitet.

O'Rourke, James J. (1974), *The Problem of Freedom in Marxist Thought*, Dordrecht: Reidel.

Papmehl, K. A. (1971), *Freedom of Expression in Eighteenth-Century Russia*, The Hague: Nijhoff.

Patterson, Orlando (1991), *Freedom. Volume I: Freedom in the Making of Western Culture*, London: I. B. Tauris.

Pavlov, A. T. (2003), 'University Philosophy in Russia', *Russian Studies in Philosophy*, 42.2: 6–20.

Plotnikov, Nikolaj (2012), '"The person is a monad with windows": Sketch of a Conceptual History of "Person" in Russia', *Studies in Eastern European Thought*, 64.3/4: 269–99.

Polunov, Alexander (2005), *Russia in the Nineteenth Century. Autocracy, Reform, and Social Change, 1814–1914*, trans. Marsahll S. Shatz, Armonk, NY: Sharpe.

Poole, Randall A. (2010), 'Vladimir Solov'ëv's Philosophical Anthropology: Autonomy, Dignity, Perfectibility', in Gary M. Hamburg and Randall A. Poole (eds), *A History of Russian Philosophy 1830–1930*, Cambridge: Cambridge University Press, 131–49.

Pushkin, Aleksandr S. (1959a), 'Ja pamjatnik sebe vozdvig nerukotvornyi (Exegi monumentum)', in *Sobranie sochinenii*, 10 vols, Moscow: Gosudarstvennoe izdatel'stvo khudozhestevennoi literatury, vol. II, p. 460.
Pushkin, Aleksandr S. (1959b), 'K Chaadaevu', in *Sobranie sochinenii*, 10 vols, Moscow: Gosudarstvennoe izdatel'stvo khudozhestevennoi literatury, vol. I, p. 65.
Rabow-Edling, Susanna (2006), *Slavophile Thought and the Politics of Cultural Nationalism*, New York: State University of New York Press.
Radishchev, Aleksandr Nikolaevich ([1790] 1958), *A Journey from St. Petersburg to Moscow*, trans. Leo Wiener, Cambridge, MA: Harvard University Press.
Russian Orthodox Church (2008), 'Basic Teaching on Human Dignity, Freedom and Rights', <https://mospat.ru/en/documents/dignity-freedom-rights/> (last accessed 24 March 2017).
Scanlan, James P. (2002), *Dostoevsky the Thinker*, Ithaca: Cornell University Press.
Schmidt, Christoph (2007), 'Freiheit in Russland. Eine begriffsgeschichtliche Spurensuche', *Jahrbücher für Geschichte Osteuropas*, 55: 264–75.
Skinner, Quentin and Martin van Gelderen (eds) (2013), *Freedom and the Construction of Europe: Religious and Constitutional Liberties*, Cambridge: Cambridge University Press.
Smith, Oliver (2014), 'Anagogical Exegesis: The Theological Roots of Russian Hermeneutics', in Patrick Lally Michelson and Judith Deutsch Kornblatt (eds), *Thinking Orthodox in Modern Russia*, Madison: University of Wisconsin Press, 196–214.
Solov'ëv, Vladimir S. (1892), 'Vol'nodumstvo', in *Ėnciklopedicheskii slovar' Brokgauza i Efrona*, vol. 7, ed. F. A. Brokgauz and I. A. Efron, Leipzig, St Petersburg: Tipo-Litografija I. A. Efrona, 136.
Solov'ëv, Vladimir S. (1900), 'Svoboda volja', in *Ėnciklopedicheskii slovar' Brokgauza i Efrona*, vol. 29, ed. F. A. Brokgauz and I. A. Efron, Leipzig, St Petersburg: Tipo-Litografija I. A. Efrona, 163–9.
Solov'ëv, Vladimir S. [1888] (1954), 'L'idée russe', in *Wladimir Solowjew. Deutsche Gesamtausgabe*, ed. Wladimir Szylkarski, Freiburg im Breisgau: Erich Wewel, 31–90.
Strickland, John (2013), *The Making of Holy Russia: The Orthodox Church and Russian Nationalism before the Revolution*, New York: Holy Trinity Publications.
Tataryn, Myroslaw I. (2000), *Augustine and Russian Orthodoxy*, Boston: International Scholars Publications.
Valliere, Paul (2000), *Modern Russian Theology: Bukharev, Soloviev, Bulgakov: Orthodox Theology in a New Key*, Edinburgh: T&T Clark.
Vodovozov, Vasily V. (1900), 'Svoboda mysli, slova', in *Ėnciklopedicheskii slovar' Brokgauza i Efrona*, vol. 29, ed. F. A. Brokgauz and I. A. Efron, Leipzig, St Petersburg: Tipo-Litografija I. A. Efrona, 172–4.
Walicki, Andrzej (1980), *A History of Russian Thought from the Enlightenment to Marxism*, Oxford: Clarendon Press.
Walicki, Andrzej (2010), 'Russian Marxism', in Gary M. Hamburg and Randall A. Poole (eds), *A History of Russian Philosophy 1830–1930*, Cambridge: Cambridge University Press, 305–25.
Wasmuth, Jennifer (2007), *Der Protestantismus und die russische Theologie: zur Rezeption und Kritik des Protestantismus in den Zeitschriften der Geistlichen Akademien an der Wende vom 19. zum 20. Jahrhundert (Forschungen zur systematischen und ökumenischen Theologie, Bd. 113)*, Göttingen: Vandenhoeck & Ruprecht.
Wenzler, Ludwig (1978), *Die Freiheit und das Böse nach Vladimir Solov'ev*, Freiburg: Verlag Karl Alber.
Werth, Paul W. (2012), 'The Emergence of "Freedom of Conscience" in Imperial Russia', *Kritika: Explorations in Russian and Eurasian History*, 13.3: 585–610.
Werth, Paul W. (2014), *The Tsar's Foreign Faiths: Toleration and the Fate of Religious Freedom in Imperial Russia*, Oxford: Oxford University Press.
Wiener, Leo (1902), *Anthology of Russian Literature from the Earliest Period to the Present Time*, 2 vols, New York: Putnam.
Wittram, Reinhard (1954), 'Das Freiheitsproblem in der russischen inneren Geschichte', *Jahrbücher für Geschichte Osteuropas*, 2: 369–86.

Yanovsky, Abel' E. (1892), 'Vol'nye ljudi', in *Ènciklopedicheskii slovar' Brokgauza i Efrona*, vol. 7, ed. F. A. Brokgauz and I. A. Efron, Leipzig, St Petersburg: Tipo-Litografija I. A. Efrona, 143–5.

Zwahlen, Regula M. (2015), 'The Lack of Moral Autonomy in the Russian Concept of Personality: A Case of Continuity across the Pre-revolutionary, Soviet and Post-Soviet Periods?', *State, Religion and Church*, 2.1: 19–43.

6

The Fetish

Roland Boer

The fetish was one of the most significant terms in nineteenth-century thought that made its way from theology and the study of religions into politics and economics. In this study, I focus on Marx's extensive development of the fetish for his own analysis of the dynamics of capitalism. But in order to set the scene, let me begin by situating the fetish in its context, which was simultaneously economic, religious and cultural (see especially Pietz 1985, 1987, 1988). When the Portuguese began sailing tentatively down the West African coast during the fifteenth century in their tiny caravels in search of a way to the 'East' that circumvented the Muslim-dominated lands of the Middle East, they encountered local people with their own cultures and religious practices. As the Portuguese established forts, refuelling stations and slaving posts, they also attempted to understand cultures that were vastly different from their own. In particular, the crucial amulets and objects, endowed with superhuman powers and keys to social exchange, had to be understood. They found the term 'idolatry' inadequate, for it had become an elaborate term in the theological tradition. Church Fathers, heresiarchs and theologians had developed a complex understanding of idolatry that went far beyond its initial biblical framework: idolatry had become a mirror of 'true religion', requiring a cultic practice, institutional structure, clergy, sacred objects, architecture and tradition. This understanding of idolatry seemed not to apply to the practices of the West Africans. Instead, the Portuguese used the term *fetisso*, the etymology of which is still disputed.[1] But they played a double game: on the one hand, the term was used to suggest that the primitive Africans were irrational, for they attributed superhuman and magical powers to simple objects of wood, stone or metal; on the other hand, the Portuguese also would swear by and even consume a fetish (where needed) to ensure a commercial exchange. In short, they derided the claim that the fetish had powers in social networking and yet they recognised such powers in their everyday interactions with the Africans.

The term 'fetish' caught on. The Dutch, French and English Protestants used it to describe Roman Catholic sacramental objects. Enlightenment intellectuals used it in the eighteenth and nineteenth centuries as the basis for a general theory of religion.[2] Notably, a certain Charles de Brosses (1760) developed a comprehensive theory of fetishism in order to understand the religion of ancient Egypt. De Brosses drew upon studies of fetishism in Western Africa and applied them – in a process that would become the norm among historians and anthropologists – to the ancient world. The argument went as follows: here too are primitives, living in our own day and time; their religious practices must be similar to those of other primitives, even if they lived millennia before our civilised society.

The crucial moment in de Brosses's argument is the search for evidence of ancient Egyptian religious practice. His primary source is the Bible, which he understood as a reliable historical source. All of the stories concerning Egyptians and their gods, magicians and beliefs, especially those clustered around the accounts of Joseph, Israelite slavery and escape under Moses in the early chapters of Exodus, became evidence for ancient fetishism. As for Canaanite practices, in which the Israelites engaged frequently when they had settled in the land, these too provided data regarding fetishism.

Marx learnt of the fetish when he read de Brosses's work (in German translation) in the early 1840s. It would become a crucial term in his work for the next forty years. In this light, I undertake two tasks: to examine the full range of Marx's constant reinterpretation and redeployment of the idea of the fetish; and to analyse the development of the idea in *Capital*, moving from the initial foray in the first volume to the completion of his argument in the third. Thus in the first part I explore the forty years over which Marx constantly rethought the idea of the fetish. This includes his youthful reading of works in the history of religions concerning fetishism among African peoples of the west coast, his repeated use of the idea through his journalistic pieces, the continual modifications in his other economic pieces, and his notes on ethnography in the last years of his life. By contrast, in the second part, I treat the 'fetishism of commodities' section in *Capital* I before focusing on the later volumes, which show that Marx's concept of the fetish moves well beyond the commodity. He begins to identify ever more forms of the fetish – such as the capitalist as a personification of capital, the landlord, socially productive powers of capital, use, exchange and surplus value, wealth,[3] interest, rent, wages and profit – until he initiates a process of distillation. This entails a focus on three key types of the fetish – capital, land and labour – and then the singular essence of capital as *Kapitalfetish*. In other words, in order to understand the inner workings of capital, Marx finds a religious, if not theological idea the most useful. At the same time, it is thoroughly transformed through his relentless dialectical approach.[4]

Forty Years of Fetishism

Marx studied and reformulated his ideas on the fetish from the early 1840s to the 1880s. In the 1840s, Marx mentions fetishism often, since he was working on a text that is now lost, *A Treatise on Christian Art*. This tantalisingly lost manuscript would have provided a much fuller picture of Marx's views on religion and aesthetics, let alone the fetish (my interest here).[5] Instead, we are left with observations and comments that appear elsewhere, reflecting fragments of his thoughts on the fetish.

Traces of the Lost Treatise on Christian Art

A few tell-tale comments appear in material from 1842 and soon afterwards – precisely when Marx was working on the treatise. They exhibit two lines of argument: first, common ideas of religious progress are highly suspect; second, fetishism involves a transfer of properties between the object fetishised and human beings, with human beings diminished to mere objects and the fetish itself gaining human properties. We see both lines in a piece that constitutes perhaps Marx's most extensive early reflection on theology, 'The Leading Article in No. 179 of the *Kölnische Zeitung*'. Marx criticises Herr Hermes, government agent and editor of a major conservative Roman Catholic journal. On fetishism, Marx writes:

> And now, indeed 'fetishism'! Truly, the erudition of a penny magazine! Fetishism is so far from raising man *above* his sensuous desires that, on the contrary, it is 'the *religion of*

sensuous desire'. Fantasy arising from desire deceives the fetish worshipper into believing that an 'inanimate object' will give up its natural character in order to comply with his desires. Hence the crude desire of the fetish-worshipper *smashes* the fetish when it ceases to be its most obedient servant. ([1842] 1975h: 189; [1842] 1975e: 177)

Hermes had proposed a rather conventional narrative of religious history that moves from sensuous animal worship, through fetishism to the highest form of Christianity, which happened to coincide with the form of Christianity in Germany at the time. In response, Marx points out that there is no progress at all, that fetishism is no advance on animal worship, for both fall into the same category (and so does Christianity). Fetishism, too, is saturated with sensuous desire, a desire that produces a fantasy that this inanimate object has magical and superhuman powers. However, when the fetish no longer provides what the worshipper wants – recovery from illness, favourable outcomes in battle, a good harvest – he smashes it in disgust. Behind Marx's argument lies a crucial assumption: with fetishism we have not two but three steps. Instead of sacralised fetish → de-sacralised object, he postulates three steps: profane object → sacralised fetish → de-sacralised object once again. The first and third stages frame the fetish itself, one as a point of origin and the other as a point of return to that state. The fetish itself is the anomaly, the break in the profaneness of the object. Marx recognises – through the quotation marks around 'inanimate object' in the quotation above – that this argument reflects his own critical perspective and not that of the fetish user, for such a user would see the object as inherently sacred in the first place. Marx's point is that any idea of progress, from a primitive religious state to one of refinement, is anything but.

As for the second argument – the transferring relation – Marx writes: 'an "inanimate object" gives up its natural character'. In other words, it ceases to be a mere object – a piece of wood, stone, metal, star or perhaps tree – and becomes something else, a god or fetish with powers it never had before. It thereby gains a whole series of attributes – able to affect human interaction, redirect nature, produce miraculous results – which it did not have before. This surrender of the object's natural properties is but one side of the inversion, for human beings too change in the process; they give up their nature as human beings to become abject worshippers and fetish users, more and more resembling lifeless objects.

Marx takes both arguments – concerning the transferring relation and the inversion of the narrative of progress – and uses them to polemical effect. For example, a couple of years later in *The Economic and Philosophic Manuscripts*, he comments on the French who are 'still dazzled by the sensuous glitter of precious metals, and are therefore still fetish-worshippers of metal money, and are not yet fully-developed money-nations' ([1844] 1975g: 312; [1844] 1990b: 552). In this case, he assumes the narrative of progress, only to turn it against the vaunted sophistication of the French: they may assume they are advanced, but they are really still savages, worshipping precious metals. The edge of this argument appears more sharply in a criticism of the Rhine Province Assembly (a pseudo-democratic gathering restricted to the nobles):

The *savages of Cuba* regarded gold as a *fetish of the Spaniards*. They celebrated a feast in its honour, sang in a circle around it and then threw it into the sea. If the Cuban savages had been present at the sitting of the Rhine Province Assembly, would they not have regarded *wood* as the *Rhinelanders*' *fetish*? But a subsequent sitting would have taught them that the worship of animals is connected with this fetishism, and they would have thrown the *hares* into the sea in order to save the *human beings*. ([1842] 1975j: 262–3; [1842] 1975k: 236)[6]

For the cultured Rhine nobles, the Cubans would indeed be seen as savages – hence the emphasis in Marx's text: 'savages of Cuba' was the nobles' phrase. But now Marx inverts the whole relation, for he purports to write from the perspective of the Cubans. To them, the mad search for gold by the Spaniards – so much so that Columbus threatened to cut off the hands of any inhabitant of Hispaniola who did not bring him gold – was much like the worship of fetishes. Marx imagines the Cubans saying: 'Let us recognise its fetish character and toss it into the sea; hopefully the Spanish too will go, perhaps diving into the sea in order to find their precious fetish.' By the time the Cubans have crossed the Atlantic and sit at the Rhine Province Assembly, the relation of savage to civilised has been fully inverted. The Cubans are now the calm, rational observers and what do they see? The nobles obsessing about wood laws, especially the move to ban the ancient practice of peasants gathering fallen wood for their cooking and heating fires. Surely wood must be their fetish, since they wish to preserve it. Or, in relation to hares, which the nobles wish to preserve from the peasants' snares, the Cubans could only conclude that the nobles are also into animal fetishism. The proper response: in order to save human beings from such terrible developments, the hares too should be thrown into the sea. And why is fetishism so deleterious for human beings? Once again the transferring relation appears: the fetish humanises – or rather, superhumanises – animals and objects while it dehumanises human beings.

I have let the story run ahead of itself, exploring possible arguments from the treatise before recounting the fate of the treatise itself. It arose from the confluence of three streams: the nature of public debate in Germany at the time, which was deeply theological, or rather, biblical; the close friendship and early collaboration with Bruno Bauer, Marx's one-time biblical teacher in Berlin; and the search for research topics and employment after Marx had finished his PhD thesis in 1841.

Concerning German public debate, the conservative nature of Prussian politics – pushed by the new king, Friedrich Wilhelm IV and his desire for a 'Christian state' – brought theology to the fore in public debate. Thus David Strauss's *Das Leben Jesu* (1835) with its democratic Christ (we may all become Christs) was the most debated work of the time. And Bruno Bauer, for a while leader of the Young Hegelians, caused a raging debate with his radical biblical criticism. He espoused atheism in the name of a free and infinite self-consciousness for which any religion, but especially that form of Christianity identified with the state, was a hubristic and brutalising particularity that claimed universal status (Bauer 1838, 1839, 1840, 1841, 1842a, 1842b, 1843, 1850–1, 1852; Moggach 2003). Both Strauss and Bauer were soon denied teaching positions as a result of their radical positions.

Marx, who had tied his fortunes to Bauer, soon knew that he had no chance of a university position. Since Bauer was a biblical scholar and theologian and since Marx set out in the first months after completing his thesis on Epicurus to collaborate with Bauer, Marx's path veered towards theology, albeit of a radical type. Their plans were audacious: a journal called *Archiv des Atheismus*, a critique of Hegel's *Philosophy of Religion*, and a series of book reviews, one at least on Karl Fischer's book, *Die Idee der Gottheit* (1839), and another on *Die menschliche Freiheit in ihrem Verhältnisse zur Sünde und zur göttlichen Gnade*, written by the Hegelian biblical critic and theologian Wilhelm Vatke – this one for Arnold Ruge's *Deutsch-Französische Jahrbücher* (see Marx [1842] 1975c; [1842] 1973d). None of these projects came to fruition, largely because the collaboration was a rocky one and because Marx's own interests began to change.

The closest the two young radicals came to publishing together was a two-volume work, to be called *Die Posaune*, or *Trumpet of the Last Judgement*. The outcome, however, was two works in Bauer's name, the first with the agreed-upon title and the second called *Hegels Lehre von der Religion und Kunst* (Bauer [1841] 1983, [1842] 1967). Although Marx has less of a role in the first volume, the second one was intended to be fully collaborative. Again, nothing came of it. In a series of letters to Arnold Ruge in 1842, we find comments by Marx on the collapse of the collaboration and his plans to produce his part of the second volume as a separate publication. It was to be called *A Treatise on Christian Art*. From Marx's other writings of the period, it seems that work would have moved from a study of the religious and fetishist art of Asia and Greece to the Christian art of the Romantics, showing how the two are connected.[7] Each time Marx mentions the manuscript in the letters to Ruge, it is one step away from completion, needing a few corrections and the writing up of a fair copy; but then he had decided to expand it and include a section on Romanticism; then it had become two volumes, one on Christian art and the other to be called *On the Romantics*; after that we hear nothing more of the treatise (Marx [1842] 1973a, [1842] 1973c, [1842] 1975b, [1842] 1902, [1842] 1975a, [1842] 1973e). Marx had clearly not learnt how to complete a manuscript (a problem that stayed with him),[8] although it did not help that he was in Trier for three months, sitting by his future father-in-law's deathbed. Herr Ludwig von Westphalen died on 3 March 1842; within a couple of months, Marx's manuscript suffered a similar fate.

There is one other piece of evidence regarding this manuscript. Apart from the letters to Ruge and the scattered comments on religion, fetishism and art from the same period, there is also a collection of reading notes from the time when Marx was working on the manuscript. In the Bonn Notebooks of 1842, excerpts from the following works appear:

Karl Friedrich von Rumohr, *Italienische Forshungen*. Bonn, 1842.
Johann Jakob Grund, *Der Malerey der Grieschen oder Enstehung, Fortschritt, Vollendung und Verfall der Malerey. Ein Versuch*. Dresden, 1810.
Charles de Brosses, *Du culte des dieux fétiches ou Parallèle de l'ancienne religion de l'Egypte avec la religion actuelle de Nigritie*. German translation by Pistorius, Berlin and Stansrund 1785. French, 1760.
C.A. Böttinger, *Ideen zur Kunstmythologie*. 2 vols. Dresden and Leipzig, 1826–36.
Christoph Meiners, *Allgemeine kritische Geschichte der Religionen*. 2 vols. Hannover, 1806–7.
Benjamin Constant, *De la religion*. Paris, 1826.
J. Barbeyrac, *Traité de la Morale des Pères de l'Église*. Amsterdam, 1728.

Marx was obviously studying a significant number of works on religion as well as art, especially when we add Gibbon, Hegel and Feuerbach, whom he was reading on the same topics. But let me focus on some key items, especially the books by Böttinger and Grund, as well as Feuerbach's discussion of *Bildlichkeit* in *The Essence of Christianity* (Feuerbach [1841] 1989: 74–9; [1841] 1986: 94–100), which Marx was also reading at the time. Among the notes Marx took, there appears the following argument: in the same way that the Greeks idealised men as gods and anthropomorphised men (especially from Böttinger), so also did Christian art produce a fetishistic anthropomorphisation of the divine while it alienated human sensuality (from Feuerbach). In short, Christianity took over the thoroughly fetishistic and pagan nature of the culture it thought it was transforming (Rose 1984: 65–9). This is a rather good argument against conventional narratives of Christian progress!

However, I am less interested in Marx's arguments concerning art or Christianity, the connections between them, or the possible links with Marx's other polemic against state censorship at the time (ibid. 61),[9] and more interested in what he read in terms of fetishism. On this matter, the work by de Brosses stands out in the collection (Marx [1842] 1976b).

Fetishism or Idolatry

In particular, I am interested in why de Brosses did not use the terms 'idol' and 'idolatry'. Instead, he subsumed idolatry within an overarching category of fetishism. The idolatries of the Egyptians, the Canaanites and even the Israelites on many occasions, were actually instances of fetishism. He may have derided fetishism as a 'stupid' and 'ridiculous' practice (Brosses 1760: 10–11), but by turning to the Bible for evidence of ancient Egyptian religious practices (there described as idolatry) and by subsuming them within a general theory of fetishism, he reinserted idolatry into discussions. Further, as a subset of fetishism, idolatry could also mean fetishism, although not vice versa. So whenever de Brosses read the word 'idol' in the Bible he assumed it was a 'fetish'.

Marx appropriated this connection from de Brosses. As evidence, one passage Marx cites with interest is a key section concerning the nature of fetishism in ancient Judah (Marx [1842] 1976b: 321–2; Brosses 1760: 27–30). Marx notes that de Brosses distinguishes between two types of fetish, the private and the public. Four types of public or 'national' fetishes appear: serpents, trees, the sea and 'a small, filthy clay image [*Bild*]' which presided over councils.[10] The key term here is *Bild*, for it translates de Brosses's *idole*. Marx goes on to make further notes from these pages by de Brosses on the roles of these four types of fetish – or idols or images – in Judah. But the elision has taken place: Marx appropriates the link between idol and fetish and in the process the idols of ancient Judah become instances of the broader category of fetishism.

Before I explore what Marx did with the idea after taking it over from de Brosses, let me make two points. To begin with, the idolatry in question was a stripped-down version, found in various biblical texts, rather than the elaborate version that came out of the theological tradition which I mentioned earlier. Second, there is a natural ideological fit between those who use the terms 'idol' or 'fetish': both come from a particular perspective, after the fact, creating a category and simultaneously making a theological and moral judgement. In the case of the biblical 'idol', the very use of the term comes much later, creating a category of religious practice that, in the very process of being created, critiqued and dismissed that category. The designation 'idol', apart from the polemic often associated with the term, was in itself a condemnation. With 'fetish' the situation is similar: the category is developed to describe what others do, imposed after the fact by an external observer. But it also contains critique and judgement, for the fetishist is mistaken, deluded, ridiculous and stupid. Marx too would assume a similar approach: 'fetish' may occasionally be a descriptive term, but more often than not it bears a negative weight. To describe something – money, commodity, capital itself – as a fetish is to imply critique on Marx's part and delusion on the part of the fetishist.

Reworking the Fetish

I have returned to my starting point, namely, Marx's early comments on fetishism: the delusion of the fetish worshipper is clear; describing an item as a fetish – gold, wood or hares – acts as a criticism; the crucial transferring relation between fetish and human being is central. Since we returned to Marx's fetishistic polemic, I can now note another connection with de Brosses. Let us recall the example of the Cubans and the Spanish fetish for gold, which Marx applied to the Rhine Province Assembly: the inversion comes from de Brosses, whom Marx cites for his own use.[11] De Brosses was clearly a crucial source, sparking Marx's interest in fetishism.

The fetish became an extraordinarily fruitful idea, appearing throughout Marx's work from the earliest journalistic pieces with the *Rheinische Zeitung* to the extraordinary economic manuscripts of the 1860s. He constantly reworked the fetish, for the purpose of analysing alienation, labour, money as mediator, the commodity form and then capital as a whole, but he ensured it kept its core concept: the transferral of powers from human beings to the object in question, to the detriment of one and the gain of the other.

For example, with alienation and labour, Marx argues in *The Economic and Philosophic Manuscripts of 1844* that the more the worker puts into the product of his labour, the greater it becomes while the worker diminishes. The basic argument would remain the same, even if the terms themselves would change:

> All these consequences are implied in the statement that the worker is related to the *product of his labour* as to an *alien* object. For on this premise it is clear that the more the worker spends himself, the more powerful becomes the alien world of objects which he creates over and against himself, the poorer he himself – his inner world – becomes, the less belongs to him as his own. It is the same in religion. The more man puts into God, the less he retains in himself [*Es ist ebenso in der Religion. Je mehr der Mensch in Gott setzt, je weniger behält er in sich selbst*]. The worker puts his life into the object; but now his life no longer belongs to him but to the object ... The *alienation* of the worker in his product means not only that his labour becomes an object, an *external* existence, but that it exists *outside him*, independently, as something alien to him, and that it becomes a power on its own confronting him. It means that the life which he has conferred on the object confronts him as something hostile and alien. ([1844] 1975g: 272; [1844] 1990b: 512)[12]

The alien objects take on lives of their own, becoming greater than the worker. The products of everyday labour swell into alien and powerful creatures because of this transferral of powers and relations. But note the analogy, for here the theological secret agent I mentioned earlier makes an appearance: 'It is the same in religion', Marx writes, and then goes on to draw the analogy: 'The more man puts into God, the less he retains in himself [*Es ist ebenso in der Religion. Je mehr der Mensch in Gott setzt, je weniger behält er in sich selbst*].'

The pattern of invoking fetishism and then using a theological analogy would remain remarkably consistent as Marx constantly reinterpreted the fetish. For example, in notes written at the same time on the French translation of James Mill's *Elements of Political Economy*, Marx uses a similar argument in connection with money. The difference now is that it is not money per se that is the issue, but the mediatory role of money: this mediating activity 'is *estranged* from man and becomes the attribute of money, a *material thing* outside man' (Marx [1844] 1975d: 212; [1844] 1990a: 446).[13] The analogy this time is with Christ, the mediator between heaven and earth. Like Christ, money as mediator acquires human properties of social interaction at the expense of such human properties. So also with the commodity relation, at which point I turn to *Capital* itself.

From the Fetishism of Commodities to *Kapitalfetisch*

In the famous passage on commodity fetishism in *Capital* I ([1867] 1996: 81–94; [1867] 1972a: 85–98), Marx attempts a dialectical leap: he argues that the transferral of powers in the commodity form – the notion that everything, no matter how different, may be exchanged in terms of its value – is both illusory and real, both mystified and concrete. The best way to see how Marx attempts his massive leap is to exegete a central passage:

> There [with commodities] is a definite social relationship between men, that assumes, in their eyes, the fantastic form of the relation between things. In order, therefore, to find an analogy, we must have recourse to the mist-enveloped regions of the religious world. In that world the productions of the human brain appear as independent beings endowed with life, and entering into relation both with one another and the human race. So it is in the world of commodities with the product of men's hands. This I call the Fetishism which attaches itself to products of labour, so soon as they are produced as commodities, and which is therefore inseparable from the production of commodities. (Ibid. 83; 86–7)[14]

At first, Marx assumes the position on fetishism with which he has worked until now: the fetish signals a transferral of attributes from human social relations to the fetish (now the commodity form) and vice versa. In earlier texts, he used this argument in relation to labour, alienation and money. The first sentence in the quotation makes the same point: the social relation between men assumes a fantastic form in the relation between things.[15]

Immediately, he faces a problem: how does the transfer of the fetish take place? Is this transference real or illusory? Three answers have been offered: (1) the transfer is, like religion, illusory; (2) the analogy with religion is misleading; and (3) Marx attempts to move dialectically beyond the opposition. The first answer argues that we suffer from a mistaken belief that the products of labour, like the fetish, gain such powers. In this case the political response is straightforward: all one need do is indicate why those beliefs are mistaken, show what the object really is – a product made by human hands – and the task is done. At times Marx seems to assume such a position,[16] sprinkling his text on the fetishism of commodities with phrases such as 'grotesque ideas', 'mystical character', 'mysterious thing', 'fantastic form', 'mist-enveloped', 'abstraction', 'social hieroglyphic', 'incarnation of abstract human labour', 'magic and necromancy', 'mystical veil', 'unsubstantial ghost', 'superstition' and 'illusions'. Commodification has become a gnostic, unreal appearance of what is actually going on (Ward 2005: 333–4; Cohen 1978: 116–17; Knafo 2002: 159–60; Iacono 1983).[17]

The problem with this argument is obvious, for it would make commodities, labour, money, exploitation and suffering a grand delusion. One puff and it comes crumbling down. Is Marx then misguided in his use of the idea of fetishism, especially in light of its religious ties? Some would suggest so, arguing that the understanding of how powers are transferred to the fetish is illusory, a product of the imagination, but that those gained by the commodity are real.[18] Marx was really showing that the perception of how those attributes are passed over to commodities is mistaken; he sets out to correct the mistake.

Marx would have done better – so the argument goes – to have used an analogy other than religious fetishism.

How exactly does the transfer take place between fetish and human beings? Marx may well argue that workers, processes of material production, social relations and the product made are real; indeed, he argues that the powers transferred and thereby gained by the product are also real and materially grounded, which then means that the effects on human beings – exploitation, suffering, ruined bodies – are equally real. But are the perceptions of this process held by workers illusory? No, for the transferral of powers between commodities and human beings appears to those producers as 'what they really are, material relations between persons and social relations between things' (Marx [1867] 1996: 84; [1867] 1972a: 87). Their bodies know perfectly well what is going on. Yet their perception of how this process works is illusory and mystified: commodities do not have this power in themselves, for it comes from the labour power of those who produce commodities. It is both/ and rather than either/or. Marx pushes at the edge of language to explain what is going on. For example, the qualities of the products of labour 'are at the same time *perceptible and imperceptible* by the senses' (ibid. 83; 86). Once again: although one may reveal the process of transferral and thereby show how value appears in the product of labour, that value appears 'just as real and final, as the fact that, after the discovery by science of the component gases of air, the atmosphere itself remained unaltered' (ibid. 85; 88). In order to get through what he is trying to argue, Marx formulates a curious phrase to express this dual character of social relations and the transferred relations between commodities: 'socially valid as well as *objective thought forms* [*gesellschaftlich gültige, also objektive Gedankenformen*]' ([1867] 1972a: 90).[19] Not only does this apply to the theories of bourgeois economists; it also applies to the very process of fetish transfer itself.[20] In other words, the process of transferral is a thought form that has become objective, utterly real. The commodity form and the value of abstracted labour it attracts are both products of thought *and* objective, imaginary and real, mysterious and concrete. As with the fetish, or indeed the idol of the religious believer, the gods may not be real, but the transfer of powers to the object made, along with the resultant effect on the worker, is very real indeed.

On three other occasions in *Capital* and its preparatory materials, Marx returns to fetishism – in the third draft of *Capital* and then twice in the third volume of *Capital*.[21] In these texts, Marx works at the question of fetishism, exploring the various means by which more and more elements of capitalism end up 'confronting living labour power [*der lebendigen Arbeitskraft gegenüber*]' (Marx [1894] 1998: 802; [1894] 1973b: 823) as alien, abstracted, all-powerful and utterly dominating. As he does so, the idea undergoes a process of expansion and distillation, so much so that the discussion of commodity fetishism in the first volume of *Capital* becomes an 'introductory framework' (Dimoulis and Milios 2004: 29). Initially, he expands the fetish to include virtually all of the dimensions of capitalism but then he distils this variety to three and then one essence.

Expanding the Fetish

In the only extant section of the third draft of *Capital*,[22] Marx identifies a whole series of items that are both the products of labour power and yet become powers independent of it. Apart from noting money, commodities, and even use and exchange value, he is particularly interested in abstractions from the social process of labour. Thus the social forms of labour are inverted and now appear as the forms of the development of capital. So also, the productive powers of social labour look like the productive powers of capital – specifically as the social combination of individual labour capacities in the workshop and as the objective conditions of labour (including machinery, fixed capital and the application of forces of nature and science). All of these seem to be immanent in the capital relation and appear to be independent of the worker. We also find the capitalist as a personification of the social character of labour, of the workshop, of capital itself, as well as items such as interest, rent, wages and profit, until the development of society as such turns out to seem as though it is the development of capital itself. All of them face the labourer as pre-existing, objective, alien realities that rule his life; they 'stand on their hind legs vis-à-vis the worker and confront him as "*capital*"' (Marx [1861–3] 1994: 457–8).[23]

In this treatment two developments have taken place. The first is to argue that the very process of 'capitalisation', which involves the extraordinary shift of properties from the social conditions of productive labour to capital, is itself a form of the fetish transfer. The significance of this initial move should not be underestimated. Let me use the example of use value, which is usually understood to be outside the zone of the fetish (at least on a reading of the first volume of *Capital*).[24] However, once use value too becomes a fetish, it throws into relief the fact that use value is an abstraction as well, that it does not have a material existence in the conventional sense of the term, that the value so attained by the product is a transfer of human powers to it. All of which means that the end of capitalism does not mean the restoration of some primal use value; rather, use value too must be destroyed in the revolution.

Second, Marx is moving inexorably to the position that the whole of capital is itself fetishised. In this third draft of *Capital*, we still have an ensemble of items that may be described as both fetishes and as undergoing the fetish transfer. When we arrive at the third volume of *Capital*, more items are added. Some are familiar, such as interest, profit, the capitalist as the personification of capital, the products of labour in all their various manifestations, or the form of the conditions of labour, which is 'alienated from labour and confronting it independently [*ihr gegenüber verselbständigte*]' (Marx [1894] 1998: 812; [1894] 1973b: 833). But others are relatively new: land as an independently producing entity, specifically in terms of ground rent; the landlord who personifies both land and this process; the abstraction of labour, which is a 'mere ghost' (the Holy Ghost, the third person of the Trinity) that somehow produces wages; those wages themselves, as a portion of the product of labour power; surplus labour → surplus value → surplus product, and thereby profit; the circulation process, since it seems as though commodities emerge from within circulation; and the collection of the world market, movements of market prices, credit, industrial and commercial cycles, alternations of prosperity and crisis – all as 'natural laws' and as 'blind necessity' (ibid. 801–18; 822–39).

Distilling the Fetish

Marx has moved well beyond commodities and the commodity form to include almost every component of capitalism. He acknowledges the shift, speaking of his earlier treatment of the fetish transfer in commodity production and money as 'the simplest categories of the capitalist mode of production' ([1894] 1998: 813; [1894] 1973b: 835). Yet I have drawn this second group of examples from a chapter called 'The Trinity Formula', where the process of distilling the fetish begins (ibid. 801–18; 822–39). A closer consideration of the list reveals a threefold pattern: capital, land and labour. Or, in more detail, a threefold formula: capital – interest, land – ground rent, and labour – wages. The key to this trinity is that relations between these terms have been obfuscated, specifically under the conditions of capitalism. Capital simply produces interest in and of itself, without any need to consider labour power, surplus labour, surplus value, commodities, production, circulation, and so on; similarly, land produces ground rent in its very nature; labour equally produces wages, for all one need do is turn up for work and wages are – naturally – forthcoming.

In each case, the fetish transfer, or 'capitalisation', is in full operation. The trinity represents, from the point of view of capitalism and classical political economy, the pure and natural essence of capitalism. In the process, the specific and particular forms of these modes under capitalism become universalised: capital is thereby equated with the produced means of production, land with land monopolised through private ownership, labour with wage-labour. Even more, the process of personification (as with Feuerbach's gods) applies not merely to the capitalist, but also to the landowner, who is now the embodiment of land, which – in a favoured metaphor – 'likewise gets on its hind legs to demand, as an independent force, its share of the product created with its help' (ibid. 811; 832–3).

Marx concludes this discussion of theo-economics:

> In capital – profit, or still better capital – interest, land – rent, labour – wages, in this economic trinity represented as the connection between the component parts of value and wealth in general and its sources, we have the complete mystification of the capitalist mode of production, the conversion of social relations into things, the direct coalescence of material production relations with their historical and social determination. It is an enchanted, perverted, topsy-turvy world, in which Monsieur le Capital and Madame la Terre do their ghost-walking as social characters and at the same time directly as mere things. (Ibid. 817; 838)

It is hardly necessary to emphasise the perpetual presence of a religious register even at this advanced level of Marx's reflections. Yet I suggest that within this trinity, God the Father-capital is still the key. From the surplus value produced through exploitation of the labourer, the landlord demands a portion for his own pockets and the worker needs a portion for the sake of (often bare) self-renewal (ibid. 809; 830). In other words, the central relation remains that of the extraction of surplus value. So now I focus on the first part of this trinitarian equation: capital – interest.

The Core of Capitalism

'The relations of capital assume their most external and most fetish-like form [*fetischartigste Form*] in interest-bearing capital' (Marx [1894] 1998: 388; [1894] 1973b: 404). So begins the twenty-fourth chapter (in section five) of *Capital* volume three.[25] Marx's concern here is the externalisation of the relations of capital, especially in the most extreme form in which social relations are left far behind. And that most 'fetish-like form' is what is now known as the financialisation of the market, in which capital creates its own surplus value, money creates money, expanding of its own accord without the mediation of the commodity. Invoking the beautifully simple formula of M–C–M', Marx argues that interest-bearing capital operates in terms of M–M'. The former at least gives the appearance of depending on social relations (the production of commodities), but the latter has dispensed with that: profit is now 'the product of a mere *thing*' (ibid. 388–9; 404).

Note what has happened to the fetishism of commodities, let alone all of the other instances of fetishism that I discussed above. In light of this argument, each of them has become a localised instance of fetishism, an example of a much more basic operation. In its pure essence, the fetish is nothing other than capital itself, and the fetish relation operates in terms of M – M', which Marx describes as 'the original starting-point of capital' (ibid. 389; 404). Capital apparently produces surplus value in and of itself, unassisted by the processes of production and circulation.

All of this is only the first step beyond the fetishism of particular elements within capitalism. The next involves expanding the very notion of fetishism, for now Marx is interested in the logical extreme of the fetish transfer. If the transfer involves the shifting of the powers and values of human social interaction to the relations between objects, then the full realisation of that transfer will result in the complete elevation of those things and the complete abasement of human relations, so much so that those relations simply disappear from the scene. The analogy with the transfer of human powers to the gods should be obvious: 'In interest-bearing capital, therefore, this automatic fetish, self-expanding value, money generating money, is brought out in its pure state and in this form it no longer bears the birthmarks of its origin.' In this pure, 'essential fetish form [*seine reine Fetishform*]' (ibid. 390; 406), capital embodies the whole process of production within itself, a 'mysterious', self-creating and self-generating source of its own increase (ibid. 389; 405). It may have various manifestations or even incarnations perhaps, as commodity, money, value, social forms of productive labour, capitalist, landlord, profit, and so on, each of them with properties acquired but now regarded as inherent, but at its heart capital is a fetish.

Once again, Marx must deal with the tension between illusion and reality, between concealment and transparency, surface and depth, external and internal, absurdity and rationality. On the one hand, capital-as-fetish is due to a topsy-turvy world. M–M', whether manifested in the form of money or commodities expanding their values independently of reproduction, is a 'perversion', a 'meaningless form' of capital, mystification 'in its most flagrant form', in short, 'the fetish form of capital and the conception of fetish capital' (ibid. 390; 405).[26] Why? While interest appears to be a primary and inherent feature of capital, it is actually a portion of the surplus value, manifested as profit, extracted from the labourer. The problem is that the real source of this surplus value is now regarded as secondary, a by-product of the supposedly primary nature of capital. That is, what is unreal is the way this pure formula of capital assumes that capital produces surplus value in and of itself – money generating money, financial speculation and volatilised markets, and so on. At the same time, the process is very real, once we bring out of concealment the process of production that generates such surplus value. But Marx goes further: M–M' may be a 'meaningless condensation', but it is also the 'original starting-point', the 'primary and general formula', the moment when the unity of production and circulation 'appears directly' (ibid. 389; 404–5).[27] Capital itself has become an 'objective thought-form' with power to oppress.

In the remaining part of this important chapter, Marx cites approvingly Luther's critique of usury[28] and then the amusing fancy of a Dr Price and his Jesus Christ sinking fund,[29] but the argument concerning fetishism has expanded far beyond that initial foray in the first volume concerning commodities, let alone the first experiments concerning Prussian laws concerning hares and fallen wood. Now all that have gone before, the full range of items from commodities through to the personification of the landlord, have become incarnations of capital's 'pure fetish form [*seine reine Fetishform*]' (ibid. 801–2; 823). Capital can exist only as parasitic, as transferral – for which the terms 'capitalisation' and 'fetishisation' equally apply – in which the means of productions are transformed into capital. Or, as he now writes towards the close of this chapter, capital and fetish elide to become one word, '*Kapitalfetisch*' ([1894] 1973b: 412).

Conclusion

From the first encounter with fetishism while reading material for his lost treatise on Christian art, Marx has used the idea in many ways: criticisms of wood (or indeed hare) theft laws and smug assertions concerning religious superiority; the development of his early theory of the alienation of labour; the identification of the mediatory role of money in social relations; and eventually commodities, value (use, exchange and surplus), wealth, profit, the capitalist, landlord, the social forms of productive labour, interest, ground rent, wages – in short, every conceivable dimension of capitalism. At each moment, a mystifying transfer takes place, in which the products of human labour gain mysterious properties and end up on the side of capital while those human beings responsible for their production lose out and suffer. Yet the theological dimension is never far from the surface of all Marx's deliberations, as we noted time and again. In the same way that fetishes, idols and even the gods produced by human hands and imaginations draw their powers from human beings, so also do the products of human labour within capitalism gain power at the expense of those human beings. As he makes this argument, Marx develops the dialectical idea of the 'objective thought form' in an effort to describe how the transfer takes place. Yet the ultimate form of the fetish turns out to be capital itself, for which Marx needed to coin a new term that captures this religious feature at the heart of capital, *Kapitalfetisch*.[30]

But why use a consistently theological term, even in all the complexity that it gains over forty years of reflection? Would not reification have been enough, speaking of the way the productive relations of human beings becomes thing-like, the relations of things? For Marx, that is hardly sufficient, since he seeks a theory that deals with both 'a personification of things and a reification of persons' ([1861–3] 1994: 457). In order to deal with that other side of the equation, the personification of things, perhaps alienation would be sufficient, or possibly abstraction, in which human powers, especially those of a socially productive nature, are sucked out of human relations. The problem is that both abstraction and even alienation are unable to explain why capital in all its many dimensions gains a life of its own, is personified, becomes an agent with immense, if not unlimited power. Only a complex theory of fetishism can explain why 'capital thus becomes a very mystic being [*sehr mystisches Wesen*]', especially 'since all of labour's social productive forces appear to be due to capital, rather than labour as such, and seem to issue from the womb of capital itself' (Marx [1894] 1998: 814, 835).[31] It is nothing less than the 'religion of everyday life [*diese Religion des Alltagslebens*]' (ibid. 817, 838).[32]

Notes

1. The word has endured many efforts to trace its etymology. It is an English translation of the pidgin *Fetisso*, connected to the Portuguese *feitiço*, which in the late Middle Ages designated 'magical practices' or 'witchcraft'. However, it has also been derived from the Latin *fatum*, signifying both fate and charm (de Brosses and Marx following him), *factitius*, linking the magic arts and the work of art (Edward Tylor) or *facere*, designating the false representation of what is sacred, beautiful or enchanting.
2. For example, for Auguste Comte fetishism becomes the first stage (followed by polytheism and monotheism) of his first great period of human history. Comte used the term in his *Système de*

politique positive (1851–4). After the theological age, of which fetishism is the first stage, we have the metaphysical and scientific stages.

3. On wealth, gold and silver, see also Marx [1859] 1987a: 387.
4. In the Marxist tradition, studies of fetishism in Marx's work have consistently appeared. For a full bibliography up to the early 1990s, see Iacono 1992. For Dimoulis and Milios, the different positions on fetishism often function 'as a point of departure for certain political strategies and as a symbol for them' (2004: 4). For a detailed treatment of these key positions – focusing on Lukács, Pashukanis, Balibar, Althusser and Gramsci – see Dimoulis and Milios 2004: 5–22. Dussell (2003: 1–16) covers Marx's early work on the fetish in a curious fashion. While his survey is somewhat comprehensive, it is also superficial and assumes that Marx was once a believer and that he sought an unalienated form of religion.
5. For studies on the aesthetic dimension of this lost treatise, see the work by Lifshitz and Rose (Lifshitz [1933] 1973, 1984; Rose 1984).
6. See also Marx's comments from an earlier article concerning the Assembly of the Estates of the Rhine Province, which has a tendency to 'canonise individuals' and to 'demand that we should bow down before the holy image of certain privileged individuals' ([1842] 1975i: 169; [1842] 1975f: 157), as well as the polemic against Louis Napoleon: 'And the cast-down, broken idol can never be set on its pedestal again. He may recoil before the storm he has raised, and again receive the benedictions of the Pope and the caresses of the British Queen' ([1859] 1980: 273).
7. A hint also appears Marx's comment to Ruge on 20 March 1842, where Marx mentions that the revised manuscript disagrees with Feuerbach's concept of religion, a disagreement that appears in the *Theses on Feuerbach*. As Marx points out in the letter, he disagrees not with the principle (projection) but the conception. It would seem that Marx was already arguing that religion is a projection of the worst in human beings rather than the best, that religion is an expression of alienation and not hope and love.
8. Marx comments to Ruge that 'the work has steadily grown into almost book dimensions, and I have been drawn into all kinds of investigations which will still take a rather long time' ([1842] 1975a: 387; [1842] 1973e: 402).
9. On pages 1–70, Rose presents an excellent contextual analysis of the artistic and very political struggles in Germany at the time between Hellenes and conservative Nazarenes on the question of religious art.
10. From the translation by Pistorius, Marx quotes: 'die Schlange, die Bäume, das Meer und ein kleines schmutziges Bild von Thon, das in den Rattsammlungen den Vorstiz hat' ([1842] 1976b: 321). De Brosses's text reads: 'le serpent, les arbres, le mer, & une vilaine petite idole d'argille qui préside aux Conseils' (1760: 27).
11. 'Die *Wilden von Cuba* hielten das *Gold* für den Fetisch der Spanier, sie feierten ihm ein Fest, tanzten und sangen um ihn und warfen es dann ins Meer, um es zu entfernen' (Marx [1842] 1976b: 322). This is an abbreviation of the account in Brosses 1760: 52–3.
12. Note also: 'Every self-estrangement of man, from himself and from nature, appears in the relation in which he places himself and nature to men other than and differentiated from himself. For this reason religious self-estrangement necessarily appears in the relationship of the layman to the priest, or again to a mediator, etc., since we are here dealing with the intellectual world' (Marx [1844] 1975g: 279; [1844] 1990b: 519; see also Marx [1857–8] 1987b: 209–10).
13. Marx would continue this line in other works: [1844] 1975g: 325–6; [1844] 1990b: 525–7; [1857–8] 1986: 154, 164, 278; [1857–8] 2005: 148, 258, 250; [1857–8] 1987b: 216; [1859] 1987a: 359; [1867] 1976a: 142–3; [1867] 1972a: 146–7.
14. Unfortunately, Philip Goodchild neglects to make full use of this treatment by Marx (2009: 264, n. 21, 271, n. 34; 2002: 80–7).
15. More fully, this transferral is a 'mysterious thing, simply because the social character of men's labour appears to them as an objective character stamped upon the product of that labour;

because the relation of the producers to the sum total of their own labour is presented to them as a social relation, existing not between themselves, but between the products of their labour' (Marx [1867] 1996: 82–3; [1867] 1972a: 86; see also Marx [1861–3] 1994: 450).

16. In the name of informal logic, Finocchiaro simply argues that Marx's argument lacks logic (1989: 237–44).
17. Pietz and Dupré also tend in this direction, suggesting that the fetish designates false consciousness (Pietz 1985: 10; Dupré 1983: 49). Nancy (2004) takes a slightly different line, arguing that Marx sought to 'dialolise' commodity fetishism, whereas the task is to re-empower the fetish, especially with regard to art. Unfortunately, the detailed and perceptive analysis of Dimoulis and Milios tends in this direction (2004: 29–32). Dussell's wayward study takes a more theological angle, seeking to show that Marx's use of fetishism is of the same ilk as the biblical criticism of idolatry (2003: 17–20).
18. See the widely quoted observation of Norman Geras (1983: 165).
19. My translation and emphasis, with thanks to Jan Rehmann for this point (personal communication). The English translations try various formulations, such as 'forms of thought expressing with social validity' or 'forms of thought which are socially valid and therefore objective' (Marx [1867] 1996: 87; [1867] 1976a: 169). Ripstein (1987) attempts a different argument, suggesting that the religious analogy is correct: in the same way that religious institutions produce religious fetishes, so also does the market produce commodity fetishes. The problem here is that he must import a third category, the institution, although he unwittingly anticipates Marx's later argument (without reading beyond volume one of *Capital*) that capitalism itself is a fetish.
20. Elsewhere Marx speaks of the 'fetishism peculiar to bourgeois political economy' ([1885] 1997: 527; [1885] 1972b: 527–8).
21. This is territory that few, if any, critics have dared to tread, preferring to stay with that mesmerising section in the first volume of *Capital* (Cohen 1978; Knafo 2002; Ripstein 1987; Finocchiaro 1989; Nancy 2004; Bennett 2001: 7–9). Baudrillard provides a slightly different approach: while staying with the fetishism of commodities, he anticipates Marx's later arguments by seeking to expand the fetish to the whole system of capitalism (1981: 90–1). Using Marx's work as a springboard, Lukács (1968, [1968] 1988) sought to develop his influential theory of reification (an 'extensive-universalising' approach), while Pashukanis ([1924] 1929) elaborates a category of legal fetishism (an 'extensive-comparative' approach). See the assessments and critique by Dimoulis and Milios (2004: 5–17). By contrast, Balibar and Althusser seek to minimise the theory of fetishism, as either a feature of bourgeois theory (Balibar) or as an example of the humanising Marx of alienation (Althusser) (see Dimoulis and Milios 2004: 17–21). So also does Mulhern (2007), who argues that fetishism is an anomaly in Marx's work, indeed that Marx over-reaches in trying to universalise the fetish. The exceptions to this studied avoidance are Dimoulis and Milios (2004: 23–31) and Düzenli (2011). I have benefited from these insightful contributions, even though I ultimately disagree.
22. Published at the close of the extensive second draft, known as the *Economic Manuscript of 1861–63* (Marx [1861–3] 1994: 455–61).
23. Or: 'They confront the workers as *shapes* of capital itself, as combinations which, unlike their isolated labour capacities, belong to capital, originate from it and are incorporated within it' (Marx [1861–3] 1994: 458). See also the description of wealth as a fetish in Marx [1859] 1987a: 387.
24. See, however, Baudrillard's argument that fetishism applies even more forcefully to use value, albeit without reference to these arguments by Marx (1981: 130–42).
25. The careful reader will have noticed that I have placed my discussion of the 'Trinity Formula', from chapter 48 of *Capital III*, before the treatment of chapter 24. The reasons for doing so should be obvious by now.
26. In the 'Trinity' chapter, Marx speaks of a perverted, enchanted and 'very mystical, social form [*sehr mystische, gesellschaftliche Form*]' ([1894] 1998: 802, 813–14; [1894] 1973b: 823, 835).

27. By giving too much weight to Marx's comments concerning mystification, perversion and meaningless condensation, Dimoulis and Milios and Düzenli interpret all of Marx's deliberations of fetishism in that light (Dimoulis and Milios 2004: 29–32; Düzenli 2011: 176–8).
28. Marx quotes Luther repeatedly from the latter's An die Pfarherrn wider den Wucher zu predigen of 1540 ([1859] 1987a: 364, 448–9; [1861–3] 1989: 531–8, 539–41; [1861–3] 1974: 516–24; [1867] 1996: 146, 203, 314, 388–9, 741; [1867] 1972a: 149, 207, 328, 619, 781; [1894] 1998: 329, 345, 391–2, 594, 605–6, 889; [1894] 1973b: 343–4, 359, 407, 613, 614–15, 911). Indeed, Marx credits Luther with providing 'an excellent picture, it fits the capitalist in general [*Allerliebstes Bild, auf den Kapitalisten überhaupt*]' ([1861–3] 1989: 539; [1861–3] 1974: 525; see further Marx [1856] 1983: 21; [1856] 1973f: 25).
29. For Price, 'One penny, put out at our Saviour's birth to 5 per cent compound interest, would before this time, have increased to a greater sum, than would be contained in a hundred and fifty millions of earths, all solid gold.' The upshot: a state would be able to 'spirit away the national debt through the mystery of compound interest', even borrowing against the future (Marx [1894] 1998: 392–3; [1894] 1973b: 408–9).
30. As Dimoulis and Milios point out, 'Marx does not expound a theory of *commodity* fetishism but a theory of the *fetishism of capital*, of capitalist relations' (2004: 27).
31. Or as Marx puts it elsewhere: 'All forms of society, in so far as they reach the stage of commodity production and money circulation, take part in this perversion. But under the capitalist mode of production and in the case of capital, which forms its dominant category, its determining production relation, this enchanted and perverted world develops still more' ([1894] 1998: 814; [1894] 1973b: 835).
32. From here it would become the basis of Walter Benjamin's oft-noted fragment, 'Capitalism as Religion' (1996: 288–91).

References

Baudrillard, Jean (1981), *For a Critique of the Political Economy of the Sign*, trans. Charles Levin, St Louis: Telos.

Bauer, Bruno (1838), *Kritik der Geschichte der Offenbarung: Die Religion des alten Testaments in der geschichtlichen Entwicklung ihrer Prinzipien dargestellt*, Berlin: Ferdinand Dümmler.

Bauer, Bruno (1839), *Herr Dr. Hengstenberg: Ein Beitrag zur Kritik der religiösen Bewußtseins. Kritische Briefe über den Gegensatz des Gesetzes und des Evangeliums*, Berlin: Ferdinand Dümmler.

Bauer, Bruno (1840), *Kritik der evangelischen Geschichte des Johannes*, Bremen: Karl Schünemann.

Bauer, Bruno (1841), *Kritik der evangelischen Geschichte der Synoptiker*, 2 vols, Leipzig: Otto Wigand.

Bauer, Bruno (1842a), *Die Gute Sache der Freiheit und meine eigene Ungelegenheit*, Zürich und Winterthur: Verlag des literarischen Comptoirs.

Bauer, Bruno (1842b), *Kritik der evangelischen Geschichte der Synoptiker und des Johannes, Dritter und letzter Band*, Braunschweig: Fr. Otto.

Bauer, Bruno (1843), *Das entdeckte Christenthum. Eine Erinnerung an das 18. Jahrhundert und ein Beitrag zur Krisis des 19. Jahrhundert*, Zürich und Winterthur: Verlag des literarischen Comptoirs.

Bauer, Bruno (1850–1), *Kritik der Evangelien und Geschichte ihres Ursprungs*, 3 vols, Berlin: Gustav Hempel.

Bauer, Bruno (1852), *Die theologische Erklärung der Evangelien*, Berlin.

Bauer, Bruno [1842] (1967), *Hegels Lehre von der Religion und der Kunst von dem Standpunkte des Glaubens aus beurteilt*, Aalen: Scientia.

Bauer, Bruno [1841] (1983), *Die Posaune des jüngsten Gerichts über Hegel den Atheisten und Antichristen: Ein Ultimatum*, Aalen: Scientia.

Benjamin, Walter (1996), *Selected Writings. Volume 1: 1912–1926*, ed. Marcus Bullock and Michael W. Jennings, Cambridge, MA: Belknap.

Bennett, Jane (2001), 'Commodity Fetishism and Commodity Enchantment', *Theory and Event*, 5.1: 1–28.

Brosses, Charles de (1760), *Du culte des dieux fétiches ou Parallèle de l'ancienne religion de l'Égypte*, Paris.
Cohen, G. A. (1978), *Karl Marx's Theory of History: A Defense*, Princeton: Princeton University Press.
Dimoulis, Dimitri and John Milios (2004), 'Commodity Fetishism vs. Capital Fetishism: Marxist Interpretations vis-à-vis Marx's Analyses in *Capital*', *Historical Materialism*, 13.2: 3–42.
Dupré, Louis (1983), *Marx's Social Critique of Culture*, New Haven: Yale University Press.
Dussell, Enrique (2003), 'The Concept of Fetishism in Marx's Thought (Elements for a General Marxist Theory of Religion)', *Radical Philosophy Review*, 6: 1–28.
Düzenli, Faruk Eray (2011), 'Introduction: Value, Commodity Fetishism, and Capital's Critique', *Rethinking Marxism*, 23.2: 172–9.
Feuerbach, Ludwig [1841] (1986), *Das Wesen des Christentums*, Stuttgart: Reclam, Ditzingen.
Feuerbach, Ludwig [1841] (1989), *The Essence of Christianity*, trans. George Eliot, Amherst, NY: Prometheus Books.
Finocchiaro, Maurice A. (1989), 'Fetishism, Argument, and Judgement in Capital', *Studies in Soviet Thought*, 38.3: 237–44.
Fischer, Karl Philipp (1839), *Die Idee der Gottheit: Ein Versuch den Theismus speculativ zu begründen und zu entwickeln*, Stuttgart: Liesching.
Geras, Norman (1983), 'Fetishism', in Tom Bottomore (ed.), *A Dictionary of Marxist Thought*, Oxford: Blackwell, 165–6.
Goodchild, Philip (2002), *Capitalism as Religion: The Price of Piety*, London: Routledge.
Goodchild, Philip (2009), *Theology of Money*, Durham, NC: Duke University Press.
Iacono, Alfonso M. (1983), 'Sul Concetto di "Feticismo" in Marx', *Studi Storici*, 24.3/4: 429–36.
Iacono, Alfonso M. (1992), *Le fétichisme. Histoire d'un concept*, Paris: Presses universitaires de France.
Knafo, Samuel (2002), 'The *Fetishizing* Subject in Marx's *Capital*', *Capital and Class*, 76: 145–76.
Lifshitz, Mikhail [1933] (1973), *The Philosophy of Art of Karl Marx*, trans. Ralph B. Winn, New York: Pluto.
Lifshitz, Mikhail (1984), *Collected Works*, Moscow: Progress.
Lukács, Georg (1968), *Geschichte und Klassenbewusstsein*, Neuwied und Berlin: Hermann Luchterhand.
Lukács, Georg [1968] (1988), *History and Class Consciousness: Studies in Marxist Dialectics*, trans. Rodney Livingstone, Cambridge, MA: MIT Press.
Marx, Karl [1842] (1902), 'Marx an Arnold Ruge in Dresden, den 20ten März 1842', in *Marx Engels Werke*, vol. 27, Berlin: Dietz, 399–401.
Marx, Karl [1867] (1972a), *Das Kapital. Kritik der politischen Ökonomie. Erster Band Buch I: Der Produktionsprozeß des Kapitals*, Marx Engels Werke, vol. 23, Berlin: Dietz.
Marx, Karl [1885] (1972b), *Das Kapital. Kritik der politischen Ökonomie. Zweiter Band Buch II. Der Zirkulationsprozeß des Kapital*, Marx Engels Werke, vol. 24, Berlin: Dietz.
Marx, Karl [1842] (1973a), 'To Arnold Ruge in Dresden, March 5, 1842', in *Marx and Engels Collected Works*, vol. 1, Moscow: Progress, 382–3.
Marx, Karl [1894] (1973b), *Das Kapital. Kritik der politischen Ökonomie. Dritter Band Buch III. Der Gesamtprozeß der kapitalistischen Produktion*, Marx Engels Werke, vol. 25, Berlin: Dietz.
Marx, Karl [1842] (1973c), 'Marx an Arnold Ruge in Dresden, den 5ten März 1842', in *Marx Engels Werke*, vol. 27, Berlin: Dietz, 397–8.
Marx, Karl [1842] (1973d), 'Marx an Arnold Ruge in Dresden, den 10ten Februar 1842', in *Marx Engels Werke*, vol. 27, Berlin: Dietz, 395–6.
Marx, Karl [1842] (1973e), 'Marx an Arnold Ruge in Dresden, den 27. April 1842', in *Marx Engels Werke*, vol. 27, Berlin: Dietz, 402–3.
Marx, Karl [1856] (1973f), 'Marx an Engels 5. März 1856', in *Marx Engels Werke*, vol. 29, Berlin: Dietz, 23–9.
Marx, Karl [1861–3] (1974), *Theorie über den Mehrwert (Vierter Band des 'Kapitals'). Dritter Teil*, Marx Engels Werke, vol. 26.3, Berlin: Dietz.

Marx, Karl [1842] (1975a), 'To Arnold Ruge in Dresden, April 27, 1842', in *Marx and Engels Collected Works*, vol. 1, Moscow: Progress, 387–8.
Marx, Karl [1842] (1975b), 'To Arnold Ruge in Dresden, March 20, 1842', in *Marx and Engels Collected Works*, vol. 1, Moscow: Progress, 383–6.
Marx, Karl [1842] (1975c), 'To Arnold Ruge in Dresden, Trier, February 10, 1842', in *Marx and Engels Collected Works*, vol. 1, Moscow: Progress, 381–2.
Marx, Karl [1844] (1975d), 'Comments on James Mill, Éléments d'économie politique', in *Marx and Engels Collected Works*, vol. 3, Moscow: Progress, 211–28.
Marx, Karl [1842] (1975e), 'Der leitende Artikel in Nr. 179 der "Kölnische Zeitung"', in *Marx Engels Gesamtausgabe*, vol. 1.1, Berlin: Dietz, 172–90.
Marx, Karl [1842] (1975f), 'Die Verhandlungen des 6. Rheinischen Lantags. Erster Artikel: Debatten über Preßfreiheit und Publikation der Landständischen Verhandlungen', in *Marx Engels Gesamtausgabe*, vol. 1.1, Berlin: Dietz, 121–69.
Marx, Karl [1844] (1975g), 'Economic and Philosophic Manuscripts of 1844', in *Marx and Engels Collected Works*, vol. 3, Moscow: Progress, 229–346.
Marx, Karl [1842] (1975h), 'The Leading Article in No. 179 of the *Kölnische Zeitung*', in *Marx and Engels Collected Works*, vol. 1, Moscow: Progress, 184–202.
Marx, Karl [1842] (1975i), 'Proceedings of the Sixth Rhine Province Assembly. First Article: Debates on Freedom of the Press and Publication of the Proceedings of the Assembly of the Estates', in *Marx and Engels Collected Works*, vol. 1, Moscow: Progress, 132–81.
Marx, Karl [1842] (1975j), 'Proceedings of the Sixth Rhine Province Assembly. Third Article: Debates on the Law on Thefts of Wood', in *Marx and Engels Collected Works*, vol. 1, Moscow: Progress, 224–63.
Marx, Karl [1842] (1975k), 'Verhandlungen des 6. Rheinischen Lantags. Dritter Artikel: Debatten über das Holzdiebstahlsgesetz', in *Marx Engels Gesamtausgabe*, vol. 1.1, Berlin: Dietz, 199–236.
Marx, Karl [1867] (1976a), *Capital: A Critique of Political Economy, Volume One*, trans. Ben Fowkes, London: Penguin/New Left Books.
Marx, Karl [1842] (1976b), 'Exzerpte aus Charles de Brosses: Ueber den Dienst der Fetischengötter', in *Marx Engels Gesamtausgabe*, vol. 4.1, Berlin: Dietz, 321–2.
Marx, Karl [1859] (1980), 'A Historic Parallel', in *Marx and Engels Collected Works*, vol. 16, Moscow: Progress, 271–3.
Marx, Karl [1856] (1983), 'Marx to Engels in Manchester, London, 5 March 1856', in *Marx and Engels Collected Works*, vol. 40, Moscow: Progress, 19–25.
Marx, Karl [1857–8] (1986), *Economic Manuscripts of 1857–58 (First Version of Capital) [Grundrisse]*, Marx and Engels Collected Works, vol. 28, Moscow: Progress.
Marx, Karl [1859] (1987a), 'A Contribution to the Critique of Political Economy', in *Marx and Engels Collected Works*, vol. 29, Moscow: Progress, 257–417.
Marx, Karl [1857–8] (1987b), 'Outlines of the Critique of Political Economy (Rough Draft of 1857–58) [Second Instalment]', in *Marx and Engels Collected Works*, vol. 29, Moscow: Progress, 3–255.
Marx, Karl [1861–3] (1989), *Economic Manuscript of 1861–63 (Continuation): A Contribution to the Critique of Political Economy*, Marx and Engels Collected Works, vol. 32, Moscow: Progress.
Marx, Karl [1844] (1990a), 'Auszüge aus James Mills Buch "Élémens d'économie politique". Trad. Par J. T. Parisot, Paris 1823', in *Marx Engels Werke*, vol. 40, Berlin: Dietz, 445–63.
Marx, Karl [1844] (1990b), 'Ökonomisch-philosophische Manuskripte aus dem Jahre 1844', in *Marx Engels Werke*, vol. 40, Berlin: Dietz, 465–588.
Marx, Karl [1861–3] (1994), *Economic Manuscript of 1861–63 (Conclusion): A Contribution to the Critique of Political Economy*, Marx and Engels Collected Works, vol. 34, Moscow: Progress.
Marx, Karl [1867] (1996), *Capital: A Critique of Political Economy, Vol. I*, Marx and Engels Collected Works, vol. 35, Moscow: Progress.
Marx, Karl [1885] (1997), *Capital: A Critique of Political Economy, Vol. II*, Marx and Engels Collected Works, vol. 36, Moscow: Progress.

Marx, Karl [1894] (1998), *Capital: A Critique of Political Economy, Vol. III, Marx and Engels Collected Works*, vol. 37, Moscow: Progress.

Marx, Karl [1857–8] (2005), *Ökonomische Manuskripte 1857/1858 [Grundrisse], Marx Engels Werke*, vol. 42, Berlin: Dietz.

Moggach, Douglas (2003), *The Philosophy and Politics of Bruno Bauer*, Cambridge: Cambridge University Press.

Mulhern, Francis (2007), 'Critical Considerations on the Fetishism of Commodities', *ELH*, 74.2: 479–92.

Nancy, Jean-Luc (2004), 'The Two Secrets of the Fetish', *Journal of Visual Art Practice*, 3.2: 139–47.

Pashukanis, Evgeny [1924] (1929), *Allgemeine Rechtslehre und Marxismus*, Vienna: Verlag für Literatur und Politik.

Pietz, William (1985), 'The Problem of the Fetish, I', *Res: Anthropology and Aesthetics*, 9: 5–17.

Pietz, William (1987), 'The Problem of the Fetish, II', *Res: Anthropology and Aesthetics*, 13: 23–45.

Pietz, William (1988), 'The Problem of the Fetish, III', *Res: Anthropology and Aesthetics*, 16: 105–23.

Ripstein, Arthur (1987), 'Commodity Fetishism', *Canadian Journal of Philosophy*, 17.4: 733–48.

Rose, Margaret A. (1984), *Marx's Lost Aesthetic: Karl Marx and the Visual Arts*, Cambridge: Cambridge University Press.

Strauss, David Friedrich (1835), *Das Leben Jesu, kritisch bearbeitet*, Tübingen: C. F. Osiander.

Strauss, David Friedrich (1902), *The Life of Jesus: Critically Examined*, trans. George Eliot, London: Swan Sonnenschein.

Ward, Graham (2005), 'The Commodification of Religion, or The Consummation of Capitalism', in Creston Davis, John Milbank and Slavoj Žižek (eds), *Theology and the Political: The New Debate*, Durham, NC: Duke University Press, 327–39.

7
Evolution

Bennett Zon

The Impassible Dream: Theology, Science and the Evolution of Music

Impassibility stems from the Greek *apatheia*, and is a historical term which describes a wide range of ideas defining God's apparent inability to feel emotion. The Greek Fathers used the word pathos (passion) to describe the suffering of Christ, and so in the early church its opposite, *apathes*, came to mean an incapability to suffer, and by extension the inability to experience emotion of any kind (Culver 1998: 1). In the broadest sense, impassibility conforms to the basic principle of Platonic theodicy and divine simplicity. God is entirely self-sufficient, all-perfect, transcendent, and unchanging in substance, and therefore unable to be affected by anything outside himself (Weinandy 2000: 19). According to the rules of impassibility, since God 'is self-sufficient, he cannot be changed. Since he is perfect, he cannot change himself. Thus suffering and emotion are both incompatible with the nature of a God who never becomes, but *is*' (Bauckham 1984: 8).

According to most theologians, God remained impassible roughly from the beginning of the church until the early twentieth century, when almost overnight He emerged from the chrysalis of impassibility suddenly – and perhaps not unexpectedly – transformed into a butterfly of passibility. There was a long period of nineteenth-century gestation, however, and in the broadest sense this essay explores how music contributed to that period of evolutionary growth. Music helps us interpret this growth because it provides Victorian evolutionary scientists with a handy – if thorny – theological surrogate for divine passibility: for Darwin, the emotion of love; for Herbert Spencer, the emotion of sympathy. This essay traces the path of their ideas through long-nineteenth-century theology and evolutionary sciences of the emotions. A set of three opening sections covers theology, science and music, respectively exploring current and nineteenth-century theologies of impassibility; theological tensions over the emotions in the science of design; and the place of emotions in the aesthetic warfare over absolute and programmatic approaches to music. A main section examines music evolution through the seminal influence of Schleiermacher and the music evolutionary theories of Spencer and Darwin, and a conclusion summarises key points and reflects on the metaphysical nature of Darwin and Spencer's music evolutionary project. Ultimately, this essay claims that Darwin and Spencer attempt the impossible: they convert an impassible God into an impassible nature and then try to humanise divine passibility by channelling it into musical emotion. Theirs is the impossible, impassible dream. Like Don Quixote, who argues that dreams are more than dreams, I argue that musical emotion gives Darwin and Spencer more than just music, more than just dreams. It gives them ideas about the evolution of music which try to 'point to the ultimate and deeper reality, the presence of the divine which is in everyone and everything but which is so often obscured from our limited earthly sight' (Bradley 2004: 103). So if the Man of La Mancha can 'dream the impossible dream' exceeding the impossible dream may not be so elusive after all.

Theology

While theologians generally agree on the currency of impassibility as a principle in the early, medieval and reformation churches, current theological opinions differ widely not only on its definition but on its historical evolution as well. Following the lead of Marcel Sarot, Anastasia Philippa Scrutton suggests that impassibility is closer to the concept of invulnerability than it is literally to 'apathy', or being devoid of emotion (2008: 1:19). Rob Lister's assessment is representative of the current lack of consensus: he posits a compromise, 'qualified-impassibility model' to interpret Patristic impassibility as 'a form of divine impassibility with affirmations of divine passion' (2012: 66) – what he calls impassible and impassioned. Irenaeus, for example, may have suggested that 'the Father of all is at a vast distance from those affections and passions which operate among men' (*Adversus Haereses*, quoted in ibid. 68), but, according to Lister, he believed God was emotionally expressive. In fact, for Irenaeus divine impassibility and divine emotion (or passion) are paired in a way which does little more than establish boundaries of analogy between divine and human experience (ibid. 69). Lister is certainly not alone in pairing the paradox of divine impassibility and divine emotion. As Keating and White (2009: 1) rightly observe, the classical doctrine of impassibility has been subject to intense criticism in modern theology, much of it unable to reconcile an impassible God of the Bible with the God who suffers in Christ. Even conservative theology struggles to reassert traditional forms of impassibility. Rather than asking whether God suffers like humans, traditional impassibilists are forced to ask whether God must be free from suffering and evil in order to save us; more specifically 'does the identity of Christ assure a presence of God in the world that is capable of transcending the "inevitability of suffering"?' (ibid. 3). Jürgen Moltmann provides some logic: 'Were God incapable of suffering in any respect, and therefore in an absolute sense, then he would be incapable of love' ([1972] 1974: 230). For Moltmann and a host of other theologians, God is not simply passible, he also 'lays himself open to the suffering which love for another brings him; and yet, by virtue of his love, he remains master of the pain that love causes him to suffer' (Moltmann, quoted in Bauckham 1990: 106).

The progression from impassibility to passibility, from emotionlessness to emotionfulness, suggests an occasionally bumpy evolutionary process which collectively reinterprets the theology of emotions. Like Aaron Ben Ze'ev, Scrutton claims that emotions have no clear and definite borders (2008: 2:85; see Ben Ze'ev 1987: 393); like Amélie Rorty, that 'The history of discussion of the passions does not form a smooth continuous history, which expands or narrows the class of pathe by following a single line of thought' (Scrutton 2:85; see Rorty 1984: 545). Characteristically and perhaps predictably, most theologians tend to treat passibility as a largely modern, twentieth-century invention: 'Sometime in the modern era', Lister opines, 'the broad consensus on divine impassibility experienced a significant shift' (2012: 124). Recent studies reflect this bias, generally bypassing the period from the end of the seventeenth century to the beginning of the twentieth. The intervening period is a particular casualty of this narrative, however, and the long nineteenth century a surprising blind spot for such a transitionally significant time in theological history. The long nineteenth century is important precisely because of its intensely transitional status, marking the progression from the impassibility of antiquity to the passibility of modernity.

Reflecting one of the key impassibilist propositions of *The Westminster Confession of Faith* (1646), William Beveridge (1637–1708) innocently espouses the view that God is

> not subject to nor capable of love, hatred, joy, grief, anger, and the like, as they daily arise in us imperfect creatures; but he is always the same unmovable, unchangeable, impassible God: and therefore in all our contemplations of the Divine essence, we are not to conceive him as one passionately rejoicing or grieving for any thing, as we do, but as a pure and perfect essence, without body, parts, and passions too; as appears from scripture, reason, and fathers. (1847: 26)

But by the nineteenth century dogmatic affirmations of this kind were manifestly under siege, anticipating Moltmann by over one hundred years (Duncan 1990: 6). According to Charles Hodge (1797–1878), Presbyterian theologian and Principal of the Princeton Theological Seminary:

> If love in God is only a name for that which accounts for the rational universe; if God is love, simply because He develops himself in thinking and conscious beings, then the word has for us no definite meaning; it reveals to us nothing concerning the real nature of God. Here again we have to choose between a mere philosophical speculation and the clear testimony of the Bible, and of our own moral and religious nature. Love of necessity involves feeling and if there be no feeling in God, there can be no love. (1872: 1:428–9)

Hodge continues to register his opposition to impassibility, substantiating his claims with the Bible more specifically:

> We must adhere to the truth in its scriptural form, or we lose it altogether. We must believe that God is love in the sense in which that word comes home to every human heart. The Scriptures do not mock us when they say, 'Like as a father pitieth his children, so the Lord pitieth them that fear Him.' (Ps. ciii: 13) He meant what He said when He proclaimed Himself as 'The Lord, the Lord God, merciful and gracious, long-suffering and abundant in goodness and truth.' (Ex. xxxiv: 6) . . . The word love has the same sense throughout this passage. God is love; and love in Him is, in all that is essential to its nature, what love is in us. (Ibid. 429)

Hodge is an important theological barometer, as is his successor at Princeton, his son A. A. Hodge. Hodge junior takes a more cautious approach. Where his father espoused a God with human-like emotions, A. A. Hodge warns against the freedom of imputing God with unworthy passions consequently (Duncan 1990: 6). Hodge the younger's prevarication emblemises a concept in transition. Hodge's contemporary, W. G. T. Shedd, follows his reading of impassibility only to come unstuck over the concept of divine passion: if passion implies passivity, a simple God cannot be moved by stimulus external to his creation. However, while God is a most pure spirit without passions . . . It is important to remember this signification of the term 'passion,' and the intention in employing it. Sometimes it has been understood to be synonymous with feeling or emotion, and the erroneous and demoralizing inference has been drawn, that the Divine nature is destitute of feeling altogether. (1888: 1:170–2)

Shedd concludes by shedding (forgive the pun) impassibility:

While therefore God as a most pure spirit has no passions, he has feelings and emotions. He is not passively wrought upon by the objective universe, so that he experiences physical impressions and organic appetites, as the creature does, but he is self-moved in all his feelings. (Ibid. 1:178)

Shedd's compromise, like Lister's, is endemic across a nineteenth century debunking divine emotionlessness against an increasingly assertive backdrop of romantic humanitarianism. Thomas Thompson epitomises the transition in theological parallel in the title of his compellingly argued essay, 'Nineteenth-Century Kenotic Christology: The Waxing, Waning, and Weighing of a Quest for a Coherent Orthodoxy'. Citing the 'stampede' to kenotic models of the Incarnation, Thompson delivers a strong message about the deeply conflicted nature of contemporary thought on Christ's humanity. Nineteenth-century kenoticists like Thomasius, Ebrard, Marensen, Gess and Mackintosh run the gamut of full to empty, transcendent to immanent, absolute to relative, immutable to mutable and impassible to passible – from Christ as emphatically 'true deity, true humanity' to a logos which 'relinquishes all divine attributes, powers, prerogatives, and glory' (2006: 79, 87). Like its counterpart in impassibility, by the end of the century kenotic theory was widely deemed to be in tatters as theologians sought 'to mediate an integrally human Jesus of more modern awareness and sensitivity with the Christ of confessions' (ibid. 95).

Science

The evolution of passibility did not happen in intellectual isolation. While theology progressed from the philosophical strictures of impassibility to more humanly emollient theories of a God 'who loves and acts' (Weinandy 2000: 25) – to theologies obviating 'God's compassionate responsiveness to suffering' (Gavrilyuk 2009: 132) – science wrestled with similar issues in different ways. A principal concern of early nineteenth-century science was the fixed nature of nature, what in the history of evolutionary theory is called the Great Chain of Being. The Great Chain of Being is a scale of nature linking nature, man and (in pre-Enlightenment versions) God in a fixed and immutable hierarchical sequence from the lowest to highest creatures (see Pietsch 2012; Archibald 2014). The God of the Great Chain of Being reflected the immutable character of the sequence itself and by the seventeenth century assumed the absolute position of divine designer (McGrath 2011: 74). By the beginning of the eighteenth century, the image of God had begun to crystallise into a fixed, absolute and rational, if remote, organisational omnipresence at the creationary helm of nature; according to John Ray:

There is no greater, at least no more palpable and convincing argument of the existence of the Deity, than the admirable art and wisdom that discovers itself in the make and constitution, the order and disposition, the ends and uses of all the parts and members of this stately fabric of Heaven and Earth. (1727: 30)

The Deity continued designing into the early nineteenth century in William Paley's famous *Natural Theology* (1802), where God receives a further boost from horology (God is compared to a clock maker; his creation, a clock). Paley's Newtonian natural theology belies a nascent humanistic approach, however, by appealing to arguments focusing in part on the organisational principles of human anatomy. The human body has become an integrated element of nature; as Alastair McGrath notes, 'Nature does not merely include stars, trees and rivers: it embraces humanity' (2006: 1:252). No sooner had Paley introduced humanity into a nature designed by God than theologians extended his evidence into the realm of mind, where correlations between rationalism and a Designing Deity were deemed to be apposite. Steeped in Augustinian thought, Henry Brougham (1778–1868), for example, asks: ought we not 'to consider the phenomena of the mind as more peculiarly adapted to help this inquiry, as bearing a nearer relation to the Great Intelligence which created and which maintains this system?' (1835: 54)

By the time Brougham arrived at his conclusions on the 'phenomena of the mind', scientific understanding had already absorbed almost a century of changing attitudes towards them. Starting, arguably, with David Hume's work on animal reason and feeling, the previously firm theological line dividing humans and animals began to erode as the immutable nature of divine absolutism and the Great Chain of Being yielded to the more inherently mutable hermeneutics of human relativism. For Hume, in both animals and humans there are original impressions of sensation (bodily pains and pleasures) and secondary or reflective impressions of passion and emotion. Passions subsequently divide into those arising directly from pain and pleasure (such as desire, aversion, grief and joy), and passions arising from pain and pleasure but more complex in cast (such as pride, humility, ambition and vanity) (Spencer 2013: 31). For Hume:

> We may observe, not only that love and hatred are common to the whole sensitive creation, but likewise that their causes . . . are of so simple a nature, that they may easily be suppos'd to operate on mere animals. There is no force of reflection or penetration requir'd. Every thing is conducted by springs and principles, which are not peculiar to man, or any one species of animals. ([1739] 2003: 282)

Hume's significance is both intrinsic and contextual: first, he is among the earliest philosophers of mind to put humans and animals on the same emotional footing; and second, he was read closely by Darwin. While Hume contends that 'reason is but a wonderful and unintelligible instinct in our souls' (ibid. 128), Darwin claims that 'our necessary notions follow as consequences on habitual or instinctive assent to propositions which are the result of our senses, our experience' ([1838–9] 2016). Darwin would generalise: 'the mind is [a] function of the body' (ibid.). If Hume provided the language of emotion Darwin's immediate antecedents would provide the increasingly secularised vocabulary – Thomas Brown (1778–1820) being perhaps the most significant. Brown made the terminological transition from the 'active powers' – appetites, passions, desires and affections – to the emotions (Dixon 2003: 13). It is not without interest that Brown and Brougham were amongst scientists who in 1797 founded the pointedly a-religious Academy of Physics in Edinburgh, organised amongst other things to explore 'The physics of mind, or the philosophy of mind, excluding religious controversies and party politics' (Welsh 1825: 499).

This was, of course, symptomatic of a more general change in attitude towards theology extending Protestant individualism to an even more seemingly self-sufficient proposition. As Dixon so aptly puts it:

> This opposition to Scholastic forms of knowledge ... combined with a passion for religious toleration and inclusivity, led to the construction of an atheological psychology in which authority was given to individual consciousness and mental science rather than religion or theology. (2003: 117)

Brown may have used terms like 'physiology of the mind', 'mental science', intellectual physics' and 'the physical investigation of the mind', but in fact his work is strictly philosophical (ibid. 118); neither is his writing dogmatically Christian. He was a natural theologian in the Broughamian, Paleyian mould and attributed to God conventionally providential terms like 'eternal Author of the universe' or 'the one designing Power' (Brown 1828: 277, 434) – precisely the terminology Darwin would later renounce and 'shedd' unceremoniously as impassibility was transferred from God to nature, and passibility from the affections to the emotions. Darwin's part in this evolutionary progress was to deny a designing God, drain emotion of its theological authorship and attribute to the expression of emotion the status of a vestigial characteristic. If man was designed purposefully by God, and by their very nature vestigial characteristics lacked purpose, the expression of emotions could not have been designed by God. Darwin's plot to unseat natural theology begins with a refutation of the work of Charles Bell, author of *Expression: Its Anatomy and Philosophy* (1824). Because, according to Bell, 'the Creator' established relations between the mind and environment, he also

> implanted, or caused to be generated in us, various higher intellectual faculties. He has raised in every intelligent being emotions that point to him, affections by which we are drawn to him, and which rest in him as their end ... These feelings cannot be traced to any source, they rise spontaneously, they are universal, and not to be shaken off; furnishing an instance of that adaptation of the mind to its various relations. (1824: 16)

Although Darwin rejected Bell's transcendentalism, he did accept certain features of his research, not least the principle of 'serviceable associated habits'. These are actions (expressions) which became habitually associated with a certain emotional state but later, shorn of their original purpose, continue to produce an expression without any environmental reason. In accepting Bell's point of view, Darwin's response was fairly predictable: habits can become instincts (Richards 1987: 232), and instincts can be expressed through the emotions. There is a potentially interesting twist, however: although, according to natural theology, God designed man perfectly, both Darwin and St Augustine believed that he was enslaved by the ostensibly useless urges of his physical body – Darwin through inheritance and Augustine through sin (Dixon 2003: 177). In other words, as anti-religious as Darwin may well have been, there is a kind of trace universalism subsisting within his theory of the emotions (Plamper and Tribe 2015: 169), and, although much contested, it proves that his fundamentally non-cognitive, materialistic approach spoke of a shared immutability at the genetic core of human and animal identity – an immutability recognisable in the relationship between mechanisms of expression and the experience of an emotion, between the impassible process of evolutionary formation and the passible experience of its expression in man.

Music

Music was no bystander to these theological and scientific developments. While theology progressed from impassibility to passibility and science from passion to emotion, music evolved a narrative of its own. In eighteenth- and nineteenth-century musical composition, this involved a general, if at times inconsistent, movement from absolute music to programme music – from the fixed, predetermined forms used in the symphony, sonata, concerto and suchlike (absolute music) to forms replicating in music the structural characteristics of extra-musical influences drawn from the arts like poetry, literature or painting (programme music). The term 'absolute music' was coined in 1846 by Wagner who used the opportunity of writing programme notes for Beethoven's ninth (choral) symphony to criticise the idea of purely instrumental music without reference to the world (Bonds 2014: 1–2). Absolute music has a complex pedigree in the language of transcendentalising immutability. For Carl Dahlhaus, 'If instrumental music had been a "pleasant noise" beneath language to the common-sense estheticians of the eighteenth century, then the romantic metaphysics of art declared it a language *above* language' (Dahlhaus [1978] 1989: 9). Contemporary music critic, Eduard Hanslick, describes it in similar terms: 'In music there is both meaning and logical sequence, but in a *musical* sense; it is a language we speak and understand yet are unable to *translate*' (Hanslick [1854] 1891: 171); moreover:

> the term 'music,' in its true meaning, must exclude compositions in which words are set to music. In vocal or operatic music it is impossible to draw so nice a distinction between the effect of the music, and that of the words, that an exact definition of the share which each has had in the production of the whole becomes practicable. An enquiry into the subject of music must leave out even compositions with inscriptions, or so-called programme music. Its union with poetry, though enhancing the power of music, does not widen its limits. (Ibid. 45)

The opposite camp – the programmaticist camp – was equally vocal (or 'instrumental' it might be said). One – if not *the* – main exponent of progammaticism was Franz Liszt. Liszt expressed the opposite opinion to concepts of the absolute; for him, music was at its most expressive not when content arbitrarily filled a predetermined form, but when the form and content were co-equally purposeful:

> In program music, the recurrence, variation, alteration, and modulation of motifs are determined by their relationship to a poetic idea. Here one theme no longer begets another ... Though not ignored, all exclusively musical considerations are subordinated to the treatment of the subject at hand. Accordingly, the treatment and subject of this symphonic genre demand an engagement that goes beyond the technical treatment of the musical material. The vague impressions of the soul are elevated to definite impressions through an articulated plan, which is taken in by the ear in much the same manner in which a cycle of paintings is taken in by the eye. The artist who favors this kind of artwork enjoys the advantage of being able to connect with a poetic process all those affects which an orchestra can express with such great power. (Liszt, *Berlioz und seine 'Harold-Symphonie'* (1855), quoted in Bonds 2014: 211)

Liszt aims to touch an absolutist nerve: whereas the experience of absolute music produces merely 'vague impressions of the soul', programme music conversely generates estimably 'definite impressions'. The difference between vague and definite impressions is not inconsequential, because it locates Liszt's transitional project in changing theories of musical expression and emotion. Roger Scruton locates differences between absolute and programme music in features of representation; for Scruton, programme music attempts to depict objects and events, and

> to derive its logic from that attempt. It does not merely echo or imitate things which have an independent reality; the development of programme music is determined by the development of its theme. The music moves in time according to the logic of its subject and not according to autonomous principles of its own. (2016)

Accurate as this definition may be at the surface level of representation, it does not, however, describe its deeper ideological intentions to crystallise emotion into something more psychologically identifiable and cathartically beneficial. Liszt is not alone in complaining about the expressive vagaries of absolute music in contrast to the emotional depths of programme music. Music critic and Liszt protégé, Peter Cornelius, astutely summarises the difference between camps:

> The first [absolutist camp] considers music a fantastical play of tones according the rules of euphony and aesthetic laws derived from the specifically musical works of Haydn, Mozart, and Beethoven . . . such as unity in variety, clarity and proportion of forms and means, etc. According to this party, music achieves its effect through itself, without the mediation of accessory ideas; it elevates the soul out of the narrowness of life to ideal heights, rinsing away through its waves of tone, as it were all the rot and triflings of life . . . [The second programmaticist camp] is no longer content to arouse vague feelings in the lay person . . . It desires instead to take as its material the rich treasures of myth, of the Bible, or history, drawing on the inexhaustible source of one's own heart, the inner circumstances of its love, its passions, its struggles with the world . . . It seeks to renounce the freedom of absolute music and its associated servitude to conventional forms in order to win a freedom of form by giving itself over to a specific poetic object. Even if the representation of a specific object runs the risk of remaining imperfect in certain respects . . . this camp considers such effort more beneficial than a constant refilling of superseded forms with vague feelings. (Cornelius, 'Review of Richard Würst, *Preis-Sinfonie*, Op. 21', 8 December 1854, quoted in Bonds 2014: 215)

Cornelius and Liszt express what many had felt by the 1850s: the impassibility of absolute music had been superseded by the passibility of programme music, and this is obvious from the way both camps expressed their opinion. Absolute music attracted transcendentalising language of a semi-religious kind. Hegel writes that:

> [music's] own proper element is the inner life as such, explicitly shapeless feeling which cannot manifest itself in the outer world and its reality but only through an external medium which quickly vanishes and is cancelled at the very moment of expression. Therefore music's content is constituted by spiritual subjectivity in its immediate subjective inherent unity, the human heart, feeling as such. ([1823] 1975: 2:626)

Dahlhaus sees this as representative of a process of spiritual inwardisation, withdrawing from the spatial and material exteriority into a 'prevailing self-awareness of the time, into "feeling'" (Dahlhaus [1978] 1989: 96) and Hegel himself claims that 'absolute inwardness, is not capable of freely expanding in its independence, so long as it remains within the mould of the bodily shape' ([1823] 1930: 1:107). Of course, Hegel is also paradoxically responsible for redirecting impassibility into passibility by 'killing' God Christologically. As Robert Williams and others suggest, for Hegel the death of God in Christ also meant the death of death and the consequent death of an impassible, apathetic divinity (Williams 2012: 1; see Caron 2005). Hegel's contribution to the evolution of musical passibility appears to be ignored by musicologists, however, who even in aesthetic contexts tend to focus on historicism and truth-content rather than feeling and emotion (see Hamilton 2007: 72–5; Schnädelbach 2010). Yet it is theologians, Keating and White, who hint – perhaps inadvertently – at a musicological methodology when they alight on Hegel's dialectal synthesis: 'This process is simultaneously in some way constitutive of the divine itself. God himself becomes in and through history, a history of dialectic, in an almost musical interplay of thesis, antithesis, and synthesis' (2009: 8). As an exemplar of programmaticism, Liszt's view of Hegel was by no means monochrome; indeed his preface to the *Hungarian Rhapsodies* (1846–53) uses Hegelian dialecticism to ascribe absolute spiritual, if not relative physical, musical nationhood to the Gypsies (Saul 2007: 13), even if he deemed their lives to be 'at once caused and consoled by four elements of sensuality and exaltation: love, song, dance, and drink' (Liszt [1861] 1926, discussed in Locke 2009: 143). Liszt's changeable attitude towards Hegelian absolutism may reflect the transitional nature of Hegel's own position on dialectical passibility, but even at his most seemingly abstract – in the *Transcendental Etudes* (1852), for example – Liszt could not restrain himself from giving most of the movements characteristically emotive titles. The progression from impassibility to passibility, passion to emotion, and absolute to programme was under way.

Music Evolution

Nineteenth-century evolutionary theories about music provide an unexpectedly rich meeting place for issues over emotion. Dominated by the two diametrically opposing propositions of Herbert Spencer and Charles Darwin, those propositions are joined by, and rooted in, theories of emotion which not only reveal an essential commonality but also betray their theological and scientific origins. The theological origins of music evolution have an ancient biblical pedigree in the Old Testament, especially in relation to the psalms and their ability to recapitulate the emotional and genealogical experience of both individuals and communities. The psalms bear an essential, if particularly heavy emotional inscription: 'When turned into song, Psalms are grasped with a heightened intensity, the conjunction of word and music linking mind and emotion in an especially potent way' (Begbie 2007: 107). Begbie speaks for the many when he obviates the emotional content and purpose of the psalms. For some, they are a school of prayer, teaching worshippers how to express their emotions to God (Bracken Long 2014: 546). Calvin himself maintains that 'there is no other book in which we are more perfectly taught the right manner of praising God, or in which we are more powerfully stirred up to the performance of this religious exercise' (Calvin, *Commentary on the Book of Psalms*, quoted in Long 2014: 557) and for Luther, in psalms message and music combine 'to move the listener's soul' (quoted in Leaver 2007: 317). But the emotional content of the psalms – and hymns, perhaps to a lesser extent – reflects more than the singer's expression of feeling about and towards himself and God. The psalms are experiential time capsules, and embed the individual and shared histories of a people's emotional narrative. Walter Breuggemann claims that the psalms 'with few exceptions, are not the voice of God addressing us. They are rather the voice of our own common humanity, gathered over a long period of time' (1984: 15). In some way or other, the psalms provide 'genetic' evidence of our shared musical and emotional ancestry; they are theological evidence of the first comprehensive theories of music evolution.

This genetic quality of music, of a type exemplified in the psalms, did not go unnoticed by nineteenth-century theorists of musical evolution for whom religion and science were not so easily separable; for them music not only afforded expression but embodied deeply felt emotions coordinating historical experience in a spiritual present. If the evolution of music evolved over time, over the course of the nineteenth century it is probably Schleiermacher who, through concepts of feeling, inadvertently gave music evolution its greatest theological impetus. Schleiermacher subscribed to an Aristotelian concept of *poiesis* (production) in which works rooted in man's nature, such as music, also transform his nature: 'Music's anthropological root actually does reach back to the emotions' (Scholtz 2010: 58). Scholtz touches upon an interesting scientific issue without observing its relationship to proto-evolutionary thinking: music evolves from a matrix of moderated and humanised feelings, creating the unity of a timeless oneness of life; that unity, combined with the need to express mood, stimulates the imagination to generate music out of its inner ear and inner voice; a process of ordering establishes a primal image which then becomes the organisational principle of the work; the work evolves from 'elementary perfection' to a combination of unity and diversity expressing 'organic perfection' (ibid. 58–9). Layered behind this evolutionary process there is another evolutionary process, however, for Schleiermacher claims that the composer's 'greatest triumph, it is true, is when he bids adieu to language altogether and embodies, in this endlessly changing wealth of tonal sequences and harmonies, all the tremors of life that can pass through the soul' ([1831–2] 1984: 174). Implicit in Schleiermacher's fundamentally absolutist (and surprisingly impassibilist) perspective is a conception of music as progressively liberated from the emotional restrictions imposed by language. Indeed, music is not only a language *above* languages, it is also an assertion of progressive spiritual unity within the disparate constraints of human ontology. To produce music is to speak (or sing) of individual feelings welling up into mutual collectivity beyond the communicative powers of language, while at the same time collective musical expressions of feelings embody the historical progress of religion. In *Christmas Eve* (1805), Schleiermacher uses storytelling to make his point, voicing the religious *Gefühl* (feeling) through Eduard, one of the story's main protagonists, but the cosy, localised interiority of the narrative belies its more profound implications for the history of religion. *Christmas Eve* is the history of the church in microcosm:

> I feel overflowing with the joy of pure serenity, which I think could withstand anything that might happen to me ... A full consciousness of this mood, however, and an apt appreciation of it, I feel I owe in part to the fact that our little one has invited us to express it in music. For every fine feeling comes completely to the fore only when we have found the right musical expression for it. Not the spoken word, for this can never be anything but indirect – a plastic element, if I may put it that way – but a real, uncluttered tone. And it is precisely to religious feeling that music is most closely related ... What the word has declared, the tones of music must make alive, in harmony conveying it to the whole inner being of its hearers and holding it fast there. ([1805] 1967: 46)

On the surface it would seem as if Schleiermacher's musical evolutionism is entirely self-contained theologically. Religious feeling progresses towards music as it rises above language. But this is to simplify the profound philosophical implications of his evolutionary process for later, more apparently secularly minded theorists of music evolution for whom emotion lies at the root of being, such as Victorian polymath, public intellectual and caustic verbalist, Herbert Spencer. Where in his *Speeches* Schleiermacher propounds a commonplace teleological evolutionism – religion progresses from (a) chaos to (b) plurality without unity to (c) unity within plurality – Spencer suggests progression from undifferentiated homogeneity to differentiated heterogeneity to differentiated homogeneity (Krech 2010: 72). In parallel, Spencer, like Schleiermacher, also espouses a theory of musical evolutionism which uses feeling to drive language ineluctably towards music. Spencer believes that music is effectively 'impassioned speech' evolving through emotion from speech to music:

> These vocal peculiarities which indicate excited feeling *are those which especially distinguish song from ordinary speech*. Every one of the alterations of voice which have found to be a physiological result of pain or pleasure *is carried to an extreme in vocal music* . . . in respect alike of *loudness, timbre, pitch, intervals*, and *rate of variation*, song employs and exaggerates the natural language of the emotions; it arises from a systematic combination of those vocal peculiarities which are physiological effects of acute pleasure and pain. (1951: 57–8)

Like Schleiermacher's history of religion, Spencer's musical evolutionism also coordinates teleological trajectory in history. While through emotion music progresses from language to music, through progressive integration it also develops into the differentiated homogeneity of historical narrative, from the undifferentiated homogeneity of simple forms to the differentiated homogeneity of more complex ones:

> In music progressive integration is displayed in numerous ways. The simple cadence embracing but a few notes, which in the chants of savages is monotonously repeated, becomes, among civilized races, a long series of different musical phrases combined into one whole; and so complete is the integration that the melody cannot be broken off in the middle nor shorn of its final note, without giving us a painful sense of incompleteness. When to the air, a bass, a tenor, and an alto are added; and when to the different voice-parts there is joined an accompaniment; we see integration of another order which grows naturally more elaborate. And the process is carried a stage higher when these complex solos, concerted pieces, choruses, and orchestral effects are combined into the vast ensemble of an oratorio or a musical drama. (1867: IXV/§114)

Like Schleiermacher, Spencer also postulates an emotional agent of evolutionary propulsion, but where for Schleiermacher that agent reveals Christian religion, in Spencer it exposes man's favourable adaptation of human sympathy. Sympathy, in Spencer's terms, is not unlike Schleiermacher's concept of 'immediate self-consciousness'. This refers to the form self-knowledge assumes when, through the collapse of subjective and objective relationships to God, man becomes cognisant of his individual relationship to the greater whole (Scholtz 2010: 51). Feelings create that 'timeless oneness of life' which both propitiates and exemplifies meaningful unity. In Spencer's terms, emotions conduce to generate a productive unity of people; music in particular evolves emotions in a process of increasingly integrated differentiation leading ultimately towards human happiness:

> In its bearings upon human happiness, this emotional language which musical culture develops and refines is only second in importance to the language of the intellect; perhaps not even second to it. For these modifications of voice produced by feelings are the means of exciting like feelings in others. Joined with gestures and expressions of face, they give life to the otherwise dead words in which the intellect utters its ideas, and so enable the hearer not only to *understand* the state of mind they accompany, but to *partake* of that state. In short they are the chief media of sympathy. (1951: 73–4)

As a facilitator of sympathy, music would also help lead Spencer to develop a theory of altruism, itself a deeply contested and religiously opaque term (unlike benevolence or charity) (Dixon 2008: 196). Spencer was immutable on the subject of altruism's evolutionary origins in survival – for him, altruistic feelings were all 'sympathetic excitements of egoistic feelings' (1855: 2:612) – and he was equally hostile to religion and certain brands of utilitarianism (Dixon 2008: 200). But then Spencer was ultimately self-conflicted towards the origins of altruism, as he was with the cosmos in general, and dallied unadvisedly with concepts of a transcendental Absolute – what in 'Religion: A Retrospect and Prospect' (1884) he would describe (infelicitously, judging from the harshness of his critics) as 'an Infinite and Eternal Energy, from which all things proceed' (1884: 12). The progression from emotion to sympathy, itself masking a progression from language to music, is not without theological and metaphysical precedent, therefore; indeed, the role of sympathy in Spencer's musical evolutionism recapitulates the nineteenth century's transitional uncertainties over the humanising theologies of impassibility and passibility, the science of passions and emotions, and the advance of programmaticism from the shackles of philosophically tyrannical musical absolutism. That Spencer resorted to mysticism to explain 'the Great Enigma' or the 'Ultimate Reality transcending human thought' (ibid.: 12) is treated with misgivings by his philosophical contemporaries; nothing suggests that scientifically minded music critics like John Stainer, C. Hubert H. Parry and Henry Hadow did not share their feelings (Zon 2018). But then the language of Spencer's uncertainties is characteristic of the anxieties of an age uncertain over the spiritual effect changes in evolutionary thought would have on emotion. For Spencer music is the *idealised* language of emotion, so if we take him at his word and there has genuinely 'little by little arisen a wide divergence between this idealized language of emotion [music] and its natural language [speech]' (1951: 69), then perhaps music is more transcendental than he intended to suggest after all, and contradictorily more impassible than passible, more passionate than emotional, more absolute than programmatic. Such are the evolutionary inconsistencies of satirist George S. Carr's 'very apostle of Altruism' (1895: 37).

Darwin was arguably less inconsistent in his musical evolutionism, because unlike Spencer he resisted the temptation to transcendentalise emotion into a higher form of sympathy. Instead, for Darwin music reproduces in man emotions once associated with the more rudimentary functions of survival and procreation, rivalry and courtship. As elsewhere in his work on emotion in music evolution, Darwin attributes to the expression of emotion the status of a vestigial characteristic, postulating that 'sensations and ideas excited in us by music, or by the cadences of impassioned oratory, appear from their vagueness, yet depth, like mental reversions to the emotions and thoughts of a long-past age' (1871: 2:336); indeed, music recalls in a vague and indefinite manner, those strong emotions which were felt during long-past ages, when, as is probable, our early progenitors courted each other by the aid of vocal tones. And as several of our strongest emotions – grief, great joy, love, and sympathy – lead to the free secretion of tears, it is not surprisingly that music should be apt to cause our eyes to be suffused with tears, especially when we are already softened by the tenderer feelings. (1872: 219)

Amongst these emotions, one has survived more than others, however – love, the true emotion of courtship: 'Love', Darwin claims, 'is still the commonest theme of our own songs' (1871: 2:336). Love is a problematical emotion for Darwin, for, although all emotions are equally atavistic, their function is not equally important to survival; in fact, Darwin appears to tacitly hierarchise love at the top of a Great Chain of Emotional Being by suggesting it has achieved emotion's greatest survival. In the process, he muddles cause and effect when the emotion of love is placed within the construct of larger evolutionary considerations like the development of language. In Darwin's world, music does not really evolve in a teleological, Spencerian way but captures emotions later found as traces embedded in language. Where, therefore, Spencer believes that music evolved from impassioned speech, Darwin propounds the opposite to be true; indeed it could be argued that for Darwin language is innately impassioned by music. Writing in *The Descent of Man*, he suggests that Spencer

> concludes that the cadences used in emotional speech afford the foundation from which music has been developed; whilst I conclude that musical notes and rhythm were first acquired by the male or female progenitors of mankind for the sake of charming the opposite sex. Thus musical tones became firmly associated with some of the strongest passions an animal is capable of feeling, and are consequently used instinctively, or through association, when strong emotions are expressed in speech. Mr. Spencer does not offer any satisfactory explanation, nor can I, why high or deep notes should be expressive, both with man and the lower animals, of certain emotions. (Ibid. 2:336)

If music is distinguished by its pre-linguistic status, it is also distinguished by its unique capacity to differentiate and promote a range of emotional expressions. Darwin clearly aims to distinguish emotional instincts of love and sympathy from passions of a more rudimentary nature, and uses evolution to repudiate the idea that morality assumes that human nature is invariably and congenitally selfish (Dixon 2008: 132). For Darwin, 'disinterested love for all living creatures, [is] the most noble attribute of man' (1871: 1:105). In evolutionary terms, music is the perfect carrier of love precisely because it is so congenitally preponderant – even universal. Darwin claims:

> The capacity and love for singing or music, though not a sexual character in man, must not here be passed over. Although the sounds emitted by animals of all kinds serve many purposes, a strong case can be made out, that the vocal organs were primarily used and perfect in relation to the propagation of the species. (Ibid. 2:330)

The universality of music and its capacity to convert sexual passion from the very rudiments of animal propagation into the highest expression of human love reflects an indisputably contemporary scientific model of emotional progressionism, and, as we know, Darwin would struggle to abandon his rather Lamarckian teleological inclinations despite seeming to overcome his theological beliefs: 'natural selection', he maintains in every edition of the *Origin of Species*, 'works solely by and for the good of each being, all corporeal and mental endowments will tend to progress towards perfection' (1859: 489). Music is implicated in this process or progress not only because sexual selection operates in conjunction with natural selection, but because it helps man tend towards perfection through the emotion of love. George Levine capitalises on this confusion more generally when he cheekily paraphrases the ubiquitous evangelical bumper sticker 'Jesus loves you' into the title of *Darwin Loves You* (2006). But, as with Darwin, there is a theological fly even within Levine's own incontestably scientific ointment: Levine's subtitle is metaphysically recidivistic and curiously Spencerian – *Darwin Loves You: Natural Selection and the Re-enchantment of the World*, and the sacralisation of secularisation is irrepressibly present in its aspirational absence. As Levine admits, even Daniel Dennett 'calls this secular world "sacred." Darwinian enchantment entails an attitude of awe and love toward the multiple forms of life' (2006: 250). Predictably, Levine and Dennett (and many similarly minded others) aim to fulfil what Darwin himself struggled to do by replacing an impassible God with an impassible Scientist:

> The scientist's tendency to love the world he or she is committed to describe as impartially, with as little affect as possible, is not an aberration at all. It is what happens to any of us when . . . we really learn to see something with great clarity, to understand its workings. (Ibid. 253)

The impassible God and the impassible Scientist are not as dissimilar as Levine would have us believe, and Darwin's understanding of music helps us to explain that. If Darwin's theory of musical origins revolves around the perfectibility inherent in the emotion of love, then the love of music would itself have an evolutionary purpose. The love of music and the music of love are intimately related, therefore, expressing an interrelationship between cause and effect with origins in the earliest and most primordially genitive attributes of man. And as man is a relative newcomer to evolutionary history, Darwin looks to simpler forms and expressions in the natural world to identify musical origins. Birdsong is Darwin's evolutionary trump card, at least in theory. Male birds sing to attract a mate, and mates are attracted by the quality of their song. The best song produces the best likelihood of reproduction, that is, survival of the fittest. But birdsong is not as straightforward as that, however, because it is difficult to extrapolate the passibility of love from the impassibility of sexual selection. At some evolutionary point in history, sex became love, but exactly when did that happen and what did music have to do with it? Nineteenth-century ornithology provides an answer, or at least a plausible explanation. Darwin wrote on *The Descent of Man* and *The Expression of the Emotions in Man and Animals* when, like most science, ornithology was fledging from its theological nest. But the field of ornithology struggled to cut its roots in natural theology, and many aspirationally scientific ornithologists clung unrepentantly to their atavistic theological tendencies. Henry Drummond encapsulates this strand of thinking:

> What goes on then in the animal kingdom is this – the Bird-Life seizes upon the bird-germ and builds it up into a bird, the image of itself . . . The visible bird is simply an incarnation of the invisible Bird-Life . . . As the Bird-Life builds up a bird, the image of itself, so the Christ-Life builds up a Christ, the image of Himself, in the inward nature of man. (1896: 292–3)

Drummond's conflation of ornithology and incarnational theology – effectively ornitheology – is commonplace at the time, and although Darwin sedulously avoids it, he cannot overcome the unassailably redemptive lens it focuses on man's relationship to man. And that lens is invariably trained on the development of love. The Rev. W. E. Evans invokes the constancy of the woodlark as an example:

> While the other larks congregate in flocks during the Winter, and fly from field to field, this, for the most part, is stationary; or, if joining the others for a time, soon separates to return and sing in its accustomed haunts. Type of the Christian with his pure and holy home... Type, too, of the spirit whose home is with God... where all its hopes and all its love are centred! (1845: 37)

It can be no surprise, therefore, that when it came to the evolution of music, Darwin struggled to extricate himself from the redemptive ornitheological language of the time, and in fact embraced the music of its form without embracing the language of its content: to paraphrase Levin, enchantment is, after all, en-chant-ment.

Conclusion

Darwin is at his most en-chant-ing when using music evolution to elevate the faceless passion of sexual selection into the intensely human emotion of love, and in this respect he does more than simply impassion music with love. Spencer may consider music to catalyse the emotion of sympathy (which in turn enhances survival), but for Darwin, as Schleiermacher, musical emotion expresses evolutionary commonalities which universalise human history within the totality of natural creation. Compare *Christmas Eve* with the magisterial ending of the *Origin of Species*:

> Only in immediate relation to [that which is] the highest in our lives – to religion, and to some distinct form of it – does music have enough concrete reference, without being tied to some mere contingency, to be intelligible. Christianity is a unique theme presented in endless variations. Yet these variations are conjoined by a single law intrinsic to each, which gives them a distinct character overall. (Schleiermacher [1805] 1967: 104)

> There is a grandeur in the view of life, with its several powers, having been originally breathed [by the Creator, editions 2 to 6] into a few forms or into one; and that, whilst this planet has gone cycling on according to the fixed law of gravity, from so simple a beginning endless forms most beautiful and most wonderful have been, and are being, evolved. (Darwin 1859: 490)

Despite his vacillation over the existence of a Creator, Darwin never relinquished his transcendental explanation of creation, and neither did his view on music and emotion change substantially over the course of his life. What did change were the ideas revolving around him, as passions and design were gradually replaced by emotions and natural selection in a cultural shift away from theological agency and towards scientific mechanism. Paradoxically, however, Darwin's mechanistic universe produced the very same cosmic impassibility which natural selection sought to humanise. Tortured by the existence of pain and suffering in the world, Darwin sought to reconcile its moral burden by preferring senseless suffering to suffering ostensibly willed or permitted by God (Fleming 1961:

230–1). Like many other theologians, John Haught responds to this acutely Darwinian dilemma by citing the need for a kenotic approach involving a passible, self-emptying God who participates in the suffering of the world – a God 'who suffers along with creation [and affirms] that the agony of living beings is not undergone in isolation from the divine eternity' (2001: 49–50). In evolutionary terms, Darwin's theory of musical origins encapsulates this conflict. Music, for Darwin, aspires to an emotional condition of love in the same way that, for Walter Pater, 'all art constantly aspires to the condition of music' ([1873] 1986: 86). Unlike Spencer, for whom 'evolution is a process which, in itself, generates value' (Ruse 1995: 231), Pater's evolutionary aspirations begin on an entirely less materialistic basis; indeed, one might even say that the opposite is true. For Pater, evolution is a process of becoming which value generates:

> It is the art of music which most completely realises this artistic ideal, this perfect identification of matter and form. In its consummate moments, the end is not distinct from the means, the subject from the expression; they inhere in and completely saturate each other; and to it, therefore, to the condition of its perfect moments, all the arts may be supposed constantly to aspire. ([1873] 1986: 88)

It does this because for Pater 'evolution is neither futuristic nor chiliastic; it is historical. The beginning and end of becoming are of no significance beside the actual process of change' (Iser [1960] 1987: 77).

Is, therefore, Darwin's theory of musical origins actually a metaphysical (or even theological) theory of becoming rather than a scientific theory of evolution? Alister McGrath provides some help answering this question. According to McGrath (and others), without incarnational theology 'we cannot trace a straight and narrow trajectory, proceeding directly from the present empirical reality that we call "nature" and the ideal that we call "the good," identifying observations of natural patterns and processes with explicit moral values or norms' (McGrath 2008: 306; see Rice 2000: 48–63). Darwin – and perhaps even Spencer – sought to do the impossible, and tried to use science to substitute musical emotion for the impassible God they replaced with impassible nature. Theirs was the impassible dream – an attempt to use music to transcend transcendence at the very core of human emotional origins – in a sense, to help us understand and attain what Schleiermacher would call 'immediate self-consciousness', or Pater simply 'music'. Of course, Darwin and Spencer were not alone in exploiting musical emotion to overcome a defiantly impassible absolute. Unlike programmaticists such as Liszt who sought to reflect the nature of life in the structure and content of their compositions, Darwin and (perhaps to a lesser extent) Spencer sought to interpret the nature of life through the structure and content of their human reflections – and they did this without recourse to denominational theology, whether projecting the evolution of music towards love or sympathy. If, according to Spencer, music is the idealised language of emotion, for Darwin there is nothing idealised about it, or evolution for that matter. According to Darwin, musical emotion is part of creation in its deepest, most remotely human and animal form, but there it remains, like a soul, within the very material stuff of our genetic make-up. There is no teleological progression towards perfection – only a driving reproductive force uniting our emotions to nature, as Hume would suggest. Musical emotion problematises the idea of an impassible God by creating passibility even at the heart of impassibility, whether natural or divine, scientific or theological. The very existence of music proclaims the impossibility of impassibility, and music evolution bears witness to its truth. Jürgen Moltmann claims that by virtue of his love God 'remains master of the pain that love causes him to suffer' (Moltmann, quoted in Bauckham 1990: 106), but for Darwin and Spencer this is precisely what music is evolved to do – to express what seems impossible: to dream the impossible dream and sing the impassible song.

References

Archibald, J. David (2014), *Aristotle's Ladder, Darwin's Tree: The Evolution of Visual Metaphors for Biological Order*, New York: Columbia University Press.
Bauckham, Richard (1984), 'Only the Suffering God Can Help: Divine Passibility in Modern Theology', *Themelios*, 9.3: 6–12.
Bauckham, Richard (1990), 'In Defence of the *The Crucified God*', in Nigel M. de S. Cameron (ed.), *The Power and Weakness of God*, Edinburgh: Rutherford House Books, 92–118.
Begbie, Jeremy (2007), *Resounding Truth: Christian Wisdom in the World of Music*, Grand Rapids: Baker.
Bell, Charles (1824), *Essays on the Anatomy and Philosophy of Expression*, 2nd edn, London: John Murray.
Ben Ze'ev, Aaron (1987), 'The Nature of Emotions', *Philosophical Studies*, 52: 393–409.
Beveridge, William (1847), *Ecclesia Anglicana Ecclesia Catholica: Or, The Doctrine of the Church of England, Consonant to Scripture, Reason, and Fathers*, 3rd edn, Oxford: Oxford University Press.
Bonds, Mark Evan (2014), *Absolute Music: The History of an Idea*, New York: Oxford University Press.
Bracken Long, Kimberly (2014), 'The Psalms in Christian Worship', in William P. Brown (ed.), *The Oxford Handbook of the Psalms*, New York: Oxford University Press, 545–56.
Bradley, Ian (2004), *You've Got to Have a Dream: The Message of the Musical*, London: SCM Press.
Breuggemann, Walter (1984), *The Message of the Psalms: A Theological Commentary*, Minneapolis: Augsburg.
Brougham, Henry Lord (1835), *A Discourse of Natural Theology, Showing the Nature of the Evidence and Advantages of the Study*, London: Charles Knight.
Brown, Thomas, M.D. (1828), *Lectures on the Philosophy of the Human Mind*, n.p.
Caron, Maxence (2005), 'Passion du Fils et Impassibilité du Père: La Solution de Hegel et ses Limites', *Revue des Sciences Philosophiques et Théologiques*, 89.3: 485–99.
Carr, George S. (1895), *Social Evolution and the Evolution of Socialism: A Critical Essay*, London: W. Stewart.
Culver, Robert Duncan (1998), 'The Impassibility of God: Cyril of Alexandria to Moltmann', *Christian Apologetics Journal*, 1.1: 1–12.
Dahlhaus, Carl [1978] (1989), *The Idea of Absolute Music*, trans. Roger Lustig, Chicago: University of Chicago Press.
Darwin, Charles (1859), *On the Origin of Species, By Means of Natural Selection, or the Preservation of Favoured Races in the Struggle for Life*, London: John Murray.
Darwin, Charles (1871), *The Descent of Man, and Selection in Relation to Sex*, 2 vols, London: John Murray.
Darwin, Charles (1872), *The Expression of the Emotions in Man and Animals*, London: John Murray.
Darwin, Charles [1838–9] (2016), *Notebook N*, ed. Paul Barrett, *Darwin Online*, <http://darwin-online.org.uk/>.
Dixon, Thomas (2003), *From Passions to Emotions: The Creation of a Secular Psychological Category*, Cambridge: Cambridge University Press.
Dixon, Thomas (2008), *The Invention of Altruism: Making Moral Meanings in Victorian Britain*, Oxford: Oxford University Press.
Drummond, Henry (1896), *Natural Law in the Spiritual World*, London: Hodder and Stoughton.

Duncan, J. Ligon (1990), 'Divine Passibility and Impassibility in Nineteenth-Century American Confessional Presbyterian Theologians', *Scottish Bulletin of Evangelical Theology*, 8: 1–15.
Evans, The Revd. W. E. (1845), *The Songs of the Birds; Or, Analogies of Animal and Spiritual Life*, London: Francis and John Rivington.
Fleming, Donald (1961), 'Charles Darwin, the Anaesthetic Man', *Victorian Studies*, 4.3: 219–36.
Gavrilyuk, Paul L. (2009), 'God's Impassible Suffering in the Flesh: The Promise of Christology', in James F. Keating and Thomas Joseph White (eds), *Divine Impassibility and the Mystery of Human Suffering*, Grand Rapids: Eerdmans, 127–49.
Hamilton, Andy (2007), *Aesthetics and Music*, London: Continuum.
Hanslick, Eduard [1854] (1891), *The Beautiful in Music: A Contribution the Revisal of Musical Aesthetics*, trans. Gustav Cohen, London: Novello.
Haught, John (2001), *God after Darwin: A Theology of Evolution*, Boulder: Westview Press.
Hegel, G. W. F. [1823] (1930), *The Philosophy of Fine Art*, 2 vols, trans. F. O. B. Osmaston, London: Bell.
Hegel, G. W. F. [1823] (1975), *Aesthetics: Lectures on Fine Arts*, 2 vols, trans. T. M. Knox, Oxford: Clarendon Press.
Hodge, Charles (1872), *Systematic Theology*, 3 vols, New York: Scribners.
Hume, David [1739] (2003), *A Treatise of Human Nature*, Mineola, NY: Dover.
Iser, Wolfgang [1960] (1987), *Walter Pater: The Aesthetic Moment*, trans. David Henry Wilson, Cambridge: Cambridge University Press.
Keating, James F. and Thomas Joseph White (eds) (2009), *Divine Impassibility and the Mystery of Human Suffering*, Grand Rapids: Eerdmans.
Krech, Volkhard (2010), 'Schleiermacher's Contested Place in Religious Studies Today', in Brent W. Sockness and Wilhelm Gräb (eds), *Schleiermacher, the Study of Religion and the Future of Theology: A Transatlantic Dialogue*, Berlin: de Gruyter, 69–80.
Leaver, Robin A. (2007), *Luther's Liturgical Music: Principles and Implications*, Grand Rapids: Eerdmans.
Levine, George (2006), *Darwin Loves You: Natural Selection and the Re-enchantment of the World*, Princeton: Princeton University Press.
Lister, Rob (2012), *God Is Impassible and Impassioned: Toward a Theology of Divine Emotion*, Nottingham: Inter-Varsity Press.
Liszt, Franz [1861] (1926), *The Gipsy in Music*, trans. Edwin Evans, London: William Reeves.
Locke, Ralph (2009), *Musical Exoticism: Images and Reflections*, Cambridge: Cambridge University Press.
Long, Thomas G. (2014), 'Preaching Psalms', in William P. Brown (ed.), *The Oxford Handbook of the Psalms*, New York: Oxford University Press, 557–68.
McGrath, Alister E. (2006), *A Scientific Theology*, 3 vols, rev. edn, London: T&T Clark.
McGrath, Alister E. (2008), *The Open Secret: A New Vision of Natural Theology*, Oxford: Blackwell.
McGrath, Alister E. (2011), *Darwinism and the Divine: Evolutionary Thought and Natural Theology*, Oxford: Wiley-Blackwell.
Moltmann, Jürgen [1972] (1974), *The Crucified God: The Cross of Christ as the Foundation and Criticism of Christian Theology*, San Francisco: Harper and Row.
Pater, Walter [1873] (1986), *The Renaissance: Studies in Art and Poetry*, ed. Adam Phillips, Oxford: Oxford University Press.
Pietsch, Theodore W. (2012), *Trees of Life: A Visual History of Evolution*, Baltimore: Johns Hopkins University Press.
Plamper, Jan and Keith Tribe (eds) (2015), *The History of Emotions: An Introduction*, 2nd edn, Oxford: Oxford University Press.
Ray, John (1727), *The Wisdom of God Manifested in the Works of the Creation*, 9th edn, London: Royal Society.
Rice, Hugh (2000), *God and Goodness*, Oxford: Oxford University Press.

Richards, Robert J. (1987), *Darwin and the Emergence of Evolutionary Theories of Mind and Behaviour*, Chicago: University of Chicago Press.

Rorty, Amélie (1984), 'Aristotle on the Metaphysical Status of Pathe', *Review of Metaphysics*, 38: 521–46.

Ruse, Michael (1995), *Evolutionary Naturalism*, London: Routledge.

Saul, Nicholas (2007), *Gypsies and Orientalism in German Literature and Anthropology of the Long Nineteenth Century*, London: Legenda.

Schleiermacher, F. D. E. [1805] (1967), *Christmas Eve: Dialogue on the Incarnation*, trans. Terence N. Tice, Richmond: John Knox.

Schleiermacher, F. D. E. [1831–2] (1984), *Ästhetik: Über den Begriff der Kunst*, ed. Thomas Lehnerer, Hamburg: Felix Meiner.

Schnädelbach, Herbert (2010), 'Hegel', in Stefan Lorenz Sorgner and Oliver Fürbeth (eds), *Music in German Philosophy: An Introduction*, Chicago: University of Chicago Press, 69–93.

Scholtz, Gunter (2010), 'Schleiermacher', in Stefan Lorenz Sorgner and Oliver Fürbeth (eds), *Music in German Philosophy: An Introduction*, Chicago: University of Chicago Press, 47–68.

Scruton, Roger (2016), 'Programme Music', *Oxford Music Online*, <http://oxfordindex.oup.com/view/10.1093/gmo/9781561592630.article.22394>.

Scrutton, Anastasia Philippa (2008), *God, Emotion and Impassibility*, 2 vols, Durham University PhD dissertation.

Shedd, William G. T. (1888), *Dogmatic Theology*, 3 vols, New York: Scribners.

Spencer, Herbert (1855), *The Principles of Psychology*, 2 vols, London: Williams and Norgate.

Spencer, Herbert (1867), *First Principles*, 2nd edn, London: Williams and Norgate.

Spencer, Herbert (1884), 'Religion: A Retrospect and Prospect', *Nineteenth Century*, 15 (January): 1–12.

Spencer, Herbert (1951), *Literary Style and Music: Including Two Short Essays on Gracefulness and Beauty*, New York: Philosophical Library.

Spencer, Jane (2013), '"Love and Hatred are Common to the Whole Sensitive Creation": Animal Feeling in the Century before Darwin', in Angelique Richardson (ed.), *After Darwin: Animals, Emotions, and the Mind*, Amsterdam: Rodopi.

Thompson, Thomas R. (2006), 'Nineteenth-Century Kenotic Christology: The Waxing, Waning, and Weighing of a Quest for a Coherent Orthodoxy', in C. Stephen Evans (ed.), *Exploring Kenotic Christology: The Self-Emptying of God*, Oxford: Oxford University Press, 74–111.

Weinandy, Thomas G. (2000), *Does God Suffer?*, Notre Dame: University of Notre Dame Press.

Welsh, The Rev. David (1825), *Account of the Life and Writings of Thomas Brown M.D.*, Edinburgh: W. & C. Tait.

Williams, Robert R. (2012), *Tragedy, Recognition, and the Death of God: Studies in Hegel and Nietzsche*, Oxford: Oxford University Press.

Zon, Bennett (2018), 'Spencer, Sympathy and the Oxford School of Music Criticism', in Jeremy Dibble and Julian Horton (eds), *British Music Criticism 1850–1950*, Woodfield: Boydell and Brewer.

8

Miracles

Ruth Barton

Introduction: The Miraculous as Problem in Victorian England

Miracle and prophecy are losing their influence over the minds of men; they are no longer put forward as the impregnable bulwarks of religion, but are withdrawn to a more secure place in the background . . . The imagination may still linger over the ancient and pleasing fictions, so long intertwined with the religious feelings of all the nations who have drawn their creeds from Palestine; but calm reason is unable to acknowledge them longer as facts. A dispassionate examination persuades us that there is no sufficient ground for believing that that land, more than others, has witnessed interruptions or suspensions of the laws of nature: . . . the sun and moon have, in all probability, ever pursued their regular course over the valleys of Judea; [the] attraction of gravitation has probably never ceased to operate on the sea of Galilee. (Hennell 1839: 1)

This is not the rhetoric of T. H. Huxley, although 'calm reason' was a favourite trope of his. Rather, it is the opening paragraph of a small book on *Christian Theism* written by Charles Hennell in 1839, when Huxley was but a youth of fourteen, beginning a medical apprenticeship in Coventry. Hennell had links to Coventry; his sisters were members of the Unitarian circle among whom Marian Evans 'lost' her evangelical faith and expanded her intellectual horizons. As Adrian Desmond (1994) presents him, Huxley's philosophical, religious and political commitments were also shaped by Unitarians in Coventry.

Understanding of miracles underwent a sea change in Victorian England. At the end of the eighteenth century, miracles and fulfilled prophecy were regarded by many, even Joseph Priestley, the renowned chemist and Unitarian advocate of rational Christianity, as good evidence for the truth of the Christian revelation. Over the following century, miracles were subject to sceptical analysis. By the end of the nineteenth century, bishops of the Church of England had to decide if they were willing to ordain as priests men who doubted the central miracles of the Christian gospel (Chadwick [1970] 1980: 145–6); this implies that doubts on lesser miracles were acceptable.

This essay takes three examples of critical analysis of the miraculous from the Victorian period. First, Charles Hennell, cited above, who argued in his 1838 *Inquiry Concerning the Origin of Christianity* that the miracles apparently reported in the New Testament had not occurred and were later elaborations or interpretations of natural events. Hennell was largely ignored, but my second example, the Rev. Professor Baden Powell, was too well known to be easily ignored. Through the 1840s and 1850s, culminating in his contribution to the notorious *Essays and Reviews* (1860), he argued that, in the contemporary stage of intellectual development, miracles had no evidential value in convincing doubters of the truth of Christian belief. Many considered that Powell himself denied miracles and accused him of heresy, but Powell's own beliefs are not easily characterised. The third case study examines a small number of papers on miracles presented to the secretive Metaphysical Society in the mid-1870s. In the Society, brilliant representatives of many occupations and beliefs debated the central metaphysical, epistemological and moral concerns of their day.[1]

This essay was initially framed as a study of interactions between naturalistic science and theology, or the advocates of naturalistic and theological understandings of the world. But science and theology do not represent two distinct groups of people, as the examples of Hennell and Powell clearly demonstrate. The 'conflicts' of an older historiography were as much within individual minds as between two 'armies' of Science and Religion, as James Moore (1979) pointed out. In Moore's terms, miracles produced cognitive dissonance for many Victorians and, as the opening example illustrates, this was not something felt uniquely strongly by scientific men. The case studies here illustrate the development of naturalistic arguments; individually they are contributions to neglected topics in the history of theological argument and literary studies.

The resulting argument takes sides on a major historiographic divide in the history of science, a long-standing difference of interpretation on the roots of naturalistic science. Following Frank Turner (1974b), interpretations of naturalistic thinking in Victorian England have focused on the so-called scientific naturalists, who based their naturalistic interpretations on the authority of science rather than the more rationalistic, Enlightenment-rooted anti-supernaturalism of the early nineteenth century. As Gowan Dawson and Bernard Lightman paraphrase Turner, the proponents of scientific naturalism were scientific 'because nature was interpreted according to three major mid-century scientific theories, the atomic theory of matter, the conservation of energy, and evolution' (2014: 11). Some historians, of whom Lightman is one, use the descriptor 'evolutionary naturalism' to 'foreground the contribution of Darwin' (ibid. 9). Against this tradition of interpretation, Robert Young ([1970] 1985) argued that Darwin should be understood as a participant in a longer tradition of naturalistic thinking that went back at least as far as his grandfather, and drew on rationalistic arguments and on much less respectable sciences, such as phrenology, mesmerism and Owenite socialism. The argument developed here supports the interpretations of Young. The case studies show that naturalistic arguments against miracles had no uniquely strong association with science.

This essay is a highly selective account of Victorian discussions over miracles. My topic is not 'miracles', as in the title, but, as elaborated in the subtitle of the introduction, 'the miraculous as problem' in Victorian England. I omit devotional understanding (hundreds, if not thousands, of articles on 'the miracles of our Lord'), theological elaboration and reinterpretation, elaborations of scientific understandings of the order of nature which allowed space for miracles, and vigorous Catholic–Protestant debate over contemporary miracles, such as the reported healings at Lourdes. These omissions risk reinforcing 'the old "triumphalist history of the secular"' (Talal Asad, quoted in LaPorte 2013: 277). As LaPorte argues (ibid. 278), the kind of account given here ignores the extent and power of conventional religion, and risks enshrining honest doubters as heroes. By making this limitation explicit I hope to partially counter the implicit prejudice. A broader range of contemporary reflection on the relationship of natural/divine order and divine intervention has entered mainstream scholarship on the seventeenth century; for the nineteenth century, Crosbie Smith's research (1998) on physicists and engineers around William

Thomson opens up alternative scientific understandings of divine free will and the miraculous; and the broad comparative perspective of *The Cambridge Companion to Miracles* (Twelftree 2011) escapes the narrowness of Western secularist perspectives.

Charles Hennell: The Unitarians and German Theology

Charles Christian Hennell (1809–50) was a home-grown, Unitarian critic of the miraculous. According to the leading historian of Victorian Unitarianism, R. K. Webb, 'in the latter part of the eighteenth century, Unitarians accepted and confidently defended miracles; by the end of the nineteenth century, miracles had been largely explained away; but in the roughly one hundred years in between, they were a problem' (2000: 113). Among Unitarians, Hennell was one of the first thoroughgoing critics of the miraculous aspects of Christian faith.

Hennell is a much-overlooked figure. Although he is well known to scholars of George Eliot's life as one of the Coventry circle among whom she turned away from her strict evangelical faith, he merges into that group. Previous analyses of Unitarian critiques of the miraculous (Dodd 1981; Webb 2000) have focused not on Hennell, but on Unitarian responses to David Strauss's *Das Leben Jesu* (1835–6).[2] This emphasis gives the mistaken impression that Strauss was the chief stimulus to Unitarian rethinking on miracles. The general neglect may be because few sources are available. A memoir by Hennell's sister, Sara (1899), which was privately printed, is extremely rare. The fullest account of Hennell is Basil Willey's study of Hennell as one of the 'formative influences' on George Eliot ([1949] 1966: 207–20). An even older classic, J. M. Robertson's *History of Freethought in the Nineteenth Century* (1929), is a valuable addition to the limited literature because he draws on Sara Hennell's *Memoir*. Ian Sellers justifiably protests, in the *Oxford Dictionary of National Biography* entry on Hennell, that Hennell, and his sisters, should be considered 'in their own right and not merely an episode in the intellectual development of George Eliot' (2004: 375).

Hennell's *Inquiry Concerning the Origin of Christianity* (1838) was a response to the concerns of his sister Caroline. In 1835, Caroline married Charles Bray, 'free thinker and social reformer', an advocate for phrenology, philosophical necessity and cooperation (Lee 2004: 401). He took d'Holbach's *System of Nature* and Volney's *Ruins of Empires* on honeymoon, expecting to persuade Caroline of his sceptical and deterministic views. Instead, she was shocked at the extent of his religious scepticism, and appealed to her brother to counter Bray's arguments and defend the fundamentals of their Unitarian faith. It was Charles Hennell who was persuaded by Charles Bray, rather than vice versa.

Hennell presented himself in the preface to his *Inquiry* (1838) as a sincere enquirer. He began, he said, from the hypothesis admitted by many previous critics, that 'there is a mixture of truth and fable in the four Gospels'; he wished to determine the extent to which Christianity had a divine origin, or, to what extent the miraculous narratives were credible (1838: iii). His method he described as the same method of 'free investigation' that led Priestley and Thomas Belsham to throw doubt on the opening chapters of Matthew and Luke (ibid. iii). Priestley had argued that the early chapters of Luke, asserting Christ's miraculous conception, were later interpolations, inserted in support of Trinitarian claims; they were not in the oldest manuscripts. But although Priestley and Belsham rejected a few particular miracles, they believed, like other Protestants, that miracles were a sign of Christ's divine mission. As Webb paraphrases Belsham:

> What man of understanding ... could be satisfied with explaining the stilling of the tempest as settling a quarrel between the disciples and the boatmen or the ascension

as an imposture? 'Must they not certainly know, that to deny the miracles of Christ is to deny his divine mission, which is itself a miracle; and that, in fact, it is downright infidelity?' (2000: 120)

In this tradition, Hennell expected to find that 'the principal miraculous facts supposed to lie at the foundation of Christianity would be found impregnable' (1838: iii). Instead, he became convinced that 'the life of Jesus Christ, and of the spread of his religion' could be explained solely by 'the operation of human motives and feelings, acted upon by the peculiar circumstances of [that] age and country' (1838: iv). Although the argument presented in *Inquiry* is often circular, as if he assumed that miracles could not occur, the biographical account supports his claim to be a sincere enquirer. He had not begun from the assumption that miracles could not happen, although that was the conclusion he reached. Moreover, Hennell's arguments were no simple extension of traditional Unitarian arguments. Priestley had argued about corruptions and interpolations in ancient manuscripts; Hennell offered a more complex account of the authorship and dating of the New Testament books and an account of Jesus's self-understanding as shaped by the hopes of the Essenes for the overthrow of the Roman overlords. My objectives here are to examine the arguments used by Hennell and make some preliminary suggestions about his sources, preliminary because there is little prior research which would enable me to locate Unitarian theological traditions within the history of biblical criticism.

Hennell's *Inquiry* was both a life of Jesus and a history of the early church. He asked: where did Jesus come from? How did he understand himself and his mission? What did his followers expect? According to Hennell, from the time of the Babylonian captivity the Jews 'compensated themselves for their present insignificance with the expectation of future greatness' (1838: 1). They looked for a future prince who would overthrow the Romans. Jesus grew up in Galilee where Essene passions led to occasional insurrections; he came to share the widespread hopes that a Jewish state would be established and saw himself as having a crucial role in bringing about a new righteous order:

> The perception of his own mental elevation over those around him led him to indulge the idea, not unnatural to any ardent Israelite, that he himself was to be the prophet and prince, like unto Moses, who should fill the restored throne of David. (Ibid. 21)

Jesus began preaching, in conformity with Jewish tradition and the emphases of the Essenes, against the corruptions of the age. He shared the notions of his time that 'mental superiority' would give him some power over the natural world and when implored by the crowds, sought 'to heal their maladies' and had 'apparent success' (ibid. 24). He gained a following in Galilee, but events did not turn out as he hoped. No influential towns supported him; both Roman and Jewish authorities considered him a threat to public order. Rather than retreat into obscurity and failure, Jesus decided to proclaim his message in Jerusalem, knowing that he risked martyrdom. He began to tell his followers that the Messiah would suffer before he reigned (ibid. 28–30). This, in outline, is how Hennell gave a psychologically coherent account of Jesus's self-understanding.

The major part of Hennell's argument is closer to the familiar German tradition of biblical criticism. He discussed the possible sources for the gospels, the differences and disagreements between them, and the order of their writing. At the heart of his argument was the general finding, or assertion, applied to all the canonical New Testament books, that the later the date of composition, the more miraculous the events recounted; and, conversely, those books closer in time to the events recounted fewer marvellous events. The epistles, most of which were written before the gospels, make few allusions to miracles (ibid. 209–10). There are fewer miracles recorded in Acts, which dates from before the gospels, than in the gospels. This is especially true of those latter parts of Acts where Luke was himself a participant in events (ibid. 100). Close analysis of the gospels shows the same pattern. John's Gospel, written late in the first century, includes miracles 'of a more bold and marvellous character' than those in the other gospels, most notably the raising of Lazarus from death (ibid. 106, 181–4).

At times, when the correlation between late date of writing and more numerous or more marvellous miracles failed, Hennell's argument became less straightforward, as in his comparison of Matthew and Mark. In Hennell's chronology, Matthew was first (ibid. 64), Mark drew on Matthew and some other source or sources (ibid. 87), and Luke drew on Matthew, Mark and other sources (ibid. 95). (Luke was last, written after the destruction of the temple in Jerusalem in AD 71, because, as it quoted Jesus as saying that the temple would be reduced to a pile of stones, it must date from after the fact.) Hennell admitted that, against the general thesis, Mark omitted, rather than elaborated, some miracles recounted by Matthew. He omitted Jesus's miraculous birth, the dream of Pilate's wife and the earthquake at Jesus's death because, Hennell explained, 'he did not believe them and did not expect to be believed if he related them' (ibid. 89–90). Similarly, differences between Luke and the earlier synoptics show that Luke did not consider Matthew and Mark 'the best authorities' (ibid. 96). Thus when the later gospel omits a miracle, Hennell used the omission to throw doubt on the authority of the earlier.

After many chapters of such arguments about both miracles and the parallel topic of fulfilled prophecies, Hennell concluded that Jesus was an enthusiast, a revolutionary, a reformer and 'a moral and religious leader' (ibid. ch. 16), a man of his own time and place. Except, and it was a big exception, 'the Prophet and Martyr of Galilee' is a representative of human virtue, especially in 'his benevolent doctrine, attractive character, and elevated designs' (ibid. 333). The evidences of a supernatural birth, miraculous works, a resurrection or an ascension are not sufficient to distinguish these tales from fictions, to be 'classed amongst the fables of an obscure age' (ibid. 358–9). Nevertheless, through these mistaken beliefs, Christianity has 'consolidated the moral and religious sentiments into . . . [an] influential form . . . which has worked powerfully towards humanizing and civilizing the world' (ibid. 362).

Hennell's theological and critical sources are not easily determined.[3] Most of his references are to classical sources and the Church Fathers. Joseph Priestley accepted the same traditional authority when he emphasised in the preface to his *History of Early Opinions Concerning Jesus Christ* that he argued from 'original writers, without even looking into any modern author whatever' (1786: x). But Priestley admitted that he checked modern authorities to see how their opinions differed from his own, and to identify any sources he had missed (1786: xi), thus his emphasis on ancient sources refers to his evidence being from original writers and cannot be taken to mean that he took no ideas from contemporary authors. It may also be that the historic appeal to the early church and its traditions was intended to carry more weight with readers than any admitted acknowledgement of modern criticism. Hennell's gospel chronology (Matthew, Mark, Luke) was argued from internal evidence and the Church Fathers, rather than any contemporary German theological authorities, and his account of the Essenes relied generally on Josephus and does not mention the then-notorious accounts of Bahrdt and Venturini (to be discussed below).

Modern scholarship offers only a few clues to more contemporary sources for Hennell. John Rogerson's study of Old Testament criticism (1984) has implications for biblical criticism in general, for he identifies Unitarians who provided links between German biblical criticism and English. As a young man, Heinrich Paulus visited England in 1788 and was entertained by leading Unitarians at Cambridge (Rogerson 1984: 159). The *Critical Review*, although edited by an Anglican, reviewed important German biblical criticism in the 1790s (ibid. 159–61). Other scholars have identified William Taylor (1765–1836) as a significant link between the *Critical Review* and German biblical criticism in the early nineteenth century (Chandler 1997, 2004; Christensen 1959). Taylor, who was from a Norwich Unitarian merchant family, contributed to English knowledge of German literature. In preparation for commercial life, he had learned European languages and travelled widely in Europe, including an extended visit of a year to Germany in 1781–2. When trade declined during the Napoleonic wars, he was happy to turn from commerce to literature (Chandler 2004; 1997: 362–6). Through numerous articles in the *Monthly Review*, *Critical Review* and *Monthly Magazine*, and by lending books from his own extensive library, he played a major role in bringing German literature to the English-speaking world (Chandler 1997, 2004; Christensen 1959: 180–1). Belsham, for example, was familiar with German historical criticism (Webb 2000: 120).

It may be that Taylor had more interest in German literature than German theology (as Chandler implies), and it appears that he developed his own theological views more fully on Old than New Testament criticism (Christensen 1959: 184–92), but it is the latter, on which he reviewed German works rather than writing independent analyses, that is most relevant here. His lengthy review of Heinrich Paulus's *Philologische-kritischer und historischer Commentar über die drei ersten Evangelien* (1800–2) is a significant example. Taylor intended to write three articles. The first and second articles, thirty and twenty-five pages long, respectively, summarised volumes I and II section by section (Taylor 1809a, 1809b). The outcry against heresy was so great that the *Critical Review* discontinued publication and Taylor turned the third article into a provocative pamphlet. I list just three points of interpretation relevant to Hennell. The order of the Gospels was Matthew, Luke, Mark according to Paulus, but Taylor thought Mark was closest to an earlier original. On two issues Taylor agreed with Paulus: Christianity grew out of a Messianic sect among the Jews, possibly the Essenes; and Zechariah was the father of Jesus (Christensen 1959: 189–92).

The Taylor–Paulus connection shows, first, that among Unitarian writers there was knowledge of German biblical criticism and that this was publicly available through major reviews in the early nineteenth century. Second, it provides a possible source for Jesus-as-Essene, the most unusual of Hennell's interpretations. Third, although Taylor and Paulus are possible sources, this rapid outline suggests that Hennell was thinking independently. His gospel chronology followed neither the German, Paulus, nor his English reviewer; he did not propose Zechariah as father of Jesus; he greatly elaborated the Essene theory.

The Essene theory can be traced back to Baron d'Holbach, Karl Friedrich Bahrdt and Karl Heinrich Venturini. In his sarcastic 1778 *Ecce Homo: Histoire critique de Jésus-Christ*, d'Holbach asserted that Jesus drew upon the doctrines of the Essenes (chs 3 and 17; 1778: 51, 184–5). According to Bahrdt (in a lengthy work published c. 1784–92), the Essenes were seeking to spiritualise the political Messianic hopes of the Jewish masses. Alexandrian Jews marked out Jesus soon after his birth and endeavoured to shape his education; Nicodemus and Joseph of Arimathea were powerfully placed members of the order who assisted in faking Jesus's death and resurrection (Schweitzer [1906] 1954: 39–44). Venturini, in a provocatively titled *Natürliche Geschicte des grossen Propheten von Nazereth*

(1800–2), also interpreted the Essenes and Jesus as turning Messianic expectations in more spiritual directions, but his chief actors were less underhand. In Egypt, Essene brothers had watched over the child, back in Palestine his education by the Essenes included the use of herbal remedies, but Jesus out-grew the Essenes and his independent actions roused concern among Roman and Jewish authorities. The Essenes did not plan his arrest and crucifixion; the Essene brothers thought him dead; his survival was a joyful surprise (Schweitzer [1906] 1954: 44–7). In Paulus's interpretation of Jesus's ambitions, as summarised by Taylor, it was Mary who was the source of Messianic hopes for Jesus, she brought him up with these hopes, and this destiny was believed within the family circle (Taylor 1809a: 454–9, 466–7). He was probably educated 'in some *Midrash*, or convent school of the Essenes', where he would have acquired some healing arts (ibid. 469), and so it continues. The particular Essene-story promulgated by Hennell was different: Jesus's messianic ambitions originated in his own observations of local political and religious life. Hennell's interpretation avoids all elements of conspiracy or deception. Schweitzer's accusation that Hennell is only Venturini 'tricked out with a fantastic paraphernalia of learning' ([1906] 1954: 161) is unjustified. This excursion into long-rejected theories provides no firm evidence as to whom Hennell read or admired. Given Bray's book choices, he had probably read d'Holbach, he had access to Paulus's theories through Taylor's summary, but he searched the original sources for himself and, as he emphasised to his sister Sara, his chief sources were Josephus and the Old Testament (Robertson 1929: 65).

Hennell's gospel chronology of Matthew, Mark, Luke, followed decades later by John was the traditional but outdated chronology. Since J. J. Griesbach's *Synopsis Evangeliorum* (1776) the received order was Matthew, Luke, Mark (Kümmel [1970] 1973: 75). On the other hand, Hennell emphasised that the Gospel of John, with its strong theological interpretations, was later and quite different from the synoptics, a theory that was established by Griesbach.

A conspiracy of silence greeted Hennell's book. According to his sister Sara, Unitarian ministers agreed that the most effective response was to avoid any allusion that might bring the book to public attention (Robertson 1929: 142). Seven years later a Unitarian critic used this silence to prove the book's unimportance: 'We are not aware that this volume has been *deemed worthy* of public attention' (ibid. 142). There are few traces of any responses: Tractarians at Oxford described it as 'miserable blasphemy', an Italian translation was put on the index, although, in the United States, Emerson reviewed it 'respectfully' (ibid. 142). It cost twelve shillings, which limited its readership, but even expensive books could be widely reviewed. I have found only one review, and that of the second, 1841 edition.

The *Inquiry* was reviewed extremely critically in the first, 1845, number of the Unitarian's new *Prospective Review*. Historians of Unitarianism emphasise that nineteenth-century Unitarianism was divided (for the fullest account, see Short 1968). The tradition of Priestley was dogmatically anti-Trinitarian and propagandist. It claimed to represent rational Christianity; sought to persuade others to identify as 'Unitarian', and moved to optimistic determinism and anti-miraculous interpretations. (Research is needed to identify how views such as Hennell's emerged from the defence of miracles by Priestley and Belsham.) A reaction against this exclusive version of Unitarianism was led in the 1840s by James Martineau, John Hamilton Thom and J. J. Tayler. They emphasised broad inclusive Christianity, an approach more characteristic of the pre-Priestley, English Presbyterianism of the eighteenth century; but took up the Coleridgean emphasis on internal conviction or religious feeling as more important than rational proof of the truth of Christian belief (ibid. 252–60). The *Prospective Review* represented the new school and Thom was the anonymous reviewer.

The review damned the argument, although not the author. The argument was 'a case of constructive treason, . . . a mixture of history, criticism, and *pure fiction*' ([Thom] 1845: 19). The fiction was Hennell's explanation of Jesus's ministry by Essenean ideals; his presentation of this account as an alternative to any '*supposition of miracle*, which he thinks he has excluded' (ibid. 19). Thom picked out two principle features of the account as unsatisfactory: the entirely speculative character of the Jesus-as-Essene story and the assumption that all miraculous elements of the gospels must be explained away. Nevertheless, he admitted that the review was written in an 'earnest and reverent' spirit (ibid. 48). This was an important qualification: Hennell was not to be classed with d'Holbach, Thomas Paine or the Rev. Richard Tayler whose accounts of Jesus and his followers were designed to give offence.

The review indicates that the conspiracy of silence against the book had not been entirely successful. 'We should not have been tempted to meddle' with such a book 'had we not heard certain rumours of the book being considered, in some quarters, unanswerable because unanswered' (ibid. 48). Thus seven years after first publication and four years after the Unitarian controversy over Strauss, Hennell's book had gained a following in some unspecified circles. As the next case study shows, arguments like Hennell's were discussed among theists, respectable free thinkers and even some Anglicans.

Baden Powell: From Anglican Orthodoxy to Unorthodoxy

Baden Powell (1796–1860) is best known among scholars for his contribution to the notorious *Essays and Reviews* of 1860. 'On the Study of the Evidences of Christianity' ([1860] 2000) was widely regarded as a repudiation of the possibility of miracles (for examples, see Shea and Whitla 2000: 72–3, 687). That an ordained clergyman and Oxford professor attacked the possibility of miracles was a theological and political scandal. The Reverend Professor Baden Powell was no young Unitarian, whose heresy could be ignored. Many of Powell's earlier books and articles with similar arguments had been severely criticised. After the publication of his *Essays on the Spirit of the Inductive Philosophy* (1855), the Bishop of London had forbidden Powell to preach in his diocese, but had to bow to higher authority when Powell was repeatedly invited to preach before the Royal family at Kensington Palace (Corsi 1988: 205). According to a non-conformist reviewer of *Christianity without Judaism* (1856), the work was both dangerous in itself and evidence of dangerous tendencies within the established church:

> If it were the work of some Unitarian divine, or of some laydisciple of Theodore Parker or Francis Newman, a very cursory notice would be all that its intrinsic merits would call for. But coming from a clergyman occupying Professor Powell's position in the Church of England, it acquires portentous significance. ([Reynolds] 1858: 414)

Powell's understanding of the miraculous went through significant changes, as Pietro Corsi shows in a substantial intellectual biography. In Powell's early works of the 1820s, he followed a long Protestant tradition, appealing to miracles and fulfilled prophecy as the basis of rational belief. By 1838, he allowed that miracles carried conviction only to those who already admitted the existence of a powerful god. He sought, unsuccessfully argues Corsi (1988: 188–9), to show that natural theology could provide persuasive evidence of the existence of God. He was critical of traditional natural theological arguments, for example, those arguments from design that relied on specific examples of design, attributing design to phenomena not explained by known laws. Rather, he argued, it was the universal uniformity of nature, which underlay all inductive science, that pointed to the existence of God. By the 1840s, instead of being evidence for the truth of Christian belief, Powell identified miracles as a problem, a hindrance to belief for many contemporaries. Analysis of the uniformity of nature as a philosophical principle and the extent to which it provided evidence of a transcendent mind or intelligence was at the heart of his later apologetic.

Although the function of miracles in Powell's apologetics changed significantly, much did not change. To the end of his life, Powell emphasised that good reasons must be given for belief. Throughout his life too, and here my emphasis differs from Corsi's, he insisted that some aspects of faith belong to the domain of revelation. Although he came to accept that something could be learned of God from nature, this was strictly limited. For the Christian believer there are also truths of revelation. At the end of his life, in the notorious essay of 1860, he wrote: 'In nature and from nature, by science and by reason, we neither have nor can possibly have any evidence of a Deity *working miracles*: – for that we must go out of nature and beyond reason' (Shea and Whitla 2000: 260). The task I set myself here is, by examining earlier and more elaborated statements about the truths of revelation and beliefs beyond reason, to clarify what he may have meant by this statement. This is to add a theological dimension to Corsi's analysis of Powell. As Corsi shows, Powell's preoccupations were philosophical and apologetic but, as I shall argue, he did not reject theological knowledge.

Baden Powell grew up among the Hackney Phalanx, or Clapton Sect (so named after the areas to the north-east of London where they lived), a group of wealthy, High Church Anglicans who were concerned at the expansion of Dissent in general and the aggressiveness of the Unitarians in particular. The Hackney Phalanx wanted to reaffirm Anglican privilege but believed that the church needed to re-establish its social and intellectual credibility in order to claim its due position. They criticised the isolationism and authoritarianism that characterised the contemporary Church of England. The church must respond to social change; it must establish its position by good works and good arguments. In keeping with these principles, Powell's mentors promoted the education of the poor, the building of local churches, higher education for the clergy – and sent young Baden Powell to Oriel College (Corsi 1988: 20, 74–5). At a time when Oxford University in general was intellectually and spiritually weak, Oriel was making a reputation for its scholarly and spiritual aspirations (ibid. 75). Powell graduated with first class honours in mathematics in 1817, having made good friendships among leading Anglican intellectuals, most notably Richard Whately, future Archbishop of Dublin.

Powell began his career in the unreformed Church of England. He was ordained a deacon at the end of 1819 and priest in 1821. He was offered, by relatives, the living of Plumstead in Kent, where he spent much of his time in experiments on light and heat and in his philosophical and theological studies (Corsi 2004). He reviewed regularly for the *British Critic*, the quarterly review promoted by the Hackney Phalanx. When Powell's wife of only three years became ill in 1824, they moved from the parish to Clapton, but Powell retained the living for the following two years, probably paying a curate some proportion of the income to perform the parish duties. In 1824 also, he was elected a Fellow of the unreformed Royal Society, and in 1827 appointed Savilian Professor of Geometry at Oxford (ibid.). At that time he had published no original scientific articles although he had reviewed works on astronomy, geology, zoology, chemistry and mechanics (see Corsi 1988: 310–13 for a bibliography). He remained at Oxford until his death in 1860.

Powell's most substantial publication from the period before his Oxford appointment indicates his Hackney inheritance: *Rational Religion Examined or Remarks on the Pretensions of Unitarianism* (1826). Here, he attacked the Unitarians' claim that they alone represented rational Christianity and argued that Anglicanism represented the tradition of 'reasonable Christianity' (Corsi 1988: 25–7, 73–4). The historic evidence of miracles and fulfilled prophecy showed the Christian revelation to be true. Against those who claimed that natural religion was sufficient, he used John Locke's argument that reason shows it is necessary to rely on Scripture. Revelation was necessary, for God could not be understood from nature; human reason could not grasp the divine. The doctrines of Unity and Trinity, and the Atonement, for example, must be accepted on the basis of revelation. Revelation was above reason but not against reason.

The situation at Oxford set new intellectual directions and political concerns for Powell. He turned his energies to improving the standard of mathematics teaching and engaged in academic politics, promoting the position of science in the curriculum, and the admission of Dissenters to the University. The intransigence of Oxford on curriculum reform and antagonism to the admission of Dissenters to the university made him increasingly impatient with church authority. Critics of the educational value of the natural sciences, including Whately, believed inductive studies had a weak epistemological status (ibid. 131). Powell devoted much of his writing over the following decades to giving, what Corsi aptly describes as, 'philosophical dignity' to science (ibid. 148, 150). He wrote on induction and causation, and elaborated what he called 'the inductive philosophy' as the heart of scientific argument (e.g. Powell 1855). On the political front, he sought to convince the educated clergy that they must take science seriously. In an 1832 pamphlet he warned: 'Scientific knowledge is rapidly spreading among *all classes* EXCEPT THE HIGHER and the consequence must be, that that Class *will no longer remain* THE HIGHER' (quoted in Corsi 1988: 116).

Powell was convinced by Thomas Arnold's *Principles of Church Reform* (1833) that the church must adapt itself to changing circumstances in order to be a truly national body. Oxford's refusal to admit Dissenters (until forced by Parliament in 1854) was further evidence of the inability of the church to respond to the modern world. The universities should benefit the nation, not only its Anglican portion, he insisted. At a time of political instability it was important that Dissenting ministers, who were in closer touch with the masses than were Anglican clergy, should be well educated (Corsi 1988: 120–1).

The Hackney emphasis on giving good reasons for Christian belief remained one of the constants in Baden Powell's theology. He quoted Scripture on the need to 'give a reason for the hope that is within us' (1857: 169; [1860] 2000: 261), or elaborated in his own, often-turgid style:

> In a religion claiming to be *true*, professing to trace its origin in historical events, and connecting itself with tangible facts, as it must be supposed that the grounds of these claims would be of a kind prominently distinguishable, and unambiguous in their character; so it might be expected that they would always be held forth by the disciples and advocates of the faith, and that the study of them would be the first object of attention, as well with consistent believers as with candid enquirers of every class. (1857: 196)

According to Powell, Tractarians, Evangelicals and the modern advocates of the authority of religious feeling all failed to give good reasons. He presented himself as a defender of rational belief, even defining faith in 1846 as 'well-founded and rational belief' (1857: 195).

Initially, in the 1830s, Powell and his friends were concerned at the authoritarianism of the Oxford Movement (Corsi 1988: 145). Telling doubters to believe because some higher or older authority said so only turned them into sceptics, he argued. The 'mystical pretensions of the prevalent theological system' produced the 'Spirit of Unbelief' (1847: 397). Those who saw themselves as on opposing sides were accused by Powell of the same error: 'High Orthodoxists' and 'earnest preachers of what is termed the Low, or Evangelical school' concur in discarding 'all use of human reason in divine things' (1857: 180). He used deliberately provocative words. The High party was no better that 'the Romanist' ([1860] 2000: 237). In the 1860 essay Powell tried to entangle his opponents in knots of their own inconsistencies. How could they object to his argument that miracles were not good evidence for faith when they themselves said it was wrong to rely on any external evidence?

Powell classified transcendentalists and others who identified inner feeling as the basis of certainty in religion in this same 'mystical' party. Coleridge might be regarded as a 'prophet' but Powell declared that he would be 'slow to trust' him (1847: 417). 'He combines extremely orthodox opinions with a kind of mystical transcendentalism not always easy to interpret, if indeed he well understood his own meaning' (1857: 180). The American transcendentalist, Theodore Parker, finds 'the first germ of all religion is represented to reside in a sort of intuitive sense of infirmity, helplessness, and dependence; to this is superadded a natural feeling of awe and veneration of the vast and unknown' (1847: 400–1). This was not Christian faith, declared Powell:

> A highly poetical religion ... is here set before us, and is described with fearless and glowing eloquence. But, instead of recognising in it the religion of the New Testament, we feel that we are looking at a series of dissolving views, which, even while we are gazing on them, make themselves air. ... Christianity is a historical religion, with supernatural attestations. Its external facts have to be verified, as well as our spiritual nature to be lifted up and set at rest. (1847: 401)

Corsi (1988: 147) argues that in the mid-1830s, through the friendship of his second wife with Blanco White, who had transitioned from Catholicism, to doubt, to Anglicanism, to Unitarianism, Powell had become open to intuitive justifications of belief. While he was undoubtedly sympathetic to doubters and alternative believers, and friendly with White, with the Unitarian William Benjamin Carpenter, and with the theist, Francis Newman, my reading of his articles on apologetics (especially those of 1846, 1847 and 1857) is that when he allowed a role for the moral sense and intuition in confirming belief, he gave those beliefs quite orthodox theological content. For example, rather than feeling some grand sense of oneness with the universe, or a mystery behind everything, when Powell appealed to internal assurance his exemplars of truths deeply felt were 'The reasonableness and sublimity of the Christian doctrines – their practical excellence, their consistency with the Divine perfections, and with the moral relations of man, and the power with which they come home to the conscience' (1846: 418).

Powell's analysis of scientific argument and his apologetic purposes came together in the consistent argument of his later works that the common ground of inductive science, the inductive philosophy as he called it, was the principle of the uniformity of nature. The basis of his entire argument, he wrote, was

> the *one grand principle of law pervading nature, or rather constituting the very idea of nature;* – which forms the vital essence of the whole of inductive science, and the sole assurance of those higher inferences, from the inductive study of natural causes, which are the indications of a supreme intelligence and a moral cause. (1859: 230)

Scientific enquiry led to ever more examples of the unity of nature, the linking together of phenomena by networks of laws, in which those of lesser scope were subordinated to others of higher generality (ibid. 229). On the one hand, this meant that those who best understood the principles of science were least likely to interpret any event as miraculous and, as he provocatively stated the problem in the 1860 essay, miracles, once seen as among 'the chief *supports* of Christianity' have become 'the main *difficulties*, and hindrances to its acceptance' (ibid. 127).

On the other hand, the utter uniformity of the laws of nature provided, Powell argued, a firm foundation for faith, a 'most philosophic defence of Revelation' (1847: 410). The order of nature demonstrated that behind it all was 'supreme intelligence', or 'universal mind and intelligence' (1857: 170, 183), 'universal reason' or, in the words cited above, 'supreme intelligence and a moral cause' (1859: 233, 230). We may not always be able to identify the relevant laws of nature but we can expect that laws will be discovered to cover those relationships still obscure: 'when we cease to trace the law, we are sure that law remains to be traced' (ibid. 231). He came to admit that different arguments appealed to different minds but, in his view, only the argument from the uniformity of nature provided rational conviction.

Powell allowed no exceptions: the moral world was as encompassed within the uniformity of nature as was the physical world. Indeed, 'the comprehensiveness of the Divine operations in the guidance of the moral as well as the physical creation' contributed to 'worthy conceptions' of God's 'interposition in the regulation of human affairs' (1847: 409). These moral laws were 'comparatively little open to our examination' – whether Powell thought this was a temporary or permanent condition is unclear – but 'the reasoning mind cannot doubt' that the moral world is governed by uniform and universal laws (ibid. 409). Many theistic writers excluded the moral realm from the natural order. Powell's inclusion of the moral within nature aligns him with the leading naturalistic thinkers of the following generation (Barton 2014: 213–14). Also, in agreement with naturalistic thinkers, Powell was willing to countenance theories of species development. He allowed that something like the slow process of *Vestiges* might have occurred. Creation though was something quite different: 'a first origin cannot be *explained* by any physical laws or causes', creation belongs to the language of theology (1857: 188–9).

Alongside his insistence on the universal operation of natural law, Powell affirmed the need for revelation. There was a domain of moral and spiritual truth on which physical science provided no insight. The foundation, in physical science 'however solidly laid, rises no higher than to the lowest basement' or, to change the metaphor, is 'just a meagre skeleton' (1855: 300). Powell constantly used theological language when summing up his conclusions. In 1847, he insisted that 'human judgements can never advance one step toward *revealed* truth' (1847: 213) and, in passing, described and by implication accepted 'the gospel, as a positive Divine revelation' (ibid. 214). Given the changes over time in Powell's views (as Corsi emphasises), it is necessary to show that this was not just a temporary opinion. I therefore emphasise that this kind of positive theological affirmation can be found even in his late publications. In 1859, he reminded his readers that though he insisted on a strict boundary between the deductions of science and 'higher truths', this was not meant 'as a *negation* of higher truths; but only that they are of *another order*'. He listed some examples of such higher truths: 'elevated spiritual views of a Deity, – a personal God, – an Omnipotent Creator, – a moral Governor – a Being of infinite spiritual perfections, – holding relations with the spirit of man; – the object of worship, trust, fear, love' (1859: 248–9). He emphasised that there had been continuity in his views: 'the point especially insisted on in the former essays was, that the extremely limited extent of strict inferences from the order of nature forms the very ground for looking to other and higher sources of information and illumination' (ibid. 249). One hundred and fifty years later, this sounds remarkably orthodox, a great deal more orthodox than Hennell, or Powell's friend, Francis Newman.

Given the serious theological allusions in Powell's mature writing, it cannot be assumed that his affirmation, in the infamous essay, that miracles should be regarded 'in a sacred light' ([1860] 2000: 260) had no meaning for him, and was merely an attempt to placate an orthodox opposition.[4] In 1847, he had tried to make sense of miracles from both a theological and a physical point of view. 'Supernatural agency' might be 'interposed in a variety of ways' (1847: 410). A marvellous occurrence might, from a physical point of view, be 'a coincidence with the pre-established order of events', while, from a theological point of view, it attested a 'moral and religious revelation' (ibid. 410). Here he alluded both to the pre-programmed surprises in orderly sequences of numbers produced by Charles Babbage's calculating machine, showing that laws can produce the unexpected, and to the long theological tradition that true miracles were defined not by reference to laws of nature but, jointly, by the wonder they evoked and by their function in attesting a new revelation. Alternatively, Powell proposed, miracles may arise in the form of 'communications between the Holy Spirit and the soul of man', such as had been promised by God (ibid. 410). In later essays, Powell criticised the wholesale reinterpretations of miracle by German rationalist theologians. Although individual miracles might be explained by the mythical interpretation of Strauss or the naturalistic explanations of Paulus, taken as a whole, the interpretations of Paulus seem 'extravagantly forced and puerile' (1859: 414) and Strauss reads as 'a caricature' (ibid. 416).

These hints and proposals and criticisms do not add up to a coherent interpretation of the miraculous. It may be that Powell, as he accused Coleridge, did not well understand his own meaning (1857: 180); more likely he knew that he had failed to make sense, for he did not develop the hints from the 1847 essay. It seems that Powell was fumbling unsuccessfully for some interpretation that gave miracles, interpreted as signs and wonders rather than as interventions in the order of nature, both physical and theological meaning. Nevertheless, he was widely judged a heretic.

The Metaphysical Society: Law, Science and Philosophy Claim Authority on Miracles

At the beginning of 1876, T. H. Huxley delivered 'The Evidence of the Miracle of the Resurrection', one of the more controversial presentations of his controversial career, to an audience of fourteen at the Metaphysical Society. It was never published (or not until 2015) as even radical Victorian editors deemed it too provocative a treatment of a sensitive topic (Desmond 1997: 84–5). According to Adrian Desmond (ibid. 84–5), it gave offence to some members of that first audience, even though the members were committed to open and courteous discussion and had heard many previous provocative arguments. The received account of the Metaphysical Society has been that discussion of Huxley's paper was extended to the following meeting of January 1876, 'the only paper so honoured' (Brown 1947: 317).

The recent publication of the Metaphysical Society's papers allows for closer assessment of the discussions about miracles, including Huxley's own presentation, at the Society, and enables a less Huxley-centric view. Huxley's paper was the third in a series of papers on miracles. First, in November 1875, the lawyer, James Fitzjames Stephen, presented 'Remarks on the Proof of Miracles', followed in December by the Unitarian physiologist, W. B. Carpenter, 'On the Fallacies of Testimony in Relation to the Supernatural', then Huxley, then the open discussion and, last in the sequence, in March 1876, a philosopher, Shadworth Hodgson, on 'The Pre-Suppositions of Miracles'. The editors of *The Papers of the Metaphysical Society* make clear that the February discussion was intended to cover all three preceding papers (Marshall et al. 2015: 2:326).

The Metaphysical Society had been founded at the end of 1869 with the intention of bringing greater understanding across all shades of religious and irreligious opinion. An initial plan to cover all shades of religious opinion in a theological society had been broadened after arguments that the naturalistic scientific men should not be defined as opposition, and the reassurance that those outside conventional religion would treat the beliefs of others with respect (Brown 1947: 21; Metcalf 1980: 214). It was agreed that discussions would be confidential, and that members would treat their opponents courteously and without personal approbation.

The 1875–6 discussions of the miraculous tried the goodwill of the participants. Lord Arthur Russell wrote to his brother that the debate after Carpenter's paper was

> brisker than usual. Frederic Harrison [positivist and lawyer] declared that he considered a belief in miracles as the commencement of insanity, and His Eminence [Cardinal Manning] replied that he considered an incapacity to believe in the supernatural as a commencement of ossification of the brain. (Marshall et al. 2015: 2:327)

It is possible to interpret this exchange as a play of wits; some members of the Society, for example W. G. Ward and T. H. Huxley, were renowned for their witticisms, but some credence must be given to the assessment of Russell, who knew the participants, that the exchange was sharper than usual.

Here, I outline the arguments of each of the four presenters and, to make my sources slightly less one-sided, I add the paper given three years previously by W. G. Ward, questioning 'Can Experience Prove the Uniformity of Nature?'. Ward was the brilliant, ebullient editor of the *Dublin Review*. In the 1830s and 1840s, he had been one of the most clubbable members of the Balliol Common Room. He moved from orthodox Anglicanism to Comtism to the Oxford Movement, and created a crisis for the Tractarians by arguing that the Thirty Nine Articles were consistent with Roman Catholic doctrine, thereby provoking an extreme reaction from the Convocation of Oxford University, which stripped him of his degrees in 1845. In the aftermath, he both married and, with his wife, converted to Roman Catholicism (O'Connell 1991: 323–5, 404–8; Gilley 2004).

Ward's informal piece on the uniformity of nature was designed to provoke discussion, rather than for publication. He argued that the strict empiricism on the basis of which opponents of the miraculous claimed to ground their arguments was completely inadequate as a foundation for the claimed principle of the uniformity of nature. If the 'phenomenists' were as empirical as they claimed, then they should investigate every alleged miracle 'with diligence and impartiality' (Ward [1872] 2015: 414). They could not claim that universal experience testifies to the uniform action of Nature if they refused to investigate claimed experiences that countered their principle. Their stated principle was therefore an 'arbitrary and ungrounded assumption' (ibid. 414). From the opposite direction, he argued that believers in the miraculous did not question the uniformity of nature, and therefore did not throw doubt on the legitimacy of inductive science. To claim a miracle was, by implication, to claim that there was 'an indubitable law of Nature which a miracle overrules' (ibid. 416).

Fitzjames Stephen was an eminent lawyer (QC 1868) and prolific journalist. He had a reputation for taking liberal causes, most notably, in the 1860s, defending one of Baden Powell's fellow essayists from heresy charges, and acting for the Jamaica Committee in accusing Governor Eyre of murder. Since 1869, he had been legal member of the Viceroy's Council in India. His paper is long and repetitive, neither incisive, nor deeply reflective. According to R. H. Hutton, a loyal attendee at meetings, Stephen's 'mighty bass' voice contributed authority to his opinions (Brown 1947: 107), and the paper may therefore have been more impressive to its original auditors than its later readers.

Stephen framed the problem of miracles as the equivalent of legal questions about the reliability of testimony. He rejected any discussion of miracles in terms of laws of nature for that would involve the critic in circularity, taking him outside the realm of fact and into the realm of cause. As a lawyer, Stephen dealt with facts and testimony. He mentioned that the English justice system was 'distinguished by the skill with which it provides for the investigation of matters of fact' ([1875] 2015: 335), a claim that was not relevant to the argument unless to establish that, as a leading lawyer, Stephen himself was an expert in determining matters of fact. His argument is a series of examples, real and hypothetical, of testimony which had been or would be insufficient to establish a legal case: an accusation of murder, from a single witness with no corroborating evidence, not even a dead body (ibid. 333); a commercial case where men of 'high character' on opposing sides gave completely contradictory evidence (ibid. 337); the ridicule with which a witness would be treated if he said an animal had provided him with information (ibid. 334); the impossibility of investigating the validity of a claim centuries after the death of the people involved (ibid. 339). (Here he revealed his literary orientation by overlooking the possibility of archaeological evidence.) He made no attempt to link his legal stories with any biblical or ecclesiastical miracles but the original audience would have noticed parallels.

Carpenter, who presented an even longer paper at the next meeting, was both man of science (a physiologist) and Christian believer, although, as a Unitarian believer, some orthodox Christians regarded him as outside the pale. On the issue of miracles he claimed to be open-minded, and in the 1840s had indeed accepted that the evidence of Christian miracles was sufficient for his assent (J. E. Carpenter 1888: 44), in spite of his friendship with Powell who was already espousing different views (Corsi 1988: 264). In 1875, his arguments often presumed that miracles did not happen. Carpenter began by citing the theist and ex-evangelical, Francis Newman, his friend of over thirty years (J. E. Carpenter 1888: 27), in support of the claim that scientific methods of enquiry applied to the study of religion would leave 'the true religious element [of belief] more pure' (W. B. Carpenter [1875] 2015: 347–8). He also made a strange opening claim that he found 'no abstract difficulty in the conception that the Author of Nature can, if He will, occasionally depart from that ordinary uniformity of sequence on which the man of Science bases his conception of the Laws of Nature' and did not 'presume to deny that there might be occasions which to His wisdom may require such departure' (ibid. 348). This was not a claim that Powell would have allowed; moreover, in the subsequent discussion he did not allow such possibilities at any point, and it therefore seems to be statement made in self-defence against potential charges of prejudice and prepossession.

Carpenter accepted Stephen's formulation of the problem as one of judging the reliability of evidence – although Stephen was not present to hear this acknowledgement. The scientist, unlike the lawyer, insisted that the validity of testimony on matters concerning the supernatural, where subjective elements loomed large, must be 'submitted to the severest scrutiny according to the strictest scientific methods' (ibid. 348), implying that the conventional methods of lawyers did not go far enough. On Carpenter's account, the scientific study of 'prepossessions' could explain the unreliability of witness statements. He placed himself in honourable company by announcing that his analysis of types of 'prepossession' paralleled 'Lord Bacon's analysis of the idols of the cave' (ibid. 347). Often, he explained, prepossessions derived from previous experience cause persons to misinterpret visual perceptions; in some cases of illness or physiological disturbance, sensations may be produced with no relationship to objective reality (ibid. 350–1). Then there are people who have waking dreams. Under this heading he placed contemporary spiritualist claims about table turning and communication with the dead, and the visions and trances of the ancient 'heathen' and Jewish worlds. Such dream-experiences were particularly common in highly imaginative people or those subject to religious enthusiasm, explained Carpenter, and were determined by the individual's prepossessions (ibid. 352). Carpenter turned his argument against modern spiritualism. People present at a séance may even see different things depending on their prepossessions. He instanced a group who saw the medium float out one window and in another while 'one honest sceptic' saw him sitting in the chair all the time (ibid. 354). (He did not raise the possibility that the sceptic could also have been suffering from 'prepossession'.) His final example was the effect of prepossession on memory or, in contemporary scientific terminology, 'memorial traces' (ibid. 356). Memories shift over time, becoming closer to what a person may have wished to have happened or with the details being shaped to fit a larger picture, a pattern of obvious relevance to the recording of the miracles of the saints or of Jesus himself.

Huxley's presentation the following month was brief and incisive, closer to the style of Ward than of Stephen or Carpenter. During discussion at the November and December meetings someone had asked that the sceptics consider a particular miracle rather than miracles in general (Huxley [1876] 2015: 366). Huxley took the challenge head-on, and prepared a paper on the miracle of the resurrection. In what seems like a Huxley egg-dance, he assured his audience that this example was not chosen with the intention of giving offence, indeed, because it was not a miracle performed by Jesus, to query the opinions held about the resurrection could be no criticism of Jesus himself (ibid. 367). Huxley was offering disingenuous explanations, which made it difficult for any opponent to accuse him of deliberate offensiveness. He emphasised that he entirely disagreed with the many who considered this miracle crucial to Christian belief (ibid. 367); however, as Huxley well knew, such a reassurance was only significant to those who, in the tradition of Hennell, considered that the moral teaching of Jesus was the only important part of Christian faith.

Huxley claimed authority on the topic because the first question at issue was 'whether the organism said to be dead was really dead'. As a biologist, he was particularly fitted to deal with death and resurrection. He had two arguments. The first was a biological distinction between somatic death and molecular death. Under the former, although the functions of the body cease, restoration is possible (ibid. 369–70), and this, he assumed, is what probably happened and that Jesus revived in the cool of the tomb. Of course, he argued, we can no longer know for sure, but this is an entirely plausible account and, he brought in one of his favourite arguments, given that we cannot be sure, it is morally wrong for a scientific man to say 'I believe' without incontrovertible proof (Barton 1983: 272). Others might have different moral standards but, he implied, these would be lower standards.

We know little of what the members thought of any of these papers. The discussion attracted eighteen members, more than the average of fourteen at the three presentations, but there are few hints of the issues discussed.[5] It is noteworthy that some of the chief protagonists were missing: Carpenter and Huxley, who had presented papers, did not attend the February discussion; Ward, the most incisive debater on the pro-miracle side, who had been at all three previous meetings, was missing; as was St George Jackson Mivart, the Catholic biologist who had likewise attended all three previous papers. It is possible that all four had other urgent engagements, but it seems likely that some of these significant participants chose to be absent.

Most of the arguments in these Metaphysical Society papers are not particularly subtle, but what stands out are the claims to authority: the lawyer had experience in deciding evidence; the scientific man followed in the steps of Bacon; science explained how honest observers could be misled by prepossession; the biologist could determine questions of death and life (even from a distance of over eighteen centuries). Cardinal Manning, according to Hutton's representation, claimed the authority of long experience for the Catholic Church. He had responded to Stephen's request for proper investigation of 'a large class of instances' of miraculous events, with the observation that, through investigations into candidates for sainthood, his church was skilled in assessing the evidence for miracles (Brown 1947: 67–8). Whether he meant this as a serious argument we cannot know; but certainly he would have known that Stephen would not take it seriously. When, the month after the open discussion, Shadworth Hodgson presented his paper on miracles, he claimed that the fundamental issue was the grounding of the principle of the uniformity of nature, and that this was to be decided by philosophy:

> I believe that we shall all of us come to hold the incapability of infringement of the axiom of uniformity. But this is because I see philosophical, though not scientific, grounds for believing that it is an universal and necessary truth. What these grounds are I will briefly attempt to indicate, thus bringing the question before its true tribunal, that of philosophy, and not that of science. (Hodgson [1876] 2015: 379)

Hodgson, although he disagreed with the defenders of miracles, agreed with those such as Ward who argued that the narrow empiricism of the scientific sceptics was an inadequate ground for their arguments. Like Fitzjames Stephen, Hodgson argued against miracles but refused to defer to scientific authority.[6]

Conclusion: Divine Action and the Uniformity of Nature

From the case studies presented, it seems that the 'problem' of the miraculous arose as much from philosophy as from science. Hennell addressed himself to the miracles of Scripture in response to the deterministic challenges of Charles Bray, his brother-in-law. Although he probably had some knowledge of the critical movements in German theology, the major stimulus to his rethinking was the materialistic, naturalistic and deterministic tradition which, Robert Young and Adrian Desmond emphasise, pre-dated Darwin. Although he was not ignorant of contemporary science – his Coventry friends were interested in mesmerism and phrenology and were friends of Robert Chambers, the anonymous author of *Vestiges* – Hennell had no particular expertise in science.

Powell was both churchman and man of science. Two chief issues bothered him: the first, how to persuade sceptical unbelievers that Christian faith was worthy of intelligent consideration. Here he argued that the post-Reformation apologetic appeal to miracles and fulfilled prophecy was no longer persuasive – to people such as Hennell and to many less educated sceptics. Second, he wanted to persuade the Anglican elite of the old universities to take science seriously. This led him into close analyses of scientific reasoning, and the relationship between 'natural and divine' knowledge. His dual concerns led him to the conclusion that God acted through law, and that the best evidence of the divine was the orderly, law-bound process of nature. His interest in apologetic came from his specific Anglican theological tradition, but the directions of his argument were shaped by discussions with Newman, White and other theist and Unitarian theological thinkers who, like Hennell, sought to adapt Christian belief to the modern world. Powell, like Hennell, was pre-Darwinian; he was willing to treat the developmental theory of *Vestiges* as a plausible hypothesis.

Similarly, in the Metaphysical Society, science was not recognised as having priority in promoting naturalistic interpretations. Certainly, Carpenter and Huxley claimed the authority of science, but it is noteworthy that Fitzjames Stephen and Shadworth Hodgson, who were both committed to naturalistic explanation, insisted, respectively, on the authority of law and philosophy, rather than deferring to science and scientific men. The number and social range of those who perceived miracles as a problem was increasing (although multitudes continued to accept the miracles of Christian tradition). These case studies suggest, although they do not prove, that doubts about the miraculous were first expressed by free thinkers, then by theists and Unitarians, before becoming plausible to a few more respectable Christian theologians. The privacy of the Metaphysical Society indicates that in the 1870s such doubts were still highly controversial.

Acknowledgements

The research for this chapter has required access to many rare or obscure books. I thank the interloan staff at the University of Auckland library for obtaining rare volumes; Peter Lineham, friend and colleague, for the enthusiasm with which he searched his own extensive library for useful items; Bernard Lightman, ever-generous colleague, for providing extracts from the just-published *Papers of the Metaphysical Society*; and the acquisitions staff at the University of Auckland library for obtaining the volumes with urgency.

Notes

1. A potential case study, focusing on the possibility of divine intervention in the present, is the critical and often satirical theological and scientific response to the proposed national prayer for relief from cattle plague, which filled the columns of the *Pall Mall Gazette* and other newspapers for a few months in 1865. The most voluble of the sceptics in this debate was the eminent physicist and flamboyant lecturer, John Tyndall (see Turner 1974a; Cragoe 2000; Barton 2018).
2. Webb justifies his choice of Strauss by noting, without elaboration, that the response to Hennell was 'more complex and less dramatic' (2000: 423, n. 26). Timothy Larsen discusses Hennell briefly in his account of British responses to Strauss (2004: 45–7). There were links between Strauss and Hennell, but only after first publication. Strauss wrote an introduction for a German translation of Hennell; Hennell read Strauss before preparing a second edition (Hennell 1841: xi).

3. Willey attributes to Hennell 'a remarkable instinctive command of the technique of textual criticism' ([1949] 1966: 210); Dodd accepts Hennell's claim that he followed Unitarian traditions of interpretation (1990: 91); Larsen can only suggest a resemblance to Thomas Paine (2004: 46).
4. Because the 1860 essay was turgid (Reardon [1971] 1995: 241) and polemical in style (an 'irritated tirade' against Whately, says Corsi 1988: 184), I focus my analysis on earlier essays where Powell's expressions were less shaped by his indignation against opponents. Shea and Whitla provide an excellent summary of the essay (2000: 66–73).
5. It is sometimes claimed that R. H. Hutton's reconstruction of a typical meeting was the discussion over miracles (e.g. Marshall et al. 2015: 2:326) but Hutton's speakers (see Brown 1947: 60–70) do not match the Minute Book account of the miracles discussion (quoted in Marshall et al. 2015: 2:326.). Hutton's fictionalised account of a meeting is a series of speeches, in which Hutton summarised the characteristic arguments of leading protagonists, and provides little insight into the process of debate. There are some hints of the previous discussions in Hodgson's paper (1876: 376–8).
6. Given his anti-miracle position, Hodgson's distinction between science and philosophy counters Bernard Lightman's recent (2014) bi-polar interpretation of the Metaphysical Society as divided into scientific naturalists and Christian metaphysicians (for Hodgson was neither), with each arguing for opposing interpretations of science. I develop an alternative interpretation of scientific naturalism and its place in the Metaphysical Society in *The X Club* (Barton 2018: ch. 6).

References

Barton, Ruth (1983), 'Evolution: The Whitworth Gun in Huxley's War for the Liberation of Science from Theology', in David Oldroyd and Ian Langham (eds), *The Wider Domain of Evolutionary Thought*, Dordrecht: Reidel, 261–87.

Barton, Ruth (2014), 'Sunday Lecture Societies: Naturalistic Scientists, Unitarians and Secularists Unite Against Sabbatarian Legislation', in Gowan Dawson and Bernard Lightman (eds), *Victorian Scientific Naturalism: Community, Identity, Continuity*, Chicago: University of Chicago Press, 189–219.

Barton, Ruth (2018), *The X Club: Power and Authority in Victorian Science*, Chicago: University of Chicago Press.

Brown, Alan Willard (1947), *The Metaphysical Society: Victorian Minds in Crisis, 1869–1880*, New York: Columbia University Press.

Carpenter, J. Estlin (1888), *Nature and Man. Essays Scientific and Philosophical by William B. Carpenter, with an Introductory Memoir*, London: Kegan Paul, Trench.

Carpenter, William Benjamin [1875] (2015), 'On the Fallacies of Testimony in Relation to the Supernatural', in Catherine Marshall, Bernard Lightman and Richard England (eds), *The Papers of the Metaphysical Society, 1869–1880, A Critical Edition*, vol. 2, Oxford: Oxford University Press, 347–62.

Chadwick, Owen [1970] (1980), *The Victorian Church*, Part II, London: A. and C. Black.

Chandler, David (1997), 'The Foundations of "Philosophical Criticism": William Taylor's Connection with the *Monthly Review*, 1792–93', *Studies in Bibliography*, 50: 359–71.

Chandler, David (2004), 'Taylor, William (1765–1836)', *Oxford Dictionary of National Biography*, 53: 997–9.

Christensen, Merton A. (1959), 'Taylor of Norwich and the Higher Criticism', *Journal of the History of Ideas*, 20: 179–94.

Corsi, Pietro (1988), *Science and Religion: Baden Powell and the Anglican Debate, 1800–1860*, Cambridge: Cambridge University Press.

Corsi, Pietro (2004), 'Powell, Baden (1796–1860)', *Oxford Dictionary of National Biography*, 45: 73–5.

Cragoe, Matthew (2000), '"The hand of the Lord is upon the cattle": Religious Reactions to the Cattle Plague, 1865–67', in Martin Hewitt (ed.), *An Age of Equipoise? Reassessing Mid-Victorian Britain*, Aldershot: Ashgate, 190–206.

Dawson, Gowan and Bernard Lightman (eds) (2014), *Victorian Scientific Naturalism: Community, Identity, Continuity*, Chicago: University of Chicago Press.

Desmond, Adrian (1994), *Huxley, the Devil's Disciple*, London: Michael Joseph.

Desmond, Adrian (1997), *Huxley, Evolution's High Priest*, London: Michael Joseph.

[D'Holbach, Paul-Henri Thiry, Baron] (1778), *Ecce Homo. Histoire critique de Jésus-Christ, ou Analyse raisonnée des Evangiles*, Amsterdam, <https://archive.org/details/histoirecritiqu00holbgoog> (last accessed 24 August 2015).

Dodd, Valerie A. (1981), 'Strauss's English Propagandists and the Politics of Unitarianism, 1841–1845', *Church History*, 50: 415–35.

Dodd, Valerie A. (1990), *George Eliot: An Intellectual Life*, Basingstoke: Macmillan.

Gilley, Sheridan (2004), 'Ward, William George (1812–1882)', *Oxford Dictionary of National Biography*, 57: 362–5.

Hennell, Charles Christian (1838), *An Inquiry Concerning the Origin of Christianity*, London.

Hennell, Charles Christian (1839), *Christian Theism*, London.

Hennell, Charles Christian (1841), *An Inquiry Concerning the Origin of Christianity*, 2nd edn, London.

Hodgson, Shadworth [1876] (2015), 'The Pre-Suppositions of Miracles', in Catherine Marshall, Bernard Lightman and Richard England (eds), *The Papers of the Metaphysical Society, 1869–1880, A Critical Edition*, vol. 2, Oxford: Oxford University Press, 376–92.

Huxley, Thomas Henry [1876] (2015), 'The Evidence of the Miracle of the Resurrection', in Catherine Marshall, Bernard Lightman and Richard England (eds), *The Papers of the Metaphysical Society, 1869–1880, A Critical Edition*, vol. 2, Oxford: Oxford University Press, 366–72.

Kümmel, Werner Georg [1970] (1973), *The New Testament: The History of the Investigation of Its Problems*, London: SCM Press.

LaPorte, Charles (2013), 'Victorian Literature, Religion, and Secularization', *Literature Compass*, 10: 277–87.

Larsen, Timothy (2004), *Contested Christianity: The Political and Social Contexts of Victorian Theology*, Waco: Baylor University Press.

Lee, Matthew (2004), 'Bray, Charles (1811–1884)', *Oxford Dictionary of National Biography*, 7: 401–2.

Lightman, Bernard (2014), 'Science at the Metaphysical Society: Defining Knowledge in the 1870s', in Bernard Lightman and Michael S. Reidy (eds), *The Age of Scientific Naturalism: Tyndall and His Contemporaries*, London: Pickering and Chatto, 187–206, 241–5.

Marshall, Catherine, Bernard Lightman and Richard England (eds) (2015), *The Papers of the Metaphysical Society, 1869–1880, A Critical Edition*, 3 vols, Oxford: Oxford University Press.

Metcalf, Priscilla (1980), *James Knowles: Victorian Editor and Architect*, Oxford: Clarendon Press.

Moore, James R. (1979), *The Post-Darwinian Controversies: A Study of the Protestant Struggle to Come to Terms with Darwin in Great Britain and America 1870–1900*, Cambridge: Cambridge University Press.

O'Connell, Marvin R. (1991), *The Oxford Conspirators: A History of the Oxford Movement 1843–1845*, Lanham: University Press of America.

Powell, Baden (1846), 'Mysticism and Scepticism', *Edinburgh Review*, 84: 195–223.

Powell, Baden (1847), 'The Study of Christian Evidences', *Edinburgh Review*, 86: 397–418.

Powell, Baden (1855), *Essays on the Spirit of the Inductive Philosophy, the Unity of Worlds, and the Philosophy of Creation*, London: Longman, Brown, Green, and Longmans.

Powell, Baden (1857), 'The Burnett Prizes: The Study of the Evidences of Natural Theology', *Oxford Essays*, 3: 168–203.

Powell, Baden (1859), *The Order of Nature Considered in Reference to the Claims of Revelation*, London: Longman, Brown, Green, Longmans & Roberts.

Powell, Baden [1860] (2000), 'On the Study of the Evidences of Christianity', in Victor Shea and William Whitla (eds), *Essays and Reviews: The 1860 Text and Its Reading*, Charlottesville and London: University Press of Virginia, 233–73.

Priestley, Joseph (1786), *An History of Early Opinions Concerning Jesus Christ, Compiled from Original Writers; Proving that the Christian Church Was at First Unitarian*, 2 vols, Birmingham.

Reardon, Bernard [1971] (1995), *Religious Thought in the Victorian Age: A Survey from Coleridge to Gore*, 2nd edn, London: Longman.

[Reynolds, H. R.] (1858), 'Christianity without Judaism', *British Quarterly Review*, 27: 414–39.

Robertson, J. M. (1929), *A History of Freethought in the Nineteenth Century*, London: Watts.

Rogerson, John (1984), *Old Testament Criticism in the Nineteenth Century: England and Germany*, London: SPCK.

Schweitzer, Albert [1906] (1954), *The Quest of the Historical Jesus: A Critical Study of ts Progress from Reimarus to Wrede*, 3rd edn, trans. W. Montgomery, London: Adam & Charles Black.

Sellers, Ian (2004), 'Hennell, Charles Christian (1805–1850)', *Oxford Dictionary of National Biography*, 26: 374–5.

Shea, Victor and William Whitla (eds) (2000), *Essays and Reviews: The 1860 Text and Its Reading*, Charlottesville and London: University Press of Virginia.

Short, H. L. (1968), 'Presbyterians under a New Name', in C. G. Bolam, Jeremy Goring, H. L. Short and Roger Thomas, *The English Presbyterians: From Elizabethan Puritanism to Modern Unitarianism*, London: George Allen & Unwin, 219–86.

Smith, Crosbie (1998), *The Science of Energy: A Cultural History of Energy Physics in Victorian Britain*, London: Athlone Press.

Stephen, James Fitzjames [1875] (2015), 'Remarks on the Proof of Miracles', in Catherine Marshall, Bernard Lightman and Richard England (eds), *The Papers of the Metaphysical Society, 1869–1880, A Critical Edition*, vol. 2, Oxford: Oxford University Press, 328–44.

[Taylor, William] (1809a), '*Commentar über das neue Testament. Von H. E. G. Paulus . . .*', *The Critical Review*, 16.5: 449–79.

[Taylor, William] (1809b), '*Kommentar über das Neue Testament, &c. . . .*', *The Critical Review*, 17.5: 449–74.

[Thom, John Hamilton] (1845), 'An Inquiry Concerning the Origin of Christianity', *The Prospective Review*, 1 (January): 19–48.

Turner, Frank M. (1974a), 'Rainfall, Plagues, and the Prince of Wales: A Chapter in the Conflict of Religion and Science', *Journal of British Studies*, 13: 46–65.

Turner, Frank M. (1974b), *Between Science and Religion: The Reaction to Scientific Naturalism in Late Victorian England*, New Haven: Yale University Press.

Twelftree, Graham H. (2011), *The Cambridge Companion to Miracles*, Cambridge: Cambridge University Press.

Ward, W. G. [1872] (2015), 'Can Experience Prove the Uniformity of Nature?', in Catherine Marshall, Bernard Lightman and Richard England (eds), *The Papers of the Metaphysical Society, 1869–1880, A Critical Edition*, vol. 1, Oxford: Oxford University Press, 412–16.

Webb, R. K. (2000), 'Miracles in English Unitarian Thought', in Mark S. Micale and Robert L. Dietle (eds), *Enlightenment, Passion, Modernity: Historical Essays in European Thought and Culture*, Stanford: Stanford University Press, 113–30, 421–5.

Willey, Basil [1949] (1966), *Nineteenth Century Studies: Coleridge to Matthew Arnold*, New York: Harper Torchbooks.

Young, Robert M. [1970] (1985), 'The Impact of Darwin on Conventional Thought', in *Darwin's Metaphor: Nature's Place in Victorian Culture*, Cambridge: Cambridge University Press, 1–22.

9

Transcendence and Immanence

Johannes Zachhuber

Introduction

The binary use of the terms 'transcendence' and 'immanence' is one of the most powerful concepts to have emerged from nineteenth-century debates about religion. It is also one of their most enduring legacies; in fact, the juxtaposition of the two terms, the assumption that they refer to an ontological, epistemic or theological duality, is today usually taken for granted and conventionally applied to the analysis of religious and other worldviews throughout history and across cultures.

The present chapter will set out by charting the historical emergence of this particular conceptual pair of opposites during the early part of the nineteenth century. Subsequently, I shall illustrate how it was used and applied in F. C. Baur, Albrecht Ritschl and Adolf Harnack. As will become clear, its widespread acceptance as descriptively valuable followed on from what was the product of rather specific philosophical developments, notably the rise of Kantian criticism and its ambivalent reception in German Idealism. Yet the reason it resonated so strongly with the wider public cannot be reduced to those academic debates. Rather, the opposition of transcendent and immanent touched a nerve of Western societies uneasy about their understanding of religion as well as its abiding importance for modern culture.

It is now widely recognised that the notion of the nineteenth century as the age of 'the secularization of the European mind' (Chadwick 1990) has been at best one-sided and more probably a misleading caricature. Yet if the nineteenth century was not a time of unmitigated religious decline, it most certainly was beset with concerns about such decline. Indifference or hostility to religion may have been less widespread than has often been assumed; very public controversies about the current state of religion certainly were one of the most characteristic features of the century.

A major reason for the increasing popularity of references to transcendence and immanence was their usefulness in those debates. To many, acceptance or denial of 'transcendence' became tantamount to acceptance or denial of religious faith as such. Thus the duality of transcendence and immanence could be invoked both by advocates of traditional religion and by its critics: the proponents of modern science could insinuate that 'transcendence' was the hypothesis that was no longer needed under a methodical approach which 'immanently' offered a full explanation of the world, while their opponents bemoaned the loss of transcendence and regarded the totalitarian dominance of immanence as the supreme expression of modernity's apostasy from religion. Some, admittedly, sought to reject this alternative, arguing instead that it was the very dualism of transcendence and immanence that caused a crisis of religious faith which, consequently, could only be overcome by moving beyond the sharp juxtaposition of the two concepts. A significant driver of nineteenth-century debates about transcendence and immanence, as we shall see, was the attempt to delegitimise this position, labelling it as pantheism and aligning it with the complete denial of transcendence.

Ultimately, the emerging popularity of the dualism of transcendence and immanence provides a fascinating insight into the close link between philosophical, theological, historical and more broadly religious concerns in the nineteenth century.

The Emergence of the Transcendent–Immanent Binary as Seen through Three Encyclopedias

The rise of the binary opposition of transcendence and immanence can be traced from the mid-eighteenth to the early nineteenth century by comparing the entries under the term 'immanent' in three major encyclopedias of the time (cf. Oeing-Hanhoff 1976): the famous *Encyclopédie* of Denis Diderot and Jean le Rond d'Alembert, published in twenty-eight volumes between 1751 and 1772; the four-volume *Allgemeines Handwörterbuch der philosophischen Wissenschaften nebst ihrer Literatur und Geschichte* authored by the eminent Kantian philosopher, Wilhelm Traugott Krug, in 1827–8; and the monumental *Allgemeine Enzyklopädie der Wissenschaften und Künste*, which was edited by Johann Samuel Ersch and Johann Gottfried Gruber in a rather astonishing 168 volumes between 1818 and 1889, but which remained incomplete nonetheless.

The *Encyclopédie* included in its eighth volume a brief and unsigned entry 'immanent' (Diderot 1765: 8:570). The article defines the term as that 'which remains within the person or which does not have an effect beyond it'. Two main contexts are given: philosophers, the author claims, distinguish between 'immanent' and 'transeunt' actions. The former are those whose end remains within the mind of the agent whereas the latter produce an effect outside the mind. Theologians, the author adds, have taken over the same distinction specifically for the actions of God. Accordingly, 'God has generated the Son and the Holy Spirit through immanent actions' whereas the creation of the world is counted as his transeunt action (ibid. 8:570).

Immanent here is clearly a concept with limited use and of no particular importance. It is a technical term whose history dates back to medieval scholasticism but without any wider claim beyond the rather narrow confines of the philosophy of mind and Christian doctrine. While it is used as part of a binary pair of opposites, it is not contrasted with 'transcendent' but with 'transeunt'. This is not because 'transcendent' is an unknown term to the editors of the *Encyclopédie*; in fact, 'transcendent' has its own entry, but the latter does not mention 'immanent' either.

One of most fateful early references to 'immanent' perfectly confirms this impression. In proposition XVIII of Part 1 of his *Ethics*, Spinoza called God the 'immanent, not the transeunt cause' of all things (1925: 2:64). While contemporary readers may be inclined to find here proof for Spinoza's alleged 'immanentist' view of the godhead, his claim is much more specific and fully in line with the usage described in the *Encyclopédie*, even though the thesis contradicts theological orthodoxy. In the act of creating the world, Spinoza urged, God does not cause an effect outside of himself but remains as much within himself as, according to Christian doctrine, in the inner-trinitarian processions.

Krug's *General Encyclopedia of Philosophical Terms* contains an article on 'immanent' in its second volume (1826: 447). Immanent is here defined as 'remaining within', but then distinguished according to three different meanings. In the first one, it is opposed to 'transcendent' and refers to the principles of cognition. The immanent use of reason remains within that which can be properly known, whereas the transcendent use claims to surpass those limits. This is Kant's own use, as we shall see in more detail later on. Second, Krug juxtaposes 'immanent' and 'transeunt' as the *Encyclopédie* did before, but defines immanent in this sense as 'contained within the human mind' or 'theoretical'. A third and, according to the author, rather specific meaning of the term is encountered in 'the pantheistic system' which, by seeing God as the world's immanent cause, ultimately identifies the two insofar as all empirical things are mere accidents of one underlying substance.

Of the three meanings only one moves decisively beyond the article in the *Encyclopédie*, and this is the very one juxtaposing transcendent and immanent. This is significant as it points to the emergence of an altogether novel interest in this duality. Yet the way Krug introduces this meaning does not suggest any broader or systematic concern for the distinction. He remains as technical and academic as the author of the earlier article in the *Encyclopédie*.

A hint towards the wider significance of the matter can only be found in Krug's reference to the 'pantheistic' use of immanent. Krug may have been unfamiliar with the earlier, theological background of Spinoza's proposition XVIII, and clearly reads him in the context of more recent controversies about 'pantheism' initiated by Friedrich Heinrich Jacobi in 1785 (Vallée 1988). Jacobi had caused public scandal by tying the half-forgotten Spinoza to the recently deceased Gotthold Ephraim Lessing, arguing that his philosophy ultimately amounted to the denial of freedom, ethical relativism and atheism. There is no evidence that the transcendent–immanent distinction was used by Jacobi himself or in the original pantheism controversy of the late eighteenth century. By the time Krug composed his *Encyclopedia* this had evidently changed.

Things look very different indeed in the much longer article 'immanent' written by the little-known philosopher Karl Hermann Scheidler (1795–1866) for the *General Encyclopedia of the Sciences and the Arts* (1839). Scheidler, who identified with conservative critics of Hegel's philosophy, such as Immanuel Hermann Fichte, considered 'the concept of the immanent together with its opposite, the transcendent, the very core or centre of [Kant's] critical philosophy' (ibid. 315). Not only is the pair important for Kantian thought, it is equally crucial for Hegel's philosophy as well (ibid. 315). Whereas, however, Kant taught a sharp dichotomy of the two and, in a way, excluded the transcendent from the realm of human knowledge, Hegel's 'doctrine claims to have full knowledge of God etc. [sic] and thus to unite immanence and transcendence' (ibid. 315).

In Scheidler's account, the opposition of transcendence and immanence finally appears as the key to recent philosophical developments. Remarkably, the earlier understanding of 'immanent', of which Krug was still aware just over ten years earlier, has entirely disappeared in Scheidler's perception. He therefore begins his overview with an extensive sketch of Kantian philosophy followed by an equally extensive description of Hegel's system. He links the latter in particular with the Spinozist heritage. Hegel himself, the article says, calls his system 'absolute idealism' but others rightly refer to it as 'pantheistic idealism or idealistic pantheism' (ibid. 316). While the article at the outset defines 'immanent' as a technical term of philosophy, the piece culminates in the observation that Hegel's 'immanent philosophy of this-worldliness fundamentally rejects . . . any faith in a higher Being, in the Beyond, or the personal immortality of the soul' (ibid. 317).

The author of this encyclopedia article goes beyond his predecessors in at least two ways: he claims the centrality of the opposition of transcendent and immanent for modern philosophy and at the same time inscribes it into contemporaneous debates about religion. The terms he uses for the latter purpose are quite telling. Those accused of insufficient recognition of transcendence deny the existence of a 'higher Being' (*ein höheres Wesen*) or 'the Beyond' (*das Jenseits*). What is at stake is not any particular doctrine of the Christian creed, but religion as such; and religion is essentially the postulation of an ontological order beyond the material realm. Faith, likewise, is conceived as the willingness to accept a worldview that involves those assumptions. In other words, the binary of transcendent and immanent corresponds to a binary of religion and non-religion, and it is the latter alternative that increasingly dominates religious debates in the nineteenth century.

Just over fifty years separate the publication of the first and the last of the three encyclopedia entries. These fifty years, admittedly, must be counted among the most eventful and transformative in the whole of Western history. Diderot and d'Alembert wrote while the *ancien régime* was still in power; Scheidler, by contrast, looks back to the French Revolution, the Napoleonic Wars and the Restoration. In fact, for him times are already heating up for the major revolutions spreading all over Europe in 1848. The intervening years were a period of radical transformation in practically all areas of culture and society. What we can conclude at this point is that the dichotomous pair of transcendent and immanent is a product of this particular intellectual transformation. Major philosophical developments played an important role in its emergence along with the evolution of a new kind of religious concern, for which the main decision was no longer one between particular doctrines or articles of faith, but more fundamentally between religion and its rejection.

Transcendence and Immanence in Kant's Philosophy

It has already become clear that Kant's critical philosophy marks a major turning point in the emergence of the transcendent–immanent binary. In fact, he is the first to use the two terms as a pair. His contribution and its significance must now be described in some more detail. In the *Critique of Pure Reason*, Kant wrote: 'We will call the principles whose application stays wholly and completely within the limits of possible experience *immanent*, but those that would fly beyond those boundaries, *transcendent* principles' (1995–: A295–6/B352[1]). Immanent and transcendent are here applied to the realm of human knowledge. Those principles of cognition that are 'within the limits of possible experience' are called immanent; those going beyond those limits are called transcendent.

In order to gauge the significance of this definition for Kant's thought but also for the wider philosophical, theological and religious debate, it is useful to recall the ultimate purpose of his most ground-breaking book. As Kant explained in the preface to the second edition of the *Critique of Pure Reason*, he was ultimately motivated by the question of why metaphysics had made less steady progress in the development towards a science than had other fields, such as mathematics and the natural sciences. His own original contribution, as he saw it, was a radical change of perspective, the celebrated Copernican turn:

> Hence let us once try whether we do not get farther with the problems of metaphysics by assuming that the objects must conform to our cognition, which would agree better with the requested possibility of an *a priori* cognition of them, which is to establish something about them before they are given to us. This would be like the first

thoughts of Copernicus, who, when he did not make good progress in the explanation of the celestial motions if he assumed that the entire celestial host revolves around the observer, tried to see if he might not have greater success if he made the observer revolve and left the stars at rest. (Ibid. Bxvi)

Given, Kant suggests, that the quest for an understanding of being qua being has not led to unequivocal results, it may be time to query our capacity for knowledge instead. By investigating the principles of our cognition, we might hope to achieve those results that have so far escaped philosophers in search of a firm metaphysical foundation.

In seeking this approach, Kant hoped to overcome the stark juxtaposition between the continental school of philosophical rationalism in the tradition of Descartes and Leibniz, in which he himself had been trained, and the British school of empiricism which had found its most brilliant representative in David Hume. Kant himself famously said that Hume's scepticism had 'first interrupted my dogmatic slumber' (ibid. 4:260). The resulting conundrum was the reason a 'critique' of pure reason was necessary.

Kant's solution lay in the insight that human cognition always depends on both sense perception and rationality. This permitted the philosopher from Königsberg to reject Hume's epistemological scepticism. Hume, he asserted, had neglected the necessarily constructive role played by human reason in all cognition. Firm and reliable knowledge was therefore possible, Kant asserted, on the basis of the successful interaction between the material provided by our senses and the formal structure imposed on it by our intellect. As long as those two went together, human cognition stood on firm ground.

The flip-side of this argument, however, was Kant's equally strongly held view that no knowledge was possible where intellectual ideas were altogether cut off from an empirical basis. He therefore rejected the traditional proofs for the existence of God or, perhaps more precisely, he took away the epistemic foundation that had made them even conceivable. For Kant, human ideas about reality could ultimately be classified in a binary way: those that fell within the boundaries of what the mind can know and those that aim to transgress those boundaries. Firm and 'scientific' knowledge is possible of the former; no knowledge is possible of the latter.

It is this precise theory that is encapsulated in Kant's use of the pair 'transcendent' and 'immanent' as expressed concisely in the above quotation. All cognition is either immanent or transcendent. Insofar as it is the former, it is verifiable and therefore in principle justified; insofar as it is the latter, the searching human mind has to guard itself against such ideas as they lead to confusion and insoluble contradictions. The terms 'transcendent' and 'immanent' are thus not merely given a novel use in Kant's first *Critique*; they are inserted into what is arguably the centrepiece of his argument. Their duality stands for the dichotomy the critical philosophy stipulates in the realm of human knowledge between legitimate and illegitimate use of reason.

It is therefore further evident that Kant's use of the distinction carries with it a normative judgement. He does not so much divide cognition into immanent and transcendent forms, but decrees that the latter of the two is deeply problematical: '[By transcendent principles] I mean principles that actually incite us to tear down all those boundary posts and to lay claim to a wholly new territory that recognises no demarcations anywhere' (ibid. A296/B352). The binary of immanent and transcendent is of such a kind that only one of the two denotes a possible form of human knowledge. Transcendent principles of pure reason are no basis for knowledge whatsoever. They are presumptuous, making empty promises that lead to no real insight. The purpose of the *Critique* is to warn against them because of their potential to mire the human mind in contradictions and hinder rather than enable the growth of human knowledge.

The negative connotations Kant associates with transcendent ideas become even clearer once we consider a German term he frequently uses as an equivalent for transcendent, the word *überschwänglich* (Zachhuber 2000). This term would now commonly be translated as 'profuse' or 'effusive' but is originally derived from the verb *schwingen*, 'to swing' which, combined with a prefix meaning 'over', suggests a movement transcending or transgressing boundaries. Kant's use of it as an equivalent for transcendent is therefore somewhat idiosyncratic but not implausible. The term has a long history in German mystical thought going back to the high Middle Ages and can be found in authors like Meister Eckhart where it signified both the ecstatic union of the mystic with God and God's superabundant being (Eckhart 1958: 55). It was later used by Lutheran pietists, such as Gottfried Arnold, who employed *überschwänglich* to translate the ontological superlative forms typical of the language of Pseudo-Dionysius the Areopagite. According to Arnold and others, *überschwänglich* cognition is such that it permits an immediate, mystical approach to God (Arnold [1703] 1969: 83).

Kant, who had a pietistic upbringing from which he later distanced himself, seems to have been aware of this specific usage (Zachhuber 2000: 147–8). This explains regular references to 'transcendent' or *überschwänglich* cognition in strongly polemical contexts. His rejection goes way beyond the measured criticism to be found in the *Critique of Pure Reason* and indicates that he associates transcendent ideas with intellectually and religiously suspicious movements.

Thus he accused opponents such as Johann Georg Schlosser (1995–: 8:398), Friedrich Heinrich Jacobi (ibid. 8:134) or Emanuel Swedenborg (ibid. 7:46) of misguided expeditions into the transcendent realm, and this claim is supported by tying them to the 'mystical-Platonic tradition' which, according to Kant, goes back to Parmenides and in particular Plato, 'the father of all enthusiasm in philosophy' (ibid. 8:398). The reference to 'enthusiasm' (*Schwärmerei*) here hints at the broader, religious background to Kant's argument. In an evidently calculated move, Kant sides with mainstream Lutheranism which over the centuries had developed a fundamental suspicion towards radical and mystical spiritualism, so much so that the term 'enthusiasts', originally used by Luther against his more radical opponents within the Reformation camp, had practically become the designation of a heresy.

At this point, it becomes possible to ascertain how Kant's use of the opposition of transcendent and immanent is also indicative of his attitude towards religion and theology. From what has been said so far, it might easily appear that his intention was simply to disown any intellectual engagement with the transcendent. Yet Kant himself famously declared that his stipulation of the boundaries of pure reason was done, at least partly, 'in order to make room for faith' (ibid. Bxxx). This corresponds with the observation that Kant's duality of immanent and transcendent principles of cognition apparently recognises that the latter exist, however much he may have warned against their inevitable abuse. Such an ambiguity, however, is not at all without precedent in theology which, on the contrary, has throughout its history grappled with the apparent tension between the affirmation that God is wholly other and any epistemic claims about the divine.

Kant's novel use of the transcendent–immanent distinction is therefore less obviously hostile towards religion than is often thought. It can perfectly well be read as a radical concession by philosophy that its potential for understanding the ultimate reality is extremely limited. In this sense, Kant's critical philosophy was met sympathetically by rather conservative theologians from the outset. An interesting example is the so-called supranaturalist theology of Gottlob Christian Storr (1746–1805), who claimed that Kant's critique of natural knowledge of God necessitated reliance on divine revelation (Storr 1794; Pannenberg 1997: 35–45). A similar use of Kant is evident in Karl Barth's early dialectical theology, especially in the second edition of his hugely influential interpretation of Paul's Epistle to the Romans ([1922] 1968). His 'theological epistemology in *Romans II* stands everywhere in the long shadow cast by Immanuel Kant' (McCormack 1995: 245). The reason is simple: Kant's radical distinction of immanent and transcendent principles of cognition *could* be read as an affirmation of a hyper-secular rejection of transcendence, but they could equally be seen to encourage a radical emphasis on divine transcendence.

This is not to say that such appropriations would have found Kant's own approval. In the realm of cognition, the division between immanent and transcendent for him was absolute. His own solution, which he presented in the *Critique of Practical Reason* and in many of his later essays, commended human practice as the realm in which the dualism of immanent and transcendent could be overcome:

> Ideas created by reason itself, whose objects (if they have any) lie wholly beyond our field of vision; although they are transcendent for speculative cognition, they are not to be taken as empty, but with a practical intent they are made available to us by lawgiving reason itself, yet not in order to brood over their objects as to what they are in themselves and in their nature, but rather how we have to think of them in behalf of moral principles. (1995–: 8:332)

As we shall see, in the early reception of Kant's philosophy, this second leg of his philosophy – the affirmation of practical religion as an alternative to the impasse on the theoretical side – remained in the background. Later, however, this was to change, and a practical solution to the transcendent–immanent dichotomy became an attractive option for theologians in the latter half of the century.

Pantheism as the 'System of Immanence'

In his encyclopedia entry, Scheidler asserted that the distinction of transcendent and immanent was equally central for the philosophies of Kant and of Hegel. This assessment is, however, more accurate for the former than the latter. In fact, none of the idealists operated with this duality. This may well be due to their monistic tendency; Hegel as well as Fichte and Schelling sought to overcome what they saw as problematical dichotomies in Kant's thought. Thus Schelling opined that 'in light of the science that we teach and distinctly perceive, immanence and transcendence are completely and equally empty words because it [sc. the science] resolves this very duality' (1856: 2:377).

It is in keeping with this observation that Krug in 1826, as we have seen, gave no indication that the duality of immanent and transcendent, which he rightly associated with Kant's critical philosophy, had subsequently been employed by his idealist heirs. He did, however, hint that 'immanent' was used in a specific sense in 'the pantheistic system'. The association of pantheism with the concept of immanence was indeed a product of the 1820s. This was an important step towards the eventual establishment of the transcendent–immanent binary, particularly important in light of the religious overtones that came to be associated with this distinction.

Pantheism was not linked to Spinoza and his philosophy until the late eighteenth century. Jacobi's writings and the ensuing 'pantheism controversy' played a major role in bringing this about. Subsequently, the term swiftly mutated into a widely used term of abuse on the philosophical–theological borderline. As a large number of thinkers with very different intellectual credentials were publicly accused of being pantheists, complaints grew that its meaning was increasingly vague and unspecific. The Enlightenment thinker, Christian Jakob Kraus, compared Herder's notion of pantheism to the sea-god Proteus who would change his shape in order to avoid answering questions directed at him (1812: 10).

In 1826, the philosopher Gottlob Benjamin Jäsche (1762–1842), known to posterity largely as the editor of Kant's lectures on logic (the so-called Jäsche Logic), sought to address this problem by composing a two-volume work entitled *Der Pantheismus nach seinen verschiedenen Hauptformen, seinem Ursprung und Fortgange, seinem speculativen und praktischen Werth und Gehalt* [Pantheism in its Various Main Forms, Its Origin and Development, Its Speculative and Practical Value and Content]. Jäsche's work is based on the assumption that pantheism is a type of philosophy going back to Greek and even Indic antiquity (Friedrich Schlegel [1808: 140–53] had already hinted at that). While acknowledging diverse varieties of pantheism, Jäsche ultimately identified its foundation as immanence: 'The reason that a conceptual difference [of God and world] cannot be held together with the basic pantheistic concept of immanence, lies in the principle itself on which all pantheism is founded' (1826: 1:33). Pantheism is thus the opposite of theism, and their main difference is identified in their respective understanding of God and world. Pantheism, according to Jäsche, denies a Godhead that is 'truly different from the world' (ibid. 1:33) whereas its alternative affirms precisely such a God.

Jäsche makes it clear in this work that for him, on the basis of this definition, all more recent versions of idealist philosophy fall into the pantheistic category (ibid. 1:42–5). In describing the current philosophical predicament, he does not hide the religious dimension of his concern. In fact, he raises the question whether or not, in light of the triumph of idealism, the 'sacred voice of conscience and religion' would have to sound a principled warning against any and all philosophy (ibid. 1:45–6). Interestingly, the philosophical antidote he recommends is a kind of Kantianism, the recognition of the boundary that 'once and for all has been set by the organism of human cognitive power for the human desire to know' (ibid. 1:46). For it is this philosophy that accepts the need for faith as a necessary addition to speculative knowledge. Conversely, pantheism is 'the only true and conceivable philosophy' (ibid. 1:47) for all those who claim for philosophy the power of complete and absolute knowledge.

Yet if Jäsche's alternative to pantheism has Kantian overtones, he ultimately sides with Jacobi and Heinrich Fries in the affirmation of a philosophy that sees 'purely reasonable faith' (*reinvernünftiger Glauben*) as being above philosophy: 'Such a philosophy, which displays itself as a theory of knowledge only in the lower regions of philosophical thought, but in its highest regions, as a doctrine of faith, must truly not be fearful of any kind of pantheism' (ibid. 1:49). The conflict between criticism and pantheism is therefore ultimately a conflict between a philosophy of faith and a philosophy of knowledge, 'which usurps rights it does not possess thereby threatening to damage religion' (ibid. 1:51).

Jäsche was not a theologian nor a fanatical polemicist. He was a professor of philosophy whose training was mainly with Immanuel Kant. In some ways, as we have seen, the opposition to his idealist contemporaries can be viewed as an outgrowth of his Kantian sympathies. Yet the overall angle he took in his work indicates a crucial shift away from

Kant's own concerns. Jäsche offers a philosophical and historical analysis, but his research is prompted by the broader sense that religion itself is under attack. One might say that the dualism we found in Kant – between immanent and transcendent principles of cognition – is now inverted, as the system of immanence is no longer, as in Kant, the one that secures reliable knowledge, but the one that transgresses its boundaries.

Interestingly, Jäsche does not make use of the binary of immanent and transcendent to characterise the dualism with which he operates. It would, arguably, be easy to ascribe it to him in practice. After all, what is the opposite of a reduction of everything to a 'system of immanence' denying a God who is separate from the world? At the same time, the fact that he does not avail himself in this situation of the duality of transcendent and immanent, is surely itself telling, for it completely confirms the impression given by Krug's nearly exactly contemporaneous *Encyclopedia*. Transcendent and immanent are established as technical terms within Kantian criticism, but there is as yet no evidence for a willingness to make more sweeping use of the pair in the interest of philosophical generalisations. This, however, was soon to change.

The Establishment of the Transcendent–Immanent Binary

Immanuel Hermann Fichte (1796–1879), son of the more famous Johann Gottlob, started where Jäsche and others had left off. A trained philosopher, he too explored the borderline territory of philosophy and theology; his first monograph was characteristically entitled *Sätze zur Vorschule der Theologie* [*Theses on the Preschool of Theology*] (1826). From the late 1820s, he emerged as a major critic of Hegel's philosophy, but whereas the Young Hegelians sought to move the Hegelian heritage away from Christian theology, Fichte Jr censured the Berlin philosopher for the incompatibility of his thought with theism. In particular, he charged that Hegel's philosophy failed to give an adequate account of the concept of personality. In spite of his claim to synthesise Spinoza's metaphysics of substance and Kant's metaphysics of the subject, Fichte argued, Hegel had in fact been unable to move beyond the former. He was ultimately a Spinozist whose one-sided focus on absolute substance prevented him from making allowance for divine or, indeed, human personality in the full sense.

If Fichte's critique of Hegel thus had similarities with Jäsche's analysis of pantheism, it was also characteristically different. Jäsche had advocated a dualism of knowledge and faith based on the quasi-Kantian insight into the boundaries of reason. Fichte, by contrast, affirmed the idealists' speculative approach and sought to perfect it. Hegel, he argued, had advanced philosophy to the point from where it could then be perfected to allow for the reality and personality of God as well as true human individuality. It is for this reason that his thought has often been described as speculative theism.

In articulating his position, Fichte initially did not draw on the distinction of immanence and transcendence. This only occurred from the mid-1830s, but then in a decisive and highly influential way. From 1833, he published a major, three-volume work, *Grundzüge zum Systeme der Philosophie* [*Foundations for the System of Philosophy*], which was not completed until 1846. The second volume, which appeared in 1836, contains a longer note under the header 'the concept of God's immanence in the world'. It is essentially a critical analysis of Hegel's philosophy of religion which, according to Fichte, is largely characterised by this very doctrine. It is clear to Fichte that this position amounts to pantheism and is in many ways identical to that of Spinoza. In spite of this damning verdict, Fichte asserts that 'in his system lies the seed from which must ultimately result the concept of transcendence, God's free and independent existence [*Fürsichsein*] above the world, which in itself contains, explains and corrects the concept of immanence' (1833–46: 2:374). Hegel's position, Fichte claims, ultimately rests on the proposition that God is not God without the world because he has his reality as Spirit only in the world (ibid. 2:376). Yet such a view, rightly thought through, must ultimately lead to the concept of a personal God who freely created the world and, in that sense, transcends it. Immanence and transcendence thus belong together, and only a philosophy that gives its due to the doctrine of divine transcendence can claim to have followed the speculative path to its end.

It might appear that Fichte has merely added to Jäsche's identification of pantheism as the 'system of immanence' the alternative of a philosophy recognising the importance of transcendence. Yet that would be oversimplifying things. For Jäsche, immanence was an ontological principle in and of itself; Fichte by contrast speaks of 'God's immanence in the world'. While he probably started from the by now conventional identification of pantheism with immanence, his focus on Hegel's philosophy of religion led him to the more specific and novel claim that pantheism was based on a view of God as 'immanent' in his creation. Only on the basis of this understanding of immanent did it then make sense for him to advance the further view that God must also, and primarily, be transcendent.

Fichte's argument provoked a furious response from Hegel's students. Hermann Friedrich Wilhelm Hinrichs (1794–1861), whom Hegel had made famous by contributing a foreword to his 1822 *Philosophy of Religion*, focused his extensive review of Fichte's book practically exclusively on this one aspect of the work (Hinrichs 1835). The charge against the master that he only taught God's immanence, not also his transcendence, was, Hinrichs urged, wholly without foundation and entirely unfair (ibid. 786). On the contrary, in emphasising this distinction, Hegel's opponents remained captive to the very dualism which his philosophy had successfully overcome. Rightly understood, Hegel's philosophy affirmed both God's immanence and his transcendence, but in a way that moves beyond their categorical juxtaposition (ibid. 787).

By phrasing the counter-argument in this way, however, Hinrichs in practice accepted Fichte's new terminological and conceptual frame, the duality of transcendence and immanence. While they disagreed on their interpretation of Hegel's philosophy as well as the most appropriate way of conceptualising the immanence as well as the transcendence of God, Fichte and his critic concurred on the suitability of this terminological pair.

A consensus on this usage was soon emerging. A good example is the writing *Das Wesen der Religion* [*The Essence of Religion*] by the liberal theologian Carl Schwarz (1812–85), published in 1847. Schwarz presents the duality of God's transcendence and his immanence as an antinomy which it is the task of the philosophy of religion to solve: 'The absolute must only be thought as transcending the world. The absolute must only be thought as immanent in the world' (1847: 1:182). In Schwarz, finally, the distinction of transcendence and immanence is presupposed as a fundamental principle of the doctrine of God. God, he argues, can legitimately be understood as transcendent:

> The world essentially exists in space and time and is thus ... a series of conditionally existing beings. The unconditional [*das Unbedingte*] must therefore be separated from them. If it were included in the totality of things that mutually condition each other, we could not call it the unconditional. (Ibid. 1:182)

On the other hand, however, there are equally plausible reasons for referring to God as immanent in the world: 'The absolute is not absolute if it has the world outside of itself.

A world, which it is not, would be its boundary; being cordoned off from finitude, the absolute itself becomes finite' (ibid. 1:182). According to Schwarz, the solution is to be found in a teleological, personal and dynamic concept of God whose immanence always carries with it a radical distinction from the world. The duality of the two is therefore as far removed from dualism as it is different from a pantheistic identification of God and world.

Ultimately, Schwarz's answer is less interesting than the evidence provided by his use of transcendent and immanent as such, which suggests that this duality had by his time become a conventional shorthand for the mapping out of possible positions in the philosophy of religion: radical dualism with a dichotomy of immanence and transcendence (Kant, Jacobi, Jäscher); pantheistic immanentism (Hegel, Schelling); speculative theism (Fichte, Scheidler, Schwarz). This corresponds to the state of affairs encountered in Scheidler's encyclopedia article written in 1839, thereby confirming that the eventual establishment of the binary use of the two terms was the result of developments from the mid-1830s.

*

At this point, we can summarily describe the emergence of the binary use of transcendence and immanence, which happened between 1781 (the year the *Critique of Pure Reason* appeared) and the mid-1830s, as the product of three overlapping intellectual and religious developments of those decades. The first is Kant's critical philosophy with its sharp distinction of transcendent and immanent principles of cognition. The second is the debate about pantheism, which was initiated by Jacobi in 1785, but was turned into a controversy about a 'system of immanence' by Jäsche's work in 1826. The third factor is the conflict over the philosophies of German idealism and in particular over Hegel which extended throughout much of the 1830s and 1840s. As we have seen, Jäsche's real targets were Schelling and Hegel, and the philosophical basis of his construction of pantheism was a philosophical cross of Kant and Jacobi. Fichte's introduction of the transcendent–immanent distinction, again, saw Kant and Hegel as equally problematical representatives of dualism and immanentism, respectively.

The result, consequently, was not one univocal understanding of this pair. Rather, the emerging duality of immanence and transcendence could serve very different ends depending on the philosophical, theological or ideological standpoint of the author. Speculative thinkers, such as Fichte and Schwarz, could appeal to the complementarity of transcendence and immanence with the aim of perfecting idealism. More apologetic theologians, however, could use the same pair of terms to signify the fundamental as well as necessary boundary between human knowledge and the realm of the divine. In this vein, for example, Carl August von Eschenmayer (1768–1852), a follower of Schelling and Jacobi, employed the distinction of transcendence and immanence to argue for a limitation of the powers of self-consciousness:

> All error is based on a lack of philosophical distinction between the immanence and the transcendence of self-consciousness. The potency of the I is sufficient ... for all that is true, beautiful and good, insofar as it falls within the immanence of self-consciousness. But this standard is insufficient for that which transcends [self-consciousness], and this is where the holy, heavenly, and divine belong. (1840: 90)

Yet others, however, could invert this logic and claim that modern science had removed the need for an appeal to the transcendent and embrace the very reduction of the world to the immanent that Eschenmayer condemns. Explaining the three stages of Auguste

Comte's philosophy of positivism, his student Émile Littré (1801–81) wrote in 1859: 'The long conflict of immanence and transcendence comes to its end. Transcendence, this is theology or metaphysics explaining the world by causes outside of itself; immanence, this is science explaining the world by causes within itself' (1859: 34). From all these discussions, religion was never far away. As we have seen, Kant himself intended his distinction between immanent and transcendent principles of cognition at least partly to delegitimise a certain brand of theological and religious thinking – one he associated with 'enthusiasm'. For Jacobi and all who came after him, the critique of pantheism was at least as much the rejection of a religious and theological position as it was an objection to particular philosophical views. Finally, the conflict about Hegel's philosophy was deeply informed by the disagreement between those who saw in him an apologist for Christianity and those who thought the opposite. Once again, the use of transcendent and immanent was directly related to this aspect of the controversy, as has been seen in Hinrich's angry rebuttal of Fichte's critique.

All these conflicts bespeak the emergence of a new frontier that was to dominate much nineteenth-century debate on religion across Europe. Increasingly, theism itself moved to the centre of public controversy. More and more, what was under scrutiny was no longer the detail of doctrine but the plausibility of belief in God as such. Religious debate became a debate about religion, and questions about its essence, its history and the role of Christianity in it consequently became urgent. The career of the duality of transcendent and immanent closely mirrors this evolving conflict line as it was perfectly suited to express and symbolise the options individuals and groups were able to choose.

What remains to be demonstrated is how this distinction, once established, was further inflected in the course of the nineteenth century. Two aspects deserve particular attention: the inscription of the transcendent–immanent distinction into historical theology in F. C. Baur's Tübingen School and its use within a more practical yet historical frame by Albrecht Ritschl and Adolf Harnack.

Transcendent and Immanent in Historical Theology: F. C. Baur

It is common today to apply the duality of transcendent and immanent as a seemingly time-invariant concept to historical analysis. The roots of this practice also lie in the nineteenth century; in fact, its origin is directly tied to the developments that have so far been described. This is partly because the latter coincided with the evolution of historicism as an intellectual paradigm and the same factors contributed to the emergence of both. This is especially true for the intellectual trajectory leading from Kant and Lessing to the idealists of the early nineteenth century. Increasingly, it was accepted that the fullest possible account of any social or cultural phenomenon was its historical contextualisation. In this sense, the history of philosophy was seen as the ultimate key to philosophy, and the history of religion likewise promised to unveil the deepest insights into the divine and its relationship with humanity (Zachhuber 2013: 7–10).

One of the most influential early proponents of historicism within Christian theology was Ferdinand Christian Baur (1792–1860). He is often presented as a theological Hegelian, but this is arguably a simplification (ibid. 51–72). While Baur, whose knowledge and understanding of contemporary philosophy and theology rivalled his expertise as a biblical and historical scholar, made no secret of his admiration for Hegel's philosophy and gave a prominent place to the presentation of his ideas in his major monographs on the history of doctrine in the 1830s and 1840s, his overarching aim was defined at a much earlier stage of his career and prior to his encounter with Hegel's philosophy. This vision consisted in a fusion of historical and philosophical theology. The truth of Christianity, he believed, could be demonstrated by inscribing its emergence into a historical trajectory that ultimately led to its full realisation in the Christian faith as the absolute religion. To attain this goal, uncompromising historical criticism was as indispensable as the most rigorous philosophical and theological analysis.

On the basis of this premise, Baur began work in the 1820s on a reconstruction of Christianity within the history of religions. His underlying conceptual framework is clearly post-Kantian, based on the duality of 'nature' and 'spirit'. This initial, conceptual dualism of nature and spirit led Baur to a historical juxtaposition of nature religions and spirit religions, and the distinction between the two is drawn, not surprisingly perhaps, on the immanence or transcendence of their deities. The duality of immanence and transcendence is thus foundational for Baur's understanding of the dynamic that moves the history of religions towards its goal. Like his idealist contemporaries, Baur sought to overcome this duality. In order for religion to come to its fulfilment, he thought, there had to be reconciliation between nature and spirit, or immanence and transcendence. This was the historic role of Christianity as the religion of reconciliation with its central feature, the Incarnation. In the person of Jesus Christ, the God-man, the dualism of nature and spirit is both preserved and solved as, according to the Chalcedonian dogma, he is fully divine and fully human, and yet one single person. In this way, Baur thought, Christianity could claim to be the 'absolute religion', the ultimate and true manifestation of what all religion was aspiring to, without however being separated and detached from the historical continuity of the history of religions.

This project inevitably led Baur to the study of the historical development of Trinitarian and Christological doctrine. For the duality of nature and spirit, immanence and transcendence is not resolved once and forever with the emergence of Christianity. Rather, it remains at the centre of theological attention throughout the history of this religion, and the development of Christianity's central dogmas is the supreme expression of this fact. Baur wrote three major monographic works on the history of Christian doctrine, *Die christliche Gnosis* [*The Christian Gnosis*] (1835), *Die christliche Lehre von der Versöhnung* [*The Christian Doctrine of Reconciliation*] (1838) and *Die christliche Lehre von der Dreieinigkeit und der Menschwerdung Gottes* The *Christian Doctrine of the Trinity and the Divine Incarnation*] (1841–3).

The last of these was published in three volumes from 1841. In line with his overall understanding of the role of Christianity in the history of religions, Baur described the overall 'theme' of the two doctrines as the relationship between God and world: 'the doctrine of God and the relationship of God to the world and to man as defined by the doctrine of the god-man' (1841–3: 1:iii). The historical development he seeks to capture on nearly 2,500 pages is driven by various attempts to conceptualise this precise relationship, leading ultimately to Baur's preferred solution in Hegel's *Philosophy of Religion*. He discusses in detail Hegel's critics who accuse him of perpetuating a system of immanence but, without failing to recognise crucial problems with Hegel's account, Baur is on the whole still willing to side with his defenders and accept that Hegel, in his view of the Spirit as the bond that overcomes the duality of immanence and transcendence, has provided the most satisfactory solution so far.

A good example of how Baur's own acceptance of the transcendent–immanent distinction coloured his interpretation of earlier thinkers is his discussion of Augustine's seminal *De trinitate* which fills the final sixty pages of the first volume of *The Christian Doctrine of the Trinity and the Incarnation*. Baur's summary of Augustine's teaching is this:

Augustine was the first to express the ... deep thought that the absolute relationship of Father and Son could only be based in the thinking mind [Geist] itself; that, as far as [this relationship] can at all be understood, it must be understood as the relationship of the thinking mind to itself. (Ibid. 1:868)

In a way that is difficult to render in English, Baur here draws on the broad meaning of the German *Geist*, which can mean both 'mind' and 'spirit'. What he takes Augustine to say, then, is that the Spirit as the common bond between Father and Son reflects the Bishop of Hippo's speculative insight in the analogy between the Trinity and the human mind. These analogies, for which *On the Trinity* is famous, indicate to Baur Augustine's awareness that the concept of mind contained the ultimate key to our understanding of the divine:

As much as Augustine time and again feels the need to remind himself that God's triune being, as it appeared to him from the doctrine of the Church, altogether transcended the mind's imagination, he could not, on the other hand, avoid the assumption, deeply rooted in the constitution of the human mind, that, if there is a key to unlock the inscrutable mystery, such a key could only lie in the rational nature of mind (*Geist*) itself. For him the spirit (*Geist*) of subjective consciousness, which initially is finite but in its finitude at the same time infinite, is the mirror of the eternal, absolute God who self-determines as the Trinity of Father, Son and Spirit. (Ibid. 1:869)

It is evident how strongly Baur's own interest in the reconciliation of immanence and transcendence informs his reading of his source. He is convinced that the Trinity has to be understood as the objective and absolute reality of mind if the dualism of nature and spirit is to be overcome. His entire approach to Augustine is determined by this premise which for him determines both Augustine's achievement and his limits.

For Baur was of course fully aware that Augustine had by no means taught the identity of the finite and the infinite spirit. Had he done so, he would hardly have achieved the status of a doctor of the church. Characteristically, Baur calls this Augustine's 'dogmatism', his concession to orthodoxy and, as such, a limitation of his investigation. By accepting on authority the truth of the Trinitarian dogma, Augustine avoided the deeper question of why God had to be thought as Trinitarian in the first place (ibid. 1:877–81). He therefore restricted his comparisons between the Trinity and the human mind to mere analogies pointing towards an understanding of the divine whose correctness was independently guaranteed by the church's magisterial teaching (ibid. 1:882). Stripping Augustine's insights of his orthodox cocoon, however, Baur suggests, reveals an even deeper truth; the parallel structure of divine spirit and human mind Augustine observed ultimately points beyond the dualism of God and world towards an understanding of God as spirit embracing and overcoming the dichotomy of immanence and transcendence.

It is arguable that Baur's criticism does not do justice to Augustine. Interestingly, the most speculative parts of the *De trinitate*, in which the Bishop of Hippo offered a probing analysis of self-consciousness, do not feature in Baur's extensive presentation of Augustine's teaching at all (Kany 2007: 314). More importantly, his reading of *On the Trinity* shows how the duality of immanence and transcendence became, soon after its establishment, a conceptual tool in historical theology and deeply influenced the reading and understanding of past religious and theological thought. Baur has been much more influential in this regard than in some of his rather questionable judgements.

Transcendence and Immanence in Albrecht Ritschl and His School

Albrecht Ritschl's (1822–89) thought took shape in the 1840s and 1850s under the influence of post-Hegelian debates about philosophy and religion. He became convinced that idealist philosophy led to pantheism and was ultimately incompatible with the theistic worldview of Christianity. At this time of his life, Hegel's critics, such as Fichte Jr, exerted considerable influence on Ritschl (Zachhuber 2013: 206–9), but in his mature thought he reached further back and Kantian insights gained considerable importance for him (Ritschl 1888: 208–11). Like Kant, Ritschl rejected epistemic claims about transcendent reality. In fact, he reserved some of his most scathing criticisms for theologians emphasising divine transcendence (ibid. 257–9). This, Ritschl thought, was incompatible with the revealed character of the Christian God.

It might then appear that Ritschl's theology was openly opposed to the very concept of transcendence. While Baur saw the role of Christianity in overcoming and reconciling the duality of immanence and transcendence, Ritschl, it could seem, rejected any reference to transcendence in the first instance as something that would lead Christians into mystical enthusiasm. Yet such an analysis would miss the main point of Ritschl's own theological position. The reason he objected to the tradition of negative theology, which he derisively called Areopagitism, is not that he rejected transcendence. Rather, he suspected that such a search for God as the other ultimately fails to recognise him as such. The God of negative theology, Ritschl claimed, is still 'nature' and as such ultimately not transcendent at all.

By contrast, it is only when conceived as purposeful will that God becomes the true representative of transcendence which Ritschl, like Baur, calls spirit (*Geist*). In other words, it is once again the duality of nature and spirit that underlies the history of religions, but the dividing line between the two is now that between the realm of physical causality and that of teleological agency (Zachhuber 2013: 180–7). And whereas Baur saw the role of Christianity in a reconciliation of nature and spirit, for Ritschl its function was to lead spirit to victory over nature whose determinism robbed humankind of its freedom and dignity.

Ritschl used Kant thus in a way characteristically different from those who appropriated him in the interest of carving out an ontological space which knowledge cannot reach but faith can. Instead, we see him draw on Kant's moral and religious thought, taking seriously the philosopher's suggestion to seek God in the context of practical reason rather than in metaphysical speculation. Yet Ritschl was not simply presenting Christianity as a religion of moral perfection. One key difference between immanent nature and transcendent spirit for him was that the former operates by means of a deterministic chain of cause and effect whereas the latter is structured by the teleology of final causes. For human beings then the former signifies the bondage of determination, while the latter promises freedom and personal flourishing. In this promise lies the specific dignity and the religious truth of Christianity which, however, has been obscured for much of its history by the fateful alliance between Christian theology and the metaphysical tradition.

The rejection of metaphysics as 'natural theology' incompatible with the spiritual and ethical character of Christianity became one of the founding principles of Ritschl's theological school. Among its members, arguably the most famous was the church historian Adolf Harnack (1851–1930). Harnack's extensive scholarly interpretation of the development of doctrine, presented most comprehensively in his *History of Dogma*, was deeply informed by Ritschl's specific version of the duality of immanence and transcendence.

Nowhere is this more apparent than in Harnack's most controversial monograph devoted to the second-century heretic, Marcion. This book was only published in 1923 but is based on material going back to Harnack's time as a student (Harnack [1923] 1990, [1870] 2003).

For Harnack, Marcion was the only theologian of the early church who understood the gospel as taught especially in Paul's letters in its radical novelty vis-à-vis the entire foregoing history of religions, pagan as well as Jewish. The utter novelty in Marcion's message, however, is nothing other than God's radical otherness and transcendence. Harnack's subtitle expresses this by describing the theme of Marcion's work as 'the gospel of the alien God'; Marcion's God is 'alien' insofar as he is not of this world and has, therefore, remained unrecognised by all prior religious history:

> [Marcion] proclaimed the *Alien* God with an entirely new 'dispositio'. He had experienced this God in Christ and only in him, therefore *he elevated the historical realism of the Christian experience to the level of the transcendent* and caught sight, beyond the dark and gloomy sphere of the world and its creator, of a new reality, that is, of a new deity. ([1923] 1990: 141)

This transcendence is not the higher sphere of metaphysical speculation. It is, as Harnack put it, the 'elevation of the historical realism of the Christian experience'; it is, in other words, the radical affirmation of the Christian God as love:

> That new reality is *love*, and nothing but love; absolutely no other feature is intermingled with this. And it is *incomprehensible* love, for out of pure mercy it accepts an entity wholly foreign to itself and, *by driving out fear*, brings to it new, eternal life. Now there is something in this world that is not of this world and is superior to it! (Ibid. 141)

This new, transcendent world is thus a future reality which, while announced and promised in Jesus Christ, will only be fully realised at the end of the current age. This alignment of the duality of immanence and transcendence with the temporal distinction of present and future was already present in Ritschl. Yet while the latter postulated a continuous and progressive historical development leading to the coming Kingdom of God, Harnack anticipates the radical eschatology of dialectical theology with a much more dualistic dichotomy of the old and the new: 'This world, together with its righteousness, its civilization, and its God, will pass away, but the new kingdom of love will abide' (ibid. 142).

Conclusion

Throughout the nineteenth century, the emergence and establishment of the duality of transcendence and immanence was largely a German story. As we have seen, it took its origin from the epistemological dualism of Kant's critical philosophy which was subsequently merged with the controversy about pantheism and applied in the tempestuous discussions about the intellectual and religious heritage of German Idealism and, specifically, of Hegel's philosophy. By the year 1840, it was conventional to inscribe current as well as historical positions in theology and the philosophy of religion into this conceptual duality. Realignments and further developments throughout the latter half of the century did little to slow its growth in popularity as a convenient shorthand for philosophical, theological and religious positions.

At the end of the century, this development entered into a new phase as the binary of immanence and transcendence gained even more ground. Perhaps the most momentous of the new contexts into which it entered at that point was Catholic thought. Maurice Blondel made the duality of immanence and transcendence the cornerstone of his theistic philosophy arguing, with clear terminological echoes of earlier debates (McNeill 1966), that Spinoza's 'principle of immanence' necessarily leads to an affirmation of transcendent truths however hostile modern rationalism seems to be to such an acknowledgement (Blondel [1894] 1997: 63). Blondel's usage was subsequently taken up by some of the most influential theologians of the twentieth century, such as Erich Przywara (1923) and Karl Rahner ([1966] 1967); the magisterial condemnation of 'immanentism' by Popes Pius X and XII furthermore indicates the significance this language gained within the Catholic Church more broadly (Denzinger et al. 2010: 3477–83, 3878).

Today, the binary of transcendence and immanence has become one of the most widely used and most evocative markers of philosophical and religious belief systems. Religious believers and theologians criticise each other for their lack of a proper acknowledgement of transcendence; secularists cite their sole reliance on the immanence of natural laws as proof for the superiority of their worldview; scholars take for granted that these two terms can be historically applied to individual and communal belief systems of the past. The purpose of this chapter is not to reject such use of these two terms, but to draw attention to the fact that its plausibility is indebted to very specific philosophical, theological and religious developments in the nineteenth century in whose long shadow we still stand.

Note

1. As is customary, page references to the *Critique of Pure Reason* correspond to the original A and B editions; page references to other works by Kant cite the *Akademie* edition numbering.

References

Arnold, Gottfried [1703] (1969), *Historie und Beschreibung der mystischen Theologie*, Stuttgart: Frommann.
Barth, Karl [1922] (1968), *The Epistle to the Romans*, trans. E. C. Hoskyns, Oxford: Oxford University Press.
Baur, Ferdinand Christian (1835), *Die christliche Gnosis oder die christliche Religions-Philosophie in ihrer geschichtlichen Entwiklung*, Tübingen: Osiander.
Baur, Ferdinand Christian (1838), *Die christliche Lehre von der Versöhnung in ihrer geschichtlichen Entwicklung von der ältesten Zeit bis auf die neueste*, Tübingen: Osiander.
Baur, Ferdinand Christian (1841–3), *Die christliche Lehre von der Dreieinigkeit und der Menschwerdung Gottes in ihrer geschichtlichen Entwicklung*, 3 vols, Tübingen: Osiander.
Blondel, Maurice [1894] (1997), 'Une des sources de la pensée moderne: l'évolution du spinozisme', in *Oeuvres complètes*, ed. C. Troisfontaine, Paris: Presses universitaires de France, 57–88.
Chadwick, Owen (1990), *The Secularization of the European Mind in the Nineteenth Century*, Cambridge: Cambridge University Press.
Denzinger Heinrich et al. (2010), *Enchiridion symbolorum definitionum et declarationum de rebus fidei et morum*, 43rd edn, Freiburg: Herder.
Diderot, Denis et al. (eds) (1765), *Encyclopédie ou dictionnaire raisonnée des sciences, des artes, et des métiers*, Neufchastel: Faulche.
Eckhart, Meister (1958), *Die deutschen Predigten*, vol. 1, ed. J. Quint, Stuttgart: Kohlhammer.
Eschenmayer, Carl August von (1840), *Grundzüge der christlichen Philosophie mit Anwendung auf die evangelischen Lehren und Thatsachen*, Basel: Spittler.

Fichte, Immanuel Hermann (1826), *Sätze zur Vorschule der Theologie*, Stuttgart: Cotta.
Fichte, Immanuel Hermann (1833–46), *Grundzüge zum Systeme der Philosophie*, 3 vols, Heidelberg: Mohr.
Harnack, Adolf von [1923] (1990), *Marcion: The Gospel of the Alien God*, trans. J. E. Steeley and L. D. Bierma, Jamestown, NY: Labyrinth Press.
Harnack, Adolf von [1870] (2003), *Marcion. Der moderne Gläubige des 2. Jahrhunderts, der erste Reformator. Die Dorpater Preisschrift*, ed. F. Steck, Berlin, New York: de Gruyter.
Hinrichs, Hermann Friedrich Wilhelm (1835), 'Review of I. H. Fichte, *Über Gegensatz, Wendepunkt und Ziel heutiger Philosophie*', *Jahrbücher für wissenschaftliche Kritik*, 97 (May): 785–98, 801–3.
Jäsche, Gottlob Benjamin (1826), *Der Pantheismus nach seinen verschiedenen Hauptformen, seinem Ursprung und Fortgange, seinem Speculativen und Praktischen Werth und Gehalt*, 2 vols, Berlin: Reimer.
Kant, Immanuel (1995–), *The Cambridge Edition of the Works of Immanuel Kant*, currently 15 vols, ed. P. Guyer and A. W. Wood, Cambridge: Cambridge University Press.
Kany, Roland (2007), *Augustins Trinitätsdenken: Bilanz, Kritik und Weiterführung der modernen Forschung zu 'De Trinitate'*, Tübingen: Mohr Siebeck.
Kraus, Christian Jakob (1812), 'Über den Pantheismus', in C. J. Kraus, *Vermischte Schriften*, vol. 5, ed. H. von Auerswald, Königsberg: Nicolovius, 1–50.
Krug, Wilhelm Traugott (1826), 'Immanent', in *Allgemeines Handwörterbuch der philosophischen Begriffe*, vol. 2, Leipzig: Brockhaus, 447.
Littré, Émile (1859), *Paroles de philosophie positive*, Paris: Adolphe Delaheys.
McCormack, Bruce L. (1995), *Karl Barth's Critically Realistic Dialectic Theology: Its Genesis and Development, 1909–1936*, Oxford: Oxford University Press.
McNeill, John J. (1966), *The Blondelian Synthesis. A Study of the Influence of German Philosophical Sources on the Formation of Blondel's Method and Thought*, Leiden: Brill.
Oeing-Hanhoff, Ludger (1976), 'Immanent, Immanenz', in *Historisches Wörterbuch der Philosophie*, vol. 4, ed. J. Ritter et al., Basel: Schwabe, 219–38.
Pannenberg, Wolfhart (1997), *Problemgeschichte der neueren evangelischen Theologie in Deutschland. Von Schleiermacher bis zu Barth und Tillich*, Göttingen: Vandenhoeck & Ruprecht.
Przywara, Erich (1923), 'Gott in uns oder Gott über uns? (Immanenz und Transzendenz im heutigen Geistesleben)', *Stimmen der Zeit*, 105: 343–62
Rahner, Karl [1966] (1967), 'Immanente und transzendente Vollendung der Welt', in *Schriften zur Theologie*, vol. 8, Zurich: Benziger, 593–609.
Ritschl, Albrecht (1888), *Die christliche Lehre von der Rechtfertigung und Versöhnung*, 3rd edn, Bonn: Marcus.
Scheidler, Karl Hermann (1839), 'Immanenz', in J. S. Ersch and J. G. Gruber (eds), *Allgemeine Encyclopädie der Wissenschaften und Künste*, vol. II/16, Leipzig: Brockhaus, 314–17.
Schelling, F. W. J. (1856), *Sämmtliche Werke*, 14 vols, ed. K. F. A. Schelling, Stuttgart: Cotta.
Schlegel, Friedrich (1808), *Über die Sprache und Weisheit der Indier*, Heidelberg: Mohr und Zimmer.
Schwarz, Carl (1847), *Das Wesen der Religion*, 2 vols, Halle: Schwetschke.
Spinoza, Benedictus de (1925), *Opera, im Auftrag der Heidelberger Akademie der Wissenschaften herausgegeben*, 4 vols, ed. C. Gebhardt, Heidelberg: Winter.
Storr, Gottlob Christian (1794), *Bemerkungen über Kant's philosophische Religionslehre*, Tübingen: Cotta.
Vallée, Gérard (1988), *The Spinoza Conversations between Lessing and Jacobi: Texts with Excerpts from the Ensuing Controversy*, trans. G. Vallée, J. B. Lawson and G. C. Chapple, Lanham: University Press of America.
Zachhuber, Johannes (2000), 'Überschwänglich. Ein Wort der Mystikersprache bei Immanuel Kant', *Archiv für Begriffsgeschichte*, 42: 139–54.
Zachhuber, Johannes (2013), *Theology as Science in Nineteenth-Century Germany: From F. C. Baur to Ernst Troeltsch*, Oxford: Oxford University Press.

10

Mediation

Andrew W. Hass

ὁ δὲ μεσίτης ἑνὸς οὐκ ἔστιν, ὁ δὲ θεὸς εἷς ἐστιν.
[Now a mediator is not {a mediator} of one, but God is one.] (Galatians 3: 20)

If the demand for mediation in the Christian theological schema is unambiguous, it is because that schema shares in traditional conceptions of the divine as a realm that, by definition, exceeds this world, and therefore exceeds human capacities. This is a question of incommensurability: the two worlds are not of the same measure, and some kind of mediating function is required to allow translation, interaction, communality, relation. If in addition that schema unfolds a human *defaulting* on what was once a unity across those worlds, a *wilful* defaulting, which puts one party out of relation with the other, then mediation is that much more required, now in the terms of reconciliation or atonement. If, further, that schema allows the one world to embody, totally and comprehensively, the realm of the other, and not merely on the level of its created order, but on the level of human experience, then mediation has been consummated in the very schema itself – the divine, as the Incarnate, both incarnates and enacts the mediatory role. This is such a foundational theological point that the Apostle Paul predicates his entire apostleship upon it (1 Timothy 2: 5–7).

But if the Christian *demand* is unambiguous, the Christian *role*, in Christ, as Christ, is less so. For the incarnation of a monotheistic God confounds the simple role of mediation between two distinct parties: it requires a mediation both between God and humanity *and* within the Godhead itself, which has disrupted its own unity for the sake of outward reconciliation by taking on human flesh. Thus Paul, in his letter to the Galatians, feels compelled to maintain that though a mediator must, by definition, mediate across more than one party, nevertheless God remains one, wholly unified. Thomas Aquinas saw the difficulty in this move. In the *Summa Theologica*, Part III, he addresses the questions 'Whether it is proper to Christ to be the Mediator of God and man?' (Question 26, Article 1) and 'Whether Christ is the Mediator of God and men?' (Question 26, Article 2). After establishing in the first Article that it is proper for Christ to be Mediator (in distinction from prophets, priests, angels and even the Holy Spirit), he then qualifies in the second Article that it is proper only for Christ as *man*, not as God. He explains:

> We may consider two things in a mediator: first, that he is a mean [*rationem medii*]; secondly, that he unites others [*officium coniungendi*]. Now it is of the nature of a mean to be distant from each extreme: while it unites by communicating to one that which belongs to the other. Now neither of these can be applied to Christ as God, but only as

man. For, as God, He does not differ from the Father and the Holy Ghost in nature and power of dominion: nor have the Father and the Holy Ghost anything that the Son has not, so that He be able to communicate to others something belonging to the Father or the Holy Ghost, as though it were belonging to others than Himself. But both can be applied to Him as man. Because, as man, He is distant both from God, by nature, and from man by dignity of both grace and glory ... And therefore He is most truly called Mediator, as man. (Aquinas [1274] 1947: 3.26.2)

In order to keep the Godhead's unity, only Christ's human side can mediate. Aquinas will elsewhere work out the Trinitarian challenges of Christ's dual nature (e.g. ibid. 3.16, 17), and affirm, along with Paul, God's internal unity. But when it comes to mediation, only something with difference can act 'in between', and it is in human nature to possess this difference.

The challenge of internal difference is at the heart of the modern philosophical project, and nowhere more exigent than in the aftermath of Kant's critical enterprise. For if the pre-Kantian subject found her difference in the objective world around her, a difference mediated by any number of forces extrinsic to her consciousness (including the sensory apparatus, rational cognition, or, still, God), the post-Kantian subject had no such recourse. For in the Kantian move that spawned the legacy of German Idealism, mediation becomes intrinsic to consciousness as such (as do sensation, rational cognition and God). It becomes less a question of what one knows as objective, and more a question of *how* one knows, and indeed how one knows *objectivity itself*. This shift is modal: both the knowing self and the objective world it intends to know are now constituted by a mode of thinking. The objective world is no longer the difference outside of us, but now our very own difference, the internal difference of the knowing self creating the objective world around it, and thereby subsuming difference as its own function. The issue in this shift then becomes, not what third party can mediate for me, as I stand over against the world, but rather what role must mediation play, if now I am the generator, and the wholly self-contained generator, of the reality I experience both within me and around me?

'Through all Kant's philosophizing runs a search for the "middle term"', writes Karl Jaspers. 'The middle term is always found by operations of the understanding – yet it is never a known object, but a mode in which something which "in itself" remains hidden is manifested to us' ([1957] 1962: 88). How exactly this hidden mediation, as a mode, manifests itself within our very own selves will be the difficult task for all subsequent Idealists to unfurl. What I want to argue in the text to follow is that the very 'transcendental' dilemma set up by Kant – how the always mediately knowing self can know itself immediately as that mediation; or how our own knowing can be known *purely* by us, before mediated experience – is the same dilemma as that encountered by Aquinas in understanding Christ the Mediator within the Godhead: the retention of unity amid difference by means of humanising mediation. And the dilemma of this dilemma is that it requires a divine act to overcome it, but an act that, in overcoming, divides its own unity. As we will see with Fichte, Schelling, Schleiermacher and Hegel, in texts that emerge on the threshold of a new century, the resulting challenge of these compounding dilemmas is not so much that the office of mediation must become human, as it is that the mediating act of the human must become divine. This challenge goes to the very heart of both Idealist and Romantic German thought, and to the theological turbulence that marked the rest of the nineteenth century.

Fichte

If the challenge for Kant was the *Ding an sich* (thing-in-itself) of the mediatory function, which would allow self-consciousness to ground its own grounding, this apparent oxymoron – the thing-in-itself is, by definition, unmediated – was overcome first and perhaps most emphatically by the most critically committed of his followers, Johann Gottlieb Fichte. For what Fichte proposed was a way for that consciousness to reach its own purity, in the same sense that Kant's 'pure reason' sought for the a priori ground of reason before experience, without giving itself over to a noumenal realm. The pure 'I', as it arises in Fichte's most celebrated and, for our purposes, most significant work, the *Wissenschaftslehre*, or *The Science of Knowledge*, first published in 1794–5,[1] is the self that does not merely *exist* in some absolute sense, but which exists by virtue of *its own self-positing*. The concept of existence, he tells us, is in fact derivative of the activity of the self in its freedom to posit itself ([1797] 1982: 69). This is to say, the self-positing precedes the posited. As he describes it later:

> *That whose being or essence consists simply in the fact that it posits itself as existing*, is the self as absolute subject. As it *posits* itself, so it *is*; and as it *is*, so it *posits* itself; and hence the self is absolute and necessary for the self. (Ibid. 98)

The circularity here means that one cannot be conscious of one's own prior existence as a substrate to that consciousness without first employing that consciousness to think or contemplate the substrate; but in that very employing, the substrate comes into existence, for 'from your self-consciousness you can never abstract' (ibid. 98).

Perhaps the best way to understand this circularity, without it reverting to a self-contradiction, is to consider the term Fichte coins here to capture the self-positing activity of the 'I' as absolute subject: *Tathandlung*. This compound word is made up of two German words for action, that of *Tat* (from the past tense of the verb *tun*, to do), and *Handlung* (from the verb *handeln*, to act, behave). Since the first is derived from the imperfect state of something already done, the *Tat* carries the sense of a 'fact', as it is rendered fully in the German *Tatsache* (literally, the 'done thing'); while the second carries the sense of ongoing behaviour in the implementation, or 'act' (originally, we presume, something resulting from *die Hände*, the hands[2]). Hence the established fact of *Tatsache* becomes the establishing fact of *Tathandlung*, or the fact/act. The auto-condition of the self is that it establishes itself as a fact – 'I', 'Ego' – whose very fact is this self-establishing. Fact and act collapse into each other, and in their convergence they become the primordial basis of a new ground, a first principle of a post-Kantian self: the self that makes itself its own fact.

The most problematic division in the Kantian scheme was, for Fichte, thus resolved, in that the two divided realms of the phenomena and noumena were now no longer required. The *Ding an sich* cannot be something that exists outside of our experience, and therefore outside our self. Only dogmatism can hold that the self is ultimately posited in some higher realm or being, without supplying on what that realm or being is grounded itself. The break that a *Wissenschaftslehre* offers as a first principle *science* is that, in the *Tathandlung*, the ground is internally supplied of its own accord. There is no need for some transcendent outside to ground all knowledge, for the *Tathandlung* self-grounds. And in doing so it collapses all other distinctions of the self into each other: subject/object, self/not-self and intuition/intellect.

In respect to the latter, Fichte could develop, directly upon the *Tathandlung*, the concept of an 'intellectual intuition' (*intellektuelle Anschauung*) that Kant himself could only acknowledge as possible in theory but not, so to speak, in practice. (The practice of the theoretical was precisely the problem.) If intuition was the reception of sense data before any conceptualising apparatus could convert it into something graspable by our understanding – before, that is, an intellectual *mediation* – then an *intellectual* intuition was, for Kant, a problem, since the intellectual was precisely the realm that *received* the sensible (as the realm that first *received* an object), and such reception, by definition, precluded conflation. Kant admits, in the first *Critique*, that God would need to conflate the two, since the intellectual, as thought, involves limitations (*Kritik* exposes the limits), and God, by definition, does not have limitations. If such a God were to exist, all his knowledge must be unmediated intuition, and therefore, as primordial being, he alone would possess intellectual intuition ([1781/7] 1929: B72). But dependent beings are dependent on the relations of things around them in space and time, relations that make their intuition derivative, and therefore all their knowledge must come by way of sensible intuition mediated by intellectual thought structures. Only God could originate an intuition in such a way that the object of that intuition and the knowledge of that intuition were one and the same, wholly unmediated. As Kant explicitly states of our sensibility: 'It is derivative (*intuitus derivativus*), not original (*intuitus originarius*), and therefore not an intellectual intuition' (ibid. B72). If we are going to have knowledge a priori, it can only come through the mode of thinking that is itself a mediating structure.

Now Fichte felt this to be a grave disservice to the knowledge we were claiming to derive, since it will always, and necessarily, preclude the thing-in-itself. In Kant, our sensibility is always already mediating, since it only receives the objects given to it as representations. The unity of those representations into a conceptual whole is then the business of the synthetic judgement of reason (the famous unity of apperception in the 'Transcendental Deduction'). To bypass somehow this mediation would be to suggest we could have an immediate consciousness of a nonsensuous entity, that is, of the thing-in-itself, and this in the Kantian scheme is simply not possible. It is even, under the *Kritik*, anathema, because it would imply that our consciousness partakes in the creation of the thing-in-itself by way of its own conceptual structures. But in Fichte's scheme as *Wissenschaftslehre*, the problem of the *Ding an sich* is done away with by shifting the question away from the existence of the object (either as given in representation or as the noumenal thing-in-itself) and towards the *Tathandlung*. 'The intellectual intuition alluded to in the Science of Knowledge refers, not to existence at all, but rather to action', he reiterates (1982: 46). It is not that the sensible, in deriving a representation, then yields to an intellectual apperception, which in turn grounds its existence as phenomenon. Rather the intellect, as self-conscious action, as *Tathandlung*, derives the possibility of all knowledge from itself, from within, which is to say it mediates the world through its own immediacy, as action.[3]

The theological implications of Fichte's position were vast, and controversial. If his predecessor, Kant himself, received official censure from the royal court upon his publication of *Religion within the Limits of Reason Alone* only a few years earlier in 1792 (and again in 1794), and published his text only by virtue of the authority granted to German universities in publishing scholarly work on religion, Fichte went one further, and under the charge of atheism was dismissed from his academic chair at Jena in 1799. Though the controversy was in relation to a separate journal article,[4] that publication was nevertheless in accordance with the principles of the *Wissenschaftslehre*, insofar as it substituted the *existence* of God for the moral *action* that brings God about. It was this kind of 'subjective idealism' that, as Jacobi disparaged it ([1799] 1987), led to nihilism, and ultimately to Fichte's dismissal. If the 'I' brings about its own fact as act, placing *Tathandlung* above *Existenz*, then humans are their own mediatory agents, and no higher mediation is required. Moreover, if what might be deemed a reality outside and unavailable to us, the *Ding an sich*, is itself no longer tenable, then Fichte did not even have recourse, as Kant did, to a back-door escape route: God might exist as such, but we are not privy to the *as such*. Fichte's science of knowledge in effect does away with theology in the traditional metaphysical sense of a divine power residing in a realm transcendent to the human experience, by means of what Thomas Pfau calls 'the inherently anthropomorphic constitution of subjectivity at the centre and circumference of all knowledge' (1994: 22). We might even say that, here in the *Wissenschaftslehre* (if not perhaps in the later works, which at times appear to reverse the immanental framework of the self-positing 'I'), a philosophy of religion that purely functions outside theology is properly born.

Schelling

In 1801 – and we must remember that the key questions concerning the philosophy and theology of mediation were being forged not in a *fin de siècle* of decadence and angst, but in a *début de siècle* of idealism and new promise – the philosopher who, at Schelling's bidding, entered the University of Jena just after Fichte's departure, G. W. F. Hegel, wrote and published *The Difference Between Fichte's and Schelling's System of Philosophy*. In it, Hegel challenged the prevailing perception of Schelling as an inheritor of Fichtean philosophy. If Fichte, in the *Tathandlung*, brought the subject as act together with the object as fact, it could do this only in the pure self-consciousness of the interior 'I'. Hegel called this a *subjective* Subject-Object identity. But there remained Nature, an absolute objectivity, yet with its own Subject-Object dynamic (whereby Nature posits its own self-subsisting reality as fact, following first Spinoza, then Kant), which Hegel rendered an *objective* Subject-Object identity. If there was going to be *absolute* identity between Subject and Object (and thus all the other pairings: self/not-self, nature/mind, empirical/conceptual, intuition/intellect, practical/theoretical, etc.) as Fichte had claimed, then there also needed to be an absolute identity, or absolute indifference, between the *subjective* Subject-Object identity and the *objective* Subject-Object identity. An identity of identities, that is. As Hegel writes:

> For absolute identity to be the principle of an entire system it is necessary that *both* subject and object be posited as Subject-Object. In Fichte's system identity constitutes itself only as *subjective* Subject-Object. [But] this subjective Subject-Object needs an objective Subject-Object to complete it . . . ([1801] 1977a: 155)

And where does one find such a unification? 'The principle of identity is the absolute principle of Schelling's system as a *whole*' (ibid. 155).

In Schelling's own *System of Transcendental Idealism* of 1800, the young Schelling put the problem this way: 'how, then, is the entire system of knowledge (e.g. the objective world with all its determinations, history, etc.) posited through the self without existing 'only for the self'? ([1800] 1978: 34). Now, on the surface it may appear that Schelling's answer comes in the form of a general commendation, even approbation, of Fichte's main principles in the *Wissenschaftslehre*: the priority of idealism over dogmatism; the understanding of self-consciousness principally as *act*, and hence the priority of act over existence; the identity of subject and object within the self, and therefore the founding formula

'I = I' or 'self = self'; the requirement of a fundamental opposition to make that formula hold, so that the self-positing 'I' must be predicated upon its not-self; the coming together of theoretical and practical philosophy; and the assumption of an intellection intuition at the heart of all these operations. But there were two fundamental differences with Fichte, which can be seen from Schelling's title alone.

The first is that of 'system' versus 'science'. It is true that Schelling acknowledged the *Wissenschaft*, the 'science' of Fichte's programme, as the groundwork for founding the first principle of all knowledge not on something extraneous to itself (as with the dogmatists) but within its own devices. And in this sense he equates his *System* with Fichte's *Wissenschaft*: 'Now every true system (such as that of the cosmos, for example) must contain the ground of its subsistence within *itself*; and hence, if there be a system of knowledge, its principle must *lie within knowledge itself*' (ibid. 15). But insofar as this *Wissenschaft* understands this knowledge purely from the starting point of the 'I', and in terms of the self's active immediacy, its self-positing does not, and cannot, take into account Nature's own knowledge, by which Nature itself can be a subject positing its own self objectively. In the language of mediacy, if the self can make immediate its own mediacy in the *Tathandlung*, how can it account for the immediacy that Nature brings, not merely for itself, but in our sensible interaction with it? This was Hegel's question, who felt that the opposing object as Nature got swallowed up in the pure subjectivity of the Absolute 'I'. For Schelling, as he had already begun to express in his *Naturphilosophie* several years earlier ([1797] 1988), if Fichte was going to abandon the Kantian dualism between phenomena and noumena, the *Wissenschaft* must at least show how the thing-in-itself can be appropriated by the 'I' in such a way as to remain not colonised by the 'I' but parallel to the 'I''s own productive act, or what Schelling called in the foreword to his *System* the 'parallelism of nature with intelligence' ([1800] 1978: 2). What this entails is therefore not so much a deductive science, and far less an explanatory science, predicated upon causality, where one side is the ground of the other. What it entails is more an *organic system*, where what is in parallel is in fact mutually productive of the other.

In the middle of the *System of Transcendental Idealism*, Schelling addresses organism itself, and states: 'The basic character of organization [as organic interrelation] is that, excluded as it were from mechanism, it subsists not merely as cause or effect, but through itself, since it is at once both cause and effect of itself' (ibid. 125–6). Now this internal conflation we saw in the *Tathandlung*, but here it is extended to all organic matter and life, not just the acting self. Indeed, we could take this as general statement of the entire *System*, whereby all oppositions (nature and intelligence, subject and object, consciousness and nonconsciousness, form and content, finite and infinite, realism and idealism, practice and theory, etc.) fall into organic interrelation, and it is the intellectual intuiting of this interrelation that makes knowledge *systematic*. Rather than being successive or progressive, the system becomes circular, leading one to its opposite but then back to its beginning point again, and it is the absolutising of this whole circular activity that Schelling is striving to articulate.

The second difference is the subtle shift from 'transcendental philosophy' to 'transcendental idealism'. If the former represents the Kantian tradition of the self abstracting the *how* of its own powers of reason through limitation and active self-positing, the latter represents, not a heightening of the abstraction into the self (as the term 'idealism' alone might suggest), but a recalibration of the *how* across the idealism–realism spectrum. Schelling says that idealism and realism – the active productivity of intuiting, and the thingness of being, respectively – necessarily presuppose each other. But, anticipating

Hegel, 'If I reflect upon *the two together*, a third view arises from both, which may be termed *ideal-realism*, or what we have hitherto designated by the name of transcendental idealism' (ibid. 41). What this ideal-realism intends to capture is not the philosophical point at which idealism becomes possible and necessary (Kant), nor even the *ideal* point at which one can know that philosophical point (Fichte), but the transcendence of the ideal that can go even beyond itself, to embrace what is not itself in a world that subsists independently around it.

In order to effect this transcendence, the system, as System, must enfold a self, as self-consciousness, that can somehow partake in this independence, and partake in it freely. (If it cannot do this freely, it loses its great Fichtean power: the ability to posit itself as its own condition, unreliant upon the conditioning of some other thing.) It needs, we might say, some mediating force or agency that is not solely its *own* power but also not exclusive of its own power. After setting up this problem in the first two parts of the argument, Schelling will go on to explicate the principles of transcendental idealism as provision for this mediation. But the mediation becomes a dialectic, as it works towards what he calls an 'absolute synthesis' between the ideal and real. And this synthesis, as dialectical product, is itself 'productivity' or 'producing' (*Producieren*) – and therefore not a static product at all. In the self's act of self-grounding self-consciousness, there is a kind of striving (Fichte's *Streben*) towards infinite and limitless productivity. But that striving is always bound by limitation (again following Fichte), which produces the products we know as things. Yet such striving (now contra Fichte) is not merely within the self, determining the self as 'I', and allowing all other things to be presented accordingly; it is also within Nature, which produces its own products, entities and events. In the dialectic of the two strivings, we find a sense of history: self-consciousness is not merely an isolated Ego operating in a self-contained vacuum, but an activity that reaches into the world, just as the world reaches into self. Thus the synthesis unfolds in 'epochs', so that self-consciousness has a history – a point Hegel will famously appropriate. But the mediating factor in the dialectical movement, the productive striving throughout its unfolding epochs, is not strictly a Fichtean self-consciousness of absolute I = I, but again, an 'I' having to give itself up to an organicism in which even consciousness yields to something outside itself. Hence, in the synthesis of self- and world-striving arises an *unconsciousness*, a striving power that is not wholly objective either to the subjective self or to Nature, but which nonetheless coincides with both, and indeed drives both. The paragon that is given at the end of the *System* is Art: there is in the depiction of the work of art a determined product or real object, but in the producing of that work there lies an unconscious realisation of the original ideal unity that exceeds both the self-conscious artist as producer and the thing that is originally depicted, as much as the self-conscious viewer who later contemplates it. The system of transcendental idealism as whole, then, is an attempt to figure this unity as it comes to light through an act of intuiting that is as much artistic as it is philosophical – a 'productive intuition', he calls it, now made universally and organically harmonised with the outer world.[5]

Near the opening of his *System*, Schelling writes that 'knowledge proper presupposes a concurrence of opposites, whose concurrence can only be a *mediated* one'. He then adds, with emphasis: '*Hence there must be some universally mediating factor in our knowledge, which is the sole ground thereof*' ([1800] 1978: 15). The system that follows, in all its formulations and intricacies, becomes an unveiling of that factor in and as productive intuition, the irreducible principle upon which the entire system of knowledge is founded. But since the mediating factor *grounds itself*, as a system, it must play more than a strictly mediating role to the system's whole. This is why he goes on directly to say, 'This principle is the mediating or indirect principle in every science, but the *immediate and direct* principle only of the *science of all knowledge*, or transcendental philosophy' (ibid. 15–16). The addition here to the Kantian and Fichtean schemes is the word 'all', in which is born transcendental idealism as a system. Critique of reason and science of knowledge both required a universal principle to mediate on their behalf; but in transcendental idealism that universal principle becomes *immediate* in the 'all' that is system, through a productive intuition that unites all, conscious and unconscious alike.

To be sure, the young Schelling is not so much interested in theology and religion here in this seminal work as the older Schelling will become. But late in the argument he does acknowledge a religious implication of his *System*. If the immediate principle in productive intuition reflects only on the unconscious (objective) side of its action, then it becomes bound to acts that are predetermined, outside the freedom of self-consciousness. This he equates with fatalism. If the immediate principle reflects only on the conscious (subjective) side of its action, then it becomes bound to arbitrary determining, outside of law and necessity. This he equates with irreligion and atheism. But if in reflection the two sides are 'elevated to that absolute which is the common ground of the harmony between freedom and intelligence, we reach the system of providence, that is, *religion* in the only true sense of the word' (ibid. 209). Here he hints at Schleiermacher.

But Schelling quickly qualifies this elevation and harmony: if the two sides were ever to fully coincide, the whole would seem to favour the side of a necessary law or necessary historical movement that justifies the whole, and so our freedom, ultimately, would become illusory. (We would simply be pawns in a larger controlled game.) The completion of this movement – that is, the manifest existence of *God* – could never take place without our freedom being jeopardised. The way out of this rather ancient theological dilemma for Schelling is (as Hegel will duly note) to keep the movement, as dialectical, ongoing, never completed or consummated, so that 'History as a whole is a progressive, gradually self-disclosing revelation of the absolute'; God is never existent in a singular point of that history, 'but He continually *reveals* Himself' (ibid. 211). The divine, then, cannot come to us in a pure and objective manifestation, or we would cease to be human in the sense of free self-consciously active beings. The divine can only come *mediated* through our own productivity: 'Man, through his history, provides a continuous demonstration of God's presence, a demonstration, however, which only the whole of history can render complete' (ibid. 211). And since the whole of history is not knowable to us, the continuous must remain continuous, and God must remain a never wholly completed revelation.

Though Schelling will later return to the question of revelation in a much more positive light,[6] here we see the conundrum of Christian mediation in new relief. If mediation presumes at least two parties, as the Apostle Paul avers, with unity forever put at risk, then the pure immediate unity of the divine, or in Schelling's terms, 'the eternal identity and the everlasting ground of harmony' (ibid. 211), can only come to us through the mediation of our own historical and cultural productivity, which means an ongoing, self-perpetuating revelation, or, to adapt Spinoza's term, a *revelata revelatans*. But this very mediation undoes the immediacy it is trying to reveal. The only way to preserve the immediacy is to reinstate it dialectically, in an ongoing and simultaneous oscillation between the conscious and unconscious, and to make that dialectical movement itself an *immediate* intuition. Schelling's tendency, however, was to err on the side of the unconscious, or of an Absolute that went beyond both sides.

Schleiermacher

A year before *System of Transcendental Idealism*, in 1799, Friedrich Schleiermacher, at the time a relatively unknown pastor and chaplain, introduced *Reden über die Religion* (*On Religion: Speeches to Its Cultured Despisers*) into this fertile period of German Idealism and Romanticism. Though less 'philosophical' in its initial look and feel, certainly compared with Kant, Fichte and Schelling, it drew heavily, if selectively, from these figures and the prevailing philosophical Zeitgeist they helped to form, and even if Schleiermacher's 'national sensation' first came out a year before Schelling's *System*, Schleiermacher would continue to revise it, and offer three more editions (1806, 1821 and 1831), so that it might be seen as very much following upon that early post-Kantian tradition, and even upon Schelling's *System*.

Given the title, and the author's own concern for those beyond the intelligentsia of philosophical esotericism – Schleiermacher was raised in the Pietist tradition, we recall – the *Speeches*, of which there are five, do not concern themselves with the specialised calibrations of philosophical minutiae. Rather they try to set out a defence of the idea of religion, perhaps even a 'philosophy of religion', in terms that the cultural despisers, or those who now feel that religion has lost its cultural credibility and currency, might readily entertain. But in doing so they offer a thinking about mediation that both confirms and expands those we have seen so far. For in his attempt to harmonise the immediacy of feeling and intuition in relation to the Deity with the mediacy of understanding and thought in relation to humanity, Schleiermacher much more forcefully and more directly embeds theology into the equation, not merely as an implication, as in the young Fichte and Schelling, but as the very point of departure.

At the opening of his First Speech, Schleiermacher affirms the problem of mediation as one between two fundamentally opposing poles, which nevertheless require each other to exist: the individual versus the Whole. But instead of beginning with the self, with an 'I' set against Nature, he begins, strikingly, with the Divine – *not* to show its eternally abiding unity, which somehow remains foreign and unavailable to us, but quite the opposite, to show its own internal *division*, which remains very much part of our experience:

> You know how the Deity, by an immutable law, has compelled Himself to divide His great work even to infinity. Each definite thing can only be made up by melting together two opposite activities. Each of His eternal thoughts can only be actualized in two hostile yet twin forms, one of which cannot exist except by means of the other. The whole corporeal world, insight into which is the highest aim of your researches, appears to the best instructed and most contemplative among you, simply a never-ending play of opposing forces. Each life is merely the uninterrupted manifestation of a perpetually renewed gain and loss, as each thing has its determinate existence by uniting and holding fast in a special way the opposing forces of Nature. ([1821] 1958: 3–4)

Now the extraordinary admission in his passage is not where it ends, the uniting of opposing forces in Nature, which is Fichte and Schelling in standard guise, but where it begins, the *divine compulsion to divide its own singular activity into opposing sides*. If the actualisation (*zur Wirklichkeit zu bringen*) of divine eternal thoughts already necessitates division, or two opposing sides (even if we are talking about an actualisation in *this world*), then we already have a sense of the young Schleiermacher's bold theology: any immediate intuition of the eternal will be of a divided impulse, and so that intuition, however immediate, will itself be divided, and will require mediation. If we are going to share in the divine, as a religious experience, we must do so through the mediation of our own intuition, which is, paradoxically, immediate. It is the fusion of these two opposites *as both instigated by and characteristic of the Divine* that marks the Speeches as so radical.

In describing how this fusion takes place, Schleiermacher opens neither with a philosophical explication of the self's epistemological groundwork, nor with a traditional Christology whereby the divided God-man is able, through his human side, to mediate on behalf of humanity the divine realms from which he also partakes. Rather, he speaks of other rarefied humans sent by God to interpret the Deity and his works and to be 'reconciler of things that otherwise would be eternally divided' (ibid. 6). These exceptional humans ('the best instructed and most contemplative among you' from the longer quote above, who, we sense, must include the very author himself), are 'ambassadors of God [*Gesandte Gottes*]' who become 'mediators between limited man and infinite humanity' (ibid. 6). And before we judge this seemingly anthropomorphic move as a stratagem to convince the sceptical without using the language of traditional theology, we need to understand this move in the larger philosophical context, that is, in the fact that revealed religion is already divided, and that the restoration of that revelation involves as much the mediation of human endeavour as it does the actions of the divine.

The entire argument of the five speeches, therefore, seeks to justify this kind of mediation, even if it centres on the immediacy that is intuition (*Anschauung*), feeling (*Gefühl*) and/or 'immediate self-consciousness [*unmittelbare Selbstbewusstein*]'. Remarkably in the course of that argument, *all* human beings, by virtue of this immediacy, become mediators, not just the chosen few. Each individual becomes a 'compendium of humanity': by working one's way back to immediate self-consciousness as intuition and feeling, one 'is no more in need of a mediator for any sort of intuition of humanity. Rather, he is himself a mediator for many' (ibid. 79). Dalia Nassar has decisively shown that this kind of mediation is both passive and active, receiving the (divided) infinite that is the Universe's, but also actively creating the (divided) infinite within the World, particularly through communication:

> Communication as community-creation is the determination of what is indeterminate, in other words the bringing of the infinite universe into the finite world, or mediation ... In communication, one is not merely communicating but, more significantly, creating a world, a 'perfect republic', that mediates the finite, or through which the infinite mediates itself. The individual is thus not a passive agent but also a creator. Through such creation, the world, as mediation, and the individual, as mediator, become mirrors of the universe. (2006: 838; see also Scott 1968: 499–512)

We can see this mediatory dynamic, especially regarding 'communication', at work in Schleiermacher's later hermeneutical thinking (between the 'comparative' and 'divinatory' methods, for example, but even within the latter alone, whereby we can come to know the author's thought and intentions better than the author herself[7]) as well as in *The Christian Faith* of 1830.[8] And even if the more mature Schleiermacher will push into view the mediating figure of Christ as Redeemer,[9] he never deviates from the indispensably dialectical role humans must play as laid out even in the first edition of the Speeches.

The crucial contribution of Schleiermacher, then, is not only to bring the Divine immediately into the mediating necessity – actualising eternal thought so that it can be experienced even in its *immediacy* requires division and mediation – but also to bring the human immediately into the divine mediating creativity. In Schleiermacher's impassioned image: 'It is the holy wedlock of the Universe with the incarnated Reason for a creative, productive embrace' ([1821] 1958: 43). This is not to say that humans are divine, nor even that the Divine is human – as such. But it is to suggest that, in making the immediate necessarily mediate, and vice versa, the absolute dependence to which humans must give themselves over in the experience of the Divine must, in a sense, go both ways.

Hegel

If, in the foregoing turn-of-the-century philosophical ferment, attempts to overcome the opposition of the mediate and the immediate were characterised by a certain dialectical movement, or striving, or productivity, which not only mediated between the two sides, but, in that mediation, offered its own immediacy, then it was Hegel who brought those attempts to their apogee.

We might first turn to the opening of Hegel's *Science of Logic* of 1812, rather than to the text that appears to follow more directly out of the line forged by his fellow philosophers, the *Phenomenology of Spirit* of 1807, to best see Hegel's move. In the *Greater Logic*, as it became known, at the beginning of Book I, 'The Doctrine of Being', Hegel states:

> that there is nothing, nothing in heaven or in nature or mind [*Geist*] or anywhere else which does not equally contain both immediacy and mediation, so that these two determinations reveal themselves to be *unseparated* and inseparable and the opposition between them to be a nullity. ([1812–16] 1969: 68)

To parse this statement, and to fully understand its advance on the previous versions of the immediacy/mediacy divide in post-Kantian thought, we need to differentiate it from Hegel's own *Phenomenology*. Hegel does this for us in the *Greater Logic*. At the opening section entitled 'With What must the Science [*Wissenschaft*] Begin?', Hegel makes it clear that the beginning point for any philosophy has tended to be thought of in terms either of an objective determinate beginning – for example, the beginning of all things is water, the one, *nous*, idea, and so on – or of a subjective criterion – for example, we must begin with thought, intuition, sensation, ego, subjectivity, and so on. More recent philosophy has focused on the *immediacy* of the latter, and its subsequent relation to objective determinations. But this immediacy does not yet penetrate to the beginning of that which allows consciousness its powers of immediate knowing in the first place. The more conventional immediate knowing, the empirical sensuous knowledge, Hegel had explicated in the *Phenomenology* in the opening chapter on sense certainty. There he tried to show how, following a tradition from Fichte to Schleiermacher, neither the object that is being sensed or intuited nor the 'I' that senses or intuits is purely immediate, 'but each is at the same time *mediated*: I have this certainty *through* something else, viz. the thing; and it, similarly, is in sense certainty *through* somethings else, viz. through the "I"' ([1807] 1977b: 59). And from this mediation he goes on to show how both sides are self-dirempted in this certainty as truth, or as he describes it in the *Greater Logic*:

> the certainty which, on the one hand, no longer has the object over against it but has internalized it, knows it as its own self – and, on the other hand, has given up the knowledge of itself as of something confronting the object of which it is only the annihilation, has divested [*entäußert*] itself of this subjectivity and is at one with its self-alienation [*Entäußerung*]. ([1812–16] 1969: 69)

But this immediacy is not yet *pure immediacy*, or what he calls 'simple immediacy', in that it does not yet get us to the beginning of the pure knowledge that knows the mediated immediacy we call sense certainty, or knows that the immediacy is always and already mediated. That pure immediacy is the pure beginning of a *logic* (vs a phenomenology) that knows not the beginning of a principle (the first principle of philosophy begins *here*, at point X – e.g. sense certainty), but rather the principle of beginning (beginning, as a principle, begins as origination). And the radical nature of *this* beginning, as origination, is not that, in its purity, it precedes or exceeds knowing (either *Glauben* or *Wissenschaft*), but precisely that it is *knowing in its purity*, knowing knowing as such, or, knowing beginning as beginning knowing.

Now how can one know pure beginning, since it is not yet here nor there, and not even, as the *Phenomenology* tell us, 'now'?[10] How can one grasp the principle of beginning in pure immediacy alone, as a moment of beginning, the beginning of principle, as beginning? The answer Hegel gives us goes back to the *Phenomenology*, yet less to its content and more to its form: one must come to the beginning by way of a passage, a journey, an odyssey that carries us through consciousness and self-consciousness back to the ground of their being (consciousness). That is, one comes to the beginning through mediation, and through mediation divesting (*entäußert*) itself of itself and becoming one with its self-alienation (*Entäußerung*) immediately. This would be the endpoint of the *Phenomenology*, absolute knowing in all its mediated form and formation, or now the beginning point of the *Science of Logic*, as pure being.

To understand this circularity, and how it fits in with our larger concerns, we need to see how Hegel here in the *Greater Logic* equates pure knowing, as the absolute beginning of simple immediacy, with pure being. This equation is as radical as the claim to know beginning as the mediately immediate. Conventional philosophy tells us that epistemology treats our capacity to know, ontology our structure of being, and logic our formal modes of cognition. Hegel asks us to rethink these distinctions. If logic consisted solely in empty formal structures into which we place content in order to arrive at knowledge or truth, then the old dualisms that began with Kant are not overcome – how we know continues to separate us from what we know. But if we want to keep the *how* and the *what* united, we must enliven the forms and make them, not merely integral to, but coincident with our living being ([1812–16] 1969: 68). In an organic manner, following Schelling, logic must *become* being. And in order for logic to become being, it must supply, following Fichte, its own content. It must be both fact and act. But in its immediacy, what content could logic possibly supply? Logic is purely formal. But in a move apposite to the coming together of immediacy and mediation, form now becomes content: *the content logic supplies is its own form*. This is to say, logic self-begets, and in this self-begetting, which makes the content of its form as well as the form of its content its own formation, logic comes into its own as being. Logic unites 'its own immanent activity' (ibid. 31) of knowing and being to become a living organism, in the organic sense of interrelation and mutual development. Logic *is* being, therefore – but in Hegel's scheme of identity this is to say that logic and being are mutually engendering of each other. In such a productive circularity lies pure knowing as absolute beginning (the coming into being), but an 'absolute' that is the same as the absolute of 'absolute knowing' – the absolutely mediated knowing on which the *Phenomenology* ends. It is in this sense that Hegel will say:

> The essential requirement for the science of logic is not so much that the beginning be a pure immediacy, but rather that the whole of the science be within itself a circle in which the first is also the last the last is also the first. (Ibid. 71)

In this very biblical circularity is the move beyond the organicism of Schelling's *Naturphilosophie*, in its identity of self and Nature through absolute synthesis. For in Schelling, both the younger and the more mature Schelling, the absolute, as Absolute, is ultimately and completely beyond the manifestations of experience. In the 'all' that is the System, productive intuition takes us to an immediate point *beyond* the oppositions, a beyond in which the oppositions are wholly consumed, as in an abyss (the *Ungrund* of *The Essence of Human Freedom*). In the *Difference* essay, Hegel calls this beyond, as Absolute, 'the night' that loses all distinctions and dichotomies (to Schelling's unease, and later chagrin) ([1801] 1977a: 93–4).[11] In the *System*, Schelling will even claim that the 'absolute synthesis is an act which takes place outside all time', and only the act of intelligence is 'an absolute beginning in time, an absolute point that is pitched and posited, as it were, into a timeless infinity, and from which all infinitude in time first commences' ([1800] 1978: 118). The unconscious is thus ever lurking as the inarticulable in this kind of immediate intuition.[12] But Hegel does not want the oppositions to be consumed out of their existence. On the contrary, it is, contra Schelling, their very existence as being (in opposition) that gives them their life and potency. When Schelling writes that 'self-consciousness is not a kind of *being* for us, but a kind of *knowing*', he wants to take us, in absolute knowing, beyond the finite (ibid. 17). But Hegel does not want to dispense with the finite – absolute knowing, as the final pages of *Phenomenology* declare, inheres in *Geist*'s externalisation back into the world as Nature: 'This last becoming of Spirit, *Nature*, is its living immediate Becoming; Nature, the externalized Spirit, is in its existence nothing but this eternal externalization of its *continuing existence* and the movement which reinstates the *Subject*' ([1807] 1877b: 492).[13] This 'living immediate Becoming' is the *end point* of self-consciousness's movement, the last as the first, so that its 'continuing existence' is what Hegel could describe later in the opening of the *Greater Logic* as a result that returns into its ground, in a circularity which keeps beginning always beginning, even throughout the process of development. In a remarkable passage of organic interrelation, Hegel writes:

> Further, the progress from that which forms the beginning is to be regarded as only a further determination of it, hence that which forms the starting point of the development remains at the base of all that follows and does not vanish from it. The progress does not consist merely in the derivation of another, or in the effected transition into a genuine other; and in so far as this transition does occur it is equally sublated again. Thus the beginning of philosophy is the foundation which is present and preserved through the entire subsequent development, remaining completely immanent in its further determinations. ([1812–16] 1969: 71)

In terms of mediacy, we could paraphrase this to say that mediation is only a further determination of the immediacy that forms the beginning, and that remains present and preserved in it. Or as Hegel offers in the very next sentence: 'Through this progress, then, the beginning loses the one-sidedness which attaches to it as something simply immediate and abstract; it becomes something mediated, and hence the line of scientific advance [*wissenschaftlichen Fortbewegung*] becomes a circle' (ibid. 71–2).

But, we ask, how does this circle maintain its circular movement? How exactly can the 'living immediate Becoming' that becomes the logic of being sustain itself? The revolutionary answer given most explicitly by the *Greater Logic*, though certainly preluded in the *Phenomenology*, is negation. The self-alienation that is at the heart of the dialectical movement between immediacy and mediation – the immediate alienating or abandoning itself in mediation; mediation alienating or abandoning itself in immediacy – is a negative movement captured in Hegel's term *Aufhebung*, which literally involves a lifting or raising up, in order to abolish the conditions from which the thing is raised, yet by means of the very conditions from which it is raised. What is so extraordinary in Hegel's development of the logic of being is that in order for the Becoming to become, in order for *anything* to self-generate, it must first negate itself. Granted, we saw this already in Fichte – self becomes not-self, as part of the making fact out of the act in *Tathandlung*. But in Hegel, the negation operates not simply to bring about a third term, a synthesis of the two opposing sides, as is commonly understood (the negative as antithesis, or one part of a triangulated dynamic). Negation is what drives the dialectical movement in the first instance, even *before* the oppositions have determined themselves. And this is why 'beginning' is so important: negation allows the movement of engendering to begin, not as an original point of departure, but as *becoming* – the beginning that remains beginning throughout the process and progress. The *Science of Logic* works this out directly after the opening from which we have been quoting above, in the movement of Being–Nothing–Becoming, where Being and Nothing are in a constant state of Becoming, so that, as Hegel says, 'the hour of their birth is the hour of their death' ([1812–16] 1969: 129). That 'hour' is a simultaneity, a constant beginning as ground, but a *resultant* ground. In order for that beginning to remain constant, a negation must continually disestablish the one and the other (as both ground and result), so that neither Being nor Nothing remains in a state of pure positivity or pure negativity. Negation is the *act* of destabilising towards perpetual Becoming, or the *making* immediate the mediation between immediacy and mediation.

The key in all this is not to see negation as a moment that requires something positive against which to act. That kind of dialectical rendering is what both Fichte and Schelling, and in some sense Schleiermacher, had held, and what Hegel felt impoverished, because it did not fully wed either side without abrogating each side. Rather, the key is to see that, as in any of the self-begetting gestures we have outlined above, what negation first and foremost negates *is itself*. This is what Hegel means by 'self-related negation' (e.g. ibid. 150, 399). Negation first acts out its powers against itself. And since immediate self-relation is being (ibid. 139), negation, in self-relating, enacts its originating and living force. Negation, ultimately, is the primordial movement of creativity, the restlessness of the negative.[14]

Now all this of course has profound theological implications. In the *Phenomenology*, before we have reached absolute knowing, but as part of the culmination of absolute knowing, self-consciousness arrives at revealed religion, and its revelation is precisely that *Geist*, as absolute Spirit, that is, as *self-knowing* Spirit, must, in its self-knowing (as self-relating), give itself over to self-alienation. This is not just the divine becoming human, but the divine, in that humanity, assuming death. 'The *death* of the divine Man, *as death*, is *abstract* negativity, the immediate result of the movement which ends only in *natural universality*' ([1807] 1977b: 475). In the movement of negation, both the natural and the abstract are negated, so that Christ, as the Mediator who dies on the cross, is also the God who dies in universal abstraction: 'The death of the Mediator is the death not only of his *natural* aspect or of his particular being-for-self, not only of the already dead husk stripped of its essential Being, but also of the *abstraction* of the divine Being' (ibid. 476). And this leads to the 'hard saying', the painful realisation 'of the Unhappy Consciousness that God Himself is dead', that the depths of the night have fully overtaken. But all is not lost there. For the absolute as Absolute now negates that night in absolute self-relation, by throwing itself back into the light of day. Thus at the very end, the language of kenosis, ironically, is invoked, as Spirit empties itself back out of death and into time as History: 'But the other side of its Becoming, *History*, is a conscious, self-*mediating* process – Spirit emptied out into Time; but this externalization, this kenosis, is equally an externalization of itself; the negative is the negative of itself' (ibid. 492).

The *Greater Logic* does not draw out these theological ramifications. But the *Lesser Logic*, or Part I of the *Encyclopaedia of Philosophical Sciences*, which first emerged in 1817, and was twice revised and expanded (1827, 1830), devotes an entire section to 'Immediate Knowing',[15] and there treats the question of God throughout. After examining the various forms and claims to immediate knowing that is God, and finding them unsatisfactory, Hegel writes:

> The general nature of the *form of immediacy* has still to be indicated briefly. For it is this form itself which, because it is *one-sided*, makes its very content one-sided, and hence *finite*. It gives the *universal* the one-sidedness of an *abstraction*, so that God becomes an essence lacking all determination; but God can only be called spirit inasmuch as he is known as inwardly *mediating himself with himself*. Only in this way is he *concrete*, living, and spirit. And that is just why the *knowing* of God contains mediation within it. ([1817] 1991: 120)

We need to read the final 'knowing of God' as a construction of both the subjective genitive and the objective genitive (what I have elsewhere called a *cogenitivity* [Hass 2014: 44–7]). Our knowing of God is mediated, but God's own knowing of himself is also mediated, and the two are interrelated, organically (this is what the cogenitive brings out). The foregoing analysis has tried to show why this must be the case: absolute knowing, as the culmination of self-consciousness as *Geist*, is a thoroughly mediated knowing, but in that thorough mediation it is brought back to its beginning, through negation, *as* negation, to its immediate becoming. Immediate knowing is mediate knowing, and the *absolute*, as absolute negation, engenders both.

We can now see that, in Hegel, the mediating act is *wholly human* and *wholly divine*. If mediation mediates between two parties, those two parties are retained, preserved, sustained in their very diremption and self-alienation from one another and from within their own internal selves. God cannot remain here an abstract unity; God is always divided through his own self-relation, which allows his determination, and his determination to be known. But what we know in that determination is a painful realisation: that God manifests himself out of, which is also to say, in, or even *as*, absolute abyss, which is nevertheless realisable, or embodied.[16]

Repercussions

The consequences of Hegel's thought, as itself a culmination of a fertile and clamorous period on the cusp of the nineteenth century, were variously understood in the decades to follow, if they were fully understood at all. We know how Left Hegelians understood his mediation in their own 'one-sided' manner, by reading *Geist*'s self-alienation from a particularly materialist or immanental point of view, which of course gave little credence to theology as traditionally conceived. And radical reconception had already begun in David Friedrich Strauss, who was the first to label Hegelians with 'Left' and 'Right' designations, and whose notorious *The Life of Jesus, Critically Examined* (1835–6) emerged only a few years after Hegel's death. The book's subtitle, *kritisch bearbeitet*, was critical less in the

Kantian sense, and more in a prejudicial appropriation of the Hegelian Spirit's historical character, so that the life of Jesus was wholly naturalised and demythologised within a realism of textual and historical empirical study. If God operated immediately in or upon the world, as the Supernaturalists maintained, it could not be at the very specific level of finite experience, where rules of cause and effect govern phenomenon incontrovertibly. It could only be on the level of the Whole, the world in its abstracted totality. But since, Strauss argued, the life of Jesus, and more directly his miracles, did not and could not operate at this abstract level, but only on a particular level, they must be seen in the more natural light of empirical causality. If divine action is thus invariably filtered through the laws of nature, which are immediate only in their totality, then the distinction between the immediate and the mediate operation of God becomes senseless, since, critically, we only ever experience the mediate. Or as Strauss put it:

> Since then our idea of God requires an immediate, and the idea of the world a mediate divine operation; and since the idea of combination of the two species of action is inadmissible: – nothing remains for us but to regard them both as so permanently and immovably united, that the operation of God on the world continues for ever and every where twofold, both immediate and mediate; which comes just to this, *that it is neither of the two, or [that] this distinction loses its value.* ([1835–6] 1860: 60; my emphasis)

Ultimately, this was not mediation in the strict Hegelian sense, or a loss of distinction through any dialectical or negative movement, but capitulation to one side, that is, to the objective reality of scientific causality to which Strauss understood the modern Hegelian trajectory to have, incontestably and irrevocably, carried us. His true Hegelian credentials were thus refuted by his peers (vociferously in some cases, such as that of Bruno Bauer, who famously won over the young Nietzsche to his anti-Strauss cause). But Strauss set in motion a strong Left Hegelian emphasis on history, which had an immense effect upon how theology was to conduct itself in the remainder of the century, in ceding to a higher (biblical) criticism and eventually to a study of religions that methodologically were shifting the ground towards, in the case of the former, historical and literary criticism and, in the case of the latter, anthropology and sociology.

The Left assault on traditional theology was perhaps no better advanced than in the person of Ludwig Feuerbach, a one-time pupil of Hegel who later, in his *The Essence of Christianity* of 1841, proffered a thoroughly humanised understanding of what many would have taken as a quintessentially Hegelian proposition: 'the object of any subject is nothing else than the subject's own nature taken objectively' ([1841] 1957: 12). There were no dialectical forces of negation at work here for Feuerbach, sublating the subject and object out of their own self-alienation towards an absolute knowledge of both the human and divine (cogenitively). This was, rather, unapologetic anthropology; as Karl Barth was later to say: 'Feuerbach wants, in the end, to help man secure his due' (1957: xii). In securing that due, in overwriting theology's transcendental claims at every level, the question of mediation was, following Strauss, reduced to the question of history – the essence of humanity as it was translated, in an ostensibly Hegelian fashion, through historical development – so that the new task of the theologian was to work out how the Divine, manifested variously in the world's religions, was revealed not *through* history but *as* history, the history of human nature in all its yearning after God's existence, yet a yearning that, in the end, *was* God's existence. Of Christianity, then, Feuerbach could write: 'The history of Christianity is the history of the Passion of Humanity' ([1841] 1957: 61). This kind of historical mediation became the solid oak of much nineteenth-century endeavour, whether in the name of theology or, increasingly, outside of theology. And its anthropocentric roots grew in their reach, and radicalised even further through the likes of Max Stirner, who felt even Feuerbach had not gone far enough. Of course, in the materialist sense it was Marx who would have the most lasting impact, in what Habermas was later to call his 'praxis philosophy' ([1985] 1987: 60ff.), whose theological dimensions were now completely eradicated in the name of an unabashed atheism (even if Marxism's own historical mediations were to resprout a liberal, or liberational, theology a century or so later).

The Right Hegelians, for their part, stuck to a 'speculative' theology, in one form or another. Here the term 'orthodoxy' prevailed: in being an orthodox Hegelian, one was being true, they maintained, to orthodox Christian theology. This was possible because the speculative nature of Hegel's thought allowed the transcendental to be happily – that is, dialectically – synthesised with the immanental, without sacrificing either side. Philipp Marheineke was perhaps foremost among these theologians, one whose adoption of Hegel came after initial influence from Schelling, and then with a personal connection to Hegel himself (Marheineke gave the university benediction at Hegel's funeral). His concern was to see divine revelation in union with human thought, by means less of a generalised world Spirit and more of the Spirit of the Christian Church, whose dogmatics could now be seen in terms of a Hegelian science. That is, the mutual interrelation of God and humans is best manifested not in the development of art, religion and philosophy across the world's various civilisations, but in the religion and tradition of the Church and its history, in what Barth called 'the form of a repetition, an analysis of the content of faith in the teaching of the Bible and the Church, an analysis which in its result is identical with revelation' ([1947] 1972: 496–7). Like Strauss, this was one way of overcoming the distinction between the immediate and the mediate, though now by upholding an orthodoxy (or as some would argue, an Augustinianism [Pattison 2013]), even if this did little to satisfy those of a more conservative bent. Others like Ferdinand Christian Baur at Tübingen, who in fact was an early teacher of Strauss, would make even more of a speculative Christian history, in an attempt, contra Strauss, to show how the development of Christian dogma, which becomes objective to itself in Christian history, is one with the essence of Spirit becoming objective to itself in world history.

The general impetus of this orthodoxy of the Right Hegelians, as a distinctly German set, was consistent with Marx in at least this much: they tended to focus on the more mature manifestation of the Hegelian 'system', especially as it emerged in the lectures and Hegel's last published text, the 1821 *Philosophy of Right*, to embrace their own onesided approach – the historical implications for the Church in society, and its salubrious marriage with the state, as confirmation of *Geist* being on the side of Protestant, or more particularly, Lutheran truth. In Habermas's view, 'The Hegelian Right suffered its shipwreck on account of its trust in the regenerative capacities of a strong state' ([1985] 1987: 70). And of course this was a German, or Prussian, state, whose mediation of theology perhaps reached its zenith when Adolph von Harnack's liberal brand of social theology led him, as General Director of the Royal Library, to sign the 'Manifesto of the NinetyThree', that document emphatically endorsing German militarism at the start of the First World War.[17]

Outside of the German-speaking world, less coordinated theological responses to Hegel's mediation were taking place. Perhaps most significantly, Søren Kierkegaard, ever the lone wolf, made a different rejoinder altogether, interpreting Hegel as an arch-absolutiser at the expense of an existentially passionate inwardness towards the eternal. He speaks of

Hegel's 'malpractice' this way: 'Perhaps it will then become evident that Hegel, who became so extraordinarily absolute in this earthly life which ordinarily is the life of relativity, would become rather relative in the absoluteness of eternal life' ([1844] 1985: 207). What Hegelianism could mediate would always preclude humanity's most interior need. In this respect, German Romanticism, whose genesis is of course coextensive with the German philosophy outlined above, perhaps had the greater reach, in that it offered what Kierkegaard (though not a Romantic) felt was so damningly missing in the Hegelian system: a way for the individual passion to emerge through the highest longings – the aesthetic, the ethical and the religious – of the self.

But none of these subsequent thinkers or movements took the centrepiece of Hegelian thought – negation – as their own beginning point. It was only at the end of the nineteenth century, in the figure of Friedrich Nietzsche, when the theological implications of creative, originating negation could truly come into their own, even if Nietzsche was not himself a devoted reader of Hegel (though a clear detractor of Strauss). Perhaps what we might say, in a Hegelian-like summary of the nineteenth century in its entirety, is that Hegel's thought, and the fecund cogitations of his predecessors at the heralding of the century, hung restlessly over the post-Hegelian camps that emerged and divided European sensibility, prodding it this way, and prodding it that way, until a *fin de siècle* could eventually express itself in a madman who announces not only the death of God, but the savage fact that *we* have killed him.

But that death would not remain unmediated. It certainly burst forth in not one but two cataclysmic world wars during the following century, which impelled Barth (against Harnack) to set up his own existential safeguards in the distancing gestures of neo-orthodoxy. But it also found voice in an ineluctable, if not uniform, shift towards a less dogmatic God: if all acts of mediation involve both human and divine interposition, and if that interposition is a destabilising not only of the positions that are being mediated, but the meta-position from which the mediation enacts its mediatory power, then God must become something other than the distinct determinations of any one religion and of their corresponding theologies. If this is a lesson the early German thinkers, so obsessed with mediation, have properly handed down to us, then perhaps we might have a new understanding of Paul's insistence in Galatians that 'God is one' – it is not that God is one as unified, nor even as universal, but that God is always, indissociably, and thus, as Kierkegaard would have it, paradoxically, a mediated One.

Notes

1. There are three basic iterations of the text: Leipzig 1794–5; Tübingen 1802; and Jena/Leipzig 1802. But there are many minor variations, which Fichte continued to make throughout his life, though none of these later refinements were published. The full title of the original was *Grundlage der gesamten Wissenschaftslehre*, or *Foundations of the Entire Science of Knowledge*.
2. Which may then lead to that which is exchanged from hand to hand, that is, *Handel* – trade, commerce, transaction – which might be ratified by the shaking of hands.
3. Having laid down this principle at the beginning in Part I, the rest of the *Wissenschaftslehre*, Parts II and III, will try to work out the intricacies of this immediate mediacy, in such terms as positing/opposing (self/not-self), interdetermination (through synthesis), striving/counter-striving (as drive), and so on.
4. 'On the Basis of Our Belief in a Divine Governance of the World', published in 1798 in *Philosophisches Journal einer Gesellschaft Teutscher Gelehrten*, which he himself co-edited.

5. In *The Philosophy of Art*, a set of lectures from 1802 and 1804, Schelling writes: '*In the ideal world, philosophy is related to art just as in the real world reason is related to the organism*', or 'art is to the ideal world what organism is to the real world' ([1802–4] 1989: 30). On the mediation of these two sides, see Yates 2013: 56ff.
6. See, for example, *Grundlegung der positiven Philosophie* [*Foundations of the Positive Philosophy*] of 1832–3, and more significantly *Philosophie der Offenbarung* [*Philosophy of Revelation*] of 1842/3, both published posthumously. For a succinct summary of that philosophy and its problems, see also Snow 1996: 214–15.
7. See, for example, Schleiermacher 1977: 175–214.
8. The opening of §3 reads: '*The piety which forms the basis of all ecclesiastical communion is, considered purely in itself, neither a Knowing nor a Doing, but a modification of Feeling, or of immediate self-consciousness*' (Schleiermacher [1831] 1999: 5).
9. This happens even in the revision of the *Speeches*, where in the explanatory notes added in 1821 Schleiermacher feels compelled to write of the immediate self-consciousness: 'But this feeling will be purest when all human limits are seen in Him from whom all limitation was banished. Hence there is no derogation from the higher mediatorship of the Redeemer' ([1821] 1958: 113).
10. '"Now"; it has already ceased to be in the act of pointing to it. The Now that *is*, is another Now than the one pointed to, and we see that the Now is just this: to be no more just when it is' (Hegel [1807] 1977b: 63).
11. In the Preface to the *Phenomenology*, Hegel will more famously speak of those who 'palm off its Absolute as the night in which, as the saying goes, all cows are black', which, he says disparagingly, is 'cognition naively reduced to vacuity' ([1807] 1977b: 9). This line will be a source of a turning point in Schelling and Hegel's relationship. At the end of the *Phenomenology*, in the final section on Absolute Knowing, he will rephrase the point less provocatively: 'nor is Spirit [*Geist*] a *tertium quid* that casts the differences back into the abyss of the Absolute and declares that therein they are all the same; on the contrary, knowing is this seeming inactivity which merely contemplates how what is differentiated spontaneously moves in its own self and returns into its unity' (ibid. 490).
12. Michael Vater summarises: 'Ultimately consciousness is put to one side and made synonymous with appearance, while the hidden Absolute is identified with the irreducibly unconscious element in self-consciousness and with the essential and indissoluble tension between the conscious and the unconscious. The unconscious as determinant activity becomes the ground of consciousness and of freedom, a ground never wholly to be clarified and translated into the light of consciousness' (quoted in Schelling [1800] 1978: xxxi).
13. Among the many different views concerning the difference between Schelling and Hegel's thought here, see, for example, Hyppolite [1952] 1997: 94–6; Bowie (1993): 159–77.
14. See Hass 2014 for a fuller explication of this paradoxical movement and force. For a fuller elaboration of the 'restlessness [*Unruhe*] of the negative', see Nancy [1997] 2002: 12 – 'But the becoming is not a process that leads to another thing, because it is the condition of every thing.'
15. As the third position of thought with respect to objectivity, the other two being metaphysics and empiricism/critical philosophy.
16. Cf. here Altizer 2003: 127–58.
17. The Manifesto ends: 'Have faith in us! Believe, that we shall carry on this war to the end as a civilized nation, to whom the legacy of a Goethe, a Beethoven, and a Kant, is just as sacred as its own hearths and homes' (Harnack et al. 1919).

References

Altizer, Thomas J. J. (2003), *Godhead and the Nothing*, Albany: State University of New York Press.
Aquinas, Thomas [1274] (1947), *The Summa Theologica*, trans. Fathers of the English Dominican Province, Benziger Bros., online edn, <http://dhspriory.org/thomas/summa/TP/TP026.html#T-PQ26OUTP1> (last accessed 26 June 2015).

Barth, Karl (1957), 'An Introductory Essay', in Ludwig Feuerbach, *The Essence of Religion*, New York: Harper & Row, iv–xliii.
Barth, Karl [1947] (1972), *Protestant Theology in the Nineteenth Century*, trans. C. E. Gunton, London: SCM.
Bowie, Andrew (1993), *Schelling and Modern European Philosophy: An Introduction*, Abingdon: Routledge.
Feuerbach, Ludwig [1841] (1957), *The Essence of Religion*, trans. George Eliot, New York: Harper & Row.
Fichte, J. G. (1982), *The Science of Knowledge*, trans. Peter Heath and John Lachs, Cambridge: Cambridge University Press.
Habermas, Jürgen [1985] (1987), *The Philosophical Discourse of Modernity*, trans. Frederick Lawrence, Cambridge: Polity Press.
Harnack, Adolph von et al. (1919), 'Manifesto of the Ninety-Three', *The North American Review*, 210.795 (August): 284–7.
Hass, Andrew W. (2014), *Hegel and the Art of Negation*, London: I. B. Tauris.
Hegel, G. W. F. [1812–16] (1969), *Science of Logic*, trans. A. V. Miller, Amherst, NY: Humanity Books.
Hegel, G. W. F. [1801] (1977a), *The Difference between Fichte's and Schelling's System of Philosophy*, trans. H. S. Harris and Walter Cerf, Albany: State University of New York Press.
Hegel, G. W. F. [1807] (1977b), *Phenomenology of Spirit*, trans. A. V. Miller, Oxford: Oxford University Press.
Hegel, G. W. F. [1817] (1991), *The Encyclopaedia Logic*, trans. T. F. Gerates et al., Indianapolis: Hackett.
Hyppolite, Jean [1952] (1997), *Logic and Existence*, trans. Leonard Lawlor and Amit Sen, Albany: State University of New York Press.
Kant, Immanuel [1781/7] (1929), *Critique of Pure Reason*, trans. Norman Kemp Smith, Houndmills: Macmillan.
Jacobi, Friedrich Heinrich [1799] (1987), 'Open Letter to Fichte', trans. Diana I. Behler, in Ernst Behler (ed.), *Philosophy of German Idealism: Fichte, Jacobi, and Schelling*, New York: Continuum, 119–43.
Jaspers, Karl [1957] (1962), *Kant*, in *The Great Philosophers: Volume 1*, ed. Hannah Arendt, trans. Ralph Manheim, London: Harcourt Brace.
Kierkegaard, Søren [1844] (1985), *Philosophical Fragments/Johannes Climacus*, ed. and trans. Howard V. Hong and Edna H. Hong, Princeton: Princeton University Press.
Nancy, Jean-Luc [1997] (2002), *The Restlessness of the Negative*, trans. Jason Smith and Steven Miller, Minneapolis: University of Minnesota Press.
Nassar, Dalia T. (2006), 'Immediacy and Mediation in Schleiermacher's *Reden Über Die Religion*', *The Review of Metaphysics*, 59.4, 807–40.
Pattison, George (2013), 'Hegelian Augustinianism: Philipp Marheineke', in Karla Pollmann and Willemien Otten (eds), *The Oxford Guide to the Historical Reception of Augustine*, Oxford: Oxford University Press, 1110–13.
Pfau, Thomas (1994), 'Critical Introduction', in *Idealism and the Endgame of Theory: Three Essays by F. W. J. Schelling*, ed. and trans. Thomas Pfau, Albany: State University of New York Press, 1–60.
Schelling, F. W. J. [1800] (1978), *System of Transcendental Idealism (1800)*, trans. Peter Heath, Charlottesville: University of Virginia.
Schelling, F. W. J. [1797] (1988), *Ideas for a Philosophy of Nature: As Introduction to the Study of this Science*, trans. E. E. Harris and P. Heath, Cambridge: Cambridge University Press.
Schelling, F. W. J. [1802–4] (1989), *Philosophy of Art*, ed. and trans. Douglas W. Stott, Minneapolis: University of Minnesota Press.
Schleiermacher, F. D. E. [1821] (1958), *On Religion: Speeches to Its Cultured Despisers*, trans. John Oman, New York: Harper and Row.

Schleiermacher, F. D. E. (1977), *Hermeneutics: The Handwritten Manuscripts*, ed. Heinz Kimmerle, trans. James Duke and Jack Forstman, Atlanta: Scholars Press.

Schleiermacher, F. D. E. [1831] (1999), *The Christian Faith*, ed. H. R. Mackintosh and J. S. Stewart, London: T&T Clark.

Scott, Charles E. (1968), 'Schleiermacher and the Problem of Divine Immediacy', *Religious Studies*, 3.2: 499–512.

Snow, Dale E. (1996), *Schelling and the End of Idealism*, Albany: State University of New York Press.

Strauss, David Friedrich [1835–6] (1860), *The Life of Jesus, Critically Examined*, trans. Marian Evans [George Eliot], New York: Calvin Blanchard.

Yates, Christopher (2013), *The Poetic Imagination in Heidegger and Schelling*, London: Bloomsbury.

11

The Historical Turn

George Pattison

Introduction

It has been commonplace to see the nineteenth century as the century in which history came into its own, and in a double sense. On the one hand, it was a century defined by epoch-making historical movements, from the French Revolution, through the emergence of new nation states (Germany, Italy, Greece and the United States, amongst others), colonialism, the industrial revolution, urbanisation, and on to its catastrophic conclusion in what is generally called the First World War. Admittedly, any century we might randomly select – the eleventh, sixteenth or eighteenth – would also be witness to profound and far-reaching changes, but it would be at least plausible to argue that what we see in the nineteenth century is a new kind of change or, more precisely, the confluence of a range of changes – social, scientific, political, cultural and technological – into a vast and new pattern.

But this is only one side of the story. The other is no less important and is arguably the presupposition of all the transformations I have just briefly sketched. This is that the nineteenth century was the moment in which human beings became conscious of themselves as historical beings who are what they are only by virtue of a process of becoming that involves both a consciousness of the past from which they have emerged and of the future towards which they must strive. Darwin's theory of evolution would provide the most all-encompassing version of this historicisation of human self-understanding, but the way to Darwin had already been well prepared by a succession of thinkers who, in a variety of ways, emphasised the historical character of human existence – German Idealism, Romanticism and Marxism being only some of the more salient moments in this historical turn.[1]

As I have indicated, the fact of historical change and the self-understanding of human life as essentially historical are not unrelated. If it is believed that a nation has a manifest destiny or that an oppressed class can be the bearer of future liberation for all or that science is intrinsically progressive, then such beliefs will themselves then play a part in furthering the relevant social or scientific change. And even if (with Marx) we regard such ideas as ideological expressions of, for example, the progressive interests of the bourgeois class, the connection is not fundamentally denied. Conversely, the experience of massive change, such as the change from an agrarian feudal society to an industrial bourgeois society, cannot but invite reflection as to what, if anything, is constant and, to use a philosophically loaded term, truly essential in human life.

These comments apply to religion no less than to other spheres of life. Here too the nineteenth century saw both radical change in the conditions and practice of religion within and (as a result of colonialism) beyond Europe and North America but also a dramatic range of new theoretical approaches, both apologetic and critical, that understood religion in historical terms. At the same time, the sphere of religion – often in alliance with restorationist political tendencies – produced some of the sharpest criticisms of the new historical consciousness. The papal Syllabus of Errors, the emergence of Protestant Fundamentalism and (in an entirely different register) the philosophy of Schopenhauer all offered religious critiques of the idea that history could bring about any significant change in the relationship between human beings and eternal truth. Yet there is one point on which, for the most part, both the proponents and the opponents of the historical turn were in substantial agreement, namely, that history was essentially unified and, as such, governed throughout by a common set of laws, truths or values. Critics of history might deny that there was genuine 'progress' in history, but mostly they did not deny its fundamental coherence as a dimension of human life.

It might be the case that this belief in the unity of history is itself a product of Jewish and Christian theology, since if it is the case that human beings are all created by the one creator God who continues to providentially rule over his creation, then it would seem to follow that human history too is united by the one divine purpose. The point is reinforced if, in the case of Christianity, it is argued that there is one person designated by God as Saviour and Judge of all. The relation to Jesus Christ therefore comes to play not just a decisive but also a unifying role in relation to the entirety of the human race. This implication is strengthened by the way in which Paul and others early on argued that not only the 'timing' of Christ's coming was providentially planned but also the way in which his life, death and resurrection could have significance for the whole of the then known world. Of course, Paul was almost certainly not thinking of the inhabitants of the Americas or Australias or even East Asia when he articulated his more universalist sayings, but the opening of the Gospel to all, emphatically *all*, made the Christian message a matter of decisive importance for all human beings at all times and places – at least in Christian self-understanding.[2]

In the centuries that followed this led inevitably to questions about the status not only of the Jews, whose God was, after all, 'the God and Father of our Lord Jesus Christ', but also of those who had lived and died without the possibility of hearing the gospel. Radical transformations in the situation of the church itself, from persecuted sect to public religion, not to mention the apparently open-ended deferral of the Parousia, further deepened and compounded the issue of how the Gospel was related to – in a loose sense – 'history'. Out of such debates the notion that all of history was shaped and moulded by a single divine providence was developed and extensively argued in works such as Eusebius' *Ecclesiastical History* and Augustine's *City of God* or, later, Bede's *History of the English Church and People*.

It is inevitably the case that Christian historiography of this kind assumes that the key to history has already been sufficiently disclosed in the Incarnation of Jesus Christ, the Word of God. He who appeared in time is also the same 'by whom all things were made' in the beginning and who will be Judge of all in the end, the Alpha and Omega. Although time is required to bring about the final fulfilment of God's purposes, these are not only sure, certain and knowable but eternally the same, 'yesterday, today, and forever'. By the Middle Ages this produced what was, for that era, a defining image of history as the mirror of eternal and timeless divine truth. What happens in time has become a 'moving image of eternity' (Plato), reinforced by the general acceptance of Boethius' doctrine of eternity as the 'complete, simultaneous and perfect possession of everlasting life'. Seen from the standpoint of eternity, events in time are like the stages of a journey along a road that can be seen in its entirety by a viewer (God) situated atop a high mountain with an open vista on the whole.

Without claiming that there was no idea of historical progress in play prior to the early modern era (the providential expansion of the church might itself, in a Christian perspective, be seen as a form of historical progress), the truth manifest in history was truth of an essentially timeless nature. Consequently, questions of history played at best a marginal role (and mostly no role) in the medieval Summas that consistently began by addressing metaphysical questions as to the existence and nature of God rather than engaging in matters of history.

An early sign that this was changing is found in Edward Stillingfleet's 1662 *Origines Sacrae or a Rational Account of the Grounds of Natural and Revealed Religion*. In his preface, Stillingfleet remarks that:

> as the tempers and geniuses of ages and times alter, so do the arms and weapons which Atheists employ against religion. The most popular pretences of the Atheists of our age, have been the irreconcileableness of the account of times in Scripture with that of the learned and ancient Heathen nations; the inconsistency of the belief of the Scriptures with the principles of reason; and the account which may be given of the origin of things, from principles of philosophy, without the Scriptures. ([1662] 1817: xiv)[3]

It is the first of these ('the irreconcileableness of the account of times') that especially leads to the most original feature of Stillingfleet's apologetic work, in that he devotes the following first part of his treatise to an extensive defence of the historical reliability of the Scriptures. The discussion of the metaphysical being of God (which, a hundred years before, would have typically stood at or near the beginning of any major apologetic work) is now postponed until the final, concluding part. Even if Stillingfleet himself does not see the matter in these terms, we can say that he adumbrates a path from history to Being that would, *mutatis mutandis*, become normative for Christian idealists of a later age. But that the study of history does indeed arrive, finally, at an understanding of Being, even, we may say, *eternal* Being, seems to be regarded as a given of any truly Christian historiography. History remains one and its unity is guaranteed by the relation between knowledge of historical life and knowledge of the one divine truth ruling over all.

When we come to the nineteenth century itself, Hegel and von Ranke have often been taken as representing two fundamentally divergent approaches to history that we might call the philosophical and the archival, respectively. But even if von Ranke does regard it as not possible to trace a line of progressive development through history, he too sees the unifying ground of history in the divine mind and that knowledge of this is the ultimate aim of historical enquiry:

> For what can be more pleasant or more welcome to the human understanding than to perceive the kernel and the deepest mystery of events and to observe how, in [the life of] one or other people, human affairs are grounded, how they gain in power, grow, and spread out? And how much more so if one gradually arrives at the point at which a just self-confidence permits one to guess or a well-practiced clarity of vision enables one to know fully, what occupied the human race at that time, what people strove for, what they gained and really achieved? For that is, so to speak, an element in the divine knowledge. But this is precisely what we are pressing on towards with the help of

historical study and such study is in its entirety moved by striving towards such knowledge. Who, then, can ask whether this is useful or not? It is sufficient to know that if there is any kind of knowledge that belongs to the perfection of the human spirit, then knowledge of this kind does so. ([1872] 1877: 285)

Consistent with this, von Ranke likewise affirms the unity of historical development itself: 'The nations can be regarded in no other connection than in that of the mutual action and reaction involved by their successive appearance on the stage of history and their combination into one progressive community' ([1881] 1884: xi–xii). Indeed, only on such presuppositions could the project of a *Universal History* such as von Ranke embarked upon in the last period of his life be at all plausible. There is no 'universal history' if the laws and conditions governing history are not themselves universal and, as such, accessible to a kind of cognition that knows more than is given in any ensemble, no matter how extensive, of concrete particulars. The essence of von Ranke's complaint against Hegel, then, is not that he offers an idealist account of history but simply that in his devotion to the *Anstrengung des Denkens* (the striving of thought) he neglects the *Anstrengung der Forschung*, that is, the rigour of concrete, archival research. Although Hegel claims that his phenomenology of spirit engages the concrete, von Ranke sees him – as, from quite differing angles, Kierkegaard and Marx also see him – as simply skipping the kind of attention to detail that supports claims as to the unitary truth informing history as a whole. Both would, however, agree that in principle true knowledge of history is knowledge that does entire justice to the concrete and particular whilst seeing the concrete and particular in the light of its universal significance.[4]

The point to be emphasised here is that underlying a range of nineteenth-century historiographies is the shared assumption that both history as the temporal sequence of individual and social actions and experiences in worldly life and history as historical science are equally governed by a unitary set of laws. Whether these laws also point us towards a discernible progress in history – scientific, material, social or moral – is a further question. But, and this is crucial, the postulation of a progressive development in history does not of itself challenge the central claim of Christian historiography regarding the fundamental unity of history. The kind of liberal Protestantism that would become widely diffused in the nineteenth century itself bears witness to this.

Some versions of the progressive view will, of course, challenge Christianity and in a variety of ways. For Feuerbach, Marx, and Comte and other secularising thinkers, Christianity now appears as only a phase in a historical development and has already been (or soon will be) superseded. Critics of progressive ideologies such as Kierkegaard or Dostoevsky's underground man found rich satirical pickings in the more naïve assertions of their contemporaries regarding the moral progress of humanity.[5] And whilst the twentieth-century theology of crisis would portray the First World War as exposing the emptiness of the nineteenth-century belief in progress, that belief was not unchallenged in the nineteenth century itself – not only by a range of Christian critics but also by decadents of various *fin-de-siècle* cultural movements and, not least, the radical atheism of a Nietzsche (to whom we shall return).

But, to repeat, progress was not really the article by which a Christian view of history stood or fell, even if it sometimes seemed like that to Christian controversialists. For whilst it is at least plausible in a preliminary kind of way to see history as being providentially guided towards a gradual realisation of the divine purposes (as Lessing had argued in his essay on 'The Education of the Human Race'), if history is not a unitary field of experience and understanding, then it is hard to see whether or how basic Christian claims regarding the universal significance of Christ's life and work make any kind of sense. Whether it is actually impossible is a matter we shall, briefly, consider at the end of this essay. First, however, we shall look at an – arguably *the* – eminent nineteenth-century attempt to develop a view of historical becoming that incorporates a unitary and developmental view and that does so as explicitly Christian, namely, Hegel's teleological phenomenology of absolute Spirit. Hegel's Christianity has, of course, been questioned from his own time down to the present, but it is not to my purposes here either to attack or defend him on this point. What is important (and why, even if he is unsuccessful in his own terms, he can still be instructive for other versions of Christian historiography) is how he attempts not only to show that history is progressive but also that this progress incorporates all those elements that would seem to disrupt it and render it into a fragmented chaotic sequence of events that are only arbitrarily or accidentally related. I shall then turn to how, just on this point, Hegel is attacked by one of his first major Christian critics, Kierkegaard. I shall then relate Kierkegaard's criticisms to the 'discovery' of eschatology amongst researchers of the 'Life of Jesus', a major focus of nineteenth-century theology's own 'historical turn'. This, in turn, will be related to the thorough-going critique of the unity of history that we find in Nietzsche's nihilism, a point on which, as so often, Nietzsche proves to be Christianity's most incisive critic. The tension between a Christian view of the unity of history and the radical disruption of the historical continuum that we find in the new eschatology and in Nietzschean pluralism then becomes one of the starting points for what would, in the early twentieth century, develop into the philosophy of existence – but that is a story that goes beyond the limits of this essay, focused as it is on the nineteenth-century development. It is also beyond the scope of this essay to reflect on the late twentieth-century debate about 'the end of history', expressly associated with a reading of Hegel and Nietzsche. Nevertheless, I shall conclude by commenting on what the nineteenth-century sources of this debate may contribute to our own current crisis of historical reason.

History as the Justification of God: Hegel

Hegel's *Phenomenology of Spirit* (1807) presents a view of Spirit as the true motor driving worldly life but doing so in a manner very different from Aristotle's unmoved mover. Hegel's Spirit does not live in immutable contemplation of its own perfection, imaged by Henry Vaughan as a 'great ring of pure and endless light'. Admittedly, there is something circular in the image of Spirit with which the *Phenomenology* closes: 'From the chalice of this realm of spirits / foams forth for Him his own infinity' (1970: 3:591; [1807] 1977: 493). Here, the essential life of Spirit is seemingly portrayed as a circular process of self-knowing but, unlike in Aristotle, this process is such as to incorporate time and therefore also all that is lived and suffered in time. Time too is a form of Spirit, albeit a deficient form – a claim that places extraordinary pressure on conventional philosophical assumptions, as the contortions of Hegel's prose make clear:

> Time is the concept itself that is there ('*da ist*') and that presents itself to consciousness as empty intuition. Consequently Spirit necessarily appears in time and continues to appear in time so long as it does not apprehend its own pure concept, that is, so long as it does not uproot time. It [time] is the pure self intuited as external to the self and not apprehended as such by it, it is the merely intuited concept. In that this [then] apprehends itself, it sublates its temporal form, grasps the intuiting act in such a way that that

act is both conceptually grasped and itself grasps [its subject] conceptually. Time thus manifests as the destiny and necessity of Spirit that is not perfected in itself . . . (Ibid. 3:584–5; 487)

But because Spirit is not simply and eternally or immutably perfected in itself, it can only come to itself through what it experiences in time, which, as the passage just quoted indicates, is to expose its own perfection to what is 'not perfected in itself' and this has potentially radical implications. As Hegel had already stated programmatically in the *Phenomenology*'s preface:

> The circle that remains self-enclosed and, like substance, holds its moments together, is an immediate relationship, one therefore which has nothing astonishing about it . . . But the life of Spirit is not the life that shrinks from death and keeps itself untouched by devastation, but rather the life that endures it and maintains itself in it. It wins its truth only when, in utter dismemberment, it finds itself . . . Spirit is this power only by looking the negative in the face and tarrying with it. (Ibid. 3:36; 18–19)

Theologically, this means that the concept of God must, as Christianity teaches, become capable of incorporating the idea that even God must suffer and die on the cross and that this demands changes in how we think of God that are far more radical than those that occurred in scholasticism's acceptance of Aristotle's unmoved, immutable and timeless deity.[6] When Hegel elsewhere speaks of a 'speculative Good Friday', it is just such a 'looking the negative in the face' that is at issue: even here, in a world momentarily derelict of God, God is to be seen.

This idea is manifest at many points in Hegel's works, as when, in the lectures on aesthetics, he describes how the timeless perfection of Greek statuary, in which the serene elevation of divine life above time is portrayed with unsurpassable beauty, must nevertheless give way to the world of Christian painting (which he calls 'Romantic art'), in which the sufferings of Christ and his saints, as well as the full range of religious emotions accompanying their dread of damnation and their hope of heaven, are depicted in vivid and living colour.

At issue, then, is something more than the challenge of integrating a mass of diverse empirical elements into the unity of the idea, although that is part of the task Hegel has set himself. What Hegel is pursuing is, in effect, nothing short of a theodicy, a justification of the possibility of God in face of all the suffering (the dismemberment and death) attendant upon history. And this is just how, in the Introduction to the *Philosophy of History*, he himself puts it:

> What we pursue in such knowledge is to gain insight into how what is intended by eternal wisdom appears in the domain of Spirit that is real and active in the world as much as in the domain of nature. What we see is to that extent a theodicy, a justification of God. This is what Leibnitz sought in his way – metaphysically and in still indeterminate, abstract categories – in order that having grasped the evil that there is in the world conceptually, the thinking spirit might be reconciled with what is amiss. In fact, there is no greater demand for such reconciliatory knowledge than in world-history. (1970: 12:28; [1837] 1956: 15)

But that, as Hegel also acknowledges, means not just acknowledging but *knowing* the way in which God providentially exercises his rule over the world. A philosophical interpretation of history is thus ultimately also theology – a point which, as we have seen, was implicitly acknowledged also by von Ranke, one of Hegel's sharpest critics. Only in the triumph of God can we be sure of the triumph of the good over all the 'perversion, corruption, and ruin of religious, ethical, and moral purposes' (ibid. 12:53; 36) that we cannot help seeing in the actual unfolding of historical life.

That being said, Hegel is by no means claiming that the philosopher has direct, unmediated access to the divine mind. Although it may be that this is, in the end, what he arrives at, he can do so only by working through the concrete mediations of the divine mind in history. Foremost amongst these are precisely the actions of those who are, in the normal human sense, the 'movers' of historical progress, those whom Hegel calls the 'world-historical individuals'. Emphasising that even the greatest of such individuals will also be moved by passions and ambitions rather than a clear philosophical grasp of their role in history, Hegel brushes aside any attempt to diminish them to the private gossip that fills the kind of biographies produced by their former servants. We all have our idiosyncratic and often petty foibles and fancies, of course – and so does any world-historical individual. But what such individuals exemplify and enact is the freedom that is able to rise above its circumstances and to direct the course of events at moments of crucial transformation in common life. It is through their actions, then, that we see adumbrated the truth that history is not just one-damned-thing-after-another but a history of freedom. Nor is it just a history of, let us say, occasional heroism. In the history of human action, we see the free actions of world-historical individuals coming together into the formation of societies in which freedom is both the birthright of all and a field of possibility for all, subject only to respect for the equal freedom of others. The religious, ethical and moral good towards which providence is gradually working its way is not just a theoretic object: it is a good that finds full realisation in the lived and living life of a common freedom.[7]

Of course, it is entirely open to discussion whether the actual execution of his phenomenology or of his philosophy of history really does justice, not only to the kind of archival detail that was a desideratum of genuine historical research according to von Ranke and his school, but also to all the suffering, dismemberment and death that is there to be seen in history. Many critics of Hegel's own time and since have doubted it. Ivan Karamazov, whose author Dostoevsky was not unfamiliar with Hegel, could not see any final harmony that could possibly justify the horrors he so powerfully describes in his 'rebellion'.[8] Nevertheless, we must at least acknowledge the significance of the step that Hegel has made in relation to the kind of metaphysical theodicy he sees in Leibniz. Theodicy cannot be founded on general considerations alone but must take with all seriousness all that is suffered in historical life. And Hegel is quite clear that 'World-history is not the domain of happiness. Periods of happiness are its empty pages' (ibid. 12:42; 26). In this connection, we might also add that, in aesthetics, Hegel's reflections on tragedy have constituted one of his enduring legacies, reflections in which Antigone played an exceptional role (he could go so far as to describe her as 'heavenly ... the most glorious figure that has ever appeared on earth ...' (a judgement which invites careful weighing in any overall estimate of Hegel's intellectual intentions) (1970: 18:509).[9]

Whether or not Hegel did justice to the suffering that he saw (and whether or not any philosophy or work of art ever *can*), he did recognise that this was a problem, and a decisive one, for philosophy. Furthermore, whilst his claim that philosophy can gain attain knowledge of the divine plan governing the progress of the world order seems hubristic, not least in relation to a certain Christian rhetoric of simple submission to an unknowable divine will, he was surely right to claim that Christianity itself, alongside its insistence on the unfathomable nature of the divine decrees, offered a certain kind of knowledge as to the divine purpose, even if this was not available to philosophy apart from faith. In other words, it is at least plausible to see Hegel's working assumptions as integral to any Christian philosophy of history – and if that is so and his project nevertheless fails, then this will therefore have serious implications for Christian philosophy of history itself.

The Moment and Eschatology: Kierkegaard to Schweitzer

Although the image of Kierkegaard as having single-handedly risen up against the Hegelian system and dealt it a mortal blow has been widely criticised in recent years, it remains the case that, as regards history and our possible knowledge of divine providence as steering history towards a future of freedom, Kierkegaard was deeply at odds with Hegel's core commitments and claims.[10] Famously, much of Kierkegaard's criticism comes coated with generous helpings of satire and humour and much of it is specifically aimed at the extravagances of the local epigones, whose claims for what the system might achieve were often less guarded than those of Hegel himself. Along with the complication of pseudonymity, this makes an exact appraisal of the philosophical issue sometimes debatable. Yet with all due allowance given to such factors, I suggest that clear differences remain and that the twentieth century was not entirely mistaken in hailing Kierkegaard as a decisive critic of Hegel's teleological historiography. But the claim that history was progressively moving towards a good end (and perhaps had already arrived there) was not the only or even the chief point at issue. Still more fundamental is the point concerning the essential unity of history and, in this regard, the twentieth century was also not wrong in seeing Kierkegaard as anticipating a view of history as essentially fragmentary.[11] But this seems paradoxical, since Kierkegaard's criticisms were made precisely in defence of what he claimed was an essentially Christian understanding of history although, as we have seen, any Christian understanding of history would seem to suppose the unity of history – even if it is able to forgo ideas of teleological progress. On this point, and that a decisive one, Hegel seems closer to what Christianity itself requires than does his Christian critic from Copenhagen. Is Kierkegaard, then (as some of his readers have from early on suspected), something of a Trojan Horse for a view of history that, in Nietzsche and others, will reveal itself as profoundly un- and even anti-Christian? Let us see.

The key elements of Kierkegaard's criticism of the Hegelian view of history are focused in the works of his pseudonym Johannes Climacus. The first of these, *Philosophical Fragments*, starts off with the fairly general question as to whether the truth can be known.[12] That the question is raised with specific regard to the kind of truth that history and historical study can attest is, however, indicated by the questions on the book's title page: 'Can a historical point of departure be given for an eternal consciousness? How can such a point of departure be of more than historical interest? Can an eternal happiness be constructed on a knowledge of history?' (1997–2013: 3:213; [1844] 1985: 1).

Avoiding direct reference to contemporary debates, Kierkegaard develops the question so as to present a choice between a Socratic and a Christian point of view. On the Socratic point of view (which turns out to have significant analogies with Hegelian and other forms of idealism), there is a continuity between life in time and eternal consciousness such that any moment in history becomes a possible starting point for recollecting the truth. Every age has the seed or germ of truth within it and the task is simply to bring this seed to full consciousness. But this also implies the essential unity of history, since the truth that is capable of being recollected at Point A (in the age of Socrates, for example) is the same truth that a modern philosopher recollects at Point B (in the 1840s, for example). In relation to such a truth, the teacher will, as Socrates said of himself, be a kind of midwife, bringing to birth the truth that each of us always and everywhere has within us.

Kierkegaard does not so much argue against this view as ask how it would look if things were to be otherwise. It is a pure 'thought-experiment'. What he immediately notes is that if the Socratic view is once abandoned, then what he calls 'the moment in time' will come to have a very different and, indeed, 'decisive' significance (ibid. 3:222; 13). History is no longer a continuum, but is marked by the rupture between being in what he calls 'untruth' and the moment in which 'truth' is revealed. There is now one moment in time that changes everything, namely, the moment when it first becomes possible for truth to be learned. But this also changes the relationship between teacher and disciple. The teacher is no longer a midwife who brings forth what is already latent or implicit in the learner's own consciousness, but one who *gives* the learner a truth that would otherwise have been unattainable. Moreover – or so Kierkegaard argues – the gap that his situation presupposes between truth and untruth is so deep as to acquire ontological significance: the learner must be born again and gain a new being, making the teacher not just a teacher but a Saviour. As the 'Christian' character of Climacus/Kierkegaard's anti-Socratic alternative emerges ever more clearly, it also becomes apparent that the 'moment' is nothing other than the moment or event of Incarnation, of God becoming human in the singular person of Jesus Christ.

However, there is one respect in which it seems that what now emerges as a Christian approach to time and history still resembles the Socratic view, at least in a strictly Platonic interpretation of the latter. For both the Socratic and the Christian point of view seem to undermine any particular privilege being granted to any particular historical epoch. It is true – indeed it is absolutely central – that on Climacus/Kierkegaard's view 'the moment' is a unique and unsubstitutable event, a caesura in history that cannot be rewritten or sublated in any way and is not a part of or moment in any progressive development. Nevertheless (and, in a sense, precisely for that reason), it thereby levels the entire range of all other historical moments such that, as Climacus/Kierkegaard puts it, there is no privilege or benefit accruing to the generation of the first disciples in comparison with any later generation. Of course, the first generation had what many would afterwards envy as the privilege of having been able to walk and talk with Jesus and to feel 'first hand' the impression of his personality, not to mention knowing the colour of his eyes, the cut of his hair, the tone of his voice and what he liked for breakfast. But, *Fragments* argues, none of this amounts to any real privilege regarding knowing the truth that is divinely revealed in him and it is clear from the historical record itself that many of those who encountered him 'in the flesh' were not only unable to see him as a bearer of truth but even regarded him as diabolically possessed – whilst others were simply uninterested.

In a later work, *Practice in Christianity*, the pseudonym Anti-Climacus makes what is essentially the same point by imagining how a range of contemporary personalities – the 'clever and reasonable' men, the clergy, the philosophers, the statesmen, the bourgeois and the mockers – would respond if they were to be confronted with Jesus now, in the midst of their own nineteenth-century world (1997–2013: 12:55–64; [1848] 1991: 42–52).[13] The outcome is that he would be no more likely to gain recognition or acceptance now than he was then. Being contemporary with Christ in a chronological sense is essentially indifferent and when, in *Fragments*, Kierkegaard/Climacus goes on to emphasise the need for each believer in whatever age he or she lives to become 'contemporary' with Christ, this means becoming contemporary with the event of Incarnation, with the singular moment that is decisive for the relationship between history and truth but which is not itself a moment 'of' history. It is a moment in time without before or after, a fragment, that is, by the same token, equally accessible and equally elusive in AD 30 and in AD 1848. Can such a moment be thought? Climacus/Kierkegaard concurs that it cannot. Is not such a moment therefore sheer paradox? Climacus/Kierkegaard concurs that it is. In an image that Karl Barth, at the time deeply impressed by his reading of Kierkegaard, would use, it is a matter of the relation between a tangent and a circle: the tangent touches the circle but is never a part of it – only, in this case, the tangent becomes the measure by which the character and identity of the entire circle is to be determined (Barth [1922] 1933: 30).[14]

All of this consistently excludes any idea of a progressive movement within history towards an ever clearer manifestation of the truth, such as we have found in Hegel, and in this regard Kierkegaard is correct to see his approach as fundamentally opposed to that of the German philosopher. To that extent, at least, the received picture of the relationship between these thinkers seems justified.

In *Concluding Scientific Postscript*, it is true that it is not, directly, the Hegelian view of history that is the focus of Kierkegaard's satirical malice. The section entitled 'The Historical Point of View' is actually concerned with the contemporary Danish Romantic theologian N. F. S. Grundtvig, whose 'universal history' was of a very different kind from Hegel's. When Kierkegaard/Climacus does engage Hegel here, it is very much with a focus on the logical and metaphysical aspects of the system, though also on what local Danish Hegelians were hailing as the congruence of Hegelian philosophy with the need of the present age. Some of Kierkegaard's darts seem misdirected if assumed to be directed against Hegel himself – his constant mockery of the self-consciously 'world-historical' character of Hegelian philosophy does not, in fact, conflict with the reservations we have heard Hegel himself attach to this term. That the existential thinker will always be motivated by the 'interest', the stake, that he himself has in existence seems to echo Hegel's own insistence on the role of passion in shaping all human action, including that of those who become figures of 'world-historical' importance. Yet even when we strip away the satire and humour and the manifold digressions that characterise the *Postscript*'s extraordinarily (not to say excessively) flamboyant style and structure, Kierkegaard's assertion, against Hegel, that we cannot know the world *sub specie aeternitatis* seems indeed to address a fundamental thesis of the Hegelian philosophy of history. But, the philosopher might riposte, in abandoning such a possibility is Kierkegaard not also abandoning the possibility of history having the kind of unity that makes such Christian claims as 'Jesus is the Saviour of the world' intelligible? If history is fundamentally ruptured in such a way that each individual can only come into a relation to the truth that is singularised out of its historical context, what is left but *fragments*? And what then is left to the historian apart from the assembling of data that have no ultimate bearing on what we might call the meaning of human life?

We shall return to such questions, but first note a further twist in the specifically theological approach to history that would, in the twentieth century, become significant also for philosophy. This is the growing realisation of the importance of eschatology in the world of the New Testament, including the outlook of Jesus himself.

One of the most important outcomes of the historical turn in nineteenth-century theology was the attempt to reconstruct the life of Jesus in the light of the best available tools of historical research. Many – often quite contradictory – 'lives' were the product of this 'Quest of the Historical Jesus'. Some, like the 'Life' by Ernest Renan, became international bestsellers, although, in this case, succeeding precisely by depicting a sentimentalised Jesus well adapted to the tastes of late nineteenth-century bourgeois culture. But although many of these Lives only too clearly saw Jesus through nineteenth-century eyes, some brought attention to what we might call the otherness of Jesus and his world, especially with regard to the eschatological and apocalyptic speculation that marked the early Jesus movement. A major breakthrough in this regard was Johannes Weiss's ground-breaking 1892 study of *The Preaching of Jesus Concerning the Kingdom of God*, which was taken up and further developed in Albert Schweitzer's apocalyptic life of Jesus.[15] Schweitzer himself concluded his magisterial study of the 'Quest of the Historical Jesus' by commenting on the implications of such an eschatological interpretation for the overall significance of Jesus's life and work. The point, as Schweitzer sees it, is that Jesus's own eschatological consciousness consigns him to a world completely different from our own. We no longer think in those categories, precisely because they devalue all that takes place within historical time and make an event that originates in an 'other' world than ours decisive for our human history. Despite their continued use by Christians, we no longer really understand or make sense of the titles 'Son of Man', 'Messiah', 'Son of God' or 'Lord' that the first century bestowed on him since they belong to a thought-world that is simply not our own. 'We can find no designation which expresses what He is for us', writes Schweitzer:

> He comes to us as One unknown, without a name, as of old, by the lake-side, He came to those men who knew Him not. He speaks to us the same word: 'Follow thou me!' and sets us to the tasks which He has to fulfil for our time. He commands. And to those who obey Him, whether they be wise or simple, he will reveal Himself in the toils, the conflicts, the sufferings which they shall pass through in His fellowship, and, as an ineffable mystery, they shall learn in their own experience Who He is. ([1906] 1954: 401)

We can no longer share the apocalyptic expectations of the first century, Schweitzer is saying (although, of course, many modern sectarians do just that), but we can – and Christians maybe must – re-enact the defining otherness of the event in which faith begins, a call from the unknown that is not simply the timeless unknown of traditional apophatic theology, but an unknown future that inscribes all historical life under the rubric of radical uncertainty and questionability. Schweitzer's starting point is that of the historian, but the conclusion at which he arrives is not unlike that reached by Kierkegaard who, in his own way, had begun with what seemed a purely philosophical question about truth.[16] For both, the historian and the philosopher, the truth of historical life emerges only in an event that breaks the continuum of historical becoming. The unity that grounds Christian claims regarding Christ's universal significance is no longer the unity of human life in its trans-generational unfolding in history but a unity that lies outside history and relates to history only by disrupting, fragmenting and, in a sense, ending it. Having done much to enculturate the view that history is essentially unified, Christian theology now returns to help unravel a secularised version of the unity it had itself proclaimed.

History as Art: Nietzsche and Burckhardt

Nietzsche never got round to reading Kierkegaard before his final breakdown overwhelmed him. Yet his quite different path of thought led him too to an equally (many would say, more) radical insight into the ultimate lack of unity in historical life. This insight is formulated with metaphysical brevity in the notes posthumously published as *The Will to Power*: 'What does nihilism mean? *That the highest values devaluate themselves*. The aim is lacking; "why?" finds no answer', he declares ([1901] 1968: 9). As he then explains, this nihilistic insight develops through three phases. The first is when we see that the world and our life in the world have no meaning apart from the reality of their actual existence. This is it and this is all it is. The second phase is when we abandon the supposition that the world constitutes a unified totality 'in' or 'underneath' its actual manifestation. Finally, there comes the realisation that there is no 'true' world behind or beyond this one: this world is the only world there is. Summing up, Nietzsche says, 'Briefly: the categories "aim," "unity," "being," which we used to project some value into the world – we *pull out* again; so the world looks *valueless*' (ibid. 13).

This realisation is the event that Nietzsche elsewhere dramatises as the death of God and, in the parable of the Madman that provides the exemplary statement of God's death, Nietzsche makes clear that this is also a caesura in the human experience of history. 'There has never been a greater deed; and whoever is born after us – for the sake of this deed he will belong to a higher history than all history hitherto', he writes ([1882] 1974: 181). And yet this 'higher' history is a history that, as the Madman has already spelled out, is without horizons, a history that moves 'backward, sideward, forward, in all directions' and therefore in no direction; it is a history without an above or a below, straying 'as through an infinite nothing' (ibid. 181).

The consequences for historiography are that the entire project of 'universal history', whether in its Enlightenment, Rankian, Hegelian, Christian or philosophical versions, is rendered otiose. There is no 'universal' by which to measure history or to which history could contribute. The history of a civilisation or a nation, of a period or of ideas or of art can still be written, but can claim no universal purchase. In this regard we might compare Nietzsche's colleague and friend, Jacob Burckhardt, with either of Hegel or von Ranke. It is not that Burckhardt does not offer the historian a wide field of endeavour:

> Only the civilized nations, not the primitive ones, are part of history in a higher sense ... Primitive peoples, however, interest us only when civilized nations come into conflict with them ... Our subject is that past which is clearly connected with the present and the future. Our guiding idea is the course of civilization, the succession of levels of culture in various peoples and within individual peoples themselves. Actually, one ought to stress especially those historical realities from which threads run to our own period and culture. There are more of them than one would think. The continuum is magnificent. The peoples around the Mediterranean and over to the Gulf of Persia are really one animate being, active humanity par excellence. In the Roman Empire, this being does attain a kind of unity. Here alone the postulates of the intellect are realized; here alone there prevails development with no absolute decline, but only a transition. (1959: 23)

'The continuum is magnificent' – indeed, but it is no longer universal and it is a continuum of which the basis is essentially only the interest that we have in it. In a sense, therefore, the fragmentation to which such a view of history leads is virtually the opposite of that to which the Kierkegaardian and eschatological interpretation led. There the telos of history was separated from history and placed outside the continuum of historical becoming. Here it is only from an inside view, *our* view, that any possible continuum becomes manifest. On this basis both history itself and the work of the historian approximate to the status of art, a subjective view of the world that expresses and reveals our manifold interest in it. It is therefore not at all coincidental that 'the civilization of the Renaissance in Italy' held such a deep attraction for Burckhardt, nor that he saw the Renaissance state precisely as 'a work of art' and its rulers as marked precisely by 'talent', a property associated with artistic creativity, as well as by patronising artists and writers to define the character of their rule (see [1860] 1944: Part 1). In these terms we return to Nietzsche, for whom the situation of nihilism meant precisely that the only 'redemption' to which history and the historical human being could now look was the illusory redemption of art:

> Art and nothing but art! It is the great means of making life possible, the great seduction to life, the great stimulant of life.
> Art as the only superior counterforce to all will to denial of life, as that which is anti-Christian, anti-Buddhist, antinihilist *par excellence*.
> Art as the *redemption of the man of knowledge* . . .
> Art as the *redemption of the man of action* . . .
> Art as the *redemption of the sufferer* . . . ([1901] 1968: 452)

On this basis a 'universal history' might again be possible, but only as a work of art on the grand scale and not as a true account of the providential unfolding of the divine purpose that is leading us progressively towards a greater good and a greater freedom. In this regard, Kierkegaard's concession that if Hegel had claimed for his system only that it was a thought-experiment rather than knowledge of absolute truth, he would have had nothing to object to is pertinent. The eschatological and the nihilistic disruptions of history are not without their common themes.[17] The perception of such commonalities is reinforced by the continuing interactions of these two tendencies in the twentieth century, in existential philosophy and theology and in critical theory.[18] But it does not follow that they are identical. Neither, of course, allows for the narration of history to play the role of theodicy that Hegel had assigned to it, nor does either allow that a single logic gives meaning to the whole (there is no knowable whole to give meaning to). Yet each does, in its way, offer a certain redemption in face of the terrors of history. Nietzsche's nihilism, as we have seen, issues in a call to live artistically and through art to give meaning to our lives, albeit it is a meaning that is self-consciously illusory and that will vary infinitely from individual to individual and age to age. The Kierkegaardian and the eschatological approach, on the other hand, dispenses with the need for artistic consolation since it is able to offer its own categorical imperative of a hope that is beyond falsification by the horrors of existence. Each seems to the other like a false consolation, and Marxism, for example, would see them both as versions of false consciousness. In this respect, despite its materialist turn, Marxism remained closer to its original Hegelian element and largely retained the Hegelian belief in the unitary teleology of history.

Conclusion

A century on from the end of the nineteenth century, Francis Fukuyama (1992) would renew the Hegelian claim that history had arrived at its consummate conclusion and that the liberal democratic state in which Hegel saw the divine purpose of universal freedom finding its best historical realisation was now the only game in the global town. Samuel P. Huntington (1996) immediately responded with the thesis of a coming 'clash of civilizations'. The various permutations on these two positions allow us to say that questions as to the unity and teleology of history remain eminently debatable. In this sense, none of Hegel, Kierkegaard, Nietzsche or others achieved (and some never intended to achieve) the kind of paradigm that would from then on be determinative for all future considerations of the subject. But what the post-1992 debate also illustrates is that all options are also loaded with direct or indirect policy implications, as, for example, how we are to evaluate neo-liberal economics or respond to radical Islam. The subject is by no means 'merely academic'. If, pace Hegel but with a nod to Kierkegaard, an essay such as this might have an edifying conclusion, then we might say – I would venture to say – that if history proves to be without a unifying purpose, it does not follow that we are handed over to an endless clash of civilisations in which the only possible peace would be the triumph of the stronger. Both Nietzschean art and Kierkegaardian hope offer something better.

Notes

1. Karl Ameriks sees the historical turn in philosophy as taking definitive shape in Karl Leopold Reinhold's response to Kant, a response that initiates the view, now more or less normal, that philosophy is not just about timeless 'questions of philosophy' but involves a reckoning with the history of philosophy to which one is heir (2006: 11). See further Part II 'Reinhold and After' (ibid. 163–206). This, then, provides a basis for the kind of full-scale historicisation of philosophy that will be seen in Hegel (see below). For a thorough discussion of the broader historicist turn in Germany, see Beiser 2011.
2. As is well known, it could still, many centuries later, be debated as to whether indigenous peoples in the Americas were to be regarded as full human beings.
3. It would go far beyond the limits of this essay to discuss how nineteenth-century historicism is to be related to the historical studies of the early modern and Enlightenment era. But if the efforts of Hume, Ferguson, Gibbon, Herder and many others contributed to making the nineteenth-century development possible, we might still have reasons to suppose that the latter saw the emergence of a significantly new paradigm of historical development and historical self-understanding.
4. It is another question as to whether such a goal is, in fact, achievable. Within the German tradition it is very plausible to see Ernst Troeltsch, one of the more significant theological inheritors of the history of religions school, as someone whose immense empirical researches ultimately overwhelmed 'the absoluteness of Christianity' that his researches were dedicated to vindicating. The story of the tensions and conflicts of combining historical research with theological affirmation is well told in Zachhuber 2013.
5. Both Kierkegaard and Dostoevsky also offer much darker warnings against what they both describe in terms of the self-divinisation of the human race. Here we might turn to Kierkegaard's *Training in Christianity* and to Dostoevsky's *Demons* as well as to Ivan Karamazov's conversation with a hallucinatory devil who reminds Ivan of his own parable of 'The Geological Cataclysm' that foretells the advent of the 'Man-God'.
6. Of course, one could put this the other way round and argue, as the Reformers would argue, that it was scholasticism that had radically changed the originally Hebrew-inflected 'God and Father of our Lord Jesus Christ' into the Aristotelian unmoved mover.
7. This invites comparison with Carlyle's doctrine of 'great men': 'Universal History, the history of what man has accomplished in this world, is at bottom the History of the Great Men who have worked here. They were the leaders of men, these great ones; the modellers, patterns, and in a wide sense creators, of whatsoever the general mass of men contrived to do or to attain; all things that we see standing accomplished in the world are properly the outer material result, the practical realization and embodiment, of Thoughts that dwelt in the Great Men sent into the world: the soul of the whole world's history, it may justly be considered, were the history of these' ([1841] 1899: 1). Carlyle's conclusion, however, focused on the exiled Napoleon, 'our last hero', is more uncertain than Hegel's. Both agree that there is a greatness and a universality in the actions of such figures that transcend their individual foibles and that make their lives meaningful for all, yet Carlyle seems more troubled, haunted, scarred even, by the negative aspects of their deeds and self-delusions.

8. 'Rebellion' is the title of the chapter in which Dostoevsky allows Ivan to give expression to the view that the suffering of children makes any kind of theodicy of history morally unacceptable. The chapter culminates in Ivan's declaration that even if forgiveness for the crimes he has listed were possible, he would not want to be a part of it and that he is justified in, as he puts it, returning the ticket to any Kingdom of Heaven procured by such means.
9. I suggest that Hegel's esteem for Antigone has to do with the fact that her action is rooted in the dialectic of acknowledgement/recognition between brother and sister, a dialectic that, in the *Phenomenology*, becomes the driving force behind the emergence of a modern state of legally binding obligations and responsibilities, albeit the way to this passes through the manifold permutations of conflicts between masters and slaves, conquerors and conquered, that intervene between Sophocles' time and our own. For discussion, see Pattison 2013: ch. 6.
10. For a robust rebuff to the older view, see Stewart 2003.
11. See, for example, Heller 1993, where Kierkegaard is presented as a precursor of such twentieth-century figures as Walter Benjamin.
12. The title itself might already seem to be pointing us towards a view of historical truth as essentially fragmentary. However, a recent translation has given us the more narrowly correct reading *Philosophical Crumbs*. The older translation, clearly well suited to the thrust of the present argument, is not, though, entirely mistaken, echoing as it does the King James Bible translation of John 6: 12, where Jesus instructs his disciples to 'gather up the fragments that remain' after the miracle of the feeding of the five thousand, where 'fragments' both carries the meaning of 'crumbs' but is also open to the kind of metaphorical extension relevant to the discussion of the meaning of history in the aftermath (as it were) of Christ's Incarnation. To anticipate the argument that follows, Kierkegaard's reading suggests that when the Incarnation becomes the measure of history, all that remains are, precisely, fragments.
13. On this point at least we should not be put off by the apparent inversion of standpoints implied in the prefix 'Anti-'.
14. The image is somewhat confused in that Barth also talks here of the 'intersection' of time and eternity.
15. See Schweitzer [1906] 1954 (Weiss is discussed on 237ff.).
16. However, it is striking that in the development of the notion of 'the moment' in *The Concept of Anxiety*, Kierkegaard expressly refers to the eschatological teaching of 1 Corinthians 15: 52 and it is arguable that his own approach is more 'eschatological' than it may at first seem.
17. In relation to this we might also mention Nietzsche's friendship with Franz Overbeck, the church historian who had also emphasised the eschatological nature of early Christianity in opposition to the views of liberal Protestant theologians. Like Kierkegaard (and, for that matter, Dostoevsky and Nietzsche himself), Overbeck would also become a source for Karl Barth's explosion of the liberal Protestant view of history in his commentary on Romans.
18. See again, for example, Heller 1993.

References

Ameriks, Karl (2006), *Kant and the Historical Turn: Philosophy as Critical Interpretation*, Oxford: Clarendon Press.
Barth, Karl [1922] (1933), *The Epistle to the Romans*, trans. E. Hoskyns, Oxford: Oxford University Press.
Beiser, Frederick C. (2011), *The German Historicist Tradition*, Oxford: Oxford University Press.
Burckhardt, Jacob [1860] (1944), *The Civilization of the Renaissance* trans. S. G. C. Middlemore, Oxford: Phaidon.
Burckhardt, Jacob (1959), *Judgements on History and Historians*, trans. Harry Zohn, London: George Allen & Unwin.
Carlyle, Thomas [1841] (1899), 'On Heroes, Hero-Worship, and the Heroic in History', in *The Works of Thomas Carlyle*, ed. E. H. Traill, vol. 5, London: Chapman and Hall, 1–251.

Fukuyama, Francis (1992), *The End of History and the Last Man*, London: Penguin.
Hegel, G. W. F. [1837] (1956), *The Philosophy of History*, trans. J. Sibree, New York: Dover.
Hegel, G. W. F. (1970), *Werke*, 20 vols, Frankfurt am Main: Suhrkamp.
Hegel, G. W. F. [1807] (1977), *Phenomenology of Spirit*, trans. A. V. Miller, Oxford: Oxford University Press.
Heller, Agnes (1993), *A Philosophy of History in Fragments*, Oxford: Blackwell.
Huntington, Samuel P. (1996), *The Clash of Civilizations and the Remaking of the World Order*, New York: Simon and Schuster.
Kierkegaard, Søren [1844] (1985), *Philosophical Fragments/Johannes Climacus*, ed. and trans. H. V. Hong and E. H. Hong, Princeton: Princeton University Press.
Kierkegaard, Søren [1848] (1991), *Practice in Christianity*, ed. and trans. Howard V. Hong and Edna H. Hong, Princeton: Princeton University Press.
Kierkegaard, Søren (1997–2013), *Søren Kierkegaards Skrifter*, ed. Niels Jørgen Cappelørn et al., 28 vols, Copenhagen: Gad.
Nietzsche, Friedrich [1901] (1968), *The Will to Power*, trans. Walter Kauffman, New York: Vintage.
Nietzsche, Friedrich [1882] (1974), *The Gay Science*, trans. Walter Kauffman, New York: Vintage.
Pattison, George (2013), *Kierkegaard and the Quest for Unambiguous Life*, Oxford: Oxford University Press.
Schweitzer, Albert [1906] (1954), *The Quest of the Historical Jesus*, trans. H. Montgomery, London: A&C Black.
Stewart, Jon (2003), *Kierkegaard's Relations to Hegel Reconsidered*, Cambridge: Cambridge University Press.
Stillingfleet, Edward [1662] (1817), *Origines Sacrae or a Rational Account of the Grounds of Natural and Revealed Religion*, Oxford: Clarendon Press.
von Ranke, Leopold [1872] (1877), *Abhandlungen und Versuche: erste Sammlung*, 2nd edn, Leipzig: Duncker and Humblot.
von Ranke, Leopold [1881] (1884), *Universal History. The Oldest Historical Group of Nations and the Greeks*, ed. and trans. G. W. Prothero, London: Kegan Paul.
Zachhuber, Johannes (2013), *Theology as Science in Nineteenth-Century Germany: From F. C. Baur to Ernst Troeltsch*, Oxford: Oxford University Press.

12

Tradition

Thomas Pfau

And what the dead had no speech for, when living,
They can tell you, being dead: the communication
Of the dead is tongued with fire beyond the language of the living,
...
We are born with the dead:
See, they return, and bring us with them. (T. S. Eliot)

This chapter's objective is twofold: first, to reconstruct the intellectual landscape in which the theological retrieval of tradition(s) unfolded during the first half of the nineteenth century, in particular Newman's distinctive and influential reappraisal of tradition as a form of 'development'. Second, I wish to explore Newman's contention that the truth of Christianity and the demands it places on every individual are inseparable from exegetical traditions and competing modes of theological inquiry to which it gave rise, as well as their subsequent, 'effective history' (*Wirkungsgeschichte*), a term I borrow from Hans-Georg Gadamer, whose account of tradition bears striking affinities to Newman's views. Right away, some methodological complications arise. For it was the nineteenth-century reappraisal of tradition that put pressure on modernity's (neo-Stoic) ethos of detached objectivity and critical prevarication as it been formulated in Descartes' sceptical and Kant's transcendental methodologies, respectively. Hence it would be question-begging for us now to scrutinise developments in nineteenth-century theology, specifically as regards the concept of tradition, by way of positivist and historicising methods when it was precisely the limitations of this type of 'critical' inquiry to which Newman and several of his contemporaries were reacting. Instead, we should keep in view Newman's alternative approach to knowledge, most fully articulated in his *Grammar of Assent* (1870), which posits 'real assent' as a more plausible point of departure for understanding a complex body of ideas and appraising its significance.

Newman, of course, was hardly alone in demurring at the prevailing tendency (variously urged by Cartesian rationalism, Humean scepticism and Kantian agnosticism) to deprive objects of inquiry (a phenomenon, a concept or a complex intellectual formation) of all narrative continuity, and to reconstitute them as discrete propositions to be probed for logical inconsistencies or procedural missteps. Yet Newman was among the first to remark how the complex, multi-layered phenomenon of Christianity in particular cannot be adequately grasped independent of the exegetical traditions and competing explanatory efforts that it has spawned over time. Neither systematic theology nor apologetics can ever disentangle themselves from the tradition of theological inquiry in which they are rooted, nor should they wish to do so. For even as a tradition is always in flux and contested as regards its meanings and overall significance, its rationality is as incontrovertible and indispensable in the realm of theology as forms of received and 'implicit' reason are in all other forms of human inquiry and social practice.

Part of what makes Newman's contribution to nineteenth-century thought so distinctive, indeed unique, is his seemingly counter-intuitive insight that eighteenth-century, common-sense empiricism, far from being the antagonist of normative theological reasoning, furnished an indispensable methodological template for it. It does so by reminding us of the fundamental mental stance with which we respond to the sheer givenness of phenomena and ideas whose necessarily partial presentation and apparent complexity solicit our fundamental assent, even as they defy instantaneous comprehension and definitive explanation. When presented with complex ideas no less than with 'every day's occurrence', Newman remarks, 'we meet them, not with suspicion and criticism, but with a frank confidence'. The default from which inquiry starts is 'faith' and 'trust', subsequently fine-tuned by ongoing reflection on the notions and realities placed before us: 'we do not begin with doubting ... [but] prove them, by using them, by applying them' ([1845] 1989: 101). It seems reasonable to draw on Newman's common-sense epistemology as our point of departure for engaging his oeuvre, namely, by taking stock of what conceptual frameworks, concerns and objectives were shaping the intellectual landscape in which he intervened.

The Legacy of the Enlightenment

In sketching the intellectual situation that, by the 1840s, prompts Newman to rethink the concept of tradition under the heading of 'development', it is necessary, however briefly, to recall how tradition was conceived in the wake of late-Enlightenment and Romantic thought. In his 1960 landmark study, *Truth and Method*, Hans-Georg Gadamer had questioned the Enlightenment's 'prejudice against prejudice', that is, its assumption that all knowledge not constructed in the here and now, and ratified by present consensus proves *ipso facto* illegitimate, simply because it draws on the authority of antecedent claims that resist definitive and objective verification. Reaffirming the view that Gadamer means to call into question, Theodor Adorno in 1966 conceives of tradition as 'subjectively desiccated' and 'ideologically corrupted' and as 'strictly speaking incompatible with bourgeois society' (1970–97: 10.1:314, 310).[1] Where the modern, autonomous individual cannot produce a compelling warrant for what it has been bequeathed by written tradition, it must reject and, if necessary, forcibly expunge all traces of such received knowledge.[2] With its distinctive mix of rhetorical hyper-ventilation and eerie prescience, Burke's *Reflections on the Revolution in France* (1790) had argued that the wholesale expurgation of all tradition was bound to radicalise the French Revolution, then just under way, and in time would bring about the utter destruction of the *ancien régime*, and of its supporting, Catholic ecclesial and monastic structures – to be supplanted by a permanently unsettled social and political culture for which the introduction, in late 1793, of a new revolutionary calendar was widely taken to be emblematic.[3]

This is not the place to rehearse the long and convoluted story of how the French Revolution's violent construal of the Enlightenment's intellectual legacy was ultimately defeated by its own Napoleonic hubris. Rather more pertinent to Newman's intellectual formation is the climate of conservatism that establishes itself in European intellectual and political culture after 1815. Integral to this shift is a certain rehabilitation of tradition, such as we find it in the political theories of Adam Müller, Friedrich Gentz (secretary to Metternich and, in 1793, the first to translate Burke's *Reflections* into German), Chateaubriand, de Maistre and, closer to home, in the 'Tory Humanism' of the later Wordsworth and the High Churchmanship of Coleridge's *On the Constitution of Church and State* (1830). Given the comprehensive political realignment of post-Waterloo Europe, it cannot surprise that the idea of tradition should have become imbued with a pathos of 'retrieval' – of lands, titles, old claims – and with the spirit of 'reaction' against most things modern. The conjoined and entrenched interests of king, church and the members of the French aristocracy – still smarting from their relatives' expropriation, exile and, in many cases, execution by the Jacobins – account for the pronounced and lasting association of tradition with a politics of stagnation, resentment and repression. A closer study of the personalities of Metternich, Charles X and a series of Tory leaders in England (Jenkinson, Canning, Goderich and Wellesley, a.k.a. Duke of Wellington) and their political vision would amply confirm how the concept of tradition in early nineteenth-century thought emerges as the very antithesis of social, political and intellectual flourishing. Indeed, the young Newman himself was not unaffected by this climate but, in his 'early political thought' exhibits 'a blend of the conservatism of Burke ... with the Nonjuring principle taught in the Anglican Homily on Wilful disobedience (1569)' (Nockles 1994: 69).[4]

If we turn from the political to the intellectual culture of European Romanticism, and more specifically to theological inquiry, additional features begin to complicate an already inauspicious picture. Caught up in that epoch's distinctive blend of exuberance and ambivalence, theological inquiry finds itself increasingly under pressure by two competing and influential frameworks: sentimentalism and historicism. Both conceptions prove sharply at odds with Newman's lifelong insistence that Christianity's original *depositum fidei* could reveal its true significance and splendour only gradually, namely, by unveiling its implications and in so doing, constitute itself as a bona fide tradition spanning nearly two millennia. By contrast, both sentimentalism and historicism posit the inherent superiority of the present as the moment when the past has been definitively overcome in the guise of objective, empirical knowledge (historicism) or, alternatively, has been wholly absorbed into the drama of Romantic inwardness (sentimentalism). Yet even as these two frameworks seem almost diametrically opposed in their respective framing of human cognition as grounded in an objective, dispassionate methodology (historicism) or in subjective epiphanies (sentimentalism), both extend the Enlightenment's strictly anthropomorphic and anti-dogmatic conception of knowledge as something not *received* but autonomously *produced*.

An amalgam of seventeenth-century Pietism and Lockean hedonism, sentimentalism had arisen in reaction against the perceived excesses of modern rationalism (Leibniz, Wolff, S. Clarke, Godwin, et al.). In time, it was to evolve into a secular fideism of sorts, one whose enduring appeal is evident in the writings of Rousseau, Hume, Smith, Macpherson (Ossian), the della Cruscans, Charlotte Turner Smith and the *Sturm und Drang* movement in Germany associated with Klopstock, Moritz, Herder, and the young Goethe and Schiller. After 1790, sentimentalism's guiding premise, namely, that the sources of human cognition can ultimately be traced to the volatile and mesmerising play of human passion, is being refracted by a resurgent awareness of the incalculable operations of irony, memory and figural language in all human expression. Cumulatively, the shift in question takes us from an orderly grammar of affect as it prevails from Thomson's *The Seasons* through Rousseau's *Nouvelle Héloïse* to Haydn's secular cantatas (e.g. *Arianna a Naxos*) to Mozart's *Idomeneo* towards a fundamentally deregulated model of free 'expression' (*Ausdruck*) such as we find it taking shape in the lyric oeuvre of the young Goethe, Novalis, Hölderlin, Wordsworth and Coleridge. For the romantic heirs of Rousseau, who had 'immensely enlarged the scope of the inner voice', accessing the as yet untapped potential of a pre-conscious past requires devising new lyric and narrative modes of expression, as well as rejecting the generic prescriptions of Augustan and Enlightenment aesthetics (Taylor 1989: 362).[5] Hence, even as sentimentalism invests the past with oblique significance, it rejects all *formal* traditions as supposedly prejudicial to the emotional and intellectual flourishing of the modern individual.

One formal innovation associated with the cultural shift just sketched, one typically said to occur between 1760 and 1800, also holds significant implications for Newman's understanding of tradition as a case of progressive retrieval. It concerns the modern *Bildungsroman*, one of Romanticism's major innovations and aimed at capturing its protagonist's social, intellectual and spiritual flourishing. At heart a revival of the Platonic motif of *anamnesis*, such narratives of personal growth and cultivation hinge on a dynamic and contingent model of aesthetic play. The inspired subject or 'genius' at the heart of such narratives appears preternaturally responsive to the vicarious summons of memory and 'chance' occurrences that 'a sensitive, and a *creative* soul' (Wordsworth [1805] 1991: Book 11, line 256) will expressively reclaim as the narrative of its own 'development' (*Bildung*).[6] Characteristic of narratives of *Bildung* is a marked tension between the oblique and distant *sources* of the self's flourishing and their gradual retrieval by an authorial voice eager to take control over its own genesis in the present. Building on Herder's 'advocacy of empathy as the condition for the connection between past and present', Goethe had remarked on an unpredictable resurgence of distant memories within individual consciousness, which thus finds itself unaccountably transformed by a 'sensibility of the past and the present in one – an intuition which brought something special into the present' (quoted in Frei 1980: 205). Similarly, Wordsworth remarks how

> The mind of Man is fram'd even like the breath
> And harmony of music. There is a dark
> Invisible workmanship that reconciles
> Discordant elements, and makes them move
> In one society.
> . . . . .
> Hard task to analyse a soul, in which,
> Not only general habits and desires,
> But each most obvious and particular thought,
> Not in a mystical and idle sense,
> But in the words of reason deeply weigh'd,
> Hath no beginning.
> ([1805] 1991: Book 1, lines 351–5, 232–7)

Well before echoing Wordsworth's passage almost verbatim in the *Apologia*, Newman had paid a late tribute to the *Bildungsroman* with his 1848 novel, *Loss and Gain*, a book perhaps most notable for the care with which its mostly dialogic action avoids the genre's frequent drift towards sentimentalism and self-absorption, tendencies that sometimes get the better of Wordsworth, and that Goethe, Stendhal and Byron could only fend off by relying on the structural principle of irony.[7] Yet the defensive mechanism of irony – a form of intellectual pride, 'false humility' (Aquinas) or 'negative mysticism' – is open only to the non-believer, as Georg Lukács had shrewdly pointed out when characterising irony as 'the highest form of freedom that can be achieved in a world without God' ([1915] 1982: 90, 93).[8]

Yet for all his fascination with the oblique, if implacable 'development' of an idea whose origins are at such distance from us, Newman remains fundamentally at odds with the sentimental absorption and ironic prevarication that variously characterise Romanticism's imaginative commerce with the past. As he puts it in 1841, 'if we attempt to effect a moral improvement by means of poetry, we shall but mature into a mawkish, frivolous, and fastidious sentimentalism' ([1872] 2004: 275). For Newman, sentimentalism's and Romanticism's preoccupation with private, subjective states and opinions is destined to expire in a relativism and agnosticism that had become integral features of early Victorian Latitudinarian culture.[9] Nowhere is this development more evident than in the widely accepted view that:

> truth and falsehood in religion are but matter of opinion; that one doctrine is as good as another; that the Governor of the world does not intend that we should gain the truth; that there is no truth; . . . that no one is answerable for his opinions; that they are a matter of necessity or accident; [and] that it is enough if we sincerely hold what we profess. ([1845] 1989: 357)

In Newman's time, the political theory implicit in late eighteenth-century sentimentalism and its Romantic successors had assumed programmatic expression under the heading of liberalism, 'that philosophy, which resolves to sit at home and make everything subordinate to the individual' (Tract 73 in [1841] 2013: 199).[10]

Newman rejects virtually every feature of modern liberalism, including a view that links Romantic sentimentalism to the rationalist and sceptical epistemologies it had contested during the previous two generations: namely, that all relevant meaning is *eo ipso* confined to the biographical time-span and private judgement of the solitary individual. Few works of Romanticism embody sentimentalism's anti-historical and anti-dogmatic stance more vividly than the young Friedrich Schleiermacher's *Addresses on Religion* (1799). Religious meaning here has been altogether absorbed into the individual's subjective, inner states, such that ecclesial structures, dogmatic meanings and even the authority of Scripture itself are all but consumed by an entirely self-certifying, individual sensibility. Here religious knowledge has increasingly merged with the subjective profession or, rather, *expression* of religious 'sentiment' (*Gefühl*). In Schleiermacher's emphatic declaration:

> for me divinity can be nothing other than a discrete type of religious intuition [*eine einzelne religiöse Anschauungsart*]. The rest of religious intuitions are independent of it and of each other. From my standpoint and according to my conceptions that are known to you, the belief 'No God, no religion' cannot occur. ([1799] 1996: 51)

Here subjective intuition no longer constitutes a subordinate, if integral, feature of humanistic and theological inquiry but, instead, has supplanted historically mindful *studiositas* altogether.

Newman's early work on the pre-Nicene Fathers and the Arian heresy had already alerted him to the hazards of a strictly subject-centred, in tendency anthropomorphic conception of Christianity. Unsurprisingly, he views the rise of rationalism in contemporary theology as an inevitable reaction against 'the revival of religious feeling during the last century ... spread, not by talents or learning in its upholders, but by their piety, zeal, and sincerity, and its own incidental and partial truth' ([1872] 2004: 241).[11] As Newman sees it, any theology that does not arise from, and in continuous response to, a rich and deep tradition will ultimately resemble the very paganism it purports to have overcome. In the last of his *Oxford University Sermons*, Newman reaffirms his early intuition of a strong nexus between Arianism and modern, liberal Protestantism forever vacillating between the ephemeral lure of sentimentalism and the arid objectivity of the Higher Criticism; such heresy, he ventures,

> has no theology; so far forth as it is heresy it has none. Deduct its remnant of Catholic theology, and what remains? Polemics, explanations, protests. It turns to Biblical Criticism, or to the Evidences of Religion, for want of a province. Its *formulæ* end in themselves, without development, because they are words; they are barren, because they are dead. ... It develops into dissolution; but it creates nothing, it tends to no system, its resultant dogma is but the denial of all dogmas, any theology, under the Gospel. ... Heresy denies to the Church what is wanting in itself. ([1843] 1997: 318)

Early in his *Development of Christian Doctrine*, Newman comments on this tendency, intrinsic to 'Protestantism as a whole, ... of dispensing with historical Christianity altogether, and of forming a Christianity from the Bible alone'. Hence it 'scarcely recognizes the fact of the twelve long ages which lie between the Councils of Nicaea and Trent'. In Newman's pithy and provocative formulation, then, 'to be deep in history is to cease to be a Protestant' ([1845] 1989: 7–8).

This last remark warrants scrutiny, however, for it points to Newman's misgivings about the other dominant framework of the Romantic era: historicism. In its dominant theological form, that of the so-called Higher Criticism first shaped by Wolf, Eichhorn, Ernesti and the Tübingen School, and subsequently extended in the controversial writings of Strauss, Feuerbach, Comte, Renan and others, historicism secures theological meanings at the expense of their relevance. Like another institutional creation of the Romantic era, the modern museum, historicism posits that to 'know' is not to participate in meanings but, rather, to quarantine them as mere past 'context' or pre-history. As Gadamer was to point out much later, historicism fundamentally re-enacts the Enlightenment's vaunted emancipation from history by arresting and inventorying the past, draining it of its relevance, and by 'reconstruct[ing] the old because it is old' ([1960] 2006: 275).[12] Nineteenth-century historicism marks the culmination of a process long in the making, involving 'a kind of detachment of the "real" historical world from its biblical description' wrought by the Enlightenment's insistence on 'a logical distinction and a reflective distance between the stories and the "reality" they depict'. Hans Frei, whom I have been quoting, has offered a compelling account of this development, noting that 'once literal and historical reading began to break apart, figural interpretation became discredited both as a literary device and as a historical argument' because it contravened 'the elementary assumption that a propositional statement has only one meaning'. The resulting historicist protocol amounts to conceptual naturalism whose 'confusion of history-likeness (literal meaning) and history (ostensive reference), and the hermeneutical reduction of the former to an aspect of the latter, meant that one lacked the distinctive category and appropriate interpretive procedure for understanding what one had actually recognized' (1980: 3–5, 12).[13]

In its methodical commitment to the attenuation of past meaning within a matrix of underlying material causes and background reference, historicism betrays its discomfort with the possibility of meanings issuing from the past and having an enduring and potentially transformative hold on the present – precisely what Newman understands by the development of an idea into a substantive tradition. Long before Gadamer was to point out that 'for the historical school there exists neither an end of history nor anything outside it' ([1960] 2006: 196), Friedrich Schlegel had objected to his contemporaries' eagerness to dissolve history into a wholly adventitious and aimless sequence of secondary causes. With characteristically searing, aphoristic wit, he skewers

> the two main principles of the so-called historical criticism . . . the Postulate of Vulgarity and the Axiom of the Average. The Postulate of Vulgarity: everything great, good, and beautiful is improbable because it is extraordinary and, at the very least, suspicious. The Axiom of the Average: as we and our surroundings are, so must it have been always and everywhere, because that, after all, is so very natural. (1996: 3)[14]

Similarly, Schelling only a few years later remarks on 'the severing of knowledge from its historical archetype by historicizing scholarship [*dieses Abtrennen des Wissens von seinem historischen Urbild durch historische Gelehrsamkeit*]' and on a growing and worrisome tendency of 'mere transmission without independent mental activity [*die bloße Überlieferung ohne selbstthätigen Geist*]' (1981: 461, 468). However cogent, and in time echoed in very different idioms, by Nietzsche, Blondel and Walter Benjamin, these initial, sharply critical responses to the ascendancy of historicist method did little to check its progress.

Conceived as a methodical unmasking and dissolving of unique 'event' into its putative background conditions, historicism 'perpetuates [the Enlightenment's] abstract contrast between myth and reason', that is, between the opacity of the past and its transparent and objective reconstruction in the present. Thus:

> the historical consciousness that emerges in romanticism involves a radicalization of the Enlightenment. For nonsensical tradition [*Überlieferung*], which had been the exception, has become the rule for historical consciousness. Meaning that is generally accessible through reason is so little believed that the whole of the past – even, ultimately . . . is understood only 'historically'. (Gadamer [1960] 2006: 275, 277)[15]

As early as the mid-1830s, Newman had begun to raise very similar questions. In Tract 73, on the 'Introduction of Rationalistic Principles into Religion' (2 February 1836), he identifies another key trait of the historical method, one that also reveals its deep continuity with Enlightenment rationalism. It concerns the presumption that a perfected historical or contextualising method ensures instantaneous and complete knowledge of its object, and that the knowledge so produced entails the utter dissolution of any tradition or 'mystery' attaching to the object in question. Peter Gordon calls this contextualism's 'premise of exhaustion', which implicitly prohibits the historian 'from imagining the possibility of semantic continuities across broad stretches of time' and waxes 'especially skeptical of the possibility that ideas from the past might still be available for *critical appropriation in the present*' (2014: 44). Given their implicit quest for definitive emancipation *from* the past, historicising and contextualising approaches to intellectual traditions tend to disrupt and quarantine the dynamic nature of complex ideas and conceptions and, ultimately, to reject process thinking altogether. Hence they tend to construe tradition in all its manifestations (religious or otherwise) as an obstacle to insight, rather than as a source of it.

Like other forms of rationalism, historicist approaches to Christian traditions disavow from the outset its most essential features: revelation and mystery. The rationalist's commitment to variously historicising and contextualising protocols of inquiry thus does not so much settle the question of tradition as beg it. For modern critical epistemologies are axiomatically committed to a strictly anthropomorphic concept of Reason; both the sources of knowledge and its eventual articulations are taken to be strictly products of *Homo faber*. For Newman, the great weakness of 'rationalist principles' is that they preclude human beings from receiving knowledge from the past and from participating within intellectual and theological traditions without first anxiously stipulating that the authority of any tradition resolves itself into finite and ultimately mundane, man-made contexts. Yet at the beginning of Western thought a nearly obverse understanding prevails, namely, of tradition as something received, not made, and of divine rather than anthropomorphic character. Thus Plato insists that tradition can only be understood as 'a gift of gods to men, ... tossed down from some divine source [θεῶν μὲν εἰς ἀνθρώπους δόσις, ὥς γε καταφαίνεται ἐμοί]'. A bequest to human communities, rather than an anthropomorphism in its own right, tradition is said both to spring from and point back to its transcendent source:

> the ancients, who were better than we and lived nearer the gods, handed down [παρέδοσαν] the tradition that all the things which are ever said to exist are sprung from one and many and have inherent in them the finite and the infinite. (1989: *Philebus* 16c)

What distinguishes the role of the ancients is not that they originated a tradition (they did not), but that they were closer in time to its source: 'anyone who accepts and "believes" that tradition is relying ... not on the "ancients", but on the gods themselves' (Pieper [1970] 2010: 28).[16] Newman evidently concurs, remarking that 'when nothing is revealed, nothing is known, and there is nothing to contemplate or marvel at; but when something is revealed and only something, for all cannot be, there are forthwith difficulties and perplexities'. What is most integral to Christianity turns out to be most vexing to modern historical method, namely, that 'revelation consists of a number of detached and incomplete truths belonging to a vast system unrevealed, of doctrines and injunctions mysteriously connected together' (Tract 73 in [1841] 2013: 188–9). Lurking behind historicism's apparent impatience with a continuously developing tradition, Newman sees the hubris of a modern secular epistemology viscerally uncomfortable with the possibility of a knowledge received on terms it does not control.

Yet to surrender the desire for dominion over what we are given is precisely what is required if traditions are to become intelligible at all. Inasmuch as it enjoins the recipient to cultivate humility and gratitude vis-à-vis what it offers, tradition fulfils what Paul Griffiths identifies as the twofold characteristic of the gift: a distinctive group of 'things [that] can be given away without being thereby lost to the giver' and that, concurrently, 'will be lost if they are not given away' (2009: 58).[17] Furthermore, what troubles Newman about the ascendancy of historical method is its propensity to fragment and disaggregate core components of Christianity that, on his view, are its indispensable and mutually supporting components (atonement, grace, justification, revelation, incarnation, et al.). Once subjected to historicising inquiry, the tradition of two millennia shrinks into just another anthropomorphism – and so reveals itself as an unwitting descendant of the Arian heresy that Newman had explored early in his career: 'it must ever be small and superficial, viewed only as received by man; and is vast only when considered as that external truth into which each Christian may grow continually' (Tract 73 in [1841] 2013: 190).[18] Newman was acutely aware of historicism's Protestant-nationalist, and implicitly secular grand narratives (e.g. Treitschke, Droysen, Ranke, Michelet, et al.) it continued to spawn – narratives that monotonously affirm the historical inevitability and superiority of the present-day, liberal-secular order and the industrial and scientific utilitarianism from which a politically dominant middle class draws both inspiration and legitimation.[19]

Meanwhile, historicism's preoccupation with philological, empirical and objective methodology forecloses precisely on what, in Newman's view, is the enduring and progressive actualisation of past teaching; hence his phrasing, precise as always, that 'to be deep *in* history is to cease to be a Protestant'. To be '*in* history' is to find oneself, not at the endpoint of it but, rather, as part of a trans-generational and open-ended process involving the reflective transmission of meanings long in the making. Put differently, knowledge of the past, of tradition, is inseparable from our considered involvement *in* that past. To *know* a tradition is to acknowledge one's hermeneutic entanglement in it as an ontological fact and, indeed, as an enabling condition. The antecedent reality and sheer richness of (exegetical, theological, philosophical) traditions exacts constant and evolving forms of hermeneutic attention that will leave the reflective agent transformed rather than, as historicism supposes, detached from the knowledge so gained. In responding to complex and deep genealogies of thought, theological inquiry also reveals the organic and fortuitous operation of memory; for 'what is memory itself, but a vast magazine of . . . dormant, but present and excitable ideas?' – that is, a progressive awakening from 'implicit to explicit reason' and to the realisation that all along one 'was possessed, ruled, guided by an unconscious idea' ([1843] 1997: 321–2). Precisely this oblique and undesigning way in which we find our way into a tradition of reasoned inquiry, Newman insists, also safeguards us against the procedural and anthropomorphic limitations of Romantic historicism and sentimentalism, respectively.

Tradition as a Hermeneutic Challenge

So much for the background conditions prompting Newman's reflections on tradition and development. None of the above, however, is meant to suggest that Newman's distinctive conception took shape merely as a reaction against Romanticism's variously elegiac, ironic or positivistic dismantling of biblical narrative and religious meaning. Rather, his main concern lies with retrieving and actively inhabiting the vast reservoir of theological reasoning that the competing frameworks of sentimentalism and historicism had either neglected or dismissed outright. As he puts it, his essay 'is directed towards a solution of the difficulty . . . which lies in the way of our using in controversy the testimony of our most natural informant concerning the doctrine and worship of Christianity, viz. the history of eighteen hundred years' ([1845] 1989: 29). While the present discussion mainly focuses on Newman's reappraisal of tradition as 'development', it bears noting that on the Continent, specifically in Germany, similar efforts had been undertaken by the Tübingen School of Catholic Theology, in particular by Johann Sebastian Drey (1777–1853), Johann Baptist Hirscher (1788–1865) and Johann Adam Möhler (1796–1838). Through its new organ, the *Theologische Quartalsschrift* (established in 1819), the Tübingen School sought to bring Catholic theology into focused dialogue with contemporary intellectual movements, such as the organic conception of historical development and a renewed emphasis on intuitive and affective sources of cognition pioneered by Fichte, Novalis,

Hölderlin and Schelling, among others (see Hinze 2010).[20] Scrutinising the arguments of Schleiermacher and Schelling in particular, Drey 'took great pains to show ... the dynamic nature of the living tradition, in the Word of God, in the scriptures, and in the binding judgment of the official teachings of the bishops in ecumenical councils' (Hinze 2010: 192). Yet Drey's three-volume *Die Apologetik als Wissenschaftliche Nachweisung der Göttlichkeit des Christentums in seiner Erscheinung* (1838–47) ends up framing tradition within a conventional, theodicy-type argument by construing the seemingly contingent historical evolution of Christianity as the temporal and incremental working-out of a divine plan. Animating the inquiry into a 'living tradition' (*eine lebendige Überlieferung*) pursued by Drey and his colleagues at Tübingen is a discomfort with the Protestant-scientific antinomy of confessional and historical knowledge, of the past as but a myth to be dispelled by philology and the inherently anthropomorphic nature of modern positivist epistemologies. Hirscher's *Die Christliche Moral* (published in three volumes, 1835–51) and, especially, Möhler's ground-breaking work on the Arian controversy (*Athanasius der Grosse und die Kirche seiner Zeit, besonders im Kampf mit dem Arianismus*, 1827) extend Drey's fundamental distinction between a strictly historical and a divine (revealed) tradition. Tradition (*Überlieferung*) is not, at least not primarily, a matter of historical retrieval but of hermeneutic participation in the discovery of meanings to be found in both endogenous and exogenous sources. Approached as a divine bequest, tradition thus 'affirms continuity and development in the doctrinal and practical identity of the church' (Hinze 2010: 199).

Yet more than Drey and Hirscher, Möhler developed an increasingly antagonistic confessional position with ultramontanist overtones. In his works after 1827, the hermeneutic challenge of a *living* tradition is ultimately subordinated to concerns with ecclesiological stability and, hence, subject to the definitive authority of the magisterium.[21] Yet in taking an increasingly strident approach to theological argument and confessional differences, Möhler loses sight of the fact that the magisterium is itself an objective and historically mutable instance of tradition and that, consequently, any authoritative appraisal of 'divine tradition' necessarily enjoins its visible representatives to engage in self-scrutiny. As a *prima facie* case of apostolic succession, ecclesiastic authority is itself a manifestation of the very tradition of which it seeks to offer an authoritative and binding appraisal. It is no accident that the major representatives of Austro-German Catholic theology (Drey, Möhler, Kleutgen and Franzelin) had significant influence on, and in some cases played an official institutional role in, the consolidation of the neo-Thomist line with which post-Vatican I Catholicism came to be associated. Arguably the most searching and extensive analysis of tradition within nineteenth-century German Catholicism is found in the work of Johann Baptist Franzelin (1816–86). In a number of major treatises (written in Latin during his years as Prefect in the German College and at other congregations in Rome), Franzelin works out his core distinction between tradition as objective content and as hermeneutic act. It is only under the auspices of the church, understood as an uninterrupted apostolic succession, that these two aspects of tradition have been organically reconciled. For Franzelin, who in 1834 joined the Society of Jesus, the reality and intelligibility of tradition constitutes a divine gift and unfolds '*sub assistentia Spiritus Sancti*'. It is a gift received rather than historically or institutionally ordained, even as its evolving interpretation depends on the visible guardianship of authorities invested by the visible church with monitoring and teaching the original *depositum fidei*. While the objective, historical record of scriptural exegesis, conciliar resolutions and church teaching renders the faith-dependent, revealed truths progressively visible and intelligible, Franzelin insists that tradition in its sheer objective-historical sense is not to be misconstrued as 'proof' of the *depositum fidei* but only as its contingent manifestation.[22]

More than some of his German Catholic contemporaries, Newman (especially in his late Anglican phase) recognises that a responsible engagement with tradition must be informed by humility and a constant awareness of it as a totality of received meanings whose ultimate significance can never be secured by discrete historical pronouncements or institutional fiat. Thus the first edition of his *Development of Christian Doctrine* (1845) honours this insight more consistently than the revised, sixth edition of 1878 with its strained defence of the new doctrine of papal infallibility of July 1870. Newman's unease with that doctrine – all but impossible to reconcile with his theory of development – is particularly evident in section II, chapters 7–8 of the 1878 edition of his *Essay*. Conceding that 'if we have but probable grounds for the Church's infallibility, ... the words *infallibility*, *necessity*, *truth*, and *certainty* ought all of them to be banished from the language', Newman's prose here verges on sophistry in a rhetorical question meant to solve his conceptual predicament: 'But why is it more inconsistent to speak of an uncertain infallibility than of a doubtful truth or a contingent necessity?' To insist that 'infallibility does not interfere with moral probation' and that 'the idea of a peremptory authority', even as it 'limits the inquiries of the individual' nonetheless 'preserves intact their probationary character' ([1845] 1989: 81, 83) is not of much help; for it leaves unexamined the role of 'individual inquiry' in a process whose scope and conclusions are definitively set by the magisterium. Moreover, even as Newman attempts to thread the needle here, one doubts that the authors of the doctrine of papal infallibility at the First Vatican Council should have intended so qualified an application for it.[23]

To clarify the tension between a dynamic concept of tradition as a hermeneutic challenge and its construal as a source of definitive, institutionally sanctioned doctrine, it helps to review the several criteria that, for Newman, are constitutive of theological inquiry as a continuously developing tradition. A first feature here is that tradition both tempers and directs human judgement. It is no accident that chapter 1 of the *Development of Christian Doctrine* opens with Newman musing on the constant propensity of human beings to form judgements. Yet in his view, such activity is not gratuitously evaluative but, on the contrary, unfolds as the continual integration of discrete aspects with one another: 'we compare, contrast, abstract, generalize, connect, adjust, classify'. Such a process has been unfolding long before the mind ventures any explicit proposition about this or that thing. 'Judgement' thus performs the work of what, in one of his *Oxford University Sermons*, Newman had called 'implicit reason'. Unlike discursive, propositional reasoning, however, the operation of judgement is inherently synthetic rather than analytic, integrative rather than disjunctive. Roughly analogous to the 'schemata' that, in Kant's first *Critique*, reconcile 'pure concepts of understanding' with 'sensible intuition', judgement in Newman's account forges connections, registers similarities, hazards preliminary classifications, and so creates a grid of mental representations that enables human beings to assimilate and respond to new phenomena as they give themselves to us.[24] Hence 'the judgments thus made ... become aspects in our minds of the things which meet us' ([1845] 1989: 33). In emphasising the oblique nature of a great deal of our mental activity, Newman already points to a trait that also characterises entire traditions of inquiry, namely, its highly adaptive and self-revising mode of operation. The vast and diverse array of representations to which judgement gives rise furnishes the very matrix that allows individuals gradually to discriminate between substantive insight and ephemeral opinion, between notions enjoying some probability and transient impressions destined to be defeated by future experience. Those representations that have persisted since first being formed, revised and tested by the trial of subsequent experience furnish us with a blueprint of what Newman understands by tradition. Hence, even as all judgement begins as *praejudicium*, its repeated testing by the passage of time also sets limits to the innate tendency of all judgement to deteriorate into purely subjective, wilful assertion.

A second feature of tradition shows its interpretive and reflective movement to extend both forward towards greater clarity and backward, in an attempt to connect present theological insight with its often distant sources. Speaking of the doctrine of the Trinity (ibid. 14ff.). Newman thus proposes that, in order 'to give a deeper meaning to their letter, we must interpret the [documents of pre-Nicaea] by the times which came after' (ibid. 16). Consistent with the organic and integrative logic of tradition, later insights 'do not reverse, but perfect, what has gone before' (ibid. 65), just as 'we elucidate the text by comment, though, or rather because, the comment is fuller and more explicit than the text' (ibid. 102). T. S. Eliot will later speak of 'a judgment, a comparison, in which two things are measured by each other' (2014: 107). For Newman, the same adaptive and self-revising logic governing individual reasoning and biographical time also structures the development of interpretive communities across many generations. Hence the historical development of an idea, which in some cases coalesces into distinctive exegetical traditions, follows the same pattern as all human judgement. For in its sheer temporal continuity, tradition shows itself to be comprised of a series of necessarily partial, though often complementary, discrete judgements such as will incrementally realise the full import of a single conception or idea. Just as ordinary object perception only ever gives us a limited and partial view of the 'thing' at any one time, so a theological idea or conception will not divulge its full import all at once. Inasmuch as 'an idea is not brought home to the intellect as objective except through ... the variety of [its] aspects' ([1845] 1989: 34), so over the course of a life and in the succession of entire generations, 'judgments and aspects will accumulate, ... one view will be modified or expanded by another, and then combined with a third' (ibid. 37). Implicitly, then, Newman's model of tradition supervenes on the modern, post-Reformation notion of a subject's putatively unconstrained private judgement in matters of faith.[25] Yet even as Newman rejects Romanticism's attempt to locate the sources of meaningful experience in the affective and emotive flux of the autonomous individual, neither does he embrace the impersonal and prevaricating stance of historicism vis-à-vis the past. While receptive to the philological discoveries of the Higher Criticism of the previous two generations, Newman sees tradition obtaining only where individuals recognise their subjective, private judgements to be steeped in, and tempered by, supra-personal and trans-generational meanings. Any considered judgement also involves our active, reasoned participation in past knowledge, just as conversely meaning and significance of a given tradition are unveiled only by our hermeneutic efforts in the present.

A third feature of tradition thus emerges, namely, that in enjoining a fusion of intellectual and ethical values long known as *studiositas*, tradition entwines knowledge with the practice of humility. Those who approach a tradition in the right spirit 'do not seek to sequester, own, possess, or dominate what they hope to know; they want, instead, to participate lovingly in it, to respond to it knowingly as gift rather than as potential possession' (Griffiths 2009: 21). Unfolding as an ongoing development of its underlying idea that can never be 'sequestered or possessed', tradition reveals its essentially interpretive and dialectical character. It constantly probes the original 'deposit of faith' or 'mystery' (Newman [1845] 1989: 59) at its core. That core had originally and crucially been revealed in

Scripture and apostolic testimony, to be sure, and those subsequently concerned with it should 'religiously adhere to the form of words and the ordinances under which [revealed truth] comes to us' (Tract 73 in Newman [1841] 2013: 193). Yet biblical testimony is rarely 'self-interpreting' but 'needs completion' (Newman [1845] 1989: 60, 62). And inasmuch as the intelligibility of the original mystery demands our trans-generational hermeneutic participation in it, the production of significant meaning pivots on a continuously developing tradition. Such is evidenced not only by some eighteen hundred years of biblical commentary but also by the typological structure of Scripture itself. Indeed, 'the whole Bible, not its prophetical portions only, is written on the principle of development' (ibid. 65), a point Newman elaborates much in the spirit of Romantic organicism:

> the earlier prophecies are pregnant texts out of which the succeeding announcements grow; they are types. It is not that first one truth is told, then another; but the whole truth or large portions of it are told at once, yet only in their rudiments, or in miniature, and they are expanded and finished in their parts, as the course of revelation proceeds. (Ibid. 64)

At the beginning of the twentieth century, Maurice Blondel echoes Newman's argument almost verbatim when characterising the testimony of Christ's 'earliest followers . . . only as an expressive but necessarily rudimentary and summary picture of the Master whose words, example and influence they reported, though unable to exhaust their meaning, perceive their implications or transmit their whole secret to others'. Consequently, 'the voice which preached the Kingdom of God inserted a *punctum movens* into the determinism of history, a word whose repercussion was so carefully calculated that the echo of it endures under a thousand harmonising forms'. In evident tribute to Newman's concept of 'antecedent probability', Maurice Blondel muses on the hubris of 'exclud[ing] even the possibility of an antecedent finality'. For when it comes to ecclesiastic and exegetical tradition, the principal 'fact' in contention – namely the manifest continuity and charismatic force of the Catholic Church over two millennia – cannot be judged a priori to be 'historical' in kind: 'the natural continuity of history does not prove that history itself can provide an explanation of it' ([1903] 1965: 245, 251). Rather, one must ask:

> Is the 'fact' in question the spiritual unity and the organic continuity of a single thought, of a single life, making the Church a single immortal being, as it were? In order to establish the truth of this it would be necessary to introduce a controlling idea into the heart of the facts, which is itself not a fact, and it alone could serve as a criterion to distinguish what was only *evolution* . . . from what is vital development, that is to say continuous creation starting from a germ which transubstantiates its own nourishment. (Ibid. 255–6)[26]

For Newman, it is already in its intricate and fecund presentation that Scripture encapsulates the principle of development and, in so doing, shapes our subsequent interpretive relation to it. For it presents us with 'a structure so unsystematic and various, and a style so figurative and indirect, that no one would presume at first sight to say what is in it and what is not' ([1845] 1989: 71). In language strongly reminiscent of Goethe's and Coleridge's organicism, Newman views Scripture as a 'germ, afterwards to be developed' (ibid. 67), a challenge that neither enthusiasm nor scientific or historical method can fully meet. What, in Newman's view, sets scientific and interpretive rationality apart is their fundamentally different outlook on risk and contingency. Scientific inquiry essentially seeks to minimise any unknown factors so as to maintain the greatest possible control over its findings. By contrast, interpretive knowledge is essentially a risk-taking and provisional endeavour. To be a rational participant in a tradition of inquiry means to put to the test the very reality of its underlying idea. Doing so involves cultivating a stance of undesigning responsiveness to what the history of articulations, which that idea has received to date, means to tell us. Hermeneutic activity can appraise the truth-value of texts issuing from the past only by admitting to the provisional and contingent nature of its own procedures and discoveries. Newman's repeated references to contingency, 'chance' (ibid. 72), and to the 'risk' (ibid. 39) that the underlying idea of a tradition might miscarry or undergo corruptions of various kinds point to an integral feature of tradition that not only cannot be eliminated but, for that very reason, also leaves our own interpretive standpoint permanently unsettled.[27]

Like evolution in the realm of biology, 'development' for Newman is an inherently adventitious process impossible to control or predict by any method that would place us outside of it. Hence Newman draws a sharp distinction between scientific method that, on Bacon's account, must reject any antecedent faith commitments, and reason as it operates in the domains of 'history, ethics, and religion'. Inasmuch as a scientific model of reason 'does not really perceive anything, but ... is a faculty of proceeding from things that are perceived to things which are not', it is clearly inapposite to ethical inquiry and scriptural exegesis, these being endeavours in which we flourish only insofar as reason 'is a living spontaneous energy within us' ([1843] 1997: 206, 257). Hermeneutic practice thus has its own rationality:

> It is not an effect of wishing and resolving, or of forced enthusiasm, or of any mechanism of reasoning, or of any mere subtlety of intellect; but comes of its own innate power of expansion within the mind in its season, though with the use of reflection, argument and original thought, more or less as it may happen, with a dependence on the ethical growth of the mind itself, and with a reflex influence upon it. Again, the Parable of the Leaven describes the development of doctrine in another respect, in its active, engrossing, and interpenetrating power. ([1845] 1989: 73–4)

Newman's distinctive fusion of cogency and eloquence, here and throughout his oeuvre, originates in his intuition that the force and appeal of philosophical and theological argument pivots on revealing to its readers how they have been implicated in it all along, and that what is truly at stake is the audience's spiritual and intellectual flourishing rather than proof of some abstract proposition. Hence the development of Christian doctrine cannot be presented as some agnostic historical account or logical sequence. Rather, it is to reveal something in which successive generations have all shared, albeit not for the sake of subjective self-fulfilment but, rather, as agents collaborating (for the most part unwittingly) in the service of a supra-personal truth.

It bears pointing out that Newman's conception of Scripture is informed by the philological German Higher Criticism's insights into the irregularity of Scripture – 'a great number of writings, of various persons, living at different times, put together into one, and assuming its existing form as if casually and by accident' ([1872] 2004: 146). Echoing Charles Lyell's transformative account of geology, Newman compares Scripture to 'the structure of the earth ... the result of (humanly speaking) a series of accidents, of gradual influences and sudden convulsions, of a long history of change and chance'. And just as geology does 'not find minerals or plants arranged within it as in a cabinet', so theology, confronting a tangle of historically discontinuous strata of meaning, 'must submit to the indirectness of scripture' (ibid. 149–51, 141). Crucially, though, the formal and material discoveries of the Higher Criticism do not, in Newman's view, constitute an argument *against* tradition but, rather, confirm its very necessity. For where 'every word requires a comment' ([1845] 1989: 65), interpretation is an inescapable entailment of 'the system of doctrine and worship, referred to but not brought out in Scripture' (ibid. 137). In its ongoing effort to 'teach things but indirectly taught in Scripture', the tradition of Scriptural interpretation mirrors the deep and convoluted profile of the Scriptural books that had called it forth. It does not aim to supplant or dispel a 'mystery' but reveals our abiding connection to it.

The key question, one on which Newman's position undergoes crucial change between 1838 and 1845, thus concerns whether what interpretation discovers 'is not all in Scripture, but part in tradition only, as the Romanists say, – or, as the English Church says, that though it is in tradition, it can also be gathered from the communications of Scripture' (ibid. 140).[28] Rightly understood, the narrative pattern wrought by tradition will be dialectical in kind; for as Alasdair MacIntyre has pointed out, 'dialectic is the instrument of enquiry which is still *in via*. . . . [Whereas] in demonstrative reasoning we argue *from* first principles, in dialectical we argue *to* first principles' (1990: 88).[29] In dialectical inquiry, the as yet unfathomable fullness (*pleroma*) of a conception that has sponsored a coherent and evolving tradition of hermeneutic reflection will itself acquire progressively greater clarity as that inquiry advances. As Socrates had put it to Glaucon:

> when the beginning is what one doesn't know, and the end and what comes in between are woven out of what isn't known . . . only the dialectical way of inquiry proceeds in this direction, destroying the hypotheses, to the beginning itself in order to make it secure. (Plato 1989: *Republic* 533c)

Being integrative rather than disjunctive in its operation, dialectical narrative advances knowledge by way of retroactive clarification. Inasmuch as it issues from the awareness that first principles are precisely what we do *not* know, the underlying ethical stance is one of reflective involvement rather than peremptory scepticism. To be a participant in the dialectical movement of a tradition is to recognise oneself as both the agent and the witness of its continued unfolding. Indeed, 'we are always situated within traditions, and this is no objectifying process – i.e., we do not conceive of what tradition says as something other, something alien. It is always part of us' (Gadamer [1960] 2006: 283).[30] Wherever individuals judge and reason about commitments, ends and goods, they do so by moving (however unwittingly) within some specific tradition of inquiry and by becoming progressively more adept in the art (*technē*) of dialogue with the past voices that such a tradition comprises. Knowledge of the past means above all 'understanding' ostensibly distant voices as they impinge on our specific situation. Whereas historicism entrusts itself to specific empirical methods so as to tabulate verifiable and supposedly value-neutral *information*, to inhabit a tradition is to acknowledge its proximity to, not distance from, us.

The conception set forth in the *Development of Christian Doctrine* anticipates Gadamer's view that 'interpretation is not an occasional, *post facto* supplement to understanding [but] rather, . . . the explicit form of understanding'. Even as he shares few if any of Newman's faith commitments, Gadamer also regards human intellectual practice as an essentially interpretive practice that can be broken down into three distinct and complementary activities or 'arts' (in the sense of Aristotelian *technē*): a *subtilitas intelligendi* or 'understanding', a *subtilitas interpretandi* or 'interpretation', and a *subtilitas applicandi* or 'application' (ibid. 306–7).[31] Specifically the last skill, that of 'application', had been both an integral feature and the ultimate aim of legal and biblical interpretation until its ill-considered marginalisation by the rise of historical method in late Enlightenment and Romantic thought. Like Newman, Gadamer considers it 'obvious that the task of hermeneutics was to adapt the text's meaning to the concrete situation to which the text is speaking' (ibid. 319). Viewed cumulatively, these countless acts of reasoned interpretation and reflected judgement intimate an underlying teleological structure. Yet they do so only in a qualified sense since the kind of knowledge incrementally yielded by our involvement in a tradition cannot be verified by some independent positivist method.

Newman's cautious epistemology implies that any imputation of teleology to doctrinal developments remains necessarily probabilistic in nature because by its very nature no finite human intelligence could ever claim to have transcended the dialectical progression by which it is constituted. In so doing, Newman takes up a fundamental challenge confronted by every theologian, namely, how to reconcile the provisional nature of empirical time with the eternal logos that ultimately sanctions any experience of meaning by finite, time-bound human beings. As Hans Urs von Balthasar observes, referencing Book XI of Augustine's Confessions, the underlying 'difficulty is the soul's experience of duration', that is, time experienced as a distinctive flow that cannot be accounted for by reference to the movement of the heavenly bodies. In the event, Newman's theory of 'development' constitutes a distinctly modern way for the finite subject to confront its inescapable experience of time as 'distension', a psychological 'spacing' or *distentio*, the latter being how Augustine renders Gregory of Nyssa's διαστασις. As Augustine had formulated the dilemma, 'I fall into dissolution amid the changing times, whose order I am yet ignorant of [*ego in tempora dissilui, quorum ordinem nescio*] (XI.29.30)'. Yet even as human beings experience time forever as sinful distension and dis-unity, their capacity for opening up to the past in the modality of patient and undesigning hermeneutic activity also furnishes a remedy of sorts. To be sure, what von Balthasar calls 'this distended attentiveness [*solche zerspannte Anspannung*]' is 'only possible if the mind, in so expecting, noting, and remembering, abides in this distension [*in dieser Anspannung verharrt*]' (1968: 7–8; translation modified).[32] That said, it would be a mistake to consider hermeneutic practice of the kind issuing in a theory of development as merely a technique belatedly introduced to sift the chaos of distended, inchoate time. Instead, scriptural exegesis and theological reflection are faithful responses to an anterior calling, itself audible in distended time, a calling that enjoins theology to seek and discern the *eschaton* inscribed within their movement through time. As Augustine notes, rather than lapsing into oblivion or nothingness, the past seems to 'be increased' precisely by our reflective encounter with it. For, as he notes, 'how does the past grow, seeing as it no longer exists [*quomodo crescit praeteritum quod iam non est*]', if not in virtue of the mind's constant 'expectancy, attention, and memory [*nisi quia in animo . . . tria sunt? Nam et expectat et adtendit et meminit*]' (XI.28.37).

To return to Newman's *Essay*, what validates the rationality and coherence of our interpretations is not some independent methodological scheme but their increasingly effective application in everyday life and reflection. Similarly, Gadamer regards legal and theological hermeneutics as exemplary cases of what it means to engage a specific tradition of inquiry; in both cases, there is an essential tension between the fixed text – the law or the gospel – on the one hand and, on the other, the sense arrived at by applying it at the concrete moment of interpretation . . . A law does not exist in order to be understood historically, but to be concretized in its legal validity by being interpreted. ([1960] 2006: 307)

It was precisely this deepening sense of the 'application' of meanings that Newman encountered during the years leading up to his 1845 conversion and his account of tradition in *The Development of Christian Doctrine* of that same year. His letters of these years, particularly those written to Catherine Froude, attest to the psychological and intellectual complexity of that journey. Newman recalls being led back 'in the course of my *regular reading* . . . to the Monophysite controversy', and finding 'more matter for serious thought in that history than in anything I had read'.[33] These explorations in Patristic theology set in motion a hermeneutic development that, while unintended, also proved almost impossible to resist:

from that time to this, the view thus brought before me has grown upon me. I had hitherto read ecclesiastical history with the eyes of our Divines, and taken what they said on faith, but now I got *a key*, which interpreted large passages of history [that] had been locked up from me. I found everywhere one and the same picture, prophetic of our present state, the Church in communion with Rome decreeing, and heretics resisting.[34]

Newman's account of his own, reluctant conversion offers *prima facie* evidence that the true warrant and consummation of philosophical and theological meanings involves their transformative 'application' both *by* and *to* the individual, rather than their detached appraisal by some impersonal method of authoritative verification.

This understanding of tradition as a gift that, if inhabited in the right spirit, may enrich the church's understanding of the *depositum fidei* would in time prompt Congar and his collaborators in the *ressourcement* project to push back against the post-Tridentine 'transformation of material tradition into formal tradition'. Echoing Newman's considered stress on the fluidity and transcendent character of tradition, Congar demurs at 'modern Catholicism's liking for the juridical approach' and a long historical 'process by which a number of theologians have come to identify tradition with the teaching of the Magisterium'. In fact, 'being carried by a living subject and . . . development', tradition crucially depends on the laity ('the faithful make a very large contribution . . . by their piety and the exercise of their religious life') ([1984] 2004: 68–9, 76).[35] Through its considered hermeneutic involvement with a specific tradition an individual joins what is in effect a trans-generational and practical community of knowledge. The active participant in a tradition necessarily transcends the confined view of biographical time and, in so doing, recognises hermeneutic practice as a form of humility rather than dominion. For Newman, to inhabit a tradition means transcending subjective, biographical time and becoming actively involved in a development that 'employs . . . minds as its instruments . . . [by] modifying and incorporating with itself existing modes of thinking and operating' ([1845] 1989: 38). Thus a specific tradition of inquiry enables an interpretive, ecclesial or legal community and the individuals that are part of it to evaluate their contingent and partial judgements and opinions against preceding conceptions, to scrutinise present intuition by the lights of past articulations, and thus learn to discriminate between the fluctuation of individual meanings and the trans-generational working-out of a truth: 'a body of thought is gradually formed without [the individual] recognizing what is going on within him'. By the adventitious play of 'external circumstances', the individual 'is led ... to trace to principles, what hitherto he has discerned by a moral perception, and adopted on sympathy; and logic is brought in to arrange and inculcate what no science was employed in gaining' (ibid. 190).

An integral feature of theological and humanistic inquiry thus shows the partial and confined knowledge achieved in the course of an individual life to be enmeshed with the long *durée* organising the development of an idea. Whereas historicist method pivots on the assumption of an epistemologically superior 'now' (*Jetztzeit*), tradition dynamically entwines two temporal planes which, drawing on Hans Blumenberg, we may identify as biographical time (*Lebenszeit*) and 'cosmic time' (*Weltzeit*), respectively:

> Only by renouncing its claim to be the measure of all things is the subject able to fathom the meaning of its existence. ... Phenomenology must recognise and describe this gradual maturation of subjectivity, understood as a balancing of resignation and fulfilment, renunciation and expectation. (Blumenberg 1996: 306; my translation)

Through what Gadamer ([1960] 2006) calls our 'immersion in a process of tradition [*Einrücken in ein Überlieferungsgeschehen*]', individuals assent to the continuing relevance and future potential of a specific tradition of inquiry and also to the authority of the interpretive community that had forged, developed and transmitted the tradition in question. To acknowledge the supra-personal authority of a tradition amounts to a holistic, ethical recognition rather than a discrete instance of notional assent to some proposition. For in its real assent to the authority of a tradition, the individual also achieves a measure of *humility*, understood not as a retreat *from* knowledge but as a distinctive form of approach *to* it. Newman's observation that 'truth is not the heritage of any individual, it is absolute and universal' not only points to insurmountable epistemological constraints on present, subjective cognition; it also treats that very fact as the ethical ground zero for all human inquiry ([1845] 1989: 50).

Hegel and Nietzsche

Already a strong implication in Newman's account, this cultivation of epistemological humility receives particular emphasis in the work of T. S. Eliot, who likewise conceives humility not as a state of passivity but as a virtue to be actively cultivated. As he argues in his 1919 essay, 'Tradition and the Individual Talent', one's proper stance vis-à-vis a given tradition is active, participatory and interpretive; there is nothing epigonal about it. Where tradition is concerned, 'blind or timid adherence should positively be discouraged'. Rather, 'you must obtain [tradition] by great labor' and, specifically, by cultivating 'a perception, not only of the pastness of the past, but of its presence' (2014: 106). A fierce and incisive critic of sentimentalism in all its Romantic guises, Eliot emphasises the impersonal, kenotic quality defining bona fide engagement of a tradition, a stance that also fundamentally informs his practice as a poet: 'What happens is a continual surrender of himself as he is at the moment to something which is more valuable.' Indeed, it is only in 'this process of depersonalization ... that art may be said to approach the condition of science' (ibid. 10).[36] Elsewhere, Eliot emphasises how the 'labor' of understanding the past is a type of structured and evolving contemplation of meanings dialogically achieved by our interaction with it. Thus:

[as a writer] matures, he becomes more like his predecessors, and more different from them. He becomes more *conscious* of them. . . . He accomplished what he did, not through a desire to express his personality, but by a complete surrender of himself to the work in which he was absorbed. . . . His personality has not been lost, but has gone, all the important part of it, into the work. (Ibid. 213–14)

Meaning here is not 'constructed' or 'imposed' but reflexively distilled inasmuch as the individual forgoes the present's spurious comforts of subjective emotion and self-possession or the detached proceduralism of historicist method. As Eliot was to put it in *Four Quartets*, 'The only wisdom we can hope to acquire / Is the wisdom of humility: humility is endless' ([1943] 1971: 27). For Newman, the epistemological analogue of such humility is found in the

characteristic of our minds, that they cannot take an object in, which is submitted to them simply and integrally. . . . Whole objects do not create in the intellect whole ideas, but are, to use a mathematical phrase, thrown into series, into a number of statements, strengthening, correcting each other, and with more or less exactness approximating, as they accumulate, to a perfect image. ([1845] 1989: 55)

To understand Newman's position here, it helps to scrutinise its seeming affinities with arguments developed, in the generation before him, by Hegel and, in the one following, by Nietzsche. On the face of it, Newman's conception of 'development' bears a marked resemblance to Hegel's idea of history as a supra-individual 'movement of the spirit' (*Bewegung des Geistes*), a progression in the course of which partial and as yet unreflected 'meanings' implicitly held and unevenly cultivated by any given individual or historical community reveal their underlying truth as they are dialectically contested and 'internalised' (*verinnerlicht*) by the labour of philosophical reflection. The Platonic motif of *anamnesis* clearly funds both Hegel's and Newman's view that any intellectual development necessarily involves a strong retroactive component whereby insights insensibly produced over time will 'of necessity come to light at a later date, and are recognized, and their issues . . . scientifically arranged' (Newman [1845] 1989: 190).

Yet, even as Hegel and Newman converge in their appraisal of 'truth' as a dynamic, integrative and trans-generational movement, they reach notably different conclusions as regards the locus of truth within the 'development' in question. For Hegel, the 'movement of the spirit' (*Bewegung des Geistes*) effectively *cancels out* (*aufheben*) its contingent origins in nature and history as well as intermittent instantiations of an idea – thus intimating the extent to which Hegel's thought stands in continuity with his Enlightenment predecessors' view of knowledge as an overcoming of, or emancipation from, past tradition. To be sure, *aufheben* also carries important connotations of 'preservation', yet even then whatever meaning is retained *from* the past will be construed as an overcoming of the idea's original lack of explicitness. Hence, in obliquely Gnostic fashion, Hegel regards all pre-modern knowledge as provisional, constrained by the vicissitudes of time and place, and hence 'self-alienated spirit' (*der sich entfremdete Geist*). The only legitimate knowledge, he insists, is one wrought by the conceptual activity of *Homo faber*. An early instance of what, later in the century, J. S. Mill will formulate under the heading of emergentism, Hegel's idea of development is a story of the *production* of meanings and, as such, remains agnostic vis-à-vis the idea of an original *depositum fidei* whose revealed meaning has ever since been clarified and consolidated as a distinctive tradition. Still, to some extent such an emergentist conception also underwrites Newman's account of development, such as in his passing remark that 'passions and affections are in action in our minds before the presence of their proper objects' ([1845] 1989: 51).

Like Hegel, Newman appears to espouse the notion of 'implicit reason' and an 'unconscious growth of ideas' (ibid. 59), even as his appraisal of 'intellectual processes ... carried on silently and spontaneously in the mind' and bound to 'come to light at a later date' (ibid. 190) is more plausibly traced to Locke on ideas, Hume on the passions and, perhaps, Hartley on associationism. Yet as soon as one remembers that Newman's dynamic view of development is inseparably woven into his understanding of faith – 'an exercise of the Reason, so spontaneous, unconscious, and unargumentative, as to seem at first sight even to be a moral act' ([1843] 1997: 279) – these similarities begin to recede. For neither does Newman regard nature and history as mere contingency and external scaffolding to be superseded in philosophical reflection, nor does he consider reflected (or 'explicit') reason as inherently superior to the 'implicit' grounds of faith from which it springs. Rather, assent to the abundant reality of knowledge received by every living being furnishes the indispensable empirical substratum *in* and *through* which alone the truth of Christianity stands to be (partially) ascertained. Far more than Hegel, that is, Newman emphasises the reciprocity of empirical practice and philosophical reflection. As Robert Pattison notes, 'it was the essence of Newmanism that belief and action are complementary' (1991: 61).

Similarly, Nietzsche's critique of historical method at first seems to bear a striking resemblance to Newman's theory of development. For Nietzsche, a principal flaw of historical method involves its tendency to drain human individuals and communities of any will to engage 'life' itself. Historicism, he argues, is prejudicial to life, for its preoccupation with method, objectivity, and verification induces 'a degree of sleeplessness, of rumination, ... which is harmful and ultimately fatal to the living thing, whether this living thing be a man or a people or a culture'. To survive and flourish, individual and entire cultures not only need a robust sense of the past but, just as importantly, a capacity for forgetting and for embracing the 'unhistorical' (*das Unhistorische*). For 'only through the power of employing the past for the purposes of life and of again introducing into history that which has been done and is gone – did man become man: but with an excess of history man again ceases to exist' ([1876] 1997: 62, 64). Much depends, Nietzsche insists, on discerning the 'boundary at which the past has to be forgotten if it is not to become the gravedigger of the present'. The limits of historical awareness are determined by whether it will enhance, rather than atrophy, life by stimulating a 'capacity to develop out of oneself in one's own way, to transform and incorporate into oneself what is past and foreign, to heal wounds, to replace what has been lost', and so forth. Simply put, 'the unhistorical and the historical are necessary in equal measure for the health of an individual, of a people and of a culture' (ibid. 62–3).

In time, Nietzsche would insist that there is, in fact, no enduring substratum or 'idea' whatsoever capable of holding together the tattered fabric of historical time against a constant onslaught of entropic and often violent change. Neither, he maintains, is it legitimate to distil a tradition as it were *ex post facto* as the supposedly hidden substrate of historical 'development'. For the Nietzsche of the *Genealogy of Morals* (1887), Platonic *anamnesis* and Hegelian 'recollection' (*Erinnerung*) are but grandiose philosophical fictions. Disputing the possibility of any meaningful history or developmental narrative, Nietzsche bluntly proclaims that 'the entire history of a "thing", an organ, a custom may take the form of an extended chain of signs, of ever-new interpretations and manipulations, whose causes ... merely follow and replace one another arbitrarily and according to circumstances' ([1887] 1996: 58).[37] Such reasoning manifestly pivots on a negative faith-commitment of sorts, an all-consuming scepticism and metaphysical naturalism for which, logically, no warrant can ever be produced. Yet in so levelling the entire conceptual framework of tradition, development and narrative meaning, Nietzsche effectively deprives himself of any conceptual resources for making qualitative discriminations of *any* kind. Just as for Nietzsche we have no warrant for claiming meaningful development over time but, instead, are faced with random 'processes', so it is no longer possible to distinguish between developments and 'corruptions' of development. Having surrendered any *terminus ad quem* or notion of a supra-personal good, Nietzsche's genealogical project of unmasking the supposed inauthenticity of all tradition and what it affirms is found to depend 'upon a set of contrasts between it and that which it aspires to overcome'. Indeed, it is 'inherently derivative from and even parasitic upon . . . that which it professes to have discarded' (MacIntyre 1990: 215).

Again, the differences with Newman's account of tradition qua 'development' prove instructive. In seeming concert with the early Nietzsche of the *Untimely Meditations*, Newman grants that the development of a tradition amounts to a distinctly agonistic process whose underlying idea 'may be interrupted, retarded, mutilated, distorted, by external violence [or] . . . enfeebled by the effort of ridding itself of domestic force'. Moreover, such vicissitudes cannot be written off as mere contingencies but, instead, are integral and necessary aspects of all historical development. For any 'great idea . . . is elicited and expended by trial, and battles into perfection and supremacy' ([1845] 1989: 39–40). Indeed, as Blumenberg points out, the Darwinian idea of 'free variation is not an end in itself but merely the means for attaining dependable invariants . . . [or] "essences" whose ultimate legitimacy we can claim' (1996: 23; my translation). In seven notes, Newman ([1845] 1989: 171–206) sets forth criteria whereby it becomes possible 'to discriminate healthy developments of an idea from its state of corruption and decay' (ibid. 171). The result is a morphology of the concepts of development and tradition that highlights Newman's unique position between a static, positivist/historicist understanding of the past and a radical naturalism/scepticism of the sort pioneered by Darwin and Nietzsche according to which development is but so much sound and fury, a sheer mindless churning of biomass either signifying nothing at all (Nietzsche) or, at most, captured by the kind of retroactive analysis that invests evolution with statistical coherence while denying it all meaning and significance (Darwin). It helps to consider at least some of Newman's criteria (nos 1–3 and 6) for a 'healthy' development, for it is in these 'Notes' that the stakes (and risks) of his theological position are thrown into sharp relief.

It is particularly in his first Note, concerned with the 'Preservation of Type', that Newman's reflections seem in some proximity, not only to Nietzsche's but also to Darwin's thought (especially [1845] 1989: 173–4, 185ff.), itself by 1845 still in a state of gestation.[38] The question here concerns the grounds justifying the claim that X has evolved over time, rather than concluding that now we are looking at Y. What guarantees the 'unity of a type' (ibid. 173) over time? Citing a few instances of doctrinal development, Newman effectively turns the tables on this very question by showing it to be animated by a self-defeating assumption. For if the underlying, formal premise be rigidly sustained – namely, that X can never develop into a variant (X^1, X^2, etc.) without, in fact, becoming something else – then X itself would from the very outset prove bereft of all intelligibility, indeed, could not even be identified *as* X. For to ground the self-identity of a thing solely in the (negative) criterion of its unchangeability does not yet tell us what X is. For that to happen, the idea or being in question would have to be observed *in actu*, just as Aristotle and Aquinas had insisted on the convertibility of Act and Being. By contrast, the rigid formalist separation of an idea's putative *essence* from its contingent *existence* in empirical time permanently traps philosophical and theological reflection within a nominalist limbo. In fact, Newman points out, human thought is essentially temporal, practical and empirical inasmuch as its grasp of things and phenomena both simple and complex pivots on observing them *in actu*. Our very capacity to *attend to* and *reflect on* a phenomenon requires detecting and capturing formal continuities in narrative and symbolic form, something that can only be accomplished against the backdrop of change and development. Just as a portrait initially 'is not striking' but over time allows us 'to see in it what we could not see at first', so all development of doctrine pivots on a gradual increase of hermeneutic focus and responsiveness. Independent of such engagement, the portrait is but an assemblage of canvas, wood and oil bereft of being and meaning alike.

Specifically with regard to theological practice, Newman thus observes that to credit an idea with an immutable essence amounts to 'an obstinate 'refusal to follow the course of doctrine as it moves on', a case of 'corruption' ([1845] 1989: 177) that, however unwittingly, ends up betraying the richness of the theological conception it means to preserve. Both in spiritual life and theological reflection, meaning is never achieved by way of sheer ahistorical repetition. Spiritual and contemplative meanings should not be confused with positions syllogistically staked out but, instead, can only be realised with undesigning hermeneutic patience with the kind of humility that a two-thousand-year-old tradition of practical reasoning enjoins. In his second Note ('Continuity of Principles'), Newman extends this fundamental point into the realm of theological conceptions and how doctrine develops over time. By 'principle' Newman understands the core axiom or underlying perspective animating the development of an idea and giving coherence to the resulting interpretive tradition. Thus 'the various sects of Protestantism' ought to be understood as so many 'applications and results' of the principle of Private Judgement (ibid. 181).[39]

Precisely because this fundamental stance shaping doctrinal views and beliefs is not made formally explicit within these views themselves, Newman insists that it ought to receive special scrutiny: 'principle is a better test of heresy than doctrine' (ibid. 181). Yet unlike Darwin and Nietzsche, Newman does not view history's agonistic progression as mere chance-based accretions and transient variations of an inherently mindless, underlying substratum. Rather, by insisting that the 'test of a true development is that it is of a *tendency conservative* of what has gone before it' (ibid. 203), Newman affirms that all change, properly understood, must be *intelligible* change, and that action and change must stand in a meaningful relation to a complex idea, conception or tradition. An absolute rupture or radical 'metanoia' cannot be understood as an instance of *change*; indeed, one could not even logically connect it to the state of things said to have preceded it. Gradualism, then, is not so much an ideological preference as it is a logical requirement of human cognition; for 'it is the rule of creation, or rather of the phenomena it presents, that life passes on to its termination by a gradual, imperceptible course of change' (ibid. 199). As Ian Ker puts it, 'what Newman has in mind is change *in continuity with the past*' (2014: 79).

By its palpable endurance across vast expanses of time, an original *depositum* or idea may grow into an increasingly coherent and fully reflected tradition, thus furnishing increasingly probability of its inherent truth. Any specific conception of meaning – including modern scepticism's attempt to subject received meanings to an intelligible critique – presupposes participation in and commitment to a coherent, communally recognised set of practices and beliefs, something that, late in his career, Newman was to scrutinise under the heading of 'real assent'.[40] He thus recognises that reason can only move towards being genuinely universal and impersonal insofar as it is neither neutral nor disinterested, that membership in a particular type of moral community, one from which fundamental dissent has to be excluded, is a condition for genuinely rational inquiry and more especially for moral and theological enquiry. (MacIntyre 1990: 59–60)

Whereas for Darwin and Nietzsche, survival is a strictly a-semantic event, one whose rationality is exclusively of a statistical kind, Newman (herein much closer to Hegel) interprets an idea's continuity over time as *prima facie* evidence of its significant and transcendent truth-value. Having outlasted virtually every known political and institutional framework of the past two millennia, Christianity and the Catholic Church, for Newman, has put paid to the 'antecedent probability' that its key tenets are not just some formally correct syllogisms but a supra-personal truth.

For Newman it follows that we cannot assert ownership of tradition but, on the contrary, are ourselves formed by its fluid and constantly evolving interpretive dynamic. Well before a rigid and often defensive concept of tradition was to find institutional expression in the neo-Thomist theology first promoted by Pio Nono (1846–78) and consolidated in the 1879 *Aeterni Patris* encyclical of his successor, Leo XIII, Newman rejects the historicist construal of tradition as a static inventory of dogmatic propositions. From the defensive politics of the European restoration after 1815 to the equally reactionary culture of reason associated with the Modernist Controversy and the (ecclesiastic) politics of *Action Française* early in the twentieth century, the misconstrual of tradition as a body of authoritative, timeless and incontestable meanings remains an enduring challenge to intellectual culture. It is no accident, then, that Maurice Blondel's letters on *History and Dogma* (1903) echo Newman's theory, formulated six decades earlier, almost verbatim. In uncompromising terms, Blondel rejects the prevailing neo-Thomism's 'inertia' (*fixisme*) and 'fatal retrogression' (*un rétrogradisme meurtrier*) for its misguided supposition that 'the Church has nothing to learn' and that the 'sacred deposit of faith is simply an aerolith, to be preserved in a glass case safe from a sacrilegious curiosity' ([1903] 1965: 278–9). Such a position, Blondel argues, is the very antithesis of what tradition asks of the theologian. For:

> dogmas cannot be rationally justified either by history alone, by the most ingenious application of dialectics to the texts, or by the efforts of the individual; but all these forces contribute, and they converge in Tradition, the authority of which, divinely assisted, is the organ of infallible expression. (Ibid. 279)[41]

Both within and beyond the precincts of systematic theology and apologetics, the debate over the nature and authority of tradition has continued, such as in von Balthasar's engagement of Barth in the Gadamer-Habermas debate of the late 1960s. To ignore the debate and its continued bearing on theological and humanistic inquiry today is to commit, by default rather than by active reasoning, to the dominant model of a hermeneutics of suspicion or, less commonly, to a purely epigonal, historical interest in the voices of the dead that, in Eliot's haunting formulation, 'bring us with them'.

Notes

1. Still, even within his narrowly secular outlook on tradition, Adorno recognises that the apparent loss of it also presents a dilemma: 'Tradition presents us with an insoluble contradiction. Though it is no longer present or susceptible of being summoned back, its utter expurgation sets us on a course for inhumanity [so beginnt der *Einmarsch in die Unmenschlichkeit*]' (1970–97: 10.1:315).
2. See Gadamer [1960] 2006: 274–8. On Newman and Gadamer, see also Pfau 2013: 53–75.
3. Burke's preoccupation with historical continuity, habit and tradition also reflects great economic anxiety about what he perceives to be an increasingly fictitious and unfathomable concept of monetary value and social wealth. See Pocock 1985.
4. Robert Pattison sees the early Newman far to the right of the Tories, viewing Peel as but 'a closet liberal in the Latitudinarian tradition. By nineteenth-century standards, Newman was not a Tory at all; he was a Jacobite in the spirit of 1745' (1991: 58).
5. On the broader cultural shift of sentimentalism, see also Taylor 1989: 248–390. On the religious crisis wrought by late Enlightenment thought, see Dupré 2005: 229–311. On tensions intrinsic to sentimental narrative, see Soni 2010: 327–73. On competing tendencies in Romantic theology, see Hedley 2014.
6. On the *Bildungsroman*, see Redfield 1996: 38–62. For the role of (aesthetic) 'play' as a catalyst of the genre's narration of progressive self-awareness, see Pfau 2011, 2010, 2007. On its post-Romantic mutation into a dystopic narrative, see Boes 2012: 73–127.
7. 'Who can recollect . . . all that he once knew about his thoughts and his deeds, and that, during a portion of his life, when, even at the time, his observation, whether of himself or of the external world, was less than before or after, by very reason of the perplexity and dismay which weighed upon him . . .' (Newman [1865] 2008: 208).
8. Quoting Augustine, Aquinas acknowledges the risk of humility being enacted as a merely pretended virtue (*falsa humilitas*). Rightly understood, humility involves a constant awareness of one's epistemological and moral limitations, or knowing one's 'disproportion to that which surpasses his capacity [*ut aliquis cognoscat id in quo deficit a proportione eius quod suam virtutem excedit*]'. The rule of this virtue thus 'is in the cognitive faculty [*regulam habet in cognitione*]' ([1274] 1947: IIa–IIae, 161, Q1; Q 2; Q 6).
9. For Newman's discussion of Latitudinarianism, see Tract 85, 'Lectures on the Scriptural Proofs of the Doctrines of the Church' (21 September 1838) ([1872] 2004: 126–41).
10. See also Newman's 'Note' on liberalism, interpolated in [1865] 2008: 359–69. As early as 1829, in a letter to his mother (13 March), Newman already surveys the spectrum of liberalism: '1. the uneducated or partially educated mass in towns, . . . 2. The Utilitarians, political economists, useful knowledge people . . . 3. The schismatics, in and out of the Church . . . 6. I might add the political indifferentists' (1978–2008: 2:130). Robert Pattison's *The Great Dissent* traces Newman's life-long, vigorous critique of modern liberalism – or 'secular divinity' (Newman 1978–2008: 5:45) – to his protracted conflict with Renn Dickson Hampden during the 1830s; see Pattison 1991: 61–95. Newman's *Development of Christian Doctrine* can be seen as yet another salvo in the Tractarian movement's prolonged contestation of Hampden's uncompromising use of privileges (some of them under dispute) associated with his position as Regius Chair of Divinity to bring to heel the Oxford Movement. See Newman [1845] 1989: 26ff. For the main tenets of the anti-Tractarian forces, see Hampden's *Lecture on Tradition*, first delivered at Oxford on 7 March 1839 ([1839] 1842).
11. Newman specifically names Schleiermacher as a key figure in this development.
12. In his structurally cognate critique of nineteenth-century 'encyclopaedism', Alasdair MacIntyre argues that 'the encyclopaedists' narrative reduces the past to a mere prologue to the rational present' (1990: 79).
13. As early as 1903, Maurice Blondel identifies the same underlying fallacy of a historical method that 'tends to accept as reality "historical" phenomena . . . as a substitute for reality itself. . . .

Historical facts will be given the role of reality itself; and an ontology ... will be extracted from a methodology' ([1903] 1965: 240). Recently, Peter Gordon has remarked on the slippage between an actual 'understanding of an idea' and its methodological confinement within a supposedly determinative 'context [which] like a discrete and holistic sphere ... englobes the idea in question and sharply delimits its capacity for movement' (2013: 39).

14. On the conceptual problems of historicism, see Pfau 1998; 2013: especially 35–52.
15. Similarly, Frei remarks how, 'with the rise of historical criticism ... the clue to meaning now is no longer the text itself but its reconstruction from its context, intentional or cultural, or else its aid in reconstructing that context, which in circular fashion then serves to explain the text itself' (1980: 160).
16. See also Congar, who notes that 'the economy begins by a *divine* transmission or tradition; it is continued in and by the men chosen and sent out by God for that purpose' ([1984] 2004: 10).
17. As Pieper notes, 'the concept of *depositum*' has a supra-personal dignity to it: 'What has been handed down to us we possess as a kind of loan' ([1970] 2010: 21).
18. Newman's arguments in favour of a Scripture and commentary as a continuous, integrative and mutually supportive tradition are already fully articulated in his first book, *The Arians of the Fourth Century* (1830), where he remarks on 'the insufficiency of the mere private study of Holy Scripture' ([1830] 2001: 50) and cautions that 'no prophet ends his subject: his brethren after him renew, enlarge, transfigure, or reconstruct it' (ibid. 58). 'Scripture being unsystematic' (ibid. 147), the literal and local interpretation of it is but 'the faith of uneducated men' (ibid. 145) and 'shallow minds' such as will 'anticipate the end apart from the course which leads to it' (ibid. 244). From the start, Newman's concept of tradition presupposes an ambitious standard of theological and philosophical literacy.
19. In 'The Tamworth Reading Room' (1841), Newman's offers a forceful critique of the liberal-secular mentality of the early Victorian era, and a sharp indictment of what he regards as the neo-pagan cult of modern state institutions; their 'chief error' lies in supposing 'that our true excellence comes not from within, but from without; not wrought through personal struggles and sufferings, but following upon a passive exposure to influences over which we have no control' ([1872] 2004: 266).
20. Given its location in predominantly Protestant Swabia and at the very heart of the seminary that produced Hegel's then dominant conception of philosophy as speculative *Wissenschaft*, Catholic theologians, Möhler in particular, soon became entangled in heated exchanges with writers like Ferdinand Christian Baur (1792–1860) eager to place theological inquiry on a rigorously scientific footing; on these debates and developments, see Zachhuber 2014: 25–63.
21. 'The authority of the Church is necessary, if Christ is to be a true, determining authority for us. ... If the Church be not the authority representing Christ, then all again relapses into darkness, uncertainty, doubt, distraction, unbelief, and superstition' (Möhler, quoted in Hinze 2010: 200).
22. For a detailed analysis of Franzelin's writings on tradition, see Gaar 1983: especially 45–123.
23. Privately, Newman is rather critical of pronouncing papal infallibility as a dogma: 'We do not move at a railroad pace in theological matters even in the 19th century. ... The tradition of Ireland, the tradition of England, is not on the side of Papal Infallibility'; and he demurs at how political schemes rather than theological discernment appear to be at the root of the dogmatic pronouncement, 'as if a dogmatic question was being treated merely as a move in ecclesiastical politics' (1978–2008: 25:93, 95).
24. See Kant [1781/7] 1965: 180–7; stressing the improvisatory and discretionary nature of the schematism, Kant notes that 'in its application to appearances and their mere form [the schema] is an art concealed in the depths of the human soul' (ibid. 183); the later *Critique of Judgement* (1790) can be read as an elaboration of his earlier, cryptic account.
25. See Newman's essay, 'Private Judgment' (1841) (1871: 2:336–74).

26. On Blondel's theory of tradition and development, see Nichols 1990: 139–54.
27. In his *Tractatus de divinia Traditione et Scriptura* (1882), Franzelin develops a strikingly similar argument; see Gaar 1983: 270–85.
28. In a note appended to the reprint of Tract 85, Newman acknowledges that in 1838 he was 'hampered by his belief in the Protestant tenet that *all* revealed doctrine is in Scripture' and, consequently, unable to say 'that, not Scripture, but history, is our informant in Christian doctrine' ([1872] 2004: 141 n.).
29. 'It is no trivial matter that all claims to knowledge are the claims of some particular person, developed out of the claims of other particular persons. Knowledge is possessed only in and through participation in a history of dialectical encounters' (MacIntyre 1990: 202).
30. Though there is no evidence that Gadamer ever read Newman, the convergence of their position is truly remarkable here: 'In tradition there is always an element of freedom and of history itself. Even the most genuine and pure tradition does not persist because of the inertia of what once existed. It needs to be affirmed, embraced, cultivated. It is, essentially, preservation, and is active in all historical change. But preservation is an act of reason, though an inconspicuous one. For this reason, only innovation and planning appear to be the result of reason. But this is an illusion . . .' (Gadamer [1960] 2006: 282).
31. See also Gadamer's 1965 supplement on 'Hermeneutics and Historicism' ([1960] 2006: 507–45); Carr 1996: 89–131.
32. Indeed, 'the mistaken idea of purely linear time could arise only when time was no longer conceived in a religious and theological way, but in secular-scientific form. . . . By contrast, religious time is . . . primarily vertical time: duration, which, because of the difference between divine eternity and the world distanced from [*von ihr abständiger Welt*] it, appears as "distension" [*Zerdehnung*]' (Balthasar 1968: 110).
33. 'Letter to Mrs. William Froude (5 April 1844)', in Newman 1978–2008: 10:196.
34. Ibid. 10:197–8; see also Newman's letters, again to Mrs. Froude, of 9 June and 15 July 1844 (ibid. 10:224, 10:243).
35. As Congar remarks later, to make the meaning of tradition contingent on the Magisterium alone risks 'reducing [theology] to a succession of isolated statements, each having its "proof" from authority, and of losing sight of the profound unity, the mutual relationship and the organic structure of all the parts' ([1984] 2004: 132).
36. As Eliot puts it elsewhere, 'the present only keeps the past alive' (2014: 215).
37. The passage in question continues: 'The "development" of a thing, a custom, an organ does not in the least resemble a *progressus* towards a goal . . . Rather, this development assumes the form of the succession of the more or less far-reaching, more or less independent processes of overpowering which affect it' (Nietzsche [1887] 1996: 58).
38. Ker sees the book as 'the theological counterpart of the *Origin of Species*' (1988: 300); recently, Hösle has argued for the ontological compatibility of Darwinian natural selection and the Christian notion of God as First Cause (2013: 24–49).
39. See also Ker (2014: 69–70), who finds strong echoes of Newman's notes in the documents of the second Vatican Council, especially *Dignitatis Humanae* (Arts 10–12).
40. See especially Newman [1870] 1979: 76–86; on 'real and unconditional assent', see also Richardson 2007: 73–84.
41. The letters on *History and Dogma* are key to understanding the *ressourcement* theology of Lubac and Congar that was to take shape in the late 1920s and 1930s; see especially Blondel's discussion of the problem of 'Extrinsicism' ([1903] 1965: 223–9). For a concise summary of the *ressourcement* project, see d'Ambrosio 1991.

References

Adorno, Theodor (1970–97), *Gesammelte Schriften*, 20 vols, Frankfurt: Suhrkamp.
Aquinas, Thomas [1274] (1947), *The Summa Theologica*, trans. Fathers of the English Dominican

Province, Benziger Bros., online edn, <http://dhspriory.org/thomas/summa/TP/TP026.html#T-PQ26OUTP1> (last accessed 24 June 2016).

Balthasar, Hans Urs von (1968), *A Theological Anthropology*, New York: Sheed & Ward.

Blondel, Maurice [1903] (1965), *The Letter on Apologetics and History and Dogma*, trans. and ed. Alexander Dru and Illtyd Trethowan, New York: Holt, Rinehart & Winston.

Blumenberg, Hans (1996), *Lebenszeit und Weltzeit*, Frankfurt: Suhrkamp.

Boes, Tobias (2012), *Formative Fictions: Nationalism, Cosmopolitanism, and the Bildungsroman*, Ithaca: Signale.

Carr, Thomas K. (1996), *Newman and Gadamer: Toward a Hermeneutic of Religious Knowledge*, New York: Oxford University Press.

Congar, Yves [1984] (2004), *The Meaning of Tradition*, trans. A. N. Woodrow, San Francisco: Ignatius Press.

d'Ambrosio, Marcellino (1991), '*Ressourcement* Theology, Aggiornamento, and the Hermeneutics of Tradition', *Communio*, 18: 530–55.

Dupré, Louis (2005), *The Enlightenment and the Intellectual Foundations of Modern Culture*, New Haven: Yale University Press.

Eliot, T. S. [1943] (1971) *Four Quartets*, London: Faber & Faber.

Eliot, T. S. (2014), *The Complete Prose of T. S. Eliot*, ed. Anthony Cuda and Ronald Schuchard, vol. 2, Baltimore: Johns Hopkins University Press.

Frei, Hans (1980), *The Eclipse of Biblical Narrative*, New Haven: Yale University Press.

Gaar, Franz (1983), *Das Prinzip der göttlichen Tradition nach Joh. Baptist Franzelin*, Regensburg: Josef Habbel.

Gadamer, Hans-Georg [1960] (2006), *Truth and Method*, trans. Donald Weinsheimer and Donald G. Marshall, New York: Continuum.

Gordon, Peter E. (2014) 'Contextualism and Criticism in the History of Ideas,' in Darrin M. McMahon and Samuel Moyn (eds), *Rethinking Modern European Intellectual History*, Oxford: Oxford University Press, 32–55.

Griffiths, Paul (2009), *Intellectual Appetite: A Theological Grammar*, Washington DC: Catholic University of America Press.

Hampden, Renn Dickson [1839] (1842), *A Lecture on Tradition*, 5th edn, London: B. Fellowes.

Hedley, Douglas (2014), 'Theology and the Revolt against the Enlightenment', in Sheridan Gilley and Brian Stanley (eds), *The Cambridge History of Christianity*, vol. 8, *World Christianities c.1815 – c.1914*, Cambridge: Cambridge University Press, 30–52.

Hinze, Bradford E. (2010), 'Roman Catholic Theology: Tübingen', in David Fergusson (ed.), *The Blackwell Companion to Nineteenth-Century Theology*, Oxford: Blackwell, 187–213.

Hösle, Vittorio (2013), *God as Reason*, South Bend: University of Notre Dame Press.

Kant, Immanuel [1781/7] (1965), *Critique of Pure Reason*, trans. Norman Kemp Smith, New York: St. Martin's Press.

Ker, Ian (1988), *John Henry Newman*, Oxford: Oxford University Press.

Ker, Ian (2014), *Newman on Vatican II*, Oxford: Oxford University Press.

Lukács, Georg [1915] (1982), *Theory of the Novel*, trans. Anna Bostock, Cambridge, MA: MIT Press.

MacIntyre, Alasdair (1990), *Three Rival Versions of Moral Enquiry: Encyclopaedia, Genealogy, and Tradition*, South Bend: University of Notre Dame Press.

Newman, John Henry (1871), *Essays Critical and Historical*, 2 vols, London: Longmans.

Newman, John Henry (1978–2008), *Letters and Diaries of John Henry Newman*, 32 vols, ed. Ian Ker et al., Oxford: Oxford University Press.

Newman, John Henry [1870] (1979), *An Essay in Aid of a Grammar of Assent*, ed. Nicholas Lash, South Bend: University of Notre Dame Press.

Newman, John Henry [1845] (1989), *An Essay on the Development of Christian Doctrine*, 6th edn, South Bend: University of Notre Dame Press.

Newman, John Henry [1843] (1997), *Oxford University Sermons*, ed. Katherine Tillman, South Bend: University of Notre Dame Press.

Newman, John Henry [1830] (2001), *The Arians of the Fourth Century*, ed. Rowan Williams, South Bend: University of Notre Dame Press.
Newman, John Henry [1872] (2004), *Discussions and Arguments on Various Subjects*, ed. Gerard Tracey and James Tolhurst, South Bend: University of Notre Dame Press.
Newman, John Henry [1865] (2008), *Apologia pro vita sua*, ed. Frank M. Turner, New Haven: Yale University Press.
Newman, John Henry [1841] (2013), *Tracts for the Times*, ed. James Tolhurst, South Bend: University of Notre Dame Press.
Nichols, Aidan, OP (1990), *From Newman to Congar: The Idea of Doctrinal Development from the Victorians to the Second Vatican Council*, Edinburgh: T&T Clark.
Nietzsche, Friedrich [1887] (1996), *On the Genealogy of Morals*, trans. Douglas Smith, New York: Oxford University Press.
Nietzsche, Friedrich [1876] (1997), *Untimely Meditations*, trans. R. J. Hollingdale, Cambridge: Cambridge University Press.
Nockles, Peter (1994), *The Oxford Movement in Context*, Cambridge: Cambridge University Press.
Pattison, Robert (1991), *The Great Dissent: John Henry Newman and the Liberal Heresy*, New York: Oxford University Press.
Pfau, Thomas (1998) 'Reading beyond Redemption: Historicism, Irony, and the Lessons of Romanticism', in Thomas Pfau and Robert E. Gleckner (eds), *Lessons of Romanticism*, Durham, NC: Duke University Press, 1–37.
Pfau, Thomas (2007), 'Of Ends and Endings: Teleological and Variational Models of Romantic Narrative', *European Romantic Review*, 18.2: 231–40.
Pfau, Thomas (2010), '*Bildungsspiele*: Vicissitudes of Socialization in *Wilhelm Meister's Apprenticeship*', *European Romantic Review*, 21.5: 567–87.
Pfau, Thomas (2011), 'The Appearance of *Stimmung*: Play as Virtual Rationality', in Anna-Katharina Gisbertz (ed.), *Stimmung: zur Wiederkehr einer ästhetischen Kategorie?*, Munich: Fink, 95–111.
Pfau, Thomas (2013), *Minding the Modern: Human Agency, Intellectual Traditions, and Responsible Knowledge*, South Bend: University of Notre Dame Press.
Pieper, Joseph [1970] (2010), *Tradition: Concept and Claim*, trans. E. Christian Kopff, South Bend: St. Augustine Press.
Plato (1989) *The Collected Dialogues*, ed. Edith Hamilton and Huntington Cairns, Princeton: Bollingen.
Pocock, J. G. A. (1985), 'The Political Economy of Burke's Analysis of the French Revolution', in *Virtue, Commerce, and History*, Cambridge: Cambridge University Press, 193–214.
Redfield, Marc (1996), *Phantom Formations: Aesthetic Ideology and the Bildungsroman*, Ithaca: Cornell University Press.
Richardson, Laurence (2007), *Newman's Approach to Knowledge*, Leominster: Gracewing.
Schelling, F. W. J. (1981), *Schriften, 1801–1804*, Darmstadt: Wissenschaftliche Buchgesellschaft.
Schlegel, Friedrich (1996), *Philosophical Fragments*, ed. Peter Firchow, Minneapolis: University of Minnesota Press.
Schleiermacher, F. D. E. [1799] (1996), *On Religion: Speeches to Its Cultured Despisers*, trans. and ed. Richard Crouter, Cambridge: Cambridge University Press.
Soni, Vivasvan (2010), *Mourning Happiness: Narrative and the Politics of Modernity*, Ithaca: Cornell University Press.
Taylor, Charles (1989), *Sources of the Self*, Cambridge, MA: Harvard University Press.
Wordsworth, William [1805] (1991), *The Thirteen-Book Prelude*, ed. Mark Reed, Ithaca: Cornell University Press.
Zachhuber, Johannes (2014), *Theology as Science in Nineteenth-Century Germany*, Oxford: Oxford University Press.

13

The Human

Steven Shakespeare

Introduction

In his account of nineteenth-century theology, Karl Barth begins by identifying its eighteenth-century presuppositions. These involved a shift to an anthropocentric worldview, a worldview which was not daunted by cosmological discoveries which seemed to reveal the marginality of human beings in the universe. Asking whether the Copernican revolution entailed the humiliation of humanity, no longer positioned at the centre of the universe, Barth answers in the negative:

> man is all the greater for this, man is in the centre of things, in a quite different sense, too, for he was able to discover this revolutionary truth by his own resources and to think it abstractly, again to consider and penetrate a world which had expanded overnight into infinity – and without anything else having changed, without his having to pay for it in any way: clearly now the world was even more and properly so *his* world! ([1947] 1972: 37–8)

The physical and metaphysical geography of the universe is no longer organised around a human fulcrum. However, the human ability to grasp this truth is the expression of a new *power* of centring: of relativising the non-human to human comprehension and control. Abstraction becomes a method of recouping the lost centre, subjecting the world to the conditions of its knowability.

Apart from the productive tension inherent in this shift, Barth is well aware of its ideological ties to the project of European imperialism. If the humiliation of the human was staved off on one level, it was embraced as a corollary of universalising dominion on the other: 'piety was practised at home, reason was criticized, truth made into poetry and poetry into truth, while abroad slaves were being hunted and sold. The absolute man really can do both' (ibid. 38–9).

The anthropocentric shift is thus a complex one. The human becomes the spiritual fulcrum of redemption, freedom and self-conscious reflection. The human is the place where spirit is manifest, incarnated and brought to bear upon the world. In some respects this represents a continuation of the Renaissance humanism, inflected via Neoplatonic and Hermetic traditions, in which the microcosm of man not only reflects the macrocosm, but is the defining point of contact between the temporal and the eternal. The difference, broadly, is that the human spirit comes to be autonomised (no longer subservient to a transcendent other), historicised (viewed as intrinsically temporal) and prioritised (as containing the founding moment and method of knowledge).

The human thus articulates a fundamental ambivalence. It is an ambivalence which is particularly significant for theology, since it takes up and mutates fundamental tropes of transcendence, evil and redemption. Not just any theology, of course: we are talking about Christian theology. It is here that the human finds its humiliation and glorification mapped out via the cruciform figure of Christ. Ironically, in an age so often allergic to the 'positivity' of particular historical faith, it is the incarnation which becomes the defining dogmatic ground upon which such opposing theological interventions as those made by Hegel, Schleiermacher, Kierkegaard and Feuerbach stake out their claims. It is the medium via which the differences between such figures are recognised as differences.

This might seem an odd and unjustified claim, given that historical revelation was so downplayed by Kant, whose long shadow lingers over the nineteenth-century debates; given too that the Trinity is a more obvious reference point for Hegel, and that Chalcedonian orthodoxy recedes or even falls by the wayside among thinkers offering a human or existential starting point for faith. However, my point is not that there is a consistent dogmatic line about Christ, but that the trope or figure of the incarnation functions, in multiple ways, to define the human and its relation to the non-human. It does so along two lines: those of reconciliation and severance. By reconciliation, I mean the harmonisation of the human with the divine, or the absolute: with that unconditioned ground from which human being arises, and which it uniquely expresses, even in its deviation from it. By severance, I mean the distinction of the human from what hinders it in achieving reconciliation. The human must be defined by its distinction from the animal, and all those to whom some form of animality is thought to cling (typically the Jew, the woman, the negro). The animal persists within what is biologically human, thereby losing any natural innocence it might have in the non-human world. When it asserts itself within human nature, the animal wears the face of the demon.

I am clearly painting in broad brush strokes here, but I wish to identify a core dynamic of those accounts of the human which significantly influence theological thinking in the nineteenth century. Inevitably this leads to some blurring of the boundaries between theology and philosophy. Romanticism and German Idealism addressed questions of absolute reality and the nature of God, for which the starting point was specifically Christian. Again, by 'specifically Christian', I do not intend a specific set of defined doctrine, but a dynamic. This dynamic is one in which reconciliation is historically achieved through the identification of what hinders it, characterised as law, externality, positivity and particularity. Conversely, the obstacles to reconciliation shape the nature of the latter: spirit and freedom (versus the letter of law); appropriation and internalisation (rather than conformity to an externally imposed revelation); and universality (as opposed to the stubbornly particular and parochial). Such values orient Kantian moral religion as much as Hegelian dialectics. They resonate in Schleiermacher's dogmatics and Feuerbach's inversion of Christianity. Even in the work of those who stand against much of the mainstream of European philosophical thought – a Kierkegaard, or a Nietzsche – the Christian dynamic of reconciliation provides a structuring backdrop.

In order to explore and test this claim, I will examine the place and importance of the human at key theological moments. I begin with a brief look at Kant's *Anthropology*, as it expresses some of the convictions and tensions of his thinking about human being which proved to be influential for what immediately follows. I then examine key themes across a number of thinkers: alterity and affectivity; the way in which redemption is figured by the abjection of the animal and the Jew; and destabilising of the human essence by something inhuman in the very notion of spirit. I will say a little more about each of these headings before going into detail.

Alterity and Affectivity

A key question for post-Kantian thought is how the human self relates to the not-self; how it recognises itself in and through its encounters with what is other. This is most evident in Hegel's dialectical attempt to do justice to the 'labour of the negative' in the process of Sprit's self-development. Far from merely presenting a totalitarian negation and assimilation of difference, the alienation of Spirit from itself is indispensable to the substantial content of what Spirit is. Hegel will not rest with a dualism which cuts the self off from the non-self (from reality 'in-itself'), but this is not in the interests of collapsing the two into monism. Of course, Hegel's resolution of this tension is not the only one. Schleiermacher, for instance, foregrounds dependency and affectivity rather than a historically mediated conceptual recognition in his account of human relatedness to its divine source. However, the key point is that the problem is crucial for articulating what it is to be human, in a way which entangles anthropology with theology. The human is human in relationship, a relationship which orients it to or expresses an encompassing divine reality.

Allied to this relationality is the concept of the historicity of human being, increasingly a feature of nineteenth-century analysis. Fichte offers us the human as essentially vocational, our moral duty expressed in a dynamic encounter of I and not-I. For Hegel, as we have already intimated, history is intrinsic to the content of developed Spirit. The temporality of human existence, and the progressive development of the human race, become vital motifs in subsequent European thought – a sense of becoming which is radicalised still further by Darwin and Marx.

The Animal and the Jew

An important undertone of the emphasis on progressive history is the echo of Christian doctrines of supercession: the displacement of the Jews by the new Israel of the church. Supercession encapsulates a progressive revelation of God, mediated through racial categories, in which 'inferior' types are surpassed, then allowed to linger as a continuing reminder of their own anachronicity, and a witness to the superiority of what has supplanted them. Redemption, and the normative definition of the human, is racialised through a Christian supercessionist lens.

The figure of the Jew thus becomes the bearer of those traits of lifeless, subservient, mechanical obedience which are a twisted reflection of the animal in the human. As the freedom of the human is progressively universalised, this comes at the cost of its abjected, non-Christian (and so subhuman) others. Without wishing to conflate it directly with Christian supercessionism, the enslavement of millions of Africans, which continued well after the British abolition of the slave trade in 1807, remains a searing testimony to the violent underpinnings of capitalist expansion and its white supremacist mission.

The Persistence of the Inhuman

The traces of the abjected inhuman are never expunged. This makes the project of realising the universal human essence problematic. With Barth, we can always suspect it of being parasitic upon strategies of both exclusion and assimilation. At the same time, this inhuman remainder becomes a theme of reflection in its own right: precisely as that which is essential to thought or its human bearer, but which stubbornly refuses to be comprehended, assimilated and put to work. From Schelling to Nietzsche, this ineradicable stain on human thought becomes a positive force of resistance to the universalising, humanising, Christianising tendency of the age. The human is a precarious surface expression of deeper subterranean forces of animality and the unconscious.

The question we will be left with is whether this movement really gets us anywhere: whether the idea of the human as both humiliated and elevated still remains, albeit in a new form, once the death of God is announced by Nietzsche. Is the human still the privileged place of revelation of the nature of the universe as it comes into awareness and expression? Even – or especially – where that expression is corrupted by pride and self-deification? Is this still an echo of a Christian theology of redemption? If so, is it because this theology is indispensable, or have we simply not yet found the exit from its echo chamber?

We begin with the hugely influential work of Kant and some of the tensions it bequeathed to subsequent reflection on the human.

Kantian Anthropology and Radical Evil

Kant begins his *Anthropology* by declaring that 'the human being is his own final end' ([1798] 2006: 3). The human is therefore the most important object of knowledge in the world. Indeed, to know the human *is* to know the world, for the human articulates and completes what the world is.

What does this mean? In Kant's case, the problem is compounded by the fact that he seems to live a double philosophical life. On the one hand, we have the three *Critiques* and related works, which are transcendental in method. They ask about the conditions which make possible our knowledge, moral striving and judgements about aesthetic beauty and purpose. Through these works, we already have a clear sense of how each question turns upon the subject rather than the object of our knowing, duty or judgement. This subject, however, is not itself available to be inspected and dissected. In terms of knowledge and experience, it is the 'transcendental unity of apperception' – the 'I think' which accompanies all perceptions. In terms of morality, it is the freely willing self which must be presupposed but never cognised.

When we get to the third *Critique*, of judgement, Kant is seeking a way to unite the disparate realms of nature and freedom. Moral will, after all, must have an effect upon the world. How can this be, if morality presumes freedom, but nature must be conceived as determined by mechanical causal laws? We cannot explore Kant's approach in detail here, but it is worth saying a little about judgements of beauty and judgements of purpose, which form the heart of his exploration.

Judgements of beauty are those of a paradoxically disinterested enjoyment. They are not merely opinions about what I personally find agreeable, but a felt pleasure in what I judge commands universal acceptance. Beautiful things present us a with a harmony that offers us no clear, knowable concept, and serves no end, other than being the catalyst for us to revel in the free play and harmony of our own different faculties of understanding and imagination: 'nature allows us to perceive in the relation of our mental powers an inner purposiveness, and one that is to be declared necessary and universally valid on the basis of something supersensible' (Kant [1790] 1987: 224). In a sense, the purpose of nature resides in the human being. The human itself cannot be purely beautiful, because we are purposive through and through. Ours is an 'ideal beauty', because we embody and express the moral law. The human, judging natural beauty, comes to realise its own transcendence of nature. The human is the end of the world, and this is confirmed for us by our felt encounters with beautiful objects.

Here, Kant's critical, transcendental philosophy rubs up against the other significant aspect of his work. For the majority of his career, Kant lectured consistently on physical geography and anthropology. His *Anthropology* is interesting in particular, for the way in which it bridges the transcendental and empirical approaches to understanding human being.

The published version of the *Anthropology* opens with this delineation of its subject matter: 'Physiological knowledge of the human being concerns investigation of what *nature* makes of the human being; pragmatic, the investigation of what *he* as a free acting being makes of himself, or can and should make of himself' ([1798] 2006: 3). Nature and freedom, irreducibly and qualitatively different, and mysteriously linked, here resurface. The human is more than a natural object; we are what we make ourselves. The human is a progressive project. The unique place of the human in the world is emphasised a little later:

> The fact that the human being can have the 'I' in his representations raises him infinitely above all other living beings on earth . . . through rank and dignity an entirely different being from *things*, such as irrational animals, with which one can do as one likes. (Ibid. 15)

This is true even for infants who have not yet learned to say 'I', for whom it has not become a thinkable concept. Human uniqueness, which is the end of the world, casts its shadow back over its inarticulate beginnings and redeems them retrospectively.

Much of what follows in the *Anthropology* catalogues the various cognitive and perceptual faculties, and the passional and volitional architecture of human desire. It ends by examining human character in general, and the characters of the different sexes and peoples in particular. Kant resists the notion that we can judge a person's character straightforwardly from their outward appearance, but he allows a more indirect approach, allowing that moral defects, for example, can by habitual expression leave their traces upon a person's face. This connection of character with physiognomy is underscored when it comes to gender:

> In all machines that are supposed to accomplish with little power just as much as those with great power, art must be put in. Consequently, one can already assume that the provision of nature put more art into the organization of the female part than that of the male; for it furnished the man with greater power than the woman in order to bring both into the most intimate *physical* union, which, in so far as they are nevertheless also *rational* beings, it orders to the end most important to it, the preservation of species. (Ibid. 204)

Without pressing the machine analogy too far, we still see here the key problematic relationship: between nature (running mechanically) and what makes human beings distinctive (their free rationality). Rational beings must procreate, which never happens without a certain lustful subordination of reason (at least on one side). The solution to this dilemma is an inbuilt inequality. The man has greater physical power, to which the woman yields. She, for her part, has greater artfulness to manipulate him and gain his protection.

It is a subject for debate whether Kant could really bring himself to admit women to full rationality. In this text at least, both man and woman are rational beings; nevertheless, the nature–freedom divide is still gendered. Woman is more closely fashioned by nature, since she lacks male physical power. Her artfulness is not primarily the manifestation of spirit, but an expression of nature, in the service of reproduction. Woman thus provides the mediation between nature and freedom: a confirmation of human distinctiveness, albeit at the cost of questioning her own full humanity.

This difficult passage from nature to freedom is replicated in Kant's account of the characteristics of different peoples. While he resists simplistic reductions of national character to the effect of climate and soil, he argues that the combination of innate features with the cultural history of a people can lead to generally well-defined features. In the *Anthropology*, Kant's ramblings are largely confined to Europe. In other texts, he takes in a wider scope: 'Humanity is at its greatest perfection in the race of the whites. The yellow Indians do have a meagre talent. The Negroes are far behind them and at the lowest point are a part of the American peoples' (quoted in Frierson 2013: 103). Negroes come in for particular attention, and Kant does not hold back in describing them as stupid and lacking all talent, whose religion 'sinks so deeply into the ridiculous as ever seems to be possible for human nature'. The very concept of humanity seems to be divided between white and black: 'So essential is the different between these two human kinds, and it seems to be just as great with regard to the capacities of mind as it is with respect to color' (quoted in ibid. 102).

These comments come from an early text of 1764, but over ten years after that, Kant published an essay, 'Of the Different Human Races', which is now credited with being a foundational work of 'scientific' racism. Here, Kant argues that humans all belong to one species. But the way in which different branches of this species are affected by the various environments within which they live creates races, defined primarily by skin colour (Mikkelsen 2013). The adaptation to different climates becomes hereditary, an observable physical and cultural trait. Dispositions become fixed, opening the door for a racist division of the world into white, black, yellow and red in which human essence is variously manifested, and hierarchically arranged. The white European is the exemplar of humanity. The others – especially the negroes – bear witness to the degeneration of humanity into a naturally determined race. The whites bear the burden of being the race that is no race, closer to the human ideal of freedom. The others represent the drag of nature on human being, against which the free white must push in order to retain their humanity. Abjection of the subhuman (especially when manifested in what is technically biologically human) is the necessary means to navigate a path to spirit.

For Kant, the elevation and subversion of humanity are closely related. His notion of radical evil brings this into focus ([1793] 1998: 45–9). Kant faces the problem of why human beings should ever do wrong: if the moral law is within us, is universal and self-legislated, how does it ever get to be subverted? The answer is that we substitute for the moral law our personal inclinations and ambitions, which inevitably are partial and self-serving. If we do this even once, it demonstrates that the moral law is not the unshakeable basis for our will, that we are capable of relativising and displacing it. And this in turn shows that the maxims which direct our will and actions are corrupted at the root. It is hard not to discern the Lutheran resonances in this. The justified sinner is at once abject before God, and yet lifted by grace to be a restored image of the divine. This operation of grace seems a long way from Kant's rational religion and his stress upon autonomy. However, Kant himself saw the need to posit supernatural assistance from the view point of practical reason's commitment to the highest good, a unity of virtue and happiness which transcends human power. Such supernatural power remains opaque to cognition, but necessary for the inner dynamic of the moral law.

From our exploration so far, some linked questions emerge: is nineteenth-century thought, in the aftermath of Kant, haunted by the return of a theology of grace? Is the human, for all its elevated status, shadowed by the inhuman, whether the drag of an animal evil or the lure of a suprahuman divine? And how do these questions bear upon the problem of the absolutisation of the white European male as the normative bearer of humanity?

Affectivity and Alterity

The contraction of epistemology and ethics into the singular point of human autonomy was not an end point, but the coiling of a spring, whose tension and release would inevitably have ripple effects on how the human being was seen in fundamental relationship to its world. Barth reads the nineteenth century as bound up with the fate of the 'absolute man'; but, while there is some validity to this, it perhaps underestimates the genuine diversity among thinkers in the wake of Kant, and the implications of their work for theology.

Hegel and Schleiermacher initiate distinctive trajectories here. For Hegel, the centrality of the human is defined by its ability to reconcile the objective and the subjective in consciousness, and it does this via religion. As Hegel puts it in his lectures on philosophy of religion: 'Religion is the consciousness of freedom and truth ... The concept of religion is universal. Religion holds this position for all peoples and persons' (2006: 76). However, this cannot remain an abstraction; the religious object cannot be an alienated transcendence, but must be realised within human consciousness: 'Religion is therefore *spirit that realizes itself in consciousness*' (ibid. 104). Religion achieves this through its representation of the divine absolute.

Hegel traces this dynamic through the gradual humanisation of religion. The human form becomes a privileged representation of the divine, freeing it from impersonal or animalistic traits:

> Insofar as spirit has natural and sensible existence, the human figure is the only way in which it can be intuited ... this is the only shape in which spirit exists; the spiritual surely cannot come forth, for example, in the shape of a lion. (Ibid. 347–9)

However, since even this humanised image remains an external ideal, it must be contested in turn through the divine alterity which reaches its apex in Judaism, and brings the human–divine relationship into crisis. Of course, for Hegel, Judaism fails to resolve this crisis, remaining stuck within a legalistic and alienated subjection to God. It is Christianity which not only proclaims but enacts the reconciliation of the divine and the human in the Man-God that is Christ. In the end, the humanisation of religion is also the deification of the human:

> In the church Christ has been called the 'God-man'. This is a monstrous compound, which directly contradicts both representation and understanding. But what has thereby been brought into human consciousness and made a certainty for it is the unity of divine and human nature ... It is the appearance of a human being in sensible presence; God in sensible presence can take no other shape than that of human being. In the sensible and mundane order, only the human is spiritual; so if the spiritual is to have a sensible shape, it must be a human shape. (Ibid. 457–8)

It is of course Feuerbach who takes this logic to its conclusion, and does so explicitly via the human/animal distinction. The opening of his *The Essence of Christianity* states that 'Religion has its basis in the essential difference between the man and the brute – the brutes have no religion' ([1841] 1957: 1). He goes on to clarify that the key difference is 'consciousness', by which he means, not merely an individual self-awareness, but a consciousness of one's species. This self-objectification, the beginning of abstract, universalising thought, is what makes higher knowledge possible. It is what gives the human its distinctive inner life.

What makes this human form of consciousness religious is its infinitude: 'Consciousness, in the strict or proper sense, is identical with consciousness of the infinite; a limited consciousness is no consciousness; consciousness is essentially infinite in its nature' (ibid. 2). Awareness of one's species-being transcends individual limitation. To think and feel the infinite is to think and feel human nature.

Here lie the seeds of Feuerbach's identification of theology with anthropology. The full realisation of this identity takes time, however, since religion begins as an indirect kind of human self-knowledge: human nature is externalised and reified:

> Hence the historical progress of religion consists in this: that what by an earlier religion was regarded as objective is now recognised as subjective; that is, what was formerly contemplated and worshipped as God is now perceived to be something *human* . . . every advance in religion is therefore a deeper self-knowledge. (Ibid. 13)

The divine nature is essentially human nature, purified and presented in its unlimited form. Feuerbach sees his task as one of fulfilling religion by overcoming the self-alienation of the human from itself (ibid. 33).

Feuerbach states that he intends no denigration of animal life, and writes of each species perceiving its own world as unlimited: 'The leaf on which the caterpillar lives is for it a world, an infinite space' (ibid. 8). Nevertheless, it is the human whose power of abstraction and feeling has a truly unlimited nature. The irony – that of course human beings perceive *their* world and nature as truly infinite, since all species do – appears to be lost on him. Indeed, for Feuerbach, the historical progress of religion is inseparable from a religious account of history as directed towards this human telos. 'Providence is the privilege of man', as Feuerbach puts it (ibid. 105). The animal has only instinct for its guide; the human alone has providence, in the sense of a miraculous interruption and cancellation of the power of nature.

In Hegel's version of this evolutionary schema, the human does not remain a simple and timeless essence, but a dynamic bridging power between nature and the divine, one that is constantly redefined by the terms it relates, even as it is the essential link between them. At the same time, the human bridge obeys an imperative: if nature and the divine are to be bridged, the traffic must be one way. That way is ascension from natural sensibility to spiritual self-awareness. The animal must not be allowed to dominate, but must be tamed, consumed, incorporated and subservient to the forward march of humanity. If the human is a bridge, it is also a cut, a breach: 'humanity as spirit is what steps forth out of natural life and passes over into a separation between its concept and its immediate existence' (Hegel 2006: 439).

When discussing religion in its 'lowest' form, that of magic, Hegel makes a startling statement: 'It is difficult to get the sense of an alien religion from within. To put oneself in the place of a dog requires the sensibilities of a dog' (ibid. 224). Given the context, it is hard to dismiss this as a dead metaphor. The lower the religion, the more animal, the less human. If alterity is key to Hegel's understanding of identity, it is also subject to this evolutionary imperative. The animal affect must be kept in its place.

Hegel, of course, was scathing about thinkers such as Jacobi or Schleiermacher, who seemed to offer an immediate awareness of the divine. They were guilty of abolishing the human, the necessary cut between immediate nature and spiritual existence. Much the same could be said of Hegel's dismissal of Schelling's philosophy of identity as the night in which all cows are black. What is pure identity but the all-consuming omnipresence of the indistinct beast?

However, if we turn to Schleiermacher, it is clear that this is a simplistic assessment. When we get to his mature work in *The Christian Faith*, the essential role played by human affectivity in apprehending God is complex. Schleiermacher affirms that 'everyone has a twofold [*doppelte*] experience' – one in which self-consciousness is attached to changing states of thinking and willing, another in which self-consciousness remains a state unchanged through various acts of thought and will ([1831] 1989: 7). Further, our self-consciousness is itself doubled, composed of an element derived from ourselves and an element from elsewhere. The latter presupposes an Other to the Ego, but 'this Other is not objectively presented in the immediate self-consciousness' (ibid. 13). This leads to the claim that there is a feeling of absolute dependence accompanying all our activity, since we are not our own origin. This feeling cannot be attributed to any given, determined instance. Instead, its Whence must be absolute, and hence can be named as God.

'Feeling' in this context is obviously not a passing emotional state, but something like the experiential manifestation of an ontological structure of human being. It is reducible to neither cognition nor volition, precisely because it unsettles the coordinates of any anthropology which takes the relationship of the subject to determined objects for granted. The relationality of absolute dependency is radical. In one sense, it therefore decentres the human. At the same time, our access to this relational structure must go via the human.

This is underlined when Schleiermacher turns to animals to clarify the nature of human consciousness:

> It is true, indeed, that the animal state is to us really entirely strange and unknown. But there is general agreement that, on the one hand, the lower animals have no knowledge, properly so called, nor any full self-consciousness which combines the different moments into a stable unity, and that, on the other hand, they are not entirely devoid of consciousness. (Ibid. 18)

Since animals (presented as an undifferentiated mass) are not entirely without consciousness, they offer a good dialectical starting point for asserting human distinctiveness.

It works like this. First, in animal life, feelings and perceptions are confused. The distinction between subject and object is not established clearly. Second, in ordinary (sensible) human self-consciousness, subjective feeling is demarcated from perceptions of objective realities. However, finally, the feeling of absolute dependence unites these contraries again. The distinction between subject and object cannot hold, not because the Other is abolished, but because it cannot be determined and objectified as anything but the source of this feeling.

The feeling of absolute dependency thus takes on some of the characteristics of the divine. It is self-identical and unchanging, whatever the varying mental states and perceptions it accompanies. It therefore coexists with the second stage of the dialectic, that of ordinary human consciousness. However, the first stage of 'animal confusion' must disappear (ibid. 22). The animal must diminish and die for the human and the divine to emerge as co-conspirators. The payoff here is that the feeling of absolute dependence is 'an essential part of human nature' (ibid. 26). This at least seems to secure a basis for a universal definition of the human. However, Schleiermacher is well aware of cultural and religious difference, as well as individual differences of temperament. How can this be accommodated without losing the self-identity of fundamental feeling? The answer is intriguing:

> Now, since the feeling of absolute dependence is in itself perfectly simple, and the conception of it provides no basis of differentiation, such a basis can be derived only from the fact that the feeling, in order to realize itself in an actual moment, must first unite with a sensible stimulation of self-consciousness, and that these sensible stimuli must be regarded as infinitely various. Now it is true that the feeling of absolute dependence in itself is equally related to all these stimulations, and is highly susceptible to them all alike. But nevertheless it may, by analogy, be assumed that this relationship in actual reality differentiates itself variously not only in individual men but also in larger masses. (Ibid. 40)

In order to become actual, the feeling of absolute dependency must be united to changing sensible forms. There must be incarnation, of a sort, but one which is dispersed across the human realm. This allows, not only for human diversity, but also for hierarchy: judgements about which human sensible forms most adequately house the absolute.

Schleiermacher is thus able to combine an openness to revelation in different religions, for example, with clear rules about which of these is superior. Revelation here is not a communication of doctrine, but an impression upon self-consciousness. Different 'impressions' are basic to different religious communities. We might say that the feeling of the divine absolute is incarnated variously in the various religious sensibilities. There is no going around these sensibilities to look at God directly, since

> Any proclamation of God which is to be operative upon and within us can only express God in His relation to us; and this is not an infra-human ignorance concerning God, but the essence of human limitedness in relation to Him. (Ibid. 52)

Nevertheless, an immanent judgement about the relative worth of religions can be made. So we read that polytheism fails to relate the human to moral ends, but remains fixed in an aesthetic relationship to nature. The different gods are depictions of inner human dispositions, and the point seems to be that these dispositions are simply accepted as natural givens, to be admired or submitted to, but not to be related to in a free and conscious manner. Among monotheistic religions, Judaism and Islam are an improvement upon this, but are still characterised by a passive element, inferior to the free moral activity of the Christian sphere. Islam especially is dubbed 'fatalistic' (ibid. 44).

Schleiermacher further argues that a religion can be distinguished by the way in which its outward unity (the relation of the community to its historical starting point and/or founding figure) is related to its inward unity (the modification of the feeling of absolute dependency which it introduces). The highest form of religion would be one in which these two unities coincide, and we are told in advance that this is Christianity. Here, the source is the divine–human unity exhibited in Christ and incorporated into the life of the believer. The implication is that other forms of religion lack this harmony (for example, by mediating the feeling of absolute dependency through nature, fate or external commands).

This hierarchy of religions is supported by a telling analogy:

> just as in the realm of Nature the species are less definite on the lower levels of life, so in this realm of religion also the uniform consummation of the outward and the inward unity is reserved for the higher development. (Ibid. 45)

Again, we are moving from the animal upward, along an evolutionary trajectory. The human is at once the presupposition of all religious feeling, but also something which is itself in process, being formed more and more perfectly by an incarnational imperative. The analogy with nature itself betrays this complex structure. Nature's hierarchy mirrors that of the religions; but religion's ultimate aim is to transcend nature, or at least to *humanise* it. The imperfection attributed to Islam, its 'fatalism', is defined as the 'subordination of the moral to the natural' (ibid. 44). Christian superiority depends upon there being this original and residual trace of the absolute within human nature. This trace may be obscured by distracting externalities, but it is consummated when the true externality of Christ appears, since here alone is the external form in perfect correspondence with the internal unity of the divine and the human.

The Animal and the Jew

For Schleiermacher, Christian apologists in the early church recognised heathen prophecies as 'a striving of human nature towards Christianity' ([1831] 1989: 62). Like Judaism, they prepare the way for Christ, since human nature is never obliterated. At the same time, Schleiermacher can say of the Old Testament that 'whatever is most definitely Jewish has least value' (ibid. 62). Jewishness represents the dead outer husk, wrapping up the inner life. The human is struggling to assert itself in relation to what remains stubbornly animalistic and natural in religion.

The attitude to other religions is thus one of colonial accommodation; to Judaism it is one of expulsion. Universal human nature provides a continuum on which religions may be placed, but it is one directed and defined by its Christian fulfilment from the start. Revelation is an originality which cannot be explained by what went before; but at the same time it must be 'the result of the power of development which resides in our human nature' (ibid. 63). The appearance of Christ is, in this sense, a natural fact: 'as certainly as Christ was a man, there must reside in human nature the possibility of taking up the divine into itself, just as did happen in Christ' (ibid. 64). Christ is the ultimate incarnation of the absolute, not only in himself but in us. He therefore reduces all other revelations to nothing.

The implications of this for Christology are beyond the scope of this essay. Suffice to say that Christ reveals the paradoxicality of human 'nature' – at once presupposed and yet always beyond what is merely natural. This is the basis upon which other religions may be judged partial expressions of the divine. The capacity to appropriate grace cannot entirely have been lost, since without it we would have no human nature. As Schleiermacher remarks in his discussion of sin:

we must not magnify our congenital sinfulness to such an extent as would involve the denial of man's capacity to appropriate redemption ... In the light of such a denial nothing would remain of those higher gifts which constitute the prerogative of human nature, and in which everything that distinguishes man from brute must have some share. (Ibid. 283)

The human affect is the mark of its distinction from the animal and potential unity with the divine. As such, it is also an intrinsically Christian, incarnational affect. The very thing which is natural to the human is its denaturalisation, and its subsequent incorporation into a teleology which is supernaturally oriented to the Christian, to the new human, to the race which is no race.

I suggest that such an anthropology leaves its marks on a wide range of theological forms in the nineteenth century, including those (such as Feuerbach and Marx) which are ostensibly anti-theological. Without wishing to minimise the distinctions between such trajectories of thought, what is at stake is the immanent transcendence which constitutes human nature, and the incorporation of this transcendence into a teleological narrative. As we have seen in Feuerbach's case, human 'species being' becomes the incarnation of the divine in the world.

A key example comes from David Friedrich Strauss. His *Life of Jesus* was seminal for critical biblical scholarship, but it culminated in a speculative statement which underlines a construal of the human which is at once immanent and spiritual:

It is Humanity that dies, rises, and ascends to heaven, for from the negation of its phenomenal life there ever proceeds a higher spiritual life; from the suppression of its mortality as a personal, national, and terrestrial spirit, arises its union with the infinite spirit of the heavens. By faith in this Christ, especially in his death and resurrection, man is justified before God; that is, by the kindling within him of the idea of Humanity, the individual man participates in the divinely human life of the species. Now the main element of that idea is, that the negation of the merely natural and sensual life, which is itself the negation of spirit (the negation of the negation, therefore), is the sole way to true spiritual life. ([1837] 1973: 780)

The human race becomes the definitive term here, and it is a race which is determined by a uniquely Christian teleo-logic of incarnation and resurrection.

Implicit in this is the overcoming of the animal and the Jew. Feuerbach saw in religion, and in the providential overcoming of nature, the essential distinction between human and animal. This process is realised most fully in Christianity, in which Christ becomes the personal unification of human and divine. Judaism must be overcome, not merely as a lower stage, but as a vicious dead-end, one which worships in God's power over nature only its own national egoism writ large: 'in the celebration of this power, the Israelite has always reference ultimately to himself' (Feuerbach [1841] 1957: 118). The Jew glories in the power of Nature as the power of God and does so in the service of an 'exclusive, monarchical arrogance' (ibid. 119).

There might seem to be an abyss between the vision of the Left Hegelians and that of Adolf Harnack later in the century, given the latter's suspicion of philosophical speculation and the malign influence of Hellenism on theology. However, they share something highly significant – a commitment to a Christian universalism which consumes all stubbornly 'positive' or 'external' excrescences:

the fact that the whole of Jesus' message may be reduced to these two heads – God as the Father, and the human soul so ennobled that it can and does unite with him – shows us that the Gospel is in no wise a positive religion like the rest; that it contains no statutory or particularistic elements; that it is, therefore, religion itself. It is superior to all antithesis and tension between this world and a world to come, between reason and ecstasy, between work and isolation from the world, between Judaism and Hellenism. It can dominate them all, and there is no factor of earthly life to which it is confined or necessarily tied down. (Harnack [1900] 1901: 63)

For Harnack, Christianity transcends the particular, the imagined, the sensed (ibid. 65). It also transcends philosophy. Whereas Plato appeals to the mind, 'Jesus Christ calls to every poor soul; he calls to every one who bears a human face' (ibid. 67). Harnack writes of the great man who enhances humankind, adding to the value of 'that race of men which has risen up out of the dull ground of Nature' (ibid. 67). He welcomes the internalisation of religion, which results in religion as humility, pure receptivity to God (ibid. 73).

Humility and domination: in this logic, they are not opposites. And whereas Hellenism might represent a rootless abstraction, Judaism – as it does for Hegel and Schleiermacher – becomes the most notable representative of externalism, and of the drag of nature upon the human race. So, even where the incarnation appears relativised by a more 'kenotic' approach, the underlying logic remains.

Indeed, it is Hegel who expresses this thought in one of its most vitriolic philosophical forms in some of his earlier texts, especially 'The Spirit of Christianity'. Here, he established Christian uniqueness via a total contrast with Judaism. The Jews are depicted as wholly passive, subservient to an alienated infinite Object, and therefore lacking human freedom and dignity. They formed a 'community of hatred' (1948: 201) and could only direct themselves to maintaining physical existence. For Hegel, the Jewish form of life is a 'total ugliness', an 'animal existence' (ibid. 202). He sums up his disdain:

> The great tragedy of the Jewish people is no Greek tragedy; it can rouse neither terror nor pity, for both of these arise only out of the fate which follows from the inevitable slip of a beautiful character; it can arouse horror alone. The fate of the Jewish people is the fate of Macbeth who stepped out of nature itself, clung to alien Beings, and so in their service had to trample and slay everything holy in human nature, had at last to be forsaken by his gods (since these were objects and he their slave) and be dashed to pieces on his faith alone. (Ibid. 204–5)

The contrast is as old as the New Testament: between the living spirit of Christ (God in person!) and the dead letter of the law. According to Hegel, rights and regulations which should be a living modification of human nature were for the Jews simply commands. Jesus therefore sets against the Jews their 'precise opposite', which is a 'human urge and so a human need' (ibid. 206).

No doubt this text can be dismissed as a relatively immature one in Hegel's oeuvre. However, he arguably never abandons its basic premise: the alienation, enslavement and anti-humanity which makes Judaism the perfect counterpoint to Christian reconciliation. And this is a logic which replicates itself throughout much nineteenth-century theology. Christianity is something inward. It is love. But it is a love predicated on hatred of the Jew, who in turn is the representative of both the animal and the machine, perversely intruding into the human realm.

There is no space to pursue this here, but this at least raises a question: when we get to the great critiques of religious alienation and slavery in Feuerbach and early Marx, how much of their redemptive response is still predicated on a historical overcoming, a universalisation and reconciliation which is racial and Christian in its form: a return to our true 'species being'?

The Persistence of the Inhuman

We began this essay with Barth's critique of the nineteenth-century anthropocentrism. He draws attention to the connection between the European deification of absolute man and the enslavement of Africans. It is not surprising that he draws the conclusion that there must be a radical gap between the human and the divine to prevent this occurring. The optimism about human nature we find in Schleiermacher, Strauss and Harnack invites the catastrophe of identifying (some) human affects, thoughts and projects with those of a divine destiny. Such a judgement can arguably be found in the midst of this nineteenth-century consensus, not least in the work of Kierkegaard. He decries 'Christendom' and the translation of Christianity into matters of birth, nationhood and race. He rejects the self-deification of the established order, insisting on the infinite qualitative difference between God and humanity.

Through Kierkegaard's web of pseudonymous voices, it is always risky to identify an authorial voice. More important for our purposes are the interconnected themes which his texts pursue: the inescapability of the finitude of human existence; the lack of coincidence and harmony between the inner and the outer nature of a human being; the separation between thought and being which denies us any speculative grasp of the absolute. The indirectness of Kierkegaard's writing is part and parcel of the way he performs these motifs. In this context, the God-man is not the culmination of an evolutionary trajectory or innate structure of human being, but a radical and paradoxical cut with sense and appearance.

Nevertheless, Kierkegaard's texts are still intertwined with the traditions they critique. In the detailed analysis of human selfhood found in *The Concept of Anxiety* and *The Sickness Unto Death*, something like the Hegelian and Schleiermachian dialectics reappear. Take the famous passage which opens *Sickness*: 'A human being is spirit. But what is spirit? Spirit is the self. But what is the self? The self is a relation that relates itself to itself or is the relation's relating itself to itself in the relation' ([1849] 1983:13). The text goes on to say that a human being is a synthesis of opposites (for example, of the temporal and the eternal), but must be more than this to qualify as a self. It must relate to itself, so implicitly rendering its synthesis dynamic and unstable. This is not the end of the matter, however, for the self is also a 'derived, established relation' which (whether it likes it or not) relates to another, to a power which has established it.

It is possible that Kierkegaard is using these formulae to satirise Hegelian language. However, there is no denying that they do set up all that follows in his analysis of the fundamental disarticulation of the self in despair. They present a self inherently ruptured, never at one with itself, and shadowed by the otherness of its source. There is an echo of earlier analyses, where anxiety plays such an important role, because it reveals the vertiginous nature of freedom. Anxiety is not the fear of any particular thing, but a terror induced by the nothingness that opens up in front of us when we choose. It is the fear of 'being-able' (Kierkegaard [1844] 1980: 44).

Kierkegaard thus takes themes of self-relation, alterity and affectivity and uses them to disrupt the narratives of reconciliation through human nature we find in different ways in

Hegel and Schleiermacher. At the same time, access to revelation is never simply a matter of passively receiving what is given from above, but always involves an immanent critique and recomposition of the forms of selfhood. Kierkegaard's indirectness is not a decorative embellishment or unfortunate detour, but an intrinsic recognition that there is no concept of God or experience of revelation which occurs with self-evident and self-authenticating authority.

There is, then, no magical escape from an immanent interrogation of the human. And the traces of a certain humanism are never simply expunged. Kierkegaard also offers us accounts of human distinctiveness from animals (based on human self-conscious reflection) and teleological justifications of Christian superiority (since it is Christianity alone which intensifies the paradoxical nature of existence to its utmost). Consider the following account of human being:

> Man is a synthesis of the psychical and the physical; however, a synthesis is unthinkable if the two are not united in a third. This third is spirit. In innocence, man is not merely animal, for if he were at any moment of his life merely animal, he would never become man. So spirit is present, but as immediate, as dreaming. (Ibid. 43)

There is a complex disavowal at work here. The human is radically distinct from the animal. No evolutionary passage from one to the other is allowed. However, the animal must still appear as a counterpoint, since it shares in the union of the psychical and physical which is also part of human nature. Here the questions mount up: what unites body and soul in the animal if not spirit? How is it that spirit in humans begins in immediacy, dreaming and darkness, if spirit is the principle of self-consciousness? The evolution from the animal to the human is displaced here by an evolution within the human, from the unconscious to the conscious. Seen in this light, spirit is experienced both as 'a hostile power, for it constantly disturbs the relation between soul and body', and as a friendly power which establishes that relation (ibid. 43).

Kierkegaard is opening up the possibility of the human self being structured by forces which are unconscious and even, in a sense, inhuman. Sprit is the apogee of human being, but it also precedes any conscious grasp or intention. It is an uncanny, destabilising factor, enabling the human to relate to the divine, but also to become demonic. It therefore never entirely escapes the shadow of the abjected animality which Kierkegaard seeks to leave behind – but cannot avoid invoking.

A major influence on Kierkegaard's work on anxiety and freedom was Schelling, especially his *Philosophical Investigations into the Essence of Human Freedom*. In that work, the sense of a dark unconscious precursor to human being is spelled out in distinction to the divine:

> Without this preceding darkness creatures have no reality; darkness is their necessary inheritance. God alone – as the one who exists – dwells in pure light since he alone is begotten from himself ... Man is formed from the maternal body; and only from the obscurity of that which is without understanding ... grow luminous thoughts. ([1809] 2006: 29)

The instability of the human is what distinguishes it both from the animal and from God. The dark principle of contraction stands in tension with the communicative, expressive, existential force of light. But without the dark ground, the light cannot emerge. It is in the human that this strange, opaque dialectic is played out to its fullest degree:

> This raising of the deepest *centrum* into light occurs in none of the creatures visible to us other than in man. In man there is the whole power of the dark principle and at the same time the whole power of the light ... Because he emerges from the Ground (is creaturely), man has in relation to God a relatively independent principle in himself; but because precisely this principle – without it ceasing for that reason to be dark according to its ground – is transfigured in light, there arises in him something higher, *spirit* ... Were now the identity of both principles in the spirit of man exactly as indissoluble as in God, then there would be no distinction, that is, God as spirit would not be revealed. The same unity that is inseverable in God must therefore be severable in man – and this is the possibility of good and evil. (Ibid. 32–3)

Revelation is dependent upon distinction. There must be a cut, there must be severance, if there is to be the articulation of spirit. Animals cannot achieve this, since they can never separate themselves from the natural unity of the forces which constitute them. The highest corruption for the human is therefore not 'becoming animal [*Tierwerdung*]', but falling *below* the animal (ibid. 40).

It is striking that, as Schelling develops these lines of thought, he is willing to go further. In *The Ages of the World* (1997), this struggle between the dark and the light is translated into God's own nature. God no longer sits above the fray, but is also defined by an internal fracture. The abyss, the dark unconscious ground of being, is a necessary magnetic pole out of which God's existence, love and personhood can emerge. They are never simply left behind, defeated or incorporated.

Both Schelling and Kierkegaard still dream of a light or a transparency within which the self can rest and humanity find consummation. But their texts invoke something that turns the humanistic and theological projects on their head. Spirit is possible because of the unspirit which births it and tracks it. An unconscious will strives for expression, not only in nature, or in the human, but in God. It looks as if the process of 'becoming animal' is not outside the human–divine spiritual nexus after all, but lodged in its very heart. With no pure access to revelation outside the detours of finite existence, has the analysis of the human in this period taken us from the end of the world to the end of God?

Conclusion: The End of the Human. The End of God?

Looking back on Kant's *Anthropology*, Foucault notes the centrality of the human in Kant's thought: 'It is from the starting point of man that the absolute can be thought' (2008: 78), since in 'man' the objectivity of the world and the free personality of God are joined. However, this anthropology is also the source of slippage. The human 'I think' of the *Critique of Pure Reason* determines reality as knowable. It retains a transcendental purity. In the *Anthropology*, by contrast, human thought is irreducibly temporal and dispersed, engaged with and defined by an irreducible empirical givenness. The human is defined by this tension between a priori structures and a reality that refuses to be transparent to thought. The analysis of the human becomes 'an impure and unthought hybrid within the internal economy of philosophy' (ibid. 106). Foucault extends this analysis in *The Order of Things* ([1966] 1974), where he explores the discursive shifts in the realms of political economy, linguistics and natural history from the eighteenth into the nineteenth century. In each case, he argues, there is a move from a 'classical' system of representation, a correspondence between signs and things, to an understanding that what appears to us is conditioned by unseen forces. So, for example, animals are no longer classified by externally visible traits, but by the internal self-affecting structure of the organism; language is not understood according the correspondence of words to things, but by the deep structures of grammar.

Famously, Foucault goes on to suggest that the concept of 'man' might itself be disappearing. The nineteenth century allowed man to appear in a different light, as strung between the unconscious darkness of the ground of being and the light of existential freedom and struggle. History became the medium of redemption which embraced human temporality. However, the figure of this man is inherently fragile, an echo of the divine purity distancing itself from its impure and hybrid origins.

The Marx of *Capital* and Nietzsche (the one who did not succumb to biologistic fantasies) articulated in different ways this precarious and transitional human state. History and language ceased to be anchored in a self-identical realm of human spirit, even one that had struggled into the light. I suggest this is ultimately the context which calls the human into question, more so even than Darwin's work. Darwin clearly called into question theological accounts of creation and human uniqueness, but his work could always be recouped by long-established evolutionary forms of thought, for which the animal ground was welcomed as a necessary basis on which to establish the human overcoming of nature.

The implications of this for theology were and are considerable. Hegel and Schleiermacher seek to understand God in and through the historicity and affectivity of human spirit, such that God is only known or experienced in or as a fundamental relationality. The divine is drawn close to human self-consciousness, at a time when that self-consciousness is itself being defined by temporal and affective alterities and ecstasies. I have argued that the attempt to maintain the identity of the human in this context works via an abjection of the animal and those with whom animality is associated. This is given a particular twist by the Christian logic of supercession. Animality is displaced on those – the negro, the Jew – who represent a threat to the human within humanity itself. The human takes on a white Christian mask, establishing its self-possession though the possession of others by right of use and force of law.

In this context, and for all Barth is right to call out the nexus of theological humanism and slavery, I suggest that a Barthian call to radical revelation is not the remedy it appears to be. The 'human as recipient of revelation' remains a theological lynchpin which ignores or underplays the displacement of the human by the forces which destructure it. As we saw with Kierkegaard and Schelling, there is no simple exit from this conundrum, and there is good reason to cease absolving the basic categories of spirit and divinity from the contaminating, hybrid forces of the unconscious.

To adapt Nietzsche's phrasing, the nineteenth-century human is a bridge; however, the ends which tether that bridge are no longer fixed or well understood. The human is stretched between the animal and the divine, but these categories are themselves falling into dispute. The human is constituted by a spirit of conscious self-relation, but a self-relation which is impossible without its inhuman, unthinkable ground. It is not therefore a matter of deciding for or against the human, any more than it is of deciding for or against the animal and/or God, since there is no pure secular or theological ground on which to do so. Indeed, dreams of such a ground often turn out to be fantasies concealing another violence.

The nineteenth century, with its hugely fertile dialogue between theology and philosophy, continues to inform an open theological project, in which the coordinates of the human are no longer given: a chance to confront the abjections which still configure our thinking of God.

References

Barth, Karl [1947] (1972), *Protestant Theology in the Nineteenth Century*, trans. C. E. Gunton, London: SCM.

Feuerbach, Ludwig [1841] (1957), *The Essence of Christianity*, trans. George Eliot, New York: Harper.

Foucault, Michel [1966] (1974), *The Order of Things: An Archaeology of the Human Sciences*, London: Routledge.

Foucault, Michel (2008), *Introduction to Kant's Anthropology*, trans. K. Briggs and R. Nigro, Los Angeles: Semiotext(e).

Frierson, Patrick (2013), *What Is the Human Being?*, London: Routledge.

Harnack, Adolf von [1900] (1901), *What Is Christianity?*, trans. T. B. Saunders, London: William and Norgate.

Hegel, G. W. F. (1948), *On Christianity: Early Theological Writings*, trans. T. M. Knox, New York: Harper.

Hegel, G. W. F. (2006), *Lectures on the Philosophy of Religion. One Volume Edition. The Lectures of 1827*, ed. and trans. P. C. Hodgson, Oxford: Clarendon Press.

Kant, Immanuel [1790] (1987), *Critique of Judgment*, trans. W. Pluhar, Indianapolis: Hackett.

Kant, Immanuel [1793] (1998), *Religion within the Boundaries of Mere Reason and Other Writings*, ed. and trans. A. Wood and G. di Giovanni, Cambridge: Cambridge University Press.

Kant, Immanuel [1798] (2006), *Anthropology from a Pragmatic Point of View*, ed. and trans. R. B. Louden, Cambridge: Cambridge University Press.

Kierkegaard, Søren [1844] (1980), *The Concept of Anxiety*, ed. and trans. R. Thomte, Princeton: Princeton University Press.

Kierkegaard, Søren [1849] (1983), *The Sickness Unto Death*, ed. and trans. H. V. Hong and E. H. Hong, Princeton: Princeton University Press.

Mikkelsen, Jon (2013), *Kant and the Concept of Race: Late Eighteenth-Century Writings*, Albany: State University of New York Press.

Schelling, F. W. J. [1809] (2006), *Philosophical Investigations into the Essence of Human Freedom*, trans. J. Love and J. Schmidt, Albany: State University of New York Press.

Schelling, F. W. J. and Slavoj Žižek (1997), *The Abyss of Freedom/The Ages of the World*, trans. J. Norman, Ann Arbor: University of Michigan Press.

Schleiermacher, F. D. E. [1831] (1989), *The Christian Faith*, ed. and trans. H. R. Mackintosh and J. S. Stewart, Edinburgh: T&T Clark.

Strauss, David Friedrich [1837] (1973), *The Life of Jesus Critically Examined*, trans. George Eliot, London: SCM.

14

The Wisdom of the East

Joseph P. Lawrence

Introduction

In a biography of Anquetil-Duperron, whose French translation of the *Zend-Avesta* appeared in 1776, Raymond Schwab had this to say about his subject:

> He goes to find in Asia a scientific proof for the primacy of the Chosen People and for the genealogies of the Bible: instead it happened that his investigations soon led to criticism of the very texts which had hitherto been considered revealed. (Quoted in Said 1984: xii–xiii)

Instead of confirming the genealogies of the Bible, the philological study of the sacred texts of the East, which assumed a central place in European universities throughout the nineteenth century, presented an alternative to them. Schwab referred to the sudden dramatic emergence of this Eastern alternative as Europe's second great Renaissance, which had been prepared by Jesuit missionaries in the 1600s who dutifully took notes while seeking the conversion of India and China. In the seventeenth century, Leibniz inferred from their accounts that China may have been the true origin of civilisation (with Chinese as the world's original language), thus giving rise to the unsettling idea that there may have been an *older* and geographically far more expansive civilisation at the bottom of both classical and biblical antiquity. If the classical Renaissance of Greek and Latin antiquity consolidated Christian Europe's sense of its own civilisational primacy, this new Renaissance undermined it. Even a discipline as inherently conservative as Christian theology would, in time, have to face this new challenge.

The marriage of Athens and Jerusalem could no longer be understood as the foundational act of global civilisation. After all, the very globalisation that from a Western perspective appears as the completion of European destiny, whether as the emergence of a rational civilisation or as the prelude to the Kingdom of God, could, from a Chinese perspective, appear as the completion of another destiny entirely, one incubated in a long history of dynasties, each of which, thanks to the wisdom of Confucius, sought to resolve the tension between the secular and divine by letting it collapse into the person of a sage-emperor who, by ruling himself, rules us all. Although it is true the Chinese experienced defeat and humiliation at the hands of Europeans, it can hardly be expected that they would regard this as the end of the story. If the first Renaissance (which gave us Christian humanism) enthroned a specifically European ideal of civilisation, the second Renaissance (which gave us a new multi-cultural humanism) dethroned the ideal by revealing its relativity. True, nineteenth-century theologians often regarded accounts of Eastern religion, whether Hindu or Buddhist, Confucian or Taoist, just as their predecessors had habitually regarded Islam – as somehow 'pagan'. Even a theologian as liberal as F. D. Maurice, whose superb work on *The Religions of the World* (1846) emphasised what Christians needed to learn from other world religions (to be both less sectarian and more spiritual), still made the chief aim of his investigations the justification of Christian missionary activity. He highlighted everything that made these religions worthy of respect as proof they were ripe for conversion.

The discovery – or, as Schwab (1984) has it, the rediscovery – that people outside of Europe possessed a wisdom older and deeper than their own was disorienting for Christian theologians, who faced the alternative of retreating behind dogmatically fortified walls or of waving (like an Emerson or Thoreau) the white flag of one Unitarianism or the other. More interesting for our purposes are thinkers such as Coleridge, Arnold, Hare, Carlyle and Maurice, sometimes identified as the Broad Church movement, who sought to find a middle way between fundamentalist reaction, on the one hand, and the abandonment of Trinitarian principles, on the other (Sanders 1942). For them, the confrontation with the East reinforced the search for the Church Universal, a Christianity freed of sectarianism and thus more catholic than Roman Catholicism ever could be. That said, the Broad Church movement accomplished little towards an understanding of Eastern religion. As Edward Said argued (1978), colonial powers such as England and France were more likely to engage in belittling caricature when looking to the East than to seek wisdom.

Given that Germany emerged much later as a colonial power, it makes sense to consider primarily the work of German thinkers and philologists when taking up our theme.[1] The father of liberal theology in nineteenth-century England was Coleridge, a disciple of Schelling. Carlyle, Arnold and Julius Hare were equally close followers of German developments. To take an example, Carlyle's inclusion of a chapter on Mohammed in *On Heroes, Hero-Worship and the Heroic in History* (1840) can be understood as a gesture towards the Goethe of the *West–East Divan*. It is hardly surprising, then, that Max Müller, the one religious thinker in England to place the encounter with the East at the very centre of his concern, was a German by birth and education. I also regard it as significant that, before taking a position at Oxford, he had been a student of that very Schelling who inspired Coleridge.

Figures such as Schelling, Coleridge and Müller are exceptional of course, especially in the light of the conservative nature of theology as a discipline. Given the general obsession with orthodoxy, even Maurice was a radical. Instead of following his lead by open-mindedly highlighting the virtues of religions as varied as Islam and Buddhism, other theologians of the day (whether neo-Lutherans in Germany or the Oxford Tractarians in England) insisted on the uniqueness of Christianity. Christianity was accustomed to think of itself in a vacuum.

Such issues remain unresolved to this day, as we can see by taking a quick look at how the three most recent Catholic popes have positioned themselves in relation to non-Christian religion. In his encyclical *Fides et Ratio* (1998), John Paul II gestured expansively to the East, defining reason so capaciously that he could begin with the words 'in both East and West', while summoning as voices of reason the Veda and Avesta, Confucius and Lao-Tze, Tirthankara and Buddha. On this broadly ecumenical basis it was easy for him to assert that Christianity faces 'new tasks of inculturation'. In other words, it does not have to speak in a specifically European way. Eight years later, John Paul's successor Benedict XVI denied exactly this. In his Regensburg Address (2006) (which triggered riots throughout the Muslim world), he contrasted the irrationality of Islam with the rationality of Christianity, insisting that Christianity is by its very nature 'Greek' and that, because the New Testament was composed in Greek, other 'inculturations' are not possible. The language of inculturation is so peculiar as to suggest that Benedict was delivering a direct response to his predecessor (Lawrence 2008). European reason, Benedict explicitly asserted, is inculturation enough, for what does it mean if not a readiness to enter into dialogue? Benedict even spoke of the specifically European character of Christianity. He drew his evidence from Acts 16: 6–10, which recounts a 'dream' that Saint Paul had that convinced him to turn his back on Asia and to go to Greece instead, quite as if he had to go there to learn the basic rules of reason from the sages of Athens. In making such an argument, there is much that Benedict ignores. Dreams, of course, are irrational. And if Paul was sent to Greece, Thomas, a fellow disciple, was sent to India. But, above all else, the synthesis of Christianity and Greek reason was not completed until Aquinas, who made no secret of how much he owed Muslim philosophers such as Avicenna and Averroes. Reason for Aquinas meant Aristotle, whose texts had long since disappeared in Europe. If they had not been preserved in Baghdad and Córdoba, Aquinas would never have been given a chance to become Aquinas. That Benedict had made a mistake to fight so publicly for a specifically 'European' Christianity (even to the point of campaigning against Turkey's entry into the European community) became all too apparent when, after his resignation, the College of Cardinals solved the problem of inculturation by making the unprecedented move of going outside Europe altogether to find his successor. The selection of Francis II, both as an Argentinian and as a Jesuit, verifies the determination of church leaders to break through to a Christianity that is more than just European.

What the theological significance of this 'more than' might mean is an issue I will take up after first providing a quick indication of how oriental studies evolved throughout a nineteenth century that began early, starting with Anquetil's publication of the *Zend-Avesta* in 1776. That there was wisdom to be gained in the East was something that had always been in the air. Plotinus, the third-century founder of Neoplatonism, born and educated in Egypt, was steeped so fully in Persian and Indian philosophy that he attached himself to a military expedition for the sake of gaining first-hand knowledge of the East. The expedition was aborted, but the lure of the Orient lived on. Augustine, a century and a half after Plotinus, was initially drawn to the prophet Mani, who peddled a synthesis of Christianity, Zoroastrianism and Buddhism, a reminder that the European world was bigger before it got smaller. It was only after the rise of Islam in the seventh century that the image of the East shrivelled into the menacing aspect of the infidel, except, of course, where an Aquinas or an Eckhart chose dialogue over opposition. When Vasco da Gama reached India in 1498, the conditions were set for an extension of such dialogue even further. Nonetheless, a truly *inner* encounter between East and West had to await two nineteenth-century developments, the work of translation and the emergence of German Idealism.

Nineteenth-Century Oriental Studies and the Emergence of Max Müller

Until 1775, the intellectual heritage of the Orient was largely restricted to the Qur'an and related Islamic texts. Despite the fact that Islam is an Abrahamic religion that shares a common Semitic root with Christianity, it had for centuries primarily served Europe as the menacing face of the other. An exotic flourish was added in 1704 when Galland published the first part of his translation (from Arabic to French) of the *Thousand and One Nights*, a project he completed in 1717, which established the background for Montesquieu's *Persian Letters*, which appeared in 1721. Montesquieu (like Voltaire after him) was mostly concerned with using a caricature of oriental despotism as a foil for highlighting similar forms of despotism holding sway in Christian Europe. A century later, whole new worlds came into view, beginning with the decipherment, early in the nineteenth century, of hieroglyphics and cuneiform, combined with the mastery of the various scripts of ancient Persia and India. By mid-century, Sinologists were at work mastering the elaborate system of Chinese characters. At the end of the century, even Japanology emerged as a discrete discipline, a development that was greatly accelerated by Japan's defeat of Russia in 1905, a startling reminder that an Eastern land might be more than just a potential colony.

All of this began, as I have said, with Anquetil's translation of the Zoroastrian scripture *Zend-Avesta*. More important (certainly for German philosophy) were the fifty Upanishads that he translated into Latin, not from the original Sanskrit, but from a seventeenth-century Persian translation. Published in 1801–2 under the title *Oupnek'hat*, they left a lasting impression on Schopenhauer in particular, who regarded them as the most sacred of all texts. Others responded similarly to the *Bhagavad Gita*, which Charles Wilkins translated from Sanskrit into English in 1785. William Jones followed with a translation of *Shakuntala* (1789), an ancient Indian fable, and the *Laws of Manu* (1794). One could not mistake the metaphysical depth, spiritual sublimity and aesthetic beauty of all of these texts. Few could deny that European culture, with roots extending to Jerusalem and Athens, had found its match – or, as most were more inclined to say, its remote and long withheld origin. The thirst for origin was so great that even though most of these works were more or less contemporary with the writings of the Old Testament, they were imagined to be much older, stretching back as long as three thousand years before the birth of Christ.

This sudden display of interest in the ancient Orient had its dark side as evinced by the English conquest of Bengal in 1757 and the Napoleonic campaigns in Egypt at the end of the eighteenth century. The study of the East was deeply entangled in the history of Western imperialism. Edward Said (1978) was right to observe that the view of the 'Orient' was often cast into the negative to justify that history, following a procedure that was based less on empirical investigation of the broad spectrum of cultures that reach across the Eurasian continent than on a vapid play of binaries: where we are democratic, they must be despotic; where we are active, they must be passive; where we are rational, they must be irrational. This was certainly the dominant Christian response to the wisdom of the East, an explanation for why religions even as void of idols as Islam and Buddhism could quickly and easily be dismissed as 'pagan'. What is odd, however, is that Said had little or nothing to say about Hinduism, where the colonial caricatures seem – at first blush – more justified, not only by the cult of many multi-armed deities, but by the rigidity of the caste system, the deference to cows, the horror of child marriages and, above all, by the burning of widows on the funeral pyres of deceased husbands. To draw attention to such images is to be struck by the vigour with which Max Müller, the greatest orientalist of them all, chided the English for fixating on them, ignoring to their spiritual detriment the depths of the Indian soul.

Employed at Oxford, Müller was proudly German:

> A scholar who studies Sanskrit in Germany is supposed to be initiated in the deep and dark mysteries of ancient wisdom, and a man who has travelled in India, even if he has only discovered Calcutta, or Bombay, or Madras, is listened to like another Marco Polo.

In England a student of Sanskrit is generally considered a bore ... and runs the risk of producing a count-out. ([1883] 2007: 3)[2]

If the English were concerned with the question of how to administer the natives, unruly inhabitants of a dark and malaria-infested land, the Germans were intent on uncovering lost wisdom, seeking 'light' from the East. To this degree, Bernard Lewis's complaint (1982) that Said should not have ignored the history of German philology, which took place outside of the context of colonialism, has merit. Consider the general sweep of oriental studies in the nineteenth century. The first chairs for the study of Sanskrit and Chinese were established, it is true, in Paris (in 1814). England did not follow through with its first chair for Sanskrit for another twenty years. Meanwhile, under the guidance of Wilhelm von Humboldt, chairs in Sanskrit philology were established throughout the various German states: in Jena in 1817, Bonn in 1818, Würzburg and Berlin in 1821. Others quickly followed: Erlangen, Göttingen, Königsberg, Munich, Tübingen, Breslau, Leipzig and Marburg. By the 1850s, oriental studies had been institutionalised from Paris to Moscow, but above all in Germany. If the study of Chinese lagged behind the study of Sanskrit, the interest was still there. Abel Rémusat in Paris had a number of close readers, most of them German. August and Friedrich Schlegel joined Wilhelm Humboldt in deriving from Rémusat bold speculations about the difference between inflected and non-inflected languages. The philosopher Schelling drew from Rémusat in his portrayal of China as representing the form of a universal humanity (Schelling 1857: 521–68). If Sinology came late to Germany, it was first there that it flourished as a discipline. Oriental studies were largely a German affair (though the love affair such work spawned reached as far as the New England of Emerson, Thoreau and Whitman). When Max Müller accepted his position at Oxford University in 1850, it was German philology he brought with him. It was German philology that made possible the publication of the *Sacred Books of the East* (1879–1910), the fifty-volume set of English translations that Müller oversaw and that constituted the culmination not only of his own long and esteemed career, but of the combined philological effort of nineteenth-century orientalists in Germany and throughout Europe.

Müller is central to our theme, standing at the crossroads not only between Germany and England, but between philosophy and philology. It was Schelling who had encouraged the then twenty-one-year-old Müller to embark upon the translation of the Upanishads and the entire Rig Veda. His philological work always took place in a philosophical context. Indeed, it was no accident that he translated Kant's *Critique of Pure Reason* in addition to the Veda. Like Schopenhauer, he regarded them as parallel texts. That said, his primary guide always remained Schelling. Evidence for this is the consistency with which he derived language and religion from the same deep source, joining them so closely that he reconstructed the history of religion through etymology (primarily the etymology of the names of the gods). The origin as such he understood as the pre-linguistic intuition of the eternal. But in contrast to Schopenhauer, who set eternity apart from time as a place of escape, Müller followed Schelling in regarding eternity as the living source of time. Commonly accredited with creating the field of comparative religion, Müller was guided by the intuition that lies at the basis of the Upanishads, the identity of Brahman and Atman, or God and Soul. From this perspective, all of the various historical religions of the world could be regarded as corruptions of a primordial religious intuition first given form in ancient India. Traditional theism is a form of idolatry, just as any other. Gods external to the soul are mythological images of the one divinity that is soul as such. Not only did this idea guide his theoretical endeavours, it was the basis of his conviction that India, mired in idolatry and superstition, could be saved by the restoration of the spirit of the Upanishads. It was in this spirit that he joined the Tagore family in India to help create the Brahmo Samaj movement as a new religious alternative in India, a kind of Indian Unitarianism, that would be caste- and creed-free, and would realise the true spirit of Christianity precisely by realising the true spirit of the Upanishads (Müller 1876: 269–71). It was with this idea that Müller stepped forth as the most radical spokesman of the Broad Church movement. As we shall see, the vision he propounded is closely related to what Schelling called philosophical religion.

The Germanic Orient

If we are to understand why Germany played such a central role in oriental studies (Marchand 2009), we have to begin (and here the criticisms of Said are particularly apt) precisely with what kept them so long from embarking on imperialist adventures – the fact that Germany achieved unification first in 1871. With Fichte's *Addresses to the German Nation* (1808) ringing in their ears, Germans engaged themselves in a frantic search for self-identity. In a very interesting way, this search led them to India. One can get a glimpse of how this happened by starting with what may appear to be a purely academic discussion – and one with no plausible connection to the Orient – the heated debate about the relative merits of Shakespeare and Racine. To understand the passion with which German Romantics turned to Shakespeare to define their new aesthetics, it helps to recall the fight with Napoleon. The classical unities that Aristotle had defined in his *Poetics* and that Racine embodied in his plays were regarded as restrictive, just as the Napoleonic Code was restrictive. If the English saw in Shakespeare the lofty culmination of the Renaissance, the Germans saw a literary rebel who would let any number of actors walk across the stage, while weaving comic intrusions into even the most serious tragedy. The Classicism of the Renaissance was better represented by the Neoclassicism of Racine. Shakespeare, from the German point of view, was the first Romantic. Indeed, he was Gothic, a throwback to the Germanic Middle Ages. The Romantics, masters of *big* ideas, took joy in making such broad and sweeping connections, while challenging even the most basic understanding of history. On their view, the barbarian hordes who swept into Rome were courageous freedom fighters who brought down a repressive empire, enacting just revenge on Caesar's brief intrusion across the Rhine. If the rules of aesthetics meant nothing to the creative genius of Shakespeare, the Romantic imagination duplicated his brazenness by assimilating him to the image of angry Huns who smashed apart a classical antiquity that had grown rigid and repressive.

After the disclosure that the Classic had a Gothic underbelly, a second move became possible: the disclosure of Asia behind Europe. Consider one month in the life of Friedrich Schlegel, the father of German Romanticism. During March of 1808 he published *Über die Sprache und Weisheit der Indier*, his great contribution to orientalism. Within two weeks he and his wife converted (in a very public way) to Catholicism. With this highly symbolic act, Schlegel joined medieval Catholicism to the ancient wisdom of India, anticipating something that came later: the idea of an 'Aryan' wedding of Germany and ancient India. By mid-century this gave rise to perhaps the oddest juxtaposition of all, the intertwining of the ancient *Veda* with the *Nibelungenlied*. What was little more than a medieval fairy tale was now associated with the sublime wisdom of the Upanishads; India had become Germanic. *Incipit* Wagner.

The assimilation of the Indic into the medieval and Germanic began with Herder's preoccupation with the purity of origin, the basis for a philosophy of history rooted as much in the Bible as in Rousseau. Humanity was born in paradise – and was united by a shared language and a secure belief in the one, true God. Already in his early *Treatise on the Origin of Language* (1772), Herder had ventured the guess that original humanity arose in the East – and that language itself emerged spontaneously out of an attentive listening to the sounds of nature together with an attentive awareness of the differences between things, quite as if the mystery of the origin of language could be discerned in the practice of deep meditation, the art of restoring the purity of an empty but attentive mind, an art consistently cultivated throughout Asia. To this, Herder joined reflections about various oriental languages, reflections developed more fully in the *Outlines of the Philosophy of History of Man* (1785). It is in this latter work that he ventured the assertion that India was the origin from which all history flowed forth. He even located the Garden of Eden somewhere in the valleys of Kashmir, supported by the Tibetan myth of Shambhala.

All of this said, however, Herder resisted the move that a half a century later became a commonplace among German orientalists, the decision to *replace* the biblical account of origins with the oriental. Instead, he unified the two by completing an orientalist reading of the Bible. The result was *The Spirit of Hebrew Poetry* ([1782–3] 1833), one of Herder's most beautiful and compelling works, published in the years just before the *Outlines*. In the centre of the work we find an interpretation of the *Book of Job*, a text that is indeed infused with the spirit of the East. Depicted as a patriarch from the mysterious land of Uz, the lesson of detachment that Job learned so painfully is so recognisably 'Eastern' in spirit that Uz might well enough be what is now called Uzbekistan, where Buddhism once reigned. But Herder himself had no need for this move. He was not tempted to push the setting eastward for the simple reason that he discerned already in the spirit of ancient Hebrew everything that drew him to the Orient.

This is where Schlegel and others departed from Herder. The mythological arc that Schlegel followed stretched from India to Greece and developed with an imaginative capacity that, on his reading, was an expression of an inflected language. Because Hebrew is non-inflected, its culture is as little mythological as the Chinese (whose language is also not inflected). Schlegel had little interest in either culture. Unlike Herder, he had mastered Sanskrit – and had a sense for how it functioned as the origin of other Indo-European (soon to be called Indo-Germanic) languages. The opening page of *Über die Sprache und Weisheit der Indier* describes this linguistic connection while evoking the vision of far-reaching migrations linking Germany with far-away India (1808: 1). Although Schlegel was as little guilty as Herder of anything like the 'Aryan' racism that came later, his act of excising the Jews from his narrative did establish the framework within which the most problematic form of orientalism later developed.

Before taking up that development, I should mention another and far more salutary dimension of the Romantic vision that helped pave the way for what I regard as the true and lasting contribution of the wisdom of the East to Christian theology. The same fascination with origins that played itself out in the elevation of the Gothic over the Classical and of the Indian over the Semitic was also responsible for elevating the Greek component of Greco-Roman classicism over the Roman. Here too it was Friedrich Schlegel who led the way, having announced the rejuvenating power of Greek poetry long before he wrote about ancient India. The German search for national identity had begun with a dramatic turn to Greece. Just as the French and the English looked to the Roman model of imperial power, central administration and a universal conception of law, Germans, lacking unity, were drawn to the fractious tangle of city states that, until the emergence of Alexander the Great, defined Greece as Greece. If Western Europe was absorbed in the pursuit of power and money, Germany would follow Greece in giving birth to poetry and philosophy. Even when Goethe, Germany's greatest poet, celebrated modernity's entanglement with power by writing *Faust*, he gave priority to culture and spirit. Faust's transformation into a man of world-historical stature required a move through the Classical Walpurgis Night, and Goethe chose for its setting the Pharsalian Fields in Greece, where Julius Caesar, by defeating Pompey, pushed Greek antiquity into the shadows. Faust was regenerated in those shadows. His journey mirrored that of Homunculus, a Google-like mind enclosed in a glass jar whose quest for rejuvenation went deeper than anything Faust could conceive. True renewal took the form not of imperial self-assertion but of its opposite, what occurs when Homunculus shattered his glass walls against the hard shell of Galatea and surrendered his spirit to the sea, letting it recapitulate in flesh and blood the billion-year evolution of life from the watery depths. Goethe's *Faust*, the poetic symbol of Europe's entanglement in power, is centred on an act of surrender that is recognisably Taoist in spirit. For Homunculus, the doorway to life is death. The glass-walled solipsism of imperial power must be shattered. Behind the Hellenistic world of Alexander was an older world that the Germans (from Hölderlin to Nietzsche) linked with the figure of Dionysus, the god who knew how to die. In *The Poet's Vocation*, Hölderlin suggested that Dionysus, perhaps as Siva, had long ago danced to Greece from India. If it was the Orient that constituted the dark and hidden centre of Greek civilisation, it was presumably the Orient that, with the help of a Dionysian community of poets and philosophers, was meant to come back to life in Germany.

But what precisely *is* the wisdom of the East that was to carry with it the power of renewal? As we shall see, there were really two very different answers given to this question. The first was given by Schopenhauer, who found in Kant a way back to ancient India that was quick and direct, requiring little in the way of a detour through Greece. The second answer, which proved ultimately of far greater importance to Christian theology, was the answer given by Schelling who had first found in the Greeks the key for disclosing the true depth of an older Asian wisdom. What Greece had to offer was given (as Hölderlin and Nietzsche separately confirmed) in the name Dionysus, the wilderness god, nature as such caught in the act of creating and manifesting itself. For Schelling, nature was alive. By conceiving nature as itself having history, Schelling was able to understand history as having roots in nature. There is an exuberant Taoism alive in his thinking that is completely missing from Schopenhauer, who regarded nature only as a monstrosity.

Schopenhauer

> If one from Asia should ask me what Europe is, I would have to reply: it is the continent utterly possessed by the unheard-of and incredible delusion that the birth of man is his absolute beginning and that he is created out of nothing. (Schopenhauer [1851] 1973: 186)

Like Schelling, Schopenhauer had a profound sense of the Dionysian core of nature, but, unlike Schelling, he saw in it nothing positive. He identified it with the Kantian thing-in-itself and called it *will*, linking it to the blind striving of nature to give birth to itself. Unlike Schelling, he failed to recognise that the will to life is always also the will to awaken. 'Indifference', for Schelling, is not simply the weary resignation of the ascetic, for it has always already been in play in the indifference with which nature itself releases into the world the creative tensions of polarity. The same indifference, moreover, is the seed of consciousness and understanding. The understanding Word unfolds out of the dark irrationality of the will so that 'the understanding is really the will in will' (Schelling [1809] 2006: 28). Whereas Schelling sought the *mediation* of darkness and light, Schopenhauer sought their separation. His fundamental intuition was gnostic: one is either entangled in the dark world or freed from it. The ultimate goal is complete annihilation of the will.

Schopenhauer insisted on the 'Eastern' character of a vision that clashes with the Christian ethical pursuit of the Kingdom of God on this earth. While recognising a certain affinity with Christian mystics such as Francis of Assisi and Meister Eckhart (Schopenhauer [1818/44] 1966: 334–7), he identified more closely with gnostic and Manichaean impulses emanating from Persia. Even more decisively, he favoured ancient works 'composed in Sanskrit' (ibid. 387). At the same time, he faulted Protestant Christianity for returning to what he called 'Jewish optimism', the idea that the world of nature is best regarded as a creation, not of blind will, but of Divine Understanding. He found particularly repulsive the idea that each individual was created ex nihilo by God, given over to a fallen nature, with a 'one-life' opportunity of achieving salvation – an opportunity so improbable that most of humanity must be regarded as condemned to everlasting hell. In one of his popular essays, Schopenhauer drew attention to what he regarded as Protestant Christianity's catastrophic rejection of the old Catholic idea of Purgatory, which he depicted as a reasonable substitute for the 'natural doctrine of metempsychosis, a doctrine which is to a certain extent self-evident and which has therefore been in all ages accepted by virtually the entire human race with the exception of the Jews' ([1851] 1973: 185). To reject metempsychosis is to deny that we arise out of the darkness of nature. The horrific consequence is that, coming from God, we ourselves must bear full responsibility for whatever darkness we are entangled in. The result is an unbridgeable gulf between the elect and the damned. Christian compassion is nullified. The odd consequence of Christian optimism is a metaphysical rationalism (A is A and not B) that makes hell everlasting. It is a motif that later led Nietzsche to assert that vengeful *ressentiment* is the true heart of Christianity ([1887] 2000: 481–8).

Schopenhauer's appropriation of Eastern religion was based on his sense that Christian asceticism did not go far enough. If suffering is evil, he hinted, it should at least play the positive function of purging the wilful pursuit of self-interest. Resignation restores our sense of connection to nature as a whole. Deep resignation prepares us to leave nature and existence behind altogether, for existence is itself nothing apart from the will to live.

While Schopenhauer cites the *Bhagavad Gita* as a Hindu text that rightly depicts life as eternal ([1818/44] 1966: 283–5), he concludes the first volume of *The World as Will and Representation* with a reference to the *Heart Sutra* of the Buddhists that is meant to show that even the eternally real, 'with all its suns and galaxies', can be intuited as – 'Nothing' (ibid. 412). More sublime than the idea of metempsychosis is the idea of this Nothing. Wisdom, then, is the recognition that the pure contemplative subject can release itself from entanglement in the will. Complete detachment (nirvana) is possible. Schopenhauer's pessimism is less severe than a Calvinism that optimistically anticipates eternal bliss, to be sure, but only for the elect who are spared the more common fate of eternal damnation:

> The Augustinian conception of the enormous number of sinners and the very small number of those who deserve eternal bliss, which is in itself a correct conception, is

also to be discovered in Brahmanism and Buddhism, where, however, the doctrine of metempsychosis robs it of its repellent character. (Ibid. 185)

What Schopenhauer derived from Eastern philosophy and religion was the hope that existence can be transcended in the end.

It was this viewpoint that informed his assessment of Western religion. Catholicism and Lutheranism, and certain sects within Islam, could all be praised for accommodating a mystical understanding missing in both Calvinism and Judaism, both of which he rejected outright. He ignored the mysticism of the Jewish Kabbalah by identifying Judaism with the religion of the Old Testament. Indeed, he assimilated the whole of Judaism to the doctrine of Creation, adding the argument that, by constituting a one-to-one relationship between the individual and God, it generated a vision of autonomous individuals forever incapable of dying into union with one another and into union with the creative will of nature. Enlightenment rationalism, destined to sap life and humanity out of the world, was, on his reading, the legacy of Jewish religion – a legacy that infected Christianity and Islam enough to make them lag behind the religions of the East.

But there too Schopenhauer saw important distinctions. He regarded Hinduism, for example, as having fallen far behind the original sublime spirit of the Upanishads, a spirit better preserved in Buddhism than in Hinduism. As for Confucianism, it was deemed too 'worldly' to merit his attention. He preferred Taoism for giving voice (in its pacifism) to the deep wisdom of resignation. At the same time, as a Gnostic, he balked at the idea that the Tao is fundamentally good, preferring the pessimism of a Buddhism that equates life with suffering.

The real strength of Buddhism, on Schopenhauer's understanding, is that it is accessible to secular reason, for his final word on religion was dismissive: 'faith and knowledge are totally different things' ([1851] 1973: 180). All the same, he did not identify knowledge with science. If Schleiermacher and Jacobi found in Kant's famous decision 'to deny *knowledge* in order to make room for faith' ([1781/7] 1998: Bxxx) a licence for a renewed fideism, Schopenhauer found in it a justification for cultivating a secularised Buddhism that could compensate for the naïve optimism of science. By stopping at the object of empirical investigation, science is left with a conception of nature that always conforms to the principle of sufficient reason. Problems can be discerned and fixed. Science gives itself over to the optimistic (and hence for Schopenhauer, the 'Jewish') religion of positivism by forgetting its inherent limit, that empirical knowledge is knowledge of the empirical alone. It fails to grasp the significance of Kant's recognition that on the far side of the object is the unknowable (and hence irrational) thing-in-itself. On the near side is the subject, which for Schopenhauer retains enough of a vision into the 'in-itself' to legitimate his declaration that reality is the irrational craving of an ever-hungry will. If positivistic atheism regards reality as the mechanical processes that science puts before us (atoms colliding with other atoms), it does so naïvely, for it derives its data solely from experience. As such, it is dream and illusion, phenomenal show void of any ground in actual reality. The world is *Maya*, the demonically spun web of deception.

Nature is not simply blind, it is cruel, as when it creates the fleeting enticement of female beauty, only to discard it once a new generation has been lured into the hellishness of life (Schopenhauer [1851] 1973: 81–2; [1818/44] 1966: 531–59). From the perspective of positivism, this hardly matters. Death will soon enough rescue us from the savage indifference of nature. For Schopenhauer, such easy rescue is impossible. Nothingness is always already the craving that generates existence. Nirvana can only be achieved in the form of a modification of the will, its completed indifference to whatever is. This is what Schelling alluded to as the understanding in the will, a deeply seated indifference that functions as origin, letting the ground of reality operate in its independence ([1809] 2006: 45). Within the will there is always already a deeper will that, resting in itself, wills nothing. Here Schopenhauer wavered, sensing a proximity to the Jewish optimism he abhorred, one that pronounced as 'good' all of the conditions of suffering humanity. Schopenhauer regarded this 'Jewish idea' as the ultimate insanity. To perceive life as yet one more incarnation of a blind will everlastingly hungry for incarnations is to entertain a vision of hell enough. But to introduce the idea of an all-powerful God who stepped out of his pre-creation nirvana to impose the awful weight of 'forever' on unsuspecting humanity is, Schopenhauer believed, something far worse. It substitutes for the innocently demonic action of blind will the morbid picture of a sadistic God who, knowing just what he is doing, creates for the pleasure of enacting 'justice', condemning anyone who, blinded by pain, refuses to echo the primordial 'it is good'.

Schopenhauer's critique of Judaism went much further. Against the sublime Christian command to 'love one's enemy', he discerned the Jewish *lex talionis* of an 'eye for an eye'. He castigated the resort to genocide as an acceptable way of clearing entry into the 'Promised Land'. With such moves, he prepared the way for an Aryan Christianity that was itself open to violence as a way of tearing out its own Jewish root. In a recent book, *The Aryan Jesus*, Susannah Heschel tells the harrowing story of the theological work done under the umbrella of the *Institut zur Erforschung und Beseitigung des jüdischen Einflusse auf das deutsche kirkliche Leben* (2008: 67–105). Christian theologians under the guidance of the Hitler regime set out to divorce the New Testament from the Old Testament. If they were not inspired by Schopenhauer directly, they operated within a tradition he helped call into being, one that includes orientalists like Paul Deussen (the boyhood friend of Nietzsche), Adolf Deissman (the author, in 1908, of *Licht vom Osten*), Paul Lagarde (the virulent anti-Semite) and, eventually, Friedrich Delitzsch, whose *Die grosse Täuschung* (1921) proposed the idea that the entire Old Testament was a deceptive ruse. While these were authors who relied on meticulous scholarship to show, for instance, that many of the Old Testament narratives had roots in Assyria, Schopenhauer's own contribution was simple and fanciful. To render plausible his assertion that 'the New Testament must be of Indian origin' ([1851] 1973: 190), he considered the possibility that the biblical flight to Egypt might have provided the young Jesus with an opportunity to engage in his own study of oriental texts (ibid. 191). His strategy, in other words, anticipated the attempt of Nazi theologians to bypass the Old Testament altogether, arguing that Christian love requires a deeper origin, a wellspring of absolute purity. That the search for such purity turned into genocide discloses the intensity of our collective need for wisdom. Envisioning Eastern wisdom as constituting a radical alternative to the self-understanding of the West had monstrous consequences. To count as wisdom, the wisdom of the East has to be integrated into that self-understanding, not placed against it. Just this was the project of Schelling.

Schelling (and Hegel)

Unlike Hegel, who inherited from Romanticism only the nationalism that made him want to define Christianity as 'German', Schelling inherited the love for origins as well. Hegel knew the importance of beginnings, it is true, but he had no love for them. Although he adopted from Herder the convention of beginning the philosophy of history in the East, he refused to romanticise it. He regarded only the Greek and the Germanic as worthy of celebration. Conceding that the ancient Upanishads uncovered the principle of civilisation by disclosing the sphere of universality as the One that gives birth to the all, Hegel went on to bemoan its emptiness – and the despotism of any culture that seeks to orient itself by it ([1837] 1975: 144–5). Indeed, by binding the principle of true religion to the ontological argument for God's existence ([1827] 1988, 181–9), he was able to exclude Oriental religion from the history of religion proper.[3] His goal was always self-consciously an absolute Eurocentrism that defines the entire movement towards globalisation in terms of a specifically European and Christian civilisation. Although his discussion of Eastern religion in his *Lectures on the Philosophy of Religion* was not only extensive but highly influential, its primary aim was to sever its connection from Christian civilisation. As such, he has little to contribute to the present discussion.

Nothing moved him to speak of the wisdom of the East. In this, he stood in sharp contrast to both Schelling and Schopenhauer. If Hegel understood the movement of history as the slow emergence of the modern state, ultimately the German state, Schelling understood the movement of history as the movement of spirit. He had a political philosophy, of course, but its central tenet was Augustinian: the purpose of the state is not to redeem humanity, but to protect human beings from their own most violent impulses with the ultimate aim of providing enough stability to make possible the life of the spirit. The state is a means, not an end. The only end of human life is to attain wisdom, the capacity to see in the world not only the evil in which it is mired, but the good towards which it strives. Schelling regarded this as eschatological hope – not the institutional structure of a human world to come. He had no use for the kind of teleological necessity that Hegel associated with the development of the modern state. Whereas Hegel's God is actuality through and through, Schelling's God is always fundamentally possibility.

Hegelian teleology is optimism in its most problematic guise, whether its utopian conclusion is understood as communism or as technological neoliberalism. Both ideals justify the abolition (oftentimes bloody) of everything that binds human beings to earth and place. From this perspective, oriental quietism, which could be understood as prudent caution, is instead an impediment to progress.

Unlike teleology, eschatological hope points beyond power. For Schelling, the free renunciation of power stands not only in the centre of Christianity, but at the centre of religion as such (1858: 193–8). As akin as it is to Schopenhauerian resignation, it does not end in gnostic denial of the world. From the eschatological point of view of the beyond, the horrific melts into death, leaving birth as the renewed opportunity to get things right. In this way, he was far from being averse to Jewish 'optimism' – but emphatically not in the form of a political utopianism. Wisdom belongs to nature rather than mind. Purposiveness grows wildly – 'without purpose'. Schelling's eschatological hope (the formless beyond) thus differs profoundly from the teleological certainty (the closed form of reason) that generates ideological fervour. It renders comprehensible a version of Eastern wisdom that is anything but weary resignation. In the spirit of Saint Paul, Schelling wove Jewish and non-Jewish religion into a coherent narrative. Like Herder, he began with the recognition within Judaism of hidden mythology (the spirit of poetry). A spirit that hovers over the primordial waters is something far different than an absolute mind that has nothing as its limit. Schopenhauer's depiction of the 'Jewish idea' was caricature: his creator God lacked a ground in nature. Schelling's was tied to the mythological process as it unfolded in the widest variety of cultures. The mystery religion of the Greeks was the resurgence of the very spirit that brought forth the Upanishads from the ancient Vedas. Its foundational insight was compatible with Semitic monotheism.

Schelling had uncovered the key to this conception while still an adolescent. In opposition to Kant, who understood intuition as turned either towards a sensible object or a mathematical form, Schelling recognised that the very existence of critical philosophy requires a purely intellectual intuition, one turned towards itself alone. The idolatry of image is undone only on the basis of an intuition that precedes and makes possible the imagination. For the imagination to spring into life, one must draw from a deeper intuition that is disentangled from every image. Schopenhauer's unsolved problem here has its solution. The 'nothing' that negates itself as nothing by the frenzy with which it wills embodiment (as expressed in the creative production of images) is itself rooted in a self-abiding emptiness that has nothing outside itself to seek. What the very young Schelling called intellectual intuition is what Eastern adepts seek in the practice of meditation.

The first fruit of Schelling's own practice was a detailed and comprehensive philosophy of nature that discerned, within the darkness of blind will, a highly structured movement of principles. One who intuits well discerns in the act of simple breathing the systole and diastole of a nothing that (to use a phrase from Max Müller's translation of the *Katha Upanishad*) is simultaneously 'smaller than small and greater than great' (Müller [1884] 1962: 11). This extends from the negative and positive poles of the electro-magnetic forces that underlie the most elementary chemical processes all the way up to the interplay of light (the entropy of an expanding universe) with gravity (the density of all that collapses into itself). While anticipating Schopenhauer's identity of nature with will, Schelling did not define that will as inherently irrational. If Schopenhauer's response to science was to oppose it to the irrationality and essential absurdity of existence as such, Schelling regarded scientific (dead, mechanical) reason as itself irrationally truncated, oblivious of the way causal connection presupposes prior identity. Science itself is Schopenhauerian to the degree that it assumes the contingency of nature while interpreting time as entropy. Assuming the irrationality of reality as such, it turns reason into an instrument with which to fix a world always on the verge of catastrophe. In contrast, Schelling's fundamental intuition is Taoist: the recognition that precisely a world in flux is a world in order. Whereas many of his contemporaries turned to the East to find the irrational complement of Western rationality, seeking, for instance, yogis who perform miracles to help fill the vacuum of a vanquished Catholic world once teeming with wonders and saints, Schelling discerned in the East the hidden face of reason, a nodal identity of Atman and Brahman so secure that death itself is its fulfilment, not its undoing.

From 1811 to 1827, Schelling wrote one version after another of what he called the *Ages of the World*, the first part of which was dedicated to the hidden past of the creator God. To penetrate such a deep past required an internal dialogue with the self that drew its inspiration from 'stories from the holy dawn of the world' ([1811] 1966: 19), by which Schelling had in mind primarily the Upanishads. Here 'nirvana' was unveiled not so much as the goal of the weary soul, but as the origin of the best in us:

> It is the calm bliss that, ecstatically oblivious of itself, is so filled and content that it has nothing to think about. It is the steady, quiet inwardness that takes joy in its own non-being. Its essence is nothing but grace, love and simplicity. It is the humanity in human beings, the divinity in God. (Ibid. 29–30)[4]

Although during the *Ages of the World* period, Schelling sought to secure such thoughts in reason and intellectual intuition, he ultimately came to regard them as the product of mythic revelation. It was then that he entered into a long, twenty-year engagement with the philological work that was being done throughout Europe. His subsequent lectures on the *Philosophie der Mythologie* and the *Philosophie der Offenbarung* contain the most sustained engagement with this work that has ever been accomplished. Not until the twentieth century was it appropriated by Christian theology. Although Schopenhauer and Nietzsche inspire those who seek in the wisdom of the East an alternative to Christianity that is spiritually satisfying while nonetheless compatible with secular reason, Schelling inspires those who look to the wisdom of the East for a confirmation of the most sublime wisdom of the West.

Schelling's emphatic non-sectarianism accounts for the theological liberalism of Max Müller, alive in the project of comparative religion. As indicated by the names of Martin Buber and Gershom Scholem, it had important consequences for Jewish as well as Christian thinking. Frithjof Schuon and Seyyed Hossein Nasr are two Muslim thinkers who have worked in the same vein. Sri Aurobindo in India and Kitarō Nishida and Keiji Nishitani in Japan showed the possibility of genuine dialogue between East and West, something that, in the wake of Edward Said, contemporary religious scholars tend to overlook when they complain that the entire project of nineteenth-century philology was a way of avoiding dialogue by privileging written texts over discourse with living representatives of ancient traditions. Against this widespread point of view, I cite Müller's translation of Buddhist texts such as the *Heart Sutra*, which he issued in fully acknowledged collaboration with Bunyiu Nanjio and Kenjiu Kasawara from the Shin Buddhist sect in Japan, a collaboration that gave rise to the Kyoto School.[5] Religion completes itself in an intuition that breaks loose from sectarian closure. This is the lesson of Schelling, who, in contrast to Schopenhauer, never played a newly conceived 'Aryan' Christianity off against Judaism. Both were simply developments of religion as such, which arises in the deeply seated intuition that the ultimate origin of reality, although it is certainly not 'mind', is just as certainly not 'chaos' – the empty heart of wisdom lies deeper still.

The open and, in the best sense of the word, *liberal* spirit that Schelling brought to Christianity has a number of notable markers, starting with Max Müller's inaugural Gifford lecture of 1884, 'What Can India Teach Us?', a lecture so generous in its conception that more Orthodox theologians campaigned to put a stop to the lecture series. If they failed, it was due to Müller's enormous popularity, the widespread perception that he had opened the window to much-needed change. Credited with founding the discipline of comparative religion, Müller's name can be linked with the double sense of Christian universalism that became an ever more prominent theme throughout the twentieth century: first, the idea that any religion, including non-Christian ones, can lead to salvation; second, the idea that hell must be purgatory in disguise, in other words, the idea that all souls may be destined for salvation so that at the end of time Satan and Christ would once again stand as brothers. The title of Hans Urs von Balthasar's little treatise, *Dare We Hope 'That All Men Be Saved'?* ([1986] 1988), is indicative of what has been a dramatic turn in twentieth-century Christian theology in general. Schelling's Church of John (a vision of an eschatologically completed Christianity) looms on the horizon once the Buddhist Bodhisattva vow to renounce salvation until all sentient beings are saved is recognised as embodying the highest aspiration of Christianity.

Conclusion

'Detachment', Krishna calls it, when instructing Arjuna in the *Bhagavad Gita*. 'Releasement', the capacity to let things be, is the parallel theme in the *Tao Te Ching*. For

Buddhists, it is the identity of form and emptiness. Wisdom, in other words, is much the same as what Socrates in the *Phaedo* indicated it must be: learning how to die – emptying the mind of what one thinks one knows.

There are those who discern a disturbing lack of consistency in what they assume must be the 'doctrine' of a work like the *Bhagavad Gita*. Like the baffled Arjuna, they find themselves asking, 'well, which is it? A life of contemplation or a life of action?' Krishna's response was to say in effect, 'it depends on who you are and the nature of your calling'. It is precisely this aspect of the text that makes it so important to the project of comparative religion. By developing a system of different 'yogas', each suitable for a different kind of character, it undercuts the dogmatic conception of religion. Schopenhauer was thus wrong to assume that the whole of Judaism is constituted by the single thought of 'creation out of nothingness' and that out of that thought consequences can be derived that he could rightly critique. The reduction of religion to ideology makes no sense when viewed through the complex lens of the *Gita*. There are those who worship images, but they can be found in any religion – and image worshippers will always disagree about which image is worth venerating. In contrast, saints are never at variance, regardless of which religion they were instructed in, for what saint mistakes God for an image? Mystical Jews stand closer to mystical Muslims or Hindus than any one of them stand to other members of their own sect.

Religion is pluralistic insofar as it resists the natural tendency towards idolatry. This is the spirit that enabled Schelling to show not only that each person of the Christian Trinity was fully and completely present in each of the major mythological traditions of Eurasia, but also that the impersonal Godhead, of interest to the mystic of any tradition, is equally present as well, yielding a truth so comprehensive that a thoughtful atheist could easily enough find a place beside the theist and the pantheist. The liberality of this vision, which we can identify with civilisation, is of course precarious. The tendency towards idolatry – and all sectarianism is idolatrous – is real. Civilisation can be held together as little by a deity as by a set of rules. It always has to be reconstituted. In the Oriental Renaissance, Christianity encountered both a threat and the possibility of reinvigoration. The encounter with Eastern wisdom, by stripping Christianity of its own tendency towards exclusion, opened up the possibility for Christianity to become Christian. The stranger I carry within myself is not set free until I recognise him in the face of the stranger who stands outside of myself. For this reason, religion cannot complete itself as religion without the help of comparative religion. The first contribution of the 'wisdom of the East' to Christian theology is given in the simple recognition that one does not have to be a Christian in order to be saved.

In the last decade of his life, Max Müller helped organise the 1893 Parliament of the World's Religions, which was held in Chicago. Unable to attend the conference, he sent Vivekananda, his Hindu friend, to represent him. The hard work of a century culminated in the appearance on a public stage of the foreign holy man. The cult of Aryanism, and the bloodshed it engendered, was not the only consequence of oriental philology. But it too had its place. Arjuna, who learned from Krishna that we are all, and in a most literal sense, brothers and sisters, was told to pick up his sword and fight. What is to be acknowledged is not only the best part of humanity, but the whole of humanity. Mythology belongs to revelation, the Old Testament to the New, and the courage of the heretic to any vibrant orthodoxy. The task of religion is not to separate heaven from hell, but to find a way of bringing them together. Hell must be made to serve its purpose: the revelation of a divinity that peers beyond good and evil into a ground of indifference that is itself a good of an entirely different order, one that can stomach the savage and painful side of finitude.

The encounter with the East forced Christian theologians to extend the ecumenical idea beyond Christianity itself. Christians, in their tendency to exclusivism, had to be put to shame by the Bodhisattva Vow of the Buddhists, the refusal to give up on life in this world until every sentient being, whether human or animal, is saved. Christians must indeed (just as Nietzsche said) overcome the spirit of vengefulness that makes them cling to the doctrine of eternal hell. Balthasar was (among other things) a Schelling scholar, just as Walter Kasper, the former head of the Pontifical Council for Promoting Christian Unity, was a Schelling scholar. The same can be said for a long range of thinkers from Paul Tillich to Jürgen Moltmann, and from Rudolf Bultmann to Karl Rahner. The recognition that a Christian must pray for universal salvation is the thought they all laboured to make clear.

The wisdom of the East was hardly new. Gregory of Nyssa had nurtured the hope for universal salvation in the generation that immediately preceded Saint Augustine. Eastern Orthodox Christianity always kept the thought alive. The world was big before it grew small. What the wisdom of the East teaches is the hope that what now is small (globalised neoliberalism) might once again grow large. The task of religion, and here the abyss between East and West is bridged, is to find a way to grow open the heart. The world is, in very many respects, just as hellish as Schopenhauer suggested it is. But salvation is not escape. It is in this world that we are to find meaning.

Paul Tillich was perhaps the greatest of the Schelling-inspired theologians. His theological dissertation ([1912] 1974) bore the title *Mysticism and Guilt-Consciousness in Schelling's Philosophical Development*. As the young Tillich conceived it, Schelling understood that Christianity represents the ideal synthesis of ethical Judaism and mystical paganism. After a stay of several months in Japan, a much older Tillich came to see that Christianity, by clinging to the idea that the Kingdom of God would be the actual outcome of history, is always more ethical than mystical. As such, it was held back from its own deepest insight, what Schelling had recognised as the true Christ in Christ, his *renunciation* of the kingdom, his surrender to the Father. After the experience of two world wars, Tillich had grown weary of Christian righteousness, particularly in its secularised forms, the cult of the nation-state, and the dreams of international communism and globalised capitalism. The self-righteous certitude that idealism will suffice to fix the world and relieve humanity of its sufferings is the source of as much evil as good. Teleological closure must be broken open by a deeper intuition, one that accords to the Taoist spirit at the bottom of every religion, a trust in a purposefulness that shows itself *only* when we let go of purpose. Religion and philosophy join together in Socratic insight, the actual knowing of our unknowing. The intuition that loosens the grip on things, letting meaning emerge as the miracle it is, does not hide away the abyss of death. Instead, it flows out of it.

Notes

1. Bernard Lewis (1982) initiated a very heated exchange with Edward Said (Said and Grabar 1982) in the *New York Review of Books* by emphasising that Said had ignored oriental studies as it was carried out in Germany, a country without an empire until the very end of the nineteenth century. What made the omission so serious, in Lewis's mind, is that Germany was the real centre of the entire enterprise.
2. Müller published this book in 1883, towards the end of his long career. It should not go without noting that, although the love he conveys for India is evident throughout this work, some of his views on India expressed in earlier years had been dismissive. One wonders whether, as a young German taking up a position in Oxford, he might have initially been inclined to speak the new language of colonialism.

3. Arvind Mandair (2006) tells this story in some detail, exposing the Hegelian (and thus Eurocentric) assumptions of New Left thinkers like Žižek and Badiou. In the process he renews Edward Said's defence of the integrity of the non-European, but on a non-secular basis that can take seriously the phenomenon of religion.
4. Schelling wrote this only shortly after the appearance of Friedrich Schlegel's *Über die Sprache und Weisheit der Indier* (1808). There is no question, then, that he was thinking explicitly of the Hindu principle of nirvana.
5. For this information, I am happy to acknowledge the response that David Keating of Memorial University of Newfoundland gave in September 2015 to a plenary address I gave on Philosophical Religion.

References

Balthasar, Hans Urs von [1986] (1988), *Dare We Hope 'That All Men Be Saved'?; With a 'Short Discourse on Hell'*, trans. David Kipp and Luther Krauth, San Francisco: Ignatius Press.
Benedict XVI (2006), *Faith, Reason and the University: Memories and Reflections (Regensburg Address)*, Vatican: Libreria Editrice Vaticana.
Carlyle, Thomas (1840), *On Heroes, Hero-Worship and the Heroic in History*, London: Chapman and Hall.
Hegel, G. W. F. [1837] (1975), *Lectures on the Philosophy of World History: Introduction*, trans. H. B. Nisbet, Cambridge: Cambridge University Press.
Hegel, G. W. F. [1827] (1988), *Lectures on the Philosophy of Religion: One Volume Edition: The Lectures of 1827*, trans. Robert F. Brown and J. M. Stewart, ed. Peter C. Hodgson, Los Angeles: University of California Press.
Herder, Johann Gottfried [1782–3] (1833), *The Spirit of Hebrew Poetry*, trans. James Marsh, Burlington, VT: Edward Smith.
Heschel, Susannah (2008), *The Aryan Jesus: Christian Theologians and the Bible in Nazi Germany*, Princeton: Princeton University Press.
John Paul II (1998), *Fides et Ratio*, Vatican: Libreria Editrice Vaticana.
Kant, Immanuel [1781/7] (1998), *Critique of Pure Reason*, trans. Paul Guyer and Allen Wood, Cambridge: Cambridge University Press.
Lawrence, Joseph P. (2008), 'Rescuing Regensburg', in Kenneth L. Parker, Peter A. Huff and Michael J. G. Pahls (eds), *Tradition and Pluralism: Essays in Honor of William M. Shea*, Lanham: University Press of America, 284–311.
Lewis, Bernard (1982), 'The Question of Orientalism', *The New York Review of Books*, 24 June.
Mandair, Arvind (2006), 'Hegel's Excess: Indology, Historical Difference and the Post-Secular Turn of Theory', *Postcolonial Studies*, 9.1: 15–34.
Marchand, Suzanne L. (2009), *German Orientalism in the Age of Empire: Religion, Race, and Scholarship*, Cambridge: Cambridge University Press.
Maurice, F. D. (1846), *The Religions of the World*, London: Macmillan.
Müller, Friedrich Max (1876), *Chips from a German Workshop*, vol. 4: *Essays Chiefly on the Science of Language*, New York: Scribner, Armstrong.
Müller, Friedrich Max [1884] (1962), *The Upanishads: Part II*, New York: Dover.
Müller, Friedrich Max [1883] (2007), *India: What Can It Teach Us?*, New York: Cosimo Classics.
Müller, Friedrich Max and Bunyiu Nanjio (1881–4), *Buddhist Texts from Japan*, Oxford: Clarendon Press.
Nietzsche, Friedrich [1887] (2000), 'Genealogy of Morals', in *Basic Writings of Nietzsche*, trans. Walter Kaufman, New York: Random House, 437–599.
Said, Edward (1978), *Orientalism*, New York: Pantheon.
Said, Edward (1984), 'Foreword', in Raymond Schwab, *The Oriental Renaissance: Europe's Rediscovery of India and the East, 1680–1880*, trans. Gene Patterson-Black and Victor Reinking, New York: Columbia University Press, xi–xix.

Said, Edward and Oleg Grabar (1982), 'Orientalism: An Exchange', *The New York Review of Books*, 12 August.
Sanders, Charles Richard (1942), *Coleridge and the Broad Church Movement*, Durham, NC: Duke University Press.
Schelling, F. W. J. (1857), 'Philosophie der Mythologie. Zweiter Theil', in *Schellings Sämmtliche Werke*, vol. 12, ed. K. F. A. Schelling, Stuttgart-Augsberg: J. G. Cotta, 135–674.
Schelling, F. W. J. (1858), 'Philosophie der Offenbarung. Zweiter Theil', in *Schellings Sämmtliche Werke*, vol. 14, ed. K. F. A. Schelling, Stuttgart-Augsberg: J. G. Cotta, 3–334.
Schelling, F. W. J. [1811] (1966), *Die Weltalter Fragmente*, ed. Manfred Schröter, Munich: C. H. Beck'sche.
Schelling, F. W. J. [1809] (2006), *Philosophical Investigations into the Essence of Human Freedom*, trans. Jeff Love and Johannes Schmidt, Albany: State University of New York Press.
Schlegel, Friedrich (1808), *Über die Sprache und Weisheit der Indier*, Heidelberg: Mohr und Zimmer.
Schopenhauer, Arthur [1818/44] (1966), *The World as Will and Representation*, trans. E. Payne, New York: Dover.
Schopenhauer, Arthur [1851] (1973), 'On Religion', in *Essays and Aphorisms*, trans. R. J. Hollingdale, London: Penguin, 95–115.
Schwab, Raymond (1984), *The Oriental Renaissance: Europe's Rediscovery of India and the East, 1680–1880*, trans. Gene Patterson-Black and Victor Reinking, New York: Columbia University Press.
Tillich, Paul [1912] (1974), *Mysticism and Guilt-Consciousness in Schelling's Philosophical Development*, trans. Victor Nuovo, Cranberry, NJ: Associated University Presses.

15

Homiletics

Joshua Cockayne

The Pulpit and the Stage

In this chapter, I explore nineteenth-century perspectives on homiletics which draw on the metaphor of the church as a stage, and the sermon as a kind of performance. The focus of the chapter will be a comparison between Søren Kierkegaard's discussion of homiletics and a view of preaching which Kierkegaard repeatedly critiques in his writings, namely, that of the Danish Bishop, Jakob Peter Mynster. For Mynster, the sermon is a performance in which the preacher presents the truths of Christianity to the congregation with the purpose of edification and upbuilding. Kierkegaard offers a detailed critique of the 'preacher as performer' view in many places in his writing: such a perspective, he thinks, leads to a kind of sham in which the preacher lacks integrity, yet presents himself as one to be followed. In contrast to this, for Kierkegaard, whilst preaching does aim at engaging each individual through edification, the role of the preacher is that of a stage prompter and not that of a performer. The prompter does not offer himself as one with authority to demonstrate the truth, but rather, as one who provokes and reminds the individual of her lines before God.

Following this, I conclude by drawing some comparisons between Kierkegaard's homiletics and the homiletics of those writing as part of the Oxford Movement in nineteenth-century Britain. As we will see, there are certain points of congruence between the theology of preaching found in Tractarian writers such as John Henry Newman and what Kierkegaard writes about preaching. Both Newman and Kierkegaard claim that the sermon should not be understood in rationalist terms – that is, preaching is not predominantly a method of teaching doctrine or theology. Instead, both maintain the sermon should seek to transform the everyday lives of the congregation and increase their devotion to God. Despite these points of similarity, the predominant difference between Kierkegaard's homiletics and that of the Tractarians is found in their approaches to authority. The Oxford Movement sought to re-emphasise the authority of the church, so the sermon becomes one of the key methods of propagating Christian truth. For Kierkegaard, in contrast, the preacher has no authority and the individual must seek to experience God's presence as a single individual. As I will show, this differing approach to religious authority is reflected in the accounts of preaching which are developed.

The Preacher as Performer: Mynster's Homiletics

From a contemporary perspective, it is undoubtedly Kierkegaard who is remembered as the prominent contributor to nineteenth-century Danish theology. However, this is not a fair reflection on how this period would have been perceived from within. As Koch and Kornerup note, Bishop Jakob Peter Mynster (1775–1854) 'more than any other became the central and representative figure in Danish theology and ecclesiastical life in the first half of the nineteenth century' (1954: 6:141, translated in Thompson 2015: 195). Mynster's influence, as Tolstrup describes it (2009: 267), is as 'the architect behind the transformation from the State's Church to the People's Church'. Although the Danish Church had been officially separated from the Roman Catholic Church since 1536, the state enjoyed control over the running of the church until the writing of the 1849 constitution in which the authority was distributed to a public administration (Thompson 2015: 194). This change in structure of the church, which Mynster was instrumental in bringing about, was a movement inspired by Pietism and the emphasis on the faith of each individual member.[1] As Niels Thulstrup describes it, Mynster's importance to the nineteenth-century Danish Church lay in

> his activities as Church administrator, ecclesiastical politician, theological and edifying writer, and, in particular, preacher ... He was a bearer of tradition and an outstanding representative of a culture in which humanism and Christianity were united, a culture that was going into decline. (1984: 32)

Those familiar with Kierkegaard's writings will be familiar with Mynster as a figure of critique and ridicule,[2] yet equally someone for whom Kierkegaard had a great deal of admiration.[3] We know that Kierkegaard was made to read Mynster's sermons as a child by his father (Thompson 2015: 198) and continued to count them amongst his devotional readings (Pattison 2012: 172). Moreover, before becoming Bishop of Zealand, Mynster was a parish priest in the church attended by the Kierkegaard family, and confirmed Søren and his older brother Peter Christian (Thulstrup 1984: 22). So, Kierkegaard was very familiar with Mynster's preaching and his approach to homiletics.

Much of what Kierkegaard writes about homiletics can be seen as a reaction to the practice of preaching in nineteenth-century Copenhagen, and it is often Mynster who bears the brunt of these critiques.[4] However, as we will see, it is possible to read both Mynster's and Kierkegaard's contributions to the discussion of preaching as attempts to address the challenge of modernity which the nineteenth-century church in Denmark faced. The influence of Enlightenment rationalist thought on Danish culture resulted in a closely connected church and academy; many of the senior figures in the church were former or current theologians and professors at the University of Copenhagen. The challenge, then, was to demonstrate how Christianity and rationalist philosophy were related and to make the case for the importance of Christianity in an increasingly secular environment. There are some striking similarities in the way that both Kierkegaard and Mynster approach this challenge, despite their disagreements. As George Pattison notes:

> Even if, from Kierkegaard's point of view, Mynster had never grasped the gravity of the contemporary challenge to Christianity, it is clear that, despite his conclusions being essentially optimistic, Mynster was in his own way aware that Christianity could not simply take its place and role for granted. It is also striking that he sees the Christian response as needing to restore the dimension of inwardness and the heart as a counter-move to a certain kind of philosophy and a tendency to substitute literature for warm, personal relations. (2012: 178)

Let us now consider Mynster's contribution to the study of preaching in more detail. Mynster was not only known for his influential preaching, he also contributed to the study of homiletics. Before being installed as Chaplain Vor Frue Kierke, Mynster wrote the treatise, *Remarks Concerning the Art of Preaching* [*Bemærkninger om den konst at prædike*] (1810), which was well received in Danish clerical circles (Pattison 2012: 173). Here, Mynster argues that the sermon should be regarded neither as a 'mission statement' (1852: 87, translated in Pattison 2012: 174), nor as an educational tool. Preaching ought not to aim at converting unbelievers or merely educating believers by engaging only their minds. For Mynster, the purpose of preaching is a kind of personal edification for those in the congregation. To achieve this, the preacher needs to engage not only a person's understanding (Mynster writes that 'thought is a light that illuminates all that is in a person' [1852: 90, translated in Pattison 2012: 175]) but also their hearts (he continues, 'if one is to address the understanding concerning religious and ethical matters, then the feeling for religion and the ethical must first live in the heart' [1852: 90, translated in Pattison 2012: 175]). As Pattison puts it, for Mynster, preaching 'is not primarily a matter of learning new information but of being confirmed in what is already known, something that simple but honest words can achieve as well as any' (2012: 173). Mynster clearly recognises the challenge to present Christianity in a way which is personally transformative and not merely something that is part of one's cultural identity. This response to an overly intellectualised Christian faith is something that he consistently addresses in his writings; for instance, in the preface to his devotional book *Observations on the Doctrines of Christian Faith* [*Betragtninger over de christelige Troslærdomme*], he writes:

> I have wanted to give benevolent readers a devotional book that is one in which reflection might satisfy not merely the understanding but speak to the whole disposition, consequently have an impact on feeling and will. But in doing this not merely that particular religious representation might be made clear and living, such as can take place in the usual collection of sermons and other writings for edification, but that the most important doctrines might be developed in a thorough-going coherence, and thus the particular representations be gathered into a whole, which – this was the author's desire and endeavour – might make a contribution towards the conveyance of a complete, thorough and efficacious knowledge of Christianity. (1846: iii–iv, translated in Thompson 2015: 196)

In response to the challenge posed by rationalism, Mynster recognises that rational thinking alone cannot arrive at the kind of truth with which Christianity is concerned (1852: 95). And, thus, the preacher should not aim at the development of rational argument which engages the intellect alone and neglects the importance of the heart and the conscience. However, in contrast to the kind of extreme separation of philosophy and Christianity which we find in places in Kierkegaard's writing (the pseudonymous author Johannes Climacus writes that 'Science and scholarship want to teach that becoming objective is the way, whereas Christianity teaches that the way is to become subjective' ([1846] 1992a: 130), for example), Mynster writes that truth 'demands the unscientific as well as the scientific' (1852: 96, translated in Pattison 2012: 176). So, for Mynster, whilst preaching must not be a merely academic pursuit, it is not entirely distinct from it in the way that we find in much of Kierkegaard's writings.

Rather than using argument to convince or persuade the congregation, Mynster saw the preacher's task as one of presenting truth to the individual ('to set forth the highest objects before the eyes of men, to open their eyes to see what is in front of them' [1852: 98, translated in Pattison 2012: 176]). The preacher's role is to make the object of preaching 'visible' and 'to invite each person to come and see it as it is' (1852: 99, translated in Pattison 2012: 176). For Mynster, the role of the preacher is to engage the individual in a kind of personal reflection, and there is a certain skill to this; it is notable that Mynster writes of the 'art' (*konst*) of preaching – preaching is something which the preacher must craft in a particular way to engage the individual. This is a craft which involves the preacher's use of 'similes and figurative words, his personifications, his manner of address, now to the whole company, now to each individual in particular, his frequent question . . .' (1852: 99–100, translated in Pattison 2012: 176). This picture of preaching is akin to a kind of performance. As Pattison describes it:

> Mynster insists the preaching is primarily a 'live' or 'performance' art. It is part of the regrettable assimilation of preaching to a more academic kind of discourse that the preacher organizes his material into a series of 'points', also evidenced by the growing custom for people to leave the service after the sermon and the fashion for printed sermons that readers can 'study' at leisure. But the written text of a sermon is 'only preparatory not the work itself.' . . . The 'live' speaker will adapt his words and ideas to his particular audience, and not simply give free rein to what he wants to say and how he wants to say it. (2012: 177, quoting Mynster 1852: 113)

What is lacking from the written presentation of the sermon is the kind of engagement between preacher and congregation which aims at showing truth. For Mynster, this is wrapped up in how the sermon is delivered and not just the content of what is written. Although Mynster describes preaching as a kind of performance, this is not a task which requires pretence (although, as we will see, this is precisely Kierkegaard's problem with him) – the preacher himself must be engaged in the task of preaching: "Tis not preaching the gospel but ourselves', Mynster writes. 'For my own part, I had rather direct five words point blank to the heart' (1852: 105, translated in Pattison 2012: 175). The preacher must be engaged personally in his task of preaching, yet, in contrast with Kierkegaard's repeated claims to be 'one without authority', for Mynster, 'the preacher is not ashamed either of his authority or of his "I" and Mynster's sermons duly make plentiful use of the "I" of one who, as an ordained pastor, is entitled to speak authoritatively in his own voice to his flock' (Pattison 2012: 189).

The Preacher as Stage Prompter: Kierkegaard's Homiletics

The idea of discussing Kierkegaard's homiletics might strike some as strange. Throughout his writings, Kierkegaard critiques the church and questions the very idea of the ordained pastor.[5] Thus, rather than giving a theology of ecclesiastical practice, Kierkegaard appears to be deeply sceptical of the whole enterprise. Furthermore, he repeatedly insists that his own religious writings are not sermons at all, but rather 'discourses'.[6] The implication appears to be that Kierkegaard's religious texts exist to be read in a certain way and not delivered by a pastor or someone who claims to have authority. As Kierkegaard puts this point in his journals:

> A Christian discourse deals to a certain extent with doubt – a sermon operates absolutely and solely on the basis of authority, that of Scripture and of Christ's apostles . . .

A sermon presupposes a pastor (ordination); a Christian discourse can be by a layman. (1999: VIII¹, A 6)

As well as this difference in the kind of authority associated with a sermon, there is also a difference in form between the discourse and the sermon. Whilst the sermons of Mynster were often reproduced in written form, as we have seen, for Mynster there is something lacking from the written discourse which can only be achieved through the performance of preaching. Kierkegaard, in contrast, lays emphasis on his writings as pieces of written text from which the reader is encouraged to 'read aloud, if possible' ([1851] 1990: 2).

In light of these issues, it may seem that Kierkegaard is not interested in giving a theology of preaching at all. Yet, this would be an oversimplification of the issues involved. We know, for instance, that, despite his criticism of preaching, Kierkegaard occasionally delivered some of his 'discourses' in church services.[7] So, whilst he clearly still regarded himself as a layman without authority, he occasionally delivered his discourses orally to a congregation. Additionally, as Sylvia Walsh notes in reference to Kierkegaard's 'Communion Discourses':

> In jotting down text for possible communion discourses in his journals, Kierkegaard sometimes refers to them as Friday sermons (*Fredags-Prædikener*) and sometimes as Friday discourses (*Fredags-Taler*). The identification of the communion addresses as discourses rather than sermons in his published works clearly reflects Kierkegaard's idiosyncratic view of them in conformity with the claim that he wrote and spoke without authority. (2011: 15)

To complicate matters further, as Pattison tells us (2012: 174), we know that Mynster saw no real difference between the sermon and the discourse. The word that is used for preaching by Mynster (*taler*) is the same word used by Kierkegaard to refer to his discourses. And, in praising a volume of Kierkegaard's discourses, Mynster writes that Kierkegaard's discourses really are sermons (ibid. 174). So it is far from clear that the distinction between discourse and sermon is as obvious as Kierkegaard makes out.

Central to Kierkegaard's refusal to call his discourses sermons is his scepticism about the authority of the established church. This is an issue which there will not be space to explore in detail here – the topic of this chapter is that of homiletics and not of ecclesiology. However, without going into Kierkegaard's views on ecclesiology in detail, we can see that there is still much in his writings that can inform the study of homiletics. Even for those who do not share Kierkegaard's scepticism of the established church, much of what he writes about preaching can help inform a contemporary study of homiletics.

A great deal of what Kierkegaard writes regarding preaching is framed negatively as criticism of his contemporaries in the Danish Lutheran Church. As we have seen, Kierkegaard clearly expresses some admiration for Mynster and valued much of his work; however, he is also very critical of Mynster's preaching in many places. For Mynster, preaching is a kind of performance art, and so we also find the metaphor of stage and performance in relation to preaching in many places in Kierkegaard's writings. However, unlike Mynster, Kierkegaard uses this analogy to critique existing views on preaching, rather than to endorse them. For instance, in a journal entry, Kierkegaard writes that,

> In paganism the theater was worship – in Christendom the churches have generally become the theater. How? In this way: it is pleasant, even enjoyable, to commune with

the highest once a week by way of the imagination. No more than that. And that actually has become the norm for sermons in Denmark. Hence the artistic distance – even in the most bungled sermons. (1999: IX, A 39)

This short passage illustrates much of what Kierkegaard finds troubling about the performative view. First, this kind of preaching makes Christianity into an act of enjoyment in which the sermon is part of a person's comfortable, everyday life and the true challenge of Christianity is never realised. The preacher's role in Christendom is to entertain, whereas, as we will see, for Kierkegaard the preacher's role ought to be to challenge and provoke the listener to exist as a single individual before God. Second, the sermon as an art of performance brings with it a kind of 'distance'. As I will explain in more detail shortly, Kierkegaard thinks that the preacher in Christendom is a kind of actor who performs for his congregation, but fails to live up to these standards himself. This kind of preacher is compared to a swimming coach who cannot swim, yet still stands at the side and shouts instructions to those in the pool (ibid. IX, A 198). I will consider each of these points in turn, before going on to consider what Kierkegaard suggests as an alternative model for homiletics.

First, then, one of the issues Kierkegaard raises with preaching in Christendom is that it fails to engage each individual in a manner which is personally transformative in the way that, he claims, Christianity requires. The importance of becoming a single individual before God is a theme which pervades Kierkegaard's entire authorship and not just his writing on preaching. For instance, in *The Sickness Unto Death*, the pseudonymous author Anti-Climacus writes: 'Christianity teaches that this individual human being – and thus every single individual human being, no matter whether man, woman, servant girl, cabinet minister, merchant, barber, student, or whatever – this individual human being exists *before God*' ([1849] 1980: 85). Additionally, in the *Point of View of My Work as an Author*, he writes that one of the primary aims of his authorship is this task of provoking others to realise their position as a single individual before God ([1859] 1998: 118). Problematically, most preaching fails to engage the congregation in this kind of reflection on their own existence before God. The result of the nationalised Lutheranism which Kierkegaard critiques is a lapsed and 'cheap' Christianity in which being a Christian can be combined easily with being a thief or an adulterer ([1851] 1990: 188–9).

One of the most striking discussions of how Kierkegaard thinks that preaching in Christendom has distorted true Christianity is in his parable of the preaching geese. Kierkegaard imagines a group of geese who gather every Sunday to hear one of the other geese preach:

The gist of the sermon was as follows: What a high destiny geese have, to what a high goal the creator – and every time this word was mentioned the geese curtsied and the ganders bowed their heads – had appointed geese. With the help of their wings they could fly away to distant regions, blessed regions, where they really had their homes, for here they were but aliens.

It was the same every Sunday. Thereafter the assemblage dispersed and each one waddled home to his family. And so to church again the next Sunday, and then home again – and that was the end of it. They flourished and grew fat, became plump and delicate – were eaten on St. Martin's Eve – and that was the end of it.

That was the end of it. Although the Sunday discourse was so very lofty, on Monday the geese would tell each other what had happened to one goose who had wanted to make serious use of the wings given by the creator and intended for the high goal set before it – what happened to it, what horrors it had to endure. The geese had a shrewd mutual understanding about this. But of course they did not talk about it on Sunday; that, after all, was not appropriate, for then, so they said, it would be obvious that our Sunday worship actually makes a fool of God and of ourselves. (1999: XI^2, A 210)

Just like the goose-preacher, Kierkegaard thinks that those who preach do attempt to provoke and challenge their hearers to take seriously the claims of Christianity, but for some reason, this never translates into transformative action. The sermon is a focus for entertaining the masses on a Sunday, but makes little difference to the individual come Monday morning. As Kierkegaard explains it, the culture of Christendom is one which

we play, allow our imagination to amuse itself in a quiet hour of Sunday daydreaming, and otherwise stay right where we are – and on Monday regard it as a proof of God's grace to get plump, fat, delicate, get layered with fat – that is, accumulate money, get to be somebody in the world, beget many children, be successful, etc. (Ibid. XI^2, A 210)

Whilst this is clearly a problem which is symptomatic of the culture as a whole, and not only as the result of poor preaching, Kierkegaard does suggest that the preacher has a specific role in counteracting or encouraging this 'fatty' kind of Christianity in which challenge is never actualised. In part, this problematic culture is down to the preacher's trivialising of the challenge of Christianity. For instance, Kierkegaard writes that 'Everywhere in life's trivialities they find analogies to the highest. Someone has had a loss, and presto! – the preacher refers to it as the Isaac whom Abraham *sacrifices*. What nonsense!' (ibid. VIII^1, A 629). To take another example, Anti-Climacus contends that the sermon-presentation encourages the congregation to be admirers of Christ and not imitators ([1850] 1991: 237). This results, Anti-Climacus tells us, from the preacher's use of observation:

The 'observation' does not come too close to either speaker or the listener; the observation very reliably guarantees that it will not become a matter of personal remarks . . . Whether or not you, the listener, do what is said does not concern me, and scarcely yourself; it is observation and at most it is a question of the extent to which the observation has satisfied you. (Ibid. 236)[8]

The preacher's use of observation encourages the kind of culture which is exemplified in the geese parable, namely, a church which is encouraged and entertained by the preacher's performance, but never takes seriously the challenge of Christianity. The preacher as an observer encourages an admiration for Christ, but fails to enable individuals to realise that Christ requires they be like him through imitation. As Anti-Climacus puts it, 'no admirer has ever wanted . . . to become just as poor, despised, insulted, mocked, and if possible even a little more' as Christ (ibid. 241). Kierkegaard thought that the view of preacher as a performer constructs a sham image of what it is to be a Christian and thus distorts the most challenging aspects of Scripture. To take another example, Kierkegaard remarks that when the book of Job is preached about, the preacher rushes too speedily to the resolution in which Job gets all things back. Kierkegaard writes that, 'This is why I prefer to preach about the preceding period' (1999: IX, A 191).[9]

So, one of the key problems Kierkegaard has with preaching as performance is the false view of Christianity which he thinks it constructs. Not only does the problem concern the congregation, however, but there is also a problem concerning the preacher himself. In his biography of Kierkegaard, Joakim Garff recounts a humorous episode in which Kierkegaard imagines replacing Mynster with a kind of music box to enact the sermon in his place; this would allow every church to benefit from Mynster's uplifting sermons, yet the benefit would be that 'there is nothing scandalous when a preaching machine does not practise what it preaches' ([2005] 2010: 655). This is a point Kierkegaard makes in many places in his writings, both in direct reference to Mynster, but also in his more general remarks concerning the act of preaching.

Again, the metaphor of performance and theatre is used to express Kierkegaard's concern with preaching; Anti-Climacus compares the preacher to an actor ([1850] 1991: 234–6), for example.[10] Whilst acting requires a kind of courage, Anti-Climacus remarks, there is something of an illusion about the actor's role; he becomes like someone else through the performance. The preacher, in contrast to this, cannot ever truly maintain this illusion of pretending to be someone he is not – even if no one else is watching, Anti-Climacus tells us, we know that 'the eye of the omniscient one is' (ibid. 235). Thus the preacher's 'task is: to be himself, and in a setting, God's house, which, all eyes and ears, requires only one thing of him – that he should be himself, be true' (ibid. 236). We can see, then, how Kierkegaard's use of performance imagery stands in contrast to Mynster's views. Whereas, for Mynster, preaching is an art of performance, for Kierkegaard, this is the very feature of preaching which he often finds so troublesome. And as we saw with the story of the music box as a replacement for Mynster's preaching, Kierkegaard also held that there was a problem with the preacher's own relationship to God. As Anti-Climacus describes this problem:

> It is a risk to preach, for as I go up into that holy place – whether the church is packed or as good as empty, whether I myself am aware of it or not, I have one listener more than can be seen, an invisible listener, God in heaven, whom I certainly cannot see but who truly can see me. This listener, he pays close attention to whether what I am saying is true, whether it is true in me, that is, he looks to see – and he can do that, because he is invisible, in a way that makes it impossible to be on one's guard against him – he looks to see whether my life expresses what I am saying. And although I do not have authority to commit anyone else, I have committed myself to every word I have said from the pulpit in the sermon – and God has heard it. Truly it is a risk to preach! (Ibid. 234)

What Anti-Climacus draws attention to here is that, through the act of preaching, the preacher distinguishes himself from the Christian masses. He puts himself forward as a single individual before God. And thus, preaching brings with it a kind of judgement that one is far from God and that one's life does not live up to the challenge of being a Christian. In this way, the act of preaching is an act of judgement – it is not that preaching gives one authority to judge others, but rather, Anti-Climacus tells us, the preacher puts himself in a place of judgement as God 'looks to see whether my life expresses what I am saying' (ibid. 234).

Although Kierkegaard is clearly critiquing Mynster, along with other members of the Danish established church, it is not clear that what he says is merely a personal attack. I think that Kierkegaard sets his sights higher than this. There is a way of reading

Kierkegaard's critique in more general terms: the problem with preaching in the way that Mynster conceives of it is a problem with authority in general. By placing oneself in a position of authority over others and by engaging in the act of preaching as performance, one puts oneself forward as someone to be followed. It is here that the difference between 'sermon' and 'discourse' becomes apparent. As Pattison puts it:

> Kierkegaard's discourses are consequently sermon-like works that are distinguished from sermons precisely by their lack of authority and by the absence of the authorial and authoritative 'I'. The work of reading the discourses is not that of deriving views and opinions second-hand from the authoritative author telling you what to think. The author, as Kierkegaard put it in one of the prefaces to the discourses, 'continually desires to be as one absent on a journey'. The aim is not to draw the reader into the fellowship of the Church ... but to leave the reader alone with God. (2012: 189, quoting Kierkegaard [1843] 1992b: 179)

According to Pattison, it is this difference in authority which can help to explain the prominence Kierkegaard gives to the written discourses read aloud, rather than spoken sermons given from a figure of authority. However, Kierkegaard's point can be generalised to homiletics in general, I think. To see this, let us consider some of Kierkegaard's positive remarks concerning the act of preaching.

As well as engaging in a comprehensive critique of the culture of Christendom and the failures of the preaching of his contemporaries, Kierkegaard does also make some positive claims about the subject in his writings.[11] The metaphor of performance and theatre which Kierkegaard uses to critique the act of preaching in Christendom is also helpful to see what he has to say positively about homiletics. In his 'Occasional Discourse on the Occasion of Confession', Kierkegaard sets aside a portion of the text to reflect on the very idea of a confession discourse. In order to avoid the kind of passive observation which Anti-Climacus described, Kierkegaard writes that 'the discourse must *decisively* require something of the listener ... that he as reader share the work with the one speaking' ([1847] 1993: 122). Note that although this passage is taken from a written discourse which is prefaced by Kierkegaard's commendation that the reader 'read aloud' (ibid. 5), the text is still presented in oral terms: Kierkegaard writes of the 'speaker' and the 'listener'. Although this may be connected to the kind of reading which Kierkegaard expects of his reader (namely, reading aloud), I think much of what is said can extend to spoken preaching.

In order to 'explain the relation between the speaker and the listener', Kierkegaard uses 'a metaphor drawn from the secular arts' (ibid. 123). He begins by making an observation regarding the relation between the actor and the stage prompter – the prompter wishes to be insignificant and overlooked and everyone's eyes are fixed on the actor. However, although the actor 'hears everything he has to say from that hidden one who sits and whispers', 'No one is so foolish as to regard the prompter as more important than the actor' (ibid. 134). Kierkegaard then goes on to apply this analogy to the act of preaching:

> Now forget the jest of art. Alas, when it comes to the religious discourse, many people are so foolish as they regard the speaker from a secular point of view and see him as an actor and see the audience as spectators who judge the artist. But this not the way it is, by no means. No, the speaker is the prompter; there are no spectators, because every listener should look inwardly to himself. The stage is eternity, and the listener, if he is

the true listener (and if he is not, it is his own fault), is standing before God through the discourse. The prompter whispers to the actor what he has to say, but the actor's rendition is the main thing, is the earnest jest of the art; the speaker whispers the words to the listener, but the main thing, the earnestness, is that the listener, with the help of the discourse and before God, in silence speaks in himself, with himself, to himself. The discourse is not spoken for the sake of the speaker, so that he may be praised or criticized, but the objective is the listener's rendition. (Ibid. 124)

We can see much of the previous critique of preaching as performance in what Kierkegaard says here. The model of the preacher entertaining the congregation as an actor entertaining his audience is fraught with the risks which I have outlined in more detail above. However, his remarks are not entirely critical here. In fact, the discussion of the preacher as a stage prompter provides us with an alternative model of homiletics which stands in stark contrast with Mynster's. Note, again, that whilst Kierkegaard presents this discourse in a written form, the metaphor of the stage prompter gives the impression that the discourse is to be spoken to the individual. Thus there is no reason why this metaphor cannot be extended to thinking more generally about homiletics, rather than narrowly focusing on what Kierkegaard describes as 'discourse'.[12]

The metaphor of preacher as stage prompter gives an entirely different perspective on the performance of preaching. Rather than observing the performance of another and looking to the preacher as example of faith, the individual in the congregation is the actor. Preaching should engage the individual in some way. Kierkegaard's confession discourse gives us some indication of what this might look like. Rather than presenting doctrine or making observation, Kierkegaard directs questions at each individual. For instance, he writes:

The discourse now asks you: *Are you living in such a way that you are conscious of being a single individual?* The question is not the inquisitive kind such as one asks about the individual with regard to distinction . . . No, it is the earnest question about what each person is according to his eternal destiny about what he is to be conscious of being, and when is this question more earnest than when before God he considers his life? (Ibid. 127)

In this way, just as the stage prompter is important and yet wants not to be noticed, the preacher should move the focus from his own observations and direct the focus to the individual in the congregation as actor on a stage.

Kierkegaard's metaphor also changes who the audience is in the act of preaching. The individual is not passive in the way that the performative view describes, but rather, she must realise that she is performing before the audience of God. As he describes it:

As soon as the religious address is viewed from the secular point of view . . . the speaker becomes an actor and the listeners become critical spectators; in that case the *religious* address is performed *secularly* before some people who are present, but God is not present any more than he is in the theater. The presence of God is the decisive element that changes everything. As soon as God is present, everyone has the task before God of paying attention to himself – the speaker during his speech has the task of paying attention to what he is saying, and the listener during the speech has the task of paying attention to how he is hearing, whether through the discourse he within himself is secretly speaking with God; otherwise the listeners would also have a task in common with God, so that God and the listeners would jointly check on the speaker and pass judgement on him. (Ibid. 125)

As with the earlier discussion of preaching, Kierkegaard suggests that preaching is an act of judgement. However, if it is the individual and not the preacher who is the performer, then it is the individual and not the preacher who is in the place of judgement. As we can see in the extract above, the most important feature of successful preaching is that the individual becomes aware of God's presence.[13] It is precisely this factor which Anti-Climacus uses to distinguish the admirer from the imitator in *Practice in Christianity*: whereas the admirer stands at a distance from Christ and avoids the challenge of coming close Christ in his abasement ([1850] 1991: 237–8), the imitator, the true Christian, experiences Christ in 'contemporaneity' (ibid. 246). As Anti-Climacus explains 'contemporaneity' earlier in the text, to experience Christ as contemporary is to experience Christ not merely as a historical figure, but also as a person whose presence is still with his believers in some way (ibid. 9).[14] In engaging with God's presence and in coming near to Christ as contemporary, transformative change is possible in the life of the individual. Unlike the waddling geese who listen but never fly, Kierkegaard's view of preaching is that it should remind the individual of God's presence, which brings with it the judgement that one is far from Christ. As he puts this in a journal entry, 'By becoming contemporary with Christ (the exemplar), you discover precisely that you don't resemble it at all. . . . From this it follows, then, that you really and truly learn what it is to take refuge in grace' (2011: 9). We can see how, on Kierkegaard's picture, the authority of the preacher becomes of very little importance. It is the presence of God which makes the difference in the life of the individual and thus, the preacher's aim is to neither teach nor entertain, but, rather, to prompt those who are gathered, or who read the discourses aloud, that they exist before God.

Much of my discussion has focused on Kierkegaard's homiletics and his critique of Bishop Mynster, which no doubt gives a fairly one-sided account. However, there is more in common between these two figures than is suggested by looking only at Kierkegaard's attacks on Christendom. Mynster clearly saw the challenge that contemporary culture posed to the Christian. In some ways, this is framed in similar terms to those used by Kierkegaard, as Thompson highlights that 'Mynster's life and writings display a complex relation to the objective and the subjective' (2015: 197). The challenge that the preacher faces, to present the truths of Christianity in a way which changes the lives and actions of individuals, is a challenge which both Mynster and Kierkegaard took seriously. Whilst both recognise that Christianity must respond to the challenges of culture and that the truths of Christianity must be realised inwardly by each individual, on the topic of homiletics there is disagreement on how to meet this challenge. For Mynster, the preacher's job is to reveal the truths of Christianity in a way which engages both the mind and the conscience. Preaching is therefore not an academic pursuit, but rather a kind of performance art which aims at engaging each individual in a personal way. In contrast to this, as we have seen, Kierkegaard is deeply sceptical of preaching as a performance; for Kierkegaard, Mynster 'had allowed the cultural forms of modernity to override those of Christianity' (ibid. 198). The speaker of the religious discourse is not a figure of authority or judgement, but rather, a person who provokes and prompts the individual to realise her existence before God. It is the presence of God alone which can change a person's actions.

Wider Perspectives on Preaching in the Nineteenth Century

By giving a detailed overview of just two views on homiletics, we have seen that the challenges faced by the nineteenth-century Danish Church forced both critics and clerics to reform and adapt their view on preaching to present Christianity as a living and transformative faith. Both Mynster and Kierkegaard attempt to provide a revised model of Christian homiletics to meet these challenges; although, as we have seen, their approaches are strikingly different. And though there is not scope for a detailed comparison, it is worth noting that the challenges faced by Mynster and Kierkegaard were not unique to nineteenth-century Danish Lutheranism. For instance, by briefly looking at the Oxford Movement in nineteenth-century Britain, we can see some parallels that reinforce this idea that views on preaching adapt to changes in culture.

Just as the Lutheran Church in Denmark was forced to respond to the challenges of modernity and the increasing secularisation of culture, those in the nineteenth-century Church of England faced a similar threat. One response to these challenges was developed in the Oxford or Tractarian Movement, initially formed around the scholar and priest John Keble and which came to include John Henry Newman, Richard Hurrell Froude, Henry Edward Manning and Edward Bouverie Pusey, amongst others. The Oxford Movement sought to call the church back to its catholic and apostolic roots, as well as to resist the political movements of the Whig and Radical politicians who wanted to subjugate or even abolish the established church (Brown and Nockles 2012: 1). As Stewart Brown and Peter Nockles describe it, the Oxford Movement

> proclaimed boldly that the Church of England represented the divine authority that society needed in order to meet the challenge of the spread of religious and political liberalism and unbelief and was a counterpoise to the growing influence of evangelical individualism with its emphasis on private judgment. In contrast to the latter, the movement's leaders promoted an unostentatious but deep spirituality which emphasised awe, obedience, reverence and the principle of reserve when communicating religious knowledge. The Tractarians placed a particular value on fasting, self-denial and asceticism. (Ibid. 2)

We can see that many of the challenges faced by the nineteenth-century Church of England were similar to those with which the Danish Church was confronted. In both cultures, the rise of secularisation, liberalism and unbelief had become an increasingly difficult challenge for the church to face. There are also some similarities in how these challenges were responded to. For instance, both Kierkegaard and Newman sought to refute the influence of rationalism on Christian thought by calling people to devotion and religious obedience.[15] However, it is clear that there are also many differences in approach: the kind of individualism which the Tractarians resisted is exemplified well by Kierkegaard's emphasis on the single individual before God. Moreover, the undermining of the church's authority which we find in Kierkegaard's writings is entirely contrary to the Tractarians' call to rediscover apostolic authority in the Church of England.

A notable similarity between those in the Oxford Movement and both Kierkegaard and Mynster is the emphasis on reforming the practice of preaching in the church in response to the challenge of modernism. We can see that many of the concerns which Mynster and Kierkegaard had with certain kinds of preaching were shared by those in the Oxford Movement. For example, as in Kierkegaard's writings, in Tractarian thought we see an emphasis on the inwardness of Christian faith and a defence of the claim that having faith is more than an assent to a set of rational doctrines. Furthermore, in agreement with both Kierkegaard and Mynster, the Tractarians gave the preacher a crucial role in the communication of faith. Newman, for instance, writes that the preacher must '*always* strive in every pulpit *so to* ... warn people that it is quite idle to pretend to faith and holiness, unless they show forth their inward principles by a pure disinterested upright line of conduct' (1891: 1:89). Similarly, Manning critiques many existing sermons as being 'too often general and unpractical' and goes on to write that:

> It is not enough that the matter of a sermon be true. It needs, so to speak, flesh and blood, human sympathy and the breath of life. The preacher must come down into the midst of his people: he must descend into the detail of every day; into the particulars of trial, the commonplace of duty, character, and personal experience. (1849: 79)

Many of those who preached during this period resist a kind of dry and overly academic teaching. As Robert H. Ellison summarises the Tractarian view, the preacher should aim 'not to bring the congregation to assent to a theological theory or set of propositions, but rather to persuade, indeed, to compel men and women to embark upon a spiritual course of action' (1998: 19). It is clear that this summary could equally be applied to the homiletic insights drawn by Kierkegaard.

However, there is much that separates the homiletics of those in the Oxford Movement from Kierkegaard's views on preaching. A key point of divergence between Kierkegaard and the Tractarians comes from their attitude to religious authority. We have seen that Kierkegaard repeatedly undermined the authority of the church – the requirement for having faith, according to Kierkegaard, is that a believer must be contemporary with Christ. Thus it is not by the church's authority or through the church's teaching that a person comes to faith, but rather, through each individual's own encounter with the person of Christ. In contrast to this, for Newman, the truth of Christianity is spread 'not as a system, not by books, not by argument, not by temporal power, but by the personal influence of such men as ... are at once teachers and patterns of it' ([1872] 1970: 91–2). And, hence, as Pattison puts it, for Newman,

> the burden of the sermon is precisely that the historical transmission of faith from person to person allows for and presupposes a fundamental analogy with the original communication of faith to the first apostles ... Newman's position presupposes that the individual's experience and judgement can, as it were, repose on what is given and experienced in the life of the Church. For Kierkegaard, however, the infallibility of the Church is just what we cannot presuppose.... Kierkegaard's call for contemporaneity is ... a way of saying that the individual's relation to the revelation of God in Jesus Christ must have a basis other than the mere fact of participation in the life of the Church. (2012: 196–7)

Clearly, there is much more to be said on the points of similarity and difference between the nineteenth-century Danish Church and the Oxford Movement in nineteenth-century Britain.[16] However, what we have seen is that the revision of the theology of homiletics is one of the key ways in which both of these traditions seek to respond to cultural challenges. Whilst the respective homiletics of these two periods of nineteenth-century theology are vastly different, in both Copenhagen and Oxford the threat which modernism and rationalism posed to the Christian faith forced a revision in this core practice of the church.

Conclusion

What has been a consistent theme throughout our consideration of nineteenth-century homiletics is that changes in culture call for changes in church practice. By looking at the role and purpose of the sermon, we have seen how those in the Danish Church sought to respond to the challenges of rationalism. All of the thinkers I have considered have held that the sermon ought to aim at transforming the actions of the individuals in a congregation and not merely their beliefs. However, Kierkegaard clearly stands out from many of the other thinkers in this period as someone who seeks not merely to revise our homiletics in response to an overly intellectualised Christendom, but rather, to entirely reform the practices of the established church and to undermine its authority. Even if we do not follow Kierkegaard's ecclesiology entirely, however, what he says regarding the sermon can be informative for homileticians. Kierkegaard's claim that it is only God who can transform lives, if true, means that preaching must primarily seek to engage those present with the presence of God. And whilst many thinkers here discussed would no doubt agree with this, the challenge with which we are left is to consider to what extent the preacher's authority facilitates or distracts from the experience of the transformative presence of God.

Notes

1. As Thulstrup notes (1984: 73), Mynster's role as the Bishop of Zealand would have given him the status of a first amongst equals.
2. Kierkegaard writes, for instance, that Mynster 'handles his office like a lawyer bureaucrat' (1999: IX, A 39) in a journal entry from 1848.
3. For instance, following his critique of the very concept of a Christian pastor, Kierkegaard writes: 'I regard Bishop Mynster very highly, and not simply because the memory of my father links me to him. No, M. expresses the purely human in the most masterful way I have ever seen' (1999: IX, A 240).
4. Although I focus almost entirely on the views of Mynster and Kierkegaard in this essay, Mynster is not the only target of Kierkegaard's attack on the church. In fact, much of Kierkegaard's disagreement is with Mynster's successor as Bishop, Hans Lassen Martensen, and occasionally, with the pastor and theologian, Nicolai Frederik Severin Grundtvig. It is the interaction between Kierkegaard and Mynster which I think can best inform a theology of homiletics. For a helpful overview of the impact of Mynster, Grundtvig and Martensen, see Thompson 2015.
5. See, for instance, Kierkegaard 1999: X^3, A 93. As Pattison puts this point, 'Kierkegaard puts the very idea of a Church as such up for question to the extent that what he effectively asks is, simply: Does Christianity actually need a Church?' (2012: 203). What follows from much of Kierkegaard's thought, as Pattison describes it, is the idea or the possibility of 'a kind of Christianity that was able to dispense with the Church' (ibid. 204).
6. For instance, Kierkegaard claims that the genre of his writings is '"discourses," not sermons, because its author does not have authority to *preach*' ([1843] 1992b: 5). He also writes that his collection of discourses 'in more than one respect are not, and thus for more than one reason are not called, *sermons*' ([1847] 1993: 215).
7. On the Communion Discourses, for instance, Kierkegaard tells us that 'Two of these discourses, which still lack something essential to be, and therefore are not called, sermons, were delivered in Frue Church' ([1848] 1995: 249).

8. This is a passage which is aimed at Mynster's preaching in particular: as Garff notes, this was one of the specific passages which sparked controversy between Mynster and Kierkegaard after the publishing of *Practice in Christianity*. Although Kierkegaard denied that the remarks on observation were aimed at Mynster, Mynster remained unconvinced ([2005] 2010: 655). Considering that one of the most widely read devotionals at the time was Mynster's *Observations on the Doctrines of Christian Faith* (1833), this accusation was hard for Kierkegaard to rebut (ibid. 655).

9. It is not merely the distortion of the challenge of Christianity which Kierkegaard remarks on. It is also the oversimplification of profound aspects of Christian doctrine. As Anti-Climacus puts this point, 'The way the pastor – and this is the same, only even more ridiculous – proves with three reasons that to pray is a bliss that "passes all understanding." What a priceless anti-climax – that something that passes all understanding – is proved by three reasons, which, if they do anything at all, presumably by no means passes all understanding. No, for that which passes all understanding – and for him who believes in it – three reasons mean no more than three bottles or three deer! – To go on, do you believe that a lover would ever think of conducting a defense of his being in love, that is, admit that to him it was not the absolute, unconditionally the absolute, but that he thought of it as being in a class with arguments against it and on that basis developed a defense; that is, do you believe that he could or would confess that he was not in love, inform against himself that he was not in love? And if someone were to suggest to a lover that he speak this way, do you not believe that the lover would consider him crazy; and if besides being in love he was also something of an observer, do you not think he would suspect that the person suggesting this to him had never known what love is or wanted him to betray and deny his love – by defending it? – Is it not obvious that the person who is really in love would never dream of wanting to prove it by three reasons, or to defend it, for he is something that is more than all reasons and any defense: he is in love. Anyone who does it is not in love; he merely pretends to be, and unfortunately – or fortunately – he is so stupid that he merely informs against himself as not being in love' ([1849] 1980: 103–4).

10. To take another example of this theatre imagery from Kierkegaard's journals: 'An actor portrays the man of nobility, the hero, the witness of the truth, and the like; he expresses all these noble, elevated, heroic feelings and thoughts. Would anyone deny that it would be jolting if the actor did this in person. But why is a pastor supposed to have the right to do this? The actor may also be a believer just like the rest of us and the pastor; to be sure, in Christendom we are all Christians, and yet our conformity is to the secular mentality. Why then is a pastor supposed to have the right to declaim in person all these wonderful virtues and continually create the confusion that he himself is the one who carries them out? A very logical mind could be tempted to make the following proposal: Completely abolish the pulpit and the clerical vestments, ordination, and the like. Arrange a little stage in the church, with the usual kind of curtain. There is no objection to using the organ if desired. A prelude is played. The curtain goes up, and "the pastor" comes out, or if a combined performance is wanted, several "pastors" come out in historical costumes. One of them would play the role of Luther. The stage director (incidentally, he could just as well be borrowed from the theater, since the Secretary for Ecclesiastical Affairs is also the Theater Secretary) has seen to the authenticity of the costume – he would declaim one of Luther's sermons. There would be some tears, of course, just as there are tears in the theater when a tragedy is presented; but for the most part crying in church is believed to be different from crying in the theater, which may well be true sometimes but as a rule is not true' (1999: X^3, A 93).

11. Kierkegaard also writes positively about specific sermons. For instance, in an entry from 1850, he writes: 'At vespers in Frelsers Kirke the other Sunday (it was my birthday) I heard a theological graduate, Clemmensen. It was a simple sermon, but the kind I like. In his sermon, probably without knowing it, he slipped in a bit of highly poetic beauty; following the Gospel text (John 16: 23–8), he had preached about life as a coming from the Father and a returning to the Father. Then came the usual part about life as a path. After that he quite effectively drew a picture of a father who sends his son into the world. Then he abandoned the metaphor for actuality, and

it became our relation to God. And then he said: And when at last, in the hour of death, the traveller's cloak is discarded and the staff laid down – *the child* goes in to the father. Superb! I wager that Clemmensen said that quite unwittingly; if he had thought about it he perhaps might even have preferred to say: the soul or the transfigured one or something similar. But no, "the child" – that is superb' (1999: X³, A 30).

12. It is also important to note that some of the features of Kierkegaard's discussion are features of the fact that the discourse is a discourse on the occasion of confession, and so not everything that is said can be assumed to extend to preaching more generally. Nevertheless, the analogy of the stage prompt contrasted with the preacher as an actor certainly seems to be relevant to much of the prior discussion.

13. Kierkegaard often stresses the importance of engaging with God's presence. For instance, in reference to preaching, he writes: 'I do not wish to be made a fool of in church. That is why I desire an empty church – then God is present, and for me at least that is more than enough' (1999: VIII¹, A 277). His discourses are often headed by short prayers which seek to make the individual aware of God's presence, for instance: 'You everywhere present One, when I was considering how I would speak and what I would say, you were present. When the single individual decided to go up into your house and went to it, you were present; but perhaps to him it was still not really being present – bless, then, our devotion that we all, each one individually, may in this hour apprehend your presence and that we are before you' (ibid. X, A 210).

14. What Kierkegaard means by 'contemporaneity' is not entirely clear. For two existing interpretations of this concept, see Stokes 2010; Cockayne 2017.

15. See Ferreira 1994 for a comparison of Newman's and Kierkegaard's accounts of faith.

16. See Pattison (2012: 194–8) for a more detailed comparison of Newman and Kierkegaard on this point.

References

Brown, Stewart J. and Peter B. Nockles (2012), *The Oxford Movement: Europe and the Wider World 1830–1930*, Cambridge: Cambridge University Press.

Cockayne, Joshua (2017), 'Contemporaneity and Communion: Kierkegaard on the Personal Presence of Christ', *British Journal for the History of Philosophy*, 25.1: 41–62.

Ellison, Robert H. (1998), *The Victorian Pulpit: Spoken and Written Sermons in Nineteenth-Century Britain*, Susquhenna, PA: Susquhenna University Press.

Ferreira, M. Jamie (1994), 'Leaps and Circles: Kierkegaard and Newman on Faith and Reason', *Religious Studies*, 30: 379–97.

Garff, Joakim [2005] (2010), *Søren Kierkegaard: A Biography*, trans. Bruce H. Kirmmse, Princeton: Princeton University Press.

Kierkegaard, Søren [1849] (1980), *The Sickness Unto Death*, ed. and trans. Howard V. Hong and Edna H. Hong, Princeton: Princeton University Press.

Kierkegaard, Søren [1851] (1990), *For Self-Examination and Judge for Yourself*, ed. and trans. Howard V. Hong and Edna H. Hong, Princeton: Princeton University Press.

Kierkegaard, Søren [1850] (1991), *Practice in Christianity*, ed. and trans. Howard V. Hong and Edna H. Hong, Princeton: Princeton University Press.

Kierkegaard, Søren [1846] (1992a), *Concluding Unscientific Postscript to* Philosophical Fragments, 2 vols, ed. and trans. Howard V. Hong and Edna H. Hong, Princeton: Princeton University Press.

Kierkegaard, Søren [1843] (1992b), *Eighteen Upbuilding Discourses*, ed. and trans. Howard V. Hong and Edna H. Hong, Princeton: Princeton University Press.

Kierkegaard, Søren [1847] (1993), *Upbuilding Discourses in Various Spirits*, trans. Howard V. Hong and Edna H. Hong, Princeton: Princeton University Press.

Kierkegaard, Søren [1848] (1995), *Christian Discourses and The Crisis and a Crisis in the Life of an Actress*, ed. and trans. Howard V. Hong and Edna H. Hong, Princeton: Princeton University Press.

Kierkegaard, Søren [1859] (1998), *The Point of View*, ed. and trans. Howard V. Hong and Edna H. Hong, Princeton: Princeton University Press.

Kierkegaard, Søren (1999), *Søren Kierkegaard's Journals and Papers*, 7 vols, 2nd edn, ed. and trans. Howard V. Hong and Edna H. Hong, assisted by Gregor Malantschuk, Bloomington: Indiana University Press.

Kierkegaard, Søren (2011), *Søren Kierkegaard's Journals and Notebooks Volume 5*, ed. Niels Jørgen Cappelørn et al., Princeton: Princeton University Press.

Koch, Hal and Bjørn Kornerup (eds) (1954), *Den Danske Kirkes Historie*, 7 vols, Copenhagen: Gyldendal.

Manning, Henry Edward (1849), *A Charge Delivered at the Ordinary Visitation of the Archdeaconry of Chichester in July, 1849*, London.

Mynster, Jakob Peter (1846), *Betragtninger over de christelige Troslærdomme*, Copenhagen: Deichmanns.

Mynster, Jakob Peter (1852), *Blandede Skrivter af Dr. J. P. Mynster*, 6 vols, Copenhagen: Gyldendal.

Newman, John Henry (1891), *Letters and Correspondence of John Henry Newman*, 2 vols, ed. Anne Mozley, London.

Newman, John Henry [1872] (1970), *University Sermons*, London: SPCK.

Pattison, George (2012), *Kierkegaard and the Theology of the Nineteenth Century*, Cambridge: Cambridge University Press.

Stokes, Patrick (2010), '"See For Your Self": Contemporaneity, Autopsy and Presence in Kierkegaard's Moral-Religious Psychology', *British Journal for the History of Philosophy*, 18.2: 297–319.

Thompson, Curtis L. (2015), 'Shapers of Kierkegaard's Danish Church: Mynster, Grundtvig, Martensen', in Jon Stewart (ed.), *A Companion to Kierkegaard*, Chichester: Wiley Blackwell, 193–206.

Thulstrup, Niels (1984), *Kierkegaard and the Church in Denmark*, Copenhagen: C. A. Reitzel.

Tolstrup, Christian Fink (2009), 'Jakob Peter Mynster: A Guiding Thread in Kierkegaard's Authorship?', in Jon Stewart (ed.), *Kierkegaard and His Danish Contemporaries, II: Theology*, London: Routledge, 267–87.

Walsh, Sylvia (2011), 'Introduction', in Søren Kierkegaard, *Discourses at the Communion on Fridays*, trans. Sylvia Walsh, Bloomington: Indiana University Press, 1–35.

16

Deification

Katya Tolstaya

Introduction: The Missing Link in Dostoevsky Studies

To most, nineteenth-century Russian Orthodox theology is known primarily through the novels of Fyodor Mikhailovich Dostoevsky (1821–81). Ever since their first publication, philosophers and theologians, as well as Dostoevsky scholars, have incessantly returned to the religious, anthropological and ethical issues raised therein. A number of images and figures from the novels have become particularly emblematic: for example, the idea that 'beauty will save the world' from the *Idiot* (1972–90: VIII:436),[1] the idea from *Crime and Punishment* and *The Brothers Karamazov* that 'if there is no God, everything is permitted', even murder (ibid. XIV:240),[2] and its counter-idea in *The Brothers Karamazov* that 'everybody is guilty for everybody else and I am the guiltiest of all' (ibid. XIV:65, 240).[3] Often scholars have implicitly or explicitly related these ideas to Russian Orthodoxy.

Since the *perestroika*, the field of Dostoevsky studies has become increasingly interested in the Christian motives in his oeuvre, particularly now that scholars from post-Soviet countries have joined the global discussion. In view of the post-Soviet religious revival, special attention has been given to the motif of spiritual eldership (*starchestvo*) found in *The Devils* and *The Brothers Karamazov*. Owing to the fact that *starchestvo* is associated with the doctrine and practice of deification (*theosis*) – one of the most fashionable theological *topoi* at the moment – these motifs of spiritual eldership and Orthodox mystical practice in Dostoevsky's work have now become central to the research field. In what follows, I look to a missing link in discussions of deification both in Dostoevsky research and in theological discourse generally: the idea of the unity of creation. I will argue this link is of core importance to both the study of nineteenth-century theology and scholarship on 'religion' in Dostoevsky.

First, I will sketch the reception and influence of hesychasm or Palamism in Russia during the nineteenth century. Second, I will consider the scholarship on Dostoevsky that finds traces of hesychasm in his novels where in fact it cannot be found. Third, I will focus on an element of hesychast spirituality that *can* be found in Dostoevsky's novels – more specifically in the figure of the elder Zosima from *The Brothers Karamazov* – that is, the idea of the unity of creation. Finally, I will begin to explore the unity of creation as the missing link in contemporary theological discourse on *theosis*. That is, it is not just Dostoevsky scholars but theologians at large who fail to establish a link between the hesychast tradition and the idea of the unity of creation. The main aim of this chapter is thus to rectify this lack in our understanding of Russian Orthodoxy in the nineteenth century.

Palamism in Russia: A Brief Sketch

Before looking at the reception of *theosis* in Dostoevsky, let us first briefly sketch the situation of its reception in Russia.

It took the Orthodox Church more than a thousand years to make *theosis* a dogma. The official doctrine of *theosis* began to be formed as a result of a number of early controversies,[4] and was then accepted as dogma by the local councils of Constantinople in 1347 and 1351. Its seeds are to be found in the First and Second General Councils, and for example in Athanasius' claim that 'God became man so that man might become God',[5] as well as in the teachings of the Cappadocian Fathers of the fourth century (Gregory of Nyssa and Basil the Great). The doctrine underwent a crucial development in Maximus the Confessor, and spread further as a form of mystical practice – hesychasm – from the late seventh century onward.

It was particularly due to the practices of the Byzantine monks from Mount Athos in the thirteenth and fourteenth centuries, and especially to one of the main representatives of the Athonine monasticism, Gregory Palamas, that hesychasm became widely known throughout the Eastern Orthodox world (Meyendorff 1959; cf. Lossky 2005; Mantzaridis [1963] 1984; and especially Williams 1999). The dogmas that were accepted at the local Constantinople councils of 1347 and 1351 were the result of the 'synthesis' formulated by Palamas of church tradition, the patristic legacy and the theotic practices of the previous centuries.

Scholarship is divided as to the question of the reception of 'Palamism' in Russia. On the one hand, some argue that 'Palamitic' ascetic writings like the *Hymns of Divine Love* by Symeon the New Theologian, the *Mirror* by Philip Monotropos from the end of the eleventh century and *The Ladder of Divine Ascent* of St John Climacus, written around 600, reached Moscow via other spiritual centres, like Kiev, Novgorod and Pskov, and so formed a constitutive part of Russian Orthodox spirituality (Paert 2010: 25). Mazour-Matusevich summarises the influence of this spirituality on Byzantium and then Russia as follows:

> The most important consequences of Palamas' victory were the absolutization of Hesychasm's influence within Byzantine society as well as rapid geographical propagation of the practice outside Byzantium proper. Palamas' teachings became fundamental not only in Byzantium's ecclesiastical but also its secular life. The latter is particularly important. Hesychasm began to realize and fulfil its universal potential ... its universal anthropological strategy. In other words, it began to apply its spiritual experience, initially limited to the monastic, to all aspects of human life and society. From this point on, the Hesychast movement also began to quickly spread into all countries of Byzantine influence, becoming the bond between the Eastern monks, their very identity, for centuries to come. (2014: 301; cf. Gavrilyuk 2013: 481)

On the other hand, Paert is more nuanced in her representation of the history of hesychasm in Russia. While noticing the popularity of the Slavonic translations of hesychast texts, the 'religious revival of the thirteenth and fourteenth century' (2010: 25), and the influence of Nil Sorskii (1433–1508) and Paisii Velichkovskii (1722–94), she observes 'a rising popularity of hesychast theology' only in the nineteenth century, in the face of 'the long-embedded prejudice against ... Gregory Palamas' (ibid. 104).

Even more rigorous is Kenworthy, who speaks of a total neglect of Palamas in Russia:

the theology of Gregory Palamas had fallen into complete neglect in prerevolutionary Russia; the revival of hesychast spirituality in nineteenth-century Russia was not accompanied or informed by a revival of Palamite theology, which was virtually unknown either in monastic circles or among Russian theologians. (2014: 98)[6]

From the above, it becomes clear that we should distinguish between (Palamitic) hesychasm – including the corpus of texts included in the Palamitic synthesis – and Palamism as the corpus of Palamas' own writings. It can be concluded with certainty that the former contributed to the formation of Russian Orthodox spirituality, or, more specifically, its attitude in contemplating God and his creation, at least from the fourteenth century onward. As far as the texts of Palamas himself go, it would require far more study of their theological-historical reception to identify precisely what Russian theologians seemed to object to.

The roots of contemporary fascination with *theosis* lie indeed in the (re)discovery of the Orthodox mystical tradition of hesychasm in late nineteenth-century Russian spirituality. The general perception of this revival is discernible in the following passage from Christine Worobec:

> Hesychasm was a 'mystical tradition based on monological prayer', such as the Jesus-Prayer, as well as on knowledge of mystical and ascetic texts based on the writings of the Athonite monk Gregory Palamas (1296–1359). Those texts were revived and revised in the 18th century by Paisii Velichkovskii. Monks who practiced hesychasm in the Russian revival [of the nineteenth century] became spiritual elders to other monks as well as the laity. The Optina Hermitage emerged as a major center of hesychasm and spiritual eldership. (2006: 336)

After the death of his three-year-old son Alyosha in 1878, and when his work on *The Brothers Karamazov* had already started, Dostoevsky visited the Optina Hermitage, the bulwark of Russian hesychast revival. In particular, the teachings of the elder Zosima, one of the main characters of the novel, and one of the few 'positive' characters in Dostoevsky's oeuvre, have been connected to hesychasm. A vivid example of this perception can be found in claims made repeatedly by Grillaert: 'Although there is in Zosima's discourse no explicit use of hesychastic terminology, there are some undeniable references to and echoes of the practice and spirituality of hesychasm throughout his teachings' (2011: 67; cf. 2008). In the following, I will argue that while Dostoevsky scholarship claims to find elements of hesychasm in Dostoevsky that are not to be found there, it ignores an important aspect of Orthodox spirituality that is in fact central to the teachings and the worldview of Zosima.

Absences of Hesychastic Practice in Dostoevsky

To see what it is that cannot be found in Dostoevsky, let me first briefly circumscribe what hesychasm actually involves. Theologically speaking, within Eastern Orthodox theology, deification is a soteriological consequence of the anthropological and ontological presuppositions of the doctrine of man as God's image and likeness (Meyendorff 1997).[7] In line with this doctrine, Eastern Orthodoxy emphasises the possibility of being one with and in God during one's earthly life. Nevertheless, it is precisely this focus on 'being' that qualifies any discourse on *theosis*. In the first place, deification is a practice and thereby belongs to the realm of existentiality:

> Divine life is a gift, but also a task which is to be accomplished by a free human effort. This polarity between the 'gift' and the 'task' is often expressed in terms of the distinction between the concepts of 'image' and 'likeness'. In Greek, the term *homoiōsis*, which corresponds to 'likeness' in Genesis 1: 26, suggests the idea of dynamic progress ('assimilation') and implies human freedom. (Meyendorff 1983: 139)

As already suggested above, the human person is able to achieve unity with God and thus acquires knowledge of God only in synergism – that is, in co-working with God. This makes for a dynamic view of the relation between God and the human person (Yannaras 1975). The human person as created by God forms a unity of spirit and matter. According to Palamas, man is at the centre of creation, and hierarchically – this echoes Gregory of Nyssa – above the angels, who only possess the spirit.

Hesychast synergism starts with the spiritual practice of overcoming passions through achieving humility, through fighting the passions through the intellect, and through constant repetition of the 'Jesus prayer', otherwise called the 'prayer of the heart': 'Lord, Jesus Christ, Son of God, have mercy upon me [a sinner].' This ascetic effort demands the whole person: 'when the hesychasts speak of drawing the intellect into the heart, then, they have in mind not only the achievement of a mental state of tranquillity and concentration, but a transformation that affects a person's whole being' (Bradshaw 2004: 231).

Hence, beginning from the idea that every action of Jesus Christ calls for imitation, hesychasts see Jesus's transfiguration on Mount Tabor as an ideal that can and should be achieved by any person. This transfiguration of a practitioner, deification, is the goal of hesychastic practice. Imitation of Christ is the way of returning to the Heavenly Father in correspondence with the apostle Paul's expression: 'I have been crucified with Christ; it is no longer I who live, but Christ who lives in me' (Galatians 2: 20). A. N. Williams makes a concise observation:

> As Evdokimov puts it: 'The image [of God] predestines humanity to theosis.' On the divine side, it requires a portrait of a God who can be self-communicating without compromising transcendence, and this the Orthodox tradition came to articulate, largely because of Palamas' theology, as the distinction between divine essence and energies. (1999: 15)

In a nutshell, as a mystical practice, hesychasm has deification as its ultimate goal. To achieve this goal, three core elements are continually required of the whole person: contemplation in inner silence (*hesychia*), asceticism and permanent repetition of the Jesus prayer.

From this general description of hesychasm, we can return to Dostoevsky. Van den Bercken dismisses Grillaert's arguments that Zosima unmistakeably represents hesychastic spirituality as an 'unjustified "orthodoxification"' (2011: 81). For example, Grillaert reads Zosima's own version of the hesychast Jesus prayer, 'O Lord, have mercy on all those who have appeared before You this day' (Dostoevsky 1972–90: XIV:288–9) as a 'revised, more universal version of the original Jesus prayer' (Grillaert 2008: 65–85; cf. Grillaert 2010: 198–9; 2011: 73). Van den Bercken objects: 'This is a contradictory conclusion, since his prayer is no longer typically hesychast or Orthodox, exactly because Zosima prays in more universal terms' (2011: 81). Against such an unjustified orthodoxification, van den Bercken points out that 'Zosima's *nouveauté* is precisely that he teaches the primacy of the Bible, which is analogous to the whole of Christianity, especially the heterodox

Protestants' (ibid. 81). It is indeed problematic to consider the ideas of a character as specifically Orthodox when these ideas can similarly be found in other Christian denominations. But we should pursue this question further, as it is exhausted by neither van den Bercken's nor Grillaert's position.

Indeed, it brings us to one of the most fundamental and widespread problems in the reception of Dostoevsky – interpreting him according to a more or less fixed version of a religious tradition or mode of thought (for example, Russian Orthodoxy or German Idealism, or early dialectical theology). Thus any attempt to 'directly link hesychasm with Dostoevsky's theology and anthropology' (Taylor 2005: 72) or to 'apply hesychastic themes and motives' in the name of 'a dostoevskian hesychastic anthropology' (Baciu 2013: 4) makes sense neither methodologically nor substantively.

Methodologically, it would risk *Hineininterpretierung*: imposing an idea or concept on the writer that is not substantively there in his works. Obviously, this method would affect one's understanding of the content. Elsewhere I have shown that, however tempting it may be to ascribe a certain theology, ideas and views to Dostoevsky based on his novels, one should first scrutinise the ideas and views which are expressed in his 'egodocuments' – texts written in the first person singular – such as letters, diary entries, and also Dostoevsky's *Diary of a Writer*. Furthermore, since Dostoevsky was not a theologian and never wrote down his religious ideas in any systematic form, we have to pay attention to the many lacunae we encounter in our reconstructions of his 'belief'; it is not easy – even based on the egodocuments – to answer the question of his religious convictions. The egodocuments testify to the existential elusiveness of faith for Dostoevsky as a living person – and for that matter, for that of his characters – rather than to a systematic religious doctrine.

The theme of deification is exemplary of these more general methodological observations. One of the most important egodocuments for the purposes of scrutinising Dostoevsky's belief is his Gospel, which he received in 1850, on his way to forced labour in Siberia. This Russian translation of the New Testament was the only book that Dostoevsky constantly kept with him during his four years of penal servitude.[8] The many notes and markings in this New Testament – with pencil, pen and fingernail – make it clear that the writer read this book again and again (cf. Kjetsaa 1984; Tolstaya 2013: 60).

The fact that some of the Pauline texts on which the practice of *theosis* is based – for example Romans 7: 22, 2 Corinthians 4: 16, Ephesians 3: 14–19 – are marked in the Gospel[9] might serve as an indication that Dostoevsky was attentive to hesychast mystical practice. Moreover, the notes for *The Brothers Karamazov* contain an allusion to Christ's transfiguration on Mount Tabor that was not included in the novel itself: 'Your flesh will change. (The Taborian light.)' (1972–90: XV:245). This shows that Dostoevsky was thinking of a specific Orthodox, and not a general Christian position for his character.

However, traits of Orthodox spirituality that can be discerned in Dostoevsky's artistic world testify to a peculiar, personal spirituality. While it is informed predominantly by Orthodox elements, these coexist with a variety of fragments from other religious and secular traditions. Thus Zosima's variation on the Jesus prayer aims not at deification with a Taborian-like change of flesh, but at commemoration of the deceased. It should be read in relation to his perception of love, which – as we will see in the next section – is an integral part of his worldview. This worldview is grounded on an element of Orthodox spirituality that all discussions in Dostoevsky studies seem to omit. I would argue that it is this underlying element in Zosima's worldview that brings all the other heterogeneous elements into a higher unity, and also constitutes an element of hesychasm. Yet, by excluding this underlying element to which I will turn in the rest of the chapter, all one can say of everything else is that, 'all this is "not far" from hesychasm and partly "in tune" with it, rather than immediately and directly belonging to hesychast tradition' (Horujy 2008: 4). The focus of the whole person on deification with its requisite strict asceticism in overcoming passions, *hesychia*, and ongoing repetition of the Jesus prayer is found in neither Dostoevsky nor his characters.

The Unnoticed Orthodox Element in Zosima's Worldview

To see what we *can* find in Dostoevsky, let us first look at a position which, in addition to flagging up a number of methodological problems, shows the direction I intend to take in what follows. Aaron Taylor writes:

> The doctrine of the immanent energies of God as manifested in Dostoevsky's work has often led to a confusion of his theology with Western panentheism. George Maloney [1978: 130] has pointed out the resemblance between Whitehead's primordial/ consequential distinction and the essence/energies distinction as elucidated by St. Gregory Palamas and the Greek Fathers. However, it makes more sense to discuss Dostoevsky's theology of God's immanence in terms of a theological tradition – Orthodox hesychasm – with which he actually had contact than in terms of one which Russian thinkers did not discover until around the turn of the century. Julia Kristeva, in *Black Sun: Depression and Melancholia*, does an excellent job of directly linking hesychasm with Dostoevsky's theology and anthropology. (2005: 71–2)

It would indeed be odd to connect Dostoevsky's spirituality to Whiteheadian idiom, of which he was unaware, especially as there is a link to a tradition which was known to the writer. But, as I argued above, 'directly linking hesychasm with Dostoevsky's theology and anthropology' is no less problematic, as precisely the content of this link has yet to be established. Moreover, as he was not a theologian nor had a systematic outlined anthropology, it is even inaccurate to speak of 'Dostoevsky's theology and anthropology'.

Nevertheless, I am interested in something that Taylor does observe, namely, the link of Dostoevsky to panentheism, and the reference to Gregory Palamas in this regard. This link is exactly the point of this chapter, and in the scholarship known to me this reference is rather exceptional if not unique. Unfortunately, Taylor makes this connection in passing (in a note), and does not elaborate on it. What is more, Taylor's statement that Julia Kristeva makes a similar link to hesychasm is surprising: nowhere does Kristeva connect Dostoevsky with hesychasm; in chapter 7 of her *Black Sun* (1989), she connects Dostoevsky's spirituality with what *she* sees as Eastern Orthodox pneumatology of the procession of the Son *per filium* as opposed to the Catholic *filioque*. It would be a different question whether this connection is justified in regard to Dostoevsky. But as it is, Kristeva provides no theological-historical sources to support her position, so that her claim appears to be a brilliant impressionistic sweep which does not substantively engage with theological discourse, nor with hesychasm.

What then is this link between Dostoevsky and hesychastic panentheism?

The core of the answer lies in the idea of the unity of creation. In *The Brothers Karamazov*, this idea is represented by the figure of Zosima, who is inspired by the insights he gained before the untimely death of his elder brother Markel. It is summarised in the words of Zosima: 'everything is like an ocean, everything flows and is connected, you touch it in one place – it reverberates at the other end of the world' (1972–90: XIV:290). This holistic worldview is anchored in the Palamitic doctrine that the whole of creation is penetrated by divine energies. This doctrine forms the basis, a *modus vivendi* for the hesychast practice of deification.

In Palamas' view, God is inaccessible and incomprehensible – that is, wholly transcendent, totally Other.[10] True knowledge of God in his essence cannot be acquired through reasoning[11] or through empirical observations. The way to know God is not philosophy but practice. Palamas' concept of God is consequently transcendent–immanent: God's presence in the world is immanent through his uncreated 'energies', which pervade every entity, material and immaterial. The notion of the penetration of creation by divine energies presupposes the ontological unity of creation. There is Otherness within everything and thence the interconnection of everything through the Other. Orthodox theology is very cautious about formulating anything positive concerning the divine energies, and restricts itself to very few utterances. One of them is that the divine energies are the grace of God. Grace is therefore viewed as life in God, which is the only goal of creation.[12] I will touch upon the topic of the relation of the penetration of creation by divine energies and the unity of creation further in the last section of this chapter; initially, however, I consider how it functions in Dostoevsky.

To do so, it is necessary to begin by expounding the relation of the author to his characters. Based on Dostoevsky's writings, a scholar cannot determine his 'lived' faith; as already mentioned, this faith always eludes the fixed image in the texts that the scholar has to rely on. With this in mind, one has to compose an image of Dostoevsky's religious conviction as a precondition for appropriately judging the religious dimension in his writings. The seminal studies of Bakhtin on Dostoevsky (1963) offer an unrivalled methodological framework for doing this.

Bakhtin defined Dostoevsky's novels as a new genre, 'polyphony'. In the polyphonic novel, there is no dominant authorial instance, no omniscient narrator or author who conveys a definite judgement about any character. The 'polyphony of voices' within a novel means that each character has its own voice, independent of the narrator, of the author and of the reader. Even the characters themselves do not speak the final word. For this reason, for Bakhtin, the dialogue – the most significant characteristic of any polyphonic novel – is never concluded. This openness characterises both the form and the content of Dostoevsky's novels. This specific polyphonic form of Dostoevsky's novels, Bakhtin points out, is one reason for their numerous divergent interpretations.

Bound by Soviet state-proclaimed atheism, Bakhtin was forced to limit himself to the discourse of literary theory. If we were to then render his thoughts explicit on the religious sphere in Dostoevsky, which he himself later called 'the most important thing' (Bocharov 1996: 71–2), it follows that each character possesses its own individual and autonomous belief.

The question of the relation between each character and God is a puzzling one. There is a kind of twofold relation: paradoxically, although every character in the novel is fictional, he or she stands in an open relation to the real God (insofar as God's ontic reality is presumed). Dostoevsky is able to depict the personal dimension of faith, without the reader's being able to determine its essence. In other words, the reader may try to define the faith of a character and describe it, but as soon as she does this, the human core of this faith slips away. In a sense, for the reader, the image of the character's faith is as evasive as the faith of the author. The crucial difference is, of course, the author's real and the character's fictional existence.[13] Once again, we only can analyse particular 'static' elements from a worldview. This elusiveness of the 'lived' faith is another reason for only trying to analyse what is actually in the text.

Zosima is clearly the spiritual centre of *The Brothers Karamazov*. Dostoevsky saw his 'entire novel' as an 'answer' to the 'powerful denial of God' (1972–90: XXVII:48) which he had put into the narrative of the 'Grand Inquisitor' in Book Five and into the preceding chapter, where the two brothers Ivan and Alyosha discuss possible responses to God on the question of human suffering, particularly the suffering of innocent children tortured to death. In an egodocumentary note from 1881, Dostoevsky assesses his artistic achievement:

> The Inquisitor and the chapter about the children … Even in Europe there cannot be found such strong atheistic *expressions* and *they never existed*. Not as a boy do I thus believe in Christ and profess him, but in the great *melting-pot of doubts* my *hosanna* was purified … (Ibid. XXVII:85)

Zosima's worldview helps us to understand what Dostoevsky meant when he wrote that the rest of the book can be regarded as an answer to the conversation between Ivan and Alyosha. It can perhaps be described as follows: creation is full of disharmony, but nevertheless it is intrinsically connected by the divine presence. The attitude that follows from this worldview is love, the key element in Dostoevsky's own faith (Tolstaya 2013). In the most important egodocument for his religious beliefs, written on 16 April 1864 after the death of his first wife, Dostoevsky expresses the hope that in the afterlife it will be possible to love *everything* as your own self. Zosima proclaims for earthly life what Dostoevsky hoped for the afterlife in 'the 1864 entry'.[14]

Dostoevsky himself usually talks about neighbourly love precisely in the context of belief in God and the soul's immortality; for example, in 'the 1864 entry', where he connects this topic to the question of whether he will see his wife again (1972–90: XX:172). Similarly, in the November issue of *A Writer's Diary*, he again calls the commandment 'Love thy neighbour as thyself' 'the only formula of man's salvation stemming from God and proclaimed to him through revelation' (ibid. XXVI:90). In *Winter Notes on Summer Impressions*, Dostoevsky explicitly addresses it when he urges people to do good without counting on a reward. The idea of remuneration becomes like the thought of 'a polar bear', which you constantly think about when you forbid yourself to think about it (ibid. V:80).

In Zosima's worldview, love encompasses all creation. A theological expression for this, as I indicated above, could be the Orthodox doctrine of the penetration of God's energies throughout creation. But Zosima never mentions energies, so it would be more appropriate to restrict the description of his perception to divine presence, thus avoiding a too direct reference to 'the doctrine of the immanent energies of God as manifested in Dostoevsky's work' (Taylor 2005: 71). Starting from an insight into the unity of creation and by *performing* the love commandment, the human person arrives at harmony. Zosima extends this idea even to non-living objects, such that love comprehends all of creation:

> Brothers, fear not human sin, love man even in his sin, for this is already a likeness of divine love and it is the highest love on earth. Love all God's creation, both the whole, and every grain of sand. Love every leaf, every ray of God's sun. Love animals, love plants, love everything. If you love everything, you will also understand God's mystery in things. Once you have understood it, you will also start to know it more and more deeply every day, continually. And then you will finally love the whole world with an all-embracing, universal love. Love animals: God has given them the principle

of thought and untroubled joy. Do not disturb it [their joy], do not torture them, do not take away their joy, do not resist God's thought. Man, do not raise yourself above the animals: they are without sin, whereas you, with your grandeur, make the earth fester by your presence and leave your festering mark behind you – sadly this is true of almost every one of us! Love little children in particular, for they are also without sin, like angels, and live for our tenderness, for the cleansing of our hearts and as a kind of instruction to us. (1972–90: XIV:289)

In Zosima's teaching, the divine is omnipresent, without God coinciding with the world. In the notes for the second chapter of *The Brothers Karamazov*, Dostoevsky writes in an 'NB': 'All things and everything in the world are unfinished for man, though the meaning of all things of the world is contained in man himself' (ibid. XV:208, 417). This does not follow from God's absolute transcendence, but rather precedes it. Key here is the practice of 'active love' as an outflow of Zosima's panentheistic worldview.

Zosima's counterpart, and the mouthpiece of atheistic doubts in the novel, Ivan Karamazov, is unable to arrive at true love and consequently at harmony in Zosima's sense, partly because of his rationally attuned mind. In his discussion with Alyosha, Ivan starts the exposition of his worldview with a confession: 'I could never understand how it is possible to love your neighbour. In my opinion it is precisely those near to us that you cannot love, perhaps this is only possible from a distance' (ibid. XIV:215). Alyosha, who is a novice in Zosima's monastery and his spiritual child,[15] objects that he has often heard the same from Zosima, but that this opinion results from a lack of experience in love. From his own experience, Alyosha knows that a great deal of love can be found to compare with Christ's love. Ivan counters that he has not 'yet' found this kind of love. He also cites the impossibility of identifying with the suffering of the other: 'Let's assume that I, for instance, can suffer deeply, but the other can never find out to what degree I suffer, because he is another and not me' (ibid. XIV:216).

Ivan distinguishes various forms of suffering. Physical suffering evokes pity more readily than spiritual suffering or suffering for an idea, because people often have notions about how a certain kind of suffering for an idea should be externally displayed and what kind of attitude goes with it. If the external characteristics of suffering do not fit their idea, people will not be able to work up feelings of pity. These thoughts seem at odds with Ivan's compassion for the suffering of children. For he goes on to tell a series of horrifying 'anecdotes' about the torture of children, which describe a terrible worldview full of pointless suffering without any relief. He says that he *can* love children close by, regardless of their appearance or social status. They have 'not yet eaten of the fruit', declares Ivan, who apparently rejects original sin.[16]

All of Ivan's anecdotes are based on real events carefully collected by Dostoevsky: 'All the stories about the children occurred, took place, were printed in the newspapers, and I can show where. Nothing has been invented by me' (Letter of 10 May 1879, ibid. XXX$_1$:64). Although Ivan wants to confine himself mainly to the suffering of children, his rebellion is aimed against pointless suffering in creation as a whole. Dostoevsky explains the position of this character in the same letter: 'My hero takes up a theme that *I think* irrefutable – the senselessness of the suffering of children – and derives from it the absurdity of all historical reality' (ibid. XXX$_1$:63).

To understand how the novel as a whole serves as an answer to Ivan, it needs to be noticed that, though all of Ivan's anecdotes are real, they are second-hand experiences. This is analogous to a problem of scholarly discourse: objectifying reflections on facts or experiences in a certain sense always fail to do justice to these facts or experiences. This problem is also analogous to the problem of the relation between text and living person outlined above.

Whereas Ivan, in the face of these sufferings, cannot see a way (or a reason) to engage with creation, Zosima begins from his idea of the unity of creation and from those *practices* that he calls 'active love'. Ivan cannot find a real connection to the world; Zosima recounts his own experience that led him to his worldview that everything is connected. This worldview leads to an awareness that everybody is guilty for everybody.

Ivan does not (yet?) realise that he must start with himself. He cannot devote himself to an 'active' love of his fellow men. Zosima does not gloss over the evil in the world. What matters to him are the ethics of active love. Zosima places the emphasis on the unity of creation in which he participates. Precisely because he simultaneously perceives all phenomena in their particularity, both the good and the evil, material and non-material creation, he does not call God to account for suffering, but himself.

Practising active love is, for example, the reason why the Elder sends Alyosha from the monastery out into the world. In this light, it is easier to understand why Alyosha says to Ivan that he has not yet advanced far enough in active love. The Elder also advises active love to another character, the capricious Madam Khokhlakova. She confesses to a great love for mankind, and dreams of becoming a sister of mercy. But she declares that there is a condition to her active love: she wants an 'immediate reward' for her actions: 'that is to say, recognition for myself and payment of love for love. Otherwise I will never be able to love!' (1972–90: XIV:52–3). Such a calculating love is opposed to the unconditional love of the first and the second commandment (Matthew 22: 37–9).

In Zosima's teachings, love connects all the elements of a theological system, for instance the conception of sin and anthropology, or the doctrines of creation and salvation. Love of man, even in his sin, is not just a question of the love commandment; rather, the commandment is the likeness of God's love: it expresses the unity of creation and the ethical responsibility of mankind saved by Christ. Thus love is very much the means by which the unity of creation is expressed.

Zosima's vision of hell is also closely connected to his vision of love: 'Fathers and teachers, I reflect: "What is hell?" I argue thus: "It is the suffering caused by not being able to love anymore"' (ibid. XIV:292). In the notes for *The Brothers Karamazov*, too, Zosima preaches love for man even in his sin (ibid. XV:244–5). In this Zosima deviates from the Eastern Orthodox doctrine that one should love man but hate his sins. The view of the unity of creation can also be found explicitly in Dostoevsky's notes on Zosima. His aim is to express '[i]n the words of the elder the idea [f]rom the individual organism to the general organism' (ibid. XV:243). In the same note, he writes of wanting to use '[a] story' that illustrates his idea 'that everybody will merge' (ibid. XV:243). Moreover, these notes are found alongside the reference to the Taborian light mentioned earlier in this essay.

In a paradoxical way, the solipsistic-rationalistic view of evil in Ivan Karamazov's argumentation is thereby transfigured. The awareness of 'being guiltier than others', rooted in the unity of creation, requires the whole person who – in the face of evil – does not point to others, but starts with him- or herself. This strictly individual responsibility for evil is propagated on the basis of both a metaphysical connection with Christ and an ethical orientation to Christ, the yardstick of moral action.[17] If we look to the context in which these connections occur, it is easier to place Zosima's teaching. Within the novel this teaching entails that all four brothers Karamazov are somehow responsible for the patricide – the detective plot around which the novel is built.

Dostoevsky Scholarship and Zosima's View of the Unity of Creation

As mentioned in the previous section, Zosima's view of the unity of creation has escaped the explicit attention of Dostoevsky scholarship. This is all the more striking in view of the renewed interest in hesychasm. In fact, scholars often seem to sense this idea without fully thinking it through. For example, Perevesentsev makes the same connection between the idea that everyone is guilty for everyone and the idea of the unity of creation, illustrated by Zosima's metaphor of the ocean:

> One of the ways (and the most important one) of opposition to evil is personal repentance. 'Young man, my brother, – says the elder Zosima, – has asked the birds to forgive him: that sounds senseless, but it's true, because everything is like an ocean, everything flows and is connected, you touch it in one place – it reverberates at the other end of the world ... Everything is like an ocean, I am telling you'. The idea of universal guilt is a striking consequence of the great idea of universal human unity. (2007: 179)

Zosima's view of the unity of creation is not anthropocentric; in fact, it implies that humanity is not the central point in creation. It would only take one step for Perevesentsev to go beyond the anthropocentric 'idea of universal human unity'. For Zosima there is joy at salvation throughout the whole of creation: all of creation, in one movement, is both 'otherworldly' and 'this-worldly'. It is precisely this way of looking at the world that gives rise to a personal sense of guilt.

In a similar vein, Gacheva infers from Zosima's teaching on guilt the necessity of general resurrection of the justified as well as sinners:

> The main thing that becomes clear from the conversations and teachings of Zosima ...: the sense of guilt and responsibility of all for all, the understanding that 'everything is like an ocean, everything flows and is connected, you touch it in one place – it reverberates at the other end of the world ... Everything is like an ocean, I am telling you', excludes the possibility of Judgment and division in God's Kingdom. 'Everybody is guilty for everybody' – means either that everybody must perish or be saved, but it cannot be the case that only a part will be saved, for such a salvation of a part will not be real. (2007: 255–6)

Gacheva connects Zosima's statement with the ideas of the philosopher, N. F. Fedorov, in whom Dostoevsky was interested in 1876–8, because of Fedorov's idea of the duty of descendants to resurrect their ancestors. However, it is Fedorov, and not Dostoevsky, who indeed finds support for his ideas in the eschatology of Gregory of Nyssa and Origen's doctrine of general *apokatastasis*, the restoration of all people without exception in the resurrection. Still, the theme of *apokatastasis* does indeed seem to loom in some of Dostoevsky's egodocuments and in the novels; at least the reader might wonder how Zosima would have responded to such an idea. One argument against the suggestion that Zosima's worldview entails *apokatastasis* would be that Dostoevsky, and certainly Fedorov, who thoroughly incorporated scientific findings into his philosophy, intended to thereby suggest some kind of resurrection enabled by scientific progress. Neither of them engaged in theological debates on soteriology. Nevertheless, we have to remind ourselves once more that the exact convictions of Dostoevsky – and in a sense, those of Zosima – remain incomplete on this matter (Tolstaya 2013).

Zakharov gives a very plausible ethical explanation of Zosima's worldview – though, again, without connecting it to the whole of creation:

> In his wise conviction, 'everything is like an ocean, everything flows and is connected, you touch it in one place – it reverberates at the other end of the world', he teaches repentance. There is no sin that is another's or just one's own. Everyone is responsible for everyone. Everyone is guilty not only for what he did, but also for what he did not do, did not foresee, did not save. Zosima teaches: 'make yourself defendant for all men's sins. Friend, but this is really so, for as soon as you sincerely make yourself defendant, you will see at once that it is really so, and that you are to blame for every one and for all things'. He lives according to the commandment 'Love thy neighbour as thyself.' He is able to love his enemy. (2007: 706)

This neglect of the deeper spiritual layer of the unity of creation that actually serves as a basis for following the love commandment in Zosima is the reason behind the fact that one of the prominent Orthodox contemporaries of Dostoevsky, the religious philosopher and monk Konstantin Leont'ev (who lived at the Optina Hermitage), saw Zosima merely as a teacher of morality, and called Dostoevsky's interpretation of Christianity 'rose-coloured' (Leont'ev 1997: 282). On the other hand, an intermediate interpretation that lies between mysticism and rationalism is given by Tarasov, who speaks of an 'ontological' guilt of everyone for everyone:

> [Dostoevsky's] favourite idea of the guilt of the individual before the others (not legal guilt, but ontological) is based on the recognition of initial imperfections [of the social milieu] and at the same time on complicity with everything that is going on in the world. Everyone is guilty in proportion to the lack of light and goodness in his own soul. Consequences of mental darkness and self-interest, which humans cannot fully expel, extend by invisible paths around us. And the tiniest of our evil thoughts, words and deeds invisibly imprint in the hearts of the others, pushing the other to envy or pride, to slavery or tyranny ('if I would have been righteous myself, – elder Zosima says, – perhaps there would have been no criminal standing before me'. Thus, negative spiritual potential grows and accumulates, feeding the world's evil. After all, 'everything is like an ocean, everything flows and is connected, you touch it in one place – it reverberates at the other end of the world'. And 'try to separate yourself from the other, try to determine where your personality ends and another begins?' (2007: 756)

Zosima's outlook on life presents another way of accommodating the particularity of evil in relation to God than presented by Tarasov. For this we have to look at the place of salvation in the teaching of Zosima. This resides in the belief that all things are without sin except human beings – that is to say, only humans need to be saved:

> Truly . . . everything is good and magnificent, because everything is truth. Look . . . at the horse, the great animal that stands at man's side, or at the ox, sad and reflective, that feeds him and works for him, look at their faces: what humility, what devotion to man, who often beats them mercilessly, what gentleness, what trust and what beauty in their faces. It is in fact moving to know that they have no sin in themselves, since

everything is perfect, everything except man is without sin and Christ is with them even before he is with us . . . Every tiny leaf desires the Word, praises God and weeps for Christ, unconsciously for itself, through the mystery alone of its sinless existence. (1972–90: XIV:267–8)

In Zosima's view, creation is united by something divine/transcendent that is undoubtedly positive. In Tarasov we find a striking reverse of the 'ontology' of 'good' and 'evil'. Humanity is united by transcendent evil. This again is due to an anthropocentric perversion of Zosima's holistic/panentheistic view. Evidently, the idea of the unity of creation precedes everything that is discussed in systematic-theological terms, such as, for example, ethics, soteriology, anthropology, and so on, and so it has to be thought in relation to (the ontological status of) evil, alongside everything else. However, this is a discussion of a theological *locus* – that is, a dogmatic theme such as the concept of God, ontology, anthropology, Christology, soteriology, epistemology, and so on – that we have to articulate and to justify in relation to other *loci*, not of a worldview of a fictitious character. Once again, we are determined by the methodological boundaries in interpreting a novel. Even though openness is the main characteristic of the polyphonic novel, this openness concerns primarily the dialogical aspect of the genre. In regard to the nature of being, openness within the novel is fundamentally different from openness within real life. I have already pointed to the distinction between the author and the character – that the author has his ontic existence, and lends ontological (fictional) existence to the character. Therefore, contrary to much literary interpretation, there is a limited amount of meaning (epistemological, noetic, axiological, factual knowledge, and so on) that the author can give to each character.

As we have seen in all the examples in this section, no justice is done to the text of the novel and to its meaning when additional meanings are identified (such as, for example, transcendence of evil in the case of Tarasov), rather than the meanings that are actually present in the text.

In order to discern what is specific to Dostoevsky's spirituality, and (in another sense) to Zosima's spirituality, one can apply theological discourse only with the highest caution. This also goes for discussing Orthodox spirituality in Dostoevsky or in Zosima. As discussed above, the divine light is one of the main characteristics of the hesychast experience. One of the major motivations behind Palamas' writings was his defence of the experience of perception of the divine light acquired by the hesychast monks of Mount Athos. It is in this context that Palamas had to formulate his view on the nature of this light in its relation to God's essence. Palamas begins from the fact that someone who lives ascetically can achieve a new state of deification, in which she not only transforms her spirit and soul but also her body, and thus opens herself up to the effect of divine energies.

Zosima often mentions light and rays of sun as witnesses to the divine pervasion of creation. We have already heard him proclaiming the love for every 'ray of God's sun'. It is also important to note a particularly strong memory from his youth:

It was a clear day and I . . . see as it were anew how the incense rose from the thurible and floated up, and how God's rays poured down on us in church from on high through the narrow window in the cupola. (1972–90: XIV:264)

On another occasion Zosima says: 'I bless the daily sunrise and my heart still sings to it, but now I love more the sunset, its long slanting rays' (ibid. XIV:268). And further: 'Lord, send peace and light to your people!' (ibid. XIV:270). (Sun)light also plays a role in the perception of creation in its relation to the Creator: 'and the sun still shines, the tiny leaves are still joyful, and the birds, the birds still praise God' (ibid. XIV:270).

When considering possible links to hesychasm and deification, it would be easy (or tempting) to 'directly' connect these references to light with the Taborian light which is essential to the practice of *theosis* and to Palamas' elaboration, especially given the reference in Dostoevsky's notes for *The Brothers Karamazov* (see above). But this would be the same misapplication of theological concepts – even if they refer to and derive from practice – like *apokatastasis* or hesychasm. The difference between hesychast practice and Zosima's teaching lies in the way they involve the whole person. According to Zosima, the awareness of 'being guiltier than others' requires the whole person in active love, which is lived from the experience of the unity of creation. In hesychasm, the whole person is turned towards ascetic practice and the Jesus prayer.

I want to end this section with reference to Rowan Williams's renowned study on Dostoevsky (2009), for, in his analysis, Williams comes very close to getting at that unity of creation which is the core of Zosima's worldview and the basis for his idea of the responsibility of everyone for everyone:

> the Word of God is addressed to and reflected in all things, and everything except humanity is naturally turned in yearning toward God (interestingly, he refers to a saint taming a bear, which suggests that he may have known at least some of the traditions around Serafim of Sarov, of whom this story is told). Responsibility is at least the acknowledgement of a fractured relation between humanity – specifically each person's human soul – and the rest of creation, a fracture for which human beings have to take the blame. (2009: 165)

In a similar way to Zakharov, Williams stresses the ethical dimension in Zosima's teaching. However, without the idea of the unity of creation, Zosima's Christianity remains too 'rose-coloured', not only idiomatically, but also on the level of content. Without this idea it may become superficial, and therefore incapable of adequately coping with the question of evil – that is, of serving as the answer to Ivan's challenge that inevitable eternal harmony is 'not worth one little tear from one single little tortured child' (1972–90: XIV:223).

There is no place here for a thorough examination of Williams' interpretation of the theme of guilt in relation to the concept of creation. It is worth mentioning, however, that surprisingly he does not seek to establish any link to Palamism. The reason why seems to be implied in the following argument:

> Asking forgiveness from the natural order shows that the isolated self has acknowledged its given limits, its *locatedness* and materiality, and so the inescapably other character of what it encounters ... What sets this apart from the 'pantheism' some have detected is precisely the emphasis on forgiveness; what is happening is not a natural process, an absorption in cosmic harmony, but one that involves decisions, awareness, attention, just that attention to the prosaic and specific that we have repeatedly seen to be in the novels a sign of grace. (2009: 165)

Williams defends Dostoevsky from suspicions of pantheism, but not on the grounds that Eastern Orthodox spirituality is in essence panentheistic. Instead, he defends him from the perspective of a very different theological *locus*. The question whether Dostoevsky (and for that matter Orthodoxy) can be dubbed pantheistic and the discussion how it is rather panentheistic belongs to the fields of theological epistemology (primarily), the doctrine of God, cosmology and the doctrine of creation. To treat it from the perspective of ethics and theological anthropology – as Williams does – deprives it of its core content, as well as being formally a sort of category mistake. It is the notion of the unity of creation that encompasses both theological epistemology (the doctrines of God, creation and other) and theological anthropology. In theological discourse, it should function as a systematic link between the two. Here, by contrast, one *locus* is substituted for another, and the crucial link is missing. It almost seems as if Williams himself maintains that Eastern Orthodoxy, including Palamism, has never been able to escape pantheism (see Williams 1977: 36).

Pantheism is a common objection to the idea of the divine penetration in creation. As Papanikolaou summarises, 'the main objection [to Palamism] is its pantheistic overtones. If the energies are God, then everything is God. If everything is not God, then the energies are less than God' (2006: 27). In the next section I would like to briefly elaborate on these theological aspects of the Eastern-Orthodox notion of the union of creation.

The Missing Link in Theological Discourse

In these concluding paragraphs, I want to provide some observations on the theological sources of the notion of the unity of creation, and pose some questions about its place in recent accounts of nineteenth-century and contemporary theology.

From the end of the nineteenth century onwards, 'theosis began to regain a central position in the consciousness of Orthodox Christians as the context and goal of the Christian life' (Russell 2009: 17); nevertheless, various elaborations of this doctrine have emerged in all Christian confessions. Contemporary interest in *theosis* is so widespread that it has been suggested as 'perhaps *the* hype of twenty-first century theology' (Wisse 2011: 301, 301–12; cf. Williams 1999: 142).[18]

Strikingly, most discussions, regardless of denomination, follow two parallel lines, which seem never to impact on each other. Either the discussion touches on *theosis* as a personal practice and thus concerns theological anthropology; or attention is given to God's wholly transcendent and unknowable essence and the divine immanent energies that penetrate creation and make participation in God possible, and thus concerns theological epistemology.

Not only do both these lines of thought remain distinct in discourse on *theosis*, remarkably the situation is very similar to that of the field of Dostoevsky studies. The crucial link between the doctrine and/or practice of deification and the union of creation seems to be missing in theological and literary studies alike. In contemporary discussions of personal co-working with God as a means of deification, the focus is on the individual practice and thus concepts such as 'person' and 'individual'. Consequently both discussion and practice remain anthropocentric, detached from creation. As Stoeckl observes:

> The renaissance of Palamism inspired a theology of the person, in which the concept of the individual as a closed entity, as an 'essence', was opposed by the notion of personhood, an energetic expression of being that is evoked only in relation. (2006: 253)

However, the link between deification and the unity of creation is fundamental to patristic thought and practice. From the desert and Cappadocian Fathers, through St Maximus the Confessor to Gregory Palamas, with their respective teachings on the divine *logoi* and *energeia* that penetrate creation, and above all throughout Eastern Orthodox spirituality, this individual practice of deification is embedded in the idea of the unity of creation as summarised in the words of the Orthodox liturgy: 'God is everywhere present and fillest all things.'

Moreover, as in the nineteenth century with Zosima, this idea still very much pertains to Orthodox spirituality. In the first half of the twentieth century, Sergii Bulgakov wrote: 'The world is completely transparent for God; it is penetrated through and through by divine energies that form the basis of its being' (Bulgakov 2012: 154; cf. Collins 2010). And one of the greatest Orthodox theologians of the twentieth century, Olivier Clément, adduces this spirituality as the core of Orthodox faith:

> In Orthodoxy, I was attracted by many things: the importance of the resurrection, the idea of deification of man through the incarnation of God, the idea of the Trinity, theology of divine energies emanating from the transfigured Christ and penetrating all of creation. The latter gave Christianity, in my eyes, a cosmic character. (1991)

However, this spirituality does not find elaboration in scholarly discourse. In fact, no secondary source on *theosis* thematises the unity of creation, or the penetration of creation by energies/*logoi* in a theological sense.[19]

The missing link of the unity of creation is, perhaps, not totally surprising when one considers the cultural- and theological-historical context of the 'turn to the subject' in which the doctrine of deification was rediscovered in Russian Orthodox spirituality in the eighteenth century, and then reinvented theologically from the late nineteenth century onwards. In this context, *theosis* is explained as personal participation in God and personal deification through a life of prayer and asceticism. That the perception of the union of creation could be linked to personal soteriology in nineteenth-century Russian spirituality can only really be gleaned from Dostoevsky, and especially in terms of Zosima's influence on some Orthodox figures in the twentieth century: Fr Seraphim Rose (1934–82) and Fr Sophrony (Sakharov, 1896–1993), to name but two.[20]

My thesis, then, has been that without this link to the unity of creation, *theosis* is hollowed out, and easily omits its fundamental theological and existential layer. With David Bradshaw, I can indeed conclude that 'It is surely surprising that their [i.e. the Cappadocian Church Fathers of the fourth century] distinction between the divine essence and energies, God in Himself and as He "reaches down to us," has played so little role in Western theology' (2006: 292). Even more surprising is that Orthodox theologians who lay claim to some continuity with the patristic tradition have yet to discover the potential of systematic elaboration of this notion that is intrinsic to the theology they claim continuity with.

Notes

1. This is the alleged statement of Prince Myshkin that he never actually makes in the novel, but which is attributed to him by Aglaya Yepanchina. All quotes from Russian have been originally translated from the source texts.
2. This idea does not figure literally in *Crime and Punishment*, but is connected to Raskolnikov's idea that a strong person is not bound by general moral laws: 'I killed for myself, just for me

... I had to know ... whether I'm a louse, like everybody else, or a man ... Am I a trembling creature or do I have the *right* ...' (Dostoevsky 1972–90: VI:322).
3. This idea also occurs earlier in *A Writer's Diary* (1876), and already in 1873 (see Tolstaya 2013: 131).
4. Roughly: in the first phase with Barlaam of Calabria, in the second phase with the group led by Gregory Akindynos, in the third phase with Nicephorus Gregoras, and in the fourth and last phase with Prochorus Cydones. See, for example, Russell 2004: 304–9.
5. 'Αὐτὸς γὰρ ἐνηνθρώπισεν, ἵνα ἡμεῖς θεοποιηθῶμεν' (Athanasius 1857: 54 [192B]).
6. Cf. the discussion of the positions of Kallistos Ware and Martin Jugie in Williams 1999: 150. Ware also speaks of a neglect of Palamism, and Jugie takes the seventeenth century as starting point for this neglect in Russia.
7. For Eastern Orthodoxy and the Reformation, Meyendorff refers to a shared rejection of the Roman Catholic view of grace as a created inner quality and of the related problems of human freedom, justification and merits. At the same time, he sees one of the great differences in the fact that the Reformation upholds the Augustinian idea of God as the (static) Highest Good, which originates in Plato.
8. Dostoevsky mentions this in the chapter 'Old People' in *A Writer's Diary* (1873) (1972–90: XXI:12). Grossman mentions that during his hard labour Dostoevsky rejected the books which his visitors brought along. He only made an exception for two novels by Dickens (1922: 9).
9. This New Testament with markings can be found on the internet (Dostoevsky n.d.).
10. A reference to two theologians from different traditions, Karl Barth and John Zizioulas, may suffice for the use of this term. God as the *ganz Andere* is one of the central ideas of Barth's theology. Zizioulas (2006), however, is reluctant to connect this link between man as the image of God, the pervasion of creation with divine energies and his ontology of otherness. A much deeper investigation would reveal whether an ontological otherness of the uncreated energies would serve his argument better than his insistence on the ontology of otherness, which he seems to borrow from Western (post)modern philosophical discourses (particularly Levinas). In this dialogue with philosophy, he is constantly speaking *to* the Orthodox (dogmatic, patristic) tradition and seems often to artificially justify his usage of 'otherness' in respect to this tradition and to almost all dogmatic *loci*.
11. Eschatologically speaking, however, Palamas expects more clarity (Meyendorff 1959: 270).
12. In Orthodoxy, the doctrine of justification is secondary.
13. For a brief discussion of the status of fictional objects such as fictional characters, and for further reading, see Hanley 2009.
14. On this egodocument, see extensively Tolstaya 2013: ch. 5.
15. 'Spiritual child' is a common expression for a relation between an Orthodox spiritual elder and his pupil.
16. Orthodoxy always takes a personal view of guilt; guilt is bound up with freedom of choice. In Dostoevsky, children are generally still frank and open in their approach to the good.
17. Van den Bercken (2011: 73) points to the aspect of collective guilt as being more of a 'Western' doctrine, and quotes Ivan Esaulov (2004), who interprets Dostoevsky's idea as 'communal guilt', linking it to the conception of *sobornost'*. Such an interpretation seems both to overstate the 'Orthodoxy' in Dostoevsky (a tendency against which van den Bercken argues throughout his book) and to neglect the foundation of this strictly *individual* guilt for 'everything and everybody' in Orthodox tradition. I intend to develop this spiritual aspect in traditional Orthodoxy in following studies.
18. Wisse expresses a common opinion (2011: 302) that 'Lossky introduced Eastern Orthodox theology to Western readers as early as the 1950s.' It was, however, M. Lot-Borodine who in a series of articles introduced the Orthodox concept of deification in the West in 1932–3. See Russell 2004: 4; Zorgdrager 2012.
19. I intend to discuss secondary sources on theosis – a discussion that lies outside the scope of the present volume – in a separate book chapter.

20. One of the questions yet to be answered is whether we are indeed dealing with the same Orthodox spirituality in Zosima and the Church Fathers. I have showed that it is difficult to claim this without imposing theological concepts on Zosima, or of an 'objectified' discourse which is substituted for living experience/practice.

References

Athanasius (1857), 'De incarnatione Verbi', in J. P. Migne, *Patrologia Graeca*, vol. 25, Paris, 95–196.
Baciu, N.-G. (2013), 'Hesychastic Themes and Motives in the Universal Literature: Tolstoy, Sadoveanu, Dostoevsky', <http://phdthesis.uaic.ro/PhDThesis/Baciu,%20Nicoleta-Ginevra,%20Hesychastic%20themes%20and%20motives%20in%20the%20universal%20literature%20-%20Tolstoi,%20Sadoveanu,%20Dostoievski.pdf> (last accessed 26 June 2016).
Bakhtin, M. M. (1963), *Проблемы творчества Достоевского* [*Problems of Dostoevsky's Poetics*], Moscow: Sovetskiĭ pisatel'.
Bercken, W. van den (2011), *Christian Fiction and Religious Realism in the Novels of Dostoevsky*, London: Anthem Press.
Bocharov, S. (1996), «Леонтьев и Достоевский» ['Leont'ev and Dostoevsky'], in N. F. Budanova (ed.), *Достоевский: материалы и исследования* [*Dostoevsky: Materials and Studies*], 12: 162–89.
Bradshaw, D. (2004), *Aristotle East and West: Metaphysics and the Division of Christendom*, Cambridge: Cambridge University Press.
Bradshaw, D. (2006), 'The Divine Glory and the Divine Energies', *Faith and Philosophy*, 23.3: 279–98.
Bulgakov, S. (2012), *Unfading Light*, Grand Rapids: Eerdmans.
Clément, O. (1991), «Почему я православный христианин. Из интервью «Континенту»» ['Why I am an Orthodox Christian. From the Interview in "Continents"'], <http://azbyka.ru/otechnik/Olive_Kleman/pochemu-ja-pravoslavnyj-hristianin/> (last accessed 3 July 2016).
Collins, P. M. (2010), 'Between Creation and Salvation: Theosis and Theurgy', in V. Kharlamov (ed.), *Theosis: Deification in Christian Theology*, vol. 2, Cambridge: James Clarke, 192–204.
Dostoevsky, F. M. (1972–90), *Полное собрание сочинений в тридцати томах* [*Complete Collected Works*], 30 vols, ed. V. G. Bazanov et al., Leningrad: Nauka.
Dostoevsky, F. M. (n.d.), *Евангелие Достоевского* [*Dostoevsky's Gospel*], <http://www.fedordostoevsky.ru/biography/evangelie/?> (last accessed 16 June 2016).
Esaulov, I. A. (2004), *Пасхальность русской словесности* [*The Easter-Likeness of Russian Literature*], Moscow: Krug'.
Gacheva, A. G. (2007), «Проблема всеобщности спасения в романе «Братья Карамазовы» (в контексте эсхатологических идей Н. Ф. Федорова и В. С. Соловьева)» ['The Problem of Universal Salvation in the Novel "The Brothers Karamazov" (in the Context of the Eschatological Ideas of N. F. Fedorov and V. S. Solovyov)'], in T. A. Kasatkina (ed.), *Роман Ф. М. Достоевского «Братья Карамазовы»: Современное состояние изучения* [*F. M. Dostoevsky's Novel 'The Brothers Karamazov': State of the Art*], Moscow: Nauka, 226–82.
Gavrilyuk, P. L. (2013), 'Nineteenth- to Twentieth-Century Russian Mysticism', in J. Lamm (ed.), *The Blackwell Companion to Christian Mysticism*, Oxford: Wiley-Blackwell, 489–501.
Grillaert, N. (2008), 'Hagiographical Discourse in "The Brothers Karamazov": A Resurrected Consciousness in Starec Zosima's Creed', *Slavica Gandensia*, 35: 65–85.
Grillaert, N. (2010), 'Dostoevskij's Portrait of a "Pure, Ideal Christian": Echoes of Nil Sorskij in the Elder Zosima', *Russian Literature*, 67.2: 185–217.
Grillaert, N. (2011), '"Raise the people in silence": Traces of Hesychasm in Dostoevskij's Fictional Saint Zosima', *Dostoevsky Studies*, 15 (New Series): 47–88.
Grossman, L. (1922), *Семинарий по Достоевскому* [*Seminars on Dostoevsky*], Petrograd: Delo.
Hanley, R. (2009), 'Fictional Objects', in R. Le Poidevin, P. Simons, A. McGonigal and R. P. Cameron (eds), *The Routledge Companion to Metaphysics*, London: Routledge, 357–69.

Horujy, S. S. (2008), ««Братья Карамазовы» в призме исихастскойантропологии» ['"The Brothers Karamazov" in the Prism of Hesychast Anthropology'], 8 April, <http://www.synergia-isa.org/article/bratya-karamazovy-v-prizme-isihastskoy-antropologii> (last accessed 8 April 2017).

Kasatkina, T. A. (ed.) (2007), *Роман Ф. М. Достоевского «Братья Карамазовы»: Современное состояние изучения* [*F. M. Dostoevsky's Novel 'The Brothers Karamazov': State of the Art*], Moscow: Nauka.

Kenworthy, S. M. (2104), 'Archbishop Nikon (Rozhdestvenskii) and Pavel Florenskii on Spiritual Experience, Theology, and the Name-Glorifiers Dispute', in P. L. Michelson and J. D. Kornblatt (eds), *Thinking Orthodox in Modern Russia: Culture, History, Context*, Madison: University of Wisconsin Press, 85–107.

Kjetsaa, G. (1984), *Dostoevsky and His New Testament*, Atlantic Highlands: Humanities Press.

Kristeva, J. (1989), *Black Sun: Depression and Melancholia*, trans. L. S. Roudiez, New York: Columbia University Press.

Leont'ev, K. (1997), «О всемирной любви (Речь Ф. М. Достоевского на Пушкинском празднике)» ['On Universal Love (F. M. Dostojevski's Speech at the Pushkin Festival)'], in A. N. Strizhov (ed.), *Ф. М. Достоевский и Православие* [*F. M. Dostoevsky and Orthodoxy*], Moscow: Otchiĭ Dom, 261–97.

Lossky, V. (2005), *The Mystical Theology of the Eastern Church*, 3rd edn, Cambridge: James Clarke.

Maloney, G. A. (1978), *A Theology of 'Uncreated Energies'*, Milwaukee, WI: Marquette University Press

Mantzaridis, G. I. [1963] (1984), *The Deification of Man: St Gregory Palamas and the Orthodox Tradition*, trans. L. Sherrard, Crestwood, NY: St Vladimir's Seminary Press.

Mazour-Matusevich, Y. (2014), 'Historical Roots of Russian Silence', *CrossCurrents Magazine: Association for Religion and Intellectual Life*, 64.2: 295–311.

Meyendorff, J. (1959), *Introduction à l'étude de Gregoire Palamas*, Paris: Éditions du Seuil.

Meyendorff, J. (1983), *Byzantine Theology: Historical Trends and Doctrinal Themes*, 2nd edn, New York: Fordham University Press.

Meyendorff, J. (1997), «Значение реформации как события в истории христианства» ['The Meaning of the Reformation as an Event in the History of Christianity'], in *Православие в современном мире* [*Orthodoxy in the Modern World*], Moscow: Put', 129–48.

Paert, I. (2010), *Spiritual Elders: Charisma and Tradition in Russian Orthodoxy*, DeKalb: Northern Illinois University Press.

Papanikolaou, A. (2006), *Being with God: Trinity, Apophaticism, and Divine–Human Communion*, Notre Dame: University of Notre Dame Press.

Perevesentsev, V. (2007), «Бунт Ивана Карамазова (оправдание Бога и мира в романе Ф. М. Достоевского «Братья Карамазовы»)» ['Ivan Karamazov's Revolt (Justification of God and World in F. M. Dostoevsky's Novel "The Brothers Karamazov")'], in T. A. Kasatkina (ed.), *Роман Ф. М. Достоевского «Братья Карамазовы»: Современное состояние изучения* [*F. M. Dostoevsky's Novel 'The Brothers Karamazov': State of the Art*], Moscow: Nauka, 161–79.

Russell, N. (2004), *The Doctrine of Deification in the Greek Patristic Tradition*, Oxford: Oxford University Press.

Russell, N. (2009), *Fellow Workers with God: Orthodox Thinking on Theosis*, Crestwood, NY: St Vladimir's Seminary Press.

Stoeckl, K. (2006), 'Modernity and Its Critique in 20th Century Russian Orthodox Thought', *Studies in Eastern European Thought*, 58: 243–69.

Tarasov, B. N. (2007), «Художественное завещание Достоевского» ['Dostoevsky's Artistic Testament'], in T. A. Kasatkina (ed.), *Роман Ф. М. Достоевского «Братья Карамазовы»: Современное состояние изучения* [*F. M. Dostoevsky's Novel 'The Brothers Karamazov': State of the Art*], Moscow: Nauka, 732–64.

Taylor, A. (2005), 'Encountering the Incarnate Subject: Dostoevsky's Fiction as an Embodiment of and Contribution to Orthodox Theology', in J. E. Barnhart (ed.), *Dostoevsky's Polyphonic Talent*, Oxford: Oxford University Press, 41–76.

Tolstaya, K. (2013), *Kaleidoscope: F. M. Dostoevsky and Early Dialectical Theology*, Leiden: Brill.
Williams, A. N. (1999), *The Ground of Union: Deification in Aquinas and Palamas*, New York: Oxford University Press.
Williams, R. (1977), 'The Philosophical Structures of Palamism', *Eastern Orthodox Review*, 9: 27–44.
Williams, R. (2009), *Dostoevsky: Language, Faith, and Fiction*, New York: Continuum.
Wisse, M. (2011), *Trinitarian Theology beyond Participation: Augustine's De Trinitate and Contemporary Theology*, New York: T&T Clark.
Worobec, C. (2006), 'Lived Orthodoxy in Imperial Russia', *Kritika: Explorations in Russian and Eurasian History*, 7.2 (New Series): 329–50.
Yannaras, Chr. (1975), 'The Distinction between Essence and Energies and Its Importance for Theology', *St. Vladimir's Theological Quarterly*, 19.4: 232–45.
Zakharov, V. N. (2007), «Осанна в горниле сомнений» ['Hosanna in the Crucible of Doubt'], in T. A. Kasatkina (ed.), *Роман Ф. М. Достоевского «Братья Карамазовы»: Современное состояние изучения* [F. M. Dostoevsky's Novel 'The Brothers Karamazov': State of the Art], Moscow: Nauka, 694–711.
Zizioulas, J. (2006), *Communion and Otherness: Further Studies in Personhood and the Church*, London: T&T Clark.
Zorgdrager, H. (2012), 'A Practice of Love: Myrrha Lot-Borodine (1882–1954) and the Modern Revival of the Doctrine of Deification', *Journal of Eastern Christian Studies*, 64.3–4: 287–307.

17

Mysticism

Benjamin Dawson

(as Jakob Böhme himself says of his spirit) 'what he hits, he hits' [(*wie Jakob Böhme selbst von seinem Geist sagt) 'was er trifft, das trifft er'*] (Schelling)

These are not drunk, as you suppose . . . (Acts 2: 15)

Introduction: Empiricism Anaesthetised

In the spring of 1882, the American empiricist philosopher, William James, launched a spirited attack on Hegelian idealism. At the very moment the Helmholtz generation was celebrating the final defeats of Hegelianism in Germany, its spectre seemed to be reappearing in British and American philosophy. Perturbed by these developments, James submitted his pluralistic (and indeed multiple) criticisms of Hegel to the influential journal *Mind*. They were, he said (couching the campaign in explicitly military terms), a 'skirmisher's shot' that he hoped soon to 'be followed by someone else's heavier musketry' (1882: 186).

Before the essay could appear, however, he sent the publisher a long supplementary note that was to be added as a postscript to the essay. In it, James explains:

> Since the manuscript of the preceding article was committed to the Editor's hands, I have made some observations on the effects of nitrous-oxide-gas-intoxication which have made me understand better than ever before both the strength and the weakness of Hegel's philosophy. (Ibid. 206)

After encouraging his readers to repeat for themselves his experiments with the drug, James continues: 'With me, as with every other individual of whom I have heard, the keynote of the experience is the tremendously exciting sense of an intense metaphysical illumination. Truth lies open to view in depth beneath depth of blinding evidence' (ibid. 206).

The simultaneously analgesic and sublime effects of inhaling nitrous oxide (N_2O) or 'laughing gas' had been known since the pioneering self-experiments performed at the Bristol Pneumatic Institute in the 1790s by the Romantic chemist, Humphry Davy. Whether or not James was aware of Davy's researches is uncertain. His own experiments were directly prompted by a pamphlet entitled *The Anaesthetic Revelation and the Gist of Philosophy*, self-published in 1874 by an American mystic named Benjamin Paul Blood. The precise aetiology of James's acquaintance with Blood (the man and his revelation) is obscure: my understanding is that Blood heard Henry James Sr. preach somewhere, probably of the awful 'vastation' or panic attack at the kitchen table which had converted him to Swedenborgianism in May 1844; that Blood afterwards sent him a copy of *The Anaesthetic Revelation* (an account of his own epiphany while etherised at the dentist's fourteen years previously); and that the pamphlet then fell into the hands of W. J., who was impressed enough to review it for the *Atlantic Monthly* and thence begin a lifelong correspondence.

No doubt the devil or the good God is in the details, and some of these will be considered below, but my initial interest in Blood is more general. He is significant because, as I shall try to show in this chapter, when James's gas experiment is read alongside his empiricist critique of Hegel what comes to light is nothing so much as an intersection or indistinction between empiricism and, precisely, *mysticism*. On the one hand, the body of the essay 'On Some Hegelisms' reveals the way Hegelian speculative dialectics appears within the semantic space of James's sober empiricism (or, better, it exhibits the ways in which it *cannot* appear there). On the other hand, the gas experiment recorded in the supplementary note reveals the specific, and specifically euphoric, form of idealism that emerges when that pluralistic empiricism is, in diverse senses, *anaesthetised* – which is to say, suspended yet sustained, cancelled and yet, at the same time, uplifted.

As is often the case in practices of self-experimentation, the distinction between the experimental instrument and the research object quickly becomes uncertain in James's inquiry into the effects of nitrous oxide intoxication. What begins as empirical research into the psychoactive powers of the gas morphs into a speculative investigation of metaphysical realities and logical relations revealed to the inebriated mind. By midway through the experience, any distinction between chemical effect and philosophical insight has dissolved such that, we are told, 'The thought of mutual implication of the parts in the bare form of a judgment of opposition, as "nothing but," "no more than," "only if," etc., produced a perfect delirium of *theoretic* rapture' (ibid. 206). In a subtle twist, logic or the form of thought itself seems to have become the source of James's derangement. And indeed the climax of his anaesthetic revelation is the sublime notion that 'There are no differences but differences between different degrees of difference and no difference. &c., &c., &c.', a statement which later, having regained his senses, he glosses as 'having the true hegelian ring, being in fact a regular *sich als sich auf sich selbst beziehende Negativität* [self as self to itself relating negativity]' (ibid. 206). In essence, then, the sober James claims that, under the intoxicating influence of nitrous oxide, he finally fully grasped the meaning of the governing principles of speculative dialectics, namely, self-relating or absolute negativity, and the identity of difference and identity.

Earlier in the note, while lamenting that 'It is impossible to convey an idea of the torrential character of the identification of opposites as it streams through the mind in this experience' (ibid. 206), James had gone on to list a number of these identified opposites – sober and drunk, god and the devil, shiver of ecstasy and shudder of horror, vomiting and swallowing, and so on. I shall not go through the whole list, but it is worth noting that they are largely empirical rather than logical oppositions (or at least there is no distinction drawn between these types of opposition). And it is these remnants of an empiricist way of thinking, the persistence of an empiricist *schema*, within James's temporary conversion to 'Hegelism', which is probably responsible for the specific proximity between this chemically induced idealism and certain varieties of religious experience – specifically, of mystical experience.

Here, then, various elements of a complex constellation seem already to be coming into view. The problem with James's approach to Hegel is the same on both sides – whether sober or delirious, he cannot distinguish absolute idealism from mysticism. In this, James belongs to a distinctive nineteenth-century reception history of Hegelian philosophy in the United States. The terms with which that philosophy is repudiated in the essay, and celebrated in the postscript, are indeed the same used at key points in the chapters of *The Varieties of Religious Experience* on 'Mysticism' and 'The Reality of the Unseen', and concertedly in lectures II and III of *A Pluralistic Universe*: namely, monism (James 1998: 124, 375), pantheism (ibid. 125, 459), immediate certainty or incommunicable conviction (ibid. 72, 363, 688), reconciliation (ibid. 350), absolute totality (ibid. 153), absolute fact (ibid. 125), semi-hallucinatory mono-ideism (ibid. 367), and so on. Hegel is on his mind across these pages as he is, one senses, at many points throughout James's remarkable anthology and psychological analysis of 'religious experience' (a variable he helped introduce into science). His methodology, distinguished in the influential opening chapters from both crude medical-materialist or psychiatric approaches and traditional discussions of religion as institution, dogma, ritual, theology, and so on, draws him naturally towards areas of the archive of religious discourses in which personal experiences of the divine are described or confessed. In short, as he is careful to acknowledge, his way of constructing religion as an object of science necessarily renders mystical experience its kernel and source. And for this reason he is drawn towards religious illuminations whose very 'incommunicableness' isolates the individual, individuates her by cutting her off from others, injects non-relation into the subject, singularising consciousness and directing it on or into itself (see ibid. 366).

One can quibble about the tendentiously Protestant lens of this approach (which reaches tragicomic proportions when James complains: 'the absence of strictly personal confessions is the chief difficulty to the purely literary student who would like to become acquainted with the inwardness of religions other than the Christian'! [Ibid. 363]); but this is only to note that the psychological approach to religion, indeed the very category of 'personal religious experience', however secular it may be, is scarcely non-sectarian. What is more intriguing, to me, is the constellation that arises from this work involving mysticism, empiricism, 'Hegelism', Hegel's actual philosophy, and the crucial conceptions we find there of mystical and sensuous experience. My claim is that if this complex system of relationships has a centre, it is the intersection, or point of indifference, between mysticism and empiricism – a point that, on occasion, James himself recognises: when he speaks, with a kind of aptly excessive emphasis, of 'the mystery of fact' (ibid. 345), for instance, or in his observation that, insofar as 'Mystical truth exists for the individual who has the transport, but no one else . . ., it resembles the knowledge given to us in sensations more than that given by conceptual thought' (ibid. 366). Quite!

When James reads Hegel's philosophy as the logical elaboration of mystical feeling (monism, reconciliation, etc.), he seems both to disparage and envy it. He thinks it has to do with 'belief in the Absolute', and that this belief, 'forced' on us not by logic but 'mystical feeling' (ibid. 350), is ultimately not philosophical but rather an 'immediate certainty' (ibid. 688). There is a kind of irony in this: James's philosophy is proudly empiricist, a philosophy of experience, and opposes itself to Hegelism as an idealism, a philosophy of the Concept. The irony is that, in mystical experience as he reconstructs it, it is Hegelism that has an extra-logical confirmation and anchor in experience, in 'life' (as he would say), which his own pluralistic, radically empiricist philosophy, apparently so much closer to empirical reality, is more and more felt to lack.

What I wish to do here is to trace some of the exchanges of masks at work in this complicated situation. My basic premise is that the reception of Hegel as a mystical thinker was internally related to the notion of being convertible to 'Hegelism' through sensuous or psychoactive means (N_2O); the aim is to offer an exposition of that internal relationship. My argument is both theoretical and historical.

The theoretical aspect consists of a series of claims, which may be outlined as follows: (1) the point of intersection between the version or perversion of Hegelian philosophy repudiated in James's essay and that which is temporarily championed in the note is, as already asserted, mysticism; (2) relatedly, the kind of 'Hegelism' it is possible to induce through drugs is empirical, personal and psychological rather than philosophical, dialectical and spiritual (in sum, is abstract not concrete), as its principle demands; (3) just for this reason is it (this empiricism-mysticism) precisely identifiable with the very first attitude or form of conviction elaborated in the 'science of the experience of consciousness' or *Phenomenology of Spirit*, namely, the 'sense certainty' whose mystical character Hegel himself underlines; (4) as analysis of that famous opening chapter makes clear, the mystery of sense, of the immediate, is an ineffability lying at the heart of *language*, the silence of reference in general, which comes out, above all, through its technological embodiment in writing; and, lastly and most delicately, (5) this mysticism-empiricism, whose negation is the opening of Hegelian thought but which returns as the figure of the latter appearing through the American binoculars of its empiricist rejection and intoxicated affirmation, is a permanent hallmark of Hegelian thought, not so much for systematic reasons as insofar as this thought requires a thinker, the system a consciousness.

The argument's historical dimension I am less eager or able to rehearse. It hinges on some textual details of the unfortunately small sample James supplies in the postscript of the 'sheet after sheet of phrases dictated or written during the intoxication, which', he says, 'to the sober reader seem meaningless drivel, but which at the moment of transcribing were fused in the fire of infinite rationality' (1882: 206). As we will see, this issue is more complicated than it seems, not least because one of the phrases in question pre-emptively addresses and partially refutes the possibility that the text is nonsense; but also because nonsense may be an important aspect of mysticism when viewed historically. For, so considered, the conventional epistemological problem of mystical experience, namely, its incommunicability, disappears, the styles and semantics of mysticism being just as inseparable from its essential character as any other discourse's. Nonsense, paradox, tautology, distortion, emphasis, and so on – there is definitely a semantics and a rhetoric, even a typography, of the ineffable.

That was no doubt the case for a long time, but in the age inhabited by James and Hegel there was also something else. In the connection between empiricism and mysticism – their unstable, oscillating and, as it were, rechargeable opposition – there are operations and effects belonging distinctively to the modern age. An achievement of the sixteenth century, this polarity emerged collaterally to the new procedures of, to borrow Blood's suggestively violent words, 'pounding and punching the chaos into the logos' (Letter from Blood to James on June 20, 1895 [following their first meeting], in Barton Perry 1935: 2:229). Complexly, Hegel is himself among the first to articulate the historical character of the dialectical relation between empiricism and mysticism, in a bold thesis, developed in his *Lectures on the History of Philosophy*, according to which the threshold of philosophical modernity was crossed and marked by the symmetrical yet inverse figures of Francis Bacon and Jakob Böhme. (This is all discussed, or at least further glossed, below.)

A Pluralistic Mystic

When he chanced upon a quotation from Benjamin Blood's writing in *Les philosophies pluraliste d'Angleterre et d'Amerique*, published in 1920 by Jean Wahl ('all [of whose] work is a profound meditation . . . on the *non-Hegelian* relations between affirmation and negation' [sic]), Deleuze was instantly intoxicated. 'The poet Blood expresses transcendental empiricism's profession of faith as a veritable aesthetic', he declared ([1968] 2004: 87, notes 18, 69). (Actually, the quotation in which Deleuze discovered his new Savoyard Vicar seems to be a melange of two passages, one from the *Anaesthetic Revelation and the Gist of Philosophy*, and the other from another of Blood's pamphlets, an eight-page document, also self-published, with the nice title: *Plato! Jesus! Kant!: The Flaw in Supremacy: A Sketch of the Nature, Process and Status of Philosophy as Inferring* [sic] *the Miracle of Nature, the Contingency of History, the Equation of Reason and Unreason, &c.* (1893).) The quotation reads:

> Nature is contingent, excessive and mystical essentially. . . . We have realised the highest divine thought of itself, and there is in it as much of wonder as of certainty. . . . Not unfortunately the universe is wild – game flavoured as a hawk's wing. Nature is miracle all. She knows no laws; the same returns not, save to bring the different. The slow round of the engraver's lathe gains but the breadth of a hair, but the difference is distributed back over the whole curve, never an instant true – ever not quite. (Blood, quoted in Deleuze [1968] 2004: 69)

The image of the lathe – a figure of infinitesimal difference with which Deleuze was understandably impressed – exemplifies the kind of intermittent but extreme genius that led James to fixate on Blood. Blood's gist of *Geist* was just enough to get these empiricists tipsy; but is his pluralistic mysticism truly, as each hoped, the homeopathic antidote to all known and potential Hegelisms? Or was it, on the contrary, through Blood that the Hegelian Spirit, the deep Mind of old Europe lately driven from its *Heimat*, enjoyed a fleeting comeback in the local gazettes of 'a town called Amsterdam, situated on the New York Central Railroad' (James 1998: 1294)?

> DILL HOUSE. | CHATHAM, MASS. June 28, 1896
>
> My dear Blood,
> Your letter was an 'event,' as anything always is from your pen – though of course I never expected any acknowledgement of my booklet.[1] . . . I take it no man is educated who has not dallied with the thought of suicide. – Barely more than a year ago I was sitting at your table and dallying with the thought of publishing an anthology of your works. But like many other projects it has been postponed in indefinitum. The hour never came last year, and pretty surely will not come next. Nevertheless I shall work for your fame *some* time! Count on W. J. I wound up my 'seminary' in speculative psychology a month ago by reading some passages from the 'Flaw in Supremacy' – 'game flavoured as a hawk[']s wing'. 'Ever not quite' covers a deal of truth – yet it seems a very simpl[e] thing to have said. '*There is no Absolute*,' were *my* last words. (James 2000: 157–8)

Benjamin Paul Blood's position with respect to the philosophical discourse of modernity – the constellation of pluralisms and monisms, empiricisms and mysticisms, of many and various Hegelisms – is determined not solely by the contents of his metaphysical reveries, but by a tension – a very large tension – between the message and the medium of this metaphysics:

> 'Yes! Paul is quite the correspondent!' said a good citizen of Amsterdam, from whom I inquired the way to Mr. Blood's dwelling many years ago, after alighting from the train. I had sought to identify him by calling him an 'author', but his neighbour thought of him only as a writer of letters to the journals I have named [i.e. the *Gazette* or the *Recorder* of his native Amsterdam, NY, or the *Utica Herald* or the *Albany Times*]. (James 1998: 1294)

Blood did not so much publish as print his visions; he sent them to the local paper or produced them as pamphlets at his own expense. And the meaning of these writings, as well as the dotted path of their reception, cannot be separated from their existence 'behind the curtain', as James puts it (that is, without appearing on international public-address systems) (ibid. 1294). In the midst of the age of the Author, Blood is a 'writer of letters'. And whether his philosophical reveries have 'the true hegelian ring' or are just another 'profound meditation on . . . non-Hegelian relations', or both or neither, Blood's discourse feels strange and irresistible largely because it runs diagonally to a dichotomy that, according to Michel Foucault and Friedrich Kittler, underwent a decisive reversal on the threshold of our dispensation:

> Modernity replaces the myth of the hero with the myth of the one who, previously, namelessly sang in praise of these heroes. Renown [*Namhaftigkeit*] is a historical variable. The hero had to have a name in a culture which had its law in a despotic signifier; the writer receives a name in a culture whose norm is, exactly conversely, the thoroughgoing registration of the ruled. In the course of this reversal, from the nameless enunciator of great names that vanish emerges an author. (Kittler 1980: 149)

On one level, as James saw, 'when the fit strikes him', Blood *is*, precisely, an author – indeed, with respect to the profound or romantic interiority from which his discourse appears to arise, it is hard to imagine a better incarnation of the author function. But his deep authorial intuitions and timelessly universal speculations are printed in bizarrely local organs and scarcely visible self-published pamphlets. As such, he occupies not simply a marginal but a genuinely conflicted position within the modern episteme: a self-reflecting transcendental ego who, without ceasing to announce the Concept of speculative dialectics, resists registration as an Author. This is perhaps why his utterances sounded like 'a sort of "left-wing" voice of defiance' (James 1998: 1295). Instead of addressing himself as an Author to each and all (*omnes et singulatim*), instead of speaking as the I that is We to the We that is I, Blood writes for anyone and no one, for a bunch of nobodies. And the point is: ultimately, such a context of enunciation cannot be separated from its content; outside the discourse of the university, inverted and somehow splintered by this medium of its pronunciation, the *Sache selbst* of absolute idealism presented itself as pluralistic mysticism. If his corpus represents a special pronunciation of the Concept (one that is, as we will see, almost but *not quite* unique), it is not only because nitrous oxide does not sublate but only suspends the schema of empiricism, but also because the Absolute sounds different in the local gazette, *is* different there.

The project of an anthology of Blood's writing must, for this reason, have presented a kind of dilemma to James, which perhaps explains its chronic deferral ('postponed in indefinitum'). On the one hand, in order to deliver Blood's antidote to Hegelism, his corpus of anaesthetic esoterica stood in need of an authorised version: it had to be extracted from its native hermeticism and anthologised, annotated, registered, copyrighted. 'Count on W. J.', Blood would be famous: from the students at Harvard to his neighbour at the train station, the secret gospel of 'ever not quite' would be decrypted for each and all: *'There is no Absolute.'* On the other hand, however, this enterprise threatened to backfire. For 'in these degenerate days' forces of encryption and secondary revision were guarding the entrance of the public sphere, so that there was every likelihood Blood's backstage teaching, his precariously pluralistic mysticism, would be inverted on arrival into ordinary Hegelism (which was just what had indeed happened when 'W. T. Harris of the old *Journal of Speculative Philosophy* got wind of these epistles' [ibid. 1294]).

Thus, the anthology never appeared. Instead, James published an essay on Blood, 'A Pluralistic Mystic' (1910), in which his texts are submitted to very extensive 'extraction' (James's term for quotation), accompanied by James's voiceover. James is the author, Blood the writer. Formally speaking, this late article could not stand in greater contrast to the long anti-Hegelian offensive of 'On Some Hegelisms' which, at the other end of James's authorship, proceeds – like the Hegelian spirit it attacks – altogether without citations (the essay contains only paraphrases of Hegel). 'Forgive! forgive! forgive! It will at any rate have made you *famous*', James explained to Blood in the letter accompanying a copy of the article (of which Blood had known nothing). A neat solution to the double bind, it was, James explained, 'signed by me, but written mostly by yourself' (see James 1978: 281).

Other interpretations of the Blood–Hegel–James triangle are of course possible. A psychological observer might see Blood, here, as predominantly the object of displacements, a function in an Oedipal-type psycho-drama played out between James and Hegel – the latter himself perhaps a condensation of earlier flawed supremacies: *Plato! Jesus! Kant!* – which, in a further round of the lathe, drew Deleuze into it.[2] Others might draw attention to the homoerotics: James was very impressed by a photo Blood sent of himself as a young weightlifter. What is clear, however, is that James's respect for Blood's metaphysics was not at all of the patronising type common for outsider philosophies – that is, the same as we have for an ingenious piece of homemade furniture (as Eliot remarked of William Blake's philosophy). The relationship is both more intimate (whether in a homosocial or family romance, Blood is a 'good object') and more impersonal – having to do with a historically longer-range polarity of empiricism and mysticism.

Logograph

The presence of Blood can be felt at every point of James's drug narrative, but most emphatically in a particular section of it which one could call the experiment within the experiment. For, while under the influence of the gas (ostensibly to observe its effects), James conducts a kind of secondary psychological experiment, the instrument of which is not so much the gas as language and, more specifically, the function of negative particles in certain written words. More specifically still, the writing experiment he performs involves, as James puts it, 'contrasting the same word with itself, differently emphasised, or shorn of its initial letter' (1882: 207). The result of this exercise, which he describes as the transcript of his delirium, presents an intriguing type of experimental writing (and one wonders, indeed, if his famous student, Gertrude Stein, ever came across it).

Actually, the position and status of this passage, which I am provisionally referring to as a (writing) experiment within the (drug) experiment, is slightly obscure; for it seems to be situated in a marginal space between the anaesthetic revelation itself and James's critical commentary on it. He introduces the text, which is located midway through the note, by saying he will now (i.e. in critical sobriety) 'transcribe a few sentences' of 'the mere *form* of recognising sameness in identity' via this practice of chopping off the first letter of words, and so on. Yet, despite sounding like an unquestionably textual practice, he represents the latter, cryptically, as what 'the mind went through' once the full delirium of theoretic rapture had begun to subside such that 'definite ideas to work on came slowly' (ibid. 207). The experimental writing thus appears peculiarly both inside and outside the experience, or rather somewhere in between.³

In fact, this writing experiment picks up on a thought from the main body of James's essay. There, in the course of his criticisms of Hegel, he had implied that the doctrine of the identity of opposites (which he attributes to Hegel) rests on the illegitimate ontological extension of what is, at bottom, nothing more than a trivial fact about *language*. 'We can cap every word with a negative particle', but the mere fact that 'the word *finished* immediately suggests the word *unfinished* and we know the two words together' ought not, James stresses, to lead to a conclusion such as *we know the infinite when we know the finite* (ibid. 207). Interestingly, however, what appeared to the sober James as a reason for rejecting Hegel's philosophy seems to the inebriated James as its confirmation. For it is precisely the apprehension of profound ontological significance in linguistic relations that now determines his rapture. Here is the crucial section of the transcript:

> What's mistake but a kind of take ?
> What's nausea but a kind of –ausea ?
> Sober, drunk, *-unk*, astonishment.
> Everything can become the subject of criticism – how criticise without something *to* criticise ?
> Agreement – disagreement ! !
> Emotion – motion ! ! !
> Die away from, *from*, die away (without the *from*).
> Reconciliation of opposites; sober, drunk, all the same !
> Good and evil reconciled in a laugh !
> It escapes, it escapes !
> But – –
> What escapes, WHAT escapes ?
> Emphasis, EMphasis; there must be some emphasis in order for there to be a phasis.
> No verbiage can give it, because the verbiage is *other*.
> *In*coherent, coherent – same.
> And it fades ! And it's infinite ! AND it's infinite !
> If it wasn't *going*, why should you hold on to it ?
> Don't you see the difference, don't you see the identity ?
> Constantly opposites united !
> The same me telling you to write and not to write !
> Extreme – extreme, extreme ! Within the *ex*tensity that 'extreme' contains is contained the '*extreme*' of intensity.
> Something, and *other* than that thing !
> Intoxication, and *otherness* than intoxication. (Ibid. 207)

I interrupt James here to underline the identification of sobriety and drunkenness, which recurs many times throughout the text and which may be seen further to situate it within a tradition of mystical writing and experience. For the idea of a coincidence of sobriety and drunkenness as a figure for beatific rapture, μέθη νηφάλιος, *sobria ebrietas*, extends back not only to Plutarch's description of the Dionysiac mysteries but also to Philo; referring to Ephesians 5: 18ff. ('Do not be drunk with wine which leads to debauchery. But be filled with the Spirit . . .'), it was favourite of Church Fathers from Origen to Ambrose and Augustine. According to Edgar Wind, it was also particularly dear to Renaissance Neo-Platonists; and it echoes perhaps in Henry Miller's attempts to get drunk on water, which Deleuze also recommended (Wind 1967: Appendix 9; Deleuze and Parnet [1987] 2007: 53). Closer to home, of course, we have Hegel's famous image of the true as 'a Bacchanalian revel [*ein bacchantischer Taumel*]' so excessive, *so* drunken, that it is, at the same time, perfect sobriety, '*durchsichtige und einfache Ruhe* [transparent and simple repose]' ([1807] 1988: 35).

Indeed, the clarity of James's intoxication, or rather of the text he produced therein or thereon, is exceptional. Superficially an act of distortion, his manner of cutting into words functions fortuitously – miraculously even – as an exercise of decryption. The script James produced while high on gas and Hegel is a kind of logograph.[4] It is the transcript of a faulty, technical, medial yet unmediated, noisy, local and real connection between speech and thought, consciousness and Concept:

> Every attempt at betterment, – every attempt at otherment, – is a – –.
> It fades forever and forever as we move.
> There is a reconciliation !
> Reconciliation – econciliation !
> By God, how that hurts ! By God, how it *doesn't* hurt ! Reconciliation of two extremes.
> By George, nothing but *o*thing !
> That sounds like nonsense, but it is pure *o*nsense !
> Thought deeper than speech – – !
> Medical school; divinity school, *school* ! SCHOOL ! Oh my God, oh God, oh God !
> (1882: 207)

Here, the transcript of the rapture breaks off. Its final exclamations are highly ambiguous, indicating either some even more sublime revelation or an equally ineffable horror. But the crucial line here is, I believe, 'By George, nothing but *o*thing':

> Reconciliation of two extremes.
> By George, nothing but *o*thing ! (Ibid. 207)

At first sight, it seems here that James is again applying his strategy of omitting negative particles from words. Unlike his removal of the 'dis' from 'disagreement', however, or the 'mis' from 'mistake', or the 'in' from 'infinite', and so on, here he removes only the first *letter*. That is, instead of erasing the entire negative particle, namely, the full 'no' of 'nothing' (which, we may note, would be a logical but not a properly textual practice), he deletes only the 'n'. In so doing, he generates, through the (textual) negation, not a 'thing' but a meaningless 'othing'. This nonsense word (which he then explains is not nonsense but pure '*o*nsense') points, as it were, to an indeterminate space between something and nothing. 'Othing', one can say, is the perfect reproduction in writing of concrete self-relating or self-positing negativity – of a mode of being equally opposed to the abstract negativity of 'nothing' as to the abstract positivity of 'something'. This makes it, of course, precisely and emphatically that which, according to Hegel, cannot be comprehended by ordinary phenomenal consciousness, of which James's empiricism is a philosophical reflection. For this state between something and nothing is unrepresentable, and thus ungraspable by *Verstand* (the representation-using intellect). Its utterance, here, is interpretable as a kind of abreaction, accompanied by a large affective charge and the admission to consciousness of a certain proper name ('by Georg[ ]'): an intimate and diagonal *e*conciliation of extremes.

In fact, 'othing' recalls *two* aspects of Hegel's system repressed or ignored by James in his essay: first, the self-positing, self-relating or 'subjective' quality of negativity (the overlooking of which turns Hegelism into monistic determinism, and thus exactly the kind of system Hegel's generation knew as Spinozism and, via Jacobi etc., found wanting); and, second, the *letter* of spirit, the complex relations of thought to language, and of speculative content to the media of its self-presentation.

Bacon / Böhme . . Hegel – James

Now, it so happens that, in a series of texts with which Hegel's generation was extremely familiar, the German mystic Jakob Böhme used a term which is a close parallel to James's 'othing', namely, '*Ichts*'. Böhme's '*Ichts*' was, exactly like James's 'othing', coined via the deletion of the first letter of the word that designates abstract negativity, *Nichts*. Of course, in German, the effect of the resulting neologism, '*Ichts*', is slightly different from James's 'othing' because of its proximity to the first-person pronoun, *Ich*. And indeed it is partly this which leads Hegel to fixate on this term in the course of his extensive presentation of Böhme in his lectures on the history of philosophy. Hegel glosses '*das Ichts*' in the following way:

> Wordplay on nothing, because it is just the negative; however, [it is] likewise the opposite of nothing, and therein lies the I of self-consciousness. . . . The Separator is the instigator, the distinguisher; and he [Böhme] now also names it – this *Ichts* – the *Lucifer*, the first-born Son of God, – the first-born creaturely angel. But this Lucifer is fallen, – in his place, Christ came. . . . Because the *Ichts* – the self's knowing of itself [*Sichselbstwissen*], *Ichheit* [egoity] (a word he coined[5]) – is the formation of the self within itself [*Sich-in-sich-Hineinbilden*], the inner imagination of the self within itself [*Sich-in-sich-Hineinimaginieren*], the being-for-itself [*Fürsichsein*], the fire, which devours everything within itself [*das alles in sich hineinzehrt*]. (1986: 20:108–9)

Hegel is profoundly impressed by all this. When Böhme goes so far as to locate hell and the devil internal to the Godhead, in the figure of divine wrath ('*der Zorn Gottes*'), Hegel approvingly glosses: 'that is extremely bold and speculative' (ibid. 109).

Before going any further, it is crucial to highlight where this reading of Böhme occurs, that is, where Hegel places him in the history of philosophy. In an intriguing and profound piece of intellectual historiography, Böhme appears alongside the champion of the inductive method in science, Francis Bacon, whom Hegel – in a suggestive association of empiricism with the military – enjoys calling the 'commander-in-chief of external, sensuous philosophising [*Heerführer des äusserlichen, sinnlichen Philosophierens*]' (Hegel 1986: 20:

91; cf. 20: 78). It is, indeed, these two figures, Bacon and Böhme, the English empiricist and the German mystic, the arrogant Lord Chancellor and the pious cobbler, whom Hegel positions, as two sides of a single moment, on the threshold of philosophical modernity. Opposing prototypes, they represent, to his eyes, the extremes of modern thought: one directed entirely outward, the other radically inward.

Now, like many of his generation, what seemed especially endearing and enthralling to Hegel about Böhme was that this journeyman cobbler from Görlitz lacked all formal education. The deficiency is reflected in the notoriously 'barbarous' style of Böhme's prose – a style that prompted Lichtenberg (in a remark that tickled Freud) to characterise these 'immortal works' as 'a kind of picnic, in which the author provides the words and the reader the sense'.[6] Wild, game-flavoured as a hawk's wing, Böhme's prose, the textual surface, has always been central to the reception of his mysticism, as also of the theosophical tradition which took its direction from him. But Hegel has a specific and very interesting explanation of this style. And it may help us understand how the writings of Böhme (the uneducated or 'barbarous' mystic) elucidate the experience of James (the intoxicated or anaesthetised empiricist) as well as, conversely, what new light is cast on Böhme's 'Ichts' by the anaesthetic revelation of James's 'othing'. My proposal is that these terms – which are technical insofar as they are anchored neither in traditional speech nor in any supposed lifeworld – are non-arbitrary but sub-theoretical ciphers of a similar (historical and therefore faulty) connection between consciousness and Concept, speech and thought, to that which we saw in James's logograph.

Hegel's own account of the coinage is as follows.

In a nutshell, his explanation rests on the claims that Böhme intuitively or, as it were, naturally grasped the idea of speculative philosophy (the principles of self-consciousness, absolute negativity, and the identity of difference and identity), but that, because of his lack of education, the Concept was (in him) incapable of expression in the medium of thought. So, Hegel writes, for instance: 'The principle of the Concept is, in Böhme, thoroughly alive; only, he cannot pronounce it in the form of thinking [*Das Prinzip des Begriffs ist in Böhme durchaus lebendig, nur kann er es nicht in der Form des Gedankens aussprechen*]' (ibid. 20:100). This explanation is, itself, exquisitely bold and speculative: the Concept is, Hegel claims, operating outside the form of thought, thus appearing in an alien medium, in a foreign body – hence, *as* a foreign body. This is not a standard account of the discrepancy between mystical experience and the media of communication. Hegel is claiming, rather, that what sounds like '*Nonsense*' (and this was indeed the English word used in German discussions of Böhme[7]) is in fact the sound of the expression, in sense (that is, in the medium of immediacy, positivity, outsidedness, nature, script), of pure interiority, self-relation, negativity. Non-sense within sense, the exhibition or superposition of infinity within the positivity of perception, '*Ichts*' (othing) is absolute '*onsense*'.

And this is why it becomes so appropriate to place Böhme's mysticism on the same transitional threshold as Bacon's empiricism. Bacon, for Hegel, had the *form* of thinking (i.e. scientific methodology) but a content radically alien to thinking (i.e. brute sensuous nature); Böhme, conversely, had the true speculative or spiritual content, but, because he lacked the form of thinking, this content could manifest itself only in unsettling disturbances of consciousness – illuminations, hallucinations, revelations, and so on – and could be pronounced only through disruptions of language such as '*das Ichts*' or, for instance, the plays involving the words *die Qualität* (quality), *die Quelle* (source) and *die Qual* (torture, agony). (Hegel is particularly smitten by Böhme's coinage of the terms *Inqualierung* and *Quallität* – adding an *l* to create a portmanteau with the assonant yet etymologically unconnected *Quelle* while highlighting the *Qual* within quality – as means of emphasising the original identity of determinateness and negativity, qualification and torment [ibid. 20:100].)

Böhme and Bacon represent, then, not an antithesis but, one could say, symmetrical contradictions. The contradiction of Böhme is that, although the content of his thinking is pure interiority, its form remains immersed in sensuousness; the contradiction of Bacon is that his inductive empiricism is, at bottom, a transplantation of the thoroughly formal, syllogistic thinking of medieval scholastic philosophy from the material of revelation onto the soil of physical nature (the field of radical exteriority, i.e. exterior not only to spirit but even, as Hegel puts it, to itself). Extremes of modern thought: Bacon is spiritually, Böhme spatially impoverished.

Actually, the notion that *space* might be the fundamental deficiency in Böhme's German proto-philosophy had been articulated, some years prior to Hegel, by Böhme's disciple, Friedrich Christoph Oetinger (an author in whom the young Schelling was particularly immersed). In the entry on 'Raum [Space]' in his *Biblisches Wörterbuch* (1776), Oetinger explicitly draws attention to the inadequacy of Böhme's understanding of space, which he evidently sees as the blindspot of the Böhmean thought-system. The article (which is itself an interesting piece of *Aufklärung* syncretism) constructs a theological-dynamical image of the cosmos by synthesising Newton's concept of absolute space as the divine sensorium, which Oetinger interprets as a kind of supernatural prosthesis ('Fühlungs-Werkzeug GOttes'), and the biblical idea of 'the firmament', whose definition he locates in the first line of the final Psalm, 'Praise ye God in His holy place, Praise Him in the *expanse* of His strength' (Psalms 150: 1):

> David says in the last Psalm: We should praise the LOrd in the space of his strength. This is *raqiya* [i.e. the Hebrew word עיקר (expanse, firmament)] and must be that which NEUTON calls space, Sensorium Dei, the instrument of God's feeling, with which he not only sees but feels what proceeds among the citizens of the earth. ([1776] 2013: 268)

In contrast to Luther who, sustaining a tradition of interpretation of *raqiya* in terms of its solidity – a tradition that extends from the Septuagint's *stereoma* through that word's Latinisation as *firmamentum* – had consistently translated *raqiya* as der Feste (fortress), Oetinger's translation of Psalm 150: 1 as *Raum seiner Stärke* sets up the comparison with Newton, whose divine sensorium thereby becomes an active expression of the deity (the space of God's strength, expanse of his power or force) rather than a merely passive instrument of sensuous certainty. For Oetinger, conceived in this way, space becomes 'the ultimate that one can think'; 'no vacuum of forces, it is not terrestrial, but filled with sheer divine forces' (ibid. 268). And yet 'Of this', Oetinger laments, 'BOEHM wants to know nothing; he mocks it, and regarding the concept of space he is not our teacher [or precursor; *Unterweiser*]' (ibid. 268).

From this angle, the worlds of Bacon and Böhme seem entirely congruent. 'Within the *extensity* that "extreme" contains is contained the "*extreme*" of intensity.' The space mocked and dismissed by Böhme is the same that Bacon submits to inductive inquiry; if the former's failing was not to see, beyond the space of measurement ('ein gemessener Raum'), a space which is beyond all measure or dimension ('ein[ ] Raum, der nicht zu messen ist' [Oetinger [1776] 2013: 268]), the latter was likewise oblivious to anything save the finite realm, the empirical, so-called real world which he, chief of police, was there to measure and quantify, command and control. And yet, at the very moment Bacon and

Böhme begin to square up to one another, to form a simple antithesis in this way, an inversion occurs and they seem to switch places. Where Böhme ('effectively the first German philosopher') had appeared involved in 'the most arduous struggle to bring the deep speculative [content] he has in his intuition into representation and, at the same time, to master the element of representing such that the speculative might be expressed in it' (Hegel to van Ghert, 29 July 1811, thanking him for the gift of an edition of Böhme's works [1969: 2:381]), from another angle, it is *Bacon* whose project appears on the right side of history, the bright side of the Concept, as Böhme retreats into his own private boundlessness. After all, with his formal intellect directed onto the finite space of physical nature, it is Bacon not Böhme who is performing the drudgery of the Concept, piously toiling to transform particularity into generality, contingency into necessity.

But the key point here is this: Böhme is for Hegel somewhat as Blood is for James. Each is the locus at which the philosophers respectively find or hope to find their philosophical system confirmed or supported in the subjectivity of an untutored or naïve consciousness. Böhme (the first German philosopher and last German mystic) lives out and writes down the Concept unthinkingly; Blood, scarcely less contradictory, is a pluralistic mystic (bearing in mind that James conceived monism as an essential and defining characteristic of mystical experience). Each is, so to speak, the privileged genius of his philosopher (or 'expert', as Blood referred to James), the extremity or limit of the latter's thought, at which, dallying or tarrying with an immediacy external to philosophy, the system seems in touch with its outside.

In fact, this status is beautifully marked out by Hegel himself with reference not to Böhme but to (his other bittersweet love) wine. It comes in a letter to Goethe (2 August 1821) thanking him for the gift of a wineglass – not any wineglass, mind, but the very one Goethe had used as a prism in his optical experiments. This letter contains the delightful suggestion, between a joke and a profundity, that:

> wine has already been a mighty support to the philosophy of nature which, being concerned to indicate that spirit is in nature [*Geist in der Natur ist*], therewith has, in wine, the closest and strongest document for such teaching [*somit an ihm das nächste und stärkste Dokument für solche Lehre hat*]. (Ibid. 2:275–6)

Hegel then launches into one of the headiest passages of writing in his corpus: wine mixes with the thought of wine and of its liminally spiritual, yet documentary position in nature, while the scientific functions of the glass – its use in the phenomenal production of colours, and the experimental refutation of Newton and England – are linked to a chain of hermetic and Masonic allusions excited by the sudden comprehension, which it induces, 'of my friend [G. F.] Creuzer's mystical cosmic cup [*mystische Weltbecher*]' (ibid. 2:275–6).

Hegel's interest in Böhme has long been acknowledged, but most often, including in a remarkable recent monograph on the subject (Muratori 2016), scholars have missed the precise significance, for Hegel, of the notorious obscurity of Böhme's language. No doubt this is connected to the broader conception, popular since the nineteenth century and (as we have seen) alive and well in James, of Hegel himself as a thinker one does not need to read in order to understand, of a philosophy whose principle is radically extrinsic to its presentation. In this, though, critics and disciples, skirmishers and defenders, are all alike faithful to Hegel. For, as Kittler argues, the particular notation system over which Hegel ruled and Goethe governed – namely, what he calls System 1800 – 'invented an archive in which the data, instead of being solely accessible as such, as in ROMs (Read Only Memories), could always be altered. . . . Random access [i.e. RAM] implies an absolute and arbitrary right to scan and select' (Kittler 1998: 161–2; 1995: 206–7). It is true; the labour of belittling and containing, of reducing and traducing, is a central strategic component of the Hegelian *Geist*'s speculative filing system. With, however, at least one exception . . .

Böhme's prose picnics constitute the system's limit. For while, on the one hand, in seeming to supply nothing but the sound-shells into which the reader projected the sense, on the other, conversely but for same reason, they resisted the system's paraphrastic routines. Untypically, they stood forth and demanded precision in citation, to be anthologised and possessed in smart editions. Certainly, this was partly because lack of education, in leaving Böhme's speculative intuition without resources of abstraction, had cobbled his meaning to his text; but partly also because, in these writings, it seemed not so much an author as the German language that was learning to speak philosophy. Either way, it may be Böhme whom Hegel has in mind when he comments, in his 1802 'Introduction' to the inaugural volume of the *Critical Journal of Philosophy*:

> if the pure Idea of philosophy is expressed with spirit, but naively and without scientific range – if it does not arrive at the objectivity of a systematic consciousness – we must still greet it with joy and delight; it is the printout of a beautiful soul [*Abdruck einer schönen Seele*], whose inertia guards it against falling into the original sin of thinking, but which also lacks the courage to hurl itself into that sin and to follow the path of its guilt, till the guilt is dissolved – and so it has not arrived at the intuition of itself in an objective whole of science. (Hegel and Schelling [1802] 2000: 277; translation modified)[8]

The 'path of its guilt' will be the *Phenomenology of Spirit*, of which Böhme, the natural consciousness of the first German philosopher, might as well be the protagonist.

The Ineffability of the Immediate

Striking as the comparison of Bacon and Böhme is, it in fact belongs to a series of reflections on empiricism and mysticism recurring in different forms across Hegel's books and letters and indeed, most notably, right at the opening of the *Phenomenology of Spirit*, in the famous chapter on sensuous certainty, '*Die sinnliche Gewißheit; oder das Diese und das Meinen* [Sense Certainty; Or the "This" and "Meaning"]'. Since I have been dallying with the argument of this chapter throughout this essay, a brief, direct interpretation of it is, by now, overdue.

In 'Sense Certainty', consciousness claims to be certain of what is given to it through the senses, and of the truth of the particulars it sees, hears and feels. Hegel's philosophical response to this claim is to request what he calls, with mock innocence, 'a simple experiment [*ein einfacher Versuch*]'. The experiment with/on natural consciousness consists merely in writing its so-called truth down ('Wir schreiben diese Wahrheit auf') ([1807] 1988: 71). 'Simple' as it is, the exercise is sufficient to prove that the sensuous reality consciousness takes to be immediately, concretely present to it is, in truth, precisely the opposite: not immediate, not concrete, not present. In its attempts to convey pure unmediated reference in words, consciousness makes use of radically deictic expressions: 'Now', 'Here', 'This'. But, through these expressions, it finds that the *meaning* of which it is so certain (unmediated sensuous particularity) seems rigorously unsayable. Transposed into language, the precious singularities of its senses are immediately inverted into the blandest abstractions: 'Now', 'Here', 'This'.

To the philosophical observer, however, the fascinating thing is that this monotony of floating universals, which appear on its 'piece of paper' whenever consciousness tries to express what it means, do not at all appear as *distortions* of the immediate sensuous particularity consciousness has in mind. For a consciousness that holds that the object of its certainty is an unmediated concrete positivity, the abstract universals it comes out with ('Now', 'Here', 'This') seem a derangement of its meaning. For a philosophical observer, however, those universals are recognisable as the unencrypted pronouncement (the *Klartext*, as it were) of the truth of sense certainty. 'Language', as Hegel puts it, 'is the more truthful.'[9] It is as if language had an inbuilt resistance to the self-deception of sense certainty – 'in it we immediately refute [*widerlegen*] our *meaning*' – so that, helplessly in spite of itself, consciousness speaks the truth (ibid. 71–2).

This is the inaugural dialectic of the *Phenomenology*. In its certainty of sensuous particulars, consciousness is in error, for the true object of its certainty is indeterminate, unconditioned being as such. Pure indeterminate being is the single absolutely unconditioned substance of which it, like everyone, is fundamentally convinced. The irony is that it shares this very basic truth with everyone only when it tries to express its exactly opposing, erroneous belief in its own incomparably singular meaning (immediate sensuous particularity). The mediator which, by inverting its meaning, offers up the truth, is language. 'Speaking has the divine nature of immediately inverting meaning [*die Meinung unmittelbar zu verkehren*], making it into something other, and thus never letting it come into words' (ibid. 78).

Of his deeply deep speculative/narcotic vision of the identity of opposites, James wrote: 'No verbiage can give it, because the verbiage is *other*' (1882: 207). From the account of the truth of sense certainty, we can say that Hegel would agree with the proposition that language is *other*, that is, it holds the force of the negative, but would disagree with the suggestion that this makes it an inadequate medium for the expression of the ineffable. On the contrary, as Giorgio Agamben puts it ([1991] 2006: 14), in the course of his reading of 'Sense Certainty' in *Language and Death*, *omnis locutio ineffabile fatur*, all speech speaks the ineffable – an axiom he borrows from Cusanus. The experience of a truth or illumination that is ineffable is shared by all varieties of mysticism. An ineffability that is spoken is, however, obviously not some profoundly intimate experience that, lying behind speech, cannot be translated into it. Rather, it is, to borrow sense certainty's term, the '*This*': demonstrative reference, 'meaning [*Meinen*]', or indication as such. What consciousness experiences as failure is a successful pronouncement of the ineffable, of the 'revealed mystery', the open secret of immediate sensuous experience. The medium is the message, and the message is the mystery of the immediate.

Both Agamben and, more recently, Brady Bowman, in his fine essay 'Spinozist Pantheism and the Truth of "Sense Certainty": What the Eleusinian Mysteries Tell Us about Hegel's *Phenomenology*' (2012), have highlighted an intriguing continuity and development between the argument of 'Sense Certainty' and the ode to 'Eleusis' which Hegel composed for Hölderlin ten years earlier in 1796. The invitation to read 'Sense Certainty' as the successor to the poem is provided by a passage towards the end of the former: 'those who assert this truth and certainty of the reality of sensuous objects can be told they ought to head back to the elementary school of wisdom, namely, the ancient Eleusinian Mysteries of Ceres and Bacchus'.[10] As both Agamben and Bowman point out,

Hegel's view of the Mysteries here seems very disenchanted in comparison with their high valorisation in his youthful hymn:

> Oh Ceres, you who were enthroned in Eleusis!
> Were I, drunk with inspiration [note this motif's recurrence], now to feel
> the shiver at your nearness,
> I'd understand your revelations,
> I'd construe those images' high sense, catch
> the hymns at the feasts of the gods,
> the high dictates of your counsel.–
>
> [*O Ceres, die du in Eleusis throntest!*
> *Begeistrung trunken fühlt' ich jetzt,*
> *die Schauer deiner Nähe,*
> *verstände deiner Offenbarungen,*
> *ich deutete der Bilder hohen Sinn, vernähme*
> *die Hymnen bei der Götter Mahlen,*
> *die hohen Sprüche ihres Rats.–*] (1969: 1:39)

When, a decade after these lines were composed, the first shape of natural consciousness (ostensibly the simplest, most empiricist, stone-cold-sober position) is thus sent back to the school of Bacchus in order to learn 'the secret of the eating of bread and the drinking of wine' (i.e. learn the nullity of sensuous particulars), it does seem that a reversal has occurred in Hegel's estimation of the Mysteries, for they are now demoted from the highest to the lowest wisdom – an *unterste Schule* belonging to some *Urgeschichte* before the beginning.

And yet both Agamben and Bowman convincingly argue that, rather than any repudiation of the Eleusinian revelations and the silence with which they must be guarded, the 'Sense Certainty' allusion maintains the same identical conception of the mystery (namely, the sense-dissolving experience of unconditioned being). With regard to its so-called content, the experience of consciousness in its sense-certain 'This' is utterly indistinguishable from the Eleusinian initiate's experience of the ineffable: 'I am in it [*Ich bin darin*; sc. this certainty] only as pure *This* [*nur als reines* Dieses]' (Hegel [1807] 1988: 69). Ironically, pure sense is an anaesthetic. And it is thus no accident that sense certainty resembles the 'ontological intuition' which appears to be the monistic discovery of each and every anaesthetic revelation (see, for example, James 1987: 287).

And yet there is one crucial difference between the experience of the ineffable in 'Sense Certainty' and the mysteries of Eleusis and laughing gas; for while the latter are placed outside communication, the former are inseparable from the performance of demonstrative reference or 'meaning'. The mystery of 'Sense Certainty' is, in stark contrast to the ode 'Eleusis', located not in a silence outside language but in a nothingness *within* it:

> The 'sacred law' of the Goddess of Eleusis, who, in the youthful hymn, prohibited the initiate from revealing in words what he had 'seen, heard, felt' during the night, is now subsumed by language itself, which has the 'divine nature' that prevents *Meinung* from being put into words. (Agamben [1991] 2006: 13)

Now, as it happens, the manuscript of the 'Eleusis' ode reveals that in a first draft of the poem Hegel *did* attempt to put the Mystery into words. It came out like this:

~~sense is lost in the intuition,~~
~~what I called mine fades,~~
~~I surrender to the immeasurable,~~
~~I am in it, am all, am only it.~~

[~~der Sinn verliert sich in dem Anschaun,~~
~~was mein ich nannte schwindet,~~
~~ich gebe mich dem Unermeßlichen dahin,~~
~~ich bin in ihm, bin alles, bin nur es.~~ –] (1969: 1:138)

As we can see, writing this down was clearly a bad idea, since Hegel immediately struck the passage out, so that the final draft of the poem upholds the silence it praises respecting the substance of the Mysteries. Yet, a decade later, this is precisely what, with such apparent innocence, he encourages natural consciousness to do with *its* sensuous certainty. And thus we come to have two scripts before us: one piece of paper has a rhapsodic description of pantheistic immersion or 'ontological emotion' written on it; the other has a simple affirmation of sensuous certainty, such as 'The now is night.' And the surprise is that comparison of the two texts reveals them to be in substance identical. Their shared content is, namely, the universal ground of all intuition, the being of the sensible in general. And while the first text is aware of the ineffability of the experience it nonetheless attempts to describe (before swiftly erasing), it is the second which, just because it is so convinced that what it means is sayable, effectively discloses the *suspension* of sheer sensuous being, within language, in the form of a rigorously unspeakable 'meaning' (simple indication or demonstrative reference as such) which is nonetheless operative in all utterance.

Notes

1. A reference to his pamphlet 'Is Life Worth Living?'
2. For James, one would probably need also to include here both Whitman (the paradigm of 'healthy-mindedness', of relationless, paratactic positivity – according to reports James cites, the man had a complete inability to feel evil, never experiencing even 'a transient sadness or a momentary humility' [1998: 82]) – and of course his actual father (died 1882), whose bulky and repetitive literary remains were left, unenviably, to the execution of his eldest son (see James Sr.: 1884).
3. Thanks to Isabel Rivers for a helpful question here.
4. Adapting this term from Beckett's characterisation of Stein's writing in a letter to Axel Kaun (the 'German Letter', 9 July 1937): 'Perhaps the logographs of Gertrude Stein lie closer to what I have in mind [*Vielleicht liegen die Logographen von Gertrude Stein dem näher was ich im Sinne habe*].' The context is relevant: 'logograph' is the term with which Beckett is here opposing his own writing programme to that of Joyce's *Work in Progress*, precisely insofar as the latter linguistically implements the Nolan doctrine of the identification of opposites: 'There it seems rather to concern an apotheosis of the word. It is as if ascension to heaven and falling to hell would be one and the same. How nice it would be to be able to believe it were indeed so [*Dort scheint es sich vielmehr um eine Apotheose des Wortes zu handeln. Es sei denn, Himmelfahrt und Höllensturz sind eins und dasselbe. Wie schön wäre es, glauben zu können, es sei in der Tat so*]' (Beckett 1983: 53).
5. The English word 'egoity', which is a viable translation of Böhme's *Ichheit*, seems also to have been coined by a Paracelsian, namely, the Puritan radical Noah Biggs in his polemic against quack medicine, *Chymiatrophilos, mataeotechnia medicinae praxeos: The Vanity of the Craft of Physick* (from which, relatedly, also 'febrile' and 'obesity'). As the *Oxford English Dictionary* fur-

ther indicates, Stirling used 'egoity' to render 'Ichheit' in his translation of Albert Schwegler's exposition of Fichte (1867: 261).
6. '[E]ine Art von Pickenick, wobei der Verfasser die Worte [(den Schall [the sound])] und der Leser den Sinn stellt' (Georg Christoph Lichtenberg, Heft D, quoted, without the passage in parentheses, in Freud 1905: 70).
7. See Lichtenberg's claim: 'Perhaps Böhme's book, of which an angel would judge exactly as we do, is occasionally nonsense, and occasionally in fact sublime [Vielleicht ist Böhms Buch, wovon ein Engel eben das Urteil fällen würde das wir fällen, zuweilen Nonsense, und zuweilen sogar erhaben]' (1994: 256–7, Heft D).
8. '[M]an [muß] es mit Freude und Genuß annehmen, wenn die reine Idee der Philosophie ohne wissenschaftlichen Umfang mit Geist als eine Naivetät sich ausdrückt, welche nicht zur Objektivität eines systematischen Bewußtseins gelangt; es ist der Abdruck einer schönen Seele, welche die Trägheit hatte, sich vor dem Sündenfall des Denkens zu bewahren, aber auch des Mutes entbehrte, sich in ihn zu stürzen und seine Schuld bis zu ihrer Auflösung durchzuführen, darum aber auch zur Selbstanschauung in einem objektiven Ganzen der Wissenschaft nicht gelangte' (Hegel 1986: 2:174).
9. 'Die Sprache aber ist, wie wir sehen, das Wahrhaftere.' '[A]s we see' subtly reinforces the connection between language, truth and evidence, which was established in the writing experiment and underlies the complex role of empirical experience in the refutation of sense certainty, and Hegelian phenomenology more generally.
10. '[D]enjenigen, welche jene Wahrheit und Gewißheit der Realität der sinnlichen Gegenstände behaupten, gesagt werden [kann], daß sie in die unterste Schule der Weisheit, nämlich in die alten Eleusischen Mysterien zurückzuweisen sind' (Hegel [1807] 1988: 77).

References

Agamben, Giorgio [1991] (2006), *Language and Death: The Place of Negativity*, trans. Karen E. Pinkus and Michael Hardt, Minneapolis: University of Minnesota Press.
Barton Perry, Ralph (1935), *The Thought and Character of William James*, 2 vols, London: Oxford University Press.
Beckett, Samuel (1983), *Disjecta: Miscellaneous Writings and a Dramatic Fragment*, ed. Ruby Cohn, London: Calder.
Bowman, Brady (2012), 'Spinozist Pantheism and the Truth of "Sense Certainty": What the Eleusinian Mysteries Tell Us about Hegel's *Phenomenology*', Journal of the History of Philosophy, 50.1, 85–110.
Deleuze, Gilles [1968] (2004), *Difference and Repetition*, trans. Paul Patton, London, New York: Continuum.
Deleuze, Gilles and Claire Parnet [1987] (2007), *Dialogues II*, trans. Hugh Tomlinson and Barbara Habberjam, New York: Columbia University.
Freud, Sigmund (1905), *Der Witz und seine Beziehung zum Unbewußten*, Leipzig, Vienna: Franz Deutike.
Hegel, G. W. F. (1969), *Briefe von und an Hegel*, 3 vols, Hamburg: Meiner.
Hegel, G. W. F. (1986), *Werke in Zwanzig Bänden*, 20 vols, Frankfurt am Main: Suhrkamp.
Hegel, G. W. F. [1807] (1988), *Phänomenologie des Geistes*, ed. Friedrich Wessels and Heinrich Clairmont, Hamburg: Meiner.
Hegel, G. W. F. and F. W. J. Schelling [1802] (2000), 'Introduction. On the Essence of Philosophical Criticism Generally and Its Relationship to the Present State of Philosophy in Particular', in *Between Kant and Hegel: Texts in the Development of Post-Kantian Idealism*, ed. and trans. George di Giovanni and H. S. Harris, Indianapolis: Hackett, 272–91.
James Sr., Henry (1884), *The Literary Remains of Henry James*, ed. William James, New York: Houghton Mifflin.
J[ames], W[illiam] (1882), 'On Some Hegelisms', Mind, 7.26: 186–208.
James, William (1978), *Essays in Philosophy*, Cambridge, MA: Harvard University Press.

James, William (1987), *Essays, Comments, and Reviews*, Cambridge, MA: Harvard University Press.
James, William (1998), *Writings: 1902–1910*, New York: Library of America.
James, William (2000), *The Correspondence of William James: Volume 8, 1895 – June 1899*, ed. Ignas K. Skrupskelis and Elizabeth M. Berkeley, Charlottesville: University of Virginia Press.
Kittler, Friedrich A. (1980), *Austreibung des Geistes aus den Geisteswissenschaften. Programme des Poststrukturalismus*, Paderborn: Ferdinand Schöning.
Kittler, Friedrich A. (1995) *Aufschreibesysteme 1800/1900*, Neuauflage, Munich: Wilhelm Fink.
Kittler, Friedrich A. (1998), *Discourse Network 1800/1900*, trans. Michael Metteer with Chris Cullens, Stanford: Stanford University Press.
Lichtenberg, Georg Christoph (1994), *Schriften und Briefe*, vol. 1, Munich: Carl Hanser.
Muratori, Cecilia (2016), *The First German Philosopher: The Mysticism of Jakob Böhme as Interpreted by Hegel*, trans. Richard Dixon and Raphaëlle Burns, Dordrecht: Springer.
Oetinger, Friedrich Christoph [1776] (2013), *Biblisches und emblematisches Wörterbuch*, ed. Gerhard Schäfer and Martin Schmidt, Berlin: de Gruyter.
Schwegler, Alfred (1867), *Handbook of the History of Philosophy*, trans. James Stirling, Edinburgh: Oliver & Boyd.
Wind, Edgar (1967), *Pagan Mysteries in the Renaissance*, rev. and enlarged edn, New York: Norton.

18

Language

Katie Terezakis

There will be even other wars
And again to Troy great Achilles will be sent. (Virgil, *Eclogues*, 4.34–6, quoted on the front page of Hamann's *Crusades of a Philologist*)

Introduction: J. G. Hamann, Trojan Horse at the Gates of Enlightenment

Johann Georg Hamann (1730–88) set out to do neither theology nor philosophy, yet has had a stealthy impact on both. His influence has been called 'subterranean';[1] it was recently described as seeping into the water table, 'to be drunk, consciously and unconsciously, throughout the nineteenth century' (Griffith-Dickson 2012: 55). Jacobi, Schleiermacher and Schelling vied to declare themselves his rightful heirs; Herder shaped his early projects in near-constant dialogue with Hamann; and Kant, who Hamann personally introduced to the works of Hume, famously woke from dogmatic slumber in order to secure for human judgement the authority that Hume and Hamann so troublingly challenged. With Hamann, Lutheran theology and philosophical critique converge, to yield an epistemological challenge whose severity remains unmatched. Hamann's challenge, however, plays out in writings so playful, polyphonic and resistant to appropriation – indeed, so inventively odd – that his style itself becomes both a matter of offence (most famously, to Hegel) as well as a literary model (most prominently, to Kierkegaard). During his lifetime, Hamann's writings earned him the appellative *Magus of the North*.[2] Goethe applauded their insight into the realm 'where nature and spirit meet in secret' (1961: 9:515). Yet most of Hamann's works are occasional pieces, penned in response to the letters and affairs of his friends, or to the publications of better-known theological and philosophical contenders. Hamann did not print his most consequential essays, despite willing contacts among publishers. Instead, he associated his position on both knowledge and writing with that of Socrates, the 'simpleton' who spoke 'as much about his ignorance as a hypochondriac about his imagined illness' ([1759] 1967: 161; 1949–57: 1:70) and who felt no need to become an author (ibid. 177; 1:78). Hamann's impact on the nineteenth century, therefore, was as covert as it was significant.

Owing in part to Hamann's unknown but motive force, some amazement tends to mark nineteenth- and twentieth-century rediscoveries of the eighteenth-century thinker who saw through the ideology of individual rights in his contemporary political discussions; who cautioned his transcendentally minded associates not to conflate statements about cognition with those about validity; who proclaimed that the theological and philosophical *subject* was a product of dominant discourses vying for power; and who – given his recognition that human reason was a historical achievement of linguistically socialised, physically embodied beings – proposed a dynamic view of relational, communicative rationality. If such characteristically late modern or postmodern insights were available at the dawn of the nineteenth century, why did Hamann not achieve greater prominence? Why is he absent, or merely incidentally mentioned, in most major treatments of modern theology?[3] This essay is an attempt to reconstruct the major wings of Hamann's thought; only the concluding, final section identifies, albeit briefly, explicit lines of Hamann's influence in the nineteenth century. By devoting its better part to Hamann's achievement, the present essay makes the case that Hamann's thinking plots some of the defining predicaments of nineteenth-century thought, including its questions about the historicity of both sacred texts and the human faculty that reads them, and about the epistemic status of theology in the wake of critical idealism, phenomenology and historicism. It should also allow us to speculate on the reasons for Hamann's relative inconspicuousness.

Hamann entered the public fray over the question of a faithful interpretation of Socrates, in a missive directed at the two friends labouring to return him to the fold of Enlightenment rationality – Kant and Johann Christoph Berens.[4] The ignorance Hamann declared in his *Socratic Memorabilia* (1759) proved to have a specific application: from the outset, Hamann was consumed with the conditioning context of human knowledge claims. After his earliest essay, Hamann's studies surfaced in articles aimed at the critical idealism of Kant, the emergent naturalism of Herder and the tolerant liberalism of Moses Mendelssohn. In each case, we find Hamann gripped by the insight that human rational activities are profoundly reliant upon language, and that language itself is a historical product. Language is both anchored by surfacing patterns of use, and inhabited by the particularities of its usage in the lives of situated human actors. Hamann's insights led later modern thinkers to credit him with initiating the turn to expressivist models of meaning and with embracing meaning holism, but what Hamann actually practises is something more attentive to demands for demonstrable epistemological criteria, and more difficult to categorise.[5]

Hamann seems to have been as little interested in initiating a systematic philosophy of language as he was in introducing a new field of theology. Our reliance on language is nearly confounding, for Hamann, because it offers the terms of whatever encounter with divinity we may have. Towards the end of life, he admits the agony of his position in a letter to Herder:

> If I were as eloquent as Demosthenes, I would do no more than repeat one sentence three times: Reason is language, Logos. On this marrowbone I gnaw, and will gnaw myself to death on it. There still remains darkness on the face of the deep for me; I still wait for an apocalyptic angel with a key to the abyss. (1955–75: 5:177)[6]

Condescension

The idea that anchors Hamann's authorship is one that he shares with kenotic theology, which seeks to understand the act of self-emptying by which the divine became human in the incarnation (Philippians 2: 6–7).[7] God's self-limitation (*Herunterlassung*) is crucial in Luther; the imagery of divine condescension and its consequence in the Lutheran tradition could be compared to similar concepts in a diverse set of theologies.[8] But Hamann's adoption of divine condescension is not derivative; on the contrary, he offers a concentrated meditation on the actuality of an *abasement of the Word*. Unlike his more academically minded predecessors and successors, Hamann seems uninterested in arguing the possibility of hypostatic union, or in parsing the complexities of Christ's access to his divine nature, or in expounding on soteriology. Instead, he seizes the portrayal of the *communicatio idiomatum*; he emphasises the activity of communication as a living exchange between divinity and humanity, in a language we are still speaking and in symbols we are still speaking about. Hamann dares his readers to think the full consequence of the doctrinal position that sees not just the arrival of Christ, but all of existence as a consequence of divine self-negation. A fundamentally constrained world, marked by restriction or lowering, is a world of suppressed sources and suspended ends. It is not a world we can grasp in its fullness, or as a totality within which we readily fit. While Hamann's application of condescension further opens the way to reflection on creation as an inexplicable and unearned 'act of love', he focuses on the concurrence between condescension and knowledge, by developing an account of our rational shortcomings and the radical dependency that our intellectual limits necessitate.

From the initial *Socratic Memorabilia*, Hamann makes the imagery of condescension central to his argument. Recall that by 1759, Socrates was a heroic model for Enlightenment thought. Hamann reminds his readers of a sincere Socrates, who confesses that his actions are determined by his heart and who is often inspired by his surroundings. This is the textual Socrates of Plato, who talks endlessly about the presence of the Gods, who delights in bodily beauty, and who gave up a life devoted to natural philosophy and book-learning in order to chase the hidden truth suggested by Apollo's oracle at Delphi. That oracle seemed to convey a contradiction in judging 'him as wisest who nevertheless confessed to himself that he knew nothing' ([1759] 1967: 157; 1949–57: 1:680). The transmission of a divine oracle is nothing more than naïve fantasy or literary indulgence 'for a philosopher of modern taste'. And just here we find modernity's first and founding falsehood (*proton pseudos*, a formulation that Hamann will go on to utilise). If Socrates' Apollo limited himself for people, 'because the latter were too stupid to accommodate themselves to him' (ibid. 157; 1:680), then he acted like a god who can 'Philippise or Socratise' far more effectively than humans can imitate Apollo.

Apollo must have laughed 'under his golden beard, when the ticklish task was presented to him in the days of Socrates of determining who among all the people living at the time might be wisest' (ibid. 163; 1:71). Hamann draws his readers' attention to his interpretative parataxis, placing various sayings of Socrates beside the Delphic inscription. What do we learn from the juxtaposed forms? That Apollo practised 'the attentiveness and renunciation of a tutor more ethically' than any mortal could (ibid. 163; 1:71). We learn that mortal wisdom is awareness that the source of knowledge is ever receding and that even the surest proof is tenuous. In our state of lacking, we need belief not only for an introduction into religious mysteries, but far more pervasively, we need belief – which Hamann sees as decisively related to religious faith – for the habits of thought and language through which we deal with experience altogether.

Hamann drives the point that belief (*Glaube*) is neither dependent upon proof, nor proof upon belief. The dissociation of belief and proof attests to the division of belief-as-faith (also *Glaube*) and reason. 'Faith is not the work of reason', he writes, 'and therefore cannot succumb to its attack, because faith arises just as little from reason as tasting and seeing do' (ibid. 169; 1:74). Perhaps more than anyone since the Plato who wrote Socrates, however, Hamann writes with palpable appreciation for the irony of assertions which he continues to deliver, with at least the guise of syllogistic argumentation. Just as reason goes off the rails in its analysis of faith, the reasonable argument on behalf of faith is tasked per se to admit its own absurdity.

Although we do not and cannot know the being of a God, there is an epistemic relationship between us. Its secret, Hamann writes, was one that Socrates understood even without knowing its Scriptural formulation. Hamman cites 1 Corinthians 8: 2–3 as 'the honorable seal and key' to Socrates' testimony: 'If anyone imagines that he knows something, he does not yet know as he ought to know. But if one loves God, one is known by him' (2007: 39). Hamann shifts the emphasis from knowing, in which the human subject rationally masters the world, to being known. With this reversal in mind, Hamann speaks of the divine–human bond in erotic and friendly terms:

> It is part of the unity of the divine revelation that the Spirit of God . . . humbled itself . . . the whole creation is a work of the highest humility. . . . So if the divine style of writing chooses even what is silly – superficial – ignoble, to put to shame the strength and ingenuity of all profane writers, then there is certainly a need for the illuminated, inspired, jealous eyes of a friend, a confident, a lover, to recognize in such a disguise the rays of heavenly splendor. (Ibid. 39)

Relation, not only as the logical category of mediation, but as the lived experience of fellowship, precedes and allows for discursive activity, which includes its abstract iteration as logic and reasoning. Gwen Griffith-Dickson gives the name *relational* to the Hamannian view of the 'human person [as] a creature that is fundamentally related to others – both to other humans and to God – as part of its own being' (2012: 55).[9]

Language is Hamann's supreme example of our reliance on pre-existent forms; he thus portrays language as a translation from a relatively unknown, but experienced *other*. From the *Aesthetica in Nuce*:

> The senses and passions speak and understand nothing but images. All the wealth of human knowledge and happiness consists in images. . . . Speak that I may see you! – This wish was fulfilled by creation, which is a speech to creatures through creatures. . . . To speak is to translate – from an angelic language into a human language, that is to translate thoughts into words, things into names, images into signs . . . (2007: 63–6)

Inescapably, language is translation; we find it always under way and we cannot help but find it (or find ourselves thrown into it, to borrow from another parlance). That from which language translates is a more direct experience of the world, even while a more direct experience of the world can only be grasped in a kind of language or revisioning. Hamann confronts the exiguity of self-knowledge and the confusion of tongues with Aristotle's *Nicomachean Ethics* in mind, for here we learn how the apparent impasse of self-knowledge is overcome in the friendships that allow us to mutually deliberate about our choices, and to observe our values in the lives of others.[10]

One reason that Hamann balks at the excessive dissection and categorisation that he thinks he sees in Mendelssohn and Kant involves this sense of what we might call the dialogic and social nature of subjective consciousness, which Hamann takes to be integrated in our apparently private experience. To begin with, Hamann makes the relatively uncontroversial claim that human beings learn to reason by communicating with others. Yet he also advances the position that reason itself is the lived experience of communication, and can never be distilled from the particularities of its communicative context.

Those who reflect on the securing basis of knowledge will find an endless chain of linguistic achievements, ultimately proving nothing more than the reality of logos, honed in communication.

The same logos is our only mode of access to divinity: 'this *communicatio* of divine and human *idiomatum* is a fundamental law and principle key of all our knowledge' (Hamann 2007: 99).[11] In conjunction with the idea of divine condescension and its resultant picture of a fallen, epistemically limited, and radically needy humanity, Hamann's stance requires a thoroughgoing ontological reversal. As he writes to Jacobi in 1787: 'What is called Being in your language, I would rather name the Word' (1955–75: 7:175).

The word is what is left in Hamann – all that is left for the intellect to gnaw on – because our knowledge is limited by the reality that launches it. There is no concept as such without its wording, and this applies first of all to the concept of God, which is entailed in the image of divine humility and conveyed in the inexplicable condescension of the Word made flesh. Hamann returns often to the opening lines of the Gospel of John, with its threefold assertion of a logos that is itself, is with God, and is God. For us, logos is the only possible foundation. Logos is the source of knowledge, yet it is simultaneously both an absolute bequest and a mediated exchange within which we find ourselves.

We do not know God, but by an act so generous we can barely grasp it, God knows us. And how do we know *that*? Hamann gamely admits we do not. We might, however, choose to believe it, to talk and write about it, to create and convey a tradition, and in all of that logodrama, we record and communicate our striving and our hope. Even if it is fantasy and falsity to posit divinity where we cannot know it, even if, as Hamann says, 'everything is fabricated and invented equally, nevertheless, the illusion, the imagination, and belief in them in their time and place has actually caused greater miracles and is still able to cause them' ([1759] 1967: 159; 1949–57: 1:69). Symbolic logos allows us to create traditions we can analyse, just as efficiently as it prompts our decision about whether to accept, on faith, that a deeper revelation is conveyed through tradition.

Metacriticism

In the quote that closes the above section, one might read into *illusion*, *imagination*, and *belief* (*Wahn*, *Einbildung*, *Glaube*) something akin to regulative ideas and the portrayal of transcendental illusion (*Schein*) in Kant. Hamann denies a philosophical resemblance to his friend Kant, yet in key respects his weightiest contributions amount to a deepening of the critical project. In a transcendental idealism subjected to Hamannian analysis we find an example of how modern criticism can extend its reach without hitting the stalemate of romantic irony met in Jena and without succumbing to the dread of nihilism that grasps at straws from Jacobi to the so-called Radical Orthodoxy. If Kierkegaard's and Schelling's intuitions are good, the metacritical initiative also has the resources to destabilise the hegemony of Hegelian formalism.

The Hamann who percolates the ground of the nineteenth century is the Hamann who posted the first, gravest and nearly unpublished critique of the first *Critique* in a 1782 letter to Herder. Through personal connections, Hamann had received a pre-press copy of Kant's long-anticipated work. He wrote a full *Metacritique on the Purism of Reason* by 1784 and sent that too to Herder, accepting Herder's advice not to publish it.[12] Herder published his own *Metacritique of the Critique of Pure Reason* in 1799. As John R. Betz recounts drolly (2012), it was only after the appearance of Herder's *Metacritique*, and years after Hamann's death, that Friedrich Theodor Rink published Hamann's essay (in 1800), apparently with the intent of exposing Herder as a plagiariser of Hamann.

It is not commonplace for a curt and seemingly offhanded essay to comprehend, diagnose and significantly critique a major, soon-to-be-canonical work even before its second edition publishes. Yet this is exactly what happens with Hamann's *Metacritique* of Kant's first *Critique*.[13] Quoting from his own translation of Hume, Hamann charges that despite Kant's acknowledgement of the awakening Hume afforded him, Kant has still managed to overlook Hume's most important suggestion: the language of a literally common sense.

Hamann names three purifications of human reason attempted in the first *Critique* and as hastily, in two short paragraphs that still have room for jibes at Kant's hubris, he names the misunderstandings and failures that attend them. Kant's first attempted purification:

> is an attempt to make reason independent of all tradition and custom and belief in them. The second . . . comes to nothing less than independence from experience and its everyday induction. . . . The third, highest, and as it were empirical purism is therefore concerned with language, the only, first, and last organon and criterion of reason, with no credentials but tradition and usage. (2007: 207–8)

Without justification, as Hamann goes on to claim, Kant describes a reason that functions independently of conventions, of experience and of language. For Kant, while reason might arise in conversation, or even discourses about experience and tradition, it is capable of freeing itself from these contingent involvements and executing judgements that see through to their apodictic core. In the imagery that Kant uses later in *Religion within the Bounds of Mere Reason*, the rhetoric and myth used to describe truth to immature audiences (whether that is truth about the categories of human understanding or the truths of rational theology), are a 'husk' that can be shed once the true fruits of knowledge are ripe (see Kant [1793] 1996).

Kant holds that knowledge comes from two separate sources – our receptivity to sense impressions and our spontaneous conceptual representation of objects – whose further derivation cannot be found (1901: A50/B74). Indeed, much of Kant's project stands or falls with this partition. Here Hamann detects the old 'gnostic hatred of matter or else a mystic love of form' (2007: 208). Kant is dreaming of a *mathesis universalis* (1901: A712/B740), but he fails to understand that maths itself represents nothing other than sensible intuitions, 'by whose sensibility all misunderstanding is excluded of itself'. As Hamann argues, even the ideality of concepts in geometry is fixed by empirical signs and figures, which metaphysics abuses, treating 'the word-signs and figures of speech of our empirical knowledge . . . as hieroglyphs and types of ideal relations' (2007: 209–10).

Hamann had already raised this issue in his *Cloverleaf of Hellenistic Letters* (1762), but there he leaves it undeveloped. In the Third Letter, dated 25 February 1760, he writes of finding in Blaise Pascal the idea that all languages are potentially decipherable 'because they are related to each other as one hidden script to another'. Hamann continues: 'that a head so practiced in mathematics can commit such an obvious fallacy is easy to understand [but . . .] From his proposition, precisely the opposite conclusion follows' (2007: 58–9).

Kant and Pascal are intent upon excising language from thought not only because ordinary languages cannot help but retain human error, accident and perplexity, but because the promise of an undiluted 'grammar', devoted to the synthesis and analysis of purely intellectual content, is already the promise of a formal system able to secure, store and organise all content, without being affected by it.[14] Hamann is right to detect in Kant the desire for a universal meta-language, purified from the messiness of tangible communicative forms. Hamann recognises a common denominator between languages, but now crucially, not in an identical semantic basis or syntactic activity which we can identify, in itself, through an analysis of its conversions. Were this the case, then languages could be mutually rendered without remainder; each could, in principle, be exchanged for another or for their common element of exchange, as recorded in the *Ursprache* or in the logically prior *mathesis universalis*. All languages would be commensurable and all human endeavours communicable via our shared access to reason; that is, the reason with which we grasp their shared units of measurement as shared units of measurement. This is the upshot of Kant's vision of universal communicability.

Hamann returns to the lesson he took from Hume lauding Berkeley. In the tradition Kant thinks he has radicalised, reason is ascribed the highest achievements of communicative form, by linguistic means and while simultaneously denying any essentially linguistic dependencies. In an artful elision, words are given the status of concepts and concepts the status of pure insights, freed of language.[15] The idealist confusion is manifold, Hamann explains. First, reason depends interminably on language for its propositions, its divisions, its ideals; indeed, reasoning activities require language for the sum and substance of their self-critique, their self-understanding and the 'orientation in thinking' that proves necessary for transcendental philosophy as much as for the interpretation of empirical data. We cannot posit, grasp or otherwise utilise an ideal proposition (such as an idea of reason) without the use of some actual language, bounded by its own signs and conventions. 'How is the faculty of thought possible? The faculty to think . . . with and beyond experience? No deduction is needed to demonstrate the genealogical priority of language, and its heraldry, over . . . logical propositions and inferences' (2007: 211).

Hamann is taunting the critical philosopher with a kind of ontological proof: it is self-evident that language is the being whose essence entails existence and whose invocation guarantees its presence. Hamann goes on to picture an experience in which the earliest languages must have been more like singing, with the palpable rhythms of human bodies respiring and marking out time in the process. Likewise he envisions the earliest written languages as images painted and drawn to record what was important to people, who learned experientially to delimit space with figures. Hamann is arguing that language and reason arise co-dynamically in action, and co-constitute one another as they develop. In different action contexts, including in our reflection upon the formal structure, conditions and achievement of past action, reason and language are never fully dissociated (or given a 'bill of divorce', as Hamann likes to say), because each new inquiry requires the happening together of reason and language.

Again, the matter cuts to the heart of the critical project, because the idealist denial extends to the decisive binaries of analytic–synthetic judgements as well as to sensibility–intuition, and a priori–a posteriori. Language has such a hold on reasoning activities because both reasoning and using language articulate a common, emergent resource. Playing on Kant's supposition that sensibility and understanding could 'perhaps spring from a common but to us unknown root' (1901: A15/B29), Hamann explains:

> The sensibility and the understanding arise as two stems of human knowledge from one common root, in such a way that through the former objects are given and through the latter thought: to what end is such a violent, unjustified, willful divorce of that which nature has joined together! Will not both stems wither . . . through a . . . rupture of their common root? Would not a single stem with two roots be an apter image of our

knowledge? ... The first is exposed to our sensibility whereas the latter ... must be thought by the understanding.... The evil snake in the bosom of the common, popular language gives us the finest parable of the hypostatic union of the sensible and intelligible nature. (2007: 212–13)

Hamann continues for another page or so, piling on the allusions and analogies, the passionate and teasing injunctions; then he concludes:

Words, therefore, have an aesthetic and logical faculty. As visible and audible objects they belong with their elements to the sensibility and intuition; however, by the spirit of their institution and meaning, they belong to the understanding and concepts. Consequently, words are pure and empirical intuitions as much as pure and empirical concepts. (Ibid. 215)

In the space of a couple of pages and possibly with as many successful scholarly and fictional references, word-plays and informal citations as have ever been packed into a few paragraphs, Hamann has argued that the critical project, subjected to its own standards, must give up the fundamental distinction upon which it rests. He has argued that reason cannot attain a non-linguistic vantage point and that languages tie us in to historical contexts and embedded forms of significance which should become the proper objects of criticism. He has also shown that following the very logic of a 'conditioning context', but without Kantianism's aprioristic liabilities, language is self-evidently available as both subject and condition of inquiry. The 'common but unknown to us root' to which Kant can only nod has been available and active all along, in our 'common, popular language'. As visible and audible, language belongs to sensibility and intuition, and as meanings and posited anchors for thinking, language belongs to the understanding and the world of concepts.

Hamann's metacritique of Kant aims directly at Kant's immanent framework; it takes aim at reason as the transparent guarantor of cognitive norms.[16] Hamann pushes at the Kantian notion of reason, geared to identify its own conditions. Once its alleged distillation from tradition, particular experience and language is proved a contradiction in terms, we can appreciate that the principles which appear to support the self-critique of reason are themselves supported by relatively interlocking analogies, metaphors and imaginative posits, rather than clear and distinct arguments. Critical reason, that is, or reason focused upon the conditions of inquiry, can become attuned to the dynamic relationships by which epistemological principles are constructed aesthetically and upheld normatively, as we name and repeat the tenets of our knowledge.

Just as much to the native Hamannian point, metacriticism demands an account of the criteria for securing knowledge claims.[17] Following up this demand leads to the discovery that the justification of knowledge claims must reproduce iterative dependencies through which criteria are established as criteria in the first place. We arrive, always again, at a framework for knowledge claims, but the framework is never given or grounded aprioristically; on the contrary, it shows up as a record of communicative practices. Here Hamann might be interpreted as taking a fully sceptical stance on reason, or of conceiving a fideist argument on the inscrutability of faith by reason, or of paving the way for relativism. Even without a clear sense for the moves of Hamann's metacritical initiative, Isaiah Berlin (1993) felt he had enough evidence of Hamann's rejection of reason to label him an *irrationalist* and a paragon of the *counter-* or *anti-Enlightenment*. Within a more nuanced philosophical treatment, Charles Taylor saw in this same Hamannian initiative the beginnings of an expressivist theory of meaning, which Taylor then works to distinguish from dominant truth-conditional models of language.[18]

Yet Hamann makes no movement towards protecting the realm of faith from critical assessment (as the fideist reading would have it); expresses no anxiety about a nihilism lurking within reason (as Jacobi supposes); and he skirts the claim that language directly structures experience (as in a meaning holism which claims that the limits of my language are the limits of my world). His point remains Socratic: logos names an active process of articulating hunches, hopes, sensitivities and reasons; and when its full dialogic attention is turned on itself, the dependence of reason on what it has not rationally mastered begins to come to light. When Hamann plays at being an Aristotle to Kant's Plato, he is not driving towards irrationalism, aversion to criticism or a denial of the reality of nature. Rather, Hamann consistently emphasises that concepts refer to relationships, further mediated by signs, and that naming things or studying their names is the indispensable scene of intellectual and ethical development.

Correspondingly, reason is neither a human essence, nor is the subject of reason a disembodied, fully realised, ahistorical manifestation. The subject of reason is an infant, then a child, and always a developing creature, who experiences reasoning activities in particular situations with specific needs and as part of both a community of communicators and a natural world. Philosophy and theology required generations after Kant to arrive at the possibility of a developmental, contingent social being who constitutes both self and world in discursive activity. Hamann realises that this kind of subject is a consequence of following through on the problem of criteria with which he confronts Kant.

Hamann has been lauded for resisting Kant's rational theology and for insisting on the embodied and historical site of human reasoning in language. This crediting is fair, but it tends to overlook the subtler elements of the interchange between Hamann and Kant (probably in part because Kant failed to recognise them in print). It thus overlooks the way that the traditions of post-Kantian philosophy and theology inherit an amalgam of critical and metacritical programmes. Nowhere is this more apparent than in the shifts that occur between Hamann's uncompromising rejection of the thesis that the origin of language is divine (in his *Herderschriften*) and Kant's appropriation and renovation of the divine origin thesis as the 'inconceivable ground' of morality.

I will treat Hamann's responses to Herder more thoroughly in the next section; first, I wish to flag the way that Hamann and Kant handle the very possibility of thinking an origin. For Kant, even the most intentional, situationally specific cognitions are fundamentally independent of language. For Hamann, who urges us on to the question of criteria, it is more significant that Kant requires language to make and to think this assertion of linguistic independence.

In the 1793 *Religion within the Boundaries of Mere Reason*, Kant reverses a key element of Hamann's argument in order, as usual, to erase language from it. Famously, Kant makes the case that the moral predisposition is an 'incomprehensible wonder'; that it must have a divine origination which the mind must simply venerate; and that ultimately, our choice of moral (or evil) maxims has 'no conceivable ground' (1901: 6:50ff.; see Terezakis 2006, 2007). So for Kant, it is decisively not logos but an unalloyed notion of morality which points to a divine source yet plays out in a human world. The moral law housed within the human actor is divinely given; beyond that we can say no more. Yet this is all Kant must say in order to explicate the rest of his position on a fully rational religion or moral theology. With the freedom to be moral (or immoral) secured as an ideal, the Kantian ground of morality can establish moral rightness without bias or semantic remainder.

Well before the *Religion* essay was published, Hamann had already expressed his decisive problem with Kant's so-called noncompatibilist solution to the question of morality: it relies on language for the 'ideal proposition' of a posit that should establish at once its freedom *for* moral choice and its freedom *from* language. Kant posits the logical necessity of the unconditioned, as a kind of frontier for the way we think about conditions. Hamann points out that such thinking only occurs in and as language. Kant tells us how to deduce the faculty of reason and to look for its effects in practical action; Hamann shows that without language, we can deduce and interpret nothing. Kant details the cognitive framework or architectonic that we share universally in common, and that allows for our common morality and freedom. Hamann finds that the cognitive framework cannot help but manifest its linguistic context. Moreover, the language that allows us to do transcendental philosophy keeps us linked to social practices and historically contingent happenstance, even where concepts and grammars appear to be at their most formal.

Naturalism and Politics

In a letter penned just after reading a pre-press copy of Herder's *Treatise on the Origin of Language* (1772), Hamann writes to Herder:

> God throws language *through* people – who doubts it? Who has? ... That he does not throw mystically, but through nature, animals, a pantheon of speaking lutes; that he speaks through the urgency of human needs or wishes – who has taken this up more than I? (1955–75: 3:10)

Hamann is reminding Herder of conversations they have been having since the early 1760s, when Herder was first sent to Hamann by Kant, apparently to learn English (Zammito 1992, 2002). Even then, Hamann was sceptical of attempts to deduce a supreme origin, especially where the richness of experience is supposed to be reduced, in the same way, to 'a single positive power or Entelechy' (2007: 118). Yet by the early 1770s, the question of linguistic origin, and in particular the determination of its either divine or human derivation, was taking centre stage in debates about human origins and corresponding debates over the best methodologies for more refined sciences of both art and nature. Thinkers hoped that in identifying the germinal moment of human language, they would uncover, too, the developmental key to individual cognition and social interaction. Texts on the topic were already proliferating when the Berlin Academy of Sciences offered its eminent essay prize for the worthiest response to the questions: 'Supposing people abandoned to their natural faculties, are they in a position to invent language? And by what means will they arrive at this invention?' (Herder [1772] 2002; Terezakis 2007: 75–124).[19] Herder's *Treatise* won the prize, assuring Herder public renown and an influence on a wide range of discourses to follow.

Herder mounts a ruse in the essay, though it is not clear that his equivocation is intentional. He spends the first part of the *Treatise* vibrantly exclaiming the completely human derivation of language. He proposes an empiricist methodology for identifying its natural launching point as well as for observing it in its current state of development. He offers a constructive way of thinking about linguistic origination as an activity of reflection or taking awareness (*Besinnung*).[20] Then abruptly, about two-thirds into the essay, Herder admits that 'creating Providence must have presided over the first moments of coming to conscious control' of language, and moreover, that it is not philosophy's business to explain that miracle, any more than we can ever explain the miracle of creation itself ([1772] 2002: 87–8).[21] Herder has been announcing his commitment to a pure naturalism for dozens of pages by this point; now he pivots, quoting Scripture admiringly, and offers a commonplace interpretation of the biblical account of Adam naming the animals at God's invitation. After the full confession, Herder launches back into his 'demonstrable proof' of the utterly human origin of language.

Odd as Herder's *Treatise* is, it makes a pronounced advancement over its philosophically prevaricating, religiously intransigent milieu. For our purposes, most of interest is Hamann's response to Herder, which he formulates in a series of letters and essays now known collectively as the *Herderschriften*.[22] In them, Hamann's earliest Humean sympathies meet his metacritical insights: Hamann challenges the assumptions of Herder's philosophical anthropology (along with that of his predecessors and contemporaries), finding fault with the predominant urge to unearth a faculty that proves humans to be distinctively different from non-human animals. Again playing an Aristotle to an idealising Plato, now personated by Herder, Hamann comically but unwaveringly insists on a return to the observation of nature. There, we find that the human being is more of an imitating, interpreting creature than an originating, enlightening being. Human awareness and action make sense as part of an animalistic continuum. Not only can some non-human animals understand and do more than some humans, but animals are so much better at some activities and have been doing them so much longer that human beings could only have first learned certain skills by imitating animals. The skills in question involve techniques of food storage as well as communication, both of which indicate sociality, memory, planning and need.

Herder and his precursors produce falsely reductive, one-dimensional accounts of linguistic origination, Hamann argues, insofar as they attempt to demarcate a uniquely human activity, separated from the rest of the natural world. Not only is human language an interpretative and translational activity (as Herder knows), it was first learned (and could not have been, strictly speaking, invented) in an interpretative and translational context. There is nothing magical or automatic about human awareness, marking or reason; our need to express our interests to others arises in the same context and for the same reasons shared by other animals who communicate among their kind. Hamann goes so far as to assert that the dual attraction and repulsion we still feel for animals, recorded in our historical and ongoing worship and abuse of them, begins with our ambivalence over the debt incurred by our mimicry. Hamann warns that properly studied, human language will prove not different in kind from animal languages, but only in degree; and likewise human sociality. Should we wish to pinpoint the first activity that is strictly human, we must move further from anthropology still, and into politics and institutionalised morality. Only in our ability to invest and divest authority, to make and unmake normative standards, and to organise a functioning social sphere accordingly, do we find the first inklings of an expressly human sphere (Terezakis 2007).

In human nature, then, studied naturalistically, Hamann identifies again a receding target. Attempts to account for a human essence, like a singular origin, are extensions on a badly framed question. Human language, like human freedom, is discovered under way and perpetually involved. Our desire to imitate and our ability to represent things in signs allow for creativity, innovation and education, but these do not delineate natural boundaries between pre-linguistic and linguistic abilities. Hamann's critique of Herder is worth working through in more detail, and what I recapitulate here retains no echo of Hamann's wit. But I wish to focus on two of its consequences: first, Hamann insists that naturalistically minded observation is preferable to all metaphysics, and that such explanation can get on well without accounting for foundations, origins, or guarantors of epistemic or normative authority. In fact, not only can various sciences carry on in a spirit that we would now call *antifoundationalist*, *pragmatic* and *fallibilist*, but they must do so, in order to avoid getting undermined by their own biases.

Just here is Hamann's second key conclusion, which he admits to wishing that Hume too had openly conceded. In applying criteria for verifying how the proof of linguistic origination is ascertained (and likewise any proof for any genetic source or metaphysical condition), we find no unadulterated verity, but always a redoubling back into the language of mediation, reflection, re-marking and analogy. Like the Kantian ideas of reason which can be shown, under metacritical scrutiny, to depend upon linguistic signification, the warrant of naturalism is no more than the faith-belief that repetition will establish precedents with which we can work, with an eye to interminable critical adjustment. It is this understanding of *Glaube* – an openly integrated understanding of religiously devoted faith and inductively produced conviction – that Hamann sees as the thread that connects all epistemological endeavours.

Hamann thinks that Herder knows as much, and teases his friend to that effect. Hamann supposes that Herder's *Treatise* is already built around a clumsy admission of the insight that linguistic origination cannot be pinpointed, naturalistically or otherwise. But Hamann wants to contest Herder over whether naturalism ought to be allowed to proceed as if it has fully answered the question of origination or, worse still, as if the question itself has become irrelevant. For Hamann, neither is true: Herder did not, as he promised, provide a fully human and natural account, nor could anyone. And the reason no one could produce such an account is profoundly relevant; it is applicable in the sciences and in the personal lives of every individual who can make decisions about how to live. Our desire for a rationally transparent understanding of being and of ourselves cannot be rerouted, as Kant supposed, into vigilance about the borderland between faith and reason. On the contrary, our reliance upon faith, especially as it manifests as habits and cognitive anticipations, provides the kind of deeply felt, upsetting awareness of our cognitive limitations that is necessary for critique as well as ethical responsibility.

Hamann develops his position still further in reaction against Mendelssohn. Scholars perpetually return to the so-called Pantheism Controversy between Mendelssohn and Jacobi.[23] The theoretical issues as much as the dramatic clash of personalities warrant the attention; the controversy is replete with level-headed demonstrations that continue to bear upon the character of liberal democracies, as well as bullying torrents and naked competition over the posthumous salvation of Gotthold Ephraim Lessing. The Pantheism Controversy includes too a contest over the correct interpretation of Baruch Spinoza, and the untimely death of Mendelssohn, mid-argument. For Jacobi, the controversy continued on even then, ultimately leading to his intellectual evisceration by Schelling, precisely over the matter of how poorly Jacobi had learned the lessons Hamann once offered him.[24]

My treatment is more narrowly on Hamann's endeavour. Just as Hamann's religiosity is bound to his rejection of any theology that makes propositional claims about the character of divinity, and bound as well to his development of the metacriticism of philosophy, it also sharpens into an unmasking of the conditions of state power and political authority. Jacobi first attacked Mendelssohn, in part over the matter of Lessing's alleged Spinozism, in order to advance his wider attack on the nihilistic destructiveness of secular reason. Secular reason, he found, was already on display in the complicity of the Berlin Enlightenment with the 'enlightened monarchy' of Frederick II of Prussia. Jacobi coined the term 'nihilism' to identify the necessary movement of reason, in its self-assured quest for certainty, into complete scepticism and ultimately into a form of despair for which Christianity was the only antidote.

In private correspondence, Hamann asks Jacobi how he can seriously hold that faith belongs to human experience, while analysing it with sceptical philosophical tools and in a forum encoded to favour rational argumentation as its condition (1955–75: 7:161–81). Jacobi explains the proper relationship between faith and reason only insofar as he wrongly agrees to the premise of their separation, Hamann charges. Hamann is moved to amplify his position publicly with the appearance in 1783 of Mendelssohn's *Jerusalem, Or on Religious Power and Judaism*.

Hamann's 1784 *Golgotha and Sheblimini!* serves as a critical review of *Jerusalem* in particular and of social contract theory in general. In 1786, after Mendelssohn's death, Hamann whetted his polemical blades further, with *Disrobing and Transfiguration: A Flying Letter to Nobody the Well Known*. Hamann's political insight is already on full view in the earlier piece, on which I will focus. There, Hamann redoubles his assessment of Herder's frail naturalism, for the basis of Mendelssohn's social contract theory is an assumed state of nature that Hamann finds ludicrous (2007: 165). The state of nature is at best a convenient place holder, Hamann writes, asserted for the same reasons that dogmatists proclaim a state of grace. It is a myth which explains and excuses the social status quo, and which vindicates the enshrinement of the solitary individual.

As is so often the case, Hamann achieves several extraordinary things very quickly in this essay. In the first place, he frames the proto-Marxist argument that rights are, in effect, ideological obscurants of the violent force they allow the political state to hold and exercise. As Marx was to argue in his early remarks 'On the Jewish Question', rights become necessary once we come to believe that people are essentially separate, inherently antagonistic and requiring of protection from one another (Marx and Engels 1978: 26–52). Rights arise where the state of nature is deemed essentially different from the state of society; the former brutal and dangerous and the latter compromising and peaceful. Hamann argues that the immediate effect of this misconception is the sense that whereas natural law might be enjoyed actively, we must suffer our duties passively, in order to uphold the contract that keeps us safe. Submission is therefore a necessary result of the compromise we make to live in community.

Justice, Hamann continues, is but a further idealisation, fashioned to reconcile this unhappy state of affairs. Hamann pokes fun at Mendelssohn's Leibnizian definition of justice, as 'wisdom combined with goodness', with a Socratic eye on the semantic 'swarm' given in place of a clear definition. Hamann means to showcase both the arcane combinations that pile up once Mendelssohn's initial state of nature is assumed, and to set up his alternative account, which returns to a more integrated vision of human sociality. Before he develops that, he insists that the 'perfect rights' defined within the budding liberal state merely reinforce its otherwise arbitrary coercive power. As well, rights replace our moral decision making: 'With perfect rights, physical force takes the place of moral capacity; and with perfect duties, physical necessity that has the force to extort actions. With such perfection, the speculative law of nature is ruptured and flows out into the height of injustice' (2007: 173).

What is this nature Mendelssohn defends against? Is it not, Hamann asks, the scene of a contract that pre-dates and allows for the so-called social contract? Hamann looks at the isolated, selfish individual of *Jerusalem*, who subordinates himself to the group because he must. He asks that we imagine ourselves instead as living within the nature that has always preserved us. The state of nature is already a state of law, Hamann argues, with its own rights and duties. What do we see when we imagine ourselves in a more natural state? We see that we must live in groups; must communicate well; must exercise responsibility. We see that 'all social contracts derive, according to the law of nature, from the moral capacity to say Yes! or No! and the moral necessity to make good on the word that has been given' (ibid. 175). Nature produces promising animals, able to make and honour their vows. And this yes- and no-saying depends upon the use of reason and language; our inward declarations must be 'regarded as the natural signs of our convictions' (ibid. 175).

Mendelssohn's argument, and his solitary 'Me alone' draped in rights and duties, maintains that actions and convictions must be separated; that people can learn to be pacified with activities that are different from those they initially most wanted to pursue. Hamann argues that motivated action is better explained by the passionate interests and rational undertakings of social animals, who are already mutually dependent and mutually obliged.

Hamann's metacritique of Mendelssohn returns us to human communicative action. Looking forward now to Foucault, Hamann suggests that emancipatory politics does not aim at the protection of the solitary individual, but aims to 'de-individualise' and multiply the ways that different groups communicate their interests and practise their mutual responsibilities. He concludes by drawing out the implication of historical Judaism. The most relevant difference between Mendelssohn's Judaism and Hamann's Christianity, according to Hamann, is their irreconcilable understanding of revealed religion. Mendelssohn denies the need for revelation and Hamann returns to it, for only in relation to a fundamentally unknown, revealed truth do we return to our 'childlike reliance on divine pledges and promises' (ibid. 182). Hamann's Christian, like historical Judaism, is preoccupied 'beyond all other[s] . . . with the ideal of a savior and knight, a man of might and wonder, of a goel' (ibid. 192). It is an irony that the political state which killed him is essentially the same state that *Jerusalem* defends, the 'meta-Mosaic state' that intends to shackle us in a 'more than Egyptian bondage and a more than Babylonian captivity' (ibid. 193). Hamann then begins to describe a form of association that comes close to the ethos guiding nineteenth-century experiments with Christian Socialism.

Writing the Sacred Profane

Afforded a bird's-eye view, Hamannian metacritique is the fork that branches off towards Marx's 'ruthless criticism of everything existing' as much as to the 'theological enlightenment of reason'.[25] Hamann was adept at inoculating his work against fractional annexation, yet that work demands of philosophy and theology a severe self-limitation as well as a distinctively naturalistic methodology, which neither was entirely prepared to accept even by the end of the nineteenth century. So Hamann's ideas have been arrogated after all, even in mutually irreconcilable forms.

I have alluded to Hamann's pithy but elaborate texts and his legendary wit. Not everyone shared that assessment, however. In his review of Hamann's long-awaited collected works, Hegel called Hamann's style 'sanctimonious', 'contrarious' and 'nasty' (Anderson 2008: 18, 27, 35). Hegel had his own, world-historical reasons for rejecting Hamann and did not stop at an objection to Hamann's manner. In the midst of more personal malignity than his ultimate dismissal of Hamann would seem to warrant, Hegel allows that Hamann possessed a 'deep-seeing genius' and that he had a 'spiritual depth [that] linger[ed] in completely concentrated intensity' (ibid. 31). This is Hegel's problem with Hamann, as it turns out: Hamann never developed his deep genius into a system; he denied not just the possibility but the relevance and the desirability of system-building. For Hegel, it is 'a living reality of the divine spirit' to need to become the creation, or the finite spirit that produces and comes to know itself. Hamann might have grasped a 'balled core of truth', but the real mission, Hegel maintains, was to unfold the ball 'into a system of nature, into a system of the state, of justice and morality' (ibid. 39).[26] Hamann failed to create the Hegelian system, but this failure stemmed in part from an insulting misjudgement, in that Hamann lived and wrote as if articulating his secret truth into any system was inimical to his pursuit of a genuinely spiritual life.

Hamann did not live long enough to learn of Hegel's disappointment with him, but Kierkegaard contested its domineering impulse. Kierkegaard probably first learned of Hamann as a student in Schelling's lectures in Berlin. Enough secondary literature is devoted to Kierkegaard's understanding of himself as 'Christian humorist' to justify only passing reference here. Kierkegaard openly quotes from Hamann; he takes on Hamannian modes of 'indirect communication' including the utilisation of pseudonyms, the invention of found texts, editor's notes and reviews, as well as the use of scores of euphemisms, coinages, innuendos and allusions. He experiments, like Hamann, as much with narrative periphrasis as with argumentative abbreviation. From Hamann, Kierkegaard takes over the Socratic model of irony as well as the possibility that Socratic discussion gives way to the need for a saviour. Although Hamann gives little sign of Kierkegaardian anxiety, Kierkegaard finds in Hamann the critique of the subject bound paradoxically together with the affirmation of individual experience. He finds in Hamann the endorsement of divine revelation as well as the possibility that such revelation is best signalled in ironic and paradoxical writing.

The dense coordination of references that make Hamann, in Kierkegaard's estimation, the 'greatest humorist in the world' (1967–78: 2:1543; 1980: 198) – where Christianity is at heart a folly – are yields on the concentrated study programmes to which Hamann constantly devoted himself. In addition to his fluency in French, Italian and English, the latter of which he also translated to supplement his income, Hamann's notebooks record his independent study of Chaldean, Greek, Hebrew and Arabic. For both Hamann and Kierkegaard, the linguistic debts of reason led more deeply into language and 'authorial action'.[27]

In Hamann we find simultaneously theological and literary justification for the nineteenth-century transformation of Scripture from the fundament of church authority into a vessel of numinous personal experience.[28] Hamann's rippling effects meet up with Robert Lowth's influential analyses of Scripture. Lowth confirms that the Hebrew writers were considered divinely inspired prophets (*Nabi*), and moreover, as Stephen Prickett shows, that certain forms of 'irony lay right at the structural center of Hebrew poetry' (2010: 397–8). Lowth uncovers the scene in which God becomes again the absolute author, this time through poet-prophets, and in a way that that renders writing simultaneously its material, worldly self, and the terrain of divine communication.[29]

Lowth's theses found fertile ground. They were republished in Göttingen in 1758, with a new preface by Johann David Michaelis. This is the same Michaelis whom Hamann attacks in the *Cloverleaf of Hellenistic Letters* for taking Scripture to be a reified shell of its former, culturally embedded self; a bare-bones 'dead language' in need of Michaelis's 'reviving' philological tools. (This is likewise the same Michaelis whose daughter Caroline went on momentarily to hold the centre of Jena Romanticism as August Schlegel's wife, and who later married Schelling.) Michaelis, Johann Gottfried Eichhorn, Hermann Samuel Reimarus, Herder and Lessing refer to Lowth's works as essential motivations, in particular for their accounts of how the lessons of Scripture can be embraced as humanistic moral truths. Like Lowth, Hamann excited those who returned to the Bible as a supreme literary standard. First the Jena Romantics and then William Blake, William Wordsworth, Samuel Taylor Coleridge and Percy Bysshe Shelley restore the image of the poet as divinely inspired and of the poetic narrative as the sight of spiritual vision.

Of those listed just above, only the Jena Romantics openly refer to their Hamannian influence, and even they do not do so regularly or methodically. Yet this is how we should expect to see the influence of someone who did the bulk of his writing in personal correspondence with those whose published works became better known. We should also detect, even where there is no awareness of Hamann's name, his influence on anti-confessionalist and anti-clerical expressions, as much as on those Biblicists who return to the reading of Scripture as history from an eternal standpoint.[30] Again, however, though later thinkers could hope to find no stauncher supporter of arguments against reductive rationalism, and no more interested reader of Scripture or of Luther, for Hamann the danger of reification brought about by rationalistic Enlightenment philosophy was just as present in the self-mythologisation of theology as a discipline. The interpretation of Scripture practised by Hamann invites hermeneutics, but it is always hostile to claims of expertise regarding divinity, transcendence and morality. It is inherently opposed to any expression of theology as a production of knowledge, even as it flirts, humorously and mercilessly, with the absurdity with its own apparent knowledge claims.

Schleiermacher takes from Hamann his renowned 'feeling of radical dependence', as well as the 'shiftable image' of knowledge claims in the *Dialectic* and the 'constitutive analogy' of the *Hermeneutics and Criticism*. Similarly, stripped of its metacritical application, Hamann's relational portrayal of a human being addressed by divinity and by the creation encourages the *personalism* or *philosophy of encounter* (*Begegnungsphilosophie*) of Ferdinard Ebner, Martin Buber and Franz Rosenzweig, as recent scholarship has begun to describe (Griffith-Dickson 2012).

Perhaps the most striking of Hamannian appropriations also follows one of Hamann's early Jena admirers, but in the case of F. W. J. Schelling, the Hamannian influence extends away from Romanticism and into an exceptional conception of so-called positive philosophy. As mentioned above, Schelling writes an exenterating review of Jacobi's Hamann interpretation, reclaiming Hamann's view of nature and natural bodies, of history, and of authentic religious practice (Betz 2012). Schelling also returns to a Hamannian vision of divine condescension in order to characterise his own more mature portrayal of the first and second divine potencies.

While there can be no faithful interpretation of Hamann that does not paint him as a Christian believer, Hamann's Christianity is also an indictment of Christianity as an established institution and geopolitical force. His interpretation of Scripture and his rendering of classical texts lead inexorably to the rejection of theology as an authoritative account of religious ideas or of the character of divinity. As logos, divinity gives itself and takes itself away. While some of Hamann's most devoted interpreters have been systematic theologians, his sporadic reception probably owes less to the complexity of his writing or of its relative unavailability in print, and more to the inbuilt defensive quills that render it both too damaging for theological appropriation and too exhaustively devout for piecemeal philosophical adoption.

Notes

1. Hamann frequently uses *subterranean* (*unterirdisch*) (Hamann 1955–75: 5:291; Unger 1905). Many of Hamann's commentators have used the word since.
2. Friedrich Carl von Moser was probably the first to call Hamann the *Magus in Norden* (see, for example, Moser's letter to Herder, in Hamann 1955–75: 4:480). Hamann embraced the title, as a letter to Kraus of 1784 makes clear; it was brought to life again by Isaiah Berlin (1993).
3. Hamann is conspicuously but typically absent from Paul Tillich's *Perspectives on 19th and 20th Century Protestant Theology* and nearly absent from Karl Barth's *Protestant Theology in the Nineteenth Century*. Hamann is nearly absent from recent and otherwise laudably thorough scholarly collections, including Smart 1985 and Fergusson 2010.
4. I refer again to the *Socratic Memorabilia* of 1759. The attempt to 're-convert' Hamann to reason and Enlightenment ideals after his conversion in London culminated in the text, an offering to 'Nobody' ('the public') and a response to 'the Two' (Kant and Berens). See O'Flaherty in Hamann [1759] 1967: 54–6; Betz 2009: 36–7, 84–7; Terezakis 2007: 26–8.
5. For Hamann's contribution to expressivist theories of meaning, see Taylor 1985, 1991; Lafont 1999.
6. See also Hamann [1759] 1967: 143. For analysis of the relationship between Hamann's religious conversion and his resultant empowerment for criticism, see Bayer 2012a: 148–9.
7. Haynes (quoted in Hamann 2007: vii–xxv) demonstrates Hamann's debt to Luther, underscoring the centrality of kenosis in the latter's thought. Haynes also makes the case for understanding Hamann's authorial style as an expression of kenosis, and his critical methodology as a principle of kenosis.
8. The Judaism expressed in the sixteenth-century Kabbala vision of *tzimtzum* can be compared to the Lutheran notion of *Herunterlassung*. For examination of notions comparable to divine condescension in other theological traditions, see Carman 1994; Chung 2008.
9. For more references to this same relationship, see Griffith-Dickson 2012: 56–7.
10. Anderson (2008: xxi–xlii) demonstrates how friendship, in both practice and theory, animates Hamann's life and work.
11. Here again, Hamann is appropriating this traditional concept to show its centrality in all of human experience and knowledge, rather than focusing more narrowly on the being of Christ.
12. Betz 2012: 5–32; 2004; 2009. The relationship is handled in Bayer 2002, 1988. Von Lüpke (1999) offers an account of metacritique that links it unequivocally with theology.
13. For the *Metakritik* in English, see Hamann 2007: 205–18; Griffith-Dickson 1995: 517–34. Griffith-Dickson's exegetical essays on metacriticism are ground-breaking (ibid. 271–361).
14. Elsewhere, I have shown that Kant considers language an unnecessary skin, which ideas can shed once clear (Terezakis 2006; 2007: ch. 4). For Kant, see Kant 1901: 5:217, 5:326, 6:213 and the late *Anthropology* (ibid. 7:217–20).
15. 'For me the question is not so much "What is reason?" as "What is language?" I suspect that here can be found the basis of all paralogisms and antinomies ascribed to reason. It comes from words being held to be concepts and concepts to be the things themselves' (Hamann to Jacobi in 1784, in 1955–75: 5:264–5).
16. Treatments of Hamann which use condescension and metacritique to allege a supreme theological or religious authority include Bayer 2002; Smith 1960; von Lüpke 2012. I argue that they are self-contradictory on this point. In English, Surber 2001 stands alone as a book-length collection of selections of metacritique. Surber's introduction is invaluable.
17. For a reckoning with the relationship between metacriticism and criteria, see Unger 1911: 1:526; Dahlstrom 2000, 2008; Walker 2009. For analysis of Hamann's metacritique of Kant and its consequence for the 'hermeneutics of suspicion', see Green 2000: 49–82.
18. In extending the expressivist model, Taylor (1991) is concerned with how language constitutes meaning; with how it articulates the otherwise hidden depth-structure of human consciousness;

with how it conveys not insular subjectivity but social relation; and as such, with how it contributes to constituting a public sphere.
19. On Herder's linguistic theory, see Beiser 1987; Forster 2002, 2003; Zammito 2002.
20. I argue in Terezakis 2007 that Herderian *Besinnung* makes naturalist inroads towards an account of originary logos and linguistic reproduction via acts of analogical translation between senses.
21. In Terezakis 2007, I analyse Herder's 'dual-origin thesis' and his 'ambivalent naturalism'. See Herder [1772] 2002: 99, where he claims within one page both the full naturalism of his account and its perfect compatibility with Genesis 2: 19.
22. See Griffith-Dickson's critical commentary (1995: 150–245) and translations of the *Herderschriften* (ibid. 445–503). See also Haynes's translations (Hamann 2007: 96–136).
23. For a compelling overview, see Beiser 1987.
24. After returning to Hamann's critique of human ('secular') reason, John Milbank (Milbank et al. 2001) admits to a closer affinity to Jacobi. For clarification of the more philosophically significant elements of Jacobi's position, see Dahlstrom 2008. Thoughtful analysis of Jacobi's legacy can be found in the introductory study and notes provided in Jacobi 1995. For an account of Schelling's trouncing of Jacobi, specifically over questions concerning Jacobi's understanding of Hamann, see Betz 2012.
25. The 'ruthless criticism of everything existing' is a citation from a letter of the young Marx (Marx and Engels 1978: 12–15). The 'theological enlightenment of reason' is a characteristic formulation taken from von Lüpke 2012: 180.
26. Hamann too refers to a 'clenched closed fist' which must be opened into a palm in the closing line of his *Metacritique of the Purism of Reason*. There, he invokes Cicero speaking of Zeno, who compared logic to the fist and eloquence to the open palm. Haynes provides the reference to Cicero's *Orator* 32.113 (Hamann 2007: 218).
27. Oswald Bayer (2012b) provides a nuanced account of Hamann's 'authorial action', linked to Hamann's fundamental anthropology and to the Trinitarian doctrine of creation.
28. In the century that follows, Old and New Testaments become a 'metatype of wholeness' in literature as well as a 'literary transcendent'. For a vivid account, see Prickett 2010.
29. See as well Garrett Green's resounding case (2000) for reading the contemporary hermeneutics of suspicion as native to this same ironic tradition.
30. See, for example, Karl Barth's description ([1947] 2002) of Gottfried Menken and his milieu.

References

Anderson, Lisa Marie (2008), *Hegel on Hamann*, Evanston: Northwestern University Press.
Barth, Karl [1947] (2002), *Protestant Theology in the Nineteenth Century*, trans. Brian Cozens and John Bowdon, Grand Rapids: Eerdmans.
Bayer, Oswald (1988), *Zeitgenosse im Widerspruch: Johann Georg Hamann als Radical Aufklärer*, Munich: Piper.
Bayer, Oswald (2002), *Vernunft ist Sprache: Hamanns Metakritik Kants*, Stuttgart: Frommann-Holzboog.
Bayer, Oswald (2012a), *A Contemporary in Dissent: Johann Georg Hamann as a Radical Enlightener*, Grand Rapids: Eerdmans.
Bayer, Oswald (2012b), 'God as Author: On the Theological Foundation of Hamann's Authorial Poetics', in Lisa Marie Anderson (ed.), *Hamann and the Tradition*, Evanston: Northwestern University Press, 163–75.
Beiser, Frederick C. (1987), *The Fate of Reason: German Philosophy from Kant to Fichte*, Cambridge, MA: Harvard University Press.
Berlin, Isaiah (1993), 'The Magus of the North', in Henry Hardy (ed.), *Three Critics of the Enlightenment: Vico, Hamann, Herder*, Princeton: Princeton University Press, 301–454.
Betz, John R. (2004), 'Enlightenment Revisited: Hamann as the First and Best Critic of Kant's Philosophy', *Modern Theology*, 20: 291–301.

Betz, John R. (2009), *After Enlightenment: Hamann as Post-Secular Visionary*, Oxford: Blackwell.
Betz, John R. (2012), 'Reading "Sibylline Leaves": J. G. Hamann in the History of Ideas', in Lisa Marie Anderson (ed.), *Hamann and the Tradition*, Evanston: Northwestern University Press, 5–32.
Carman, John B. (1994), *Majesty and Meekness: A Comparative Study of Contrast and Harmony in the Concept of God*, Grand Rapids: Eerdmans.
Chung, Paul S. (2008), *Martin Luther and Buddhism: Aesthetics of Suffering*, 2nd edn, Eugene, OR: Wipf & Stock.
Dahlstrom, Daniel O. (2000), 'The Aesthetic Holism of Hamann, Herder, and Schiller', in Karl Ameriks (ed.), *The Cambridge Companion to German Idealism*, Cambridge: Cambridge University Press, 76–94.
Dahlstrom, Daniel O. (2008), *Philosophical Legacies; Essays on the Thought of Kant, Hegel, and Their Contemporaries*, Washington DC: Catholic University of America Press.
Fergusson, David (ed.) (2010), *The Blackwell Companion to Nineteenth-Century Theology*, Oxford: Blackwell.
Forster, Michael N. (2002), 'Herder's Philosophy of Language, Interpretation, and Translation: Three Fundamental Principles', *The Review of Metaphysics*, 56.2: 323–56.
Forster, Michael N. (2003), 'Gods, Animals, and Artists: Some Problem Cases in Herder's Philosophy of Language', *Inquiry*, 26: 65–96.
Goethe, Johann Wolfgang von (1961), *Werke in Zehn Bänden*, ed. Reinhard Buchwald et al., Weimer: Volksverlag.
Green, Garrett (2000), *Theology, Hermeneutics, and Imagination: The Crisis of Interpretation at the End of Modernity*, Cambridge: Cambridge University Press.
Griffith-Dickson, Gwen (1995), *Johann Georg Hamann's Relational Metacriticism*, New York: de Gruyter.
Griffith-Dickson, Gwen (2012), 'God, I, and Thou: Hamann and the Personalist Tradition', in Lisa Marie Anderson (ed.), *Hamann and the Tradition*, Evanston: Northwestern University Press, 55–66.
Hamann, Johann Georg (1949–57), *Sämtliche Werke*, ed. Josef Nadler, 6 vols, Vienna: Herder.
Hamann, Johann Georg (1955–75), *Briefwechsel*, ed. Walther Ziesemer and Arthur Henkel, 8 vols, Wiesbaden: Insel.
Hamann, Johann Georg [1759] (1967), *Socratic Memorabilia*, ed. and trans. James C. O'Flaherty, Baltimore: Johns Hopkins University Press.
Hamann, Johann Georg (2007), *Johann Georg Hamann: Writings of Philosophy and Language*, ed. Kenneth Haynes, Cambridge: Cambridge University Press.
Herder, Johann Gottfried [1772] (2002), 'Treatise on the Origin of Language', in *Philosophical Writings*, trans. and ed. Michael N. Forster, Cambridge: Cambridge University Press, 65–166.
Jacobi, Friedrich Heinrich (1995), *The Main Philosophical Writings and the Novel 'Allwill'*, ed. and trans. George di Giovanni, Montreal: McGill-Queens University Press.
Kant, Immanuel (1901), *Gesammelte Schriften*, ed. Königlich-Preussischen Akademie der Wissenschaften zu Berlin, Berlin: Reimar.
Kant, Immanuel [1793] (1996), 'Religion within the Bounds of Mere Reason', in Alan Wood and George di Giovanni (eds), *Religion and Rational Theology*, Cambridge: Cambridge University Press, 39–216.
Kierkegaard, Søren (1967–78), *Søren Kierkegaard's Journals and Papers*, 7 vols, ed. and trans. Howard V. Hong and Edna H. Hong, Bloomington: Indiana University Press.
Kierkegaard, Søren (1980), *The Concept of Anxiety: Kierkegaard's Writings, VIII*, ed. and trans. Reidar Thomte, Princeton: Princeton University Press.
Lafont, Cristina (1999), *The Linguistic Turn in Hermeneutic Philosophy*, trans. José Medina, Cambridge: MIT Press.
Marx, Karl and Frederick Engels (1978), *The Marx–Engels Reader*, 2nd edn, ed. Robert C. Tucker, New York: W. W. Norton.

Milbank, John, Catherine Pickstock and Graham Ward (eds) (2001), *Radical Orthodoxy*, London: Routledge.

Prickett, Stephen (2010), 'The Bible and Literary Interpretation', in David Fergusson (ed.), *The Blackwell Companion to Nineteenth-Century Theology*, Oxford: Blackwell, 395–411.

Smart, Ninian, John Clayton, Steven Katz and Patrick Sherry (eds) (1985), *Nineteenth Century Religious Thought in the West*, 3 vols, Cambridge: Cambridge University Press.

Smith, Ronald Gregor (1960), *J. G. Hamann 1730–1788: A Study in Christian Existence*, London: Collins.

Surber, Jere Paul (2001), *Metacritique: The Linguistic Assault on German Idealism*, Amherst, NY: Humanity Books.

Taylor, Charles (1985), *Human Agency and Language*, Cambridge: Cambridge University Press.

Taylor Charles (1991), 'The Importance of Herder', in Edna Ullmann-Margalit and Avishai Margalit (eds), *Isaiah Berlin: A Celebration*, Chicago: University of Chicago Press, 40–63.

Terezakis, Katie (2006), 'Language and Immanence in Hamann', *Graduate Faculty Philosophy Journal*, 27.2: 25–50.

Terezakis, Katie (2007), *The Immanent Word: The Turn to Language in German Philosophy 1759–1801*, New York: Routledge.

Unger, Rudolf (1905), *Hamanns Sprachtheorie im Zusammenhange seines Denkens: Grundlegung zu einer Würdigung der Geistesgeschichtlichen Stellung des Magus in Norden*, Munich: C. H. Beck.

Unger, Rudolf (1911), *Hamann und die Aufklärung: Studien zur Vorgeschichte des romantischen Geistes im 18. Jahrhundert*, Jena: Eugen Diederichs.

von Lüpke, J. (1999), 'Metakritische Theologie: Überlegungen zu Gegenstand und Methode der Theologie im Gespräch mit Osward Bayer', *Neue Zeitschrift für systematische Theologie*, 41: 203–24.

von Lüpke, Johannes (2012), 'Metaphysics and Metacritique: Hamann's Understanding of the Word of God in the Tradition of Lutheran Theology', in Lisa Marie Anderson (ed.), *Hamann and the Tradition*, Evanston: Northwestern University Press, 176–81.

Walker, James (2009), Review of Daniel O. Dahlstrom, *Philosophical Legacies: Essays on the Thought of Kant, Hegel, and Their Contemporaries*, *Notre Dame Philosophical Reviews*, 10 January 2009, <http://ndpr.nd.edu/news/23878/?id=15006> (last accessed 22 March 2017).

Zammito, John (1992), *The Genesis of Kant's Critique of Judgement*, Chicago: University of Chicago Press.

Zammito, John (2002), *Kant, Herder, and the Birth of Anthropology*, Chicago: University of Chicago Press.

Index

Addams, Jane, 53–4, 61
Adorno, Theodor, 220, 242
Agamben, Giorgio, 334–5
Altizer, Thomas, 9, 23, 200
Anselm of Canterbury, 73, 74
Aquinas, Thomas, 4, 7, 11, 23, 75, 81, 182–3, 222, 239–40, 242, 267
Aristotle, 7, 11, 13, 207–8, 239–40, 247, 270, 342, 349
Arnold, Matthew, 266
Arnold, Thomas, 152
Athanasius, 228, 301, 316
Augustine of Hippo, 11, 23, 74, 97, 129, 176–7, 204, 234, 242, 280, 328

Babbage, Charles, 155
Bacon, Francis, 232, 323, 329–30, 331–2, 333
Badiou, Alain, 15, 281
Bakhtin, Mikhail, 306
Bakunin, Mikhail, 3, 9, 12, 93–4, 95
Barth, Karl, 23, 78, 82, 170, 197, 199, 212, 217, 241, 247–8, 249, 253, 260, 263, 316, 355–6
Bauer, Bruno, 108–9, 197
Baur, Ferdinand Christian, 4, 18, 164, 175–7, 178, 198, 243
Beethoven, Ludwig von, 130, 200
Belinsky, Vissarion, 92–3, 95–6, 101
Benjamin, Walter, 120, 217, 225
Berlin, Isaiah, 85, 87, 91, 94, 99, 101, 346–7, 355
Berlioz, Hector, 20–2
Blake, William, 3, 7, 9–11, 326, 354
Blondel, Maurice, 5, 180, 225, 231, 241–3, 244
Blood, Benjamin, 6, 320–1, 323–6, 332
Blumenberg, Hans, 39, 236, 239
Böhme, Jakob, 6, 323, 329–33, 336–7
Bray, Charles, 145, 149, 159
Brosses, Charles de, 105–6, 109, 110–11, 117–18
Brown, Thomas, 128–9
Buber, Martin, 278, 354
Bulgakov, Sergei, 101, 315

Bultmann, Rudolf, 18, 23, 280
Burckhardt, Jacob, 4, 35, 81, 214–15
Burke, Edmund, 220, 242

Calvin, John, 132, 273
Campbell, Thomas, 47
Carlyle, Thomas, 216, 266
Carpenter, William Benjamin, 153, 156–8, 159, 160
Catherine II, 87, 88
Chaadaev, Petr, 92
Chateaubriand, François-René, 5, 221
Chernyshevsky, Nikolai, 97
Chicherin, Boris, 91, 99, 100
Coleridge, Samuel Taylor, 3, 5, 29, 39–41, 42, 149, 153, 155, 221–2, 231, 266, 354
Comte, Auguste, 9, 12, 35, 42, 117–18, 174–5, 206, 224
Congar, Yves, 243–4
Constant, Benjamin, 109
Coxey, Jacob, 51

d'Alembert, Jean le Rond, 165, 167
D'Costa, Gavin, 66, 69–70, 73–4, 76–80, 81–2
D'Holbach, Paul-Henri Thiry, 145, 148–9, 150
Darwin, Charles, 1, 4, 22–3, 48–9, 124–5, 128–9, 132, 135–40, 144, 159, 203, 239–41, 244, 249, 263
Davy, Humphry, 320
de Maistre, Joseph, 5, 221
Deleuze, Gilles, 324, 326, 328
Delitzsch, Friedrich, 275
Descartes, René, 7, 11, 12, 15, 168, 219
Diderot, Denis, 165, 167
Dostoevsky, Fyodor, 3, 5, 20–2, 92, 93, 97, 206, 209, 216–17, 300–17
Drey, Johann Sebastian, 71, 80, 227–8
Droysen, Johann Gustav, 227

Eckhart von Hochheim, 169, 273
Eliot, George, 3, 29, 33–6, 38–9, 42, 143, 145

INDEX

Eliot, Thomas Stearns, 7, 219, 230, 236–7, 244, 326
Emerson, Ralph Waldo, 22–3, 269
Eschenmayer, Carl August, 174–5

Fedorov, Nikolai, 310
Feuerbach, Ludwig, 9, 109–10, 115, 118, 197–8, 206, 224, 248, 254, 258, 260
Fichte, Immanuel Hermann, 166, 172–4, 175, 178
Fichte, Johann Gottlieb, 4, 13, 39, 67, 68, 70, 75, 170, 183, 184–5, 187, 188–9, 190, 192, 193, 195, 199–200, 227, 249, 270
Foucault, Michel, 262–3, 325, 352
Franzelin, Johann Baptist, 5, 228–9, 243, 244
Frei, Hans, 222–4, 243
Freud, Sigmund, 330
Froude, Catherine, 235
Froude, Richard Hurrell, 294

Gadamer, Hans-Georg, 5, 36–7, 219, 220, 224, 225, 233–5, 236, 241, 242, 244
Gladden, Washington, 3, 51, 55, 58
Goethe, Johann Wolfgang, 200, 221–2, 231, 272, 332, 339
Gogol, Nikolai, 95
Graham, Sylvester, 47
Gregory of Nyssa, 243, 280, 301, 303
Grundtvig, Nicolai, 296

Habermas, Jürgen, 198, 241
Hagenbach, Karl Rudolf, 71
Hamann, Johann Georg, 6, 339–56
Harnack, Adolf von, 55, 61, 69, 77, 78, 164, 175, 178–9, 198, 199, 200, 258–9, 260
Hegel, Georg Wilhelm Friedrich, 3, 4, 5, 6, 7, 9–10, 12–15, 17, 23, 68–9, 91–3, 108–9, 131–2, 166, 170, 172–3, 174, 175–6, 178–9, 183, 186, 187–8, 189, 192–9, 200, 205–6, 207–10, 212, 214–16, 217, 237–8, 248, 249, 253–5, 259, 260–1, 263, 280–1, 320–37, 352–3
Heidegger, Martin, 7, 17
Hennell, Charles, 4, 143–50, 158, 159–60
Herder, Johann Gottfried, 91, 171, 216, 221–2, 271, 275–6, 339, 343–4, 348–51, 354, 355–6
Hermes, Georg, 68, 80
Herron, George, 51
Herzen, Alexander, 85, 86, 92, 93–4, 95, 99, 100
Hinrichs, Hermann Friedrich Wilhelm, 173
Hirscher, Johann Baptist, 227–8
Hodge, Charles, 126
Hodgson, Shadworth, 157, 159, 160, 161
Hölderlin, Friedrich, 222, 227, 272
Humboldt, Alexander von, 72
Humboldt, Wilhelm von, 67–8, 269

Hume, David, 7, 12, 128, 168, 216, 219, 221, 339, 344–5, 349
Huxley, Thomas Henry, 143, 155–60

Ioann, Archimandrite Sokolov, 98–9

Jacobi, Friedrich Heinrich, 166, 169, 171, 174, 175, 255, 274, 347, 350–1, 356
James, Henry, 320, 336
James, William, 6, 320–9, 330, 332, 334, 336
Jäsche, Gottlob Benjamin, 171–2, 173, 174
Jones, William, 268
Josephus, 147, 149
Jowett, Benjamin, 74, 81

Kant, Immanuel, 1, 7, 8, 12–13, 47, 90, 91, 97, 99, 101, 164, 166, 167–70, 171–2, 174, 175, 178, 179, 183, 184–6, 188–9, 197, 200, 216, 219, 229, 243, 248, 249–53, 262–3, 269, 272, 274, 277, 324, 326, 339–40, 342–8, 350, 355
Keble, John, 294
Khomiakov, Aleksei, 94–5
Kierkegaard, Søren, 4, 5, 9, 10, 18–19, 23, 36, 198–9, 206, 207, 210–12, 213, 214–16, 217, 248, 260–2, 263, 283–98, 339, 343, 353
Kingsley, Charles, 3, 29–33, 38
Kireevsky, Ivan, 94–5
Kittler, Friedrich, 325, 332–3
Krug, Wilhelm Traugott, 165–6, 170, 172

Lagarde, Paul, 76–7, 275
Lamarck, Jean-Baptiste, 136
Laruelle, François, 28, 41
Leibniz, Gottfried Wilhelm, 13, 168, 208, 209, 221, 265, 351
Lenz, Max, 64–5, 69
Leo XIII, 57, 241
Lessing, Gotthold Ephraim, 166, 175, 206, 350, 354
Lichtenberg, Georg Christoph, 330, 337
Liszt, Franz, 130–2
Locke, John, 152, 221, 238
Löwith, Karl, 15, 39
Luther, Martin, 18, 20, 116, 120, 132, 169, 252–3, 340–1, 354, 355
Lyell, Charles, 232

MacIntyre, Alasdair, 233, 239, 240–1, 242, 244
Mackintosh, Charles Henry, 127
Maimon, Salomon, 3, 12–15
Manning, Henry Edward, 294, 295
Marcion, 179
Marheineke, Philip, 198
Martensen, Hans Lassen, 296
Marx, Karl, 3–4, 93–4, 100, 105–20, 198, 203, 206, 249, 260, 263, 352, 356
Maurice, Frederick Denison, 52, 266

INDEX

Mazzini, Giuseppe, 52
Mendelssohn, Moses, 342, 350–2
Metternich, Klemens, 221
Milbank, John, 39, 356
Mill, James, 111
Mill, John Stuart, 2, 237
Möhler, Johann Adam, 227–8, 243
Moltmann, Jürgen, 125–6, 139–40, 280
Müller, Adam, 221
Müller, Friedrich Max, 76–7, 266, 267–70, 277–80
Mynster, Jakob Peter, 283–6, 287, 290–1, 292, 293, 294–5, 296–7

Nancy, Jean-Luc, 1, 29, 119
Napoleon I, 66, 216, 268
Newman, Francis, 150, 153, 155, 157, 160
Newman, John Henry, 3, 4–5, 29–33, 38, 41–2, 65–6, 70, 73–4, 75, 76, 79–80, 81–2, 219–44, 283, 294–5, 298
Newton, Isaac, 331, 332
Niebuhr, Reinhold, 60–1
Nietzsche, Friedrich, 3, 4, 5, 7–9, 10, 15–18, 20, 23, 29, 38–9, 72, 77, 82, 197, 199, 206, 207, 210, 213–15, 217, 225, 237–41, 244, 248, 249, 263, 272
Novalis, 222, 227

Ockham, William, 7, 11
Oetinger, Friedrich Christoph, 331
Overbeck, Franz, 3, 8, 9, 15–18, 19, 76–8, 217

Paine, Thomas, 150, 160
Palamas, Gregory, 300, 301–4, 306, 312–13, 314–15, 316
Paley, William, 128, 129
Pascal, Blaise, 11, 344
Pater, Walter, 139
Pattison, George, 4, 198, 203–18, 284–7, 291, 295, 298
Paulus, Heinrich, 148–9, 155
Pestalozzi, Johann Heinrich, 39
Phelps, Elizabeth Stuart, 52
Pius IX, 241
Plato, 7, 11, 124, 169, 204, 211, 226, 324, 326, 341, 347, 349
Powell, Baden, 4, 143–4, 150–5, 157, 160
Priestley, Joseph, 143, 145–7, 149
Proudhon, Pierre-Joseph, 9, 12
Pusey, Edward, 30, 294
Pushkin, Aleksandr, 92, 100

Radishchev, Aleksandr, 87–8
Ragaz, Leonhard, 58
Rahner, Karl, 280
Rauschenbusch, Walter, 3, 50, 51, 55–6, 58–9, 60

Ray, John, 127–8
Reinhold, Karl Leopold, 216
Rémusat, Abel, 269
Renan, Ernest, 212, 224
Ritschl, Albrecht, 4, 55, 61, 164, 175, 178–80
Robinson, Edward, 73
Rousseau, Jean-Jacques, 39, 221
Ruge, Arnold, 109–10, 118

Said, Edward, 265, 266, 268–9, 270, 278, 280–1
Saint Paul, 4, 17, 87, 179, 182–3, 189, 199, 204, 267, 303, 304, 320, 340, 342
Saint Simon, Henri de, 39
Savonarola, Girolamo, 34–6
Schaff, Philip, 73
Scheidler, Karl Hermann, 166–7, 170, 174
Schelling, Friedrich Wilhelm Joseph, 3, 4, 9, 13–15, 23, 70, 92, 94, 170, 174, 183, 186–9, 190, 193–4, 195, 198, 200, 225, 227, 249, 255, 261–2, 263, 266, 269, 270, 272–3, 275–80, 281, 320, 331, 333, 339, 343, 350, 353–4
Schlegel, August Wilhelm, 269, 354
Schlegel, Caroline, 353–4
Schlegel, Friedrich, 171, 225, 269, 270, 271
Schleiermacher, Freidrich Daniel Ernst, 3, 4, 9, 27–8, 29, 36–8, 42, 47, 67–8, 70–1, 74–5, 77, 124, 132–3, 138–9, 183, 189, 190–2, 195–200, 223, 242, 248, 253, 255–8, 259, 260–1, 263, 274, 339, 354
Schlosser, Johann Georg, 169
Schmitt, Carl, 11–12
Schopenhauer, Arthur, 204, 268, 269, 272–5, 276, 278
Schwab, Charles, 265–6
Schwarz, Carl, 173–4
Schweitzer, Albert, 4, 18–19, 23, 149, 213, 217
Scott, Walter, 29, 41–2
Secrétan, Charles, 96
Shedd, William, 126–7
Sheldon, Charles Monroe, 54–5
Smart, Ninian, 76, 78
Socrates, 210–11, 233, 279, 339, 341–2, 351, 353
Solov'ëv, Vladimir, 3, 86, 90, 96–7, 100–1
Spencer, Herbert, 4, 124–5, 128, 132, 134–6, 138–40
Spinoza, Baruch, 13–14, 15, 166, 171, 172, 180, 186, 189, 350
Stephen, James Fitzjames, 156–8, 159, 160
Stillingfleet, Edward, 205
Stirner, Max, 3, 9–11, 198
Strauss, David Friedrich, 18, 50, 108, 145, 150, 160, 196–7, 198, 199, 224, 258–9, 260
Strong, Josiah, 51
Svetlov, Pavel, 97–8
Swedenborg, Emanuel, 169, 321

Taubes, Jacob, 7–8
Taylor, Charles, 6, 28–9, 32, 33, 34, 222, 242, 347, 355–6
Taylor, William, 148–9
Thomasius, Gottfried, 127
Tillich, Paul, 23, 280, 355
Tolstoy, Leo, 51–2, 90, 92, 96
Troeltsch, Ernst, 216

Velichkovskii, Paisii, 301–2
Venturini, Karl Heinrich, 148–9
Virchow, Rudolf, 72
Voltaire, 12, 20, 90, 268
von Balthasar, Hans Urs, 6, 74, 234, 241, 244, 278
von Ranke, Leopold, 35, 205–6, 209, 214, 227

Wagner, Richard, 130, 270
Ward, William George, 156–7, 158, 159
Weiss, Johannes, 213
Wesley, Charles, 60
Westcott, Edward Noyes, 51–2
White, Blanco, 153, 160
Whitehead, Alfred North, 11, 305
Whitman, Walt, 23, 269, 336
Wiseman, Cardinal Nicholas, 30–2
Wolf, Friedrich August, 72, 224
Wolff, Christian, 90, 100
Wordsworth, William, 222–3, 354

Zachhuber, Johannes, 4, 80, 164–81, 216, 243

EU representative:
Easy Access System Europe
Mustamäe tee 50, 10621 Tallinn, Estonia
Gpsr.requests@easproject.com

www.ingramcontent.com/pod-product-compliance
Lightning Source LLC
Chambersburg PA
CBHW081535300426
44116CB00015B/2640